ASPEN PUBLISHERS

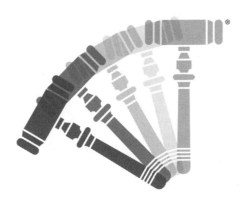

Casenote™ Legal Briefs

CONSTITUTIONAL LAW

Keyed to Courses Using

Chemerinsky's
Constitutional Law

Third Edition

Wolters Kluwer

Law & Business

AUSTIN   BOSTON   CHICAGO   NEW YORK   THE NETHERLANDS

This publication is designed to provide accurate and authoritative information in regard to the subject matter covered. It is sold with the understanding that the publisher is not engaged in rendering legal, accounting, or other professional services. If legal advice or other expert assistance is required, the services of a competent professional person should be sought.

> — From a Declaration of Principles adopted jointly by a Committee of the American Bar Association and a Committee of Publishers and Associates

To contact Customer Care, e-mail customer.care@aspenpublishers.com, call 1-800-234-1660, fax 1-800-901-9075, or mail correspondence to:

Aspen Publishers
Attn: Order Department
P.O. Box 990
Frederick, MD 21705

Printed in the United States of America.

2 3 4 5 6 7 8 9 0

ISBN 978-0-7355-7878-4

About Wolters Kluwer Law & Business

Wolters Kluwer Law & Business is a leading provider of research information and workflow solutions in key specialty areas. The strengths of the individual brands of Aspen Publishers, CCH, Kluwer Law International and Loislaw are aligned within Wolters Kluwer Law & Business to provide comprehensive, in-depth solutions and expert-authored content for the legal, professional and education markets.

CCH was founded in 1913 and has served more than four generations of business professionals and their clients. The CCH products in the Wolters Kluwer Law & Business group are highly regarded electronic and print resources for legal, securities, antitrust and trade regulation, government contracting, banking, pension, payroll, employment and labor, and health-care reimbursement and compliance professionals.

Aspen Publishers is a leading information provider for attorneys, business professionals and law students. Written by preeminent authorities, Aspen products offer analytical and practical information in a range of specialty practice areas from securities law and intellectual property to mergers and acquisitions and pension/benefits. Aspen's trusted legal education resources provide professors and students with high-quality, up-to-date and effective resources for successful instruction and study in all areas of the law.

Kluwer Law International supplies the global business community with comprehensive English-language international legal information. Legal practitioners, corporate counsel and business executives around the world rely on the Kluwer Law International journals, loose-leafs, books and electronic products for authoritative information in many areas of international legal practice.

Loislaw is a premier provider of digitized legal content to small law firm practitioners of various specializations. Loislaw provides attorneys with the ability to quickly and efficiently find the necessary legal information they need, when and where they need it, by facilitating access to primary law as well as state-specific law, records, forms and treatises.

Wolters Kluwer Law & Business, a unit of Wolters Kluwer, is headquartered in New York and Riverwoods, Illinois. Wolters Kluwer is a leading multinational publisher and information services company.

Format for the Casenote Legal Brief

Nature of Case: This section identifies the form of action (e.g., breach of contract, negligence, battery), the type of proceeding (e.g., demurrer, appeal from trial court's jury instructions) or the relief sought (e.g., damages, injunction, criminal sanctions).

Palsgraf v. Long Island R.R. Co.

Injured bystander (P) v. Railroad company (D)

N.Y. Ct. App., 248 N.Y. 339, 162 N.E. 99 (1928).

Party ID: Quick identification of the relationship between the parties.

Fact Summary: This is included to refresh your memory and can be used as a quick reminder of the facts.

NATURE OF CASE: Appeal from judgment affirming verdict for plaintiff seeking damages for personal injury.

FACT SUMMARY: Helen Palsgraf (P) was injured on R.R.'s (D) train platform when R.R.'s (D) guard helped a passenger aboard a moving train, causing his package to fall on the tracks. The package contained fireworks which exploded, creating a shock that tipped a scale onto Palsgraf (P).

Rule of Law: Summarizes the general principle of law that the case illustrates. It may be used for instant recall of the court's holding and for classroom discussion or home review.

🏛 RULE OF LAW
The risk reasonably to be perceived defines the duty to be obeyed.

FACTS: Helen Palsgraf (P) purchased a ticket to Rockaway Beach from R.R. (D) and was waiting on the train platform. As she waited, two men ran to catch a train that was pulling out from the platform. The first man jumped aboard, but the second man, who appeared as if he might fall, was helped aboard by the guard on the train who had kept the door open so they could jump aboard. A guard on the platform also helped by pushing him onto the train. The man was carrying a package wrapped in newspaper. In the process, the man dropped his package, which fell on the tracks. The package contained fireworks and exploded. The shock of the explosion was apparently of great enough strength to tip over some scales at the other end of the platform, which fell on Palsgraf (P) and injured her. A jury awarded her damages, and R.R. (D) appealed.

Facts: This section contains all relevant facts of the case, including the contentions of the parties and the lower court holdings. It is written in a logical order to give the student a clear understanding of the case. The plaintiff and defendant are identified by their proper names throughout and are always labeled with a (P) or (D).

ISSUE: Does the risk reasonably to be perceived define the duty to be obeyed?

HOLDING AND DECISION: (Cardozo, C.J.) Yes. The risk reasonably to be perceived defines the duty to be obeyed. If there is no foreseeable hazard to the injured party as the result of a seemingly innocent act, the act does not become a tort because it happened to be a wrong as to another. If the wrong was not willful, the plaintiff must show that the act as to her had such great and apparent possibilities of danger as to entitle her to protection. Negligence in the abstract is not enough upon which to base liability. Negligence is a relative concept, evolving out of the common law doctrine of trespass on the case. To establish liability, the defendant must owe a legal duty of reasonable care to the injured party. A cause of action in tort will lie where harm,

though unintended, could have been averted or avoided by observance of such a duty. The scope of the duty is limited by the range of danger that a reasonable person could foresee. In this case, there was nothing to suggest from the appearance of the parcel or otherwise that the parcel contained fireworks. The guard could not reasonably have had any warning of a threat to Palsgraf (P), and R.R. (D) therefore cannot be held liable. Judgment is reversed in favor of R.R. (D).

DISSENT: (Andrews, J.) The concept that there is no negligence unless R.R. (D) owes a legal duty to take care as to Palsgraf (P) herself is too narrow. Everyone owes to the world at large the duty of refraining from those acts that may unreasonably threaten the safety of others. If the guard's action was negligent as to those nearby, it was also negligent as to those outside what might be termed the "danger zone." For Palsgraf (P) to recover, R.R.'s (D) negligence must have been the proximate cause of her injury, a question of fact for the jury.

Concurrence/Dissent: All concurrences and dissents are briefed whenever they are included by the casebook editor.

▶ ANALYSIS
The majority defined the limit of the defendant's liability in terms of the danger that a reasonable person in defendant's situation would have perceived. The dissent argued that the limitation should not be placed on liability, but rather on damages. Judge Andrews suggested that only injuries that would not have happened but for R.R.'s (D) negligence should be compensable. Both the majority and dissent recognized the policy-driven need to limit liability for negligent acts, seeking, in the words of Judge Andrews, to define a framework "that will be practical and in keeping with the general understanding of mankind." The Restatement (Second) of Torts has accepted Judge Cardozo's view.

Analysis: This last paragraph gives you a broad understanding of where the case "fits in" with other cases in the section of the book and with the entire course. It is a hornbook-style discussion indicating whether the case is a majority or minority opinion and comparing the principal case with other cases in the casebook. It may also provide analysis from restatements, uniform codes, and law review articles. The analysis will prove to be invaluable to classroom discussion.

Quicknotes

FORESEEABILITY A reasonable expectation that change is the probable result of certain acts or omissions.

NEGLIGENCE Conduct falling below the standard of care that a reasonable person would demonstrate under similar conditions.

PROXIMATE CAUSE The natural sequence of events without which an injury would not have been sustained.

Issue: The issue is a concise question that brings out the essence of the opinion as it relates to the section of the casebook in which the case appears. Both substantive and procedural issues are included if relevant to the decision.

Holding and Decision: This section offers a clear and in-depth discussion of the rule of the case and the court's rationale. It is written in easy-to-understand language and answers the issue presented by applying the law to the facts of the case. When relevant, it includes a thorough discussion of the exceptions to the case as listed by the court, any major cites to the other cases on point, and the names of the judges who wrote the decisions.

Quicknotes: Conveniently defines legal terms found in the case and summarizes the nature of any statutes, codes, or rules referred to in the text.

Aspen Publishers is proud to offer *Casenote Legal Briefs*—continuing thirty years of publishing America's best-selling legal briefs.

Casenote Legal Briefs are designed to help you save time when briefing assigned cases. Organized under convenient headings, they show you how to abstract the basic facts and holdings from the text of the actual opinions handed down by the courts. Used as part of a rigorous study regimen, they can help you spend more time analyzing and critiquing points of law than on copying bits and pieces of judicial opinions into your notebook or outline.

Casenote Legal Briefs should never be used as a substitute for assigned casebook readings. They work best when read as a follow-up to reviewing the underlying opinions themselves. Students who try to avoid reading and digesting the judicial opinions in their casebooks or online sources will end up shortchanging themselves in the long run. The ability to absorb, critique, and restate the dynamic and complex elements of case law decisions is crucial to your success in law school and beyond. It cannot be developed vicariously.

Casenote Legal Briefs represents but one of the many offerings in Aspen's Study Aid Timeline, which includes:

- *Casenote Legal Briefs*
- *Emanuel Law Outlines*
- *Examples & Explanations* Series
- *Introduction to Law* Series
- Emanuel *Law in a Flash* Flashcards
- Emanuel *CrunchTime* Series

Each of these series is designed to provide you with easy-to-understand explanations of complex points of law. Each volume offers guidance on the principles of legal analysis and, consulted regularly, will hone your ability to spot relevant issues. We have titles that will help you prepare for class, prepare for your exams, and enhance your general comprehension of the law along the way.

To find out more about Aspen Study Aid publications, visit us online at *http://lawschool.aspenpublishers.com* or email us at *legaledu@wolterskluwer.com*. We'll be happy to assist you.

Get this Casenote Legal Brief as an AspenLaw Studydesk eBook today!

By returning this form to Aspen Publishers, you will receive a complimentary eBook download of this Casenote Legal Brief in the AspenLaw Studydesk digital format.* Learn more about AspenLaw Studydesk today at *www.AspenLaw.com.*

Name	Phone ( )
Address	Apt. No.
City	State ZIP Code
Law School	Year (check one) ☐ 1st ☐ 2nd ☐ 3rd

Cut out the UPC found on the lower left corner of the back cover of this book. Staple the UPC inside this box. Only the original UPC from the book cover will be accepted. (No photocopies or store stickers are allowed.)

Attach UPC inside this box.

Email (Print legibly or you may not get access!)

Title of this book (course subject)

ISBN of this book (10- or 13-digit number on the UPC)

Used with which casebook (provide author's name)

Mail the completed form to: Aspen Publishers, Inc.
Legal Education Division
130 Turner Street, Bldg 3, 4th Floor
Waltham, MA 02453-8901

* Upon receipt of this completed form, you will be emailed a code for the digital download of this book in AspenLaw Studydesk format. The AspenLaw Studydesk application is available as a 60-day free trial at *www.AspenLaw.com.*

For a full list of print titles by Aspen Publishers, visit *lawschool.aspenpublishers.com.*
For a full list of digital eBook titles by Aspen Publishers, visit *www.AspenLaw.com.*

Make a photocopy of this form and your UPC for your records.

For detailed information on the use of the information you provide on this form, please see the PRIVACY POLICY at www.aspenpublishers.com.

How to Brief a Case

A. Decide on a Format and Stick to It

Structure is essential to a good brief. It enables you to arrange systematically the related parts that are scattered throughout most cases, thus making manageable and understandable what might otherwise seem to be an endless and unfathomable sea of information. There are, of course, an unlimited number of formats that can be utilized. However, it is best to find one that suits your needs and stick to it. Consistency breeds both efficiency and the security that when called upon you will know where to look in your brief for the information you are asked to give.

Any format, as long as it presents the essential elements of a case in an organized fashion, can be used. Experience, however, has led *Casenotes* to develop and utilize the following format because of its logical flow and universal applicability.

NATURE OF CASE: This is a brief statement of the legal character and procedural status of the case (e.g., "Appeal of a burglary conviction").

There are many different alternatives open to a litigant dissatisfied with a court ruling. The key to determining which one has been used is to discover *who is asking this court for what*.

This first entry in the brief should be kept as *short as possible*. Use the court's terminology if you understand it. But since jurisdictions vary as to the titles of pleadings, the best entry is the one that addresses who wants what in this proceeding, not the one that sounds most like the court's language.

RULE OF LAW: A statement of the general principle of law that the case illustrates (e.g., "An acceptance that varies any term of the offer is considered a rejection and counteroffer").

Determining the rule of law of a case is a procedure similar to determining the issue of the case. Avoid being fooled by red herrings; there may be a few rules of law mentioned in the case excerpt, but usually only one is *the* rule with which the casebook editor is concerned. The techniques used to locate the issue, described below, may also be utilized to find the rule of law. Generally, your best guide is simply the chapter heading. It is a clue to the point the casebook editor seeks to make and should be kept in mind when reading every case in the respective section.

FACTS: A synopsis of only the essential facts of the case, i.e., those bearing upon or leading up to the issue.

The facts entry should be a short statement of the events and transactions that led one party to initiate legal proceedings against another in the first place. While some cases conveniently state the salient facts at the beginning of the decision, in other instances they will have to be culled from hiding places throughout the text, even from concurring and dissenting opinions. Some of the "facts" will often be in dispute and should be so noted. Conflicting evidence may be briefly pointed up. "Hard" facts must be included. Both must be *relevant* in order to be listed in the facts entry. It is impossible to tell what is relevant until the entire case is read, as the ultimate determination of the rights and liabilities of the parties may turn on something buried deep in the opinion.

Generally, the facts entry should not be longer than three to five *short* sentences.

It is often helpful to identify the role played by a party in a given context. For example, in a construction contract case the identification of a party as the "contractor" or "builder" alleviates the need to tell that that party was the one who was supposed to have built the house.

It is always helpful, and a good general practice, to identify the "plaintiff" and the "defendant." This may seem elementary and uncomplicated, but, especially in view of the creative editing practiced by some casebook editors, it is sometimes a difficult or even impossible task. Bear in mind that the *party presently* seeking something from this court may not be the plaintiff, and that sometimes only the cross-claim of a defendant is treated in the excerpt. Confusing or misaligning the parties can ruin your analysis and understanding of the case.

ISSUE: A statement of the general legal question answered by or illustrated in the case. For clarity, the issue is best put in the form of a question capable of a "yes" or "no" answer. In reality, the issue is simply the Rule of Law put in the form of a question (e.g., "May an offer be accepted by performance?").

The major problem presented in discerning what is *the* issue in the case is that an opinion usually purports to raise and answer several questions. However, except for rare cases, only one such question is really the issue in the case. Collateral issues not necessary to the resolution of the matter in controversy are handled by the court by language known as *"obiter dictum"* or merely *"dictum."* While dicta may be included later in the brief, they have no place under the issue heading.

To find the issue, ask *who wants what* and then go on to ask *why did that party succeed or fail in getting it*. Once this is determined, the "why" should be turned into a question.

The complexity of the issues in the cases will vary, but in all cases a single-sentence question should sum up the issue. *In a few cases,* there will be two, or even more rarely, three issues of equal importance to the resolution of the case. Each should be expressed in a single-sentence question.

Since many issues are resolved by a court in coming to a final disposition of a case, the casebook editor will reproduce the portion of the opinion containing the issue or issues most relevant to the area of law under scrutiny. A noted law professor gave this advice: "Close the book; look at the title on the cover." Chances are, if it is Property, you need not concern yourself with whether, for example, the federal government's treatment of the plaintiff's land really raises a federal question sufficient to support jurisdiction on this ground in federal court.

The same rule applies to chapter headings designating sub-areas within the subjects. They tip you off as to what the text is designed to teach. The cases are arranged in a casebook to show a progression or development of the law, so that the preceding cases may also help.

It is also most important to remember to *read the notes and questions* at the end of a case to determine what the editors wanted you to have gleaned from it.

HOLDING AND DECISION: This section should succinctly explain the rationale of the court in arriving at its decision. In capsulizing the "reasoning" of the court, it should always include an application of the general rule or rules of law to the specific facts of the case. Hidden justifications come to light in this entry; the reasons for the state of the law, the public policies, the biases and prejudices, those considerations that influence the justices' thinking and, ultimately, the outcome of the case. At the end, there should be a short indication of the disposition or procedural resolution of the case (e.g., "Decision of the trial court for Mr. Smith (P) reversed").

The foregoing format is designed to help you "digest" the reams of case material with which you will be faced in your law school career. Once mastered by practice, it will place at your fingertips the information the authors of your casebooks have sought to impart to you in case-by-case illustration and analysis.

B. Be as Economical as Possible in Briefing Cases

Once armed with a format that encourages succinctness, it is as important to be economical with regard to the time spent on the actual reading of the case as it is to be economical in the writing of the brief itself. This does not mean "skimming" a case. Rather, it means reading the case with an "eye" trained to recognize into which "section" of your brief a particular passage or line fits and having a system for quickly and precisely marking the case so that the passages fitting any one particular part of

the brief can be easily identified and brought together in a concise and accurate manner when the brief is actually written.

It is of no use to simply repeat everything in the opinion of the court; record only enough information to trigger your recollection of what the court said. Nevertheless, an accurate statement of the "law of the case," i.e., the legal principle applied to the facts, is absolutely essential to class preparation and to learning the law under the case method.

To that end, it is important to develop a "shorthand" that you can use to make margin notations. These notations will tell you at a glance in which section of the brief you will be placing that particular passage or portion of the opinion.

Some students prefer to underline all the salient portions of the opinion (with a pencil or colored underliner marker), making marginal notations as they go along. Others prefer the color-coded method of underlining, utilizing different colors of markers to underline the salient portions of the case, each separate color being used to represent a different section of the brief. For example, blue underlining could be used for passages relating to the rule of law, yellow for those relating to the issue, and green for those relating to the holding and decision, etc. While it has its advocates, the color-coded method can be confusing and time-consuming (all that time spent on changing colored markers). Furthermore, it can interfere with the continuity and concentration many students deem essential to the reading of a case for maximum comprehension. In the end, however, it is a matter of personal preference and style. Just remember, whatever method you use, underlining must be used sparingly or its value is lost.

If you take the marginal notation route, an efficient and easy method is to go along underlining the key portions of the case and placing in the margin alongside them the following "markers" to indicate where a particular passage or line "belongs" in the brief you will write:

N   (NATURE OF CASE)
RL   (RULE OF LAW)
I   (ISSUE)
HL   (HOLDING AND DECISION, relates to
         the RULE OF LAW behind the decision)
HR   (HOLDING AND DECISION, gives the
         RATIONALE or reasoning behind the
         decision)
HA   (HOLDING AND DECISION, APPLIES
         the general principle(s) of law to the facts
         of the case to arrive at the decision)

Remember that a particular passage may well contain information necessary to more than one part of your brief, in which case you simply note that in the margin. If you are using the color-coded underlining method instead of margin notation, simply make asterisks or checks in the margin next to the passage in question in the colors that indicate the additional sections of the brief where it might be utilized.

The economy of utilizing "shorthand" in marking cases for briefing can be maintained in the actual brief writing process itself by utilizing "law student shorthand" within the brief. There are many commonly used words and phrases for which abbreviations can be substituted in your briefs (and in your class notes also). You can develop abbreviations that are personal to you and which will save you a lot of time. A reference list of briefing abbreviations can be found on page xii of this book.

C. Use Both the Briefing Process and the Brief as a Learning Tool

Now that you have a format and the tools for briefing cases efficiently, the most important thing is to make the time spent in briefing profitable to you and to make the most advantageous use of the briefs you create. Of course, the briefs are invaluable for classroom reference when you are called upon to explain or analyze a particular case. However, they are also useful in reviewing for exams. A quick glance at the fact summary should bring the case to mind, and a rereading of the rule of law should enable you to go over the underlying legal concept in your mind, how it was applied in that particular case, and how it might apply in other factual settings.

As to the value to be derived from engaging in the briefing process itself, there is an immediate benefit that arises from being forced to sift through the essential facts and reasoning from the court's opinion and to succinctly express them in your own words in your brief. The process ensures that you understand the case and the point that it illustrates, and that means you will be ready to absorb further analysis and information brought forth in class. It also ensures you will have something to say when called upon in class. The briefing process helps develop a mental agility for getting to the *gist* of a case and for identifying, expounding on, and applying the legal concepts and issues found there. The briefing process is the mental process on which you must rely in taking law school examinations; it is also the mental process upon which a lawyer relies in serving his clients and in making his living.

Abbreviations for Briefs

acceptance	acp	offer	O
affirmed	aff	offeree	OE
answer	ans	offeror	OR
assumption of risk	a/r	ordinance	ord
attorney	atty	pain and suffering	p/s
beyond a reasonable doubt	b/r/d	parol evidence	p/e
bona fide purchaser	BFP	plaintiff	P
breach of contract	br/k	prima facie	p/f
cause of action	c/a	probable cause	p/c
common law	c/l	proximate cause	px/c
Constitution	Con	real property	r/p
constitutional	con	reasonable doubt	r/d
contract	K	reasonable man	r/m
contributory negligence	c/n	rebuttable presumption	rb/p
cross	x	remanded	rem
cross-complaint	x/c	res ipsa loquitur	RIL
cross-examination	x/ex	respondeat superior	r/s
cruel and unusual punishment	c/u/p	Restatement	RS
defendant	D	reversed	rev
dismissed	dis	Rule Against Perpetuities	RAP
double jeopardy	d/j	search and seizure	s/s
due process	d/p	search warrant	s/w
equal protection	e/p	self-defense	s/d
equity	eq	specific performance	s/p
evidence	ev	statute of limitations	S/L
exclude	exc	statute of frauds	S/F
exclusionary rule	exc/r	statute	S
felony	f/n	summary judgment	s/j
freedom of speech	f/s	tenancy in common	t/c
good faith	g/f	tenancy at will	t/w
habeas corpus	h/c	tenant	t
hearsay	hr	third party	TP
husband	H	third party beneficiary	TPB
in loco parentis	ILP	transferred intent	TI
injunction	inj	unconscionable	uncon
inter vivos	I/v	unconstitutional	unconst
joint tenancy	j/t	undue influence	u/e
judgment	judgt	Uniform Commercial Code	UCC
jurisdiction	jur	unilateral	uni
last clear chance	LCC	vendee	VE
long-arm statute	LAS	vendor	VR
majority view	maj	versus	v
meeting of minds	MOM	void for vagueness	VFV
minority view	min	weight of the evidence	w/e
Miranda warnings	Mir/w	weight of authority	w/a
Miranda rule	Mir/r	wife	W
negligence	neg	with	w/
notice	ntc	within	w/i
nuisance	nus	without prejudice	w/o/p
obligation	ob	without	w/o
obscene	obs	wrongful death	wr/d

Table of Cases

The Federal Judicial Power

Quick Reference Rules of Law

Marbury v. Madison

Justice (P) v. Secretary of State (D)

5 U.S. (1 Cranch) 137 (1803).

NATURE OF CASE: Writ of mandamus to compel delivery of commission.

FACT SUMMARY: President Jefferson's Secretary of State, Madison (D), refused to deliver a commission granted to Marbury (P) by former President Adams.

🏛 RULE OF LAW
The Supreme Court has the power, implied from Article VI, § 2 of the Constitution, to review acts of Congress and if they are found repugnant to the Constitution, to declare them void.

FACTS: [On March 2, 1801, the outgoing President of the United States, John Adams, named forty-two justices of the peace for the District of Columbia under the Organic Act passed the same day by Congress. William Marbury (P) was one of the justices named. The commissions of Marbury (P) and other named justices were signed by Adams on his last day in office, March 3, and signed and sealed by the Acting Secretary of State, John Marshall. However, the formal commissions were not delivered by the end of the day. The new President, Thomas Jefferson, treated those appointments that were not formalized by delivery of the papers of commission prior to Adams leaving office as a nullity. Marbury (P) and other affected colleagues brought this writ of mandamus to the Supreme Court to compel Jefferson's Secretary of State, James Madison (D), to deliver the commissions.] John Marshall, the Chief Justice of the Supreme Court, delivered the opinion.

ISSUE: Does the Constitution give the Supreme Court the authority to review acts of Congress and declare them, if repugnant to the Constitution, to be void?

HOLDING AND DECISION: (Marshall, C.J.) Yes. The Supreme Court has the power, implied from Article VI, § 2 of the Constitution, to review acts of Congress and if they are found repugnant to the Constitution, to declare them void. The government of the United States is a government of laws, not of men. The President, bound by these laws, is given certain political powers by the Constitution, laws that he may use at his discretion. To aid him in his duties, he is authorized to appoint certain officers to carry out his orders. Their acts as officers are his acts and are never subject to examination by the courts. However, where these officers are given by law specific duties on which individual rights depend, any individual injured by breach of such duty may resort to his country's laws for a remedy. Here, Marbury (P) had a right to the commission, and Madison's (D) refusal to deliver it violated that right. The present case is clearly one for mandamus. However, should the Supreme Court be the court to issue it? The Judiciary Act of 1789 established and authorized United States courts to issue writs of mandamus to courts or persons holding office under U.S. authority. Secretary of State Madison (D) comes within the Act. If the Supreme Court is powerless to issue the writ of mandamus to him, it must be because the Act is unconstitutional. Article III of the Constitution provides that the Supreme Court shall have original jurisdiction in all cases affecting ambassadors, other public ministers and consuls, and where a state is a party. In all other cases, the Supreme Court shall have appellate jurisdiction. Marbury (P) urged that since Article III contains no restrictive words, the power to assign original jurisdiction to the courts remains in the legislature. But if Congress is allowed to distribute the original and appellate jurisdiction of the Supreme Court, as in the Judiciary Act, then the constitutional grant of Article III is form without substance. But no clause in the Constitution is presumed to be without effect. For the Court to issue a mandamus, it must be an exercise of appellate jurisdiction. The grant of appellate jurisdiction is the power to revise and correct proceedings already instituted; it does not create the cause. To issue a writ of mandamus ordering an executive officer to deliver a paper is to create the original action for that paper. This would be an unconstitutional exercise of original jurisdiction beyond the power of the court. It is the province and duty of the judicial department to say what the law is. And any law, including acts of the legislature, which is repugnant to the Constitution is void.

▶ ANALYSIS

Judicial review of legislative acts was a controversial subject even before the Constitution was ratified and adopted. Alexander Hamilton upheld the theory of judicial review in the Federalist Papers. He argued that the judiciary, being the most vulnerable branch of the government, was designed to be an intermediary between the people and the legislature. Since the interpretation of laws was the responsibility of the judiciary, and the Constitution the supreme law of the land, any conflict between legislative acts and the Constitution were to be resolved by the court in favor of the Constitution. But other authorities have attacked this position. In the case of *Eakin v. Raub*, Justice Gibson dissented, stating that the judiciary's function was limited to interpreting the laws and should not extend to scrutinizing the legislature's authority to enact them. Judge Learned Hand felt that judicial review was inconsistent with the separation of powers. But history has supported the authority of judicial review of legislative acts. The

Continued on next page.

United States survives on a tripartite government. Theoretically, the three branches should be strong enough to check and balance the others. To limit the judiciary to the passive task of interpretation would be to limit its strength in the tripartite structure. *Marbury* served to buttress the judiciary branch making it equal to the executive and legislative branches.

■■■

Quicknotes

JUDICIAL REVIEW The authority of the courts to review decisions, actions or omissions committed by another agency or branch of government.

■■■

District of Columbia v. Heller

District of Columbia (D) v. Would-be handgun owner (P)

128 S. Ct. 2783 (2008).

NATURE OF CASE: Review of federal appeals court judgment.

FACT SUMMARY: The District of Columbia (D) appealed to the Supreme Court after a federal appeals court ruled that the District's (D) gun control laws were unconstitutional.

🏛 RULE OF LAW
The D.C. Code's (1) general bar against the registration of handguns, (2) prohibition against carrying a pistol without a license, and (3) requirement that all lawful firearms to be kept unloaded and either disassembled or trigger locked violate rights of individuals under the U.S. Constitution's Second Amendment, which permits individuals to keep handguns and other firearms for private use in their homes, even though they are not affiliated with any state-regulated militia.

FACTS: The District of Columbia (D) passed a law that barred the registration of handguns, requiring licenses for all pistols and mandating that all legal firearms must be kept unloaded and disassembled or trigger locked. A group of private gun owners, represented in this case by Dick Heller (P), sued the District (D). They claimed that the laws violated their right to bear arms under the Second Amendment of the U.S. Constitution. A federal trial court refused to grant the plaintiffs relief, holding that the Second Amendment applies only to regulated militias and not to private gun ownership. But the U.S. Court of Appeals for the District of Columbia Circuit disagreed and held that the Second Amendment does protect private gun owners. The District (D) appealed, arguing that the Second Amendment should not apply to D.C. because it is a federal enclave rather than a state, and that the D.C. legislation regulates, but does not prohibit, gun ownership. Heller (P) disagreed on the merits and urged the Court to review the case in order to clearly define the relationship between federal gun control laws and the Second Amendment.

ISSUE: Do the D.C. Code's (1) general bar against the registration of handguns, (2) prohibition against carrying a pistol without a license, and (3) requirement that all lawful firearms to be kept unloaded and either disassembled or trigger locked violate rights of individuals under the U.S. Constitution's Second Amendment to keep handguns and other firearms for private use in their homes, even though they are not affiliated with any state-regulated militia?

HOLDING AND DECISION: (Scalia, J.) Yes. The D.C. Code's (1) general bar against the registration of handguns, (2) prohibition against carrying a pistol without a license, and (3) requirement that all lawful firearms to be kept unloaded and either disassembled or trigger locked violate

rights of individuals under the U.S. Constitution's Second Amendment, which permits individuals to keep handguns and other firearms for private use in their homes, even though they are not affiliated with any state-regulated militia. The Second Amendment protects an individual right to possess a firearm unconnected with service in a militia, and to use that firearm for traditionally lawful purposes, such as self-defense within the home. The text of the Second Amendment, as well as applicable language in state constitutions adopted soon after the Second Amendment, support that conclusion. The operative clause of the Second Amendment— "the right of the people to keep and bear Arms, shall not be infringed"—is controlling and refers to a pre-existing right of individuals to possess and carry personal weapons for self-defense and intrinsically for defense against tyranny. In addition, the prefatory clause, which announces a purpose of a "well regulated Militia, being necessary to the security of a free State," is consistent with the meaning of the operative clause and refers to a well-trained citizen militia, which "comprised all males physically capable of acting in concert for the common defense," as being necessary to the security of a free people. Finally, none of the Supreme Court's precedents forecloses the Court's interpretation.

DISSENT: (Stevens, J.) The Second Amendment protects only the rights of individuals to bear arms as part of a well-regulated state militia, not for other purposes, even if they are lawful.

DISSENT: (Breyer, J.) Even if possession were to be allowed for other reasons, any law regulating the use of firearms would have to be "unreasonable or inappropriate" to violate the Second Amendment. The D.C. laws at issue in this case were both reasonable and appropriate.

▶ ANALYSIS

This is a landmark case since it is the first Supreme Court case in United States history to address directly whether the right to keep and bear arms is a right of individuals, in addition to being a collective right that applies only to state-regulated militias. Robert A. Levy, a senior fellow at the Cato Institute, originally began the case by soliciting plaintiffs for a planned Second Amendment lawsuit that he would personally finance. He was a constitutional scholar with an academic interest in the subject. Shelly Parker, Tom Palmer, Gillian St. Lawrence, Tracey Ambeau, George Lyon and Dick Heller were the original plaintiffs. All plaintiffs but Heller were found to not have standing by the court of appeals, since Heller was the only plaintiff who had been denied a permit for a handgun.

■━■

Ex parte McCardle

Federal government (P) v. Newspaper editor (D)

74 U.S. 506 (1868).

NATURE OF CASE: Appeal from denial of habeas corpus.

FACT SUMMARY: McCardle (D) appealed from a denial of habeas corpus to the Supreme Court, but Congress passed an act forbidding the Court jurisdiction.

🏛 RULE OF LAW
Although the Supreme Court derives its appellate jurisdiction from the Constitution, the Constitution also gives Congress the express power to make exceptions to that appellate jurisdiction.

FACTS: After the Civil War, Congress imposed military government on many former Confederate states under authority of the Civil War Reconstruction Acts. McCardle (D), a Mississippi newspaper editor, was held in military custody on charges of publishing libelous and incendiary articles. McCardle (D) brought a habeas corpus writ based on a congressional act passed in 1867. The act authorized federal courts to grant habeas corpus to persons held in violation of constitutional rights, and also gave authority for appeals to the Supreme Court. The circuit court denied McCardle's (D) habeas corpus writ, but the Supreme Court sustained jurisdiction for an appeal on the merits. However, after arguments were heard, Congress passed an act on March 12, 1868 that repealed that much of the 1867 act, which allowed an appeal to the Supreme Court from the circuit court and the exercise by the Supreme Court by jurisdiction on any such appeals, past or present.

ISSUE: Does Congress have the power, under the Constitution, to make exceptions to the appellate jurisdiction of the Supreme Court?

HOLDING AND DECISION: (Chase, C.J.) Yes. Although the Supreme Court derives its appellate jurisdiction from the Constitution, the Constitution also gives Congress the express power to make exceptions to that appellate jurisdiction. The appellate jurisdiction of the Supreme Court is not derived from acts of Congress, but is conferred by the Constitution with such exceptions and regulations as Congress shall make. And though Congress has affirmatively described in the Act of 1789 the regulations governing the exercise of the Supreme Court's appellate jurisdiction, with the implication that any exercise of that jurisdiction not within the purview of the Act would be negated, the exception to the appellate jurisdiction in the present case is not to be inferred from such affirmations. The exceptions in this case are express. That part of the 1867 Act giving the court appellate jurisdiction in habeas corpus cases is expressly repealed. The effect is to take away the court's jurisdiction, dismissing the cause. When a legislative act is repealed, it is as if it had never existed except to transactions past and closed. Thus, no judgment can be rendered in a suit after repeal of the act under which it was brought. But this does not deny forever the court's appellate power in habeas corpus cases. The Act of 1868 affects only such appeals from circuit courts brought under the Act of 1867.

▶ ANALYSIS

McCardle is clearly an example of judicial restraint. The authority of Congress to control the jurisdiction of the Supreme Court is not unlimited. This was proved in *Marbury v. Madison*, 5 U.S. (1 Cranch) 137 (1803), where the Court, faced with an extension by Congress of its original jurisdiction as granted under the Constitution, refused to accept the constitutionality of the congressional act. While this specifically limited the Supreme Court's original jurisdiction, it provided Marshall with the ideal arena to assert the doctrine of judicial review. But in *McCardle*, the Court backed away from confrontation with Congress due to current-day political crises that followed the Civil War. Thereafter, the Court sought to limit congressional power by the power of judicial review announced in *Marbury*. The Court held on several occasions that certain congressional attempts to delimit its jurisdiction were unconstitutional attempts to invade the judicial province. Such congressional actions were considered a violation of the separation of powers. Today, it is doubtful that *McCardle* would be sustained.

■▬■

Quicknotes

HABEAS CORPUS A proceeding in which a defendant brings a writ to compel a judicial determination of whether he is lawfully being held in custody.

■▬■

United States v. Klein

Parties not identified.

80 U.S. 128 (1871).

NATURE OF CASE: Appeal of compensation awarded for property destroyed by the Union army during the Civil War.

FACT SUMMARY: Klein was awarded compensation for property destroyed by the Union army because a presidential pardon he received presumptively showed that he had been loyal, loyalty being a condition of receiving such an award. On appeal, he challenged a congressional enactment that directed federal courts to find that a pardon was proof of disloyalty and that denied the court jurisdiction over the claim.

🏛 RULE OF LAW
A statute violates the separation of powers by commanding a court to draw a certain conclusion from evidence before it and by directing the court to dismiss an appeal for lack of jurisdiction when it encounters such evidence.

FACTS: In 1863, Congress passed a law that provided that individuals whose property was seized during the Civil War could recover the property or be compensated for it upon proof that they had been loyal during the war. The Supreme Court subsequently held that a presidential pardon was proof of such loyalty. [Klein received a presidential pardon for his role in the Civil War and received a compensatory award. While the government appealed Klein's award], Congress enacted a law that provided that a pardon without an express disclaimer of guilt was proof of disloyalty. The law also provided that, upon proof of a pardon, the court's jurisdiction would cease, and directed the court to dismiss the claim. [Klein contended that this law was an unconstitutional violation of the separation of powers.]

ISSUE: Does a statute violate the separation of powers by commanding a court to draw a certain conclusion from evidence before it and by directing the court to dismiss an appeal for lack of jurisdiction when it encounters such evidence?

HOLDING AND DECISION: (Chase, C.J.) Yes. This law does not regulate the courts' appellate power as permitted by the Constitution. If the law simply denied the right of appeal in a certain class of cases, it would be constitutional. However, under the statute, the court does have jurisdiction up to the point where there is proof of a pardon. At that point, the statute requires the court to declare that its jurisdiction has ceased and to dismiss the case. This directs the court how to decide a case, and allows the legislative branch to dictate to the judicial branch rules of decision. By attempting to dictate to the courts how they must decide a particular case, Congress has violated the separation of powers, given that it already granted jurisdiction over such cases to the courts. In addition, the law also violates the separation of powers with regard to the executive branch by attempting to impair the effect of an executive pardon.

▶ ANALYSIS

The Supreme Court distinguished the *Klein* holding in *Robertson v. Seattle Audubon Society*, 503 U.S. 429 (1992). According to the casebook author, "The [*Robertson*] Court said that *Klein* applies in a situation where Congress directs the judiciary as to decision making under an existing law and does not apply when Congress adopts a new law."

■==■

Quicknotes

SEPARATION OF POWERS The system of checks and balances preventing one branch of government from infringing upon exercising the powers of another branch of government.

■==■

Plaut v. Spendthrift Farm, Inc.

Individual representing a class (P) v. Corporation (D)

514 U.S. 211 (1995).

NATURE OF CASE: Appeal from a judgment dismissing a motion to reinstate a previously dismissed class action for violation of federal securities law.

FACT SUMMARY: After Congress amended the Securities Exchange Act, changing the limitations periods established by case precedent and mandating reinstatement of cases dismissed as time barred, the district court denied Plaut's (P) motion to reinstate the final judgment in his case on the ground that the amendment was unconstitutional.

RULE OF LAW
Congress may not retroactively command the federal courts to reopen final judgments without violating the separation of powers doctrine.

FACTS: Plaut (P) represented the class in an action alleging that Spendthrift Farm (D) violated § 10(b) of the Securities Exchange Act of 1934 through the use of fraud and deceit in the sale of stock. The district court found that the claims were untimely under the limitations periods established in *Lampf, Pleva, Lipkind, Prupis & Petigrow v. Gilbertson*, 501 U.S. 350 (1991). When Plaut's (P) claims were dismissed with prejudice, no appeal was filed, and the judgment became final. Subsequently, Congress amended the Securities Exchange Act, changing the limitations period and mandating reinstatement of any action dismissed as time barred subsequent to *Lampf*. Based on this amendment, Plaut (P) moved to reinstate. The district court denied the motion, finding the amendment unconstitutional. The court of appeals affirmed. Plaut (P) appealed.

ISSUE: May Congress retroactively command the federal courts to reopen final judgments without violating the separation of powers doctrine?

HOLDING AND DECISION: (Scalia, J.) No. Congress may not retroactively command the federal courts to reopen final judgments without violating the separation of powers doctrine. Article III of the Constitution establishes a "judicial department" with the "province and duty to say what the law is" in particular cases and controversies. Judicial decisions in the period immediately following the ratification of the Constitution confirm the understanding that it forbade interference with the final judgments of courts. History shows that the Framers crafted this charter of the judicial department with an express understanding that it gives the federal judiciary the power not merely to rule on cases, but to decide them subject to review only by superior courts in the Article III hierarchy. With § 27A(b),

Congress has exceeded its authority by requiring the federal courts to exercise "the Judicial Power of the United States" in a manner repugnant to the text, structure and traditions of Article III. Thus, the judgment of the court of appeals is affirmed.

ANALYSIS

The Framers of the Constitution, prompted by a crescendo of legislative interference with private judgments of the courts, felt a sharp necessity to separate the legislative from the judicial power. Before and during the debates on ratification, Madison, Jefferson, and Hamilton each wrote of the factional disorders and disarray that the system of legislative equity had produced in the years before the framing. Each believed that the separation of the legislative from the judicial power in the new Constitution would solve the problems.

■=■

Quicknotes

SEPARATION OF POWERS The system of checks and balances preventing one branch of government from infringing upon exercising the powers of another branch of government.

■=■

Allen v. Wright

Parties not identified.

468 U.S. 737 (1984).

NATURE OF CASE: Appeal of order denying tax-exempt status to racially discriminatory private schools.

FACT SUMMARY: Parents (P) of black schoolchildren filed an action to compel the IRS (D) to deny tax-exempt status to racially discriminatory private schools, in conformity with the law.

🏛 RULE OF LAW
One does not have standing to sue in federal court unless he can allege the violation of a right personal to him.

FACTS: Parents of black schoolchildren brought an action to compel the IRS (D) to deny tax-exempt status to private schools that discriminate, an illegal practice. It was alleged that the practice promoted segregated schools and made desegregation more difficult. The court of appeals held in favor of the parents (P).

ISSUE: Does one have standing to sue in federal court if he cannot allege a violation of a right personal to him?

HOLDING AND DECISION: (O'Connor, J.) No. One does not have standing to sue in federal court if he cannot allege a violation of a right personal to him. Federal courts are not designed to air generalized grievances. A plaintiff must allege injury traceable to a defendant's conduct likely to be redressed by the requested relief. It has long been held that the "right" to have the Government act in accordance with the law will not confer standing; something more personal is required. To do this would constitute an excessive intrusion of the judiciary into the executive branch of government. In the area in question, a plaintiff must show that he himself has been denied equal treatment in order to have standing. This has not been shown here. The allegation that the conduct of the IRS (D) promotes segregation is purely speculative. No allegation is made that withdrawal of the funds would make a difference in public school integration. Since no personal injury traceable to the IRS's (D) conduct has been alleged, no standing exists.

DISSENT: (Stevens, J.) The plaintiffs allege that the conduct of the IRS (D) promotes the exodus of white children who would otherwise attend integrated schools. This is a sufficient concrete injury to confer standing.

▶ ANALYSIS

The requirements of standing are based on both textual and nontextual concerns. The "case or controversy" requirement is a basis for standing requirements. Also forming a basis are prudential concerns such as not unnecessarily interfering with other branches.

■■■

Quicknotes

STANDING The right to commence suit against another party because of a personal stake in the resolution of the controversy.

■■■

Massachusetts v. Environmental Protection Agency

State (P) v. Federal agency (D)

127 S. Ct. 1438 (2007).

NATURE OF CASE: Appeal challenging a federal agency's alleged refusal to enforce the federal Clean Air Act against motor-vehicle emissions.

FACT SUMMARY: A state and several other parties challenged the Environmental Protection Agency's (EPA) (D) failure to enforce the Clean Air Act against motor-vehicle emissions.

🏛 RULE OF LAW
A plaintiff has standing if it demonstrates a concrete injury that is both fairly traceable to the defendant and redressable by judicial relief.

FACTS: The Environmental Protection Agency (EPA) (D) refused to enforce the Clean Air Act against motor-vehicle emissions. Massachusetts (P) and several other parties appealed the EPA's (D) refusal [by petitioning the Court of Appeals for the District of Columbia Circuit to review the Agency's (D) decision. The appellate court did not affirmatively hold that Massachusetts (P) had standing, but a majority of that court did uphold the EPA's (D) decision. Massachusetts (P) petitioned the Supreme Court for further review.]

ISSUE: Does a plaintiff have standing if it demonstrates a concrete injury that is both fairly traceable to the defendant and redressable by judicial relief?

HOLDING AND DECISION: (Stevens, J.) Yes. A plaintiff has standing if it demonstrates a concrete injury that is both fairly traceable to the defendant and redressable by judicial relief. The jurisdiction of federal courts is limited to "cases" and "controversies," and Massachusetts (P) has satisfied that threshold hurdle here. As a state, Massachusetts (P) proceeds in its quasi-sovereign capacity, and caselaw supports applying different standards of justiciability for such litigants. The particularized injury for Massachusetts (P) in this case is the damage to the State's (P) coastline that will, and will continue to, occur. Further, the injury to that coastline is fairly traceable to the EPA's (D) inaction; even small effects on an injury in fact satisfy the causation requirement in federal standing analysis. Finally, Massachusetts's (P) injury can be redressed judicially, even though the outcome of a judicial remedy might be delayed while new motor-vehicle emissions are implemented. Accordingly, Massachusetts (P) has standing. [Reversed and remanded.]

DISSENT: (Roberts, C.J.) Any redress of the injuries in this case should be left to the political branches. Relaxing standing requirements for a state exists nowhere in this Court's precedents. Under normal standing analysis, Massachusetts's (P) injury fails to satisfy the requirement of a "concrete and particularized" injury; injuries to "humanity at large" do not suffice. Also, any causal connection between the EPA's (D) inaction and damage to the coastlines is so tenuous and speculative that it cannot support a finding of standing. Further, Massachusetts (P) cannot satisfy the redressability factor because emissions from other countries are likely to dwarf any reduction in emissions that might result from the EPA's (D) enforcement of the Clean Air Act. Diluting the appropriate standing requirements only permits courts to encroach upon authority that is properly committed to Congress and the President.

▶ ANALYSIS

The three factors in the standing analysis announced by *Lujan v. Defenders of Wildlife*, 504 U.S. 555 (1992), are very clear: the complaining party must have suffered (1) an injury in fact (2) that is fairly traceable to the defendant and (3) that can be redressed by judicial relief. As the Court's 5-4 decision in this case shows, however, what is not so clear is how those three factors should apply to any specific dispute. The fundamental importance of justiciability, as Chief Justice Roberts notes in dissent, resides in the most basic questions about the kinds of disputes that courts should—and should not—hear.

■=■

Quicknotes

REDRESSABILITY Requirement that in order for a court to hear a case there must be an injury that is redressable or capable of being remedied.

■=■

Singleton v. Wulff

State health official (D) v. Physician (P)

428 U.S. 106 (1976).

NATURE OF CASE: Action for declaration of the unconstitutionality of a state statute that excludes abortions that are not "medically indicated" from the purposes for which Medicaid benefits are available to needy persons.

FACT SUMMARY: Physicians brought suit on behalf of welfare patients who were eligible for Medicaid payments, challenging a state statute that excluded abortions that were not "medically indicated" from the purposes for which Medicaid benefits were available to needy persons.

🏛 RULE OF LAW
A litigant has standing to bring suit where the litigant's relationship with a third party whose rights he wishes to assert is very close and where there are genuine obstacles to the third party's suing on its own behalf.

FACTS: Missouri enacted a statute that excluded abortions that were not "medically indicated" from the purposes for which Medicaid benefits were available to needy persons. Wulff (P) and another plaintiff were Missouri-licensed physicians who performed nonmedically indicated abortions for needy women who were eligible for Medicaid payments. The physicians brought suit challenging the statute as an unconstitutional interference with the decision to have an abortion. The physicians' standing to maintain the suit was challenged.

ISSUE: Does a litigant have standing to bring suit where the litigant's relationship with a third party whose rights he wishes to assert is very close and where there are genuine obstacles to the third party's suing on its own behalf?

HOLDING AND DECISION: (Blackmun, J.) Yes. A litigant has standing to bring suit where the litigant's relationship with a third party whose rights he wishes to assert is very close and where there are genuine obstacles to the third party's suing on its own behalf. As a preliminary matter, the physicians alleged "injury in fact," i.e., a sufficiently concrete interest in the outcome of their suit to make it a case or controversy subject to the district court's Article III jurisdiction. If Wulff (P) and the other physician were to prevail in their suit to remove the statutory limitation on reimbursable abortions, they would benefit by receiving payment for the abortions and the state would be out of pocket by the amount of the payments. Second, as a prudential matter, the physicians were proper proponents of the particular rights on which they based their suit. Though ordinarily one may not claim standing to vindicate the constitutional rights of some third party, here the underlying justification for that rule is absent. A woman cannot safely secure an abortion without a physician's aid, and a poor woman cannot easily secure an abortion without the physician's being paid by the state. Aside from the woman herself, the physician is uniquely qualified, by virtue of his confidential, professional relationship with her, to litigate the constitutionality of the state's interference with, or discrimination against, the abortion decision. Moreover, there are genuine obstacles to the woman's assertion of her own rights, in that the desire to protect her privacy may deter her from herself bringing suit, and because her claim will soon become at least technically moot if her indigency forces her to forgo the abortion.

▶ ANALYSIS

Generally, a plaintiff must state that s(he) has suffered an injury, not that a third party has suffered an injury. However, the Supreme Court in *Singleton* recognized exceptions to the general rule. The author of the casebook notes that there is a third exception to the third-party standing rule: "In addition to the two exceptions discussed in *Singleton*, there is a third exception: the overbreadth doctrine. A defendant to whom a law constitutionally may be applied may challenge a law as regulating substantially more speech than the Constitution allows to be regulated."

Quicknotes

STANDING The right to commence suit against another party because of a personal stake in the resolution of the controversy.

Elk Grove Unified School Dist. v. Newdow

School district (D) v. Parent (P)

542 U.S. 1, 124 S. Ct. 2301 (2004).

NATURE OF CASE: Constitutional challenge to a state law requiring teachers to lead willing students in recitation of the Pledge of Allegiance.

FACT SUMMARY: The father (P) of a California kindergarten student objected to the School District's (D) rule requiring all teachers to lead students in recitation of the Pledge of Allegiance at the beginning of each school day. The father (P) shared physical custody of the student with the student's mother, but the mother was judicially declared to have sole legal custody, which included the right to make all final decisions relating to the education of her daughter. Nevertheless, the father (P) sued the School District, claiming that the School District's (D) policy violated his daughter's First Amendment rights.

🏛 RULE OF LAW
A parent with uncertain custody status lacks standing to sue in federal courts on behalf of his or her child because the federal courts will refrain from intervention in a case involving distinct domestic relations questions.

FACTS: Michael Newdow (P), an atheist, objected to the Elk Grove School District's (D) requirement that each elementary school teacher lead her students in a daily recitation of the Pledge of Allegiance. Newdow's (P) objection arose because of the words "under God" in the Pledge. Newdow (P) claimed that this recitation constituted forced religious indoctrination of his kindergartener daughter in violation of her First Amendment rights. Newdow (P) sued individually and as his daughter's "next friend." Newdow (P), however, shared physical custody of his daughter with his daughter's mother, but the mother was judicially declared under state law to be final decision-maker in all matters related to the daughter's education. The Court of Appeals for the Ninth Circuit, in its first opinion, held that the Newdow (P) had standing to sue, and that both the School District's (D) policy and the 1954 Act, through which the words "under God" were inserted into the Pledge of Allegiance, violated the Establishment Clause of the First Amendment. After that decision, the daughter's mother sought to intervene or have the case dismissed, arguing that she had legal custody of the child and that she alone made the final decisions regarding the child's education. The mother also claimed that the daughter was a Christian and did not object to the Pledge of Allegiance on religious grounds, contrary to Newdow's (P) assertions. The court then held, in a second opinion, that the fact that the mother had sole legal custody of her daughter did not deprive Newdow (P) of standing to sue as a noncustodial parent. The Supreme Court granted certiorari to decide the preliminary issue of standing and the First Amendment issue.

ISSUE: Does a parent with uncertain custody status lack standing to sue in federal courts on behalf of his or her child?

HOLDING AND DECISION: (Stevens, J.) Yes. A parent with uncertain custody status lacks standing to sue in federal courts on behalf of his or her child because the federal courts will refrain from intervention in a case involving distinct domestic relations questions. Domestic relations is an area of the law wholly reserved to the states, and the State of California's domestic-relations law defined Newdow's (P) parental status. Newdow's (P) custody status at the time of the lawsuit was uncertain. Newdow (P) could communicate with the girl and had shared physical custody, but was not entitled to make the final decisions as to her education because her mother had sole legal custody. Because the only standing he could assert would have derived through his parental status with regard to his daughter, and because the state court determined that his relationship was of a noncustodial nature, Newdow (P) lacked standing to sue on this issue in federal court. Newdow (P) did not have standing to sue individually, either. Since this Court determined that Newdow (P) does not have standing to sue, the Court need not reach the First Amendment issue. Reversed.

CONCURRENCE IN PART AND DISSENT IN PART: (Rehnquist, C.J.) The District's (D) policy that requires teachers to lead willing students in reciting the Pledge of Allegiance does not violate the Establishment Clause of the First Amendment, and Newdow (P) does have standing to sue. The majority does not dispute that Newdow (P) satisfies the requirements of Article III standing, but erects a new standing requirement that expands the prudential prohibition on third-party standing, and it improperly bases this new standard on the domestic-relations exception and the abstention doctrine, as well as criticism of the Court of Appeals's construction of state law. The domestic-relations exception is not a prudential limitation on federal jurisdiction, but limits federal diversity jurisdiction in domestic-relations cases. Since this case does not involve diversity jurisdiction, and Newdow (P) does not ask for a divorce, alimony, or child custody decree, the domestic-relations exception does not apply. Instead, this case involves a substantial federal question about the constitutionality of the District's (D) policy requiring the leading of the Pledge of Allegiance, and the substantial federal question is the source of this Court's jurisdiction. Finally, the Court of Appeals twice concluded that Newdow (P) had the requisite standing to bring the

Continued on next page.

suit, and deference to those two opinions is required since this Court has a policy of deferring to regional court construction of state law.

▶ *ANALYSIS*

This case divided the country politically and caused religious furor as atheists and Christians squared off. Had the Supreme Court affirmed the Ninth Circuit, school districts across the country would have been unable to require recitation of the Pledge but it still could have been offered as an "opportunity." Most people who did object to the Pledge objected to the 1954 insertion into the Pledge of the words "under God," but supporters argued that those words were meant to express a part of this country's religious history rather than supporting any one religion. At the end of the day, though, it was the contentious custody battle between the girl's parents that decided the case, which leaves the First Amendment issue for future battles.

■━■

Quicknotes

STANDING The right to commence suit against another party because of a personal stake in the resolution of the controversy.

■━■

United States v. Richardson

Federal government (D) v. Federal taxpayer (P)

418 U.S. 166 (1974).

NATURE OF CASE: Action seeking declaration that secret CIA expenditures violated the public accounting clause of Article I, § 9 of the Constitution.

FACT SUMMARY: Richardson (P) brought suit as a federal taxpayer seeking a declaration that the Central Intelligence Agency Act was unconstitutional insofar as it violated the public accounting clause of Article I, §9 of the Constitution. His standing to bring the suit in his capacity as a taxpayer was challenged.

🏛 RULE OF LAW
A taxpayer does not have standing to bring a generalized grievance challenging a statute regulating a federal agency's accounting and reporting procedures.

FACTS: Richardson (P) brought an action as a federal taxpayer alleging that certain provisions of the Central Intelligence Agency Act of 1949 violated Art. I, § 9, cl. 7 of the Constitution, which requires a public accounting of the receipts and expenditures of public money. However, he made no claim that funds were being spent in violation of constitutional limitations on the taxing and spending power. Rather, he was seeking to compel the government to give him information on how the CIA spends its funds.

ISSUE: Does a taxpayer have standing to bring a generalized grievance challenging a statute regulating a federal agency's accounting and reporting procedures?

HOLDING AND DECISION: (Burger, C.J.) No. A taxpayer does not have standing to bring a generalized grievance challenging a statute regulating a federal agency's accounting and reporting procedures. First, there is no logical nexus between Richardson's (P) asserted status as a taxpayer and the claimed failure of Congress to require disclosure of the CIA's expenditures. He is not asserting that funds are being spent in violation of the taxing and spending power, but rather is seeking to air his generalized grievances about the conduct of government. He claims that without detailed information on CIA expenditures, he cannot fulfill his function as a citizen and member of the electorate. This is the kind of generalized grievance that is common to all members of the public. Thus, he has not alleged that, as a taxpayer, he will suffer a particular injury from the operation of the statute. Ultimately, the citizen's remedy for such a claim is through the political process.

DISSENT: (Stewart J.) The nature of Richardson's (P) claim is that the Constitution gives him a right to receive, and imposes on the government a correlative duty to provide, an accounting of how public money is spent. Courts of law exist for the resolution of such right-duty disputes, and, therefore, when a plaintiff seeks a judicial determination that a defendant owes him a duty, the plaintiff has standing to litigate the existence of such a duty once he has shown that the defendant declined to honor his claim.

▶ ANALYSIS

The author of the casebook notes that "[t]he prohibition against generalized grievances prevents individuals from suing if their only injury is as a citizen or a taxpayer concerned with having the government follow the law." According to the author of the casebook, taxpayer standing is permitted only "to challenge government expenditures as violating the Establishment Clause of the First Amendment, the provision that prohibits Congress from making any law respecting the establishment of religion." See *Flast v. Cohen*, 392 U.S. 83 (1968).

■=■

Quicknotes

STANDING The right to commence suit against another party because of a personal stake in the resolution of the controversy.

■=■

Flast v. Cohen

Federal taxpayer (P) v. Government official (D)

392 U.S. 83 (1968).

NATURE OF CASE: Challenge to constitutionality of statute providing federal financial aid to religious schools.

FACT SUMMARY: Flast (appellant) and other federal taxpayers claimed that the appropriation of funds that, under a federal statute, were being used to support instruction in religious schools was unconstitutional. The taxpayers' standing to bring the suit was challenged.

🏛 RULE OF LAW
Federal taxpayers have standing to challenge government expenditures that are claimed to violate the Establishment Clause.

FACTS: Flast (P) and other taxpayers alleged that federal funds had been disbursed by federal officials (D) under the Elementary and Secondary Education Act of 1965 to finance instruction and the purchase of educational materials for use in religious schools in violation of the Establishment and Free Exercise Clauses of the First Amendment. The government moved to dismiss the complaint on the ground that appellants lacked standing to maintain the action. The taxpayers alleged proper standing based solely on their status as federal taxpayers.

ISSUE: Do federal taxpayers have standing to challenge government expenditures that are claimed to violate the Establishment Clause?

HOLDING AND DECISION: (Warren, C.J.) Yes. Federal taxpayers have standing to challenge government expenditures that are claimed to violate the Establishment Clause. There is no absolute bar in Article III of the Constitution to suits by federal taxpayers challenging allegedly unconstitutional federal taxing and spending programs. To maintain an action challenging the constitutionality of a federal spending program, individuals must demonstrate the necessary stake as taxpayers in the outcome of the litigation. If the taxpayers can satisfy a two-part nexus test, they will be deemed to have such a stake. First, the taxpayer must establish a logical link between the status as a taxpayer and the type of legislation attacked, and, thus, taxpayers are limited to challenging exercises of the congressional power under the taxing and spending clause. Second, there must be a link between that status and the precise nature of the constitutional infringement alleged. Taxpayers must show that the statute exceeds specific constitutional limitations on the exercise of the taxing and spending power and not simply that the enactment is generally beyond the powers delegated to Congress by Art. I, § 8. The taxpayer-appellants here have satisfied this double-nexus test because they have alleged that tax money is being spent in violation of a specific constitutional protection against the abuse of legislative power, i. e., the Establishment Clause of the First Amendment.

DISSENT: (Harlan, J.) The majority's double-nexus test does not measure a taxpayer's personal interest or stake in the outcome of any suit: a taxpayer's interest in a suit challenging a public expenditure does not vary according to the constitutional provision under which he states his claim. Moreover, permitting standing for such public actions will upset the balance of power among the branches of the federal government.

▶ ANALYSIS

Flast represents a narrow exception to the general rule that taxpayers do not have standing to bring generalized grievances about governmental conduct. Even in the context of the Establishment Clause, *Flast* has not been extended beyond challenges to expenditures.

■══■

Quicknotes

ESTABLISHMENT CLAUSE The constitutional provision prohibiting the government from favoring any one religion over others, or engaging in religious activities or advocacy.

STANDING The right to commence suit against another party because of a personal stake in the resolution of the controversy.

■══■

Hein v. Freedom from Religion Foundation

Federal government (D) v. Taxpayer (P)

127 S. Ct. 2553 (2007).

NATURE OF CASE: Appeal from federal court of appeals.

FACT SUMMARY: A nonreligious nonprofit organization (P) challenged the Bush administration's executive orders related to faith-based initiatives. The government (D) argued that the organization (P) did not have standing to sue.

🏛 RULE OF LAW
Taxpayers do not have standing to bring an Establishment Clause challenge against executive branch actions funded by general appropriations rather than by any specific congressional grant.

FACTS: President George W. Bush issued executive orders that created the Office of Faith-Based and Community Initiatives, a program aimed at allowing religious charitable organizations to compete alongside nonreligious ones for federal funding and which instructed various executive departments to hold conferences promoting the Faith-Based Initiative. The Freedom from Religion Foundation (P) sued, alleging that because the conferences favored religious organizations over nonreligious ones, they violated the Establishment Clause of the First Amendment of the Constitution. The government (D) argued that the Foundation (P) had no standing to sue because there was no case or controversy as required by Article III of the Constitution, and because the Foundation (P) had not been harmed in any way by the conferences. The Foundation (P) argued that exceptions to the general rule that individuals do not have standing to challenge a federal program simply because of their status as taxpayers have been made for Establishment Clause challenges, and that they apply here. The district court ruled that the Foundation (P) lacked standing, holding that the exceptions covered only challenges to specific congressional expenditures, not executive-branch actions funded by the general funds allotted to the executive departments. The Court of Appeals for the Seventh Circuit reversed, ruling that any taxpayer has standing to bring an Establishment Clause challenge against an executive-branch program, whether funded by a specific congressional grant or by a discretionary use of a general appropriation.

ISSUE: Do taxpayers have standing to bring an Establishment Clause challenge against Executive Branch actions funded by general appropriations rather than by any specific congressional grant?

HOLDING AND DECISION: (Alito, J.) No. Taxpayers do not have standing to bring an Establishment Clause challenge against Executive Branch actions funded by general appropriations rather than by any specific congressional grant. Relevant caselaw—specifically *Flast v. Cohen*—presents a narrow exception to the general rule that taxpayer status does not grant standing to sue the government (D), and *Flast* did not support the Seventh Circuit's broad interpretation. In order to have standing under *Flast*, a taxpayer must not only challenge a policy on the basis of the Establishment Clause, but also bring the challenge against a congressional expenditure. Since no specific congressional appropriation was implicated in the suit, there was no case or controversy under the *Flast* exception. To extend *Flast* to executive actions would threaten the separation of powers by relaxing the doctrine of standing and turning federal courts into "general complaint bureaus."

CONCURRENCE: (Scalia, J.) The plurality's distinction is "utterly meaningless," and *Flast* should be overruled.

DISSENT: (Souter, J.) Taxpayers suffer injury when executive agencies spend identifiable sums of tax money for religious purposes, no less than when Congress authorizes the same thing.

▶ *ANALYSIS*

Critics of this case found it denies Americans with "legitimate" church-state grievances access to court to challenge public funding of religion, regardless of which branch of government is spending the money. But it is important to note that this ruling applies to only a few situations. Most lawsuits involving church-state issues, including those challenging congressional appropriations for faith-based programs, will not be affected.

■═■

Quicknotes

ESTABLISHMENT CLAUSE The constitutional provision prohibiting the government from favoring any one religion over others, or engaging in religious activities or advocacy.

STANDING The right to commence suit against another party because of a personal stake in the resolution of the controversy.

■═■

Poe v. Ullman

Contraceptive seekers (P) v. State's attorney for Connecticut (D)

367 U.S. 497 (1961).

NATURE OF CASE: Constitutional challenge to state statute prohibiting use and the provision of medical advice on contraceptive devices.

FACT SUMMARY: Plaintiffs sought medical advice on the use of contraceptives but could not receive it because of Connecticut statutes prohibiting the use of and dispensation of medical advice about contraceptives. Plaintiffs challenged the statutes' constitutionality under the Fourteenth Amendment.

🏛 RULE OF LAW
Criminal statutes that are not enforced are not ripe for constitutional adjudication.

FACTS: Paul and Pauline Poe (P), a married couple, lost three children in infancy and determined that contraceptive methods were necessary to prevent a fourth pregnancy. The third plaintiff, Jane Doe, needs contraceptives to prevent a second pregnancy that could be life threatening. Connecticut statutes from the late 1800s prohibit the use of and the dispensation of medical advice about contraceptives. Plaintiffs challenged the constitutionality of the statutes under the Fourteenth Amendment.

ISSUE: Are unenforced criminal statutes ripe for constitutional adjudication?

HOLDING AND DECISION: (Frankfurter, J.) No. Criminal statutes that are not enforced are not ripe for constitutional adjudication. The criminal statutes have only been enforced in one case in 1940. No prosecutions are recorded and nothing has been threatened concerning plaintiffs. The plaintiffs are concerned with the threat of enforcement, not the actual application of the statutes to them. Thus, there is nothing for this Court to adjudicate because this Court does not address actions with no immediacy.

DISSENT: (Douglas, J.) The physicians and patients should not have to flout the law to get information on contraceptives, regardless of the enforcement history of these statutes. The constitutional rights at issue should be determined without forcing the arrest of one of the parties.

▶ ANALYSIS

This was a test case for family planning clinics wishing to open their doors in Connecticut. The opinion here resulted in the clinics opening their doors and facing arrest because of the laws' existence or being ignored because of the laws' nullity. The majority's opinion raises the question of whether or not laws should be ignored simply because they haven't been enforced in some time. Encouraging citizens to engage in criminal behavior should not be the aim of the Supreme Court.

■=■

Quicknotes

RIPENESS A doctrine precluding a federal court from hearing or determining a matter unless it constitutes an actual and present controversy warranting a determination by the court.

■=■

Abbott Laboratories v. Gardner

Drug manufacturer (P) v. Government official (D)

387 U.S. 136 (1967).

NATURE OF CASE: Declaratory action seeking to enjoin enforcement of federal regulations claimed to have been issued in excess of the authority granted to the federal agency issuing them.

FACT SUMMARY: Drug manufacturer (P) claimed that a federal agency that issued drug-labeling regulations, effective in the future, exceeded its authority.

🏛 RULE OF LAW
A pre-enforcement review of challenged regulations is ripe for judicial determination where the issue involved is a purely legal one and the impact of the regulation on the challenger is direct and immediate.

FACTS: Congress amended the Food, Drug, and Cosmetic Act to require the "established" name of drugs to be included on all drug labels. The "established" name is a government-issued drug name, while the prescription drug manufacturers used "proprietary names" to market the drugs. The same drugs marketed under proprietary names were often available for less money under the established names, and Congress wanted prescribing physicians to be aware of this fact. Numerous drug manufacturers and their trade association challenged the regulations on the ground that the Commissioner exceeded his authority under the statute, seeking a pre-enforcement judicial declaration to that effect as well as an injunction of the regulations.

ISSUE: Is a pre-enforcement review of challenged regulations ripe for judicial determination where the issue involved is a purely legal one and the impact of the regulation on the challenger is direct and immediate?

HOLDING AND DECISION: (Harlan, J.) Yes. Pre-enforcement review of challenged regulations is ripe for judicial determination where the issue involved is a purely legal one and the impact of the regulation on the challenger is direct and immediate. The issue is fit for judicial decision because the issue involved is a purely legal one, i.e., whether the Commissioner properly construed the statute. Also, the impact of the regulations on the drug manufacturers is sufficiently direct and immediate to make it appropriate for judicial review at this stage. These regulations purport to give an authoritative interpretation of a statutory provision that has a direct effect on the day-to-day business of all prescription drug companies. The manufacturers are thus placed in a dilemma: either they comply and incur the considerable cost of compliance, or they refuse to comply and risk incurring criminal prosecution.

▶ ANALYSIS

Abbott Laboratories has been applied to pre-enforcement review of statutes although it was meant to apply only to pre-enforcement review of regulations. This expansion beyond its original purpose has served to protect legislative efforts that could have been chilled by a constant stream of pre-enforcement reviews initiated by disgruntled constituents.

■━■

Quicknotes

RIPENESS A doctrine precluding a federal court from hearing or determining a matter unless it constitutes an actual and present controversy warranting a determination by the court.

■━■

Friends of the Earth, Inc. v. Laidlaw Environmental Services

Environmental watchdog group (P) v. Permit holder corporation (D)

528 U.S. 167 (2000).

NATURE OF CASE: Citizen suit for injunction and declarative judgment.

FACT SUMMARY: Plaintiff environmentalists sued the defendant corporation in a citizen suit on grounds that the corporation was violating the mercury-discharge limits of its National Pollutant Discharge Elimination System (NPDES) permit.

> 🏛 **RULE OF LAW**
> Voluntary compliance moots a case only if the improper behavior is not capable of being repeated.

FACTS: Laidlaw Environmental Services (D) operated a plant that discharged mercury. The Clean Water Act authorized the issuance of National Pollutant Discharge Elimination System (NPDES) permits to corporations such as Laidlaw (D) so as to limit the amounts of certain discharges. Friends of the Earth, Inc. (P) sued Laidlaw (D) in a citizen suit, claiming that Laidlaw (D) was violating its mercury-discharge limits. During the appeals process, Laidlaw (D) came into compliance with the Clean Water Act limits and then proceeded to shut the offending plant. Laidlaw (D) claimed that its compliance and subsequent plant closure mooted the case.

ISSUE: Does voluntary compliance moot a case if the improper behavior is capable of being repeated?

HOLDING AND DECISION: (Ginsburg, J.) No. Voluntary compliance moots a case only if the improper behavior is not capable of being repeated. The burden is on the party claiming mootness to demonstrate to the Court that the behavior cannot be repeated. Simply coming into compliance is insufficient because the corporation could easily fall out of compliance once the case is dismissed for mootness. Whether or not future violations are possible is a disputed question of fact, especially because Laidlaw (D) retains its NPDES permit. Remanded.

▶ ANALYSIS

Commentators have noted with interest that the Court did not rule that Laidlaw had met its burden under the mootness doctrine by closing the offending plant. Perhaps the Court believed that a plan existed to reopen the plant allowing the violations to once again occur. It is difficult to imagine what a defendant would have to demonstrate in order to meet its burden under this mootness doctrine if the actual closing of the business is insufficient.

Quicknotes

MOOT Judgment on the particular issue has previously been decided or settled.

■═■

United States Parole Commn. v. Geraghty

Federal agency (D) v. Federal prisoner (P)

445 U.S. 388 (1980).

NATURE OF CASE: Action brought on behalf of a class of federal prisoners challenging the U.S. Parole Release Guidelines.

FACT SUMMARY: Geraghty (P) brought suit challenging the validity of the U.S. Parole Release Guidelines on behalf of all federal prisoners eligible for parole. Class certification was denied and Geraghty (P) was released from prison while his appeal was pending.

RULE OF LAW
An action brought on behalf of a class does not become moot upon expiration of the named plaintiff's substantive claim, even though class certification has been denied.

FACTS: Geraghty (P), after twice being denied parole from a federal prison, brought suit against petitioners in district court challenging the validity of the U.S. Parole Commission's Parole Release Guidelines. The district court denied respondent's request for certification of the suit as a class action on behalf of a class of "all federal prisoners who are or who will become eligible for release on parole," and granted summary judgment for the defendants on the merits. Plaintiff was released from prison while his appeal to the court of appeals was pending. [The court of appeals nonetheless reversed the denial of class certification and remanded to the district court. The court of appeals's ruling was appealed to the Supreme Court.]

ISSUE: Does an action brought on behalf of a class become moot upon expiration of the named plaintiff's substantive claim, even though class certification has been denied?

HOLDING AND DECISION: (Blackmun, J.) No. An action brought on behalf of a class does not become moot upon expiration of the named plaintiff's substantive claim, even though class certification has been denied. The controversy between the prisoners and the Parole Commission (D) is still a "live" one and there can be a substitute for the named representative. The imperatives of a dispute capable of judicial resolution—sharply presented issues in a concrete factual setting and self-interested parties vigorously advocating opposing positions—can exist with respect to the class certification issue notwithstanding that the named plaintiff's claim on the merits has expired. Such imperatives are present in this case, where the question whether class certification is appropriate remains as a concrete, sharply presented issue, and Geraghty (P) continues vigorously to advocate his right to have a class certified. Thus, the proposed representative retains a "personal stake" in obtaining class certification.

ANALYSIS

The majority emphasized that the formalistic view of Art. III jurisprudence, while perhaps the starting point of all inquiry, is riddled with exceptions, and that its opinion, in creating such an exception, looked to practicalities and prudential considerations. The resulting mootness doctrine is thus a flexible one.

Quicknotes

MOOT Judgment on the particular issue has previously been decided or settled.

Baker v. Carr

Resident (P) v. State (D)

369 U.S. 186 (1962).

NATURE OF CASE: Action seeking a declaration of the unconstitutionality of a state law and injunctive relief.

FACT SUMMARY: Baker (P) alleged that because of population changes since 1901, the 1901 State Apportionment Act was obsolete and unconstitutional, and that the state legislature refused to reapportion itself.

🏛 RULE OF LAW
The fact that a suit seeks protection of a political right does not mean it necessarily presents a political question.

FACTS: [Between 1901 and 1961 Tennessee's population had substantially grown and has been redistributed. Baker (P) alleged that because of the population changes and the state legislature's failure to reapportion voting districts by itself since, the 1901 Apportionment Act was unconstitutional and obsolete. Baker (P) also alleged that because of the makeup of the legislature resulting from the 1901 Act, redress in the form of a state constitutional amendment was difficult or impossible.]

ISSUE: Does a constitutional challenge to a state apportionment act present a political question?

HOLDING AND DECISION: (Brennan, J.) No. The fact that a suit seeks protection of a political right does not mean it necessarily presents a political question. The primary reason that political questions have been held to be nonjusticiable is the separation of powers. An analysis of any case held to involve a political question will reveal: (1) a history of the issue's management by another governmental branch; (2) a lack of judicially manageable standards for resolving it; (3) the impossibility of deciding the case without an initial policy determination calling for nonjudicial discretion; (4) the impossibility of resolving it without expressing lack of respect due other government branches; (5) an unusual need for unquestioning adherence to a political decision already made; or (6) the potentiality of embarrassment from a variety of announcements by different governmental departments on one question. The mere fact that a suit seeks protection of a political right does not mean that it involves a political question. The Court cannot reject as involving a political question a real controversy as to whether a certain action exceeded constitutional limits. Here Baker (P) alleges that a state's actions violate his right to equal protection. None of the above-mentioned characteristics of a political question are present. Further, the nonjusticiability of claims arising under the Guarantee Clause can have no bearing on the justiciability of the equal protection claim presented here.

DISSENT: (Frankfurter, J.) A long line of cases has held that the Guarantee Clause is not enforceable through the courts. The present case involves all of the elements that have made the Guarantee Clause cases nonjusticiable. The Equal Protection Clause provides no clearer guide for judicial examination of apportionment statutes than would the Guarantee Clause. What is actually asked here is for the Court to choose among competing theories of representation, and ultimately, among competing political philosophies, to establish an appropriate frame of government for Tennessee. To find the Court's power to make such a choice in the broad guarantee of the Equal Protection Clause is to rewrite the Constitution.

▶ ANALYSIS

Baker v. Carr is the most important case on political questions. Traditionally, the Court refused to review cases arising from state apportionment statutes, since they were all said to present political questions. In *Colegrove v. Green*, 382 U.S. 549, it was contended that the fact that apportioned districts were not of approximate equality in population rendered the state apportionment act unconstitutional. The Court held that a political question was presented and so the case was nonjusticiable. However, in *Gomillion v. Lightfoot*, 364 U.S. 339, the Court showed some willingness to enter the area of apportionment. There a statute apportioned a district with the obvious purpose of excluding black votes. The Court held that a justiciable violation of equal protection had been alleged. In distinguishing *Colegrove*, it stated that there the complaint alleged only a dilution of the strength of the appellants' votes as a result of legislative inaction over a number of years, whereas in *Gomillion*, the petitioners complained that affirmative legislative action had deprived them of their votes.

■═■

Quicknotes

EQUAL PROTECTION CLAUSE A constitutional provision that each person be guaranteed the same protection of the laws enjoyed by other persons in like circumstances.

JUSTICIABILITY An actual controversy that is capable of determination by the court.

■═■

Vieth v. Jubelirer

Democratic voter (P) v. Party not identified (D)

541 U.S. 267 (2004).

NATURE OF CASE: Constitutional challenge and injunction to redistricting plan.

FACT SUMMARY: The Commonwealth of Pennsylvania drew redistricting maps in such a way that favored the majority Republican Party. Vieth (P), a Democrat, challenged the redistricting as unconstitutional political gerrymandering.

🏛 RULE OF LAW
Political gerrymandering claims are nonjusticiable.

FACTS: The 2000 census resulted in two fewer representatives for the Commonwealth of Pennsylvania and the political districts had to be redrawn. Under pressure from the national Republican Party the majority republicans in the Pennsylvania government drew the districts in such a way that the Republican Party was favored over the Democrats. Vieth (P), a democrat voter in Pennsylvania, challenged the redistricting as unconstitutional political gerrymandering and sought to enjoin the redistricting plan's implementation. The district court dismissed plaintiffs' claims and the Supreme Court granted certiorari.

ISSUE: Are political gerrymandering claims nonjusticiable?

HOLDING AND DECISION: (Scalia, J.) Yes. Political gerrymandering claims are nonjusticiable. The judicial branch must refrain from passing judgment on political questions with "a lack of judicially discoverable and manageable standards for resolving" them. As this Court held in a four-justice plurality opinion in *Davis v. Bandemer* (1986), no discoverable and manageable standards to decide political gerrymandering claims exist. *Bandemer* expressed the hope that a standard could be determined in the future, but that hope has never been realized, and this Court now finds that *Bandemer* was wrongly decided. After eighteen years, no standard has been discerned and claims are brought with no hope of resolution. Justice Kennedy would like to keep the issue open in case a future Court arrives at an appropriate standard, but this would leave the lower courts with no guidance. No constitutional judicially enforceable limit exists for redistricting. The plaintiffs' claim must be dismissed.

CONCURRENCE: (Kennedy, J.) The judicial branch simply cannot become so intimately involved in the American political process as to order the redrawing of district plans, so the plurality opinion is correct. While the issue currently remains nonjusticiable, nothing suggests that an appropriate standard could not arise in the future. The Court should not shut the door on all future claims of partisan gerrymandering.

DISSENT: (Stevens, J.) Policymakers have a duty to remain impartial and political gerrymandering is a violation of that duty. The Court should not foreclose all future claims because a standard to evaluate the violation of the duty of impartiality has not yet been found.

DISSENT: (Souter, J.) Voters are entitled to substantial equality and drawing districts in such a way to favor one voter over another is a denial of that entitlement. The Court should have taken the opportunity today to develop a standard of review for political gerrymandering claims. A prima facie case could consist of five elements: (1) plaintiff's identification with a cohesive political group; (2) traditional districting principles were not applied to plaintiff's district; (3) specific correlations between the nonapplication of traditional principles and the population of plaintiff's district; (4) presentation of a hypothetically appropriate district; and (5) intentional action on the part of the defendants to affect plaintiff's political group.

DISSENT: (Breyer, J.) An equal protection violation could be advanced here to remedy the districting. Courts need not intervene, however, where a minority group has entrenched itself and uses the political process to maintain power, because the unhappy majority will use the same political process to remove the minority. That is a remediable abuse. In cases like today's, the Court should be able to fashion a remedy.

▶ ANALYSIS

The result of the holding in *Vieth* is that displeased voters should take the claims of political gerrymandering through the political process as opposed to through the judicial process. In the case of *Vieth*, however, national leaders were the ones pressuring state leaders to draw the gerrymandering districts. If the national leaders participate in the gerrymandering and the judicial branch cannot become involved, where is the dispute to be taken? Some commentators suggest that the only viable solution is to have a nonpartisan body draw all political districts.

■■■

Quicknotes

GERRYMANDERING To create a civil division of an unusual shape for an improper purpose such as redistricting a state so that a maximum number of the elected representatives will be of a particular political party.

JUSTICIABILITY An actual controversy that is capable of determination by the court.

■■■

Powell v. McCormack

Congressman (P) v. Speaker of the House (D)

395 U.S. 486 (1969).

NATURE OF CASE: Action for declaratory judgment and injunction.

FACT SUMMARY: Congress denied Representative Adam Clayton Powell, Jr. (P) his seat on the ground that he had made improper use of government funds.

🏛 RULE OF LAW
The House of Representatives may not deny a duly elected official his seat so long as the official meets the standing constitutional requirements for a representative.

FACTS: In November 1966, Adam Clayton Powell, Jr. (P) was elected to the 90th Congress. Certain allegations, however, had been lodged against him during the 89th Congress alleging certain improprieties in his use of federal funds for his and his staff's "travel expenses." By resolution, the 90th Congress refused to swear him in until after an investigation. A select investigating committee recommended that Powell (P) be seated and fined $40,000, but the House as a whole rejected the recommendation and voted to exclude Powell (P) from the House. Powell (P) thereupon filed this action against McCormack (D), speaker of the House, and several House employees, seeking a declaratory judgment that his exclusion had been illegal and a mandatory injunction requiring payment of his back salary. Prior to resolution of this action, however, the 90th Congress ended and Powell (D) was elected to the 91st Congress and permitted to take his seat. On appeal, McCormack (D) alleged that the Supreme Court lacks the power to review Congress's expulsion on several grounds enumerated below.

ISSUE: May the House of Representatives deny a duly elected official his seat, even though the official meets the standing constitutional requirements for a representative?

HOLDING AND DECISION: (Warren, C.J.) No. The House of Representatives may not deny a duly elected official his seat so long as the official meets the standing constitutional requirements for a representative. Article 1, § 5 does not provide authority to the House to deny a duly elected official his seat. A review of legislative history and the Framers' intent brings us to such a conclusion. The government should not have the authority to exclude a person whom the people have elected as their representative when that elected official meets the qualifications prescribed by the Constitution, namely age, citizenship, and residence. The House does have the authority to expel a member with a two-thirds majority vote and that is sufficient authority.

▶ ANALYSIS

This case primarily points up two of the most difficult and vague areas of the scope of judicial review: "mootness" and "political questions." As a general rule, the disposition of the key issue in a controversy will render it moot unless it is shown to be either (1) "capable of repetition yet evading review," *Hall v. Beals*, 396 U.S. 45 (1969), or (2) it involves possible adverse collateral consequences, *Sibron v. New York*, 392 U.S. 40 (1968). *Powell* falls into the latter category. Article I, § 5 states that "each House shall be the judge of the elections, returns, and qualifications of its members." *Powell*, however, stands for the proposition that this power cannot be exercised arbitrarily. Note that if Congress had merely ruled on Powell's (P) residency qualifications (for example) the textual commitment of the Constitution of such consideration by Congress would have been dispositive.

■■■

Quicknotes

MOOT Judgment on the particular issue that has previously been decided or settled.

POLITICAL QUESTION An issue that is more appropriately left to the determination of another governmental branch and which the court declines to hear.

■■■

Goldwater v. Carter

Congressman (P) v. President (D)

444 U.S. 996 (1979).

NATURE OF CASE: Action challenging the constitutionality of executive treaty cancellation.

FACT SUMMARY: Goldwater (P) and other members of Congress claimed that President Carter (D) had no constitutional power unilaterally to terminate a treaty with Taiwan.

RULE OF LAW
The Supreme Court will not decide nonjusticiable political questions or those not ripe for judicial review.

FACTS: President Carter (D) had acted alone in terminating a treaty with Taiwan, and several members of Congress, including Senator Goldwater (P), questioned his constitutional power to do so without congressional approval. After a judgment in the court of appeals favorable to Goldwater (P), President Carter (D) petitioned the Supreme Court for a writ of certiorari.

ISSUE: Will the Supreme Court decide nonjusticiable political questions or questions not ripe for judicial review?

HOLDING AND DECISION: (Rehnquist, J.) No. Nonjusticiable political questions will not be decided by the court, nor will issues which are not ripe for judicial review. Since a majority of the justices view this case as falling within one of these doctrines, the petition is granted and the case remanded with directions to dismiss the complaint.

CONCURRENCE: (Powell, J.) A dispute between Congress and the President is not ripe for judicial review unless and until each branch has taken action asserting its constitutional authority and such has yet to happen in this case. So, I concur in the result but am compelled to note my disagreement that this case falls within the political question doctrine.

DISSENT: (Brennan, J.) The court should not confront the President's decision to terminate the treaty with Taiwan when the Congress has not yet done so. The dismissal was proper here. Justice Rehnquist's contention concerning the "political question" issue is incorrect. He would argue that this Court should not address the issue at hand because of it is a political question. The Constitution does not, however, unequivocally confer such a termination power upon the President. Traditional judicial interpretation tools could be employed to evaluate the President's decision in this case. Finally, the judicial branch may certainly intervene where the other two branches may be encroaching upon each other. Far from being an untouchable political question, it would be this Court's duty to decide this case if it was ripe.

ANALYSIS

Baker v. Carr, 369 U.S. 186, 217 (1962), sets forth the three basic inquiries to be made in determining if the political question doctrine applies in a particular case as follows: first, does the issue involve the resolution of questions committed by the text of the Constitution to a coordinate branch of government; second, would resolution of the question demand that a court move beyond areas of judicial expertise; and third, do prudential considerations counsel against judicial intervention?

Quicknotes

JUSTICIABILITY An actual controversy that is capable of determination by the court.

MOOT Judgment on the particular issue that has previously been decided or settled.

POLITICAL QUESTION An issue that is more appropriately left to the determination of another governmental branch and which the court declines to hear.

RIPENESS A doctrine precluding a federal court from hearing or determining a matter unless it constitutes an actual and present controversy warranting a determination by the court.

Nixon v. United States

Former judge (P) v. Federal government (D)

506 U.S. 224 (1993).

NATURE OF CASE: Appeal of conviction upon impeachment for high crimes and misdemeanors.

FACT SUMMARY: Nixon (P), a former judge, alleged that a Senate impeachment rule pursuant to which he was impeached was unconstitutional because it prohibited the full Senate from taking part in the impeachment evidentiary hearings.

> ## 🏛 RULE OF LAW
> An action is nonjusticiable where there is a textually demonstrable constitutional commitment of the issue to a coordinate branch of government or a lack of judicially discoverable and manageable standards for resolving it.

FACTS: Nixon (P), a former federal district court judge in Mississippi, was convicted of making false statements to a grand jury and sent to prison. He was subsequently accused in a bill of impeachment of high crimes and misdemeanors by the House of Representatives and convicted by the Senate under Senate Rule XI. That rule delegated to a Senate committee the task of hearing the testimony of witnesses in the impeachment trial. Nixon (P) filed suit, arguing that the rule was unconstitutional because it delegated the duty to try him to a committee, prohibiting the full Senate from taking part in the trial in violation of the Impeachment Trial Clause. The district court held the claim nonjusticiable and the court of appeals affirmed. The Supreme Court granted review.

ISSUE: Is an action nonjusticiable where there is constitutional commitment of the issue to a coordinate branch of government or a lack of judicially discoverable and manageable standards for resolving it?

HOLDING AND DECISION: (Rehnquist, C.J.) Yes. An action is nonjusticiable where there is a textually demonstrable constitutional commitment of the issue to a coordinate branch of government or a lack of judicially discoverable and manageable standards for resolving it. Article I, § 3, clause 6 of the Constitution provides: "The Senate shall have the sole Power to try all Impeachments." Because it is subject to a variety of definitions, the use of the word "try" cannot be interpreted as an implied limitation on the method by which the Senate might proceed in trying impeachments. Various reasons support finding the impeachment procedure nonjusticiable. The imposition of the requirements that the members be under oath and that there be a two-thirds vote to convict suggests that the Framers did not intend to impose limitations by the use of the word "try." The use of the word "sole" also suggests that the Framers intended to commit the issue exclusively to the Senate. The Framers provided for both the impeachment trial and a separate criminal trial to avoid bias and insure independent judgment. Further, judicial review would be inconsistent with the Framers' creation of impeachment as the only check on the judicial branch by the legislature. Finally, judicial review of the process could potentially expose the country's political life to periods of chaos.

CONCURRENCE: (White, J.) The Framers intended the use of the word "sole" to be a limitation on potential interference by the House and not on review by the judiciary. Further, to say that the use of the word "try" does not present a judicially manageable standard is insupportable where one would intuitively expect that the Framers used the word in its legal sense.

CONCURRENCE: (Souter, J.) Not all judicial interference with the impeachment process is inappropriate, and such could be necessary if the Senate were to act in a manner seriously threatening the integrity of its results.

▶ ANALYSIS

In political question cases the Court is in large part concerned with the respect it owes to the legislative branch. This concern takes on different forms depending on the aspect of the doctrine at issue. The "textually demonstrable commitment of the issue to a coordinate political department" aspect is primarily a separation of powers question. The "lack of judicially discoverable and manageable standards" aspect is a question of Court's competence or ability to resolve the issue even if it is not committed to another branch.

■■■■

Quicknotes

JUSTICIABILITY An actual controversy that is capable of determination by the court.

POLITICAL QUESTION An issue that is more appropriately left to the determination of another governmental branch and which the court declines to hear.

SEPARATION OF POWERS The system of checks and balances preventing one branch of government from infringing upon exercising the powers of another branch of government.

■■■■

The Federal Legislative Power

Quick Reference Rules of Law

McCulloch v. Maryland

Bank cashier (D) v. State (P)

17 U.S. (4 Wheat.) 316 (1819).

NATURE OF CASE: Action arising out of violation of a state statute.

FACT SUMMARY: McCulloch (D), the cashier of the Baltimore branch of the U.S. Bank, issued bank notes in violation of a Maryland (P) statute providing that no bank, without authority from the state, could issue bank notes except on stamped paper issued by the state.

🏛 RULE OF LAW
(1) Certain federal powers, giving Congress the discretion and power to choose and enact the means to perform the duties imposed upon it, are to be implied from the Necessary and Proper Clause.
(2) The federal Constitution and the laws made pursuant to it are supreme and control the constitutions and the laws of the states.

FACTS: [A Maryland (P) statute prohibited any bank operating in the state without state authority from issuing bank notes except upon stamped paper issued by the state. The law specified the fees payable for the paper, and provided for penalties for violators. An act of Congress established a U.S. Bank. McCulloch (D), the U.S. Bank's cashier for its Baltimore branch, issued bank notes without complying with the Maryland (P) law.]

ISSUE:
(1) Does Congress have the power to incorporate a bank?
(2) Does a state have the power to impose fees on the operation of an institution created by Congress pursuant to its constitutional powers?

HOLDING AND DECISION: (Marshall, C.J.)
(1) Yes. Certain federal powers, giving Congress the discretion and power to choose and enact the means to perform the duties imposed upon it, are to be implied from the Necessary and Proper Clause. It is true that this government is one of enumerated powers. However, the Constitution does not exclude incidental or implied powers. It does not require that everything be granted expressly and minutely described. To have so required would have entirely changed the character of the Constitution and made it into a legal code. The enumerated powers given to the government imply the ordinary means of execution. The power of creating a corporation may be implied as incidental to other powers, or used as a means of executing them. The Necessary and Proper Clause gives Congress the power to make "all laws which shall be necessary and proper, for carrying into execution" the powers vested by the Constitution in the U.S.

Government. Maryland (P) argues that the word "necessary" limits the right to pass laws for the execution of the granted powers to those that are indispensable. However, in common usage, "necessary" frequently means convenient, useful, essential. Considering the word's common usage, its usage in another part of the Constitution (Article 1, § 10), and its inclusion among the powers given to Congress, rather than among the limitations upon Congress, it cannot be held to restrain Congress. The sound construction of the Constitution must allow Congress the discretion to choose the means to perform the duties imposed upon it. As long as the end is legitimate and within the scope of the Constitution, any means that are appropriate are plainly adapted to that end, and those that are not prohibited by the Constitution, but are consistent with its spirit, are constitutional. A bank is a convenient, useful, and essential instrument for handling national finances. Hence, it is within Congress's power to enact a law incorporating a U.S. bank.

(2) No. The federal Constitution and the laws made pursuant to it are supreme and control the Constitutions and the laws of the states. Maryland (P) is incorrect in its contention that the powers of the federal government are delegated by the states, which alone are truly sovereign. The Constitution derives its authority from the people, not from the states. Here, Maryland's (P) statute in effect taxes the operation of the U.S. Bank, a bank properly created within Congress's power. The power to tax involves the power to destroy. Here it is in opposition to the supreme congressional power to create a bank. Also, when a state taxes an organization created by the U.S. Government, it acts upon an institution created by people over whom it claims no control. The states have no power, by taxation or otherwise, to impede, burden, or in any manner control the operations of constitutional laws enacted by Congress. The Maryland (P) statute is, therefore, unconstitutional and void.

▶ ANALYSIS

Federalism is the basis of the Constitution's response to the problem of governing large geographical areas with diverse local needs. The success of federalism depends upon maintaining the balance between the need for the supremacy and sovereignty of the federal government and the interest in maintaining independent state government and curtailing national intrusion into intrastate affairs. The U.S. federal structure allocates powers between the nation

Continued on next page.

and the states by enumerating the powers delegated to the national government and acknowledging the retention by the states of the remainder. The Articles of Confederation followed a similar scheme. The Constitution expanded the enumerated national powers to remedy weaknesses of the Articles. The move from the Articles to the Constitution was a shift from a central government with fewer powers to one with more powers.

■═■

Quicknotes

FEDERALISM A scheme of government whereby the power to govern is among a central and localized governments.

NECESSARY AND PROPER CLAUSE, ARTICLE I, SECTION 8 OF THE U.S. CONSTITUTION Enables Congress to make all laws that may be "necessary and proper" to execute its other, enumerated powers.

■═■

Gibbons v. Ogden

Ship operator (D) v. Ship operator (P)

22 U.S. (9 Wheat.) 1 (1824).

NATURE OF CASE: Action seeking an injunction to protect an exclusive right to operate ships between New York City and New Jersey.

FACT SUMMARY: Ogden (P), after acquiring a monopoly right from the State of New York to operate ships between New York City and New Jersey, sought to enjoin Gibbons (D) from operating his ships, licensed by the federal government, between the same points.

🏛 RULE OF LAW
If a state law conflicts with a congressional act regulating commerce, the congressional act is controlling.

FACTS: [The New York legislature granted an exclusive right to Robert Livingston and Robert Fulton to operate steamboats in New York waters. Ogden (P) obtained an assignment from Livingston and Fulton to operate his ships between Elizabethtownport, New Jersey, and New York City. Gibbons (D) was also running two boats between these points and his boats had been enrolled and licensed under the laws of the United States for carrying on the coasting trade. Ogden (P) obtained an injunction stopping Gibbons (D) from operating his ships between the points for which Ogden (P) had received an exclusive right to operate his own ships. The case was appealed to the Supreme Court.] Ogden (P) claimed that the federal government did not have exclusive jurisdiction over commerce, but that the states had retained power by which they could regulate commerce within their own states and that the exclusive right to operate his ships only concerned intrastate commerce. Gibbons (D) contended that Congress had exclusive power to regulate interstate commerce and that New York had attempted to regulate interstate commerce by granting the exclusive right and enforcing it with the injunction.

ISSUE: If a state law conflicts with a congressional act regulating commerce, is the congressional act controlling?

HOLDING AND DECISION: (Marshall, C.J.) Yes. If a state law conflicts with a congressional act regulating commerce, the congressional act is controlling. Congress has the power to regulate navigation within the limits of every state and, therefore, the regulations that Congress passed controlling navigation within the boundaries of New York were valid. Ogden (P) argued that the states, through the Tenth Amendment, have the power to regulate commerce with foreign nations and among the states because the power that the states gave up to Congress to regulate commerce wasn't absolute and the residue of that power remained with the states. But Congress was given all the power to regulate interstate commerce, although it is possible for the states to pass regulations that may affect some activity associated with interstate commerce. In that case, states must base such regulations on some other source of power than the commerce power (such as the police power of the state). Regardless of the source of the state power, any time a state regulation conflicts with a federal regulation, the state regulation must yield to the federal law. Since in this case the law of New York conflicted with a federal regulation dealing with interstate commerce, the New York law is not valid. Accordingly, the Court dismissed Ogden's (P) suit to obtain an injunction against Gibbons (D).

▶ ANALYSIS

The federal commerce power is concurrent with state power over commerce within the state. Hence, the Court has been asked many times to define the line between federal and state power to regulate commerce. During the early history of the United States, the court was not often called upon to determine the scope of federal power under the Commerce Clause. Instead, the early cases generally involved some state action that was claimed to discriminate against or burden interstate commerce. Hence, the Commerce Clause operated as a restraint upon state powers. Most of these cases did not involve any exercise of the commerce power by Congress at all. Large-scale regulatory action by Congress began with the Interstate Commerce Act in 1887 and the Sherman Antitrust Act in 1890. Challenges to these statutes initiated the major modern confrontations between the Court and congressional authority regarding commerce.

■■■

Quicknotes

COMMERCE CLAUSE Article 1, Section 8, clause 3 of the U.S. Constitution, granting Congress the power to regulate commerce with foreign countries and among the states.

■■■

United States v. E.C. Knight Co.

Federal government (P) v. Corporation (D)

156 U.S. 1 (1895).

NATURE OF CASE: Antitrust action against corporation that acquired a monopoly in sugar refining.

FACT SUMMARY: American Sugar Refining Company acquired several sugar refineries, giving it nearly complete control of the refining of sugar in the United States. The federal government (P) brought an antitrust action to set aside the acquisitions.

🏛 RULE OF LAW
The Commerce Clause does not empower Congress to regulate manufacturing.

FACTS: The American Sugar Refining Company acquired four sugar refineries, giving it almost total control of the refining of sugar in the United States—an undeniable monopoly. The federal government (P) brought an antitrust action under the Sherman Antitrust Act to set aside the acquisitions, but its complaint was dismissed.

ISSUE: Does the Commerce Clause empower Congress to regulate manufacturing?

HOLDING AND DECISION: (Fuller, C.J.) No. Assuming a monopoly in manufacturing was acquired, the power to control manufacturing is secondary and incidental to the power to control commerce. "Commerce succeeds to manufacture, and is not a part of it." Congress could control a monopoly of commerce, but because manufacturing is not commerce, Congress may not control a monopoly of manufacturing.

DISSENT: (Harlan, J.) Congress has the power to remove any restraints on interstate commerce, and an exercise of such power will not interfere with the autonomy of the states, but will protect the safety of the states. Any monopoly that interferes with interstate commerce affects directly, and not incidentally, the people of all the states. Therefore, the remedy for such a monopoly is in the federal government's power, which should not be narrowly interpreted.

▶ ANALYSIS

During this laissez faire period of the Court's jurisprudence, with its attendant hostility to government economic regulation, a similar view was taken with regard to other "precommercial" activities, such as mining, agriculture, and insurance. Adopting a formal category of "commerce," however artificial, meant that entire categories of human industry were outside of the commerce power.

Quicknotes

COMMERCE POWER The power delegated to Congress by the U.S. Constitution to regulate interstate commerce.

Carter v. Carter Coal Co.

Stockholder (P) v. Corporation (D)

298 U.S. 238 (1936).

NATURE OF CASE: Stockholder suit to enjoin company from complying with requirements of the Coal Conservation Act.

FACT SUMMARY: The Coal Conservation Act attempted to regulate certain aspects of coal production. Carter (P) brought suit to enjoin his company (D) from complying with the Act.

RULE OF LAW
Production or manufacture of goods that may or may not be shipped out of state is not interstate commerce and not subject to federal regulation.

FACTS: The Coal Conservation Act of 1935 established a tax on coal production. Producers would receive a reduction of this tax by accepting coal codes that were to be formulated. These codes would establish minimum prices for coal, wages, and hours for workers, and would require that producers recognize their employees' right to organize and bargain collectively. Carter (P) brought this action to enjoin Carter Coal Co. (D) from complying with these requirements and from paying the tax.

ISSUE: Is the production of coal that may or may not be shipped across state lines "interstate commerce," which would allow federal regulation?

HOLDING AND DECISION: (Sutherland, J.) No. The attempted federal regulation of coal production is not sustainable as within Congress's power to regulate interstate commerce or as within a more general power to regulate for the public welfare. The preamble of the Act states that the production of coal "directly affects interstate commerce" and that regulation is necessary to protect the public interest in maintaining an adequate supply of coal and promoting fair producer-employee relations. It has always been held that Congress can only exercise powers that were specifically delegated to it by the Constitution; therefore, this Act cannot be sustained merely on the ground that it promotes the general welfare. The Act, then, can only be upheld if it is within the powers granted the federal government by the Commerce Clause. In manufacturing a product that it subsequently ships into interstate commerce, a manufacturer engages in two separate activities: first, the manufacture or production of a product (which is purely local and only subject to state regulation); second, the actual shipment of the goods across state lines, which is subject only to federal regulation. Since production is purely local, and this Act purports to regulate the employer/employee relationship in production, the Act is not a valid exercise of Congress's power to regulate interstate commerce, and cannot be sustained.

ANALYSIS

The *Carter* case, like *Schecter*, is based on a strict geographical definition of interstate commerce. If the act in question, here the production of coal, takes place at all times within a single state, it cannot be interstate commerce and cannot be regulated. Although the Court admits that coal production has an effect on interstate commerce, it was only an indirect, not a direct effect. The weakness of this argument is pointed out in the dissent: intrastate acts can have such a great influence on interstate commerce, even in the absence of a direct effect, that the literalistic direct/indirect distinction serves no purpose.

∎≡∎

Quicknotes

COMMERCE POWER The power delegated to Congress by the U.S. Constitution to regulate interstate commerce.

∎≡∎

Houston, East & West Texas Railway Co. v. United States
(The Shreveport Rate Cases)

Railroad companies (Appellants) v. Federal government (Appellee)

234 U.S. 342 (1914).

NATURE OF CASE: Appeal from an order of the Interstate Commerce Commission (ICC).

FACT SUMMARY: Railroad freight rates for intrastate shipment were lower than for interstate shipment. The ICC, finding that the lower intrastate rates discriminated against interstate commerce, ordered that this price discrimination cease. Railroad companies handling freight traffic within the state appealed.

🏛 RULE OF LAW
Congress has the power to regulate intrastate commerce when it impacts interstate commerce.

FACTS: Railroad freight rates set by the Texas Railroad Commission for shipment within Texas were lower than maximum rates set by the ICC for shipment between Texas and points outside the state. The ICC found that the lower Texas rates discouraged interstate shipping and so established rates for the interstate shipments that were the same as those established by the Texas Railroad Commission for intrastate shipments. The affected railroad companies appealed the ICC's order, arguing that Congress lacked authority to regulate, through the ICC, intrastate freight rates.

ISSUE: Does Congress have the power to regulate intrastate commerce when it impacts interstate commerce?

HOLDING AND DECISION: (Hughes, J.) Yes. Congress's authority, which applies to instruments of interstate commerce, such as the railroads here, extends to the intrastate activities of such instruments of commerce when those activities have a close and substantial relation to interstate traffic. Whenever the interstate and intrastate activities of carriers are closely related, such that the regulation of one affects the other, it is Congress, and not the state, that has the final say. Thus, Congress may control intrastate commerce to protect interstate commerce.

▶ ANALYSIS

This case, also known as the *Shreveport Rate Case*, embodied the principle that in time came to be known as the "protective principle," namely that Congress has the authority to regulate intrastate commerce for the protection of interstate commerce.

Quicknotes

COMMERCE POWER The power delegated to Congress by the U.S. Constitution to regulate interstate commerce.

A.L.A. Schechter Poultry Corp. v. United States

Poultry slaughterhouse (D) v. Federal government (P)

295 U.S. 495 (1935).

NATURE OF CASE: Constitutional challenge to the employment regulations of the Live Poultry Code.

FACT SUMMARY: The "Live Poultry Code" required sellers to sell only entire coops or half-coops of chickens, and made it illegal for buyers to reject individual chickens. The Code also regulated employment by requiring collective bargaining, prohibiting child labor, and by establishing a 40-hour work week and a minimum wage. The slaughterhouse (D) was convicted of violating the employment regulations of the Live Poultry Code, and on appeal, challenged its constitutionality.

🏛 RULE OF LAW
The federal government has no authority to regulate intrastate transactions having an indirect effect on interstate commerce.

FACTS: Live chickens are shipped to New York and Philadelphia from all over the country. The A.L.A. Schechter Poultry Corp. ("A.L.A.") (D) purchased the live chickens from vendors in New York and Philadelphia and trucked the chickens to its Brooklyn slaughterhouse. Once at the slaughterhouse, the chickens were slaughtered and sold to local retailers who sold directly to consumers. The A.L.A. (D) did not sell poultry in interstate commerce. The Live Poultry Code governed the sale of live poultry, as well as the employment conditions within the slaughterhouses. The Code required sellers to sell only entire coops or half-coops of chickens, and made it illegal for buyers to reject individual chickens. The Code also regulated employment by requiring collective bargaining, prohibiting child labor, and by establishing a 40-hour work week and a minimum wage. The federal government (P) sought indictments against the A.L.A. (D) for violations of the employment regulations of the Code, and the A.L.A. (D) was convicted. On appeal, the A.L.A. (D) argued that the Code does not apply because the A.L.A.'s (D) activities were wholly intrastate and the federal government (P) may only regulate interstate transactions.

ISSUE: Does the federal government have authority to regulate intrastate transactions having an indirect effect on interstate commerce?

HOLDING AND DECISION: (Hughes, C.J.) No. The federal government has no authority to regulate intrastate transactions having an indirect effect on interstate commerce. The chickens arrived in New York or Philadelphia through interstate commerce and the A.L.A.'s (D) purchase of those chickens did have an indirect effect on interstate transactions. The A.L.A.'s (D) activities, however, were wholly intrastate once the chickens arrived at the Brooklyn slaughterhouse. The transactions that occurred after the chickens were in state were

between A.L.A. (D) and local retailers, who sold to primarily local consumers. The simple fact that the chickens were once in the interstate "stream of commerce" does not automatically place the A.L.A. (D) under federal regulations. If the federal government is granted the authority to regulate even indirect effects on interstate commerce, the entire purpose behind state sovereignty is rendered moot. The distinction between direct and indirect effects of intrastate activities on interstate commerce must be of vital importance.

▶ ANALYSIS

This case is commonly known as the "sick chicken case" and was one in a series of cases intolerant of Franklin D. Roosevelt's New Deal economic legislation. The fear at the time was that the federal government was overreaching and that the states would not retain any authority over themselves. The Supreme Court issued a similar decision in *U.S. v. Lopez* in 1995.

■■■

Quicknotes

COMMERCE POWER The power delegated to Congress by the U.S. Constitution to regulate interstate commerce.

■■■

Hammer v. Dagenhart

Employment (D) v. Parent (P)

247 U.S. 251 (1918).

NATURE OF CASE: Appeal from a decree enjoining enforcement of the Child Labor Act.

FACT SUMMARY: Congress passed a law prohibiting the shipment in interstate commerce of any products of any mills, mines, or factories that employed children.

🏛 RULE OF LAW
Congress cannot, under its commerce power, pass a law prohibiting the transportation in interstate commerce of products of companies that employed children as laborers in violation of the terms of the law.

FACTS: A congressional act prohibited the shipment in interstate commerce of the product of any mill, cannery, workshop, or factory that employed children under the age of 14 or employed children between the ages of 14 and 16 for more than eight hours a day, or more than six days a week, or before 6 A.M. or after 7 P.M. Dagenhart (P) brought this action on behalf of his two minor children after being informed by the company where they worked of their impending discharge on the effective date of the act. Hammer (D), the U.S. Attorney General, and the company that had employed Dagenhart's (P) children were named as defendants.

ISSUE: Can Congress, under its commerce power, pass a law prohibiting the transportation in interstate commerce of products of companies that employed children as laborers in violation of the terms of the law?

HOLDING AND DECISION: (Day, J.) No. Congress cannot, under its commerce power, pass a law prohibiting the transportation in interstate commerce of products of companies that employed children as laborers in violation of the terms of the law. It is argued that the power of Congress to regulate commerce includes the power to prohibit the transportation of ordinary products in commerce. Here, the thing intended to be accomplished by this act is the denial of interstate commerce facilities to those employing children within the prohibited ages. The goods shipped are of themselves harmless. The production of articles intended for interstate commerce is a matter of local regulation. The making of goods and the mining of coal are not commerce, nor does the fact that these things are to be afterwards shipped or used in interstate commerce make their production a part thereof. It is also argued that congressional regulation is necessary because of the unfair advantage possessed by manufacturers in states that have less stringent child labor laws. However, Congress has no power to require states to exercise their police powers to prevent possible unfair competition. The

act is unconstitutional, and the decree enjoining its enforcement is affirmed.

DISSENT: (Holmes, J.) Precedent has established that a law is not beyond Congress's commerce power merely because it affects matters of state control. States are free to control within their borders, but once transportation extends beyond the borders, Congress may certainly intervene. Indirect effect on State action should not curtail congressional directives.

▶ ANALYSIS

After the *Hammer* decision, Congress sought to regulate child labor through the taxing power. That law was invalidated in *Bailey v. Drexel Furnishing Co.*, 259 U.S. 20 (1922). Subsequently, Congress submitted to the states a proposed constitutional amendment that authorized a national child-labor law. The amendment has not been ratified, but the need for it has largely disappeared in view of *U.S. v. Darby*, 312 U.S. 100 (1941), which overruled *Hammer*.

■===■

Quicknotes

COMMERCE POWER The power delegated to Congress by the U.S. Constitution to regulate interstate commerce.

■===■

Champion v. Ames

Interstate transporter (D) v. Government (P)

188 U.S. 321 (1903).

NATURE OF CASE: Appeal from dismissal of a petition for a writ of habeas corpus after indictment for conspiracy to violate a lottery law.

FACT SUMMARY: The Federal Lottery Act prohibited transporting lottery tickets from one state to another.

🏛 RULE OF LAW
Under its power to regulate commerce, Congress may, for the purpose of guarding the morals of the people and protecting interstate commerce, prohibit the carrying of lottery tickets in interstate commerce.

FACTS: Champion (D) was indicted for conspiracy to violate the Federal Lottery Act. The law prohibited importing, mailing, or transporting from one state to another any lottery ticket. The indictment charged shipment by Wells Fargo Express of a box containing lottery tickets. Champion (D) challenges the constitutionality of the Act.

ISSUE: May Congress, under its commerce power, prohibit the transporting of lottery tickets in interstate commerce?

HOLDING AND DECISION: (Harlan, J.) Yes. Congress may, under its commerce power, prohibit the transporting of lottery tickets in interstate commerce. The power to regulate commerce among the states has been expressly given to Congress. By this statute, Congress does not interfere with traffic or commerce carried on exclusively within the limits of a state. It is only regulating interstate commerce. As a state may, for the purpose of guarding the morals of its people, forbid all sales of lottery tickets within its limits, so Congress, for the purpose of guarding public morals and protecting interstate commerce, may prohibit transporting lottery tickets in interstate commerce. "We should hesitate long before adjudging that an evil of such an appalling character . . . cannot be met and crushed by the only power competent to that end."

▶ ANALYSIS

Early twentieth-century reformers seeking a constitutional basis for broader federal police measures were encouraged by the lottery decision. The decision is an example of one in which the court treats the commerce power as analogous to a federal police power, The lottery-case precedent sustained a variety of early twentieth-century laws excluding objects deemed harmful from interstate commerce. Examples include the Mann Act prohibiting the transportation of women for immoral purposes, a statute banning interstate transportation of adulterated or misbranded articles, and a statute banning interstate transportation of goods made in violation of state law or possession of which violated state law.

■■■

Quicknotes

COMMERCE POWER The power delegated to Congress by the U.S. Constitution to regulate interstate commerce.

HABEAS CORPUS A proceeding in which a defendant brings a writ to compel a judicial determination of whether he is lawfully being held in custody.

■■■

National Labor Relations Board v. Jones & Laughlin Steel Corp.

Federal agency (P) v. Steel company (D)

301 U.S. 1 (1937).

NATURE OF CASE: Action alleging unfair labor practice under the National Labor Relations Act.

FACT SUMMARY: Jones & Laughlin Steel Corp. (D), a manufacturing company with subsidiaries in several states and nationwide sales, was charged with an unfair labor practice under the National Labor Relations Act. In defense, Jones & Laughlin (D) claimed that the Act was an unconstitutional attempt to regulate intrastate production.

🏛 RULE OF LAW
Under the Commerce Clause, Congress has the power to regulate any activity, even intrastate production, if the activity has an appreciable effect, either direct or indirect, on interstate commerce.

FACTS: Pursuant to a complaint filed by a labor union, the National Labor Relations Board (P) found that Jones & Laughlin Steel (D) had engaged in "unfair labor practices." The Board (P) issued a cease and desist order to Jones & Laughlin (D) to stop using discriminatory and coercive practices to prevent union organization at two steel plants in and around Pittsburgh. Jones & Laughlin (D) operates its subsidiaries in multiple states, forming one integrated company. The thousands of employees were involved in the wholly owned subsidiaries. The company refused to comply and the Board (P) went to court for judicial enforcement of its order under the authority of the National Labor Relations Act of 1935. Jones & Laughlin (D) contended that the order was an unconstitutional exercise of the Board's (P) authority, since the plants were not engaged in interstate commerce, being totally manufacturing facilities. The court of appeals upheld the company's position and refused enforcement of the order on the ground that the order "lay beyond the range of federal power."

ISSUE: Do the manufacturing portions of a large, integrated multistate corporation fall within the constitutional meaning of the term "activities affecting commerce" so as to allow federal regulation thereof?

HOLDING AND DECISION: (Hughes, C.J.) Yes. The manufacturing portions of a large, integrated multistate corporation fall within the constitutional meaning of the term "activities affecting commerce" so as to allow federal regulation thereof. Under the Commerce Clause, Congress has the power to regulate any activity, even intrastate production, if the activity has an appreciable effect, either direct or indirect, on interstate commerce. The act of the Board (P) in ordering Jones & Laughlin (D) to cease interfering with its employees' rights of self-organization and collective bargaining, is an exercise of the congressional power to regulate interstate commerce. The definitions in the Act restrict the Board's (P) actions to protecting interstate commerce in the constitutional sense, and the Board (P) is given the power to determine if the practice in question affects commerce in such a way as to be subject to federal control. Congress has the power to protect interstate commerce by all appropriate types of legislation, and the controlling question is the effect on interstate commerce, not the source of the interference. Although such legislation may result in the regulation of acts that are intrastate in character, Congress still has the power to regulate if the intrastate acts bear such a close and substantial relation to interstate commerce that control is appropriate for the protection of commerce. Congress is forbidden only from regulating acts that have a remote and indirect effect on interstate commerce. Here, even though the application of the National Labor Relations Act results in the regulation of labor practices at Jones & Laughlin's (D) manufacturing plants, the circumstances indicate the required substantial effect on interstate commerce. If production were interrupted at one of the plants due to a labor dispute, the extensive nationwide operations of Jones & Laughlin (D) indicate that there would necessarily be an immediate effect on interstate commerce. Therefore, the National Labor Relations Act as applied to the facts of this case is a proper exercise of Congress's power to regulate interstate commerce.

DISSENT: (McReynolds, J.) Although employees may only be involved in production operations, those operations still affect interstate commerce and the labor practices of the company fall under federal purview. This is a broad statute with wide-sweeping consequences because nearly every industry can be viewed as having interstate operations due to out-of-state shipments of production lines.

▶ ANALYSIS

With this case the Supreme Court retreated from its strict geographical definition of interstate commerce and the direct/indirect approach that it used in *Schecter* and *Carter*. *Jones & Laughlin* states that under the Commerce Clause Congress has the power to regulate any activity that has a significant effect on interstate commerce, regardless of whether that effect is direct or indirect. This new concept is often called the "affectation doctrine." Although the Court cited prior cases in its opinion and said it was not creating new law, *Jones & Laughlin* is, in

Continued on next page.

effect, a reversal of the *Schecter* line of cases. The Court now bases its opinions on a combination of the Commerce Clause and the Necessary and Proper Clause: power to regulate interstate commerce extends to control over intrastate activities when necessary and appropriate to make regulation of interstate commerce effective.

■≡■

Quicknotes

COMMERCE CLAUSE   Article 1, section 8, clause 3 of the U.S. Constitution, granting Congress the power to regulate commerce with foreign countries and among the states.

COMMERCE POWER   The power delegated to Congress by the U.S. Constitution to regulate interstate commerce.

■≡■

United States v. Darby

Federal government (P) v. Manufacturer (D)

312 U.S. 100 (1941).

NATURE OF CASE: Criminal prosecution for violation of Fair Labor Standards Act.

FACT SUMMARY: Darby (D) was a lumber manufacturer, some of whose goods were later shipped in interstate commerce. He was indicted for violation of the wage and hour provisions of the Fair Labor Standards Act and defended on the ground that as an intrastate producer he was not subject to federal regulation.

🏛 RULE OF LAW
Congress has the power to regulate the hours and wages of workers who are engaged in the production of goods destined for interstate commerce and can prohibit the shipment in interstate commerce of goods manufactured in violation of the wage and hour provisions.

FACTS: Darby (D) was a manufacturer of finished lumber, and a large part of the lumber he produced was shipped in interstate commerce. The purpose of the Fair Labor Standards Act was to prevent the shipment in interstate commerce of certain products produced under substandard labor conditions. The Act set up minimum wages and maximum hours and punished the shipment in interstate commerce of goods produced in violation of the wage/hour requirements and also punished the employment of persons in violation of those requirements. Darby (D) was arrested for both shipment of goods in violation of the Act and employment of workers in violation of the Act. [The trial court dismissed the indictment on the ground that the Act was an unconstitutional regulation of manufacturing within the states.]

ISSUE: Does Congress have the power to prohibit shipment in interstate commerce of goods produced in violation of the wage/hour provisions of the Labor Standards Act and the power to prohibit employment of workers involved in the production of goods for interstate shipment in violation of the wage/hour provisions of the Labor Standards Act?

HOLDING AND DECISION: (Stone, J.) Yes. Congress has the power to prohibit shipment in interstate commerce of goods produced in violation of the wage/hour provisions of the Labor Standards Act and the power to prohibit employment of workers involved in the production of goods for interstate shipment in violation of the wage/hour provisions of the Labor Standards Act. Both prohibitions are a constitutional exercise of Congress's commerce power. Although manufacturing itself is not interstate commerce, the shipment of goods across state lines is interstate commerce and the prohibition of such shipment is a regulation of commerce. Congress has plenary power to exclude from

interstate commerce any article that it determines to be injurious to public welfare, subject only to the specific prohibitions of the Constitution. In the Fair Labor Standards Act, Congress has determined that the shipment of goods produced under substandard labor conditions is injurious to commerce and therefore has the power to prohibit the shipment of such goods, independent of the indirect effect of such prohibition on the states. The prohibition of employment of workers engaged in the production of goods for interstate commerce at substandard conditions is also sustainable, independent of the power to exclude the shipment of the goods so produced. The power over interstate commerce is not confined to the regulation of commerce among the states, but includes regulation of intrastate activities that so affect interstate commerce as to make regulation of them an appropriate means to the end of regulating interstate commerce. Here, Congress has determined that the employment of workers in substandard conditions is a form of unfair competition injurious to interstate commerce, since the goods so produced will be lower priced than the goods produced under adequate conditions. Such a form of competition would hasten the spread of substandard conditions and produce a dislocation of commerce and the destruction of many businesses. Since Congress has the power to suppress this form of unfair competition, and the Act is an appropriate means to that end, the wage/hour provisions are within Congress's power. It is irrelevant that only part of the goods produced will be shipped in interstate commerce. Congress has power to regulate the whole factory even though only a part of the products will have an effect on interstate commerce.

▶ ANALYSIS

Darby is an example of the application of the affectation doctrine. It had long been the law that Congress had the power to exclude from interstate commerce harmful objects or immoral activities, such as erroneously labeled goods or lottery tickets. This case extends the power to exclude articles produced under conditions that Congress considered harmful to the national welfare. Even though production of lumber was an entirely intrastate activity, it was a part of an economic process that led to the eventual sale of lumber across state limits, affecting interstate commerce. The federal commerce power extends to purely interstate transactions; the effect on commerce, not the location of the regulated act, is the basis for the exercise of the federal power. This case overruled the earlier case of *Hammer v. Dagenhart,* 247 U.S. 251 (1918), which held

Continued on next page.

unconstitutional an attempt by Congress to exclude articles made by child labor from interstate commerce.

■━■

Quicknotes

COMMERCE POWER The power delegated to Congress by
the U.S. Constitution to regulate interstate commerce.

■━■

Wickard v. Filburn

Department of Agriculture (P) v. Farmer (D)

317 U.S. 111 (1942).

NATURE OF CASE: Action to enjoin enforcement of penalty provisions of the Agricultural Adjustment Act.

FACT SUMMARY: Filburn (D) was ordered to pay a penalty imposed by the Agriculture Adjustment Act for producing wheat in excess of his assigned quota. He argued that the federal regulations could not be constitutionally applied to his crops because part of his crop was intended for his own consumption, not for interstate commerce.

🏛 **RULE OF LAW**
Farm production that is intended for consumption on the farm is subject to Congress's commerce power, since it may have a substantial economic effect on interstate commerce.

FACTS: The purpose of the Agriculture Adjustment Act was to control the volume of wheat moving in interstate commerce to avoid surpluses and shortages that would result in abnormally high or low prices and thereby obstruct commerce. Under the Act, the Secretary of Agriculture would set a national acreage allotment for wheat production, which would be divided into allotments for individual farms. Filburn (D) was the owner and operator of a small farm. In the past he had grown a small amount of wheat of which he sold part, fed part to poultry and livestock (some of the livestock were later sold), used part in making flour for home consumption, and kept the rest for seeding the next year. In 1940, his wheat production exceeded the maximum he was allowed under the Agriculture Adjustment Act and he was assessed a penalty for the excess. Filburn (D) refused to pay on the ground that the Act was unconstitutional in that it attempted to regulate purely local production and consumption that, at most, had an indirect effect on interstate commerce. The government argued that the Act regulated not production and consumption, but only marketing (which was defined in the Act to include the feeding of the wheat to livestock which was later sold), and even if interpreted to include production and consumption, it was a legitimate exercise of the Commerce Clause and the Necessary and Proper Clause.

ISSUE: Does Congress, under the Commerce Clause, have the power to regulate the production of wheat that is grown for home-consumption purposes rather than for sale in interstate commerce?

HOLDING AND DECISION: (Jackson, J.) Yes. Under the Commerce Clause, Congress has the power to regulate the production of wheat that is grown for home-consumption purposes rather than for sale in interstate commerce. Farm production that is intended for consumption on the farm is subject to Congress's commerce power, since it may have a substantial economic effect on interstate commerce. A local activity, such as production, may be reached under the Commerce Clause if it exerts a substantial economic effect on interstate commerce. The Act was enacted because of the problems of the wheat market: there had been a decrease in export in recent years, causing surpluses that in turn caused congestion in the market and lower prices. It has been repeatedly held that the commerce power of Congress includes the power to regulate prices and practices affecting prices. Wheat destined for home consumption has an effect on the interstate price of wheat and is, therefore, subject to regulation. As the market price of wheat climbs, farmers will sell more of their crop that was intended for home consumption on the market causing a decrease in prices. Even if the wheat is never sold, there still is a substantial effect on interstate commerce because it reduces demand for wheat; the wheat that Filburn (D) produces for his own use means that he will buy less wheat on the market. Although the actual effect of Filburn's (D) overproduction will be small, the combination of all such producers does cause a substantial effect on commerce.

▶ *ANALYSIS*

Wickard is yet another application of the "affectation doctrine." The Court focuses not on the nature of the regulated activity (e.g., whether it is local) but on the final economic effect of that activity. Here, although the effect of Filburn's (D) excess wheat production was insignificant on the national market, there still was some effect, at least in theory, and thus regulation was allowed. The Court in *Wickard* expressly rejected the old formulas for determining the extent of the commerce power such as direct/indirect and production/commerce.

Quicknotes

COMMERCE POWER The power delegated to Congress by the U.S. Constitution to regulate interstate commerce.

NECESSARY AND PROPER CLAUSE, ARTICLE I, SECTION 8 OF THE U.S. CONSTITUTION Enables Congress to make all laws that may be "necessary and proper" to execute its other, enumerated powers.

Heart of Atlanta Motel, Inc. v. United States

Local business (P) v. Federal government (D)

379 U.S. 241 (1964).

NATURE OF CASE: Declaratory judgment action regarding enforcement of a federal civil rights act.

FACT SUMMARY: The applicability of the 1964 Civil Rights Act to a business local in scope was challenged as unconstitutional.

RULE OF LAW
Congress, under the Commerce Clause, may regulate businesses local in scope, if their business activities have some impact on interstate commerce.

FACTS: In 1964, Congress passed the Civil Rights Act, which forbade, among other things, racial discrimination in public accommodations. Heart of Atlanta Motel, Inc. (P), which operated a single motel in Atlanta, brought an action seeking a declaration that enforcement of the law was unconstitutional against a local business such as it. The court of appeals upheld the Act's validity, and the Supreme Court granted review.

ISSUE: May Congress under the Commerce Clause regulate businesses local in scope if their business activities in some way have an impact on interstate commerce?

HOLDING AND DECISION: (Clark, J.) Yes. Under the Commerce Clause, Congress may regulate businesses local in scope if their business activities in some way have an impact on interstate commerce. The Commerce Clause allows Congress to regulate commerce among the several states. That a particular business is local in character does not impact on Congress's ability to regulate it, provided that the business in some manner impacts interstate commerce. The 1964 Civil Rights Act may be applied to a business local in scope. Here, Congress found that racial discrimination in public lodging had a deleterious effect on the interstate movement of persons and goods, a conclusion that it could rationally make. Also, the fact that Congress's primary motivation in enacting the law might have been moral rather than economic is of no moment; as long as a valid commercial motivation for a law exists, moral concerns are irrelevant.

CONCURRENCE: (Douglas, J.) The Commerce Clause should not be the sole justification for the Court's opinion. The Fourteenth Amendment may be more apt here. Individual constitutional rights should be of more importance than the interstate transportation of products.

▶ ANALYSIS

It has been argued that this case represented the de facto end of the federal system of government instituted by the nation's Founders. This case established the principal that the scope of the Commerce Clause was so broad that almost any sort of activity could be touched thereby. Essentially, after this case, Congress's regulatory power has been unlimited, a result almost certainly not intended by the Constitution's Framers.

Quicknotes

COMMERCE CLAUSE Article 1, section 8, clause 3 of the U.S. Constitution, granting Congress the power to regulate commerce with foreign countries and among the states.

Katzenbach v. McClung, Sr. & McClung, Jr.

Attorney General (D) v. Restaurant owner (P)

379 U.S. 294 (1964).

NATURE OF CASE: Action seeking injunctive relief and attacking the validity of Title II of the Civil Rights Act of 1964 as applied to a restaurant.

FACT SUMMARY: Ollie's Barbeque refused sit-down service to Negroes. The lower court found that a substantial portion of the food served in the restaurant had moved in interstate commerce.

🏛 RULE OF LAW
Although an activity is local and may not be regarded as commerce, it may still be reached by Congress if it exerts a substantial economic effect on interstate commerce.

FACTS: Ollie's Barbeque is a family-owned restaurant situated on a state highway, eleven blocks from an interstate highway and a somewhat greater distance from railroad and bus stations. It has a take-out service for Negroes but refuses to serve them in its dining rooms. The lower court found that a substantial portion of the food served in the restaurant had moved in interstate commerce. It is argued that Congress legislated a conclusive presumption that racial discrimination in restaurants serving food, which has been transported in interstate commerce, affects such commerce. Congress made no formal findings on this issue.

ISSUE: May Congress, pursuant to its commerce power, prohibit racial discrimination in a restaurant that serves food that was transported in interstate commerce?

HOLDING AND DECISION: (Clark, J.) Yes. Pursuant to its commerce power, Congress may prohibit racial discrimination in a restaurant that serves food that was transported in interstate commerce. Although an activity is local and may not be regarded as commerce, it may still, whatever its nature, be reached by Congress if it exerts a substantial economic effect on interstate commerce. Further, although an individual defendant or plaintiff's own effect on commerce may be slight, if their contribution taken together with that of many others similarly situated is substantial, then the individual's activity may be regulated. Hence, although the amount of food served at Ollie's may be insignificant when compared with the amount of food transported in interstate commerce and although Ollie's may appear to be local, Congress may still regulate it if there is a rational basis for its finding the Civil Rights Act to be necessary to the protection of commerce. It is true that Congress did not make any formal findings as to the effect upon commerce of racial discrimination in restaurants. However, Congress did conduct prolonged hearings on the Act and the record is replete with testimony of the burdens placed on commerce by discrimination in restaurants. Diminished spending by Negroes resulting from discrimination practiced by restaurants and the total loss of such customers has, regardless of the absence of direct evidence, a close connection to interstate commerce. Also, there was testimony that discrimination in restaurants had a direct and restrictive effect upon interstate travel by Negroes. This testimony afforded ample basis for the conclusion that restaurants practicing discrimination sold less interstate food, travel was obstructed, and business in general suffered due to the practice of racial discrimination in restaurants. Hence, Congress had a rational basis for finding that such discrimination had a direct and adverse effect on the free flow of interstate commerce. The Act, as applied to restaurants and to Ollie's, is constitutional.

▶ ANALYSIS

Prior to the 1964 Act, the Court had found that general provisions of the Interstate Commerce Act prohibited racial discrimination by interstate carriers. *Henderson v. U.S.*, 339 U.S. 816 (1950), held that these provisions prohibited segregation in railroad dining cars. In *Boynton v. Virginia*, 364 U.S. 454 (1960), the Court reversed a trespass conviction of a black interstate bus passenger who had been refused service at a bus terminal restaurant. Though, like the Interstate Commerce Act, the National Labor Relations Act and the Railway Labor Act contain no provisions specifically addressed to racial discrimination, interpretations have made them applicable to the civil rights area. In *Steele v. Louisville & Nashville R.R. Co.*, 323 U.S. 192 (1944), it was held that a union's status as exclusive bargaining agent under the Railway Labor Act carried the implied duty to represent all members in the bargaining unit without discrimination.

■≡■

Quicknotes

COMMERCE POWER The power delegated to Congress by the U.S. Constitution to regulate interstate commerce.

■≡■

National League of Cities v. Usery

Cities (P) v. Labor Secretary (D)

426 U.S. 833 (1976).

NATURE OF CASE: Action for declaratory judgment.

FACT SUMMARY: Congress, in 1974, extended the minimum wage and overtime provisions of the Fair Labor Standards Act to cover all state and municipal employees.

🏛 RULE OF LAW

The Tenth Amendment prohibits Congress to enact any legislation designed to "operate to directly displace the states' freedom to structure integral operations in ... traditional government functions," and, as such, Congress may not employ the Commerce Power to interfere with any state activity, the performance of which can be characterized as an "attribute of sovereignty."

FACTS: In 1938, Congress passed the Fair Labor Standards Act to regulate minimum wage and overtime pay in private industry. The Act was valid under the commerce power. In 1974, the Act was amended to apply to public employees. Usery (P) contends that Congress exceeded its authority when it applied the Act to regulate the states as public employers.

ISSUE: May Congress, acting pursuant to the Commerce Power, regulate the labor market insofar as it concerns state and municipal government employees?

HOLDING AND DECISION: (Rehnquist, J.) No. Pursuant to the Commerce Clause, Congress may not regulate the labor market insofar as it concerns state and municipal government employees. The Tenth Amendment prohibits Congress from enacting any legislation designed to "operate to directly displace the states' freedom to structure integral operations in ... traditional governmental functions," and, as such, Congress may not employ the Commerce Power to interfere with any state activity, the performance of which can be characterized as an "attribute of sovereignty." Though the Commerce Power is correctly characterized as plenary, it is not without other constitutional limitations. One such limitation, the Tenth Amendment, protects the states against any intrusion into sovereign state activities. There can be little doubt that the amendments challenged here interfere with "attributes of sovereignty" of the states. The increased costs to the states coupled with the necessary interference in the delivery of service (which will certainly be occasioned by the work adjustments which these amendments will cause) clearly interfere with the right of the states to manage their own affairs.

CONCURRENCE: (Blackmun, J.) The virtual balancing approach adopted today for determining when the Commerce Power must give way to the Tenth Amendment is essential to federalism.

DISSENT: (Brennan, J.) This Court has held the Commerce Power to be absolute since *Gibbons v. Ogden*. The abstraction manufactured by the Court is no more viable today than when it was rejected by the Court in the late 1930s when dealing with New Deal legislation.

DISSENT: (Stevens, J.) The federal government already regulates state employment activities in such things as fair hiring, environmental guidelines, and transportation limitations. It is difficult to understand that the federal government cannot regulate state wages.

▶ ANALYSIS

This case points up one more example of the Burger Court's policy of restricting federal power while expanding the "sovereign" powers of the states. Note that it overrules the 1968 case of *Maryland v. Wirtz*, 392 US 183 (1968), in which early 1960s amendments to the FLSA (dealing with extensions of the act to public employees "engaged in commerce" and/or working in state hospitals, schools, and other institutions) were sustained by the Court under the Commerce Power. Note also that the rationale of the Court is identical to the later discredited rationale of the early 1930s Court, which invalidated much of the early New Deal legislation (*Carter v. Carter Coal*, [298 U.S. 238 (1936)], *Hammer v. Dagenhart*, *U.S. v. Butler*, etc.).

■==■

Quicknotes

COMMERCE CLAUSE Article 1, section 8, clause 3 of the U.S. Constitution, granting Congress the power to regulate commerce with foreign countries and among the states.

COMMERCE POWER The power delegated to Congress by the U.S. Constitution to regulate interstate commerce.

TENTH AMENDMENT The Tenth Amendment to the U.S. Constitution reserves those powers therein, not expressly delegated to the federal government or prohibited to the states, to the states or to the people.

■==■

Garcia v. San Antonio Metropolitan Transit Authority

State department (P) v. Public transportation agency (D)

469 U.S. 528 (1985).

NATURE OF CASE: Appeal from denial of application of federal labor standards to state operations.

FACT SUMMARY: Garcia (P) appealed from a decision for San Antonio Metropolitan Transit Authority (SAMTA) (D) holding that municipal ownership and operation of a mass transit system is a traditional governmental function and thus, according to the test established in National League of Cities v. Usery, 426 U.S. 833 (1976), its system was immune from the requirements of the Fair Labor Standards Act (FLSA).

🏛 RULE OF LAW
The test for determining state immunity from federal regulation under the Commerce Clause is not whether the state activity sought to be regulated is a traditional state function, but rather whether the regulation as applied to the state activity is destructive of state sovereignty or violative of any constitutional provision.

FACTS: SAMTA (D) is the public mass transit authority that provides transportation in the San Antonio metropolitan area. The Wage and Hour Administration of the Department of Labor (P) found that SAMTA's (D) operations were not immune from the application of the minimum wage and overtime requirements of FLSA. SAMTA (D) filed an action for declaratory judgment, seeking a ruling that pursuant to the earlier decision in *National League of Cities v. Usery*, its activities comprised a traditional governmental function and were thus immune from the requirements of the FLSA. During the appeals of this case, the Supreme Court decided a case that found that the provision of a commuter rail service was not a traditional governmental function and thus did not enjoy constitutional immunity from congressional regulation under the Commerce Clause. The case was remanded to the district court in light of this case, which adhered to its original view and entered judgment in favor of SAMTA (D). From this decision, Garcia (P) appealed.

ISSUE: Does the test for determining whether a state activity is immune from federal regulation under the Commerce Clause continue to include a determination of whether the activity is a traditional state governmental function?

HOLDING AND DECISION: (Blackmun, J.) No. The test for determining state immunity from federal regulation under the Commerce Clause is not whether the state activity sought to be regulated is a traditional governmental function, but rather whether the regulation as applied to the state activity is destructive of state sovereignty or violative of

any constitutional provision. The prerequisite for governmental immunity under *National League of Cities v. Usery*, that the federal statute infringes on traditional governmental functions, has proved to be an unworkable standard. The *National League* case gave no indication of how to determine whether a function was a traditional or nontraditional one. The decisions of the lower courts, which have made elusive constitutional distinctions in order to find some functions traditional and others nontraditional, indicate the difficulty in applying the standard. This Court has previously rejected the notion that a governmental function could be determined to be traditional on a purely historical basis, since this basis does not allow accommodating changes in the historical functions of states. Any distinction that purports to separate out important governmental functions is inconsistent with the role of federalism in a democratic society, which allows states to engage freely in any activity not forbidden to them under the Constitution, since allowing unelected federal judiciaries to determine which functions may be important disserves the principles of democratic self-government. The manner in which the states are insulated from congressional regulation under the Commerce Clause is found in the limitations imposed by the Constitution under Article I and in the structure of the federal government itself, which in giving the states considerable influence over both branches of the Congress and the executive branch, affords the states protection against the unbridled regulation of the federal government under the Commerce Clause. The constitutional scheme developed to protect the "states as states" is thus one of process, not one of result. It is sufficient to say that in the present case the application of the minimum wage and overtime requirements of the FLSA to SAMTA (D) is not destructive of state sovereignty or violative of any constitutional provision, and that therefore SAMTA (D) is not immune from the application of the FLSA. *National League of Cities v. Usery* is overruled. Reversed and remanded.

DISSENT: (Powell, J.) The Court in the present case works a substantial alteration of the federal government and the states, allowing Congress to assume a state's sovereign power free from judicial review. The Framers intended the states to retain sovereignty in some matters at least and the majority completely ignores that intention. The majority offers no explanation as to how the states will protect their sovereignty simply through their role in the electoral process.

DISSENT: (Rehnquist, J.) Either approach suggested by the dissents is preferable to the Court's actions in the

Continued on next page.

present case, and under either approach, the judgment of the district court should be affirmed.

▶ *ANALYSIS*

The continuing validity of *National League of Cities v. Usery* had always been in doubt, and the scope of that particular opinion had uncertain limits. For example, it was not clear that Congress would be prohibited from affecting traditional governmental function of the states under various powers delegated to Congress, such as the war power or the civil rights enforcement power, and it was not clear whether that decision would apply to regulatory conditions attached to federal grants disbursed through the spending power.

■══■

Quicknotes

COMMERCE POWER The power delegated to Congress by the U.S. Constitution to regulate interstate commerce.

■══■

United States v. Lopez

Federal government (P) v. Student (D)

514 U.S. 549 (1995).

NATURE OF CASE: Appeal from order reversing federal firearms-law violation conviction.

FACT SUMMARY: Lopez (D) was convicted under the 1990 federal Gun-Free School Zones Act, which prohibited guns near schools.

🏛 RULE OF LAW
The 1990 federal Gun-Free School Zones Act exceeded Congress's Commerce Clause regulatory powers.

FACTS: The 1990 federal Gun-Free School Zones Act made it a federal offense for a student to carry a gun onto campus. Lopez (D) was charged and convicted under the Act. On appeal, he contended that the Act was beyond Congress's powers under the Commerce Clause. The Fifth Circuit agreed and reversed. The Supreme Court granted review.

ISSUE: Did the 1990 Federal Gun-Free School Zones Act exceed Congress's Commerce Clause regulatory power?

HOLDING AND DECISION: (Rehnquist, C.J.) Yes. The 1990 federal Gun-Free School Zones Act exceeded Congress's Commerce Clause regulatory powers. It must be remembered that the federal government is one of limited, enumerated powers. For Congress to legislate, it must do so under an express constitutional provision. Since the 1930s, the Commerce Clause has been the source of most of Congress's legislative power. However, this clause is not a general grant of police power. A law passed under this Clause must relate to: (1) a channel of interstate commerce; (2) an instrumentality of interstate commerce; or (3) an activity having a substantial effect on interstate commerce. In this case, the regulated activity, carrying a gun to school, has no such effect. It is a purely local matter. Granted, if one is willing to accept a lengthy series of interferences and assumptions, such an activity may affect interstate commerce. Any activity can do so. However, if the concept of limited federal government is to have any meaning, Congress's legislative power must be cut off somewhere. That somewhere is the point at which a regulated activity does not substantially affect interstate commerce, and that point has been passed here.

CONCURRENCE: (Kennedy, J.) It is only with great care that this Court should intervene in matters relating to the Commerce Clause, as it is a matter best left to the political sectors of government. However, when an exercise of power under the Clause unduly upsets the balance of power between the states and the national government, as does the law at issue here, it is proper for the Court to intervene.

CONCURRENCE: (Thomas, J.) The substantial effects test is a New Deal innovation that goes far beyond the original intent of the Framers, who had a much narrower view of what commerce could be regulated. In fact, it grants Congress something approaching a general police power, a result clearly at odds with the Tenth Amendment.

DISSENT: (Stevens, J.) The education of our youth has a major impact on the national economy and is a proper subject for Commerce Clause regulation.

DISSENT: (Souter, J.) The Court's approach today constitutes a step backward towards the excessive judicial activism that characterized judicial review of congressional enactments during the first third of this century.

DISSENT: (Breyer, J.) In determining whether a regulated activity has a significant impact on interstate commerce, it is necessary to consider not a single example of the regulated activity, but rather the cumulative effects of all similar instances of that conduct. Here, it is clear that the cumulative impact of the possession of weapons by students on campus will, over time, have a significant impact on the national economy.

▶ ANALYSIS

Since 1937, the scope of congressional regulatory power under the Commerce Clause has grown enormously. By the 1960s, Congress's power under the Clause had increased to a level approaching a general police power. The present case represents the first significant break in this pattern and may signal a states' rights trend.

■≡■

Quicknotes

COMMERCE CLAUSE Article 1, section 8, clause 3 of the U.S. Constitution, granting Congress the power to regulate commerce with foreign countries and among the states.

■≡■

United States v. Morrison

Federal government (P) v. Students (D)

529 U.S. 598 (2000).

NATURE OF CASE: Suit alleging sexual assault in violation of the Violence Against Women Act.

FACT SUMMARY: Brzonkala (P) brought suit against two football-playing male students (D) and Virginia Polytechnic University under the Violence Against Women Act.

🏛 RULE OF LAW
Commerce Clause regulation of intrastate activity may be upheld only where the activity being regulated is economic in nature.

FACTS: Brzonkala (P), a student at Virginia Polytechnic Institute, complained that football-playing students Morrison (D) and Crawford (D) assaulted and repeatedly raped her. Virginia Tech's Judicial Committee found insufficient evidence to punish Crawford (D), but found Morrison (D) guilty of sexual assault and sentenced him to immediate suspension for two semesters. The school's vice president set this aside as excessive punishment. Brzonkala (P) then dropped out of the university and brought suit against the school and the male students (D) under the Violence Against Women Act, 42 U.S.C. § 13981, providing a federal cause of action of a crime of violence motivated by gender.

ISSUE: May Commerce Clause regulation of intrastate activity be upheld only where the activity being regulated is economic in nature?

HOLDING AND DECISION: (Rehnquist, C.J.) Yes. Commerce Clause regulation of intrastate activity may be upheld only where the activity being regulated is economic in nature. The Court considered whether either the Commerce Clause or the Fourteenth Amendment authorized Congress to create this new cause of action. There are three main categories of activity Congress may regulate under its Commerce Clause power: (1) the use of channels of interstate commerce; (2) regulation or protection of the instrumentalities of interstate commerce or persons or things in interstate commerce, though the threat may come from intrastate activities; and (3) the power to regulate those activities having a substantial relation to interstate commerce. Brzonkala (P) argued that § 13981 fell under the third category. In *Lopez*, this Court concluded that those cases in which federal regulation of intrastate activity (based on the activity's substantial effects on interstate commerce) has been sustained have included some type of economic endeavor. Gender-motivated crimes of violence are not economic activities. While § 13981 is supported by numerous findings regarding the serious impact that gender-motivated violence has on victims and their families, the existence of congressional findings is not sufficient in itself to sustain the constitutionality of Commerce Clause legislation. Whether a particular activity affects interstate commerce sufficiently to come under the constitutional power of Congress to regulate is a judicial question. The Court also rejects the argument that Congress may regulate noneconomic, violent criminal conduct based solely on that conduct's aggregate effect on interstate commerce. The regulation and punishment of intrastate violence that is not directed at the instrumentalities of interstate commerce is reserved to the states.

CONCURRENCE: (Thomas, J.) The notion of a substantial effects test is inconsistent with Congress's powers and early Commerce Clause jurisprudence, perpetuating the federal government's (P) view that the Commerce Clause has no limits.

DISSENT: (Souter, J.) Congress has the power to legislate with regard to activities that in the aggregate have a substantial effect on interstate commerce. The fact of the substantial effect is a question for Congress in the first instance and not the courts. Here, Congress assembled a mountain of data demonstrating the effects of violence against women on interstate commerce.

▶ ANALYSIS

The primary issue here is that the federal government is seeking to regulate areas traditionally regulated exclusively by the states. The majority concludes that the regulation and punishment of intrastate violence that is not directed to the instrumentalities of interstate commerce is the exclusive jurisdiction of local government. What the dissent argues here is that Congress in this case has amassed substantial findings to demonstrate that such intrastate violence does have an effect on the instrumentalities of commerce.

■=■

Quicknotes

COMMERCE CLAUSE Article 1, section 8, clause 3 of the U.S. Constitution, granting Congress the power to regulate commerce with foreign countries and among the states.

■=■

Pierce County, Washington v. Guillen

Municipal government (D) v. Decedent's spouse (P)

573 U.S. 129 (2003).

NATURE OF CASE: Constitutional challenge to federal information confidentiality statute.

FACT SUMMARY: Guillen's (P) wife died in a car accident at a known dangerous intersection. Pierce County, Washington (Pierce County) (P) had attempted to get federal funding to make the intersection safer, but had been denied. Guillen (P) challenged the constitutionality of the federal privacy statute that protected the documentation of Pierce County's efforts to obtain federal funding.

🏛 RULE OF LAW

Congress's commerce power authorizes legislation aimed to improve the safety of the channels of interstate commerce.

FACTS: Congress passed legislation meant to assist states in identifying highways in need of safety improvements and allocated federal funds to implement those improvements. States were concerned that publicly obtaining and documenting the information that certain highways and intersections were unsafe would increase their liability prior to implementing the safety measures. The federal government responded to the concerns by passing additional legislation prohibiting the release of the gathered highway information. Pierce County (D) attempted to obtain federal funds to address the dangerousness of a certain intersection within its county, but the funds were initially denied. Ignacio Guillen's (P) wife was killed at that intersection before the application for funds could be renewed. The second application was approved. Guillen (P) sued Pierce County (D) and sought to discover the applications and information surrounding the safety of the intersection. Pierce County (D) claimed the protection of the federal privacy statute. Guillen (P) challenged the constitutionality of the statute as an improper exercise of congressional power.

ISSUE: Does Congress's commerce power authorize legislation aimed to improve the safety of the channels of interstate commerce?

HOLDING AND DECISION: (Thomas, J.) Yes. Congress's commerce power authorizes legislation aimed to improve the safety of the channels of interstate commerce. The states were reluctant to provide the necessary safety information about the condition of their highways because of liability issues. The federal government is within its rights and authority to provide protections that would encourage the production of that information. Congress may regulate interstate commerce under the Commerce Power, and that regulation includes control over the channels of interstate commerce, such as highways. The privacy

provision will result in greater safety on the nation's highways. The statute is constitutional.

▶ ANALYSIS

States could abuse the privacy statute by withholding all information about any accidents at a given intersection, but the overall effect of the statute is to increase highway safety nationwide. Although disclosure is usually preferred in litigation, confidentiality for the benefit of the people generally should trump the need for disclosure in one individual's case.

Quicknotes

COMMERCE CLAUSE Article 1, section 8, clause 3 of the U.S. Constitution, granting Congress the power to regulate commerce with foreign countries and among the states.

Gonzales v. Raich

Attorney General (D) v. Medicinal user of marijuana (P)

545 U.S. 1 (2005).

NATURE OF CASE: Suit for injunctive and declaratory relief challenging the validity of the federal Controlled Substances Act as applied to the medicinal use of marijuana.

FACT SUMMARY: Two sufferers of serious physical ailments sought to grow and use marijuana for medicinal purposes as permitted by California law.

🏛 RULE OF LAW

The Commerce Clause permits Congress to criminalize local cultivation and medicinal use of marijuana even if those uses otherwise comply with a state's laws.

FACTS: Congress enacted the Controlled Substances Act (CSA), which could be interpreted to proscribe possessing, obtaining, or manufacturing marijuana for personal medicinal use. Angel Raich (P) and Diane Monson (P), California residents who suffered from serious medical conditions, wanted to use marijuana for medicinal purposes, a use permitted by California law. Raich (P) and Monson (P) sued the Government (D) for injunctive and declaratory relief to prohibit the CSA from being enforced against them.

ISSUE: Does the Commerce Clause permit Congress to criminalize local cultivation and medicinal use of marijuana even if those uses otherwise comply with a state's laws?

HOLDING AND DECISION: (Stevens, J.) Yes. The Commerce Clause permits Congress to criminalize local cultivation and medicinal use of marijuana even if those uses otherwise comply with a state's laws. Congress may regulate local economic activities that substantially affect interstate commerce. As applied to Angel Raich (P) and Diane Monson (P), the CSA would comply with that standard: the statute would regulate home-grown, home-used marijuana, an activity that would substantially affect the nationwide market for marijuana. The decisions in *United States v. Morrison*, 529 U.S. 598 (2000), and *Lopez v. United States*, 514 U.S. 549 (1995), are inapposite because those cases decided challenges to entire statutes, and they involved no economic activity; the proposed use here seeks only to invalidate local enforcement of the CSA for a very specific purpose, and the use is also an economic activity. Vacated and remanded.

CONCURRENCE: (Scalia, J.) By itself, the Commerce Clause is not sufficient to support the CSA's application against Raich (P) and Monson (P). The CSA has the essential additional support, however, in the Necessary and Proper Clause, which permits Congress to regulate local, noneconomic activity if the regulation is necessary to effectuate valid legislation enacted pursuant to the Commerce Clause.

Here, Congressional regulation of Raich's (P) and Monson's (P) proposed use of marijuana should be permitted as a necessary part of the CSA's overall regulatory scheme.

DISSENT: (O'Connor, J.) The Court today denies California citizens the ability to serve as a national laboratory on the question of medicinal use of marijuana. Contrary to precedent, the majority has upheld federal law under the Commerce Clause without any proof that the proposed use of marijuana constitutes economic activity or that the use substantially affects interstate commerce even if it is economic activity. Today's definition of "economic activity" is effectively unlimited because the marijuana at issue here was never remotely involved in interstate commerce. Moreover, there was no evidence that in-home medicinal use of marijuana makes up a large enough proportion of the national market for marijuana to be detected at all, let alone to be seen as "substantially affecting" the national market. Regardless of how this Court might assess the wisdom of California's laws, that state's citizens should be permitted to conduct the local experiment that they chose.

DISSENT: (Thomas, J.) This decision means that Congress can regulate almost anything under the Commerce Clause. Today's decision is wrong because merely possessing an item for personal use is not economic activity within the meaning of the Commerce Clause. The CSA fares no better under the Necessary and Proper Clause because regulating these proposed uses is not "necessary" based on some failure of California's law. The regulation also is not "proper" because it would undermine federalism and states' rights.

▶ ANALYSIS

The majority in *Raich* uses contemporary Commerce Clause analysis, as it must do, in distinguishing *Morrison* and *Lopez*. By grounding this decision in *Wickard v. Filburn*, 317 U.S. 111 (1942), though, the *Raich* majority seems to have restored much of the gigantic breadth of the Commerce Clause power that existed before *Lopez* was handed down in 1995.

■=■

Quicknotes

COMMERCE CLAUSE Article 1, section 8, clause 3 of the U.S. Constitution, granting Congress the power to regulate commerce with foreign countries and among the states.

INJUNCTIVE RELIEF A court order issued as a remedy, requiring a person to do, or prohibiting that person from doing, a specific act.

■=■

New York v. United States

State (P) v. Federal government (D)

505 U.S. 144 (1992).

NATURE OF CASE: Appeal of dismissal of suit for declaratory judgment.

FACT SUMMARY: New York (P) sought a declaration that the Low-Level Radioactive Waste Policy Amendments Act (1985 Act) was unconstitutional.

🏛 RULE OF LAW
The federal government may not order a state government to enact particular legislation.

FACTS: Three states had disposal sites for radioactive waste. After study and negotiation, the National Governors' Association (NGA) devised a plan that became the 1985 Act. The 1985 Act set deadlines for every state to join a regional waste compact, develop in-state disposal, or find another way to dispose of its own waste. The 1985 Act assured the sited states they would not have the entire nation's waste burden, and gave the other 47 states seven more years of access to active sites. The 1985 Act provided three incentives for state compliance: (1) Congress authorized sited states to impose a surcharge, part of which would go into federal escrow, with funds to be returned to complying states; (2) Congress empowered sited states to deny access to states not in compliance; and (3) any state not in compliance by 1992 had to either take title to all waste generated in their state or else become liable to in-state waste generators for all damages. As of 1990 New York (P) had not joined a regional waste compact. Unable to settle on an in-state site, New York (P) sought to invalidate the 1985 Act as violative of state sovereignty principles of the Tenth Amendment. The sited states intervened as defendants. The district court dismissed, the court of appeals affirmed, and New York (P) appealed.

ISSUE: May the federal government order a state government to enact particular legislation?

HOLDING AND DECISION: (O'Connor, J.) No. The federal government may not order a state government to enact particular legislation. The federal government may provide incentives for states to regulate in a certain way by tying funding to acceptance of a federal plan or by giving states a choice between enacting a federal plan or having state law preempted by federal law. The burden should fall on the waste generators and not on the states. The take title provision, the third incentive of the federal plan, crosses the line to coercion. Whether a state "chooses" to take title to waste or to accept liability for disposal, the burden of not enacting the federal plan falls on the state. The strength of the federal interest is irrelevant. Federal courts may issue directives to state officials, but the Constitution expressly grants that authority. Such authority is outside Congress's enumerated powers and, for that reason, also infringes on state sovereignty reserved by the Tenth Amendment. While the 1985 Act was a creation of and compromise among the states, the states may not constitutionally consent to give up their sovereignty.

CONCURRENCE AND DISSENT: (White, J.) The Acts were the product of cooperative federalism. The states bargained among themselves to solve an imminent crisis and achieve compromises for Congress to sanction. New York (P) reaped the benefits of the 1985 Act, an agreement that it helped formulate, and should not be able to sue now. The majority wrongly finds that states cannot consent to relinquish some sovereignty. Tenth Amendment restrictions on the commerce power are procedural limits, designed to prevent federal destruction of state governments, not to protect substantive areas of state autonomy.

CONCURRENCE AND DISSENT: (Stevens, J.) The notion that Congress may not order states to implement federal legislation is incorrect and unsound. The federal government regulates state railroads, schools, prisons, and elections, and in time of war, Congress undoubtedly could command states to supply soldiers.

▶ ANALYSIS

Under the Articles of Confederation, the federal government could act only by ordering states to enact legislation. The Framers decided that the federal government needed power to regulate citizens directly and so drafted the Constitution. The Court interpreted the Framers' decision as a rejection of federal power to order states to enact legislation.

■■■

Quicknotes

TENTH AMENDMENT The Tenth Amendment to the U.S. Constitution reserves those powers therein, not expressly delegated to the federal government or prohibited to the states, to the states or to the people.

■■■

Printz v. United States

Parties not identified.

521 U.S. 898 (1997).

NATURE OF CASE: Review of judgment upholding the constitutionality of the Brady Act.

FACT SUMMARY: Two chief law enforcement officers (CLEOs) (P) filed actions challenging the constitutionality of several interim provisions of the Brady Act, which required that they perform background checks on prospective gun purchasers.

🏛 RULE OF LAW
The federal government may neither issue directives requiring the states to address particular problems, nor command the states' officers, or those of their political subdivisions, to administer or enforce a federal regulatory program.

FACTS: The Gun Control Act of 1968 (GCA) established a detailed federal scheme governing the distribution of firearms. In 1993, Congress amended the GCA by passing the Brady Act, which required the attorney general to establish a national instant background check system by November 30, 1998, and immediately put into place certain interim provisions. The interim provisions required that any firearms dealer who proposed to sell a handgun must receive identifying information from the buyer and provide that information to the CLEO of the buyer's residence. The CLEO must make a reasonable effort to ascertain within five business days whether receipt or possession of the firearm would be in violation of any local, state, or federal law. Printz (P) and Mack (P), the CLEOs for counties in Montana and Arizona, respectively, filed separate actions challenging the Brady Act's interim provisions. They argued that the congressional action compelling state officers to execute federal laws and pressing them into service was unconstitutional. The government (D) countered that Congresses have been enacting statutes since the country's formation that required the participation of state officials in the implementation of federal laws. The district courts held that although the provisions were unconstitutional, they were severable from the remainder of the Act. On appeal, the holdings were reversed and all of the interim provisions were found to be constitutional. The Supreme Court granted review.

ISSUE: May the federal government issue directives requiring the states to address particular problems, or command the states' officers, or those of their political subdivisions, to administer or enforce a federal regulatory program?

HOLDING AND DECISION: (Scalia, J.) No. The federal government may neither issue directives requiring

the states to address particular problems, nor command the states' officers, or those of their political subdivisions, to administer or enforce a federal regulatory program. Although early Congresses may have been empowered to impress state judges into service, there is no evidence that they commanded the states' executive officers absent a particularized constitutional authorization. More recent federal statutes requiring the participation of state or local officials have been linked with federal funding measures unlike the one at issue here. Furthermore, the structure of the Constitution explicitly confers upon Congress the authority to regulate individuals, not the states. Finally, this Court, as well various circuit and appellate courts, have consistently concluded that Congress may not compel the states to enact or enforce a federal regulatory program. Neither may Congress circumvent this prohibition by issuing directives to conscript state officers directly.

CONCURRENCE: (Thomas, J.) Such wholly point-of-sale, intrastate transactions as the intrastate sale of firearms is not to be regulated by the federal government. The majority is correct in holding that the Brady Act violates the Tenth Amendment, but it must be emphasized that the federal government has no regulatory control whatsoever over wholly intrastate transactions. In addition to the lack of authority to control, it is arguable that the Second Amendment also prevents federal government regulation as it pertains to transactions involving firearms.

DISSENT: (Stevens, J.) The Brady Act was passed in response to what Congress described as an "epidemic of gun violence," in essence, a national emergency. When Congress exercises the powers delegated to it by the Constitution, it may impose affirmative obligations on executive and judicial officers of state and local governments as well as ordinary citizens. This conclusion is firmly supported by the text of the Constitution, the early history of the nation, decisions of this Court, and a correct understanding of the basic structure of the federal government.

▶ ANALYSIS

The majority and dissent both found numerous justifications, from mostly similar sources, of why the Brady Act's provisions should or should not stand. Justice Stevens perhaps brought up the most current and compelling argument: the necessity of addressing a serious and growing national problem. When evaluating a solution to a "national

Continued on next page.

epidemic" it would seem that finding a workable remedy would be most imperative.

■═■

Quicknotes

TENTH AMENDMENT The Tenth Amendment to the U.S. Constitution reserves those powers therein, not expressly delegated to the federal government or prohibited to the states, to the states or to the people.

■═■

Reno v. Condon

U.S. Attorney General (D) v. State Attorney General (P)

528 U.S. 141 (2000).

NATURE OF CASE: Appeal from challenge to federal statute as violative of the Tenth Amendment.

FACT SUMMARY: A federal statute regulated the disclosure of private information contained in state motor vehicle department records. The statute was challenged as violating the Tenth Amendment's principles of federalism.

▦ RULE OF LAW
Congress may regulate the states' activities where the regulation does not require the states in their sovereign capacity to regulate their citizens.

FACTS: The Driver's Privacy Protection Act of 1994 (DPPA) regulated the disclosure and resale of personal information—such as a person's name, address, telephone number, Social Security number, etc.—contained in the records of state motor-vehicle departments. South Carolina's law conflicted with the DPPA's provisions, and the state challenged the law as violating the Tenth Amendment. [The District Court held for the state, and the Court of Appeals affirmed.]

ISSUE: May Congress regulate the states' activities where the regulation does not require the states in their sovereign capacity to regulate their citizens?

HOLDING AND DECISION: (Rehnquist, C.J.) Yes. Congress may regulate the states' activities where the regulation does not require the states in their sovereign capacity to regulate their citizens. The information in the state motor vehicle department records is a "thing in interstate commerce" because it is used by insurers, manufacturers, direct marketers and others engaged in interstate commerce. Accordingly, Congress presumptively has authority to regulate it under the Commerce Clause. However, the analysis of the statute's constitutionality does not stop there and must address federalism concerns. Here, the DPPA does not implicate the Tenth Amendment because, even though the state may have to devote time and effort to complying with the statute, the statute does not require the state to regulate its own citizens, to enact legislation, or to assist in the enforcement of federal statutes regulating private individuals.

▶ ANALYSIS

This case distinguished *New York v. United States*, 505 U.S. 144 (1992), and *Printz v. United States*, 521 U.S. 898 (1997), which had held that federal statutes were invalid because they had commandeered the state legislative process. Those cases protected the process of autonomous state lawmaking, holding that Congress could not require the

states to do Congress's work for it. Here, the Court protected Congress's substantive authority to regulate a certain field and displace the states from regulation.

■═■

Quicknotes

COMMERCE CLAUSE Article 1, section 8, clause 3 of the U.S. Constitution, granting Congress the power to regulate commerce with foreign countries and among the states.

TENTH AMENDMENT The Tenth Amendment to the U.S. Constitution reserves those powers therein, not expressly delegated to the federal government or prohibited to the states, to the states or to the people.

■═■

United States v. Butler

Federal government (D) v. Receivers (P)

297 U.S. 1 (1936).

NATURE OF CASE: Action challenging the constitutionality of the Agricultural Adjustment Act of 1933.

FACT SUMMARY: [The Agricultural Adjustment Act of 1933 stated that there was a national economic emergency arising from the low price of agricultural products in comparison with other commodities. To remedy this situation, a tax would be collected from processors of an agricultural product. The revenue raised would be paid to farmers who curtailed their production of that product.]

🏛 RULE OF LAW
Congress may not, under the pretext of exercising the taxing power, accomplish prohibited ends, such as the regulation of matters of purely state concern and clearly beyond its national powers.

FACTS: [The Agricultural Adjustment Act of 1933 declared that a national economic emergency had arisen due to the disparity between the prices of agricultural and other commodities, resulting in the destruction of farmers' purchasing power. To remedy this situation, a tax would be collected from processors of agricultural products. The revenue raised thereby would be paid to farmers who voluntarily curtailed their production of those crops used by the processors. The Secretary of Agriculture was to determine the crops to which the Act's plan would apply. In July 1933, the Secretary determined that the Act's plan should be applied to cotton. A tax claim was presented to Butler (P) as receivers of the Hoosal Mills Corp., as cotton processors. The district court held the tax to be valid.]

ISSUE: Is a tax on the processing of agricultural products valid where the revenue raised by the tax is to be paid to farmers who voluntarily curtail their production of crops?

HOLDING AND DECISION: (Roberts, J.) No. Congress may not, under the pretext of exercising the taxing power, accomplish prohibited ends, such as the regulation of matters of purely state concern and clearly beyond its national powers. First, Butler (P) has standing to question the validity of the tax because it is but a part of the unconstitutional plan of the Agricultural Adjustment Act. The Spending Power in Article I, § 8 is a distinct federal power limited in that it must be exercised for the general welfare of the people. Section 8 is not to be used to authorize legislation passed for the general welfare of the people. The Act seeks to regulate and control agricultural production, a matter beyond the power of the federal government. The farmer who chooses not to comply with the plan loses benefits, which relieves the Act of any semblance of voluntary compliance. The federal government is attempting to regulate wholly state activity through the Spending Power as an enforcement mechanism. The Spending Power is not an end run around state regulatory power.

DISSENT: (Stone, J.) Courts are to be concerned only with the power to enact statutes, not with their wisdom. The constitutional power of Congress to tax the processing of agricultural products is not questioned. The tax is held to be invalid because it is a step in a plan to regulate agricultural production. Nothing indicates, however, that this is an unconstitutional delegation of legislative power and it certainly is a legitimate use of the taxing and spending power. Such a limitation is contradictory and destructive of the power to appropriate for the public welfare, and is incapable of practical application. Congress's spending power is not subordinate to its legislative powers. The Act is not unconstitutional merely because it seeks to defray an expenditure for the welfare of the people rather than use taxes to support another government function.

▶ ANALYSIS

The *Butler* decision contributed greatly to the pressure that produced the court-packing plan a few months later. It is called the landmark case in the area of federal regulation of local matters through taxation. However, if the tax and the appropriation provisions had not been so closely tied together, it is doubtful that the court would have invalidated the tax. The tax appeared to have a valid revenue-raising purpose, and once separated from the taxing provisions, there would have been no one with standing to attack the appropriation.

■===■

Quicknotes

SPENDING POWER The power delegated to Congress by the U.S. Constitution to spend money in providing for the nation's welfare.

TAXING POWER The authority delegated to Congress by the U.S. Constitution to impose taxes.

■===■

Sabri v. United States

Real estate developer (D) v. Federal government (P)

541 U.S. 600 (2004).

NATURE OF CASE: Constitutional challenge to federal antibribery statute.

FACT SUMMARY: Defendant developer offered bribes to a city councilman to ease his real estate building plans. He was convicted for violating the federal antibribery statute, which he now challenges as unconstitutional.

🏛 RULE OF LAW
The absence of a nexus between federal funding and prohibited conduct does not result in a statute's presumed unconstitutionality.

FACTS: Basim Omar Sabri (D), a real estate developer, sought to ease the process for his development by bribing a city councilman on three separate occasions. The federal government (P) indicted Sabri (D) for violating 18 U.S.C. § 666(a)(2), which criminalizes bribing officials of organizations that receive over $10,000 in federal funds. After Sabri (D) was convicted, he challenged the constitutionality of § 666. Sabri (D) claimed that the section was unconstitutional because there was no requirement to prove the connection between the federal funds and the bribe. The Supreme Court granted certiorari.

ISSUE: Does the absence of a nexus between federal funding and prohibited conduct result in a statute's presumed unconstitutionality?

HOLDING AND DECISION: (Souter, J.) No. The absence of a nexus between federal funding and prohibited conduct does not result in a statute's presumed unconstitutionality. The defendant's argument is easily disposed of. Nothing requires such a connection so long as the federal government is acting within its legitimate authority under the Necessary and Proper clause. The Spending Power permits the federal government to condition the provision of federal funding upon certain conditions, such as the prohibition of accepting bribes. A direct correlation between the funds going through the entity and the bribe being accepted may not be able to be found and is not necessary to establish as an element of the crime.

CONCURRENCE: (Thomas, J.) The Necessary and Proper clause does not give the federal government unfettered power. A connection between the corrupt transaction and the federal benefit should have to be shown. This case should have been decided on Commerce Clause jurisprudence, but the judgment was correct nonetheless.

▶ ANALYSIS

It is appropriate for the federal government to ensure that its funds are being spent for the general welfare and not given away in response to bribes. The federal government commonly conditions grants to state governments and the Supreme Court usually affirms the conditions.

■■■■■

Quicknotes

NECESSARY AND PROPER CLAUSE, ARTICLE I, SECTION 8 OF THE U.S. CONSTITUTION Enables Congress to make all laws that may be "necessary and proper" to execute its other, enumerated powers.

SPENDING POWER The power delegated to Congress by the U.S. Constitution to spend money in providing for the nation's welfare.

■■■■■

South Dakota v. Dole

State (P) v. Federal Government (D)

483 U.S. 203 (1987).

NATURE OF CASE: Appeal from decisions upholding federal highway funding requirement.

FACT SUMMARY: Congress passed a law withholding federal highway funds to states with a minimum drinking age of less than 21 years.

🏛 RULE OF LAW
Congress may withhold federal highway funds to states with a minimum drinking age of less than 21 years.

FACTS: In 1984, Congress enacted 23 U.S.C. § 158, which directed the Secretary of Transportation to withhold 5 percent of federal highway funds to states with a drinking age of less than 21 years of age. [This was based on the perception that border states with drinking ages of less than 21 encouraged drinking and driving.] South Dakota (P) sought a declaration that the law was unconstitutional. [The district and circuit courts upheld the law, and the Supreme Court granted review.]

ISSUE: May Congress withhold federal highway funds to states with a minimum drinking age of less than 21 years?

HOLDING AND DECISION: (Rehnquist, C.J.) Yes. Congress may withhold federal highway funds to states with a minimum drinking age of less than 21 years. It is well recognized that Congress may use its spending power to induce cooperation by states in areas that it cannot necessarily regulate directly. Therefore, even if Congress could not directly legislate state drinking ages, it can use the threat of withheld funds to achieve its regulatory goal. South Dakota (P) argued that alcohol is a special case, as the Twenty-First Amendment specifically leaves the regulation of drinking to the states. However, this leads the analysis back to its point of origin, namely, that Congress can indirectly regulate through its spending power. That is all it has done here.

DISSENT: (Brennan, J.) The Twenty-First Amendment expressly reserves the regulation of alcohol to the states.

DISSENT: (O'Connor, J.) Section 158 cannot be justified as reasonably related to the federal highway system. It is an attempt to regulate alcoholic beverages, something Congress may not do.

ANALYSIS

It is not uncommon for Congress to attempt to regulate "with a carrot" rather than by direct regulation. The present case is one such action. Probably the most controversial area where this has been subject to constitutional consideration is in the area of abortions. Cases such as *Maher v. Roe*, 432 U.S. 464 (1977), and *Rust v. Sullivan*, 500 U.S. 173 (1991), have established Congress's right in this area.

Quicknotes

SPENDING POWER The power delegated to Congress by the U.S. Constitution to spend money in providing for the nation's welfare.

United States v. Morrison

Federal government (P) v. Accused rapist (D)

529 U.S. 598 (2000).

NATURE OF CASE: Constitutional challenge to the Violence Against Women Act.

FACT SUMMARY: Defendant was accused of sexually assaulting a freshman student at a Virginia university and the victim sued the defendant for civil damages under the Violence Against Women Act (VAWA). The defendant challenged the constitutionality of the civil damages portion of VAWA.

🏛 RULE OF LAW
The Fourteenth Amendment does not support the enforcement of the civil damages remedy of the Violence Against Women Act.

FACTS: Ms. Brzonkala alleged that defendant Morrison (D) sexually assaulted her when she was a freshman at Virginia Tech University. Brzonkala sued Morrison (D) in federal civil court seeking damages under the Violence Against Women Act (VAWA). Morrison (D) challenged the constitutionality of the VAWA, contending that Congress had no authority to enact the VAWA. The federal government (P) argued that Congress had the authority under the Fourteenth Amendment.

ISSUE: Does the Fourteenth Amendment support the enforcement of the civil damages remedy of the Violence Against Women Act?

HOLDING AND DECISION: (Rehnquist, C.J.) No. The Fourteenth Amendment does not support the enforcement of the civil damages remedy of the Violence Against Women Act. Congress may address discriminatory conduct through § 5 of the Fourteenth Amendment, subject to certain limitations. If the congressional laws are directed toward conduct of private persons, the laws exceed Congress's limits, as this Court held in the Civil Rights Cases. The remedy Ms. Brzonkala seeks must be found in Virginia state courts and not the federal courts.

DISSENT: (Breyer, J.) Congress was not seeking to regulate private persons' conduct through § 5, but rather, was regulating state conduct when states did not provide sufficient remedies for gender-motivated violence.

▶ ANALYSIS

Critics argue that Congress was really reaching when it determined that gender-motivated violence against women affected interstate commerce. One of the justifications was that women were afraid to travel out of fear of assault. This case is one in a line in which the Supreme Court had to curtail congressional efforts to regulate more conduct using its power to regulate interstate commerce. The Court emphasizes that Congress may regulate only economic activities that substantially affect interstate commerce.

■=■

Quicknotes

FOURTEENTH AMENDMENT Amendment to the U.S. Constitution; declares that no state shall make or enforce any law that shall abridge the privileges or immunities of citizens of the United States. No state shall deny to any person within its jurisdiction the equal protection of the laws.

■=■

Katzenbach v. Morgan & Morgan

Registered voters (P) v. State attorney general (D)

384 U.S. 641 (1966).

NATURE OF CASE: Challenge to constitutionality of federal statute.

FACT SUMMARY: As part of the Voting Rights Act, Congress inserted a provision that prohibited restrictions on the right to register to vote because of the applicant's inability to read and write English where the applicant had at least a sixth-grade education in a Puerto Rican school where instruction was primarily in Spanish. New York had a statutory requirement of an ability to read and write English as a prerequisite to voter registration.

🏛 RULE OF LAW
A federal statute enacted pursuant to the Enabling Clause of the Fourteenth Amendment supersedes any state constitutional or statutory provision that is in conflict with the federal law.

FACTS: New York had a statute that required all persons seeking to register to vote be able to read and write the English language. In the Voting Rights Act of 1965, Congress inserted a provision that prohibited a requirement of English reading and writing ability where the person seeking to vote had completed at least a sixth-grade education in Puerto Rico, where the language of instruction is primarily Spanish. This suit was instituted by a group of registered voters in New York who challenged that provision of the federal statute insofar as it would prohibit enforcement of the New York requirement. At issue were the several hundred thousand Puerto Rican immigrants in New York who were prevented from voting by the New York statute, but who would be qualified under the federal law. The Attorney General of New York filed a brief in which he argued that the federal legislation would supersede the state law only if the state law were found to violate the provisions of the Fourteenth Amendment without reference to the federal statute. Also advanced was the argument that the federal statute violated the Equal Protection Clause of the Fourteenth Amendment, since it discriminated between non-English-speaking persons from Puerto Rico and non-English-speaking persons from other countries.

ISSUE: Does a federal statute enacted pursuant to the Enabling Clause of the Fourteenth Amendment supersede a conflicting state law by reason of the Supremacy Clause of the U.S. Constitution?

HOLDING AND DECISION: (Brennan, J.) Yes. A federal statute enacted pursuant to the Enabling Clause of the Fourteenth Amendment supersedes any state constitutional or statutory provision that is in conflict with the federal law. There is no need to determine if the New York English

literacy law is violative of the Fourteenth Amendment Equal Protection Clause in order to validate the federal law respecting voter qualifications. If Congress were limited to restricting only those state laws that violated the amendment, there would be no need for the federal law, since the state law could be invalidated in the courts. Rather, the test must be whether the federal legislation is appropriate to enforcement of the Equal Protection Clause. Section 5 of the Fourteenth Amendment is to be read to grant the same powers as the Necessary and Proper Clause of Article I, § 8. Therefore, the federal statute must be examined to see if it is "plainly adapted to that end" and whether it is not prohibited by but is consistent with "the letter and spirit of the Constitution." It was well within congressional authority to say that the need to vote by the Puerto Rican community warranted intrusion upon any state interests served by the English-literacy test. The federal law was "plainly adapted" to furthering the aims of the Fourteenth Amendment. There is a perceivable basis for Congress to determine that this legislation was a proper way to resolve an inequity resulting from Congress's evaluation that an invidious discrimination existed. As to the contention that the federal law itself violates the Equal Protection Clause, the law does not restrict anyone's voting rights, but rather extends the franchise to a previously ineligible group. This was a reform measure and, as we have previously held, Congress need not correct an entire evil with one law but may "take one step at a time, addressing itself" to that problem which seems most pressing. We hold, therefore, that the federal law was a proper exercise of the powers granted Congress by the Fourteenth Amendment and that the Supremacy Clause prevents enforcement of the New York statute insofar as it is inconsistent with the federal law. Reversed.

DISSENT: (Harlan, J.) The majority has confused the question of legislative enforcement power with the area of proper judicial review. The question here is whether the state law is so arbitrary or irrational as to violate the Equal Protection Clause. And that is a judicial, not legislative, determination. The majority has validated a legislative determination by Congress that a state law is violative of the Constitution. There is no record of any evidence secured by Congress to support this determination. The judiciary is the ultimate arbiter of constitutionality, not Congress.

▶ *ANALYSIS*

As has occurred before, there was a footnote to the decision that caused as much controversy as the decision

Continued on next page.

itself. In this footnote, the court stated that Congress could enact legislation giving force to the Fourteenth Amendment that expanded the rights provided in the Amendment, but could not dilute or restrict the Amendment by legislation. In other words, Congress can make determinations of constitutionality so long as they expand rights but cannot make those determinations if they restrict rights. However, there is serious debate as to whether allowing Congress to take an independent role in interpreting the Constitution can be justified under any circumstances in view of *Marbury v. Madison*. Once loosed in this area, can any restraint be thereafter imposed? Congress has traditionally tried to stay within judicially circumscribed bounds of constitutionality. But if it has an "independent role" in this area, the restraints are removed. An example of this may be seen in the Omnibus Crime Control Act, wherein Congress made legislative inroads to judicially granted rights as expressed in the *Miranda* decision. The court can always rule on these inroads, but is it not better that Congress not be encouraged to embark on them in the first instance?

■═■

Quicknotes

ENABLING CLAUSE OF THE FOURTEENTH AMENDMENT A provision in the U.S. Constitution granting the power to implement and enforce the law.

EQUAL PROTECTION CLAUSE A constitutional provision that each person be guaranteed the same protection of the laws enjoyed by other persons in like circumstances.

NECESSARY AND PROPER CLAUSE, ARTICLE I, SECTION 8 OF THE U.S. CONSTITUTION Enables Congress to make all laws that may be "necessary and proper" to execute its other, enumerated powers.

■═■

City of Boerne v. Flores

City (D) v. Archbishop (P)

521 U.S. 507 (1997).

NATURE OF CASE: Review of judgment sustaining the constitutionality of the Religious Freedom Restoration Act of 1993.

FACT SUMMARY: After the city of Boerne (D) denied Archbishop Flores (P) a building permit to expand a church, he contended that the permit denial violated the Religious Freedom Restoration Act (RFRA).

🏛 **RULE OF LAW**
The RFRA unconstitutionally exceeds Congress's enforcement power under the Due Process Clause of the Fourteenth Amendment.

FACTS: The Religious Freedom Restoration Act (RFRA) prohibited the government from substantially burdening a person's exercise of religion, even if the burden is the result of a generally applicable law, unless the government has a compelling interest and is using the least restrictive means. Boerne (D) enacted a city ordinance requiring city preapproval for any construction on any of the city's historic landmarks. Archbishop Flores (P) sought a building permit to expand his church, a historic landmark. Boerne (D) denied the permit and Flores (P) sued, invoking the RFRA. The district court determined that the RFRA exceeded congressional power, but the Fifth Circuit reversed, holding the Act constitutional. Boerne (D) appealed.

ISSUE: Does the RFRA unconstitutionally exceed Congress's enforcement power under the Due Process Clause of the Fourteenth Amendment?

HOLDING AND DECISION: (Kennedy, J.) Yes. The RFRA unconstitutionally exceeds Congress's enforcement power under the Due Process Clause of the Fourteenth Amendment. Here, Congress, with the RFRA, attempts to replace, with the compelling-interest test, this Court's decision asserting that the compelling-interest test is inappropriate in cases involving general prohibitions with free exercise challenges. See *Employment Div., Dept. of Human Resources of Oregon v. Smith*, 494 U.S. 872 (1990). Such an action violates the long tradition of separation of powers established by the Constitution. The judiciary is to determine the constitutionality of laws, and the powers of the legislature are defined and limited. While Congress can enact remedial, preventive legislation that deters violations, the RFRA is not a preventive law. Instead, the RFRA redefines the scope of the Free Exercise Clause and nothing in our history extends to Congress the ability to take such action. The RFRA is so out of proportion to a supposed remedial or preventive object that it cannot be regarded as a response to unconstitutional behavior. Reversed.

DISSENT: (O'Connor, J.) Because the Court relies on the incorrectly decided *Smith* to establish the yardstick of the Free Exercise Clause, I dissent.

DISSENT: (Souter, J.) Because the Court relies on *Smith* to establish the yardstick of the Free Exercise Clause, and the appropriateness of the *Smith* standard was neither briefed nor argued, the case should be reargued.

▶ ANALYSIS

The Religious Freedom Restoration Act was one of the four federal laws overturned by the Supreme Court during its 1997 term. Although the Court has endorsed judicial restraint in recent years, it has not hesitated to quash improper intrusions on its authority to set unconstitutional standards. The Court, however, chose not to revisit the religious freedom issue in its *Boerne* decision, leaving intact the ruling in *Smith* that inspired Congress to pass the RFRA. In *Smith*, the Court approved Oregon's use of its ban on peyote to prohibit the drug's use in Native American religious rituals. The RFRA was intended to guarantee religious observance a higher degree of statutory protection than the *Smith* Court thought necessary.

Quicknotes

DUE PROCESS CLAUSE Clauses found in the Fifth and Fourteenth Amendments to the U.S. Constitution providing that no person shall be deprived of "life, liberty, or property, without due process of law."

FREE EXERCISE CLAUSE The guarantee of the First Amendment to the U.S. Constitution prohibiting Congress from enacting laws regarding the establishment of religion or prohibiting the free exercise thereof.

Fitzpatrick v. Bitzer

State employees (P) v. State official (D)

427 U.S. 445 (1976).

NATURE OF CASE: Class action brought against state alleging discrimination based on sex in violation of the Civil Rights Act of 1964.

FACT SUMMARY: Male state employees (P) brought in federal court a class action against a state (D) alleging that certain provisions of the state's statutory retirement-benefit plan discriminated against them because of their sex in violation of the Civil Rights Act of 1964.

🏛 RULE OF LAW

Congress may use its enforcement power under the Fourteenth Amendment to abrogate the states' sovereign immunity and to permit private suits against the states in federal court.

FACTS: Present and retired male employees (P) of the State of Connecticut brought in federal district court a class action alleging that certain provisions of Connecticut's statutory retirement plan discriminated against them because of their sex, in violation of Title VII of the Civil Rights Act of 1964, which extends coverage to the states as employers. The district court held in part for the claimants, but rejected their request for back pay on Eleventh Amendment grounds, and the court of appeals affirmed in part and reversed in part, holding that a private federal action for retroactive damages is not a constitutionally permissible method of enforcing Fourteenth Amendment rights.

ISSUE: May Congress use its enforcement power under the Fourteenth Amendment to abrogate the states' sovereign immunity and to permit private suits against the states in federal court?

HOLDING AND DECISION: (Rehnquist, J.) Yes. Congress, using its enforcement power under § 5 of the Fourteenth Amendment, in Title VII of the Civil Rights Act of 1964 authorized federal courts to award money damages to private individuals against state governments that subject the individual to employment discrimination. The issue is thus whether the Eleventh Amendment shields the states from such suits. The Eleventh Amendment, and the sovereign immunity from suits that it confers, are limited by the Fourteenth Amendment's enforcement provisions. The Fourteenth Amendment's substantive provisions by themselves impose significant limitations on state authority, and thus, when Congress acts under the enforcement provisions, not only is it exercising legislative authority, but it is also exercising authority under a constitutional amendment whose other sections also limit state authority. Therefore, Congress may determine that private suits against states are appropriate to enforcing the Fourteenth

Amendment, whereas such suits might not be permissible in other contexts.

▶ ANALYSIS

In addition to abrogation by Congress of the states' sovereign immunity to suit, under § 5 of the Fourteenth Amendment, the states themselves may waive their sovereign immunity from suit, but such waiver must be explicit. However, Congress may not authorize suits against states in state courts, without their consent, even for violations of federal law.

■═■

Quicknotes

ELEVENTH AMENDMENT The Eleventh Amendment to the U.S. Constitution prohibits the extension of the judicial powers of the federal courts to suits brought against a state by citizens of another state, or of a foreign state, without the state's consent.

FOURTEENTH AMENDMENT The Fourteenth Amendment to the U.S. Constitution declares that no state shall make or enforce any law that shall abridge the privileges or immunities of citizens of the United States. No state shall deny to any person within its jurisdiction the equal protection of the laws.

■═■

Seminole Tribe of Florida v. Florida

Indian tribe (P) v. State (D)

517 U.S. 44 (1996).

NATURE OF CASE: Appeal from decision dismissing a suit brought pursuant to the Indian Gaming Regulatory Act.

FACT SUMMARY: Florida (D) claimed it was immune from a suit under the Indian Gaming Regulatory Act although Congress had expressly provided federal courts with jurisdiction.

🏛 RULE OF LAW
Congress may not abrogate the states' immunity from suits.

FACTS: Congress enacted the Indian Gaming Regulatory Act providing that Indian tribes may conduct gaming activities following an agreement with the state in which the activities are located. The Act imposes upon the states a duty to negotiate with the tribes and authorizes tribes to bring suit against a state in federal court to compel the negotiations. In 1991, the Seminole Tribe (P) brought suit against Florida (D) for failing to negotiate. Florida (D) moved to dismiss the suit, arguing that the suit violated Florida's (D) sovereign immunity. The district court denied the motion, but the Eleventh Circuit reversed, holding that the Eleventh Amendment barred the suit. The Supreme Court granted certiorari.

ISSUE: May Congress abrogate the states' immunity from suits?

HOLDING AND DECISION: (Rehnquist, C.J.) No. Congress may not abrogate the states' immunity from suits. The Eleventh Amendment provides that the states are immune from suits by the citizens of the United States. Congressional intent to abrogate the states' immunity from suit must be obvious from a clear legislative statement. In the present case, the Indian Gaming Regulatory Act includes an unmistakably clear statement of the intent to abrogate. The next consideration is whether the law was passed pursuant to a constitutional provision giving Congress that power. The only such provisions this Court has found to give Congress the power to abrogate are the Fourteenth Amendment and the Commerce Clause. Since the case that ruled that the Commerce Clause can give Congress the power to abrogate arose from an incorrect rationale, it is hereby overruled. The Eleventh Amendment prevents congressional authorization of suits against states even where the Constitution has vested Congress with authority over a particular area of law.

DISSENT: (Stevens, J.) The majority decision is a sharp break from precedent and may be read to prevent Congress from providing a federal forum for a broad range of actions against states, such as those sounding in copyright, patent, and bankruptcy law.

DISSENT: (Souter, J.) The Eleventh Amendment does not bar federal-question jurisdiction in the federal courts involving a state as a party. *Hans v. Louisiana*, 134 U.S. 1 (1890), misunderstood this fact and mischaracterized the purpose and structure of the Eleventh Amendment. A careful review of the history of sovereign-immunity in England and in early America as well as the Framers' intent leads to this conclusion. The majority today compounds the error in *Hans* by constitutionalizing the holding in *Hans* when Congress has chosen to abrogate it.

▶ ANALYSIS

In allowing the abrogation power for the Fourteenth Amendment only, the majority placed considerable weight on the fact that it was passed after the Eleventh Amendment. On the other hand, the majority believed that the Eleventh Amendment took away any authority that the Commerce Clause may have provided because it came afterward. As Justice Stevens pointed out, this case could carry significant ramifications for the relationship between the states and the federal government.

Quicknotes

COMMERCE CLAUSE Article 1, section 8, clause 3 of the U.S. Constitution, granting Congress the power to regulate commerce with foreign countries and among the states.

ELEVENTH AMENDMENT The Eleventh Amendment to the U.S. Constitution prohibits the extension of the judicial powers of the federal courts to suits brought against a state by citizens of another state, or of a foreign state, without the state's consent.

United States v. Georgia

Prisoner (P) v. State (D)

546 U.S. 151 (2006).

NATURE OF CASE: Review of federal appeals court judgment.

FACT SUMMARY: A paraplegic prisoner, Tony Goodman (P), sued the state prison (D) for discrimination. The state (D) claimed it was immune from such suits.

🏛 RULE OF LAW
(1) Title II of the Americans with Disabilities Act of 1990 abolished state sovereign immunity for suits by prisoners with disabilities claiming discrimination by state prisons.
(2) Title II was a proper exercise of Congress's power under § 5 of the Fourteenth Amendment, as applied to the administration of prison systems.

FACTS: Tony Goodman (P) was a paraplegic held in a Georgia state prison, and he sued the state of Georgia (D) in federal court for maintaining prison conditions that allegedly discriminated against disabled people and violated Title II of the Americans with Disabilities Act (ADA). Georgia (D) claimed it was immune from the suit under the Eleventh Amendment of the U.S. Constitution. The district court ruled for Georgia (D), but the Court of Appeals for the Eleventh Circuit reversed. Before the Eleventh Circuit ruled in the case, the United States sued Georgia (D), arguing that the ADA's Title II abolished state sovereign immunity from monetary suits. Congress could do this, the U.S. argued, by exercising its Fourteenth Amendment power to enforce equal protection.

ISSUE:
(1) Did Title II of the Americans with Disabilities Act of 1990 abolish state sovereign immunity for suits by prisoners with disabilities claiming discrimination by state prisons?
(2) Was Title II a proper exercise of Congress's power under § 5 of the Fourteenth Amendment, as applied to the administration of prison systems?

HOLDING AND DECISION: (Scalia, J.)

(1) Yes. Title II of the Americans with Disabilities Act of 1990 abolished state sovereign immunity for suits by prisoners with disabilities claiming discrimination by state prisons. Title II abrogates sovereign immunity in cases where violations of the Eighth Amendment are alleged. The Fourteenth Amendment incorporates the Eighth Amendment by making it apply to the states.
(2) Yes. Title II was a proper exercise of Congress's power under § 5 of the Fourteenth Amendment, as applied to

the administration of prison systems. Congress can enforce the Fourteenth Amendment against the states "by creating private remedies against the States for actual violations" of its provisions, which can involve abrogating state sovereign immunity.

⏵ ANALYSIS

Note that the Court did not address the question of whether Title II validly abrogates sovereign immunity when the Eighth Amendment is not involved.

■■■

Quicknotes

EIGHTH AMENDMENT The Eighth Amendment to the federal constitution prohibits the imposition of excessive bail, fines, and cruel and unusual punishment.

ELEVENTH AMENDMENT The Eleventh Amendment to the U.S. Constitution prohibits the extension of the judicial powers of the federal courts to suits brought against a state by citizens of another state, or of a foreign state, without the state's consent.

■■■

Alden v. Maine

State employees (P) v. State (D)

527 U.S. 706 (1999).

NATURE OF CASE: Suit brought by state employees (P) against state (D) to enforce overtime provisions of federal labor statute.

FACT SUMMARY: State employees (P) sued in state court their employer, the State (D), claiming it had violated overtime provisions of a federal labor statute.

🏛 RULE OF LAW
Congress's Article I power does not authorize it to abrogate the states' immunity from suit on federal claims in their own courts.

FACTS: Probation officers (P) sued in Maine's trial court the State of Maine (D), claiming that it violated the provisions of the Fair Labor Standards Act of 1938 (FLSA) and sought compensation and damages. The State (D) had not consented to such suit, and the trial court dismissed on the basis of sovereign immunity. The Maine Supreme Judicial Court affirmed, and the Supreme Court granted review.

ISSUE: Does Congress's Article I power authorize it to abrogate the states' immunity from suit on federal claims in their own courts?

HOLDING AND DECISION: (Kennedy, J.) No. Immunity from suit was a fundamental aspect of sovereignty that the states enjoyed before the ratification of the Constitution and that they retained after ratification. The states' sovereignty is confirmed by the Tenth Amendment and the history that led to the enactment of the Eleventh Amendment (a reaction to *Chisolm v. Georgia*, 2 U.S. 419 (1973)), a Supreme Court case that held that a citizen of one state could sue another state without its consent). Rather than looking narrowly at the literal text of the Eleventh Amendment, the Court looks to the history and structure of the Constitution—the constitutional design—which support the inference that the Constitution preserves the states' traditional immunity from suit absent an express waiver. The power given to Congress in Article I and by the Supremacy Clause may override sovereign immunity only when doing so is in keeping with the constitutional design. Again, the history and structure of the Constitution do not permit an inference that the states could be stripped of their sovereign immunity in their own courts. This historical analysis encompasses early congressional practice and the Court's earlier decisions that described sovereign immunity in sweeping terms. Also, the principles of federalism and the role of the state courts in the constitutional design support this conclusion. Otherwise, the states would be forced, through their courts, to turn against themselves and would provide the federal government

with a power to control state governmental processes. Moreover, allowing private suits against the states could potentially force the states to become debtors and could severely burden the states' financial integrity. The constitutional system, with its recognition of the essential sovereignty of the states, strikes a balance between the supremacy of federal law and the states' sovereignty. The states still must obey federal laws that adhere to the constitutional design, and are subject to suits brought pursuant to Congress's enforcement power under § 5 of the Fourteenth Amendment. In addition, municipalities and state officers are not protected by sovereign immunity. Thus, the proper balance is struck between ensuring compliance with valid federal laws and respect for the states' sovereignty.

DISSENT: (Souter, J.) The majority's historical analysis is wrong. "Sovereign immunity" at common law was defeasible by statute and was not an unalterable right. The Constitution when first framed did not even mention sovereign immunity. The Colonies did not enjoy sovereign immunity, and some Framers thought it had no place in a republic. Some states initially did not see themselves as immune from suit, whereas others did. In any event, at the ratifying convention, no one was espousing an indefeasible, natural law view of sovereign immunity. Thus, the majority's rationale for its holding, which is based on a conception of sovereign immunity as fundamental to sovereignty or inherent in statehood, finds no support in the thinking of the Founders. The majority's other rationale, based on principles of federalism, also is flawed. That is because the states are not sovereign with respect to national objectives. Once a state has created courts of general jurisdiction, the Supremacy Clause requires those courts to entertain federal claims. Although the majority might respond that the federal government may bring suit in federal court against a state for violations of federal law, the reality is that it would be unlikely for the federal government to enforce private rights of close to five million state employees. The majority's ruling thus would have the same effect as not allowing state tort victims to sue unless they have a federal attorney. Ultimately, the majority's conception of state sovereign immunity is true neither to history nor to the Constitution's structure.

▶ ANALYSIS

Some, like the dissent, see *Alden* as part of a developing body of state sovereign-immunity jurisprudence that they compare to the Court's turn-of-the-century laissez faire

Continued on next page.

due process doctrines. The similarity lies in what these critics see as the Court's imputing immutable constitutional status to doctrines that are not based on truth or reality. The Court is clearly split into two factions in this area by a doctrinal rift.

■■■

Quicknotes

ELEVENTH AMENDMENT The Eleventh Amendment to the U.S. Constitution prohibits the extension of the judicial powers of the federal courts to suits brought against a state by citizens of another state, or of a foreign state, without the state's consent.

SOVEREIGN IMMUNITY Immunity of government from suit without its consent.

SUPREMACY CLAUSE Article VI, section 2 of the U.S. Constitution, which provides that federal action must prevail over inconsistent state action.

TENTH AMENDMENT The Tenth Amendment to the U.S. Constitution reserves those powers therein, not expressly delegated to the federal government or prohibited to the states, to the states or to the people.

■■■

The Federal Executive Power

Quick Reference Rules of Law

Youngstown Sheet & Tube Co. v. Sawyer

Steel companies (P) v. Federal government (D)

343 U.S. 579 (1952).

NATURE OF CASE: Suit for declaratory and injunctive relief from a presidential order.

FACT SUMMARY: Faced with an imminent steel strike during the Korean War, the President ordered governmental seizure of the steel companies to prevent the strike. The companies challenged his power to take such action as being without constitutional authority or prior congressional approval.

🏛 RULE OF LAW
The President, as leader of the executive branch, is bound to enforce the laws within the limits of the authority expressly granted to him by the Constitution, and he cannot usurp the lawmaking power of Congress by an assertion of an unspecified aggregation of his specified powers.

FACTS: As a result of long, but unsuccessful, negotiations with various steel companies, the United Steelworkers of America served notice of intent to strike in April, 1952. Through the last months of the negotiations the President had utilized every available administrative remedy to effect a settlement and avert a strike. Congress had engaged in extensive debate on solutions but had passed no legislation on the issue. By order of the President, the Secretary of Commerce seized the steel companies so that steel production would not be interrupted during the Korean War. The steel companies sued in federal district court to have the seizure order declared invalid and to enjoin its enforcement. The government asserted that the President had "inherent power" to make the order and that it was "supported by the Constitution, historical precedent and court decisions." The district court granted a preliminary injunction that was stayed the same day by the court of appeals. The Supreme Court granted certiorari and ordered immediate argument.

ISSUE: May the President, relying on a concept of inherent powers, and in his capacity as Commander-in-Chief, make an order that usurps the lawmaking authority of Congress on the basis of a compelling need to protect the national security?

HOLDING AND DECISION: (Black, J.) No. There is, admittedly, no express congressional authority for these seizures, and so, if any authority for the President's act can be found, it must come from the Constitution. In the absence of express authority for the President's act, it is argued that the power can be implied from the aggregate of his express powers granted by the Constitution. This order cannot be justified by reliance on the President's role as Commander-in-Chief. Even though the term "theater of war" has enjoyed an expanding definition, it cannot embrace the taking of private property to prevent a strike. The President's powers in the area of legislation are limited to proposing new laws to Congress or vetoing laws that he deems inadvisable. This order is not executive implementation of a congressional act but a legislative act performed by the President. Only Congress may do what the President has attempted here. The Constitution is specific in vesting the lawmaking powers in Congress, and we, therefore, affirm the district court's decision to enjoin the enforcement of this order.

CONCURRENCE: (Jackson, J.) The power of the President to act can be viewed as three separate categories of circumstances. First, the President's power is at its maximum when he acts pursuant to express or implied congressional authority. Second, in the absence of a congressional grant of power, the President acts solely on the basis of his powers as specified in the Constitution. Third, when the President acts in contravention of congressional action, he may do so only where it can be shown that Congress has exceeded its constitutional powers and the President is acting in his own sphere of authority. It is in this last area where presidential acts are subject to the closest scrutiny. This order is clearly not in the first category. His act cannot be justified in the second category since Congress has limited seizure powers to specific instances not embracing this order. The constitutional grant of powers to the President is in specific terms that do not permit any loose aggregation to create powers not specified. There is little question that Congress could have authorized those seizures and this very power denies the same authority to the President.

CONCURRENCE: (Douglas, J.) The only branch of government that may authorize seizures is the branch that must authorize compensation, i.e., the Congress.

CONCURRENCE: (Frankfurter, J.) This decision does not attempt to define the limits of presidential authority. The President cannot act in contravention of an express congressional act, nor may he act where Congress has done nothing. Were this a case of a long history of congressional acquiescence to presidential practice our decision might be different, but no such showing has been made.

DISSENT: (Vinson, J.) The majority's opinion has left the President powerless to act at the very time the need for his independent and immediate action is greatest. The President's seizure in this case is in accord with congressional intent to support the resistance of aggression in the world and is in furtherance of his duty to execute the laws

Continued on next page.

of this nation. The executive is the only branch of government that may, by design, act swiftly to meet national emergencies. This decision emasculates that necessary power.

▶ *ANALYSIS*

This cases is popularly known as "The Steel Seizure Case." Justice Black's broad language was criticized by many scholars as being overly expansive for the case presented. However, other authorities pointed out that the broad arguments advanced by the government required a broad response. During oral argument before the court, the government counsel stated that while the Constitution imposed limits on congressional and judicial powers, no such limits were imposed on the presidency. While supplemental briefs were filed modifying this position, the damage may already have been done. The Court was faced with a paucity of judicial precedents. The President and Congress have traditionally preferred political rather than judicial solutions to their conflicts. This practice avoids the limitations imposed on future actions by binding judicial precedents. And, as can be seen by the cases of *Marbury v. Madison* (1803) and *United States v. Nixon* (1974), the executive branch has not fared well when it has submitted to judicial jurisdiction.

■■■

Quicknotes

EXECUTIVE BRANCH The branch of government responsible for the administration of the laws.

■■■

United States v. Richard M. Nixon, President of the United States

Federal government (P) v. President (D)

418 U.S. 683 (1974).

NATURE OF CASE: Certiorari granted after denial of a motion to quash a third-party subpoena duces tecum.

FACT SUMMARY: Nixon (D) challenges a subpoena served on him as a third party requiring the production of tapes and documents for use in a criminal prosecution.

🏛 RULE OF LAW
Absent a claim of need to protect military, diplomatic, or sensitive national security secrets, an absolute, unqualified presidential privilege of immunity from judicial process under all circumstances does not exist.

FACTS: After the grand jury returned an indictment charging seven defendants with various offenses relating to Watergate, Special Prosecutor Jaworski moved for the issuance of a subpoena duces tecum to obtain Watergate-related tapes and documents from Nixon (D). Jaworski claimed that the materials were important to the government's proof at the criminal proceeding against the seven defendants. The subpoena was issued, and Nixon (D) turned over some materials. His lawyer then moved to quash the subpoena. Nixon (D) contended that the separation of powers doctrine precludes judicial review of a presidential claim of privilege and that the need for confidentiality of high-level communication requires an absolute privilege as against a subpoena.

ISSUE: Does the President possess an absolute executive privilege that is immune from judicial review?

HOLDING AND DECISION: (Burger, C.J.) No. Absent a claim of need to protect military, diplomatic, or sensitive national security secrets, an absolute, unqualified presidential privilege of immunity from judicial process under all circumstances does not exist. First of all, Nixon (D) claimed the court lacks jurisdiction to issue the subpoena because the matter was an intrabranch dispute within the executive branch. However, courts must look behind names that symbolize the parties to determine whether a justiciable case or controversy exists. Here, the Special Prosecutor, with his asserted need for the subpoenaed material, was opposed by the President with his assertion of privilege against disclosure. This setting assures that there is the necessary concreteness and adversity to sharpen the presentation of the issues. Against Nixon's (D) claim of absolute privilege immune from judicial review, this court reaffirms the holding of *Marbury v. Madison* (1803) that "it is emphatically the province and duty of the Judicial Department to say what the law is," and this is true with respect to a claim of executive privilege. Absent a claim of need to protect military, diplomatic, or sensitive national security secrets, neither the doctrine of the separation of powers nor the generalized need for the confidentiality of high-level communications, without more, can sustain an absolute unqualified presidential privilege. Now that the Court has decided that legitimate needs of judicial process may outweigh presidential privilege, it is necessary to resolve those competing interests in this case. It is true that the need for confidentiality justifies a presumptive privilege for presidential communications. However, our criminal justice system depends on a complete presentation of all relevant facts. To ensure this presentation, compulsory process must be available. Here, Jaworski has demonstrated a specific need at a criminal trial for the material sought. Nixon (D) has not based his claim of privilege on the military or diplomatic content of the materials but rather on a generalized interest in confidentiality. The allowance of this privilege based on only a generalized interest in confidentiality to withhold relevant evidence in a criminal trial would cut deeply into the guarantee of due process and cannot prevail.

⏵ *ANALYSIS*

On July 16, 1973, Alexander Butterfield testified before the Senate Select Committee on presidential campaign activities that conversations in President Nixon's offices had been recorded automatically at Nixon's direction. Nixon declined to comply with requests for the tapes from Special Prosecutor Cox and the Senate Select Committee. Nixon maintained that the tapes would remain under his personal control. When a subpoena for the tapes was issued, Nixon replied that he asserted executive privilege and that the President is not subject to compulsory process from the courts. The grand jury then instructed the Special Prosecutor to seek an order for the production of the tapes. It was that enforcement proceeding which produced the first ruling in the case. Judge Sirica ordered the President to produce the items for in-camera inspection. The court of appeals affirmed. *Nixon v. Sirica*, 487 F.2d 700 (1973).

■═■

Quicknotes

EXECUTIVE PRIVILEGE The right of the executive branch to refuse to disclose confidential communications if such exemption is necessary for the effective discharge of its official duties.

SUBPOENA DUCES TECUM A court mandate compelling the production of documents under a witness' control.

■═■

William J. Clinton, President of the United States v. City of New York

Parties not identified.

524 U.S. 417 (1998).

NATURE OF CASE: Challenge to the constitutionality of new presidential powers.

FACT SUMMARY: The Line Item Veto Act of 1996 allowed the president to cancel provisions that have been signed into law. Parties affected by President Clinton's cancellation of a provision of the Balanced Budget Act of 1997 challenged the constitutionality of the Act.

🏛 **RULE OF LAW**
The cancellation provisions authorized by the Line Item Veto Act are not constitutional.

FACTS: President Clinton used his authority under the Line Item Veto Act of 1996 to cancel a provision of the Balanced Budget Act of 1997. This forced New York to repay certain funds to the federal government under the Medicaid program and removed a tax benefit to food processors acquired by farmers' cooperatives. New York City and several private organizations challenged the constitutionality of the Medicaid cancellation, and the Snake River Potato Growers (a farmers' cooperative) challenged the food processors provision.

ISSUE: Are the cancellation provisions authorized by the Line Item Veto Act constitutional?

HOLDING AND DECISION: (Stevens, J.) No. The cancellation provisions authorized by the Line Item Veto Act are not constitutional. The Line Item Veto Act gives the President the power to "cancel in whole" three types of provisions that have already been signed into law: (1) any dollar amount of discretionary budget authority; (2) any item of new direct spending; or (3) any limited tax benefit. With respect to each cancellation, the President must determine that it will (i) reduce the Federal budget deficit; (ii) not impair any essential government functions; and (iii) not harm the national interest. A cancellation takes effect upon receipt by Congress of the notification of the cancellation. However, a majority vote of both Houses is sufficient to make the cancellation null and void. Although the Constitution expressly authorizes the President to veto a bill under Article I, § 7, it is silent on the subject of unilateral Presidential action that repeals or amends parts of duly enacted statues as authorized under the Line Item Veto Act. Constitutional silence should be construed as express prohibition. If there is to be a new role for the president in the procedure to determine the final text of a law, such a change must come through the amendment procedures and not by legislation.

CONCURRENCE: (Kennedy, J.) Separation of powers was designed to protect liberty, because the concentration of power in any single branch is a threat to liberty.

DISSENT: (Breyer, J.) Given how complex our nation has become, Congress cannot divide bills into thousands or tens of thousands of separate appropriations bills, each of which the President would have to veto or sign separately. Therefore, the Line Item Veto may help representative government work better.

▶ *ANALYSIS*

The majority did not comment on the wisdom of the Line Item Veto Act, because they found this step unnecessary given their finding that the Act was unconstitutional. Justice Kennedy did not let that stop him, since he felt that the Line Item Veto Act affected the separation of powers which in turn threatened liberty.

■━■

Quicknotes

LINE ITEM VETO ACT Act authorizes a government official to veto specified items in appropriation bills.

SEPARATION OF POWERS The system of checks and balances preventing one branch of government from infringing upon exercising the powers of another branch of government.

■━■

A.L.A. Schechter Poultry Corp. v. United States

Criminal defendant (D) v. Federal government (P)

295 U.S. 495 (1935).

NATURE OF CASE: Criminal action for violation of codes created by business groups acting under authority of power delegated to the President by Congress.

FACT SUMMARY: A corporation was indicted for alleged conspiracy and violations of a code that prescribed labor standards and other regulations for industry. The code, created by a business group delegated this authority by a federal law, was challenged as the product of an unconstitutional delegation of legislative power.

🏛 RULE OF LAW
Congress cannot delegate its legislative power to the President.

FACTS: The National Industrial Recovery Act delegated to the President the power to regulate various industries by redelegating to business groups and boards of the various industries authority to create codes of conduct for the industries. However, the statute itself did not prescribe standards to guide the creation of these codes. Schechter Poultry Corp. (D) was indicted for violating one of these codes that regulated the poultry industry in the New York City area. The code was challenged as having been created by an unconstitutional delegation of legislative power.

ISSUE: Can Congress delegate its legislative power to the President?

HOLDING AND DECISION: (Hughes, C.J.) No. Congress cannot delegate to the President legislative power to make whatever laws he thinks are necessary to achieve a certain end. The key is that the President's discretion must not be unfettered. Here, with minor exceptions, the proponents of a code have virtually unfettered discretion as to the rules they pass, and the President likewise may approve or disapprove the codes as he sees fit. The statute provides no standards or guidelines for creating the codes. Instead, it just authorizes the creation of the codes to create such standards. Because the President's discretion is unfettered by Congressional standards, the code-making authority is an unconstitutional delegation of legislative power.

▶ ANALYSIS

This case, along with *Panama Refining Co. v. Ryan*, 293 U.S. 388 (1935), was a prime example of the Court's enforcement of the non-delegation doctrine. The Court, using this doctrine along with others to strike down key New Deal legislation, precipitated Roosevelt's Court-packing plan, which, although never implemented, brought about a change in the Court's jurisprudence. *Schechter* and *Panama Refining* have not been followed since they were decided.

Quicknotes

DISCRETION The authority conferred upon a public official to act reasonably in accordance with his own judgment under certain circumstances.

Panama Refining Co. v. Ryan

Regulated business (P) v. Federal officials (D)

293 U.S. 388 (1935).

NATURE OF CASE: Action to enjoin enforcement of federal industry regulations.

FACT SUMMARY: A business subject to federal industry regulations that were issued by the President, acting under authority of Congress, sought to enjoin the regulations on the ground that they were an unconstitutional delegation of Congress's legislative power.

RULE OF LAW
Congress cannot delegate its powers to the President or his agencies without providing policy standards and guidance for the delegated powers.

FACTS: The President, acting under authority of the National Industrial Recovery Act (Act), by executive order, prohibited the transportation in interstate and foreign commerce of petroleum and petroleum products produced in excess of amounts allowed by the states. Panama Refining Co. (P), as an owner of an oil refinery, brought suit to restrain federal officials (D) from enforcing the regulations that issued under the Act. The district court granted a permanent injunction against enforcement, but the court of appeals reversed. The Supreme Court granted review.

ISSUE: Can Congress delegate its powers to the President or his agencies without providing policy standards and guidance for the delegated powers?

HOLDING AND DECISION: (Hughes, C.J.) No. Here the Act did not provide any policy guidelines for prohibiting or not prohibiting the transportation of petroleum production in excess of state allowances. Congress was silent as to any policy considerations and did not require the President to make findings or even choose between which objectives he was pursuing. The President's discretion was unfettered; Congress left the matter to him "to be dealt with as he pleased." Under the Constitution, Congress is not allowed to abdicate or transfer its essential legislative powers. Although Congress may authorize others to make rules, for the sake of practicality and flexibility, it can do so only if it provides policies and standards for the establishment of such rules. When it does not provide such standards, it lets others perform its lawmaking functions.

▶ *ANALYSIS*

Our increasingly complex world has demanded increasingly broad delegations of authority from Congress to other agencies. The Court has acceded to such delegations, and since *Panama Oil* and *Schechter*, 295 U.S. 495 (1935), were handed down, no federal law has been held to be an impermissible delegation of legislative power.

■=■

Quicknotes

EXECUTIVE ORDER An order issued by the President, or another executive of government, which has the force of law.

■=■

Whitman v. American Trucking Assn., Inc.

Administrator of the Environmental Protection Agency (D) v. Trucking company (P)

531 U.S. 457 (2001).

NATURE OF CASE: Constitutional challenge to the Clean Air Act.

FACT SUMMARY: The Administrator of the Environmental Protection Agency (EPA) (D) was to review and revise the National Ambient Air Quality Standards (NAAQS). The plaintiff trucking company objected to such review and revisions as unconstitutional.

🏛 RULE OF LAW
(1) Providing agencies some level of discretion in setting regulations is not an unconstitutional delegation of law.
(2) Financial impacts are not to be taken into consideration when environmental regulations are promulgated.

FACTS: The Clean Air Act requires the EPA to promulgate NAAQS and then for the Administrator of the EPA, Whitman, (D) to review and revise those as necessary. Several industries and the American Trucking Assn., Inc. (P) filed suit, claiming that the financial impact of implementing such standards should have been considered by the EPA and that the Clean Air Act did not provide an "intelligible principle" to guide the EPA in promulgating the NAAQS. The district court found that the Clean Air Act's requirements were an unconstitutional delegation of legislative power to Whitman (D), but argued that the EPA could bypass the constitutional issue by restricting its interpretation of the sections of the Clean Air Act at issue. The Supreme Court granted certiorari.

ISSUE: (1) Is providing agencies some level of discretion in setting regulations an unconstitutional delegation of law? (2) Should financial impacts be taken into consideration when environmental regulations are promulgated?

HOLDING AND DECISION: (Scalia, J.) No. (1) Providing agencies some level of discretion in setting regulations is not an unconstitutional delegation of law. (2) No. Financial impacts are not to be taken into consideration when environmental regulations are promulgated. The Clean Air Act does not have to set numeric guidelines for the EPA to promulgate NAAQS. Article I, § 1 prohibits Congress from delegating legislative authority to agencies, and decision-making authority may be delegated only when accompanied by an "intelligible principle" to guide the decision-maker. The Clean Air Act's limitations on Whitman's (D) decision-making ability is similar to language this Court has upheld in the past and is sufficient to

survive a constitutional challenge. It is appropriate for Whitman (D) to have a certain degree of discretion. What Whitman (D) does not have is the authority to take financial impact into consideration. Absolutely nothing in the Clean Air Act allows for costs to be part of the decision-making process.

▶ ANALYSIS

Critics argue that independent agencies have too much authority already considering the Constitution is completely silent as to their existence, much less to their formal role in government. Giving agencies discretion to make decisions affecting hundreds of industries seems too much unless one considers the rather stringent requirements of an "intelligible principle." That principle is determined by Congress and is a strict guideline for what agencies may or may not do. If these guidelines are not followed, judicial review is available as a check and balance for the unofficial fourth branch of government.

■=■

Quicknotes

DISCRETION The authority conferred upon a public official to act reasonably in accordance with his own judgment under certain circumstances.

■=■

Immigration & Naturalization Service v. Jagdish Rai Chadha

Federal agency (D) v. Illegal immigrant (P)

462 U.S. 919 (1983).

NATURE OF CASE: Consolidated actions challenging the constitutionality of a federal statute.

FACT SUMMARY: Chadha (P) and others challenged the constitutionality of a federal statute that purported to authorize one House of Congress, by resolution, to invalidate the decision of the Attorney General (made under authority delegated by Congress) to allow a particular deportable illegal immigrant to remain in the United States.

🏛 RULE OF LAW
Because it constitutes an exercise of legislative power and is thus subject to the bicameralism and presentment requirements of Article I of the Constitution, the federal statute purporting to authorize a one-house veto of the Attorney General's decision to allow a particular deportable alien to remain in the United States is unconstitutional.

FACTS: Three cases consolidated on appeal all presented the question of the constitutionality of a federal statute that authorized either House of Congress, by resolution, to invalidate the decision of the Attorney General (made pursuant to authority delegated by Congress) to allow a particular deportable alien to remain in the United States. After such a one-house veto effectively overturned the Attorney General's decision to let Chadha (P) and certain other individuals remain in the United States, each initiated an action challenging the constitutionality of the aforesaid statute. Chadha (P) filed a petition for a review of his deportation order, with the INS (D) actually agreeing with his contention that the statute was unconstitutional. The court of appeals held that the statute violated the doctrine of separation of powers.

ISSUE: Is it constitutional for Congress to statutorily authorize a one-house veto of a decision the Attorney General makes, under authority delegated to him by Congress, to allow a particular deportable alien to remain in the United States?

HOLDING AND DECISION: (Burger, C.J.) No. The Constitution does not permit Congress to statutorily authorize a one-house veto of a decision the Attorney General makes, pursuant to authority delegated to him by Congress, to allow a particular deportable alien to remain in the United States. Such an action is clearly an exercise of legislative power, which makes it subject to the bicameralism and presentment requirements of Article I of the Constitution unless one of the express constitutional exceptions authorizing one

House to act alone applies. None of them applies. Thus, to accomplish what has been attempted by one House of Congress in this case requires action in conformity with the express procedures of the Constitution's prescription for legislative action, passage by a majority of both Houses, and presentment to the President (for his signing or his veto). Such requirements were built into the Constitution to act as enduring checks on each branch and to protect the people from the improvident exercise of power by mandating certain prescribed steps. In attempting to bypass those steps, Congress has acted unconstitutionally.

CONCURRENCE: (Powell, J.) This case should be decided on the narrower ground that Congress assumes a judicial function in violation of the principle of separation of powers when it finds that a particular person does not satisfy the statutory criteria for permanent residence in this country. The Court's broader decision will apparently invalidate every use of the legislative veto, which is a procedure that has been much used by Congress and one it clearly views as essential to controlling the delegation of power to administrative agencies. While one may reasonably disagree with Congress's assessment of the veto's utility, the respect due its judgment as a coordinate branch of government cautions that our holding should be no more extensive than necessary to decide this case.

DISSENT: (White, J.) Today's decision sounds the death knell for nearly two hundred statutory provisions in which Congress has reserved a "legislative veto," which has become a central means by which Congress secures the accountability of executive and independent agencies. Without this particular tool, Congress faces a Hobson's choice: either to refrain from delegating the necessary authority, leaving itself with a hopeless task of writing laws with the requisite specificity to cover endless special circumstances across the entire policy landscape, or, in the alternative, to abdicate its lawmaking function to the executive branch and independent agencies. Absent authority to use the legislative veto, Congress must write hundreds of laws specific to every special circumstance that may arise or abdicate its legislative responsibilities to the executive branch and independence agencies. Congress relies on the legislative veto as a control over lawmaking and as a means of defense against unrestricted power. Congress is not bypassing the requirements of presentation and bicameralism with the veto but is merely providing a check against edicts from the executive branch.

Continued on next page.

The majority now leaves open the possibility that an appointed executive will make legislative decisions rather than the elected body as representatives of the people.

▶ *ANALYSIS*

It is only within the last 50 years that the legislative veto has come into widespread use. When the federal government began its massive growth in response to the Depression, the legislative veto was "invented" as one means of keeping a check on the sprawling new structure. While many commentators, after the Court's announcement of this decision, opined that the result was a major shift of power from the legislative branch to the executive branch, Congress, through more restrictive draftsmanship, should actually see minimal diminishment of its control of those areas over which it desires to retain control.

■═■

Quicknotes

BICAMERALISM The necessity of approval by a majority of both houses of Congress in ratifying legislation or approving other legislative action.

LEGISLATIVE VETO A resolution passed by one or both legislature houses that is intended to block an administrative regulation or action.

PRESENTMENT The act of bringing a congressional decision before the President for his approval or veto.

■═■

Alexia Morrison, Independent Counsel v. Theodore B. Olson

Independent counsel (P) v. Federal employees (D)

487 U.S. 654 (1988).

NATURE OF CASE: Appeal from reversal of denial of motion to quash subpoenas.

FACT SUMMARY: Morrison (P) appealed from a decision reversing a district court decision upholding the constitutionality of the independent-counsel provisions of the Ethics in Government Act and denying Olson's (D) motion to quash subpoenas, contending in part that those provisions were not violative of the Appointments Clause of the Constitution.

🏛 RULE OF LAW

The independent-counsel provisions of the Ethics in Government Act are not violative of the Appointments Clause of the Constitution.

FACTS: Sections 591-599 of the Ethics in Government Act (Act) allow for the appointment of an "independent counsel" to investigate and prosecute appropriate certain high-ranking government officials for violations of criminal laws. The Attorney General conducts an initial investigation, and only if the Attorney General applies to the special division, created by the Act, for appointment of independent counsel, is independent counsel appointed. The special division appoints independent counsel and defines his prosecutorial jurisdiction. Within this jurisdiction, the independent counsel is granted full power and independent authority to exercise all powers of the Department of Justice. The Attorney General and the Department of Justice are required to suspend all proceedings regarding matters within independent counsel's jurisdiction. Independent counsel's tenure is governed by two provisions. The first provision allows the Attorney General, on his own personal action, to remove independent counsel for good cause. Independent counsel can seek judicial review of this decision. The other provision allows termination of independent counsel's office when he informs the Attorney General he has substantially completed his investigations or prosecutions undertaken under the Act, or when the special division so determines. Finally, the Act provides for congressional oversight of independent counsel's activities. [In 1984, the House Judiciary Committee began an investigation into the Justice Department's role in an EPA document-production controversy. The chairman requested that the Attorney General seek the appointment of an independent counsel to investigate the role of Olson (D), Schmults (D), and Dinkins (D). The Attorney General applied for appointment of independent counsel with respect to Olson (D) only.] McKay (D) was appointed independent counsel, and Morrison (D) succeeded him. After unsuccessfully attempting to have the Committee's allegations against Schmults (D) and Dinkins (D) furnished,

Morrison (D) subpoenaed them and Olson (D) pursuant to the Olson (D) investigation. All three moved to quash the subpoenas, claiming the independent-counsel provisions were unconstitutional, and that therefore Morrison (D) had no authority to proceed. The district court disagreed and denied the motions to quash. The court of appeals reversed, and from that decision, Morrison (P) appealed, contending in part that the independent-counsel provisions of the Act were not violative of the Appointments Clause of the Constitution.

ISSUE: Are the independent-counsel provisions of the Ethics in Government Act violative of the Appointments Clause of the Constitution?

HOLDING AND DECISION: (Rehnquist, C.J.) No. The independent-counsel provisions of the Ethics in Government Act are not violative of the Appointments Clause of the Constitution. Once the special division determines to appoint independent counsel and defines that counsel's prosecutorial jurisdiction, the independent counsel's rights and responsibilities are indeed broad. The rights and responsibilities are still limited by what is authorized by the special division. The counsel's tenure, however, is limited by statute and allows for removal for good cause or removal once the actions or prosecutions are complete. Morrison (P) is subject to removal by a higher executive branch officer, is restricted in jurisdiction and tenure, and is limited to authorized duties. These characteristics of the office of independent counsel confirm that Morrison (P) is an inferior and not a principal officer. Reversed.

DISSENT: (Scalia, J.) The inarguable fact is that the President has sole discretion in conducting criminal prosecution and the law in question deprives the executive branch of its right to exercise sole discretion. This being so, the law violates separation of powers and thus should be invalidated.

▶ ANALYSIS

Other cases have upheld the federal court's power to appoint private attorneys to prosecute contempt of court orders, justifying the decision in part on the need for the Judiciary to have the power to independently vindicate its own authority. Justice Scalia, the author of the dissent, concurred in this judgment. See *Young v. United States ex rel. Vuitton et Fils S.A.*, 107 S. Ct. 2124 (1987).

■■■

Continued on next page.

Quicknotes

APPOINTMENTS CLAUSE Article II, Section 2, clause 2 of the U.S. Constitution conferring power upon the President to appoint ambassadors, public ministers and consuls, judges of the Supreme Court and all other officers of the United States with the advice and consent of the Senate.

■══■

United States v. Curtiss-Wright Export Corp.

Federal government (P) v. Export company (D)

299 U.S. 304 (1936).

NATURE OF CASE: Action to prosecute company that violated embargo authorized by Congress and proclaimed by the President.

FACT SUMMARY: Curtiss-Wright (D) challenged a joint resolution from Congress authorizing the President to prohibit the sale of arms to Bolivia and Paraguay as an unconstitutional delegation of legislative power.

RULE OF LAW
The constitutional powers of the federal government regarding foreign affairs are more expansive than those regarding domestic affairs.

FACTS: Congress passed a joint resolution authorizing the President to prohibit the sale of arms to Bolivia and Paraguay, countries that were involved in an armed conflict in Chaco. The President believed that such a prohibition would increase the chances of reestablishing peace in the region and declared an embargo. Curtiss-Wright Export (D) was indicted for violating the terms of the embargo, but the lower court found that the joint resolution was an unconstitutional delegation of legislative power. The United States (P) appealed the ruling.

ISSUE: Are the constitutional powers of the federal government regarding foreign affairs more expansive than those regarding domestic affairs?

HOLDING AND DECISION: (Sutherland, J.) Yes. The constitutional powers of the federal government regarding foreign affairs are more expansive than those regarding domestic affairs. The President's powers over international relations are not restricted by the Constitution to the same extent as those regarding domestic affairs. Although the Constitution's enumerated powers set strict limits on all branches of the federal government, these limits apply only to internal affairs. The President has exclusive and plenary power as the sole organ of the federal government in international relations. The President has the power to speak or listen as a representative of the country, and he alone negotiates treaties. Furthermore, the nature of foreign relations and the conditions of war necessitate that different rules apply under these conditions. Therefore, the lower court erred in finding that the resolution was an unconstitutional delegation. Reversed.

▶ ANALYSIS

Because the Constitution does not specifically assign powers regarding international affairs, so the specifics have been worked out over time with the help of the President, Congress, and the Supreme Court. This case has received criticism because the Court seemed to indicate that the President's power is virtually limitless. While this is not entirely accurate, the balancing of the gray areas is continuously being negotiated.

■■■

Quicknotes

PLENARY Unlimited and open; as broad as a given situation may require.

■■■

Dames & Moore v. Regan, Secretary of the Treasury

Creditor (P) v. Federal government (D)

453 U.S. 654 (1981).

NATURE OF CASE: Review of appeal of decision issuing an order of attachment pursuant to a breach of contract.

FACT SUMMARY: Dames & Moore (P) filed suit to recover funds owed on a contract with the government of Iran, but the order of attachment was voided by an executive agreement.

🏛 RULE OF LAW
The president lacks the plenary power to settle claims against foreign governments through an executive agreement; however, where Congress at least acquiesces in the president's actions, the president can settle such claims.

FACTS: In November of 1979 President Carter, acting pursuant to the International Emergency Economic Powers Act (IEEPA), froze Iranian assets in the United States after Americans were taken hostage in Tehran. The Americans held hostage were subsequently released on January 20, 1981 pursuant to an executive agreement entered into the day before. The agreement included a promise to settle all claims and litigation between the countries through arbitration. Dames & Moore (P), holders of an attachment order against Iranian assets, took exception with this agreement and filed suit. The litigation eventually reached the Supreme Court.

ISSUE: Does the president possess plenary powers to settle claims against foreign governments through an executive agreement?

HOLDING AND DECISION: (Rehnquist, J.) No. The president lacks the plenary power to settle claims against foreign governments through an executive agreement; however, where Congress at least acquiesces in the president's actions, the president can settle such claims. When Congress implicitly or explicitly authorizes presidential action, the action is given the greatest presumption of validity. Here, while the President's exact decision was not contemplated in the IEEPA, substantial powers to seize and handle foreign assets was conferred in the President by Congress. Dames & Moore (P) would have to show that the government as a whole lacks the power to settle claims with foreign entities when it is in the interest of the United States to do so; such a heavy burden has not been met. There is a long history of congressional acquiescence to international agreements settling claims between citizens of the United States and nationals of other countries. However, there is no independent source of presidential authority to settle such claims. Had Congress not implicitly approved of the action, the President would have been beyond his bounds. But, in this case, he acted under the implied authority of Congress.

▶ ANALYSIS

In *Youngstown Sheet & Tube Co. v. Sawyer*, 343 U.S. 579 (1952), Justice Jackson divided presidential authority into three categories: express or implied grants of power from Congress, actions in the face of congressional silence, and actions in direct contravention to congressional legislation. When acting against the wishes of Congress, the president's power was limited to express constitutional grants in Article II. At the other extreme, presidential power was at its greatest when acting with congressional approval, as Justice Rehnquist found to be the case here.

■═■

Quicknotes

BREACH OF CONTRACT Unlawful failure by a party to perform its obligations pursuant to contract.

EXECUTIVE AGREEMENT An agreement with a foreign nation that is binding on the country, entered into by the President without Senate approval.

PLENARY Unlimited and open; as broad as a given situation may require.

■═■

Hamdi v. Rumsfeld

Alleged enemy combatant (D) v. U.S. Secretary of Defense (P)

542 U.S. 507, 124 S. Ct. 2633 (2004).

NATURE OF CASE: Habeas petition from designation and detention as an enemy combatant.

FACT SUMMARY: Hamdi (D) was charged as an enemy combatant and detained by the U.S. military. He challenged his status and the constitutionality of holding him without formal charges or proceedings.

🏛 RULE OF LAW
A United States citizen designated and detained as an enemy combatant has a due process right to challenge the underlying factual support for that designation before a neutral arbitrator.

FACTS: On September 11, 2001, al Qaeda terrorists attacked the United States and caused the deaths of 3,000 American citizens. In response, the President, authorized by Congress, sent military troops to Afghanistan to locate and subdue the terrorists and the Taliban regime supporting them. Yaser Esam Hamdi (D) was born in America but had lived most of his life in Saudi Arabia. He was captured by allied troops while fighting with the Taliban and turned over to the U.S. military. The government classified Hamdi (D) as an "enemy combatant" and determined to hold him indefinitely without formal charges or proceedings. Hamdi (D) challenged this designation as unconstitutional. The Fourth Circuit held that no further hearing was required and the Supreme Court granted certiorari.

ISSUE: Does a United States citizen designated and detained as an enemy combatant have a due process right to challenge the underlying factual support for that designation before a neutral arbitrator?

HOLDING AND DECISION: (O'Connor, J.) Yes. A United States citizen designated and detained as an enemy combatant has a due process right to challenge the underlying factual support for that designation before a neutral arbitrator. This Court finds that Congress did in fact authorize the detention of persons such as Hamdi (D) because Hamdi (D) was detained pursuant to an act of Congress. Contrary to the Fourth Circuit's holding, it is not undisputed that Hamdi (D) was captured in a combat zone because all that is certain is that Hamdi (D) resided in that area. Hamdi (D) has thus not made any concessions abdicating his rights, if any, to further hearing. The Government next argues that the Court should only consider whether broader authorization existed for the detention and not whether an individual detainee is entitled to further proceedings. A citizen, however, has a right to be free from unlawful detention without due process of law. The Court must weigh the governmental interest in confining enemy combatants against the individual liberty rights of the detainee. After due consideration, it is not necessary to provide initial due process hearings for captures, but those who must be detained further are entitled to further proceedings. The detainee must have an opportunity to demonstrate that the government's factual assertions are untrue.

CONCURRENCE AND DISSENT: (Souter, J.) The judgment of the plurality is correct, but the reasoning about the authorization for detentions is entirely wrong. Congress did not specifically authorize the imprisonment of individuals and the government's interpretation of the authorization is too broad. The due process considerations need not be reached because of the absence of a further act of Congress.

DISSENT: (Scalia, J.) The government must prosecute for treason or another crime in federal court unless wartime allows for the enactment of the Suspension Clause. As no one contends this is a Suspension Clause situation, nothing allows for the detention of this man without due process proceedings. This is especially true given that this man is a U.S. citizen and not a foreign-born captive.

DISSENT: (Thomas, J.) This case is within the federal government's war powers, and Hamdi's (D) habeas claim should fail without necessitating a remand. Hamdi (D) has not been denied due process because the President acted within his rights to detain him and no further process is owed.

▶ ANALYSIS

While the Court did not directly address presidential authority to designate and detain enemy combatants, it did temper the government's attempts to unilaterally control wartime captures as they related to American citizens. Although many supported the President's actions after the terrorist attacks of 2001, many more recognized the danger in resting too much power in the executive branch even in wartime. Mistakes can be made and captured U.S. citizens should be entitled to place their case before an objective party.

▪■▬▪

Quicknotes

DUE PROCESS The constitutional mandate requiring the courts to protect and enforce individuals' rights and liberties consistent with prevailing principles of fairness

Continued on next page.

and justice and prohibiting the federal and state governments from such activities that deprive its citizens of life, liberty, or property interest.

HABEAS CORPUS A proceeding in which a defendant brings a writ to compel a judicial determination of whether he is lawfully being held in custody.

■≡■

Boumediene v. Bush

Guantanamo detainees (P) v. Federal government

128 S. Ct. 2229 (2008).

NATURE OF CASE: Review of federal appeals court judgment.

FACT SUMMARY: Lakhdar Boumediene (P) and other detainees (P) held at Guantanamo Bay, Cuba, petitioned the court for a writ of habeas corpus. The federal appeals court ruled in favor of the U.S. government (D).

🏛 **RULE OF LAW**

(1) The Military Commissions Act of 2006 strips federal courts of jurisdiction over habeas petitions filed by foreign citizens detained at Guantanamo Bay.

(2) Detainees are not barred from seeking habeas or invoking the Suspension Clause simply because they had been designated as enemy combatants or held at Guantanamo Bay.

(3) The Military Commissions Act of 2006 is a violation of the Suspension Clause of the Constitution.

FACTS: Bosnian police captured Lakhdar Boumediene (P) and five other Algerian natives after U.S. intelligence officers suspected them of plotting to attack the U.S. embassy there. The U.S. government (D) classified the men as enemy combatants in the war on terror and held them at the Guantanamo Bay. Boumediene (P) filed a petition for a writ of habeas corpus, claiming that the U.S. government (D) violated the Due Process Clause of the U.S. Constitution, various statutes and treaties, the common law, and international law. A district court judge granted the government's (D) motion to have all of the claims dismissed on the ground that Boumediene (P), as an alien held at an overseas military base, had no right to a habeas petition. The Court of Appeals for the D.C. Circuit affirmed, but the Supreme Court reversed in *Rasul v. Bush*, holding that the habeas statute extends to noncitizen detainees at Guantanamo. In 2006, Congress passed the Military Commissions Act of 2006 (MCA), which withdrew the jurisdiction of federal courts to hear habeas applications from detainees classified as enemy combatants under the Detainee Treatment Act of 2005. The case was appealed to the D.C. Circuit for the second time, and this time the detainees (P) argued that the MCA did not apply to their petitions, and that if it did, it was unconstitutional under the Suspension Clause. The D.C. Circuit ruled in favor of the government (D) on both points, holding that the MCA applied to "all cases, without exception," that pertain to aspects of detention. One of the purposes of the MCA, according to the court, was to overrule the Supreme Court's opinion in *Hamdan v. Rumsfeld*, 548 U.S. 557 (2006), which had allowed petitions like Boumediene's (P) to go forward. The D.C.

Circuit held that the Suspension Clause protects only the writ of habeas corpus as it existed in 1789, and that the writ would not have been understood in 1789 to apply to an overseas military base leased from a foreign government. Constitutional rights do not apply to aliens outside of the United States, the court held, and the leased military base in Cuba does not qualify as inside the geographic borders of the U.S. The Supreme Court granted certiorari after initially denying review, three months earlier.

ISSUE:

(1) Does the Military Commissions Act of 2006 strip federal courts of jurisdiction over habeas petitions filed by foreign citizens detained at Guantanamo Bay?

(2) Are detainees barred from seeking habeas or invoking the Suspension Clause simply because they had been designated as enemy combatants or held at Guantanamo Bay?

(3) Is the Military Commissions Act of 2006 a violation of the Suspension Clause of the Constitution?

HOLDING AND DECISION: (Kennedy, J.)

(1) Yes. The Military Commissions Act of 2006 strips federal courts of jurisdiction over habeas petitions filed by foreign citizens detained at Guantanamo Bay. If the MCA is considered valid, its legislative history requires that the detainees' cases be dismissed.

(2) No. Detainees are not barred from seeking habeas or invoking the Suspension Clause simply because they had been designated as enemy combatants or held at Guantanamo Bay. The Suspension Clause provides that the "Privilege of the Writ of Habeas Corpus shall not be suspended, unless when in Cases of Rebellion or Invasion the public Safety may require it." The Framers thought the writ was an essential mechanism in the separation-of-powers scheme. Moreover, the Suspension Clause applies to Guantanamo, despite the fact that the United States (D) does not claim sovereignty over the place of detention. Even when the United States (D) acts outside its borders, its powers are subject to the Constitution.

(3) Yes. The Military Commissions Act of 2006 is a violation of the Suspension Clause of the Constitution. Because the procedures laid out in the Detainee Treatment Act are not adequate substitutes for the habeas writ, the MCA operates as an unconstitutional suspension of that writ. Reversed.

CONCURRENCE: (Souter, J.) Two additional points are worth mentioning: First, the jurisdictional question

Continued on next page.

answered in this case would be answered in the same way in purely constitutional cases. Second, the prisoners involved in this case have been held at Guantanamo for six years, without habeas scrutiny, and while the military should handle such cases within some reasonable period of time, it was appropriate for the courts to step in where the military had failed after six years.

DISSENT: (Roberts, C.J.) The procedural protections offered aliens who are detained by this country as enemy combatants were generous under the Detainee Treatment Act, and the court rejects them out of hand without stating what due process rights the detainees hold. The majority also fails to delineate the procedures that should be followed by the judiciary in reviewing cases deemed appropriate. The majority's opinion is not really about the detainees, but about control of federal policy regarding enemy combatants.

DISSENT: (Scalia, J.) The court's grant of constitutional right to habeas corpus to alien enemies detained abroad by military forces occurs in the course of an ongoing war, but the writ of habeas corpus does not, and never has, run in favor of aliens abroad. The Suspension Clause has no application, and the court's intervention is ultra vires.

▶ *ANALYSIS*

President Bush agreed to honor the ruling. At a June 2008 town hall meeting, then-Republican presidential nominee John McCain said the ruling was "one of the worst decisions in the history of this country." He said that "[t]hese are people who are not citizens. They do not and never have been given the rights that citizens in this country have." Then-Democratic presidential nominee Barack Obama described the ruling as "a rejection of the Bush administration's attempt to create a legal black hole at Guantanamo" and "an important step toward re-establishing our credibility as a nation committed to the rule of law."

■■■

Quicknotes

DUE PROCESS The constitutional mandate requiring the courts to protect and enforce individuals' rights and liberties consistent with prevailing principles of fairness and justice and prohibiting the federal and state governments from such activities that deprive its citizens of life, liberty, or property interest.

DUE PROCESS CLAUSE Clauses found in the Fifth and Fourteenth Amendments to the U.S. Constitution providing that no person shall be deprived of "life, liberty, or property, without due process of law."

HABEAS CORPUS A proceeding in which a defendant brings a writ to compel a judicial determination of whether he is lawfully being held in custody.

SUSPENSION CLAUSE A clause found in Article I of the U.S. Constitution that protects against arbitrary suspensions of the writ of habeas corpus.

■■■

Richard Nixon v. A. Ernest Fitzgerald

President of the United States (D) v. Executive employee (P)

457 U.S. 731 (1982).

NATURE OF CASE: Wrongful termination action seeking civil damages from former President.

FACT SUMMARY: Fitzgerald (P) was fired from his job in the Air Force. Allegedly, he was terminated by the President (D) in retaliation for revealing to Congress information that was embarrassing to the Department of Defense.

🏛 RULE OF LAW
The president of the United States has absolute immunity from civil damages liability for all official actions taken while in office.

FACTS: Fitzgerald (P) was a management analyst with the Air Force, who, to the embarrassment of his supervisors, testified to Congress about severe cost-overruns and technical difficulties relating to the development of a transport plane. During the presidency of Richard M. Nixon (D), Fitzgerald was dismissed from his job during a departmental reorganization and reduction in force, in which his job was eliminated. Suing in district court for civil damages, and naming President Nixon as a defendant, Fitzgerald alleged that his separation represented unlawful retaliation for his congressional testimony. The court ruled that Nixon was not entitled to claim absolute presidential immunity. The court of appeals dismissed summarily on the immunity issue. The Supreme Court granted review.

ISSUE: Does the president of the United States have absolute immunity from civil damages liability for all official actions taken while in office?

HOLDING AND DECISION: (Powell, J.) Yes. As a matter of public policy rooted in the structure of government mandated by the separation of powers principle, the President has absolute immunity from civil damages liability predicated on his official acts. This results from the president's unique position in the constitutional scheme and the great importance of his duties. Unlike other executives (e.g., governors) who have only qualified immunity, the president's role in the federal government is so important, and affects so many people, that to divert his energies with concerns of private lawsuits would imperil the effective functioning of government. There are also other formal and informal checks on the president, including impeachment, that can ensure that the president is not above the law.

DISSENT: (White, J.) Giving the office of the president absolute immunity, rather than attaching such immunity only to particular acts the president might perform, places the president above the law. The majority's holding essentially gives the president sovereign immunity, and does so as a matter of public policy, not as a reasoned judicial decision based on precedent.

▶ ANALYSIS

Nowhere does the Constitution explicitly provide the president or other executive branch officials with immunity. As with other Court-created rights, the Court has implied immunity from Constitutional doctrine—here, the doctrine of separation of powers. This immunity, however, does not extend to acts that occurred before the president took office, and suits relating to such acts will not even be temporarily stayed during the presidency.

■■■■

Quicknotes

EXECUTIVE IMMUNITY Exemption of the President from suit for decisions made pursuant to his official duties.

SEPARATION OF POWERS The system of checks and balances preventing one branch of government from infringing upon exercising the powers of another branch of government.

■■■■

William Jefferson Clinton v. Paula Corbin Jones

President (D) v. State Employee (P)

520 U.S. 681 (1997).

NATURE OF CASE: Appeal of order reinstating trial in suit for damages against the President.

FACT SUMMARY: President Clinton (D), who was sued by Jones (P) following an alleged incident that occurred in 1991 before his election to the office of President, sought to have all litigation on the matter suspended until after his term has concluded.

> 🏛 **RULE OF LAW**
> The doctrine of separation of powers does not require federal courts to stay all private actions against the president until he leaves office.

FACTS: Clinton (D) was elected to the presidency in 1992, and re-elected in 1996, with his term of office expiring on January 20, 2001. In May 1991, while serving as the governor of Arkansas, he delivered a speech at an official conference held at the Excelsior Hotel in Little Rock, Arkansas. Paula Jones (P), a state employee working at the registration desk of the conference, alleged that she was persuaded to leave her desk and visit Clinton (D) in a business suite at the hotel where he made "abhorrent" sexual advances that she vehemently rejected. In May 1994, Jones (P) filed suit against Clinton (D), seeking damages and alleging deprivation and conspiracy to deprive her of federal civil rights under color of state law, and state-law torts of intentional infliction of emotional distress and defamation. Clinton (D) filed a motion to dismiss on grounds of presidential immunity, and requested the court to defer all other pleadings and motions until after the immunity issue was resolved. The district court denied the motion to dismiss on immunity grounds and ruled that discovery could proceed, but ordered any trial stayed until the end of Clinton's (D) presidency. Jones (P) and Clinton (D) appealed, and the appellate court affirmed the denial of the motion to dismiss, but reversed the order postponing the trial. The Supreme Court granted certiorari.

ISSUE: Does the doctrine of separation of powers require federal courts to stay all private actions against the president until he leaves office?

HOLDING AND DECISION: (Stevens, J.) No. The doctrine of separation of powers does not require federal courts to stay all private actions against the president until he leaves office. The principal rationale for affording certain public officials immunity from suits for money damages arising out of their official acts is inapplicable to unofficial conduct. Although Clinton (D) argues that the doctrine of separation of powers places limits on the authority of the judiciary to interfere with the executive branch, it does not follow that these principles would be violated by

allowing Jones's (P) action to proceed. There is no suggestion that the judiciary is being asked to perform any function that might in some way be described as executive, or that this decision will curtail the scope of official powers of the executive branch. Furthermore, only three sitting presidents have been subjected to suits for their private actions, and it is unlikely that this decision will result in a deluge of such litigation. If Congress deems it appropriate to afford the president stronger protection, it may respond with appropriate legislation. Affirmed.

▶ ANALYSIS

The president is absolutely immune from civil damages liability for his official acts in office. *Nixon v. Fitzgerald*, 457 U.S. 731 (1982). In *Fitzgerald*, the Court noted that because of the singular importance of the president's duties, diverting his energies by concern about private lawsuits would raise unique risks to the effective functioning of the government. Clinton (P) argued, albeit unsuccessfully, that he too would be distracted from his public duties by participation in Jones's (P) lawsuit. But the *Fitzgerald* Court's central concern was not the distraction of participating in a trial, but the worry and caution attendant to the possibility of damages actions stemming from any particular official decision.

■═■

Quicknotes

EXECUTIVE IMMUNITY Exemption of the President from suit for decisions made pursuant to his official duties.

SEPARATION OF POWERS The system of checks and balances preventing one branch of government from infringing upon exercising the powers of another branch of government.

■═■

Limits on State Regulatory and Taxing Power

Quick Reference Rules of Law

Lorillard Tobacco Co. v. Reilly

Tobacco advertiser (P) v. State attorney general (D)

533 U.S. 525 (2001).

NATURE OF CASE: Suit challenging state regulations of advertising for tobacco products.

FACT SUMMARY: The Massachusetts Attorney General (D) promulgated regulations of advertising for cigarettes, smokeless tobacco, and cigars. Lorillard Tobacco Co. (P) sued to invalidate the regulations, arguing in part that the Federal Cigarette Labeling and Advertising Act (FCLAA) expressly preempted the state regulations of outdoor and point-of-sale advertising of cigarettes.

RULE OF LAW

The FCLAA expressly preempts state regulation of outdoor and point-of-sale cigarette advertising by unequivocally prohibiting such regulation by the states.

FACTS: Congress enacted the FCLAA in 1965 and broadened the Act's express preemption provision in 1969. That provision prohibits states from further burdening advertising or promotion of cigarettes whose packages comply with the FCLAA's own advertising and promotional requirements for cigarettes. In 1999, Reilly (D) promulgated regulations restricting, among other things, outdoor and point-of-sale advertising of cigarettes.

ISSUE: In the FCLAA, did Congress expressly preempt state regulation of outdoor and point-of-sale cigarette advertising by unequivocally prohibiting such regulation by the states?

HOLDING AND DECISION: (O'Connor, J.) Yes. The FCLAA preempts state regulation of outdoor and point-of-sale cigarette advertising by unequivocally prohibiting such regulation by the states. Congress intended to bar state regulation in this area even if concern for smoking and health motivate the regulations. Additionally, the Massachusetts regulations are preempted because the asserted attempt to regulate the location, and not the content, of cigarette advertising has no foundation in the FCLAA. Because the FCLAA prohibits states from imposing additional burdens on cigarette advertising, the FCLAA preempts the Massachusetts regulations.

DISSENT: (Stevens, J.) Where congressional intent to preempt the states' traditional police powers is ambiguous, the Court must read a preemption provision narrowly. In this case that principle means that, in the FCLAA, Congress did not intend to preempt states from regulating the location of cigarette advertising. The FCLAA restricts state regulation of the content, not the location, of cigarette advertising. Even if this reading were wrong, the FCLAA's preemption provision is, at best, ambiguous, and the Court therefore should defer to the presumption favoring the traditional police powers of the states.

ANALYSIS

Grounded in the Supremacy Clause in Article VI, § 2 of the Constitution, the preemption doctrine ensures that national laws shall have national application whenever the national voice, such as in Congress, so requires. The problem, as the sharply divided Court on the preemption issue in *Lorillard* illustrates, lies in determining exactly when Congress intends to preempt state regulation, even when the preemption seems to be express. The dissenters in *Lorillard*, however, stretch the ordinary meaning of the words in the FCLAA too far: "No requirement . . . imposed under State law" applies to all locations and thus clearly expresses congressional intent to preempt.

Quicknotes

PREEMPTION Doctrine holding that matters of national interest take precedence over matters of local interest; the federal law takes precedence over state law.

Florida Lime & Avocado Growers, Inc. v. Paul, Director, Dept. of Agriculture of California

Farmers (P) v. State officer (D)

373 U.S. 132 (1963).

NATURE OF CASE: Action to enjoin state agricultural statute on ground that it is preempted by federal regulations.

FACT SUMMARY: Producers of avocados in Florida sued to enjoin enforcement of a California statute that prohibited transportation or sale in California of avocados based on oil content. They argued that federal marketing regulations that gauged the maturity of avocados without reference to oil content preempted the California statute.

🏛 RULE OF LAW
A federal law that sets a minimum standard does not preempt a stricter state law.

FACTS: California's Agricultural Code gauged the maturity of avocados by oil content and prohibited the sale or transportation in California of avocados that did not meet a certain standard. In contrast, the federal marketing orders approved by the secretary of Agriculture gauged the maturity of avocados grown in Florida by standards that did not reference oil content. Avocado growers in Florida sued to enjoin the California statute insofar as it could be applied to exclude from California those Florida avocados that, although mature by federal standards, did not meet the California oil-content standard.

ISSUE: Does a federal law that sets a minimum standard preempt a stricter state law?

HOLDING AND DECISION: (Brennan, J.) No. A federal law that sets a minimum standard does not preempt a stricter state law. Where compliance with both federal and state regulations is a physical impossibility, federal law preempts state law, and no inquiry into congressional intent is necessary. However, where, as here, it is possible to comply with both laws—Florida avocados could have met the California standard if given more time to grow—there is no inherent conflict between the two laws, even though they are dissimilar.

▶ *ANALYSIS*

The type of preemption presented in this case is known as conflicts preemption. The straightforward rule for conflicts preemption is that it occurs when courts determine there is an actual conflict between the state and federal laws. An actual conflict occurs when it is impossible to comply with both the federal and state law (they are mutually exclusive) or the state law stands in the way of giving effect to the federal law.

Quicknotes

PREEMPTION Doctrine holding that matters of national interest take precedence over matters of local interest; the federal law takes precedence over state law.

■===■

Pacific Gas & Electric Co. v. State Energy Resources Conservation & Development Commn.

Electric utility company (P) v. State agency (D)

461 U.S. 190 (1983).

NATURE OF CASE: Action seeking a declaratory judgment.

FACT SUMMARY: Pacific Gas (P) maintained that certain provisions of California's Warren-Alquist Act were invalid because it was preempted by Congress's passage of the Atomic Energy Act of 1954.

🏛 RULE OF LAW
In passing the Atomic Energy Act of 1954, Congress preempted state regulation of the radiological safety aspects involved in the construction and operation of nuclear plants but intended for the states to retain their traditional responsibility in the field of regulating electrical utilities for determining questions of need, reliability, cost, and other related state concerns.

FACTS: In challenging the validity of various provisions of California's Warren-Alquist State Energy Resources Conservation and Development Act, Pacific Gas (P) claimed that such regulation as it attempted was preempted by the Atomic Energy Act, which Congress enacted in 1954. Of particular concern was a provision imposing a moratorium on the certification of new nuclear plants until the State Energy Resources and Conservation Commission (Energy Commission) (D) "finds that there has been developed and that the United States through its authorized agency has approved and there exists a demonstrated technology or means for the disposal of high-level nuclear waste." Disposal was defined as a "method for the permanent and terminal disposition of high-level nuclear waste," a goal that was not even close to being reached. The district court held that the aforementioned nuclear moratorium provision was not preempted because it saw in certain sections of the Atomic Energy Act congressional authorization for states to regulate nuclear power plants "for purposes other than protection against radiation hazards."

ISSUE: Has Congress, in passing the Atomic Energy Act of 1954, totally preempted any state regulation of nuclear power or power plants?

HOLDING AND DECISION: (White, J.) No. The intent of Congress in passing the Atomic Energy Act of 1954 was to give the federal government exclusive regulatory power over the radiological safety aspects involved in the construction and operation of a nuclear plant. It did not intend to preempt the states from exercising their traditional responsibility in the field of regulating electrical utilities (nuclear or otherwise) for determining questions of need, reliability, cost, and other related state concerns.

California has maintained that its moratorium provisions are aimed at economic problems, arguing that without a permanent nuclear-waste disposal system the nuclear-waste problem could become critical and lead to unpredictably high costs to either contain the problem or shut down reactors. Accepting this avowed economic purpose as the rationale for enacting the moratorium provision, the statute lies outside the occupied field of nuclear safety regulation. It does not conflict with federal regulation of nuclear waste disposal. In fact, its very words accept that it is the federal responsibility to develop and license such technology and it nowhere seeks to impose its own state standards on nuclear-waste disposal. It does not conflict with the Nuclear Regulatory Commission's decision to continue licensing reactors despite the uncertainty surrounding the waste-disposal problem or with Congress's recent passage of legislation directed at that problem. The NRC's imprimatur indicates only that it is safe to proceed with such plants, not that it is economically wise to do so. Since the NRC order does not and could not compel a utility to develop a nuclear plant, compliance with both it and California's challenged statutory provision is possible. Furthermore, because the NRC's regulations are aimed at insuring that plants are safe, not necessarily that they are economical, California's statutory provision does not interfere with the objective of the federal regulation. Finally, there is little doubt that a primary purpose of the Atomic Energy Act was and is the promotion of nuclear power. But, as the court of appeals noted, the promotion of nuclear power was not intended by Congress to be accomplished "at all costs." The elaborate licensing and safety provisions and the continued preservation of state regulation in traditional areas belie that. Thus, it cannot be said that California's statutory provision "frustrates" the Atomic Energy Act's purpose of developing the commercial use of nuclear power. Quite simply, there has been no preemption with regard to the type of provision California enacted.

▶ ANALYSIS

There are instances in which Congress explicitly preempts state authority by expressly stating as much in the federal statute itself. More often, however, Congress's intent to supersede state law altogether is to be found: (1) from a "scheme of federal regulation so pervasive as to make reasonable the inference that Congress left no room to supplement it"; or (2) because "the Act of Congress touches a field in which the federal interest is so dominant that the

Continued on next page.

federal system will be assumed to preclude enforcement of state laws on the same subject;" or (3) because "the object sought to be obtained by the federal law and the character of obligations imposed by it may reveal the same purpose." *Fidelity Federal Savings & Loan Ass'n v. de la Cuesta*, 458 U.S. 141 (1982).

■═■

Quicknotes

PREEMPTION Doctrine holding that matters of national interest take precedence over matters of local interest; the federal law takes precedence over state law.

■═■

Hines, Secretary of Labor & Industry of Pennsylvania v. Davidowitz

State official (D) v. Aliens (P)

312 U.S. 52 (1941).

NATURE OF CASE: Appeal from order enjoining enforcement of state law that regulated alien registration.

FACT SUMMARY: Pennsylvania enacted a law that regulated alien registration, and a year later Congress passed a similar law. Aliens (P) challenged the state law on various constitutional grounds, including preemption by the federal law.

🏛 RULE OF LAW
A federal law that regulates alien registration preempts all similar state laws.

FACTS: Pennsylvania passed the Alien Registration Act in 1939. The act provided a comprehensive alien registration scheme for aliens in Pennsylvania. Davidowitz and other aliens (appellees) challenged the law as denying equal protection to aliens, and on other constitutional grounds. A federal district court found for the aliens (appellees) and enjoined enforcement of the act, and that decision was appealed to the Supreme Court. Then, in 1940, during the pendency of the appeal, Congress passed a federal Alien Registration Act, which also provided a comprehensive alien registration scheme.

ISSUE: Does a federal law that regulates alien registration preempt all similar state laws?

HOLDING AND DECISION: (Black, J.) Yes. The basic subject of the state and federal laws is identical: the registration of aliens. Congress has supremacy in the area of foreign affairs, including immigration, naturalization, and deportation. Any law passed by Congress in this area is the supreme law of the land. One of the most sensitive matters in this area has to do with the protection of a country's nationals while they are in another country, and Congress has entered into many treaties regarding aliens. Consequently, the regulation of aliens is inherent in the responsibilities of the national government. Thus, where both Congress and a state act in this area, even though the state law does not actually conflict with the federal law, the federal law is supreme and the state law cannot add to or complement it in any way. Otherwise, the state law and its requirements could negatively impact on foreign relations.

DISSENT: (Stone, J.) Congress has not explicitly preempted this field, and, therefore, the Court should not do what Congress could have done, but failed to do. State powers should not be diminished based on what Congress might have intended but did not express, unless the state law violates a right granted to the federal government by the Constitution.

▶ ANALYSIS

This case exemplifies the concept of field preemption, whereby Congress preempts an entire field, even though it has not expressly preempted the state law and the state law does not actually conflict with the federal law. Immigration and foreign affairs are areas that the Court has long held are the exclusive province of Congress.

■===■

Quicknotes

PREEMPTION Doctrine holding that matters of national interest take precedence over matters of local interest; the federal law takes precedence over state law.

■===■

H.P. Hood & Sons, Inc. v. Du Mond, Commissioner of Agriculture & Markets of New York

Milk distributor (P) v. Milk commissioner (D)

336 U.S. 525 (1949).

NATURE OF CASE: Action challenging the constitutionality of a New York milk-dealer licensing law.

FACT SUMMARY: Hood (P), a Boston milk distributor, obtained milk from New York. He was denied a license to establish a receiving depot in New York on the basis of a New York law that makes a condition of the issuance of a license that such issuance will not tend to be destructive of competition in a market already "adequately served."

🏛 **RULE OF LAW**
Restrictions imposed for the avowed purpose and with the practical effect of curtailing the volume of interstate commerce to aid local economic interests will not be sustained.

FACTS: Hood (P) was a Boston milk distributor who obtained his supply of milk from producers in New York State. He had established three milk receiving and processing depots in New York under licenses from that state. When he applied for a license to open a fourth depot, he was denied. The basis for the denial was that issuance would tend to create destructive competition in an area already adequately served. In his denial, the milk Commissioner (D) stated that the fourth depot would draw milk supplies away from other existing processing plants and would tend to deprive the local market of an adequate supply of milk.

ISSUE: May a state constitutionally enact restrictions with the purpose and effect of curtailing the volume of interstate commerce for the benefit of local economic interests?

HOLDING AND DECISION: (Jackson, J.) No. Restrictions imposed for the avowed purpose and with the practical effect of curtailing the volume of interstate commerce to aid local economic interests will not be sustained. There is a distinction between the power of the state to shelter its people from menaces to their health or safety, even when those dangers emanate from interstate commerce, and its lack of power to retard, burden, or constrict the flow of such commerce for their economic advantage. *Baldwin v. G.A.F. Seelig* 294 U.S. 511 (1935), is a recent explicit condemnation by this Court of economic restraints an interstate commerce for local economic advantage. "Our system, fostered by the Commerce Clause, is that every farmer and every craftsperson shall be encouraged to produce by the certainty that he will have free access to every market in the Nation, that no home embargoes will withhold his export, and no foreign state will by customs duties or regulations exclude them. . . . Such was the vision of the Founders; such has been the doctrine of this Court which has given it reality." Since the statute, as applied to Hood (P), violates the Commerce Clause and is not authorized by federal legislation pursuant to that Clause, it cannot stand.

▶ **ANALYSIS**

In *Milk Control Board v. Eisenberg*, 306 U.S. 346 (1939), a New York milk dealer who bought milk from Pennsylvania producers challenged a Pennsylvania law. The law set the minimum price to be paid by dealers to milk producers. The Supreme Court upheld the law, stating that it did not attempt to regulate shipment to or sale in New York. It also found that the activity affected was essentially local in Pennsylvania, since only a fraction of the milk produced in that state is shipped out of state. The effect on interstate commerce was found to be incidental. *Baldwin* was not controlling. The Court stated that that decision "condemned an enactment aimed solely at interstate commerce, attempting to affect and regulate the price of milk in a sister state" and amounted, in effect, to a tariff.

■══■

Quicknotes

DORMANT COMMERCE CLAUSE The regulatory effect of the Commerce Clause on state activity affecting interstate commerce, where Congress itself has not acted to control the activity; a provision inferred from, but not expressly present in, the language of the Commerce Clause.

■══■

Aaron B. Cooley v. The Board of Wardens of the Port of Philadelphia

Ship consignee (D) v. State board (P)

53 U.S. (12 How.) 299 (1851).

NATURE OF CASE: Action for violation of a state local-pilot law.

FACT SUMMARY: Cooley (D) violated a Pennsylvania law requiring all ships using the port of Philadelphia to engage a local pilot.

🏛 RULE OF LAW
The states may regulate those areas of interstate commerce that are local in nature and do not demand one national system of regulation by Congress.

FACTS: In 1803, Pennsylvania passed a law that required every ship entering or leaving the port of Philadelphia to use a local pilot. The law imposed a penalty of half the pilotage fee paid to the Board of Wardens (P) and put in a fund for retired pilots and their dependents. Cooley (D), who was a consignee of two ships that had left the port without a local pilot, was held liable under the law. Cooley (D) challenged the right of the state to impose regulations on pilots because it interfered with interstate commerce. The Board of Wardens (P) relied on an Act of Congress in 1789, which stated that all pilots in the rivers, harbors, and ports of the United States shall continue to be regulated in conformity with the existing laws of the states and such laws as the states shall enact for that purpose, until Congress enacts legislation to the contrary.

ISSUE: Is the grant of power to Congress to regulate interstate and foreign commerce an exclusive grant prohibiting the states from legislating, even in areas of primarily local concern?

HOLDING AND DECISION: [Judge not stated in casebook excerpt.] No. The states may regulate those areas of interstate commerce that are local in nature and do not demand a uniform national system of regulation by Congress. The regulation here, requiring overall half-pilotage fees, is consistent with the overall regulations on the subject. When the State of Pennsylvania enacted § 2 of the 1832 act, the State was not indirectly legislating upon other subjects besides pilotage. On the contrary, that section is consistent with the 1803 law at issue here; the section of the 1832 act merely specifies pilotage requirements, by tonnage, of vessels and the trades in which they are engaged. Rather than unfairly favoring ships in the coal trade, those requirements properly apply to all ships entering the Philadelphia port. The Act of 1803 is a lawful exercise of the Pennsylvania legislature's discretion in our federal system. The congressional Act of 1789 unequivocally defined such matters as local, not national, in character. Congress therefore deemed them to be most appropriately regulated through multiple systems of laws instead of through one national system that fails to account for local differences.

▶ ANALYSIS

The local interest versus the national interest test is still used by the court today. In applying this test, the Court balances the national interest against the local interest and also determines if the local regulation discriminates against interstate commerce. If the local interest outweighs the national interest and the regulation does not discriminate against interstate commerce, the states are allowed to regulate that subject of commerce. If it appears that the state regulation has placed a burden on interstate commerce, the Court has drawn the line and refused to hold the state regulations valid even though a local subject may be involved.

■■■

Quicknotes

DORMANT COMMERCE CLAUSE The regulatory effect of the Commerce Clause on state activity affecting interstate commerce, where Congress itself has not acted to control the activity; a provision inferred from, but not expressly present in, the language of the Commerce Clause.

■■■

South Carolina State Highway Dept. v. Barnwell Bros., Inc.

State agency (D) v. Interstate truckers (P)

303 U.S. 177 (1938).

NATURE OF CASE: Appeal from order enjoining enforcement of state statute regulating the weight and width of trucks within the state.

FACT SUMMARY: A South Carolina law prohibited trucks exceeding a certain width and weight from using the state's highways. Interstate truckers (P) challenged the law as an unconstitutional burden on interstate commerce.

🏛 RULE OF LAW
A state law regulating the weight and width of trucks using its highways does not unconstitutionally burden interstate commerce.

FACTS: South Carolina prohibited trucks from using its highways if their width exceeded 90 inches and if their total weight exceeded 20,000 pounds. Interstate truckers (P) challenged these prohibitions as imposing an unconstitutional burden on interstate commerce. A district court enjoined enforcement of these prohibitions, finding that they would seriously impede motor truck traffic passing to and through the state and would increase its cost, and would otherwise impose an undue burden on interstate commerce. The Supreme Court granted review.

ISSUE: Does a state law regulating the weight and width of trucks using its highways unconstitutionally burden interstate commerce?

HOLDING AND DECISION: (Stone, J.) No. Congress has not decided to regulate the width and weight of motor vehicles in interstate motor traffic and has left intact the states' authority to regulate in this area. The Commerce Clause itself prohibits discrimination by states against interstate commerce, as where state laws are nominally of local concern, but in reality are aimed at gaining a local advantage. Here, however, the object of state regulation is of great local concern. Unlike state control of the railroads, which is subject to the Commerce Clause, the safe and economical use of highways is a prime concern of the states, which own and maintain their own highways, and nondiscriminatory regulations of interstate commerce that ensure such use are permitted. Where Congress has not acted, it is not for the courts to decide what are suitable motor vehicle size regulations—that is a legislative choice and not a judicial one. South Carolina's regulations are within its legislative power and do not infringe the Fourteenth Amendment. Therefore, the resulting burden on interstate commerce is not forbidden.

▶ ANALYSIS

As this case illustrates, modern decisions approach the Dormant Commerce Clause with an amalgam of doctrines that include a requirement that the state law in question be rationally related to a legitimate state purpose, that state laws that unjustifiably discriminate against interstate commerce are prohibited by the dormant commerce clause unless and until Congress permits the states to discriminate, and that nondiscriminatory state laws that unduly burden interstate commerce are prohibited by the Dormant Commerce Clause unless and until Congress permits the states to impose such a burden.

■■■

Quicknotes

DORMANT COMMERCE CLAUSE The regulatory effect of the Commerce Clause on state activity affecting interstate commerce, where Congress itself has not acted to control the activity; a provision inferred from, but not expressly present in, the language of the Commerce Clause.

■■■

Southern Pacific Co. v. Arizona ex rel. Sullivan, Attorney General

Railroad company (D) v. State (P)

325 U.S. 761 (1945).

NATURE OF CASE: Action to recover statutory penalties for violation of the Arizona Train Limit Law.

FACT SUMMARY: The Arizona Train Limit Law prohibited the operation within the state of passenger trains more than 14 cars long and freight trains more than 70 cars long.

RULE OF LAW
In deciding whether a state law places an unreasonable burden on interstate commerce, and hence cannot be sustained, the Court must balance the nature and extent of the burden which would be imposed by the statute against the merits and purposes to be derived from the state regulation.

FACTS: The Arizona Train Limit Law made it unlawful to operate within the state a train of more than 14 passenger cars or 70 freight cars. It authorized the state to recover a money penalty for each violation. Arizona (P) brought this action against Southern Pacific (D) to recover the statutory penalties for operative trains within the state in violation of the law. The trial court decided for Southern Pacific (D) on the basis of detailed findings. The state supreme court reversed. It thought that the statute was enacted within the state's police power and that it bore some reasonable relation to the health, safety, and well-being of the state's people. Hence, the Court thought, the statute should not be overturned notwithstanding its admittedly adverse effect on interstate commerce.

ISSUE: In determining whether a state law imposes an unallowable burden on interstate commerce, is it for the courts to balance the burden to be imposed against the merits and purposes to be derived from the law?

HOLDING AND DECISION: (Stone, C.J.) Yes. Wide scope has been left to the states for regulating matters of local concern, but such regulation must not materially restrict the free flow of interstate commerce or interfere with it in matters requiring national uniformity. The courts must determine the nature and extent of the burden that a state regulation would impose on interstate commerce, and then balance that burden against the benefits and merits to be derived from the regulation. In this case, the findings show that the operations of trains of more than 14 passenger cars and more than 70 freight cars is standard practice of the major U.S. railroads. If train length is to be regulated, national uniformity in regulation, such as only Congress can impose, is "practically indispensable to the operation of an efficient and economical national railway system." The findings leave no doubt that the Arizona Train Limit Law imposes a serious burden on interstate commerce. The

practical effect of the law is to control train operations beyond the boundaries of the state because of the necessity of breaking up and reassembling long trains before entering and leaving the regulating state. Further, the Arizona law has no reasonable relation to safety. It in fact makes train operation more dangerous, as is demonstrated by the increase in accidents due to the increase in the number of trains. The purpose of the Act was to cut down on "slack action accidents." Slack action is increased as train length is increased. However, the trial court found that such accidents occurred as frequently in Arizona as in Nevada, where train length is unregulated. Hence, the total effect of the law as a safety measure in reducing accidents is so slight as to not outweigh the national interest in keeping interstate commerce free from substantial interference and from subjection to local regulation that does not have a uniform effect on the interstate train journey which it interrupts. Here, Arizona's (P) safety interest is clearly outweighed by the national interest in an adequate, economical, and efficient railway system. The state supreme court's decision sustaining the statute is reversed.

ANALYSIS

The following are examples of regulations that were held not unreasonably to burden commerce (or where a national interstate commerce interest did not outweigh the state's benefits). A requirement that all persons operating trains within the state (even those in purely interstate movement) be licensed to insure their skill and fitness was upheld. Likewise, the Court upheld "full crew" laws defining the size of train crews. Laws prescribing reasonable safety and comfort devices and others limiting the speed of trains within city limits, as well as those regulating grade crossing, were also upheld.

Quicknotes

DORMANT COMMERCE CLAUSE The regulatory effect of the Commerce Clause on state activity affecting interstate commerce, where Congress itself has not acted to control the activity; a provision inferred from, but not expressly present in, the language of the Commerce Clause.

City of Philadelphia v. New Jersey

State (P) v. State (D)

437 U.S. 617 (1978).

NATURE OF CASE: Appeal from decision upholding the constitutionality of a state commerce statute.

FACT SUMMARY: The New Jersey Supreme Court upheld a New Jersey law prohibiting the importation of waste originating in another state into New Jersey (D) on the basis that it protected a legitimate health interest of the state of New Jersey (D).

🏛 RULE OF LAW
State laws that are basically protectionist in nature unduly burden interstate commerce and thus are unconstitutional.

FACTS: New Jersey enacted a statute that prohibited the importation of solid or liquid waste which was collected or originated in another state. The law was challenged by private landfill owners in New Jersey (D), and the trial court held that it unduly burdened interstate commerce by discriminating against products from other states. The New Jersey Supreme Court reversed, holding the law advanced legitimate health and safety concerns and thus did not unduly burden interstate commerce. The U.S. Supreme Court granted certiorari.

ISSUE: Do state laws that are basically protectionist in nature unduly burden interstate commerce?

HOLDING AND DECISION: (Stewart, J.) Yes. State laws that are basically protectionist in nature unduly burden interstate commerce and are unconstitutional. Even if New Jersey's (D) ultimate purpose was to protect the health and safety of its citizens, it may not accomplish this by discriminating against articles of commerce coming from outside the state. Discrimination must be based on some property of the goods other than geographic origin. This law treats inherently similar products differently based solely on place of origin. As a result, it improperly discriminates against out-of-state production and unduly burdens interstate commerce.

DISSENT: (Rehnquist, J.) New Jersey (D) recognized the health and safety problems associated with the use of landfills in disposing of waste. Under its inherent police power, that state could validly limit the amount of waste its citizens had to deal with by limiting the use of its land as a dump site for any other state.

▶ ANALYSIS

This case reaffirms the Court's holding in *Dean Milk Co. v. Madison*, 340 U.S. 349 (1951). It recognizes that waste is an element of commerce, and its disposal must be regulated as is all commerce. Because no federal regulation exists on the interstate transport and disposition of waste, states may regulate it only if done in a way that is not unduly burdensome. Since the *Dean Milk* decision, discrimination based on point of origin has been held unduly burdensome.

■══■

Quicknotes

DORMANT COMMERCE CLAUSE The regulatory effect of the Commerce Clause on state activity affecting interstate commerce, where Congress itself has not acted to control the activity; a provision inferred from, but not expressly present in, the language of the Commerce Clause.

■══■

C&A Carbone, Inc. v. Town of Clarkstown, New York

Recycling center (D) v. Municipality (P)

511 U.S. 383 (1994).

NATURE OF CASE: Review of municipal ordinance regulating solid-waste disposal.

FACT SUMMARY: The town of Clarkstown (P) mandated that all solid waste leaving the city be processed through a particular transfer station.

🏛 RULE OF LAW

Discrimination against interstate commerce in favor of local businesses is per se invalid unless the municipality can demonstrate under rigorous scrutiny that it has no other means to advance a legitimate local interest.

FACTS: The Town of Clarkstown (P) entered an arrangement with a local contractor that the latter would build and operate a solid-waste transfer station, which, in five years, would be sold back to the Town (P). In order to amortize the cost of the facility, the Town (P), by ordinance, mandated that all solid waste leaving the Town (P) be processed through that station. When C&A Carbone (D), a recycling center in town, attempted to ship its nonrecyclable waste to another state in order to save money, the Town (P) sought an injunction to force Carbone (D) to comply with the ordinance. Carbone (D) challenged the ordinance as contrary to the Commerce Clause. The state courts rejected the challenge, and the Supreme Court granted review.

ISSUE: Is discrimination against interstate commerce per se invalid?

HOLDING AND DECISION: (Kennedy, J.) Yes. Discrimination against interstate commerce is per se invalid. Any ordinance that deprives nonlocal businesses from access to local markets discriminates against interstate commerce and is invalid under the dormant Commerce Clause. With respect to waste, the commodity at issue is not the waste itself but rather the service of processing it and/or transporting it. When a city designates a particular commercial entity as the sole provider of such services, nonlocal providers of the service are effectively shut out. Local governments may not use their regulatory power to favor local businesses by prohibiting patronage of out-of-state competitors. Here, the town (P) has shut out nonlocal solid waste operators, although it has a number of nondiscriminatory alternatives that would satisfy its environmental and fiscal concerns, and thus its ordinance is unconstitutional.

DISSENT: (Souter, J.) The Town (P) here is regulating a traditional government function, something it may legitimately do.

▶ ANALYSIS

The essential vice in discriminatory ordinances that mandate local processing is that they bar the import of the processing service. These laws hoard a local resource—be it shrimp, milk, or solid waste—for the benefit of local businesses that treat it. Clarkstown's (P) ordinance was even more egregiously protectionist than most such laws since it favored a single local proprietor.

Quicknotes

DORMANT COMMERCE CLAUSE The regulatory effect of the Commerce Clause on state activity affecting interstate commerce, where Congress itself has not acted to control the activity; a provision inferred from, but not expressly present in, the language of the Commerce Clause.

United Haulers Assn., Inc. v. Oneida-Herkimer Solid Waste Management Authority

Private hauler of trash (P) v. County waste authority (D)

127 S. Ct. 1786 (2007).

NATURE OF CASE: Suit challenging a county's "flow control" ordinance under the dormant Commerce Clause.

FACT SUMMARY: A county's "flow control" ordinance required haulers of trash to deliver the trash to facilities owned and operated by a state-created public benefit corporation.

🏛 RULE OF LAW

An ordinance requiring that trash be delivered to a state-created public benefit corporation does not violate the dormant Commerce Clause.

FACTS: The Oneida-Herkimer Solid Waste Management Authority (WMA) (D) adopted an ordinance requiring that all trash be delivered to a state-created public benefit corporation. [United Haulers Association (P) sued the WMA (D), alleging that it could deliver trash to out-of-state facilities at lower costs than those required by the WMA's (D) ordinance. The trial court agreed with United Haulers' (P) Commerce Clause argument and enjoined the WMA (D) from enforcing the ordinance. The intermediate appellate court reversed, reasoning that the ordinance was permissible because it benefited a public entity instead of private businesses.] United Haulers (P) petitioned the Supreme Court for further review.

ISSUE: Does an ordinance requiring that trash be delivered to a state-created public benefit corporation violate the dormant Commerce Clause?

HOLDING AND DECISION: (Roberts, C.J.) No. An ordinance requiring that trash be delivered to a state-created public benefit corporation does not violate the dormant Commerce Clause. The distinction between private and public facilities is constitutionally significant because laws benefiting local government may serve several legitimate purposes instead of economic protectionism. To hold otherwise—that is, to treat public and private facilities equally under the dormant Commerce Clause—would lead to much interference by federal courts in state and local affairs. Also worth noting is that the injury alleged by United Haulers (P)—more expensive waste disposal—will be borne by local citizens, not by citizens of other states. Typically, the dormant Commerce Clause is enforced to prohibit shifting expenses out of state instead of keeping them at home. United Haulers' (P) proper remedy is therefore through the local political process, not through the federal courts. [Affirmed.]

CONCURRENCE: (Scalia, J.) The so-called "negative" Commerce Clause is an unjustified judicial invention not to be expanded beyond its existing domain, but nevertheless applies in the interest of stare decisis against state law that facially discriminates against interstate commerce and against state law that is indistinguishable from a type of law previously held unconstitutional. The flow-control law at issue in this case benefits a public entity performing a traditional local-government function and treats all private entities precisely the same way.

CONCURRENCE: (Thomas, J.) The negative Commerce Clause has no basis in the Constitution. The Court has no policy role in regulating interstate commerce, and the negative Commerce Clause jurisprudence should be discarded. But the judgment is correct because the power to regulate interstate commerce is a power given to Congress and not the Court.

DISSENT: (Alito, J.) Benefiting public facilities does not meaningfully distinguish this ordinance from the ordinance struck down in *C&A Carbone, Inc. v. Clarkstown*, 511 U.S. 383 (1994). The difference is merely formal because the waste facility in *Carbone* was "private" only in the most technical sense of the term: when that suit was filed, the facility's title was in the process of transferring to the town of Clarkstown. Further, the WMA's (D) ordinance here violates the market-participant doctrine, which prohibits local governments from discriminatorily regulating markets in which they participate. The ordinance here also fails to serve "legitimate goals unrelated to protectionism" because it clearly benefits local employees of the public facilities and local businesses who supply those facilities. Such preference is economic protectionism by any other name and thus deserves strict scrutiny. Finally, the fact that the WMA's (D) ordinance applies equally to in-state and out-of-state private businesses is not persuasive because caselaw squarely provides that such an equality of burdens cannot save legislation under the dormant Commerce Clause.

▶ ANALYSIS

The dormant Commerce Clause usually prohibits state and local regulations that impose relatively direct, overt burdens on interstate commerce. Here, the WMA's (D) ordinance clearly imposed direct, overt burdens on interstate commerce, but it did so for public benefit. That distinction with cases that bar interstate commerce to protect local private businesses saved the WMA's (D) ordinance under the dormant Commerce Clause.

■■■

Continued on next page.

Quicknotes

DORMANT COMMERCE CLAUSE The regulatory effect of the Commerce Clause on state activity affecting interstate commerce, where Congress itself has not acted to control the activity; a provision inferred from, but not expressly present in, the language of the Commerce Clause.

INTERSTATE COMMERCE Commercial dealings between two parties located in different states or located in one state and accomplished through a point in another state or a foreign country; commercial dealings transacted between two states.

STRICT SCRUTINY Method by which courts determine the constitutionality of a law, when a law affects a fundamental right. Under the test, the legislature must have had a compelling interest to enact the law and measures prescribed by the law must be the least restrictive means possible to accomplish its goal.

■══■

Hughes v. Oklahoma

Operator of minnow business (D) v. State (P)

441 U.S. 322 (1979).

NATURE OF CASE: Appeal from a conviction for violating an Oklahoma statute.

FACT SUMMARY: Hughes (D) was convicted under an Oklahoma (P) statute forbidding the transportation for sale outside the state of minnows seined or procured from Oklahoma (P) waters.

🏛 RULE OF LAW
It constitutes a violation of the Commerce Clause of the Constitution for a state to statutorily provide that no person can ship for sale out-of-state fish or wildlife procured within that state.

FACTS: Oklahoma (P) passed a statute providing that no person could transport or ship minnows for sale outside the state that were seined or procured within the waters of Oklahoma (P). Convicted for violating this law, William Hughes (D), who operated a Texas commercial minnow business, appealed. He argued that the statute was repugnant to the Commerce Clause, the court of criminal appeals affirmed his conviction and he appealed again.

ISSUE: Is the Commerce Clause violated by a state statute barring the transportation or shipping for sale outside a state of fish or wildlife procured within that state?

HOLDING AND DECISION: (Brennan, J.) Yes. The Commerce Clause of the Constitution is violated by a state statute barring the transportation or shipment for sale elsewhere of fish or wildlife procured within that state. The once-embraced rule that a state owns all the wildlife within it and has the right to qualify ownership of it is now discarded. State regulations of wild animals should be considered according to the same general rule applied to state regulations of other natural resources. This rule necessitates inquiries as to (1) whether the statute regulates evenhandedly or discriminates against interstate commerce; (2) whether it serves a legitimate local purpose; and (3) whether alternative means could promote this local purpose as well without discriminating against interstate commerce. The legitimate interest in conservation is not, in this case, advanced by the least discriminatory means available. There is no attempt to limit in-state capturing and sales of minnows, only restraint on interstate transport. Thus, this statute fails to pass constitutional muster.

▶ ANALYSIS

Greer v. Connecticut, 161 U.S. 519 (1896), had held this type of state action constitutional on the theory that a state owned the animals within its borders and could therefore qualify the ownership of wild game taken within the state.

Although that doctrine was weakened in intervening years, it was not fully overruled until this decision.

Quicknotes

COMMERCE CLAUSE Article 1, section 8, clause 3 of the U.S. Constitution, granting Congress the power to regulate commerce with foreign countries and among the states.

Hunt, Governor of the State of North Carolina v. Washington State Apple Advertising Commn.

State governor (D) v. State agency (P)

432 U.S. 333 (1977).

NATURE OF CASE: Appeal from injunction and declaration that agricultural regulation is unconstitutionally discriminatory against out-of-state commerce.

FACT SUMMARY: A North Carolina law required specific grading for all closed apple containers sold or shipped into the state. Washington state had a different and more stringent system for grading its apples. Compliance with the North Carolina regulation would have significantly increased the cost of doing business for the Washington apple industry, which sought to have the regulation enjoined and declared unconstitutionally discriminatory against out-of-state commerce.

RULE OF LAW
A facially neutral law is discriminatory if it has discriminatory effects.

FACTS: North Carolina required apples sold in the state to be packed in cartons carrying only the U.S. Department of Agriculture (USDA) grade or no grade at all. Washington, a leading apple producer, had developed at a significant cost a system of grading apples that was different from, and more stringent than, the USDA standard. This standard was regarded throughout the country as superior to the USDA standard. The Washington apple industry (P) sued to have the regulation enjoined and declared unconstitutionally discriminatory against out-of-state commerce. A district court granted the relief sought, and the Supreme Court granted review.

ISSUE: Is a facially neutral law discriminatory if it has discriminatory effects?

HOLDING AND DECISION: (Burger, C.J.) Yes. The regulation, although facially neutral (applying equally to apples from outside and inside the state) has the practical effect of not only burdening interstate sales of Washington apples, but it also discriminates against them. First, the regulation raises the cost of doing business for the Washington apple industry in the North Carolina market, while leaving North Carolina counterparts unaffected. Second, it strips away from the Washington apple industry the market advantages it had earned for itself through its expensive and superior grading system. Third, by prohibiting the Washington apple industry from using its grade, the regulation had a leveling effect that operated to the advantage of local apple producers. When discrimination is found, the state has the burden of justifying its regulation both in terms of the local benefit and the unavailability of nondiscriminatory alternatives that can effect such benefit. Here, the claimed benefit of preventing consumer deception was slight and could be achieved by less discriminatory alternatives.

ANALYSIS

The *Hunt* test is sometimes considered a hybrid test that uses both the discrimination and burdens doctrines. If the balancing test of the burden doctrine alone were used, the burden would be on the party challenging the law to prove that the burden on interstate commerce outweighed the local benefit. In *Hunt*, the Court shifted the burden to the state to prove both local benefits and a lack of nondiscriminatory alternatives— a test that is more stringent than the discrimination doctrine.

Quicknotes

COMMERCE CLAUSE Article 1, section 8, clause 3 of the U.S. Constitution, granting Congress the power to regulate commerce with foreign countries and among the states.

DISCRIMINATION Unequal treatment of a class of persons.

Exxon Corp. v. Governor of Maryland

Oil companies (P) v. State governor (D)

437 U.S. 117 (1978).

NATURE OF CASE: Appeal from ruling that state law that prohibited out-of-state oil companies (P) from operating a retail service station within the state did not discriminate against out-of-state companies.

FACT SUMMARY: A Maryland law prohibited oil companies (P) from operating a retail service station within the state. Virtually all oil companies (P) were located outside of Maryland. The oil companies (P) argued that, therefore, the law had a discriminatory effect on the out-of-state oil companies (P) and impermissibly burdened interstate commerce.

🏛 **RULE OF LAW**
A facially neutral law that burdens some interstate companies with disparate impact is not discriminatory merely because it imposes such burdens.

FACTS: Maryland prohibited producers or refiners of petroleum products from operating retail service (gas) stations within the state. Virtually all petroleum producers and refiners were located outside of Maryland, and therefore these companies had to divest themselves of their Maryland gas stations and could not otherwise directly sell their product in Maryland. The oil companies (P) claimed the law had a discriminatory effect on the out-of-state oil companies and impermissibly burdened interstate commerce. At trial, the oil companies (P) prevailed on due process grounds, but the Maryland Court of Appeals reversed, upholding the law against the oil companies (P) attacks. The Supreme Court granted review.

ISSUE: Is a facially neutral law that burdens some interstate companies with disparate impact discriminatory merely because it imposes such burdens?

HOLDING AND DECISION: (Stevens, J.) No. The law does impose some burdens on the oil companies (P), but the fact that the burden of the law falls solely on interstate companies does not, by itself, establish a claim of discrimination against interstate commerce. That is because the statute creates no barrier against interstate independent dealers, nor does it prohibit the flow of interstate goods, place added costs upon them, or distinguish between in-state and out-of-state companies in the retail market. The absence of these factors distinguishes this case from those in which a state law was found to be discriminatory. Moreover, the statute does not impermissibly burden interstate commerce, even if some of the oil companies (P) were to stop selling oil products in the state. Interstate commerce is not subjected to an impermissible burden simply because an otherwise valid regulation causes some business to shift from one interstate supplier to another. The Commerce Clause protects the interstate market, not particular interstate firms, from prohibitive or burdensome regulations.

DISSENT: (Blackmun, J.) The effect of the law is discriminatory because it protects in-state retail service station dealers from the competition of out-of-state businesses. This protectionist discrimination is not justified by any legitimate state interest that cannot be achieved by less discriminatory regulation. Specifically, 99 percent of the stations protected from out-of-state competition were locally owned.

▶ *ANALYSIS*

This case is a departure from *Hunt*, 432 U.S. 333 (1977), which held that a facially neutral law can be found discriminatory if there is proof of discriminatory impact. Here, there was strong evidence of discriminatory purpose and effect, as made clear by the dissent, but nonetheless these were insufficient for a finding of impermissible discrimination.

■▬■

Quicknotes

COMMERCE CLAUSE Article 1, section 8, clause 3 of the U.S. Constitution, granting Congress the power to regulate commerce with foreign countries and among the states.

DUE PROCESS The constitutional mandate requiring the courts to protect and enforce individuals' rights and liberties consistent with prevailing principles of fairness and justice and prohibiting the federal and state governments from such activities that deprive its citizens of life, liberty, or property interest.

■▬■

West Lynn Creamery, Inc. v. Healy, Commissioner of Massachusetts Dept. of Food & Agriculture

Milk dealer (P) v. State (D)

512 U.S. 186 (1994).

NATURE OF CASE: Review of judicial rejection of legal challenge to agricultural assessment.

FACT SUMMARY: A law assessing a fee on all milk sold in Massachusetts (D), the funds of which were disbursed solely to local producers, was challenged as unconstitutional.

🏛 RULE OF LAW
An assessment scheme that levies a tax on all distribution of a good but disburses its assets to local producers only is unconstitutional.

FACTS: Massachusetts's (D) legislature, perceiving a need to protect local dairy producers, enacted an assessment system wherein a certain levy was placed on all dairy products sold in Massachusetts (D), the proceeds of which were disbursed to Massachusetts's (D) producers only. The system was challenged by West Lynn Creamery (P), a milk dealer who purchased out-of-state milk, as unconstitutional. The state courts rejected the challenge, and the Supreme Court granted review.

ISSUE: Is an assessment scheme that levies a tax on all distribution of a good but disburses its assets to local producers unconstitutional?

HOLDING AND DECISION: (Stevens, J.) Yes. An assessment scheme that levies a tax on all distribution of a good but disburses its assets to local producers of the distributed goods only is unconstitutional. A state may not enact a tariff on out-of-state goods; to do so is a clear violation of the Commerce Clause. The system at issue here, although taking two steps to achieve its goal, is a de facto tariff. While all producers pay equally into the fund, the assets go only to local producers. This is, in effect, a tariff. The fact that Massachusetts (D) could validly enact either a local subsidy or a nondiscriminatory tax is irrelevant; coupled, the two measures constitute a tariff and cannot stand, as the assessment is clear discrimination against interstate commerce.

▶ ANALYSIS

The Commerce Clause, in its dormant expression, operates on two levels. If a law directly discriminates against commerce from another state, it is per se invalid. If it only incidentally burdens interstate commerce, a court must look to the benefits of the law versus its burdens. The law at issue here was of the per se invalid type.

Quicknotes

COMMERCE CLAUSE Article 1, section 8, clause 3 of the U.S. Constitution, granting Congress the power to regulate commerce with foreign countries and among the states.

State of Minnesota v. Clover Leaf Creamery Co.

State (D) v. Dairy company (P)

449 U.S. 456 (1981).

NATURE OF CASE: Appeal from invalidation of state regulation.

FACT SUMMARY: Minnesota (D) enacted a statute prohibiting the sale of dairy products in disposable plastic containers but permitting such sales in disposable paperboard containers and Clover (P), a dairy using plastic containers, challenged the statute as violative of the Equal Protection and Commerce Clauses.

🏛 RULE OF LAW
A state statute prohibiting sales within the state of products packed in certain kinds of disposable containers for environmental reasons does not unduly burden interstate commerce nor violate the Equal Protection Clause.

FACTS: Minnesota (D) prohibited the use of plastic disposable containers for the sale of dairy products. The legislature determined that such containers were injurious to the environment, while paperboard containers were less so. Clover (P) was a dairy concern that owned equipment for the production of plastic containers for use in selling its products. Clover (P) filed an action challenging the statute as a burden upon interstate commerce and a violation of the Equal Protection Clause. The Minnesota Supreme Court affirmed the trial court's declaration of the statute as null and void for violation of these constitutional clauses, but disagreed with the lower court's determination that the actual purpose of the statute was to benefit Minnesota's (D) pulpwood industry by discriminating against the plastics industry. The U.S. Supreme Court granted certiorari.

ISSUE: Does a state statute prohibiting sales within the state of products packed in certain kinds of disposable containers for environmental reasons unduly burden interstate commerce or violate the Equal Protection Clause?

HOLDING AND DECISION: (Brennan, J.) No. A state statute prohibiting sales within the state of products packed in certain kinds of disposable containers for environmental reasons does not unduly burden interstate commerce nor violate the Equal Protection Clause. The statute does not discriminate between intrastate and interstate sellers; both are prohibited from selling products in disposable plastic containers. Neither is it a protectionist measure. Thus, our inquiry is whether the incidental burden imposed upon interstate commerce is clearly excessive in relation to putative local benefits. The change of containers is not an excessive burden upon out-of-state producers. Paperboard containers are readily obtainable. The benefits include a reduction in the amount of solid waste for disposal and an increase in the

Minnesota (D) pulpwood industry. This state statute prohibiting sales within the state of products packed in certain kinds of disposable containers, here plastic ones for environmental reasons, does not unduly burden interstate commerce nor violate the Equal Protection Clause.

▶ ANALYSIS

A state may reasonably regulate commerce within its borders with an effect outside of them if legitimate objectives outweigh incidental burdens upon interstate commerce. If there is discrimination, there must be no other reasonable means by which to protect a legitimate local interest. The determination is made by a balancing approach.

■■■

Quicknotes

EQUAL PROTECTION CLAUSE A constitutional provision that each person be guaranteed the same protection of the laws enjoyed by other persons in like circumstances.

■■■

Dean Milk Co. v. City of Madison, Wisconsin

Milk products distributor (P) v. Municipality (D)

340 U.S. 349 (1951).

NATURE OF CASE: Action challenging the validity of a city ordinance regulating the sale of milk and milk products within the municipality's jurisdiction.

FACT SUMMARY: A Madison (D) ordinance made it unlawful to sell any milk as pasteurized unless it had been processed and bottled at an approved pasteurization plant located within five miles of the city.

🏛 RULE OF LAW
A locality may not discriminate against interstate commerce, even to protect the health and safety of its people if reasonable alternatives exist which do not discriminate and are adequate to conserve legitimate local interests.

FACTS: Dean Milk Co. (P) was an Illinois corporation engaged in distributing milk products in Illinois and Wisconsin. Madison (D) is a city in Wisconsin. A Madison (D) ordinance prohibited the sale of any milk as pasteurized unless it had been processed and bottled at an approved pasteurization plant located within five miles of the city. Dean Milk (P) had pasteurization plants located 65 and 85 miles from Madison (D). Dean Milk (P) was denied a license to sell its milk products within Madison (D) solely because its pasteurization plants were more than five miles away. Dean Milk (P) contended that the ordinance imposed an undue burden on interstate commerce.

ISSUE: Can an ordinance, which in practical effect prevents out-of-state sellers from competing with local producers, be upheld?

HOLDING AND DECISION: [Judge not stated in casebook excerpt.] No. A locality may not discriminate against interstate commerce, even to protect the health and safety of its people, if reasonable alternatives exist which do not discriminate and are adequate to conserve legitimate local interests. The Madison (D) ordinance erects an economic barrier protecting a major local industry against competition from without the state. Hence, it plainly discriminates against interstate commerce. It must be decided whether the ordinance can be justified in view of the local interest and the available methods for protecting those interests. Reasonable and adequate alternatives do exist. Madison (D) could send its inspectors to the distant plants, or it could exclude from its city all milk not produced in conformity with standards as high as those enforced by Madison (D). It could use the local ratings checked by the U.S. Public Health Service to enforce such a provision. The Madison (D) ordinance must yield to the principle that "one state in its dealings with another may not place itself in a position of economic isolation."

▶ ANALYSIS

In *Nebbia v. New York*, 291 U.S. 502 (1934), the court sustained the state regulation of minimum milk prices to be paid by dealers to local producers. However, in *Baldwin v. Seelig*, 294 U.S. 511 (1935), the same law was challenged as applied to out-of-state producers. The Supreme Court held that application to be an unconstitutional burden on commerce in that it "set a barrier to traffic between one state and another as effective as if custom duties, equal to the price differential (between the out-of-state price and the minimum price set by New York) had been laid upon the thing transported." *Baldwin* was heavily relied upon in *Dean Milk*.

Quicknotes

DORMANT COMMERCE CLAUSE The regulatory effect of the Commerce Clause on state activity affecting interstate commerce, where Congress itself has not acted to control the activity; a provision inferred from, but not expressly present in, the language of the Commerce Clause.

Maine v. Taylor & United States

State (P) v. Bait dealer and Federal government (D)

477 U.S. 131 (1986).

NATURE OF CASE: Appeal from indictment under a federal statute making it a federal crime to transport fish in interstate commerce in violation of state law.

FACT SUMMARY: Taylor (D) imported live baitfish into Maine despite a Maine statute prohibiting such importation. He was indicted under a federal statute that made it a federal crime to transport fish in interstate commerce in violation of state law. Taylor (D) challenged the Maine statute as an unconstitutional burden on interstate commerce.

> **RULE OF LAW**
> A facially discriminatory law is constitutional where less discriminatory alternatives are unavailable.

FACTS: To protect its native fish, Maine prohibited the importation of nonnative baitfish. Taylor, a bait dealer, nevertheless arranged for the importation of live baitfish and was indicted under a federal statute making it a federal crime to transport fish in interstate commerce in violation of state law. Taylor moved to dismiss the indictment on the ground that Maine's law unconstitutionally burdened interstate commerce. Maine argued that there was no less discriminatory alternative to protect the state's fisheries from parasites and nonnative species that might be included in shipments of imported baitfish. The district court dismissed Taylor's motion, but the court of appeals reversed. The Supreme Court granted review.

ISSUE: Is a facially discriminatory law constitutional where less discriminatory alternatives are unavailable?

HOLDING AND DECISION: (Blackmun, J.) Yes. States may regulate matters of legitimate local concern even though interstate commerce may be affected. Where a law is discriminatory on its face, the state has the burden of showing that the law both serves a legitimate local purpose and that this purpose cannot be achieved by available nondiscriminatory means. Based on the evidence presented by Maine (P), there is no less discriminatory way to prevent significant threats to Maine's unique and fragile fisheries from parasites prevalent in out-of-state fish, but not common in Maine. Also, nonnative species inadvertently included with baitfish could pose a threat by competing with native species for food, by preying on native species, or disturbing the environment in other ways. Inspecting for commingled nonnative species, because of the small size of the fish, and for parasites is a physical impossibility. Because there is no less discriminatory way to promote a legitimate state interest—guarding against imperfectly understood environmental risks—the law is constitutional.

DISSENT: (Stevens, J.) Maine (P) is blatantly discriminating against other states, because it has a thriving baitfish population of its own, but flatly prohibits importation of baitfish from other states. The state bears a heavy burden to justify such blatant discrimination. The majority believes that Maine (P) has met its burden by relying on uncertainty about possible ecological effects from the baitfish. However, this ambiguity about ecological impact should defeat, rather than sustain, a discriminatory measure.

> **ANALYSIS**
>
> *Maine v. Taylor* is the only case thus far that has upheld a facially discriminatory law challenged under the dormant Commerce Clause. It follows from the holding in this case that laws that are discriminatory, but enacted for reasons other than shielding local interests from the effects of interstate commerce, are not invalid per se.

Quicknotes

DISCRIMINATION Unequal treatment of a class of persons.

DORMANT COMMERCE CLAUSE The regulatory effect of the Commerce Clause on state activity affecting interstate commerce, where Congress itself has not acted to control the activity; a provision inferred from, but not expressly present in, the language of the Commerce Clause.

Loren J. Pike v. Bruce Church, Inc.

State official (D) v. Farming corporation (P)

397 U.S. 137 (1970).

NATURE OF CASE: Appeal from order enjoining enforcement of a state law that required that certain fruit grown in the state be packed in the state rather than in another state.

FACT SUMMARY: Arizona required that all cantaloupes grown in Arizona be packed there. Bruce Church, Inc. (P) sent the cantaloupes it grew in Arizona in bulk to its packing facilities in California. Pike (D) issued an order prohibiting such transportation. Bruce Church, Inc. (P) filed suit to enjoin the law as an unconstitutional burden on interstate commerce.

RULE OF LAW
A nondiscriminatory law that places burdens on interstate commerce that clearly exceed the local benefits is unconstitutional.

FACTS: Arizona required that all cantaloupes grown in Arizona be packed there. Bruce Church, Inc. (P), a farming corporation with extensive operations in California and Arizona, sent the cantaloupes it grew in Arizona uncrated and in bulk to its packing facilities in California, about 30 miles away from its Arizona operations. Pike (D), an Arizona official charged with enforcing the Arizona law, issued an order prohibiting such transportation. Bruce Church, Inc. (P) filed suit to enjoin the law as an unconstitutional burden on interstate commerce, arguing that it would cost $200,000 to build and operate a plant in Arizona, the sole purpose of which would be to comply with the law. A district court granted the requested injunction, and the Supreme Court granted review.

ISSUE: Is a nondiscriminatory law that places burdens on interstate commerce that clearly exceed the local benefits unconstitutional?

HOLDING AND DECISION: (Stewart, J.) Yes. Where a nondiscriminatory law effectuates a legitimate local interest, and its effects on interstate commerce are only incidental, it will be upheld unless the burden imposed on interstate commerce is clearly excessive in relation to the putative local benefits. Thus, where there is a legitimate local interest, it must be balanced against the burden it imposes. Here, the goal of the state law, to protect and enhance the reputation of growers within the state, is a legitimate state interest. However, the Court tends to view with suspicion state statutes requiring business operations to be performed in the home state that could more efficiently be performed elsewhere. In that light, the burden on interstate commerce imposed by the state law here is unconstitutional, since Arizona's minimal interest in identifying the origin of Bruce Church, Inc.'s (P) cantaloupes to enhance the reputation of Arizona producers cannot justify subjecting it to the substantial capital expenditure of building and operating in Arizona a packing plant that it does not need.

ANALYSIS

The *Pike* inquiry requires courts to balance the local benefits against the burdens on interstate commerce. This methodology has been criticized as too subjective, given the difficulty of measuring these rather abstract concepts—benefits versus burdens—with the same scale.

Quicknotes

DORMANT COMMERCE CLAUSE The regulatory effect of the Commerce Clause on state activity affecting interstate commerce, where Congress itself has not acted to control the activity; a provision inferred from, but not expressly present in, the language of the Commerce Clause.

Bibb, Director, Dept. of Public Safety of Illinois v. Navajo Freight Lines, Inc.

State official (D) v. Interstate motor carrier (P)

359 U.S. 520 (1959).

NATURE OF CASE: Appeal from order enjoining state law that requires trucks passing through the state to have a contoured mudguard.

FACT SUMMARY: Illinois required all trucks passing through the state to use a contoured mudguard. No other state required such mudguards, and one state even made the use of such mudguards illegal. An interstate motor carrier (P) challenged the law as an undue burden on interstate commerce.

🏛 RULE OF LAW
A nondiscriminatory local safety measure that places burdens on interstate commerce that clearly exceed the local benefits is unconstitutional.

FACTS: An Illinois law required trucks and trailers using Illinois's highways to be equipped with a contoured mudguard. Arkansas required trucks to have straight mudguards, and all the other states required either type. Navajo Freight Lines, Inc. (Navajo) (P) challenged the Illinois law on the ground that it unduly burdened interstate commerce. A district court agreed that the Illinois law violated the Commerce Clause, and the court enjoined Bibb (D) and other Illinois officials from enforcing the law. The Supreme Court granted review.

ISSUE: Is a nondiscriminatory local safety measure that places burdens on interstate commerce that clearly exceed the local benefits unconstitutional?

HOLDING AND DECISION: (Douglas, J.) Yes. States have a legitimate safety interest in regulating their highways and safety measures carry a strong presumption of validity. Here, the law would add to a carrier's costs of doing business, since every truck entering interstate commerce would have to have the contoured mudguards, given the impossibility of determining at what point a particular truck would enter Illinois; trucks going to both Arkansas and Illinois would have to either avoid Illinois or stop at the border to change their mudguards; and compliance with the Illinois law would seriously interfere with "interline" trucking operations—the interchanging of trailers between carriers. Moreover, the trial court found that the contoured mudguards had no safety benefits over straight ones and actually created previously unknown hazards. These burdens on interstate commerce are "heavy" and "pass the permissible limits even for safety regulations."

▶ ANALYSIS

As with the *Pike* case, 397 U.S. 137 (1970), here the Court used a balancing test that measured the burdens placed on interstate commerce against the local benefits from the law. This is only one of a few cases that have used the balancing test to find that a nondiscriminatory safety measure placed an unconstitutional burden on interstate commerce.

■■■■

Quicknotes

COMMERCE CLAUSE Article 1, section 8, clause 3 of the U.S. Constitution, granting Congress the power to regulate commerce with foreign countries and among the states.

■■■■

Consolidated Freightways Corp. of Delaware v. Raymond Kassel

State (D) v. Common carrier (P)

455 U.S. 329 (1981).

NATURE OF CASE: Appeal from decision holding that an Iowa statute unconstitutionally burdened interstate commerce.

FACT SUMMARY: Consolidated Freightways Corp. (P) challenged the constitutionality of an Iowa statute that prohibited the use of certain large trucks within the state boundaries.

🏛 RULE OF LAW
A state safety regulation will be unconstitutional if its asserted safety purpose is outweighed by its degree of interference with interstate commerce.

FACTS: The State of Iowa passed a statute restricting the length of vehicles that may use its highways. The state law set a general length limit of 55 feet for most vehicles, and 60 feet for trucks pulling two trailers ("doubles"). Iowa was the only state in the western or midwestern United States to outlaw the use of 65-foot doubles. Consolidated Freightways Corp. (P), one of the largest common carriers in the country, alleged that the Iowa statute unconstitutionally burdened interstate commerce. The district court and the court of appeals found the statute unconstitutional and Kassel (D), on behalf of the state, appealed.

ISSUE: Will a state safety regulation be held to be unconstitutional if its asserted safety purpose is outweighed by the degree of interference with interstate commerce?

HOLDING AND DECISION: (Powell, J.) Yes. While bona fide state safety regulations are entitled to a strong presumption of validity, the asserted safety purpose must be weighed against the degree of interference with interstate commerce. Here, the State of Iowa failed to present any persuasive evidence that 65-foot doubles are less safe than 55-foot single trailers. Consolidated Freightways Corp. (P) demonstrated that Iowa's law substantially burdens interstate commerce by compelling trucking companies either to route 65-foot doubles around Iowa or use the smaller trucks allowed by the state statute. Thus the Iowa statute is in violation of the Commerce Clause.

DISSENT: (Rehnquist, J.) A sensitive consideration must be made when weighing the safety purposes of a statute against the burden on interstate commerce. A state safety regulation is invalid if its asserted safety justification is merely a pretext for discrimination against interstate commerce. The Iowa statute is a valid highway safety regulation and is entitled to the strongest presumption of validity.

▶ *ANALYSIS*

Traditionally, states have been free to pass public safety regulations restricting the use of highways and railway facilities. However, state safety regulations have been struck down when only a marginal increase in safety causes a substantial burden on interstate commerce. This case simply follows this rationale.

■══■

Quicknotes

COMMERCE CLAUSE Article 1, section 8, clause 3 of the U.S. Constitution, granting Congress the power to regulate commerce with foreign countries and among the states.

■══■

Western & Southern Life Insurance Co. v. State Board of Equalization of California

Insurance company (P) v. State agency (D)

451 U.S. 648 (1981).

NATURE OF CASE: Appeal from decision upholding retaliatory tax imposed on out-of-state insurers.

FACT SUMMARY: California imposed a retaliatory tax on certain out-of-state insurers. Western & Southern Life Insurance Co. (Western) (P) was subject to the tax and challenged it on the ground that it was discriminatory and impermissibly burdened interstate commerce.

🏛 RULE OF LAW
A discriminatory and retaliatory law is constitutional where the law is in an area that Congress has authorized the states to regulate.

FACTS: California imposed a retaliatory tax on out-of-state insurers when the insurer's state of incorporation imposed higher taxes on California insurers doing business in that state than California would otherwise impose on that state's insurers doing business in California. Western (P), an Ohio insurer doing business in California, after unsuccessfully filing administrative refund claims for California retaliatory taxes paid, brought a refund suit in California Superior Court, alleging that the retaliatory tax violated the Commerce Clause. The Superior Court ruled the tax unconstitutional, but the California Court of Appeal reversed. The Supreme Court granted review.

ISSUE: Is a discriminatory and retaliatory law constitutional where the law is in an area that Congress has authorized the states to regulate?

HOLDING AND DECISION: (Brennan, J.) Yes. Congress can regulate interstate commerce as it sees fit. In the exercise of this plenary power, Congress can give states the power to restrict interstate commerce that they would otherwise not enjoy. "If Congress ordains that the States may freely regulate an aspect of interstate commerce, any action taken by a State within the scope of the congressional authorization is rendered invulnerable to Commerce Clause challenge." Congress, in the McCarran-Ferguson Act, removed all Commerce Clause limitations on the states' authority to regulate and tax the insurance business. Therefore, there is no Commerce Clause restriction on California's authority to tax the insurance business.

▶ ANALYSIS

Even though a law may not be challenged as violating the Commerce Clause because Congress has removed Commerce Clause restrictions on a state's power, the law may nevertheless be challenged on other constitutional grounds, such as the Equal Protection Clause or Privileges and Immunities Clause. In *Western & Southern Life Ins. Co.*, the insurance company also challenged the California law as an equal protection violation.

Quicknotes

COMMERCE CLAUSE Article 1, section 8, clause 3 of the U.S. Constitution, granting Congress the power to regulate commerce with foreign countries and among the states.

EQUAL PROTECTION CLAUSE A constitutional provision that each person be guaranteed the same protection of the laws enjoyed by other persons in like circumstances.

Reeves, Inc. v. William Stake

Cement distributor (P) v. State (P)

447 U.S. 429 (1980).

NATURE OF CASE: Action to enjoin action taken by South Dakota as unconstitutional.

FACT SUMMARY: During a time of shortage, South Dakota promulgated a plan to confine the sale of the cement it produced in its plant to South Dakota residents.

🏛 RULE OF LAW
In the absence of congressional action, nothing in the Commerce Clause prohibits a state from being a market participant (as opposed to a regulator) and acting in that capacity to favor its own citizens over others.

FACTS: In 1919, South Dakota had built its own plant to produce cement. By the 1970s, some 40 percent of its output was going to out-of-state distributors. Reeves (P) was an out-of-state distributor that purchased almost all of its cement from the South Dakota plant for 20 years. In 1978, a nation-wide cement shortage arose and the Commission running South Dakota's plant decided to reaffirm its policy of supplying all South Dakota customers first and honoring all contract commitments, with the remaining volume allocated on a first-come, first-served basis. Reeves (P) was hit hard, and brought suit against the Commission challenging the constitutionality of the plant's policy favoring South Dakota buyers under the Commerce Clause. The district court enjoined the practice. However, the court of appeals reversed on the grounds that *Hughes v. Alexandria*, 426 US. 794 (1976) held a state could freely act as a market participant, as opposed to a regulator, and in that capacity act to favor its own citizens over others.

ISSUE: When acting as a market participant rather than as a regulator, is a state free to act in that capacity to favor its own citizens over others without violating the Commerce Clause?

HOLDING AND DECISION: (Blackmun, J.) Yes. The Commerce Clause does not prohibit a state from favoring its own citizens over others while acting as a market participant rather than as a regulator. The Commerce Clause responds principally to state taxes and regulatory measures impeding free private trade in the national marketplace. There is no indication of a constitutional plan to limit the ability of a state itself to operate freely in the free market, which is what South Dakota was doing here.

DISSENT: (Powell, J.) The Commerce Clause was intended to prevent just this type of economic protectionism. States certainly can participate in a market to produce goods for public needs. At the same time, the Commerce Clause prohibits states from burdening interstate commerce while they are acting as market participants.

▶ ANALYSIS

South Dakota could have steered clear of the Commerce Clause by providing that cement it produced be used only for its own public needs or that it first would go to fulfill those needs. The clause does not reach a state's action in procuring goods and services for the operation of its government, so a state can act in that way without regard to the possible effect on interstate commerce.

■═■

Quicknotes

COMMERCE CLAUSE Article 1, section 8, clause 3 of the U.S. Constitution, granting Congress the power to regulate commerce with foreign countries and among the states.

MARKET PARTICIPANT DOCTRINE Allows states acting as market participants (i.e., businesses) to be exempted from the dormant Commerce Clause.

■═■

South-Central Timber Development, Inc. v. Commissioner, Dept. of Natural Resources of Alaska

Timber company (P) v. State (D)

467 U.S. 82 (1984).

NATURE OF CASE: Appeal from finding of congressional authorization of state regulation.

FACT SUMMARY: Alaska offered to sell large amounts of state-owned timber if the buyers, including South-Central Timber (P), agreed to process it within state boundaries, but South-Central Timber (P) wanted to buy the timber and ship it to Japan for processing.

🏛 RULE OF LAW
If a state imposes burdens on commerce within a market in which it is a participant, but the burdens have a substantial regulatory effect outside of that particular market, they are per se invalid under the Federal Commerce Clause.

FACTS: Alaska offered for sale a large quantity of state-owned timber. However, it required potential purchasers to agree to process the timber within state boundaries before shipment out of Alaska. This law was enacted to protect existing timber-processing industries within the state and to obtain further revenue from the timber beyond its sale. South-Central Timber (P) wanted to buy Alaska timber and also wanted to ship it beyond Alaskan borders to Japan for processing. South-Central (P) challenged the constitutional validity of the Alaska requirement on Commerce Clause grounds. Alaska responded by asserting that the in-state processing requirement was exempt from invalidation under the Commerce Clause under the "market-participant" doctrine. The court of appeals found that Congress had authorized Alaska's processing requirement, and South-Central (P) appealed to the Supreme Court.

ISSUE: If a state imposes burdens on commerce within a market in which it is a participant, but those burdens have a substantial regulatory effect outside of that particular market, are they per se invalid under the Federal Commerce Clause?

HOLDING AND DECISION: (White, J.) Yes. The market-participant doctrine allows a state to impose burdens on interstate commerce within the market in which it is a participant but allows it to go no further. The state may not impose conditions, whether by statute, regulation, or contract, that have a substantial regulatory effect outside of that particular market. "Market" for Commerce Clause purposes is narrowly defined and precludes a state's exercise of leverage in the market in which it is directly participating in order to regulate a "downstream" market. Here, Alaska is a direct participant in the timber market but not in the processing market. Although Alaska may legitimately prefer its own residents in the initial disposition of goods, in other words, when it is a "private

trader" in the immediate transaction, it may not attach restrictions on dispositions subsequent to the goods coming to rest in private hands after Alaska no longer has a proprietary interest in them. Alaska may not govern the private, separate economic relationships of its trading partners downstream; as a typical seller, it has no say over how the product is used after sale. Because Alaska's local-processing requirement burdens interstate commerce, it is per se invalid under the Federal Commerce Clause.

DISSENT: (Rehnquist, J.) The distinction drawn in the plurality opinion between market participation and market regulation is unconvincing and artificial. Alaska could have chosen a number of constitutionally valid ways of requiring the buyers of its timber to process it within the state, all of which in substance are the same as the contractual provisions the plurality found violative of the Commerce Clause. For instance, Alaska could have chosen to sell its timber only to those companies that themselves own and operate processing plants in Alaska, or the statute itself could have paid to have the logs processed and then sold only processed, rather than unprocessed, logs. The plurality approach is unduly formalistic.

▶ ANALYSIS

The facts of this case closely resemble the facts of an earlier Supreme Court case, in which the court struck down a Louisiana law prohibiting export from the state of any shrimp from which the heads and hulls had not been removed. See *Foster-Fountain Packing Co. v. Haydel*, 278 U.S. 1 (1928). The Court rejected the claim that the fact that the shrimp were owned by the state authorized the state to impose such limitations. The case, as here, involved a natural resource that the Court noted could have been retained for use and consumption within its borders, but because Louisiana permitted its shrimp to be taken and sold in interstate commerce, it released its right to and terminated its control of the shrimp so taken.

Quicknotes

COMMERCE CLAUSE Article 1, section 8, clause 3 of the U.S. Constitution, granting Congress the power to regulate commerce with foreign countries and among the states.

MARKET PARTICIPANT DOCTRINE Allows states acting as market participants (i.e., businesses) to be exempted from the dormant Commerce Clause.

Toomer v. Witsell

Fishermen (P) v. State officials (D)

334 U.S. 385 (1948).

NATURE OF CASE: Appeal from dismissal of suit to enjoin statutes requiring a higher fishing license fee for out-of-staters on the ground that the statutes violate the Privileges and Immunities Clause.

FACT SUMMARY: South Carolina required payment of a fishing license fee for out-of-staters that was much higher than the fee imposed on in-staters. Out-of-state fishermen challenged the statutes imposing the fees as unconstitutional violations of the Privileges and Immunities Clause.

🏛 RULE OF LAW
A law that discriminates against out-of-staters violates the Privileges and Immunities Clause where there is no substantial reason for differential treatment.

FACTS: South Carolina imposed a $25 fee for commercial shrimp boats owned by South Carolinians and a $2,500 fee for the same of type of boat owned by out-of-staters. Several Georgia fishermen (P) challenged the law as violating the Privileges and Immunities Clause. South Carolina argued that the differential was necessary to conserve shrimp and to defray the cost of South Carolina's additional shrimp conservation measures attributable to outside fishing. A district court dismissed the suit, and the Supreme Court granted review.

ISSUE: Does a law that discriminates against out-of-staters violate the Privileges and Immunities Clause where there is no substantial reason for differential treatment?

HOLDING AND DECISION: (Vinson, C.J.) Yes. The Privileges and Immunities Clause is designed to insure to a citizen of State A who ventures into State B the same privileges that the citizens of State B enjoy. This constitutional provision is not absolute, however, and states may discriminate against outsiders when there is a substantial reason for differential treatment. Thus, the inquiry—giving the states ample leeway to regulate local problems—is whether such reasons exist and whether the degree of discrimination is closely related to those reasons. Here, South Carolina's objective, i.e., to conserve its shrimp supply and curtail excessive fishing, although a legitimate state interest, does not justify the discriminatory fees because nothing indicated that the outsiders were a particular source of the problem at which the statutes were aimed. Reversed.

▶ ANALYSIS

The discrimination in *Toomer* involved the ability of out-of-state fishermen to earn their livelihood. The vast majority of cases in which the Court has applied the Privileges and Immunities Clause are cases involving outsiders engaged in important economic activities, such as earning one's livelihood. Another area where the Privileges and Immunities Clause is applied is where a state discriminates against outsiders with regard to constitutional rights. However, the Court has been reluctant to apply the Privileges and Immunities Clause where the discrimination does not involve important economic activities or constitutional rights.

■═■

Quicknotes

PRIVILEGES AND IMMUNITIES CLAUSE Article IV, section 2, clause 1 of the U.S. Constitution, which states that a state cannot favor its own citizens by discriminating against other states' citizens who may come within its borders.

■═■

United Building & Construction Trades Council of Camden County v. Mayor & Council of the City of Camden

Trade council (P) v. City (D)

465 U.S. 208 (1984).

NATURE OF CASE: Appeal from judgment upholding constitutionality of a municipal residency ordinance.

FACT SUMMARY: The New Jersey Supreme Court held that a municipal ordinance, which required that 40 percent of all workers on city constructions projects be residents of the city, was not covered by the Privileges and Immunities Clause.

🏛 RULE OF LAW
The Privileges and Immunities Clause applies to municipal ordinances that discriminate on the basis of municipal residence.

FACTS: The City of Camden (D), New Jersey, enacted an ordinance requiring that contractors and subcontractors working on city construction projects employ a workforce of 40 Camden (D) residents. The Trades Council (P) sued, contending the ordinance discriminated against non-city residents in violation of the Privileges and Immunities Clause. The Supreme Court of New Jersey upheld the ordinance, holding that the Privileges and Immunities Clause did not apply to municipal ordinances that discriminate on the basis of municipal residence because the discrimination applies to both New Jersey residents outside Camden (D) as well as out-of-state residents. Therefore, no discrimination based on state residence was made by the ordinance, and it did not come under the Privileges and Immunities Clause. The U.S. Supreme Court took jurisdiction.

ISSUE: Does the Privileges and Immunities Clause apply to municipal ordinances that discriminate on the basis of municipal rather than state citizenship?

HOLDING AND DECISION: (Rehnquist, J.) Yes. The Privileges and Immunities Clause applies to municipal ordinances that discriminate on the basis of municipal residence. Ordinances are enacted under the municipality's power derived from the state. Thus, ordinances are not outside the clause merely because they are enacted by a municipality. Further, although New Jersey residents living outside of Camden (D) were affected by the ordinance along with out-of-state residents, New Jersey residents had the opportunity to expand or contract municipal power by voting in state elections. Out-of-state residents had no such power. Therefore, the clause applies. The ordinance affected the rights of nonresidents to pursue a livelihood of their choosing. This is clearly a fundamental privilege protected by the clause. Because no trial was held, it is necessary that the decision of the Supreme Court of New Jersey be reversed and the case remanded to determine whether Camden's (D)

economic problems were sufficient to justify the discrimination placed on nonresidents by the ordinance. Reversed and remanded.

▶ ANALYSIS

In this case, the court points out that although the ordinance may have been valid under the Commerce Clause, as the City was acting as a market participant, such an analysis does not apply under the Privileges and Immunities Clause. That clause imposes a direct restraint on state action in the interest of interstate harmony.

■■■■

Quicknotes

COMMERCE CLAUSE Article 1, section 8, clause 3 of the U.S. Constitution, granting Congress the power to regulate commerce with foreign countries and among the states.

MARKET PARTICIPANT DOCTRINE Allows states acting as market participants (i.e., businesses) to be exempted from the dormant Commerce Clause.

PRIVILEGES AND IMMUNITIES CLAUSE Article IV, section 2, clause 1 of the U.S. Constitution, which states that a state cannot favor its own citizens by discriminating against other states' citizens who may come within its borders.

■■■■

Lester Baldwin v. Fish & Game Commn. of Montana

Nonresident hunters (P) v. State agency (D)

436 U.S. 371 (1978).

NATURE OF CASE: Appeal from dismissal of declaratory and injunctive action seeking to hold a discriminatory elk-hunting licensing scheme in violation of the Privileges and Immunities Clause.

FACT SUMMARY: Montana imposed a much higher license fee for elk hunting on nonresidents than on residents. Nonresident hunters (P) challenged the licensing scheme as a violation of the Privileges and Immunities Clause.

RULE OF LAW
A discriminatory law regulating recreational activity does not violate the Privileges and Immunities Clause.

FACTS: A Montana statutory elk-hunting license scheme imposed substantially higher (by at least seven and one-half times) license fees on nonresidents of the state than on residents, and required nonresidents (but not residents) to purchase a "combination" license in order to be able to obtain a single elk. Nonresident hunters (P) filed suit for an injunction against enforcement of the statute and sought reimbursement of fees already paid, claiming that the statute violated the Privileges and Immunities Clause. A district court denied all relief, and the Supreme Court granted review.

ISSUE: Does a discriminatory law regulating recreational activity violate the Privileges and Immunities Clause?

HOLDING AND DECISION: (Blackmun, J.) No. Access by nonresidents to recreational big-game hunting in Montana does not fall within the category of rights protected by the Privileges and Immunities Clause. Only with respect to those "privileges" and "immunities" bearing upon the vitality of the Nation as a single entity must a state treat all citizens, resident and nonresident, equally. Here, equality in access to Montana elk is not basic to the maintenance or well-being of the Union, nor are the nonresidents deprived of a means of livelihood.

⯈ ANALYSIS

In assessing which rights are "basic to the maintenance or well-being of the Union," rather than perceiving "fundamental" rights to be natural rights, the Court views these rights as those relating to the privileges of trade and commerce. Hence the Court's determination in *Baldwin* that recreational activities are not a "fundamental" right and its emphasis on the fact that the livelihood of nonresidents was not implicated by the discriminatory statute.

Quicknotes

PRIVILEGES AND IMMUNITIES CLAUSE Article IV, section 2, clause 1 of the U.S. Constitution, which states that a state cannot favor its own citizens by discriminating against other states' citizens who may come within its borders.

Supreme Court of New Hampshire v. Kathryn A. Piper

State court (D) v. Nonresident attorney (P)

470 U.S. 274 (1985).

NATURE OF CASE: Appeal from decision that the residency requirement for the practice of law violates the Privileges and Immunities Clause.

FACT SUMMARY: Piper (P), who lived in Vermont, passed the New Hampshire bar examination, but was not admitted because New Hampshire made residency a prerequisite to admission. She challenged this requirement as a violation of the Privileges and Immunities Clause.

🏛 RULE OF LAW
A residency requirement for the practice of law violates the Privileges and Immunities Clause.

FACTS: Rule 42 of the New Hampshire Supreme Court (D) limited bar admission to state residents. Piper (P), who lived in Vermont and lived a few hundred yards from the New Hampshire border, took and passed the New Hampshire bar examination. Pursuant to Rule 42, Piper (P) was denied admission to the bar solely because she did not reside in New Hampshire. Piper (P) filed suit in federal district court alleging that Rule 42 violated the Privileges and Immunities Clause. The district court agreed with her, and the court of appeals affirmed. The Supreme Court granted review.

ISSUE: Does a residency requirement for the practice of law violate the Privileges and Immunities Clause?

HOLDING AND DECISION: (Powell, J.) Yes. The practice of law is a "privilege" under the Privileges and Immunities Clause because of its importance to the economy, as well as for noncommercial reasons. But the Privileges and Immunities Clause is not an absolute, and discrimination against nonresidents is allowed where there is a substantial reason for the differential treatment, and the discrimination bears a substantial relationship to the state's objectives. In deciding the relationship between the discrimination and objectives, the Court considers the availability of less restrictive means. Here, none of the reasons offered by the state for its refusal to admit nonresidents to the bar—nonresidents would be less likely to keep abreast of local rules and procedures, to behave ethically, to be available for court proceedings, and to do pro bono and other volunteer work in the state—meet the test of "substantiality," and the means chosen do not bear the necessary relationship to the state's objectives. Also, there are less restrictive means for achieving the state's goals.

DISSENT: (Rehnquist, J.) The practice of law is not like other business conducted across state lines. Unlike other businesses that are indistinguishable from state to state, the practice of law varies in each state, because each state establishes its own laws. Thus, a state has a substantial interest in having its lawyers, like its legislators and judges, be members of its constituency. A residency law like the one in Rule 42 accomplishes this goal. Also, the majority's less-restrictive-means analysis is not appropriate in the context of the Privileges and Immunities Clause because inevitably the Court can always think of another "less restrictive" approach, which is judicial second-guessing of the legislature. Another interest that justifies limiting bar membership to residents is the need to have attorneys available for their clients in emergency situations and even in the regular course of litigation. The majority's answer to this, the use of local co-counsel, raises more problems than it solves. Accordingly, New Hampshire has more than enough "substantial reasons" for requiring its attorneys to be residents.

▶ ANALYSIS

The essential debate between the majority and the dissent in this case revolves around what interests are sufficiently "substantial" to permit discrimination. Clearly, this is one area where reasonable minds can disagree.

■=■

Quicknotes

PRIVILEGES AND IMMUNITIES CLAUSE Article IV, section 2, clause 1 of the Constitution, which states that a state cannot favor its own citizens by discriminating against other states' citizens who may come within its borders.

■=■

The Structure of the Constitution's Protection of Civil Rights and Civil Liberties

Quick Reference Rules of Law

Barron v. Mayor and City Council of Baltimore

Wharf owner (P) v. Municipality (D)

32 U.S. (7 Pet.) 243 (1833).

NATURE OF CASE: Action to recover damages.

FACT SUMMARY: Barron (P) claimed that the City (D) made his wharf useless by diverting the streams during its construction work.

🏛 RULE OF LAW
The amendments to the Constitution were intended as limitations solely on the exercise of power by the U.S. Government and are not applicable to the legislation of the states.

FACTS: Barron (P) sued the City (D) for making his wharf in Baltimore Harbor useless. He claimed that the City (D) had diverted the flow of streams during its street construction and that this diversion had deposited earth near the wharf, causing the water to become too shallow for most vessels. Barron (P) claimed that the action violated the Fifth Amendment guarantee that property will not be taken without just compensation.

ISSUE: Is state legislation subject to the limitations imposed by the amendments to the United States Constitution?

HOLDING AND DECISION: (Marshall, C.J.) No. The amendments to the Constitution were intended as limitations solely on the exercise of power by the U.S. Government and are not applicable to the legislation of the states. The Constitution and its amendments were established by the people of the United States for themselves, for their own government, and not for the governments of the states. The people and each state established their own constitution. The constitutional amendments restrain only the power of the federal government and are not applicable to the actions of the state governments. Article I, § 10 expressly lists the restrictions upon the state governments. We find no reason why if the amendments were to apply to the states, there are not express words so stating. The amendments contain no expression indicating an intent to apply them to the states. Hence, because there is no conflict here between the City (D) and state's action and the federal Constitution, this court has no jurisdiction over this action.

▌ ANALYSIS

There were relatively few references to individual rights in the original Constitution. Its major concern was with governmental structures and relationships. The most important limitation on state power that was protective of individual rights was the Contract Clause. Nor was there a significant broader spectrum of individual rights restrictions on the national government. In response to the demand for additional constitutional protection of individual as well as states' rights, the first ten amendments were proposed and ratified. Since federal criminal decisions were not ordinarily reviewable by the Supreme Court, the Court had little occasion for interpretation of the Bill of Rights prior to the Civil War.

■═■

Quicknotes

CONTRACT CLAUSE Article 1, section 10 of the U.S. Constitution prohibiting states from passing any "law impairing the Obligation of Contracts."

■═■

Slaughter-House Cases: Butchers' Benevolent Assn. of New Orleans v. Crescent City Livestock Landing & Slaughter-House Co.

Butchers (P) v. State (D)

83 U.S. (16 Wall.) 36 (1872).

NATURE OF CASE: Appeal of state enforcement of a monopoly.

FACT SUMMARY: Louisiana created a 25-year slaughterhouse monopoly to which several butchers who were not included objected.

🏛 RULE OF LAW
The Fourteenth Amendment protects the privileges and immunities of national, not state, citizenship, and neither the Equal Protection, Due Process, nor Privileges and Immunities Clauses of that amendment may be used to interfere with state control of the privileges and immunities of state citizenship.

FACTS: A Louisiana law of 1869 granted a monopoly to one Slaughterhouse Company for the three largest parishes in that state. Butchers (P), who were not included in the monopoly, challenged the law creating it on the grounds that it violated the Thirteenth Amendment ban on involuntary servitude and the Fourteenth Amendment protections of the privileges and immunities of national citizenship and equal protection and due process of law. From a judgment sustaining the law, the butchers (P) appealed.

ISSUE: Does the Fourteenth Amendment Privileges and Immunities Clause make all privileges and immunities of citizenship federal rights subject to federal enforcement?

HOLDING AND DECISION: (Miller, J.) No. The Fourteenth Amendment protects the privileges and immunities of national, not state, citizenship, and neither the Equal Protection, Due Process, nor Privileges and Immunities Clauses of that Amendment may be used to interfere with state control of the privileges and immunities of state citizenship. The underlying purpose of all three of the post-Civil War amendments was to eliminate the remnants of African slavery, not to effect any fundamental change in the relations of the government. The Fourteenth Amendment expressly was adopted to assure only that states would not "abridge the privileges or immunities of citizens of the United States" (i.e., Negro citizens in their pursuit of national rights such as the right to protection on the high seas). Similarly, the Equal Protection and Due Process Clauses of that Amendment were drawn to protect former slaves from state denial of federal rights. No interpretation of this Amendment (or the Thirteenth, which is an even clearer case) may be used to prevent the State of Louisiana from exercising its police power here (to promote public health in

slaughterhouses) to define particular privileges and immunities of its citizens.

DISSENT: (Field, J.) Justice Field views the Fourteenth Amendment as protection for all citizens of the fundamental rights of free government from abridgment by the states.

▶ ANALYSIS

The effect of this decision was to essentially render the Fourteenth Amendment Privileges or Immunities Clause ineffectual as a means of protecting individual rights from state abridgment. In addition, it ruled out the possibility that the Bill of Rights could be enforced upon the states as privileges or immunities of national citizenship. Subsequently, of course, the court adopted the position of Justice Bradley and began selectively incorporating parts of those Amendments into the Fourteenth Amendment Due Process Clause. In addition, the Equal Protection Clause has been used extensively to prohibit state action that is discriminatory in any irrational way (i.e., the rational basis test). Note, finally, that even the Thirteenth Amendment, summarily treated above, has been expanded to bar private discriminatory action that can be identified as a badge of slavery.

■══■

Quicknotes

EQUAL PROTECTION CLAUSE A constitutional provision that each person be guaranteed the same protection of the laws enjoyed by other persons in like circumstances.

FOURTEENTH AMENDMENT DUE PROCESS CLAUSE Provides that protections mandated by the U.S. Constitution and observed by the federal government are equally applicable, and therefore must be observed by the States.

PRIVILEGES OR IMMUNITIES CLAUSE Section 1 of the Fourteenth Amendment of the U.S. Constitution prohibiting state laws that abridge the privileges or immunities of U.S. citizens.

THIRTEENTH AMENDMENT The provision that abolished slavery in the United States.

■══■

Saenz v. Roe

New state resident (P) v. State government (D)

526 U.S. 489 (1999).

NATURE OF CASE: Appeal from an order enjoining implementation of a state statute.

FACT SUMMARY: When California (D) discriminated against citizens who had resided in the state for less than one year in distributing welfare benefits, the state statute was challenged and held to be unconstitutional.

🏛 RULE OF LAW
Durational residency requirements violate the fundamental right to travel by denying a newly arrived citizen the same privileges and immunities enjoyed by other citizens in the same state, and are therefore subject to strict liability.

FACTS: In 1992, California (D) enacted a statute limiting the maximum first-year welfare benefits available to newly arrived residents to the amount they would have received in the state of their prior residence. Saenz (P) and other California residents who were eligible for such benefits challenged the constitutionality of the durational residency requirement, alleging their right to travel was violated. The district court preliminarily enjoined implementation of the statute and the court of appeals affirmed. Congress enacted the Personal Responsibility and Work Opportunity Reconciliation Act of 1996, which expressly authorized states to apply the rules (including benefit amounts) of another state if the family has resided in the state for less than twelve months. California (D) appealed, alleging that the statute should be upheld if it has a rational basis, and that the state's (D) legitimate interest in saving over $10 million a year satisfied that test.

ISSUE: Do durational residency requirements violate the fundamental right to travel by denying a newly arrived citizen the same privileges and immunities enjoyed by other citizens in the same state, and are they thus subject to strict liability?

HOLDING AND DECISION: (Stevens, J.) Yes. Durational residency requirements violate the fundamental right to travel by denying a newly arrived citizen the same privileges and immunities enjoyed by other citizens in the same state, and such requirements are therefore subject to strict scrutiny. New citizens of a state are guaranteed the same privileges and immunities enjoyed by established citizens of the state under the Privileges or Immunities Clause of Section 1 of the Fourteenth Amendment. That clause provides that a state's citizens are also citizens of the United States, and it prohibits states from making or enforcing "any law which shall abridge the privileges or immunities of citizens of the United States." As one of the fundamental rights identified by the Court in the *Slaughter-House Cases*,

83 U.S. 36 (1872), the right to travel requires strict judicial scrutiny when state laws impose burdens upon it; neither rational basis nor intermediate review will suffice when a fundamental right is at stake. In this case, the fundamental right to travel between states means that California's discriminatory classification between new and established citizens penalizes the new citizens instead of benignly protecting the state's interest in allocating welfare benefits to bona fide residents. According to the evidence, few people move to California just for its relatively high welfare benefits. Additionally, California itself represents that it did not enact the discriminatory legislation to deter people from migrating into the state for welfare benefits. Deterrence of new welfare recipients therefore is not a valid justification for the law.

DISSENT: (Rehnquist, C.J.) The Court mistakenly relies on the dormant Privileges or Immunities Clause of the Fourteenth Amendment to invalidate California's reasonable residency requirement. Nothing in the Constitution—and certainly not a clause that the Court has used only one other time, in a decision overruled just five years later—prohibits such a requirement.

DISSENT: (Thomas, J.) The majority attributes a meaning to the Privileges or Immunities Clause that likely was unintended when the Fourteenth Amendment was enacted and ratified. At that time, people understood "privileges or immunities of citizens" to be their fundamental right, rather than every public benefit established by positive law.

▶ ANALYSIS

The Court in this case found that a state violated the Privileges or Immunities Clause when it discriminated against citizens who had been residents for less than one year. The Thomas dissent alleged that this was contrary to the original understanding at the time the Fourteenth Amendment was enacted. Chief Justice Rehnquist's dissent went on to point out that a welfare subsidy is as much an investment in human capital as is a tuition subsidy and their attendant benefits are just as portable.

■=■

Quicknotes

FUNDAMENTAL RIGHT A liberty that is either expressly or impliedly provided for in the United States Constitution, the deprivation or burdening of which is subject to a heightened standard of review.

Continued on next page.

PRIVILEGES OR IMMUNITIES CLAUSE, Section 1 of the Fourteenth Amendment of the U.S. Constitution prohibiting state laws that abridge the privileges or immunities of U.S. citizens.

STRICT SCRUTINY Method by which courts determine the constitutionality of a law, when a law affects a fundamental right. Under the test, the legislature must have had a compelling interest to enact the law and measures prescribed by the law must be the least restrictive means possible to accomplish its goal.

■═■

Twining v. New Jersey

Criminal defendant (D) v. State (P)

211 U.S. 78 (1908).

NATURE OF CASE: Appeal from criminal conviction based on defendant's failure to testify.

FACT SUMMARY: Twining (D) was convicted in New Jersey (P) of fraud after he failed to testify on his behalf. New Jersey did not include in its constitution a right against compelled self-incrimination. Twining (D) challenged his conviction on the ground that the Fourteenth Amendment applied this right to the states.

🏛 RULE OF LAW
The Fourteenth Amendment does not incorporate provisions of the Bill of Rights that guarantee the right against compelled self-incrimination.

FACTS: Twining (D) [referred to as "defendant" in the opinion], was indicted in New Jersey (P) for fraud. At trial, Twining (D) refused to testify, and the jury was instructed that they could find him guilty on the basis of his failure to testify against evidence that tended to incriminate him. New Jersey was one of the few states that did not incorporate in its constitution the right against compelled self-incrimination. Twining (D) challenged his conviction, arguing that the Due Process Clause and Privileges or Immunities Clause of the Fourteenth Amendment incorporated the right against compelled self-incrimination and that, therefore, this right applied to the states. The conviction was successively affirmed by the courts of New Jersey, and the Supreme Court granted review.

ISSUE: Does the Fourteenth Amendment incorporate provisions of the Bill of Rights that guarantee the right against compelled self-incrimination?

HOLDING AND DECISION: [Judge not stated in casebook excerpt.] No. The privilege against self-incrimination was included in the first ten amendments (Bill of Rights) to the Constitution. The argument that this privilege is incorporated by the Fourteenth Amendment's Privileges or Immunities Clause, and therefore applies to state action, fails because this privilege is not a fundamental right, privilege or immunity of national citizenship. The argument that compelled self-incrimination is a denial of due process of law, and therefore incorporated by the Due Process Clause, also fails because the privilege is not an inalienable, fundamental right and historically was not part of the concept of due process.

▌ANALYSIS

The significance of this case is not so much its holding as it is the fact that this was the first case to explicitly discuss applying the Bill of Rights to the states through the process of incorporation.

Quicknotes

DUE PROCESS CLAUSE Clauses found in the Fifth and Fourteenth Amendments to the U.S. Constitution providing that no person shall be deprived of "life, liberty, or property, without due process of law."

FUNDAMENTAL RIGHT A liberty that is either expressly or impliedly provided for in the United States Constitution, the deprivation or burdening of which is subject to a heightened standard of review.

PRIVILEGES OR IMMUNITIES CLAUSE Section 1 of the Fourteenth Amendment of the U.S. Constitution prohibiting state laws that abridge the privileges or immunities of U.S. citizens.

Duncan v. Louisiana

Defendant (D) v. State (P)

391 U.S. 145 (1968).

NATURE OF CASE: Appeal from conviction of battery and sentence of 60 days with a $150 fine.

FACT SUMMARY: Louisiana's constitution granted jury trials only in cases in which capital punishment or imprisonment at hard labor may be granted.

🏛 RULE OF LAW
The right to a jury trial in serious criminal cases punishable by at least two years in prison is a fundamental right that must be recognized by the states as part of their obligation to extend due process of law to all persons within their jurisdiction.

FACTS: Duncan (D) was charged with simple battery, which in Louisiana was punishable by a maximum of two years' imprisonment and a $300 fine. His request for a jury trial was denied by the trial court because the Louisiana (P) constitution granted jury trials only in cases in which capital punishment or imprisonment at hard labor may be imposed.

ISSUE: Does the Fourteenth Amendment guarantee a right of jury trial in all criminal cases which, were they to be tried in a federal court, would come within the Sixth Amendment's guarantee?

HOLDING AND DECISION: (White, J.) Yes. The right to a jury trial in serious criminal cases punishable by at least two years in prison is a fundamental right that must be recognized by the states as part of their obligation to extend due process of law to all persons within their jurisdiction. A right to jury trial is granted to a criminal defendant in order to guard against an overzealous or corrupt prosecutor and the compliant, biased, or eccentric judge. A holding that due process assures a right to jury trial will not cast doubt on the integrity of every trial conducted without a jury.

CONCURRENCE: (Black, J.) Both total and selective incorporation of the Bill of Rights are to be preferred to assigning no settled meaning to the term "due process" as this will shift from time to time in accordance with changing theories.

▶ ANALYSIS

One commentator has suggested that, after *Duncan*, the Court, although describing its test as a "fundamental rights" approach, has actually embraced "selective incorporation" in which all of the Bill of Rights, one provision at a time, has been incorporated in fact. Nevertheless, it is still unclear whether by "specific" provisions, the Court

means only the text of the actual amendments or judicial interpretations in decisions involving those rights.

■■■

Quicknotes

DUE PROCESS CLAUSE Clauses found in the Fifth and Fourteenth Amendments to the U.S. Constitution providing that no person shall be deprived of "life, liberty, or property, without due process of law."

FUNDAMENTAL RIGHT A liberty that is either expressly or impliedly provided for in the United States Constitution, the deprivation or burdening of which is subject to a heightened standard of review.

SELECTIVE INCORPORATION Doctrine providing that the Bill of Rights is incorporated by the Due Process Clause only to the extent that the Supreme Court decides that the privileges and immunities therein are so essential to fundamental principles of due process to be preserved against both state and federal action.

■■■

The Civil Rights Cases: United States v. Stanley

Excluded citizens (P) v. Institutions (D)

109 U.S. 3 (1883).

NATURE OF CASE: Review of criminal and civil prosecutions under the 1875 Civil Rights Act.

FACT SUMMARY: In the 1875 Civil Rights Act, Congress sought to prohibit private discrimination under the Fourteenth and Thirteenth Amendments.

🏛 RULE OF LAW
Civil rights guaranteed by the Constitution cannot be impaired by the wrongful acts of individuals unless such acts are sanctioned or authorized by the state.

FACTS: Congress in 1875 passed the federal Civil Rights Act prohibiting private citizens from excluding other citizens from inns, public transportation, and places of amusement based on race. The Act was passed under the authority of the Thirteenth and Fourteenth Amendments. In four criminal prosecutions and one civil lawsuit involving exclusion of African-Americans from hotels, theaters, and railroads, those prosecuted challenged the constitutionality of the Act.

ISSUE: Can civil rights guaranteed by the Constitution be impaired by the wrongful acts of individuals if such acts are not sanctioned or authorized by the state?

HOLDING AND DECISION: (Bradley, J.) No. Civil rights guaranteed by the Constitution cannot be impaired by the wrongful acts of private individuals unless such acts are sanctioned or authorized by the state. By its express terms, Section 1 of the Fourteenth Amendment applies only to states and prohibits certain action by states. That section has no application to the private conduct of individuals, which is the province of state law. The enforcement power granted to Congress in the last section of the Fourteenth Amendment enables Congress only to pass laws prohibiting states from engaging in the form of action proscribed by Section 1 of the Amendment. Accordingly, the first two sections of the Civil Rights Act of 1875 are invalid because they seek to proscribe private, individual conduct that is properly the subject of state legislation.

DISSENT: (Harlan, J.) The majority reads the text of Section 1 of the Fourteenth Amendment more narrowly than the Framers of the Amendment intended. That Amendment was adopted with the purpose and spirit of ensuring the liberty that is inherent in American citizenship, and the Court's reading thus violates the rule of construction that requires courts to give effect to the Framers' intent.

▶ ANALYSIS

The Court's narrow reading of § 1 of the Fourteenth Amendment stands to this day. Although subsequent decisions have chipped away at it to some extent, the rule remains that the Fourteenth Amendment affects only state action. The major civil rights legislation of the 1960s came about, not through the Fourteenth Amendment, but through the seemingly unlikely jurisdictional basis of the Commerce Clause of Article III.

Quicknotes

FOURTEENTH AMENDMENT Declares that no state shall make or enforce any law that shall abridge the privileges or immunities of citizens of the United States. No state shall deny to any person within its jurisdiction the equal protection of the laws.

STATE ACTION Actions brought pursuant to the Fourteenth Amendment claiming that the government violated the plaintiff's civil rights.

Marsh v. Alabama

Jehovah's Witness (D) v. State (P)

326 U.S. 501 (1946).

NATURE OF CASE: Appeal from the affirmance of a conviction for violation of a state statute challenged as invalid under the First Amendment as applied to the state by the Fourteenth Amendment.

FACT SUMMARY: Marsh, a Jehovah's Witness, was convicted of criminal trespass in a company town for distributing literature without permission of the town's management. She appealed the conviction on First Amendment grounds.

🏛 RULE OF LAW
A state violates the First and Fourteenth Amendments by imposing criminal liability on a person who distributes religious literature on the premises of a company-owned town without permission of the town's management.

FACTS: Chickasaw, Alabama, was a company town, owned in its entirety by the Gulf Shipbuilding Corporation (Gulf), but otherwise had all the characteristics of any other American town. Marsh (D), a Jehovah's Witness, distributed religious literature in the streets of the town without Gulf's permission. She was arrested and convicted in state court pursuant to an Alabama statute that made it a crime (criminal trespass) to enter or remain on the premises of another after having been warned not to. Marsh (D) appealed her conviction, claiming that the state statute abridged her rights under the First and Fourteenth Amendments. The conviction was affirmed at the state level and the Supreme Court granted review.

ISSUE: Does a state violate the First and Fourteenth Amendments by imposing criminal liability on a person who distributes religious literature on the premises of a company-owned town without permission of the town's management?

HOLDING AND DECISION: (Black, J.) Yes. If Chickasaw had been a municipality, it would be clear that a conviction under a municipal ordinance for distributing religious literature in the streets would be unconstitutional. The state (P) argues that because Chickasaw is privately held, it has the power, enforced by the state statute, to abridge freedoms of the press and religion. However, a privately held town is not like a private homeowner, who could suppress unwanted religious expression on his property without violating the Constitution. The more an owner opens up his property for use by the public, the more the property owners' rights become limited by the constitutional rights of those who use it. In balancing the rights of property owners against the rights of those who use the property to enjoy freedom of press and religion, the latter enjoy a preferred position. Private ownership of a town, therefore, does not justify the state's permitting the owner from depriving citizens of their fundamental liberties.

▶ ANALYSIS

The public function doctrine recognizes that private persons exercising governmental powers should be regarded as state actors. In this case, the Court saw the running of a town, whether by a municipality or a private owner, as a public function. The company-owner of the town was a state actor because the town was built and operated primarily to benefit the public and its operation was essentially a public function. It was the town's public character that transformed the corporate owner from a private property owner to an agent of the state.

■══■

Quicknotes

FOURTEENTH AMENDMENT Declares that no state shall make or enforce any law that shall abridge the privileges or immunities of citizens of the United States. No state shall deny to any person within its jurisdiction the equal protection of the laws.

STATE ACTION Actions brought pursuant to the Fourteenth Amendment claiming that the government violated the plaintiff's civil rights.

■══■

Jackson v. Metropolitan Edison Co.

Customer (P) v. Utility company (D)

419 U.S. 345 (1974).

NATURE OF CASE: Federal civil rights action under 42 U.S.C. § 1983.

FACT SUMMARY: Jackson (P) claimed that Metropolitan's (D) (a privately owned utility company) action in terminating service to her for nonpayment without notice, a hearing, or an opportunity to pay, constituted state action and violated due process.

🏛 RULE OF LAW
Evidence showing a heavily regulated private utility, enjoying at least a partial monopoly in the providing of electrical service, elected to terminate service to a customer in a manner found by the state public-utilities commission to be permissible under state law does not demonstrate a sufficiently close nexus between the state and the utility's action to make that action state action.

FACTS: Metropolitan (D) is a privately owned utility that holds a certificate of public convenience issued by the state public utilities commission, empowering it to deliver electricity. It has filed a general tariff with the commission, a provision of which states Metropolitan's (D) right to terminate electricity to a user for nonpayment. Metropolitan (D) terminated Jackson's (P) electric service for nonpayment. She claims that this constituted state action and because it was done without notice, a hearing, or opportunity to pay, such action deprived her of her property (her alleged right to reasonably continuous electrical service) without due process.

ISSUE: Where a heavily regulated public utility, which enjoys at least a partial monopoly, elects to terminate service to a customer in a manner found by the state public-utilities commission to be permissible under state law, does such termination constitute state action?

HOLDING AND DECISION: (Rehnquist, J.) No. Evidence showing a heavily regulated private utility, enjoying at least a partial monopoly in the providing of electrical service, which elected to terminate service to a customer in a manner found by the state public-utilities commission to be permissible under state law, does not demonstrate a sufficiently close nexus between the state and the utility's action to make that action state action. The mere fact that a business is subject to detailed and extensive state regulation does not convert its action into state action. Nor does the fact that it enjoys a monopoly make its action state action. It's true that Metropolitan's (D) services affect the public interest. However, the actions of all businesses that affect the public interest cannot be called state action. Metropolitan (D) is not performing a public function since state law imposes no obligation on the state to furnish utility service. Hence, the evidence did not demonstrate a sufficiently close nexus between the state and Metropolitan's (D) action so that Metropolitan's (D) termination of services may be treated as state action.

DISSENT: (Marshall, J.) Metropolitan Edison's (D) method of terminating service to its customers clearly qualifies as state action. Earlier decisions have found state action where, as here, a government "insinuated itself into a position of interdependence with (the company)." *Burton v. Wilmington Parking Authority*, 365 U.S. 715 (1961). The Court also ignores established bases for state action here because Pennsylvania has sanctioned the utility as a monopoly, the State has cooperated extensively with the utility, and the utility's service is essentially a public function. Before this case, a state's authorization of a private entity's conduct sufficed for a finding of state action. The majority also overlooks the broad interaction between the state and the utility, as well as the crucial fact that Pennsylvania has specifically approved the very termination procedures that are at issue here. Metropolitan Edison (D) provides what has traditionally been an essential public function. That the state has not affirmatively required the company to provide that service should not defeat a finding of state action in this case.

▶ ANALYSIS

In *Moose Lodge v. Irvis*, 407 U.S. 163 (1972), the lodge refused service to a black guest of a lodge member. The guest claimed that although the lodge was a private club, its action was unconstitutional because it held a state liquor license. The Court held that the state was not sufficiently implicated in the lodge's discriminatory policies to make its action state action. The dissent argued that the "state was putting the weight of its liquor license, concededly a valued and important adjunct to a private club, behind racial discrimination."

Quicknotes

DUE PROCESS CLAUSE Clauses found in the Fifth and Fourteenth Amendments to the United States Constitution providing that no person shall be deprived of "life, liberty, or property, without due process of law."

STATE ACTION Actions brought pursuant to the Fourteenth Amendment claiming that the government violated the plaintiff's civil rights.

Terry v. Adams

Negro voters (P) v. White Texas Democrats (D)

345 U.S. 461 (1953).

NATURE OF CASE: Class action by Negroes (P) to enjoin a whites-only political organization (D) from holding pre-primaries, the main purpose of which was to exclude Negroes from voting.

FACT SUMMARY: A whites-only Texas political organization (D), the purpose of which was to exclude Negroes from voting, dominated county politics through its pre-primaries, with all its candidates winning Democratic primaries and general elections. Negroes (P) brought a class action to enjoin the organization under the Fifteenth Amendment.

🏛 RULE OF LAW
A political organization's exclusion of voters solely on the basis of race violates the Fifteenth Amendment where that organization's primary determines who will be elected in general elections.

FACTS: The Jaybird Democratic Association was a whites-only Texas political organization (D) that operated just like a political party. The Association held pre-primaries, and for more than 50 years, the Association's countywide candidates had invariably been nominated in the Democratic primaries and elected to office. However, the Jaybirds argued that the Association was a private club because the Association's elections were not governed by state laws and did not utilize state elective machinery or funds. Candidates elected by the Association were not certified by the Association as its candidates in the Democratic primary, but filed their own names as candidates. The admitted purpose of the organization was to exclude Negroes from voting. Negro voters (P) brought a class action to determine the constitutionality under the Fifteenth Amendment of being excluded from voting in the Association's elections solely on the basis of color and race. The district court held for the Petitioners, but the court of appeals reversed. The Supreme Court granted review.

ISSUE: Does a political organization's exclusion of voters solely on the basis of race violate the Fifteenth Amendment where that organization's primary determines who will be elected in general elections?

HOLDING AND DECISION: (Black, J.) Yes. Where the Democratic Party excluded Negroes from voting in the party's primaries, the Court held that it violated the Fifteenth Amendment. Here, the Association is run just like a political party and the qualifications of its members are the same as for all Texas voters, with the exception that they must also be white. Such a proviso in a county-operated primary would be clearly unconstitutional. Here, the state's permitting elections such as those held by the Jaybirds, which are duplicative of the state's election process, permits a flagrant abuse of those elections to circumvent the Fifteenth Amendment. The only election that has effectively counted for over 50 years has been the one held by the Jaybirds. The Democratic primary and the general election are nothing more than "perfunctory ratifiers" of the result of the Jaybird election. It is therefore immaterial that the state doesn't regulate that part of the election process that it leaves for the Jaybirds to manage; the effect of the whole process—Jaybird primary plus Democratic primary plus general election—is to strip Negroes of any influence in the voting process.

▌ ANALYSIS

Here, the Court found state action in Texas's inaction—its failure to regulate anything other than the general election. This case exemplifies the public function exception to the state action doctrine, and although a paradigm of the public function exception, would be most applicable as precedent where government chooses to stop performing a task traditionally relegated to government so as to avoid the Constitution's requirements.

■■■

Quicknotes

FIFTEENTH AMENDMENT The right of citizens of the United States to vote shall not be denied on account of race, color, or previous condition of servitude.

STATE ACTION Actions brought pursuant to the Fourteenth Amendment claiming that the government violated the plaintiff's civil rights.

■■■

Evans v. Newton

Negroes (P) v. Park managers (D)

382 U.S. 296 (1966).

NATURE OF CASE: Action to replace trustees of city park that was devised for the use of whites only.

FACT SUMMARY: Land was devised to a city for use as a park for whites only, with the city as trustee. After suit was brought to remove the city as trustee because it allowed Negroes to use the park, the city resigned as trustee and a state court appointed a private trustee to continue the exclusion of Negroes from the park. Negro (P) intervenors challenged the racial restriction as violating the Fourteenth Amendment.

🏛 **RULE OF LAW**
A private park that is municipal in character and that excludes people on the basis of color and race violates the Fourteenth Amendment.

FACTS: United States Senator Augustus Bacon devised in his will to the City of Macon, Georgia, a parcel of land that was to be used as a park for whites only. The city was named trustee, and a board of managers was created under the trust to administer the park. The city eventually opened the park to use by Negroes as well, because it was clear that it could not constitutionally enforce the racial exclusion, and individual managers (D) brought suit to remove the city as trustee so as to effectuate the Senator's will. The city resigned as trustee, and a state court appointed private trustees to continue the exclusion of Negroes from the park. Negroes (P) intervened, alleging that the racial limitation violated the Fourteenth Amendment's Equal Protection Clause. On appeal, the Georgia Supreme Court affirmed the appointment of the private trustees. The Supreme Court granted review.

ISSUE: Does a private park that is municipal in character and that excludes people on the basis of color and race violate the Fourteenth Amendment?

HOLDING AND DECISION: (Douglas, J.) Yes. The Equal Protection Clause of the Fourteenth Amendment bans state-sponsored racial inequality. What is state action and what is private action is not always easy to determine, and must be made as a factual determination. Here, the park was an integral part of the city, and the city continued to maintain and operate the park. Running the park is thus a public function, even if managed by a private entity. The services rendered by a park are municipal in nature—mass recreation through the use of parks is in the public domain—and, under the circumstances of this case, the park is subject to the equal protection requirements of the Fourteenth Amendment.

the Court has never gone that far, the Civil Rights Act of 1964 made this less necessary because the Act prohibits discrimination by places of public accommodation, such as hotels, restaurants, or amusement parks.

■■■

Quicknotes

FOURTEENTH AMENDMENT Declares that no state shall make or enforce any law that shall abridge the privileges or immunities of citizens of the United States. No state shall deny to any person within its jurisdiction the equal protection of the laws.

STATE ACTION Actions brought pursuant to the Fourteenth Amendment claiming that the government violated the plaintiff's civil rights.

■■■

▌ *ANALYSIS*

The language in this case was broad enough to make almost any place of recreation a "public function." Although

Amalgamated Food Employees Union Local 590 v. Logan Valley Plaza, Inc.

Union picketers (D) v. Shopping center (P)

391 U.S. 308 (1968).

NATURE OF CASE: Appeal from order enjoining picketing and trespassing on privately owned shopping center property.

FACT SUMMARY: Union members (D) peacefully picketed a non-union store located in a privately owned shopping center (P). A court enjoined the picketing in the shopping center (P), justifying the injunction as protecting the shopping center's property rights. The picketers (D) challenged the injunction on First Amendment grounds.

🏛 RULE OF LAW
The First Amendment protects labor picketing of a store in a privately owned shopping center.

FACTS: Weis Markets owned and operated a supermarket in a large shopping center complex owned by Logan Valley Plaza (P). In front of Weis's building there was a covered porch and a parcel pickup zone. Members of the Amalgamated Food Employees Union picketed Weis's store, confining the picketing almost entirely to the parcel pickup zone and the portion of the parking area adjacent thereto. The picketing was peaceful with some sporadic and infrequent congestion of the parcel pickup area. A Pennsylvania Court of Common Pleas enjoined picketing and trespassing on the Weis storeroom, porch and parcel pick-up area and on the Logan parking area, thus preventing picketing inside the shopping center. That court held the injunction was justified in order to protect the shopping center's property rights and because the picketing was unlawfully aimed at coercing Weis to compel its employees to join a union. The Pennsylvania Supreme Court affirmed the issuance of the injunction on the sole ground that picketers' conduct constituted a trespass on the shopping center's property. The union appealed on First Amendment grounds, and the Supreme Court granted review.

ISSUE: Does the First Amendment protect labor picketing of a store in a privately owned shopping center?

HOLDING AND DECISION: (Marshall, J.) Yes. Peaceful picketing in a public location, such as a town's business center, absent other factors involving the purpose or the manner of the picketing, is protected by the First Amendment. The issue is thus whether a privately owned shopping center is akin to such a public location. *Marsh v. Alabama*, 326 U.S. 501 (1946), held that under some circumstances private property may, for First Amendment purposes, be treated as though it is public property. The shopping center is the functional equivalent of the business block in the town involved in Marsh. Here, the shopping center serves as the community business block and is open to the public. Accordingly, the state

may not delegate the power, through the use of trespass laws, to exclude entirely those members of the public who wish to exercise their First Amendment rights on the premises in a manner and for a purpose generally consonant with the use to which the property is actually put. Nonetheless, property owners and the state can reasonably regulate the exercise of First Amendment rights on their property to prevent interference with the normal use of the property by others.

▶ ANALYSIS

The expansive language of this case, which might suggest that all privately owned shopping centers fall within the public function exception to the state action doctrine, was quickly repudiated, and the case was expressly overruled by *Hudgens v. NLRB*, 424 U.S. 507 (1976).

■■■

Quicknotes

FIRST AMENDMENT Prohibits Congress from enacting any law respecting an establishment of religion, prohibiting the free exercise of religion, abridging freedom of speech or the press, the right of peaceful assembly and the right to petition for a redress of grievances.

■■■

Lloyd Corp. v. Tanner

Shopping center (D) v. Handbill distributors (P)

407 U.S. 551 (1972).

NATURE OF CASE: Appeal from order enjoining enforcement of private shopping center's no-handbilling policy.

FACT SUMMARY: Protestors of the Vietnam War (P) distributed handbills in a private shopping center (D) and were threatened with arrest for trespassing. They challenged the shopping center's no-handbilling policy as violative of their First and Fourteenth Amendment rights.

🏛 RULE OF LAW
A shopping center does not violate the First and Fourteenth Amendments when it prohibits handbilling that is unrelated to the shopping center's operations.

FACTS: Protestors of the Vietnam War (P) distributed anti-war handbills in the mall portion of the Lloyd Center (D), a large private shopping center spanning many city blocks and surrounded by public sidewalks and streets. The center's security guards asked the protestors, under threat of arrest, to stop the handbilling, suggesting that they could resume their activities on the public streets and sidewalks adjacent to but outside the center, which the handbill distributors (P) did. The handbill distributors (P), claiming that the center's action violated their First Amendment rights, thereafter brought an action for injunctive and declaratory relief. The district court, stressing that the center is "open to the general public" and "the functional equivalent of a public business district," and relying on *Marsh v. Alabama*, 326 U.S. 501 (1946) and *Amalgamated Food Employees Union v. Logan Valley Plaza*, 391 U.S. 308 (1968), held that the center's (D) policy of prohibiting handbilling within the mall violated the handbill distributors' (P) First Amendment rights. The court of appeals affirmed, and the Supreme Court granted review.

ISSUE: Does a shopping center violate the First and Fourteenth Amendments when it prohibits handbilling that is unrelated to the shopping center's operations?

HOLDING AND DECISION: (Powell, J.) No. The handbilling had no relation to any purpose for which the center is used. The facts in this case are significantly different from those in *Logan Valley*, 391 U.S. 308 (1968), which involved labor picketing designed to convey a message to patrons of a particular store, so located in the center of a large private enclave as to preclude other reasonable access to store patrons. Here, the handbill distributors (P) could, and did, make their distributions on the public sidewalks and streets that all of the center's patrons had to use before entering or leaving the center. Thus, in *Logan Valley*, the picketers had no alternative means of communicating their message, but here the handbill distributors (P) did. Under these circumstances, the center did not lose its private character and its

right to protection under the Fourteenth Amendment merely because the public was generally invited to use it for the purpose of doing business with the center's tenants.

▶ ANALYSIS

Although the distinction between this case and *Logan Valley*, 391 U.S. 308 (1968), has a common sense basis, constitutionally it is difficult to defend. The Supreme Court long has held that the core of the First Amendment is that the government cannot regulate speech based on its content. In *Lloyd*, however, it was precisely the content of the speech (unrelated to the operation of the center) that was determinative in whether it would be allowed. Thus, under *Lloyd* speech is constitutionally protected in a shopping center only where its content is related to the center's operations.

■■■

Quicknotes

FIRST AMENDMENT Prohibits Congress from enacting any law respecting an establishment of religion, prohibiting the free exercise of religion, abridging freedom of speech or the press, the right of peaceful assembly and the right to petition for a redress of grievances.

FOURTEENTH AMENDMENT Declares that no state shall make or enforce any law that shall abridge the privileges or immunities of citizens of the United States. No state shall deny to any person within its jurisdiction the equal protection of the laws.

■■■

Hudgens v. National Labor Relations Board

Shopping center owner (P) v. Federal agency (D)

424 U.S. 507 (1976).

NATURE OF CASE: Appeal from affirmance of cease-and-desist order issued by the National Labor Relations Board (NLRB) to shopping center owner for unfair labor practices.

FACT SUMMARY: Striking union members picketed their employer's retail store in a shopping center. The shopping center (P) threatened them with arrest for trespass and they left, but filed unfair labor practices charges against the shopping center with the NLRB (D), which issued a cease-and-desist order to the shopping center.

RULE OF LAW
There is no First Amendment right to picket a store in a privately owned shopping center.

FACTS: When striking members of a union picketed in front of their employer's leased store located in petitioner's shopping center, the shopping center's general manager threatened them with arrest for criminal trespass if they did not depart, and they left. The union then filed unfair labor practice charges against the shopping center (P), alleging that the threat constituted interference with rights protected by the National Labor Relations Act (NLRA). The NLRB, concluding that the NLRA had been violated, issued a cease-and-desist order against petitioner, and the court of appeals enforced the order. The shopping center owner (P) and the union contended that the case should be decided under the criteria of the NLRA alone, whereas the NLRB (D) contended that such rights and liabilities must be measured under a First Amendment standard.

ISSUE: Is there a First Amendment right to picket a store in a privately owned shopping center?

HOLDING AND DECISION: (Stewart, J.) No. The Constitution itself does not guarantee freedom from the abridgment of free speech against private parties. Therefore, until the law is changed, the holding of *Amalgamated Food Employees Union Local 590 v. Logan Valley Plaza, Inc.* (Logan Valley), 391 U.S. 308 (1968), is expressly overturned. *Logan Valley* held that a private shopping center was the functional equivalent of a municipality and was, therefore, subject to the First Amendment. However, if the First Amendment applies to privately owned shopping centers, then the law cannot permit a distinction based on the content of the speech.

ANALYSIS

Although it is difficult to square *Hudgens* with the Court's opinion in *Marsh*, 326 U.S. 501 (1946) (that a company town is the functional equivalent of a municipality), because a shopping center is very much like a town square, on the other

hand, shopping centers are not a traditional government responsibility. Moreover, private owners generally have the ability to control their business and activities that occur on their property. Thus, although *Marsh* is still good law, its application is narrow, and it is clear that privately owned shopping centers need not comply with the First Amendment.

Quicknotes

CEASE AND DESIST ORDER An order from a court or administrative agency prohibiting a person or business from continuing a particular course of conduct.

FIRST AMENDMENT RIGHTS Rights conferred by the First Amendment to the U.S. Constitution prohibiting Congress from enacting any law respecting an establishment of religion, prohibiting the free exercise of religion, abridging freedom of speech or the press, the right of peaceful assembly and the right to petition for a redress of grievances.

Shelley v. Kraemer

Purchaser (D) v. Property owner (P)

334 U.S. 1 (1948).

NATURE OF CASE: Action to enforce a restrictive covenant in the sale of real property.

FACT SUMMARY: Kraemer (P) sought to void a sale of real property to Shelley (D) from a Mr. Fitzgerald, relying on a racially restrictive covenant.

🏛 RULE OF LAW
Judicial enforcement of a private racially restrictive covenant is considered state action for Fourteenth Amendment purposes.

FACTS: On February 16, 1911, 30 out of a total of 39 owners of property fronting both sides of Labadie Avenue between Taylor Avenue and Cora Avenue in St. Louis signed an agreement, which was subsequently recorded, providing in part that the property could not be used or occupied by anyone of the Negro or Mongolian race for a period of 50 years. This covenant was to be valid whether it was included in future conveyances or not and was to attach to the land as a condition precedent to the sale of the property. On August 11, 1945, Shelley (D), a Negro, purchased a parcel of land subject to the restrictive covenant from a Mr. Fitzgerald. Shelley (D) did not have any actual knowledge of the restrictive agreement at the time of the purchase. On October 9, 1945, Kraemer (P), an owner of other property subject to the terms of the restrictive covenant, brought suit in the circuit court of St. Louis to enjoin Shelley (D) from taking possession of the property and to divest title from Shelley (D) and revest title in Fitzgerald or in such person as the court should direct. The trial court held for Shelley (D), but on appeal the Supreme Court of Missouri reversed that decision. Shelley (D) contended that the restrictive covenant violated the Equal Protection Clause of the Fourteenth Amendment. Kraemer (P) contended that no state action was involved in the private restrictive covenant, and even if there were state action, the courts would enforce a restrictive covenant barring whites from purchasing certain land and so there was equal protection of the law. He further contended that if he was not allowed to enforce the covenant he would be denied equal protection of the law.

ISSUE: Does the Equal Protection Clause of the Fourteenth Amendment prevent judicial enforcement by state courts of private restrictive covenants based on race or color?

HOLDING AND DECISION: (Vinson, C.J.) Yes. Judicial enforcement of a private racially restrictive covenant is considered state action for Fourteenth Amendment purposes. Because the restrictive covenants did not involve any action by the state legislature or city council, the restrictive covenant itself did not violate any rights protected by the Fourteenth Amendment, since it was strictly a private covenant. But the judicial enforcement of the covenant did qualify as state action. From the time of the adoption of the Fourteenth Amendment until the present, the Court has consistently ruled that the action of the states to which the Amendment has reference includes action of state courts and state judicial officers. Therefore, in granting judicial enforcement of the restrictive agreement, the state has denied Shelley (D) equal protection of the laws and the action of the state courts cannot stand. The Court noted that the enjoyment of property rights, free from discrimination by the states, was among the objectives sought to be effectuated by the Framers of the Fourteenth Amendment.

▶ ANALYSIS

The Court in its post-*Shelley v. Kraemer* decisions has given this decision a fairly narrow reading. A broad reading of this case requires that whenever a state court enforces a private racial restrictive covenant, such action constitutes state action, which is forbidden by the Fourteenth Amendment. In cases where the ruling in this case could have been found to be applicable, the Court has used a different rationale. Some of the Court's statements suggest that state involvement, rather than evenhanded enforcement of private biases, was necessary to find unconstitutional state action. Justice Black, in a dissenting opinion, stated that the decision in this case only is applicable in cases involving property rights.

■═■

Quicknotes

FOURTEENTH AMENDMENT Declares that no state shall make or enforce any law that shall abridge the privileges or immunities of citizens of the United States. No state shall deny to any person within its jurisdiction the equal protection of the laws.

RACIALLY RESTRICTIVE COVENANT A provision contained in a deed that discriminates on the basis of race by limiting those persons entitled to use of the property.

STATE ACTION Actions brought pursuant to the Fourteenth Amendment claiming that the government violated the plaintiff's civil rights.

■═■

Lugar v. Edmondson Oil Co.

Debtor (P) v. Creditor (D)

457 U.S. 922 (1982).

NATURE OF CASE: Action brought by debtor against creditor for using a state ex parte prejudgment attachment proceeding that allegedly deprived debtor of due process of law.

FACT SUMMARY: Lugar (P) was indebted to Edmondson Oil Co. (Edmondson) (D). Edmondson sued on the debt, and, in an ancillary prejudgment ex parte proceeding, had Lugar's property attached. At a later hearing, the attachment was dismissed, and Lugar sued Edmondson as a state actor for having deprived him of due process of law.

🏛 RULE OF LAW
Constitutional requirements of due process apply to prejudgment attachment procedures whenever state officers act jointly with a private creditor in securing the property in dispute.

FACTS: Edmondson (D) filed suit in Virginia state court on a debt owed by Lugar (P), and sought prejudgment attachment of certain of Lugar's property. Pursuant to Virginia law, Edmondson (D) alleged, in an ex parte petition, a belief that Lugar (P) was disposing of or might dispose of his property in order to defeat his creditors. Acting on that petition, a clerk of the state court issued a writ of attachment, which was executed by the county sheriff; a hearing on the propriety of the attachment was later conducted, and 34 days after the levy, the trial judge dismissed the attachment for Edmondson's (D) failure to establish the alleged statutory grounds for attachment. Lugar (P) then brought an action in district court under 42 U.S.C. § 1983, alleging that in attaching his property, Edmondson (D) had acted jointly with the state to deprive him of his property without due process of law. The district court did not find state action and the court of appeals affirmed. The Supreme Court granted review.

ISSUE: Do constitutional requirements of due process apply to prejudgment attachment procedures whenever state officers act jointly with a private creditor in securing the property in dispute?

HOLDING AND DECISION: (White, J.) Yes. For a finding of state action, a two-part test must be satisfied. First, the deprivation must be caused by the exercise of some right or privilege created by the state, or a rule of conduct imposed by the state, or by a person for whom the state is responsible. Second, the party charged with the deprivation must be a state actor by virtue of being a state official, by acting together with or getting significant assistance from a state official, or because his conduct is otherwise attributable to the state. Here, the first prong is met by Virginia's prejudgment attachment procedure. The question then becomes whether the second prong is satisfied—whether Edmondson (D) was a state actor. Here, Edmondson's (D) use of the procedure makes it a state actor because of its joint participation with state officials (the sheriff). Such "joint participation" does not require something more than invoking the aid of state officials to take advantage of the state's procedures. Lugar (P) was, therefore, deprived of his property through state action, and Edmondson (D), therefore, was acting under color of state law in participating in that deprivation.

▶ *ANALYSIS*

The majority in this case prevailed by a narrow 5 to 4 vote. The dissent argued that it would be unjust to hold a private citizen who did no more than commence a legal action of the kind traditionally initiated by private parties as engaging in "state action."

■■■

Quicknotes

EX PARTE A proceeding commenced by one party.

STATE ACTION Actions brought pursuant to the Fourteenth Amendment claiming that the government violated the plaintiff's civil rights.

■■■

Edmondson v. Leesville Concrete Co.

Black tort claimant (P) v. Company (D)

500 U.S. 614 (1991).

NATURE OF CASE: Review of award of damages for personal injury.

FACT SUMMARY: Leesville (D), defendant in a civil action, allegedly exercised, during jury selections, peremptory challenges on the basis of race.

🏛 RULE OF LAW
A party in a civil action may not exercise peremptory challenges on the basis of race.

FACTS: Edmonson (P), a black, sued Leesville (D), a white, for personal injury. During voir dire, Leesville (D) allegedly excluded blacks from the jury by use of peremptory challenges. The jury returned a verdict of $18,000, much less than Edmonson (D) had wanted. Edmonson (P) appealed, contending that Leesville (D) had improperly excluded potential jurors on the basis of race. The verdict was affirmed on appeal, and the Supreme Court granted certiorari.

ISSUE: May a party in a civil action exercise peremptory challenges on the basis of race?

HOLDING AND DECISION: (Kennedy, J.) No. A party in a civil action may not exercise peremptory challenges on the basis of race. For a governmental entity to so exercise peremptory challenges would without doubt violate the Equal Protection Clause. However, when this is done by a private party, the issue arises as to whether state action sufficient to implicate the Fourteenth Amendment exists. A private party will be held to be a state actor if (1) the right of privilege exercised has its source in state power, and (2) whether the private party could fairly be described as a state actor. Here, the first criterion undoubtedly is met, as the right involved is part of the judicial system, an inherently state-related apparatus. As to the second factor, analysis compels a similar conclusion. A party to a lawsuit relies on state machinery; he is to an extent performing a governmental function, namely, the administration of justice; and the injury he may cause would be carried out through governmental authority. In light of these considerations, the necessary conclusion is that a private party exercising peremptory challenges is a state actor.

▌ *ANALYSIS*

It is a basic principle of constitutional law that the Constitution, for the most part, controls only state conduct. As the present case illustrates, however, what is and what is not state action is not necessarily an easy call. Supreme Court jurisprudence on this issue is far from clear, and decisions sometimes appear to be more result-oriented than the products of clear legal analysis.

Quicknotes

PEREMPTORY CHALLENGE Challenge brought by a party to a lawsuit of a prospective juror without the need to specify a particular reason.

STATE ACTION Actions brought pursuant to the Fourteenth Amendment claiming that the government violated the plaintiff's civil rights.

VOIR DIRE Examination of potential jurors on a case.

Burton v. Wilmington Parking Authority

Negro customer (P) v. Municipal authority (D)

365 U.S. 715 (1961).

NATURE OF CASE: Action seeking declaratory and injunctive relief for racial discrimination.

FACT SUMMARY: Wilmington Parking Authority (D) leased space in a parking facility to Eagle Coffee Shoppe for use as a restaurant, and it refused to serve Burton (P), a Negro.

🏛 RULE OF LAW
Racial discrimination by a business that is located in and constitutes part of a state-owned public facility is considered to be state action and is forbidden by the Fourteenth Amendment.

FACTS: Wilmington Parking Authority (D) was going to erect a public parking facility, but before it started construction it was advised that the anticipated revenue from the parking of cars and proceeds from the sale of its bonds would not be sufficient to finance the construction costs of the facility. To secure additional capital, the Authority (D) decided to enter into long-term leases with responsible tenants for commercial use of some of the space available in the projected garage building. A 20-year lease was entered into with Eagle Coffee Shoppe, Inc. for a space to be used as a restaurant. Even though the Authority (D) had the power to adopt rules and regulations requiring that the restaurant services be made available to the general public, the lease contained no such requirement of Eagle Coffee Shoppe. Under a Delaware statute, Eagle Coffee Shoppe was classified as a restaurant and not an inn and, therefore, was not required to serve all persons entering their shop. Burton (P) attempted to enter the restaurant but was refused service because he was a Negro. As a result, Burton (P) filed an action seeking declaratory and injunctive relief against Wilmington Parking Authority (D) claiming that as the restaurant was the Authority's (D) lessee, and the Authority (D) was an agency of the state, that the discrimination was therefore state action. However, the Supreme Court of Delaware held that Eagle was acting in a purely private capacity under its lease and that the action was not that of the Authority (D) and was not, therefore, state action. The court based its conclusion on the fact that only 15 percent of the total cost of the facility was advanced from public funds and that the revenue from parking was only 30.5 percent of the total income. Eagle had expended considerable amounts of its own funds on furnishings and there was no public entrance direct from the parking area. The only connection Eagle had with the public facility was the payment of $28,700 in rent annually. The decision was appealed to the Supreme Court.

ISSUE: Is racial discrimination by a business that leases facilities from the state considered to be state action?

HOLDING AND DECISION: (Clark, J.) Yes. The Court held that the restaurant was so closely tied in with the Parking Authority (D) that the discriminatory action by the restaurant was considered to be state action. The Court pointed out that the land and building were publicly owned and that the costs of land acquisition, construction, and maintenance were defrayed entirely from donations by the City of Wilmington from loans and revenue bonds, and from the proceeds of rentals and parking services out of which the loans and bonds were payable. The Court also noted that the restaurant operated as an integral part of a public building devoted to a public parking service and that part of the facility was open to the public while in another part Negroes were refused service. The fact that the Parking Authority (D) didn't require in the lease that the restaurant be open to the public doesn't allow the restaurant to discriminate against Negroes with impunity. By its inaction, the Authority (D), and through it, the state, made itself a party to the refusal of service. Because of the financial interdependence between the Authority (D) and the restaurant, and because of the physical relation of the facility, the discriminatory action by the restaurant cannot be considered purely private action.

▶ ANALYSIS

The Court in this case did not clearly define the requirements for a finding of state action. In subsequent cases, however, it became clearer that the critical factor in the *Burton* case was the leasing of public property to a private enterprise for its exclusive use. The City of Montgomery, Alabama rented or granted the exclusive use of certain public recreation areas to private groups that practiced racial discrimination. The Court found no difficulty in invalidating this practice. But a more troublesome problem was presented by the grant of nonexclusive permits to such groups. A case involving such nonexclusive use was remanded for further findings on how much restriction was placed on free public access by these nonexclusive permits. Finally, in *Moose Lodge v. Irvis*, 407 U.S. 163 (1972), the Court found that the granting of a liquor license to a private fraternal organization that discriminated was not sufficient state action to involve the Equal Protection Clause.

■=■

Quicknotes

EQUAL PROTECTION CLAUSE A constitutional provision that each person be guaranteed the same protection of the laws enjoyed by other persons in like circumstances.

FOURTEENTH AMENDMENT Declares that no state shall make or enforce any law that shall abridge the privileges or immunities of citizens of the United States. No state

Continued on next page.

shall deny to any person within its jurisdiction the equal protection of the laws.

STATE ACTION Actions brought pursuant to the Fourteenth Amendment claiming that the government violated the plaintiff's civil rights.

■━■

Moose Lodge No. 107 v. Irvis

Fraternal organization (D) v. Guest (P)

407 U.S. 163 (1972).

NATURE OF CASE: Appeal from an order declaring a liquor license invalid.

FACT SUMMARY: The Moose Lodge (D) refused to serve Irvis (P), the black guest of a member, solely on the basis of his race.

🏛 RULE OF LAW
Merely granting a liquor license to a private club that engages in discriminatory practices is not sufficient state action to invoke the Fourteenth Amendment.

FACTS: Irvis (P), a black, was invited by a member to dine in the private dining room of the Moose Lodge (D). The Lodge (D) refused to serve Irvis (P) solely because of his race. Irvis (P) sought to enjoin the Lodge's (D) conduct on the ground that state action under the Fourteenth Amendment existed because Lodge (D) was issued one of a limited number of liquor licenses by the state. The district court found state action based on the state's total control over the granting of licenses, its use of police powers to regulate the Lodge's (D) physical facilities, and its licensing requirements, including the submission of a list of names and addresses of all members. The Lodge (D) appealed.

ISSUE: Is the mere granting of a liquor license to a private club that engages in discriminatory practices sufficient state action to invoke the Fourteenth Amendment?

HOLDING AND DECISION: (Rehnquist, J.) No. Merely granting a liquor license to a private club that engages in discriminatory practices is not sufficient state action to invoke the Fourteenth Amendment. For state action to be found, it must be shown that the state, through an exercise of its power and authority, fostered discrimination. Merely granting a liquor license to a private club to serve liquor to members and their guests is essentially neutral conduct, even where the club's bylaws limit membership and service of guests along racial lines. It cannot be said that such conduct either fosters or encourages discriminatory practices, nor can it be maintained that the state is lending either its prestige or support to a discriminatory group.

DISSENT: (Douglas, J.) Where a state grants a limited resource to a racially discriminatory private group, it is lending its prestige to the group and is encouraging and fostering racial discrimination. The Court overlooks two considerations that require a finding of state action on this case's facts. First, the state's Regulation Section 113.09 conditions a liquor license on the licensee's compliance with its own bylaws; in this case, that requirement amounts to Pennsylvania compelling the private club here to engage in racial discrimination. Second, because no more liquor licenses can be issued in the city where the club is located, the regulation burdens the ability of blacks to purchase liquor. Accordingly, the state's liquor license serves to promote racial discrimination in a manner that should invoke the Fourteenth Amendment.

▌ *ANALYSIS*

The Court considered the issuance of a liquor license to be a neutral activity in the same sense as the state's furnishing of electricity, water, police, and fire protection. However, it would appear that a liquor license is distinguishable from basic and necessary state services that are tax supported. The Court did give minor relief, however. The state liquor regulation required the club licensee to adhere to its own construction and bylaws. Since Moose Lodge (D) incorporated racial discrimination in its constitution and bylaws, the state regulation, although neutral in its terms, invoked the sanction of the state to enforce a concededly discriminatory private rule, and that portion was declared invalid.

■═■

Quicknotes

EQUAL PROTECTION CLAUSE A constitutional provision that each person be guaranteed the same protection of the laws enjoyed by other persons in like circumstances.

FOURTEENTH AMENDMENT Declares that no state shall make or enforce any law that shall abridge the privileges or immunities of citizens of the United States. No state shall deny to any person within its jurisdiction the equal protection of the laws.

STATE ACTION Actions brought pursuant to the Fourteenth Amendment claiming that the government violated the plaintiff's civil rights.

■═■

Norwood v. Harrison

Parents of schoolchildren (P) v. State officials (D)

413 U.S. 455 (1973).

NATURE OF CASE: Class action by parents of schoolchildren to enjoin enforcement of state program that lends books to public and private schools without regard to whether the schools have racially discriminatory policies.

FACT SUMMARY: A Mississippi textbook lending program provided books to students in public and private schools. Parents of schoolchildren (P) in the state sought to enjoin the program because some of the private schools excluded children on the basis of race, and, the parents (P) alleged, the program thus provided direct state aid to racially segregated education, in violation of their constitutional rights.

🏛 RULE OF LAW
State-funded financial aid to private schools that discriminate on the basis of race supports such discrimination and thereby violates the Equal Protection Clause.

FACTS: A Mississippi statutory program, begun in 1940, loaned textbooks that were purchased by the state to students in both public and private schools, without reference to whether any participating private school had racially discriminatory policies. The number of private secular schools in Mississippi, with a virtually all-white student population, had greatly increased since the program's inception. Parents of Mississippi schoolchildren (P) filed a class action on behalf of all students in Mississippi to enjoin the textbook lending program. The parents asserted that by supplying the textbooks to the segregated private schools, the state was directly supporting segregated education, in violation of the students' constitutional rights to fully desegregated public schools. A district court upheld the lending program, and the Supreme Court granted review.

ISSUE: Does state-funded financial aid to private schools that discriminate on the basis of race support such discrimination and thereby violate the Equal Protection Clause?

HOLDING AND DECISION: [Judge not stated in casebook excerpt.] Yes. The Court as previously enjoined state tuition grants to students attending racially discriminatory private schools. A textbook lending program is not legally distinguishable from such aid. Free textbooks are a form of financial aid because they defray the cost of providing such books to the private schools themselves. If the private school discriminates, the state's aid supports such discrimination. Racial discrimination in state-operated schools is barred by the Constitution and it is also axiomatic that a state may not induce, encourage or promote private persons to accomplish what it is constitutionally forbidden to accomplish. Even though the program's intent is a laudable one—to help all children in the state—its effect is constitutionally impermissible. "A State's constitutional obligation requires it to steer clear, not only of operating the old dual system of racially segregated schools, but also of giving significant aid to institutions that practice racial or other invidious discrimination."

▶ ANALYSIS

Norwood involved a challenge to state aid for segregated private schools in Mississippi, a state with a long history of school segregation. Outside of this historical context, however, the Court has been reluctant to find that state financial aid for private schools is state action.

■══■

Quicknotes

EQUAL PROTECTION CLAUSE A constitutional provision that each person be guaranteed the same protection of the laws enjoyed by other persons in like circumstances.

FOURTEENTH AMENDMENT Declares that no state shall make or enforce any law that shall abridge the privileges or immunities of citizens of the United States. No state shall deny to any person within its jurisdiction the equal protection of the laws.

STATE ACTION Actions brought pursuant to the Fourteenth Amendment claiming that the government violated the plaintiff's civil rights.

■══■

Rendell-Baker v. Kohn

Private school teachers (P) v. Private school director (D)

457 U.S. 830 (1982).

NATURE OF CASE: Action under 42 U.S.C. § 1983 claiming that teachers at a private school (P), which allegedly was acting under color of state law, were discharged in violation of their First and Fourteenth Amendment rights.

FACT SUMMARY: A private school that educated students who could not adjust to the public schools was supported and heavily regulated by the state. The school's director (D) fired a teacher because of her speech activities. The teacher brought suit, under the theory that the school was a state actor, alleging that her constitutional rights had been violated by the school.

RULE OF LAW
A private school is not a state actor, even though it is funded and heavily regulated by the state, where it is not exercising the exclusive prerogatives of the state.

FACTS: The New Perspectives School was a private school that helped maladjusted high school students. Nearly all of the school's students were referred to it by the state; almost all of its funding came from public sources; and it was heavily regulated by the state. Rendell-Baker (P), a teacher at the school, was discharged by Kohn (D), the school's director, over a policy dispute. Later, Kohn (D) dismissed several other teachers for their support of Rendell-Baker. The teachers (P) brought suit under 42 U.S.C. § 1983 alleging that they had been dismissed, without due process under the Fourteenth Amendment, for exercising their free speech rights under the First Amendment. The district court held that the school had acted under color of state law, but the court of appeals reversed, and the Supreme Court granted review.

ISSUE: Is a private school a state actor, even though it is funded and heavily regulated by the state, where it is not exercising the exclusive prerogatives of the state?

HOLDING AND DECISION: (Burger, C.J.) No. The school is like a private contractor that has government contracts. The acts of such contractors do not become acts of the government by reason of their significant or even total engagement in performing public contracts. Here, the decision to fire the teachers (P) was not compelled or even influenced by any state regulation, and the state, despite otherwise heavily regulating the school, did not show interest in regulating the school's personnel matters. Here, although the school clearly serves a public function, that function is not one that has been traditionally the exclusive prerogative of the state. The school's actions are, therefore, not state action. Affirmed.

DISSENT: (Marshall, J.) The state delegated its duty to teach children to the school. Because the school receives almost all of its funding from the state, and because it is heavily regulated by the state, the nexus between the school and state is so substantial that the school's actions must be considered state action. The majority's analogy of the school to a private contractor is inapposite because government contractors are not strictly supervised by the government, nor do they perform a statutory duty of the government.

▶ ANALYSIS

This case exemplifies the modern requirement of the public function doctrine: private action becomes state action only when the private actor exercises powers that have been traditionally reserved to the government. This doctrine is not limited to private schools, but has been applied to other private actors, such as nursing homes (*Blum v. Yaretsky*, 457 U.S. 991 [1982]) publicly regulated utilities (*Jackson v. Metropolitan Edison Co.*, 419 U.S. 345 [1974]) and others.

Quicknotes

EQUAL PROTECTION CLAUSE A constitutional provision that each person be guaranteed the same protection of the laws enjoyed by other persons in like circumstances.

FIRST AMENDMENT Prohibits Congress from enacting any law respecting an establishment of religion, prohibiting the free exercise of religion, abridging freedom of speech or the press, the right of peaceful assembly and the right to petition for a redress of grievances.

FOURTEENTH AMENDMENT Declares that no state shall make or enforce any law that shall abridge the privileges or immunities of citizens of the United States. No state shall deny to any person within its jurisdiction the equal protection of the laws.

STATE ACTION Actions brought pursuant to the Fourteenth Amendment claiming that the government violated the plaintiff's civil rights.

Blum v. Yaretsky

State official (D) v. Nursing home patients (P)

457 U.S. 991 (1982).

NATURE OF CASE: Class action to enjoin state officials (D) from acting on transfer or discharge decisions made by private nursing homes without a hearing, on the ground that the absence of such a hearing is a violation of due process.

FACT SUMMARY: Private nursing homes transferred or discharged Medicaid patients (P) without a hearing. The patients claimed a violation of their rights to due process.

🏛 RULE OF LAW
A private nursing home's decision to transfer or discharge Medicaid-eligible patients without a hearing is not state action that violates due process.

FACTS: State policy required that private nursing home facilities receiving Medicaid funding create "utilization review committees" (URCs) to determine the level of care needed. After a decision from a URC, the state would terminate its Medicaid payments for patients without a hearing unless they were transferred from skilled nursing home facilities to less-equipped, cheaper, lower level-of-care health-related facilities. Although the state paid over 90 percent of the medical expenses of the patients, the ultimate decision rested with the private nursing homes. Nursing home patients (P) sued the nursing homes and the state officials administering the Medicaid program, claiming they should be given due process with regard to their transfer or discharge. The district court held in favor of the patients (P) and the court of appeals affirmed, finding state action. The Supreme Court granted review.

ISSUE: Is a private nursing home's decision to transfer or discharge Medicaid-eligible patients without a hearing state action that violates due process?

HOLDING AND DECISION: (Rehnquist, J.) No. The patients (P) are seeking to hold state officials (D) liable for the actions of private parties and to regulate the private parties. Although the nursing homes are heavily regulated by the state, the mere fact that a private party is subject to state regulation does not by itself turn that action into state action. Also, all the decisions regarding the transfers or discharges are made by private parties—physicians and nursing home administrators. A state normally can be held responsible for a private decision only when it has exercised such significant encouragement, either overt or covert, that the choice must be deemed to be state action as a matter of law. Here, just because the state responded to those decisions (by adjusting Medicaid payments accordingly) does not render the state responsible for those decisions, especially given that there was no indication that the decisions were influenced in any way by the state's obligation to adjust benefits based on those decisions.

DISSENT: (Brennan, J.) The majority's analysis is flawed because its factual assumption—that the decisions to transfer or discharge are purely an exercise of professional judgment by a physician—is incorrect. In fact, the level-of-care decisions have far less to do with such exercises of independent professional judgment than they do with the state's desire to save money. The reality is that it is the state's fiscal interests that drive and direct the standards by which the level-of-care decisions are made. And, there is also a very great degree of interdependence between the nursing homes and the state, which provides most of the financing for the homes. Accordingly, there is state action because the state has placed its "power, property, and prestige" behind the actions of the nursing homes.

▶ ANALYSIS

In *Blum*, as in *Rendell-Baker*, 457 U.S. 830 (1982), the almost complete subsidies by the state of private action were not enough for a finding of state action, but in cases such as *Norwood*, 413 U.S. 455 (1973), even partial aid was found to be enough for a finding of state action. These cases are most easily distinguished on the ground that in *Norwood*, the government's aid had the effect, if not the intent, of encouraging constitutional violations. On the other hand, in *Blum* and *Rendell-Baker*, the state's support was in no way intended to encourage constitutional violations.

■=■

Quicknotes

DUE PROCESS CLAUSE Clauses found in the Fifth and Fourteenth Amendments to the United States Constitution providing that no person shall be deprived of "life, liberty, or property, without due process of law."

EQUAL PROTECTION CLAUSE A constitutional provision that each person be guaranteed the same protection of the laws enjoyed by other persons in like circumstances.

FOURTEENTH AMENDMENT Declares that no state shall make or enforce any law that shall abridge the privileges or immunities of citizens of the United States. No state shall deny to any person within its jurisdiction the equal protection of the laws.

STATE ACTION Actions brought pursuant to the Fourteenth Amendment claiming that the government violated the plaintiff's civil rights.

■=■

Reitman v. Mulkey

Landlord (D) v. Prospective tenants (P)

387 U.S 369 (1967).

NATURE OF CASE: Action for injunctive relief and damages under §§ 51 and 52 of the California Civil Code.

FACT SUMMARY: Reitman (D) refused to rent the Mulkeys (P) an apartment on account of their race.

🏛 RULE OF LAW
The abandonment of a positive nondiscrimination policy by a state in favor of a neutral stance that would allow discrimination to occur in the sale and rental of private housing constitutes state action within the meaning of the Fourteenth Amendment.

FACTS: In a statewide ballot in 1964, the voters of California initiated a measure known as Proposition 14 which prevented the state from denying or limiting the right of any person to sell, lease, or rent his property to such persons as he, in his absolute discretion, chooses. Prior to the passing of this proposition, the Mulkeys (P) attempted to rent an apartment from Reitman (D), who refused to rent solely on the grounds of the Mulkeys' (P) race. As a result, the Mulkeys (P) sued under §§ 51 and 52 of the California Civil Code, which provided that all persons are free and equal and are entitled to the full and equal accommodations, advantages, facilities, privileges, or services in all business establishments of every kind whatsoever. They sought both injunctive relief and damages. Reitman (D) moved for summary judgment on the ground that §§ 51 and 52 had been rendered null and void by Proposition 14, which had been passed after the filing of the complaint. The trial court granted the motion and the case was appealed to the California Supreme Court, which held that Proposition 14, which had become Article I, § 26 of the California Constitution, was invalid as it denied the equal protection of the laws guaranteed by the Fourteenth Amendment. Reitman (D) claimed that Proposition 14 did not violate the Equal Protection Clause because it merely put the state in a neutral position by not allowing the state to interfere with the right of an individual to sell or rent his land to whomever he pleased and because the state wasn't encouraging racial discrimination simply because it was not restricting it.

ISSUE: Does the abandonment of a positive nondiscrimination policy by a state in favor of a neutral stance that would allow discrimination to occur in the sale and rental of private housing constitute state action within the meaning of the Fourteenth Amendment?

HOLDING AND DECISION: (White, J.) Yes. The abandonment of a positive nondiscrimination policy by a state in favor of a neutral stance that would allow discrimination to occur in the sale and rental of private housing constitutes

state action within the meaning of the Fourteenth Amendment. The Court gave great deference to the reasoning and conclusion of the California Supreme Court when that court invalidated Proposition 14. While the states are not required to affirmatively forbid racial discrimination, they cannot foster it. Prior to the passage of Proposition 14 as a state constitutional amendment, the state had several statutes forbidding racial discrimination in the sale or rental of private housing units. As Justice Stewart pointed out in his concurring opinion in *Burton v. Wilmington Parking Authority*, 365 U.S. 715 (1961), the state may not authorize discrimination. By abandoning its open housing statutes in favor of a supposed position of neutrality, the state has encouraged private discrimination. If California's position had always been neutral and Proposition 14 was merely a codification of that position, no issue would be presented. However, the California Supreme Court determined that the effect of Proposition 14 was to place the state in the position of sanctioning and encouraging private discrimination. While this Court undertakes no definite definition of that which would always constitute state action, there is no reason why it should reject the conclusions of the California court.

DISSENT: (Harlan, J.) This case presents no violation of the Fourteenth Amendment since Proposition 14 merely put the state in a neutral position in the area of private discrimination affecting the sale or rental of private residential property. The majority opinion was solely based on a conclusion of law and did not attempt to find any facts that pointed out that Proposition 14 actually did involve state discriminatory actions. For there to be state action sufficient to bring the Fourteenth Amendment into operation, there must be some affirmative and purposeful state action that actively fosters discrimination. There is no such action in this case.

▶ ANALYSIS

This case has been criticized because of the reasoning behind the Court's decision. Many writers felt that Proposition 14 was properly adopted and was within the power of the voters to adopt. Regardless of the views of the critics, the Court expanded the state action concept by this decision. The state cannot make lawful that which it has previously held to be discriminatory and unlawful. It was clear in this case that state action was involved, but this case does little

Continued on next page.

to indicate the scope of involvement necessary by the state to make private actions state actions.

■═■

Quicknotes

EQUAL PROTECTION CLAUSE A constitutional provision that each person be guaranteed the same protection of the laws enjoyed by other persons in like circumstances.

FOURTEENTH AMENDMENT Declares that no state shall make or enforce any law that shall abridge the privileges or immunities of citizens of the United States. No state shall deny to any person within its jurisdiction the equal protection of the laws.

STATE ACTION Actions brought pursuant to the Fourteenth Amendment claiming that the government violated the plaintiff's civil rights.

■═■

Brentwood Academy v. Tennessee Secondary School Athletic Assn.

Private secondary school (P) v. Statewide athletic assn. (D)

531 U.S. 288 (2001).

NATURE OF CASE: Suit by private secondary school regarding penalties imposed by nongovernmental statewide athletic association.

FACT SUMMARY: The nongovernmental Tennessee Secondary School Athletic Association (TSSAA) (D) penalized a private secondary school in Tennessee, Brentwood Academy (P), for violating the TSSAA's (D) rules on recruiting athletes. The school (P) sued the TSSAA (D) in federal court, arguing in part that the TSSAA's (D) penalties constituted state action under the Fifth and Fourteenth Amendments.

> ## 🏛 RULE OF LAW
> A nongovernmental statewide association's actions constitute state action if state officials are pervasively entwined in the structure of the association.

FACTS: The TSSAA (D) is not a government entity. It is a not-for-profit corporation whose purpose is to regulate interscholastic athletics in private and public secondary schools in Tennessee. The vast majority of its member schools (84 percent of them) are public schools. Some of its voting members are administrators at public schools. The State of Tennessee does not pay the TSSAA's (D) staff, but staff members are eligible for the state's public retirement program. Since the TSSAA's (D) formation in 1925, the state has expressed its support of the TSSAA (D) on several occasions, and has even designated it as the body that supervises and regulates interscholastic sports in Tennessee. The TSSAA (D) oversees, among other things, the eligibility of students to participate in sports, and it exercised that power in an enforcement action against Brentwood Academy (P), a private secondary school in Tennessee, for violating the TSSAA's (D) rules on recruiting athletes. Tennessee's State Board of Education has expressly endorsed the rule that the TSSAA (D) applied against Brentwood Academy (P). The TSSAA (D) declared sports teams at Brentwood Academy (P) ineligible for post-season participation for two years and also fined the Academy (P) $3,000. When the TSSAA imposed these penalties, all its voting members were public school administrators. The Academy (P) filed suit against the TSSAA (D) in federal court, alleging deprivations of its federal constitutional rights.

ISSUE: Do a nongovernmental statewide association's actions constitute state action if state officials are pervasively entwined in the structure of the association?

HOLDING AND DECISION: (Souter, J.) Yes. A nongovernmental statewide association's actions constitute state action if state officials are pervasively entwined in the

structure of the association. Unlike *NCAA v. Tarkanian,* 488 U.S. 179 (1988), which dealt with a nationwide nongovernmental athletic association, this case involves a nongovernmental athletic association organized and located within the same sovereign. The TSSAA (D) simply would not exist without the control and day-to-day efforts of public school officials in the state. With the State of Tennessee so pervasively entwined with the TSSAA (D), it is fair to attribute the TSSAA's (D) actions to the state for purposes of constitutional analysis.

DISSENT: (Thomas, J.) The TSSAA (D) fails all known tests for state action. It has not performed a public function; it was not created, coerced, or encouraged by the state; and it has not acted in a symbiotic relationship with the state. The Court's new "entwinement" rationale thus extends the state-action doctrine, and it extends the doctrine too far because the result in this case fails the underlying theme of our state-action jurisprudence: The TSSAA's (D) actions cannot be fairly attributed to the State of Tennessee. Failing to define "entwinement" muddies the effects of this case's holding, but that holding nonetheless clearly extends the state-action doctrine beyond the point of being fair to the states.

▌ ANALYSIS

Constitutions don't restrict only government action. California's state constitution (Article 1, Section 8) prohibits discrimination, including discrimination by private actors, in "business, profession, vocation, or employment." Montana's state constitution (Article 2, Section 4) codifies a broad fundamental state right not to be discriminated against "by any person, firm, corporation, or institution." Since the decision in *The Civil Rights Cases,* 109 U.S. 3 (1883), however, state action has been a fundamental prerequisite for invoking the protections of the Fourteenth Amendment to the U.S. Constitution. Brentwood Academy shows that that doctrine is still evolving more than a century later, although, as Justice Thomas remarks in his dissent, in ways that are not entirely clear.

■═■

Quicknotes

FIFTH AMENDMENT Provides that no person shall be compelled to serve as a witness against himself, or be subject to trial for the same offense twice, or be deprived of life, liberty, or property without due process of law.

Continued on next page.

FOURTEENTH AMENDMENT Declares that no state shall make or enforce any law that shall abridge the privileges or immunities of citizens of the United States. No state shall deny to any person within its jurisdiction the equal protection of the laws.

STATE ACTION Actions brought pursuant to the Fourteenth Amendment claiming that the government violated the plaintiff's civil rights.

CHAPTER 6

Economic Liberties

Quick Reference Rules of Law

Allgeyer v. Louisiana

Property owner (D) v. State (P)

165 U.S. 578 (1897).

NATURE OF CASE: Appeal from conviction of violating a state statute that prohibited insuring property in the state except through an insurer licensed to do business in the state, on the ground that the statute deprived a property owner of liberty without due process.

FACT SUMMARY: Allgeyer (D) purchased marine insurance from a New York insurer for his property in Louisiana (P), and was convicted of violating a Louisiana law that prohibited insuring Louisiana property except through an insurer licensed to do business in Louisiana. Allgeyer (D) challenged the conviction as a violation of the Fourteenth Amendment.

🏛 RULE OF LAW
A state law that prohibits insuring property in the state except through an insurer licensed to do business in that state violates the Fourteenth Amendment.

FACTS: Louisiana (P) prohibited insuring Louisiana property except through an insurer licensed to do business in Louisiana. Allgeyer (D) purchased marine insurance on his goods shipped from New Orleans from a New York insurer. Allgeyer was convicted of violating the law and was ordered to pay a fine. Allgeyer appealed the conviction on the ground that the Louisiana law violated the Fourteenth Amendment by depriving him of liberty without due process of law. The Louisiana courts upheld the conviction, and the Supreme Court granted review.

ISSUE: Does a state law that prohibits insuring property in the state except through an insurer licensed to do business in that state violate the Fourteenth Amendment?

HOLDING AND DECISION: (Peckham, J.) Yes. Citizens of a state have the right to enter into contracts outside of the state, including contracts for insurance. The Louisiana law interferes with that right and therefore interferes with freedom of contract by depriving property owners of their liberty without due process. The term "liberty" in the Due Process Clauses embraces "the right of the citizen to be free in the enjoyment of all his faculties; to be free to use them in all lawful ways; to live and work where he will; to earn his livelihood by any lawful calling; to pursue any livelihood or avocation, and for that purpose to enter into all contracts which may be proper, necessary, and essential to his carrying out to a successful conclusion the purposes above mentioned." Allgeyer had a right to enter into an insurance contract outside Louisiana and the Louisiana law illegally deprived him of that right without due process.

▶ ANALYSIS

Allgeyer was the first case in an era where economic regulations were struck down as violative of substantive due process. The language quoted above as to the meaning of "liberty" was repeated by the Court many times in the following four decades, until the beginning of the New Deal era in 1937, to justify invalidating state laws on due process grounds.

■━■

Quicknotes

FOURTEENTH AMENDMENT Declares that no state shall make or enforce any law that shall abridge the privileges or immunities of citizens of the United States. No state shall deny to any person within its jurisdiction the equal protection of the laws.

LIBERTY INTEREST A right conferred by the Due Process Clauses of the state and federal constitutions.

■━■

Lochner v. New York

Baker (D) v. State (P)

198 U.S. 45 (1905).

NATURE OF CASE: Appeal from conviction for violation of a labor law.

FACT SUMMARY: A state labor law prohibited employment in bakeries for more than 60 hours a week or more than 10 hours a day. Lochner (D) permitted an employee in his bakery to work over 60 hours in one week.

🏛 RULE OF LAW
To be a fair, reasonable, and appropriate use of a state's police power, an act must have a direct relation, as a means to an end, to an appropriate and legitimate state objective.

FACTS: Lochner (D) was fined for violating a state labor law. The law prohibited employment in bakeries for more than 60 hours a week or more than 10 hours a day. Lochner (D) permitted an employee to work in his bakery for more than 60 hours in one week.

ISSUE: Is a state law regulating the hours bakery employees may work a valid exercise of state police power?

HOLDING AND DECISION: (Peckham, J.) No. To be a fair, reasonable, and appropriate use of a state's police power, an act must have a direct relation, as a means to an end, to an appropriate and legitimate state objective. The general right to make a contract in relation to one's business is part of the liberty of the individual protected by the Fourteenth Amendment. The right to purchase or sell labor is part of the liberty protected by this Amendment. However, the states do possess certain police powers relating to the safety, health, morals, and general welfare of the public. If the contract is one that the state in the exercise of its police power has the right to prohibit, the Fourteenth Amendment will not prevent the state's prohibition. When, as here, the state acts to limit the right to labor or the right to contract, it is necessary to determine whether the rights of the state or the individual shall prevail. The Fourteenth Amendment limits the state's exercise of its police power; otherwise the states would have unbounded power once it stated that legislation was to conserve the health, morals, or safety of its people. It is not sufficient to assert that the act relates to public health. Rather, it must have a more direct relation, as a means to an end, to an appropriate state goal, before an act can interfere with an individual's right to contract in relation to his labor. In this case, there is no reasonable foundation for holding the act to be necessary to the health of the public or of bakery officials. Statutes such as this one are mere meddlesome interferences with the rights of the individual. They are invalid unless there is some fair ground to say that there is material danger to the public health or to the employees' health if the labor hours are not curtailed. It cannot be said that the production of healthy bread depends upon the hours that the employees work. Nor is the trade of a baker an unhealthy one to the degree that would authorize the legislature to interfere with the rights to labor and of free contract.

DISSENT: (Holmes, J.) The word "liberty" in the Fourteenth Amendment should not invalidate a statute unless it can be said that a reasonable person would say that the statute infringes fundamental principles of our people and our law. A reasonable person might think this statute valid. Citizens' liberty is regulated by many state laws that have been held to be valid, i.e., the Sunday laws.

DISSENT: (Harlan, J.) Whether or not this be wise legislation is not a question for this Court. It is impossible to say that there is not substantial or real relation between the statute and the state's legitimate goals. This decision brings under the court's supervision matters that supposedly belonged exclusively to state legislatures.

▶ ANALYSIS

From the *Lochner* decision in 1905 to the 1930's the court invalidated a considerable number of laws on substantive due process grounds, such as laws fixing minimum wages, maximum hours, prices, and law regulating business activities. The modern court claims to have rejected the *Lochner* doctrine. It has withdrawn careful scrutiny in most economic areas but has maintained and increased intervention with respect to a variety of noneconomic liberties. However, not only economic regulations were struck down under *Lochner*. That doctrine formed the basis for pulling First Amendment rights into the Fourteenth Amendment concept of liberty. *Lochner* also helped justify on behalf of other noneconomic rights such as the right to teach in a foreign language (*Meyers v. Nebraska*, 262 U.S 390 [1923]). The Court relied on *Meyers* in the birth-control decision, *Griswold v. Connecticut*, 381 U.S. 479 (1965).

◼━◼

Quicknotes

FOURTEENTH AMENDMENT Declares that no state shall make or enforce any law that shall abridge the privileges or immunities of citizens of the United States. No state shall deny to any person within its jurisdiction the equal protection of the laws.

LIBERTY INTEREST A right conferred by the Due Process Clauses of the state and federal constitutions.

Continued on next page.

SUBSTANTIVE DUE PROCESS A constitutional safeguard limiting the power of the state, irrespective of how fair its procedures may be; substantive limits placed on the power of the state.

■━■

Coppage v. Kansas

Employer (D) v. State (P)

236 U.S. 1 (1915).

NATURE OF CASE: Appeal from criminal conviction for violation of a state law that made it illegal to require employees, as a condition of employment, to agree not to join a union, on the ground that the law was a deprivation of liberty and property without due process.

FACT SUMMARY: Coppage (D) was convicted of violating a law that made it a crime to require employees, as a condition of employment, to agree to not join a union. Coppage (D) appealed his conviction on the ground that the law deprived him of liberty and property without due process of law.

RULE OF LAW
A state law that makes it a crime to require employees, as a condition of employment, to agree to not join a union violates the Fourteenth Amendment's due process provisions.

FACTS: Coppage (D) was convicted in Kansas (P) with violating a Kansas statute that made it a crime for any employer or employer's agent to require prospective or current employees to enter into an agreement not to join or remain a member of any labor union as a condition of securing employment or continuing in employment. Coppage (D) appealed the conviction on the ground that the law violated the Fourteenth Amendments as a deprivation of liberty or property without due process, and the Supreme Court of Kansas affirmed the conviction. The Supreme Court granted review.

ISSUE: Does a state law that makes it a crime to require employees, as a condition of employment, to agree not to join a union violate the Fourteenth Amendment due process provisions?

HOLDING AND DECISION: (Pitney, J.) Yes. In *Adair v. United States*, 208 U.S. 161 (1908), the Court decided that a virtually identical federal law violated the Fifth Amendment. Applying that case to the states, it is clear that if Congress is prevented from interfering with freedom of contract because of the Fifth Amendment Due Process Clause, the states are equally prevented from interfering with the freedom of contract on the basis of the Fourteenth Amendment's due process provisions. Employees and employers have the freedom of contracting with each other on terms they see fit, and the freedom to terminate the employment relationship on grounds that they agree upon. Included in the right of personal liberty and the right of private property is the right to make contracts for the acquisition of property. One of the principal forms of this type of contract is the employment contract, because most people cannot acquire property without the money they earn as employees. Only a reasonable exercise of the police power could justify interference with this right, and such a justification is not present here.

ANALYSIS

Coppage, which found freedom of contract rooted in both property and liberty, was overturned in 1941 by *Phelps Dodge v. NLRB*, 313 US 177.

Quicknotes

DUE PROCESS CLAUSE Clauses found in the Fifth and Fourteenth Amendments to the U.S. Constitution providing that no person shall be deprived of "life, liberty, or property, without due process of law."

FREEDOM OF CONTRACT A basic freedom guaranteed by Article I, section 10, clause 1, of the U.S. Constitution and which may not be denied by the state.

Muller v. Oregon

Employer (D) v. State (P)

208 U.S. 412 (1908).

NATURE OF CASE: Appeal from conviction for violating a state law that prohibited employers from requiring women to work more than ten hours a day.

FACT SUMMARY: Muller (D) was convicted of violating a state law that prohibited employers from requiring women to work more than ten hours a day. He appealed the conviction on the ground that it deprived him of the freedom to contract under the Fourteenth Amendment.

🏛 RULE OF LAW
A state law that prohibits employers from requiring women to work more than ten hours a day does not violate the freedom to contract guaranteed by the Fourteenth Amendment.

FACTS: Oregon had a statute that required that no female could be employed for more than ten hours during any one day, and that made it a misdemeanor to violate the statute. Muller (D), a supervisor at a laundry shop, was convicted of allowing one of his female employees to work more than ten hours per day. He appealed the conviction on the ground that it violated his constitutional right to freedom of contract. The Oregon Supreme Court affirmed the conviction, and the U.S. Supreme Court granted review.

ISSUE: Does a state law that prohibits employers from requiring women to work more than ten hours a day violate the freedom to contract guaranteed by the Fourteenth Amendment?

HOLDING AND DECISION: (Brewer, J.) No. There is no absolute freedom of contract, although any laws abridging such freedom must be justified by the existence of exceptional circumstances. Here those circumstances exist in the inherent difference between the two sexes, and a public interest in protecting women, who depend on men and whose "physical structure and the performance of the maternal functions place her at a disadvantage in the struggle for subsistence." Such legislation would not be necessary for men. Thus, the limits placed by the law on a woman's freedom of contract are not just for her benefit, but for the benefit of all of society.

▶ ANALYSIS

Other than being a prime example of the Court's paternalism during the *Lochner* era, (see *Lochner*, 198 U.S. 45 [1905]), this case is notable for the brief filed in the case by Louis Brandeis, who would later become a Supreme Court Justice. The brief, explicitly mentioned in the opinion, was a detailed, 113-page brief that purported to document that women's reproductive health required limiting nondomestic work.

This type of brief, which used social science data to show the need for a particular law, came to be known as the "Brandeis brief."

Quicknotes

FOURTEENTH AMENDMENT Declares that no state shall make or enforce any law that shall abridge the privileges or immunities of citizens of the United States. No state shall deny to any person within its jurisdiction the equal protection of the laws.

FREEDOM OF CONTRACT A basic freedom guaranteed by Article I, section 10, cause. 1, of the U.S. Constitution and which may not be denied by the state.

Adkins v. Children's Hospital

Government official (D) v. Employer (P)

261 U.S. 525 (1923).

NATURE OF CASE: Appeal from order enjoining enforcement of a law prescribing minimum wages for women.

FACT SUMMARY: Congress enacted a law that prescribed minimum wages for women working in the District of Columbia. Children's Hospital (P) challenged the law on the ground that it violated the Fifth Amendment's due process guarantees.

🏛 RULE OF LAW
A law that prescribes minimum wages for women violates the Due Process Clause of the Fifth Amendment.

FACTS: Congress passed a law that fixed minimum wages for women (and children) in the District of Columbia. Children's Hospital (P), which employed many women, challenged the law as a violation of the Fifth Amendment's due process guarantees, and sued to enjoin enforcement of the law. The Supreme Court of the District (the trial court) denied the requested injunctive relief, but the Court of Appeals for the District reversed. The U.S. Supreme Court granted review.

ISSUE: Does a law that prescribes minimum wages for women violate the Due Process Clause of the Fifth Amendment?

HOLDING AND DECISION: (Sutherland, J.) Yes. The Due Process Clause of the Fifth Amendment guarantees the freedom of contract. Employment contracts are covered by that freedom and the parties thereto have an equal right to obtain from each other the best terms they can. And although freedom of contract is not absolute, it is the rule, not the exception, and for a law to abridge that freedom requires exceptional circumstances. Here, there are no such exceptional circumstances. The differences between the two sexes have diminished to the point of vanishing, as evidenced by passage of the Nineteenth Amendment [guaranteeing the vote for women], and emancipated women do not need to have their freedom of contract restricted to protect them, any more than men do. Also, the argument that without a minimum wage women would be forced to earn money in an immoral manner is unfounded because it cannot be shown that well-paid women safeguard their morality any more than less-paid women. The law favors the employee but does not take into account the employer's needs. The law exacts from the employer an arbitrary payment that is not connected to the employer's business or the kind of work the employee does. For these reasons, the law violates the Constitution's due process requirements.

▶ ANALYSIS

The casebook author states: "The Court reaffirmed *Adkins* in 1936, in *Morehead v. New York ex rel. Tipaldo*, 298 U.S. 587 (1936), which also declared unconstitutional a state minimum-wage law for women. In *Morehead*, like in *Adkins*, the Court found that the minimum wage law impermissibly interfered with the freedom of contract because it did not serve a valid state police purpose."

Quicknotes

DUE PROCESS CLAUSE Clauses found in the Fifth and Fourteenth Amendments to the U.S. Constitution providing that no person shall be deprived of "life, liberty, or property, without due process of law."

FREEDOM OF CONTRACT A basic freedom guaranteed by Article I, section 10, clause 1, of the U.S. Constitution and which may not be denied by the state.

Weaver v. Palmer Bros. Co.

State official (D) v. Bedding manufacturer (P)

270 U.S. 402 (1926).

NATURE OF CASE: Appeal from order enjoining a law that prohibited the use of shoddy [a fill material made out of rags and other debris] in comfortables [bedcovers] as violative of due process.

FACT SUMMARY: A Pennsylvania law prohibited the use of shoddy in comfortables. Palmer Bros. Co. (Palmer) (P), a manufacturer, used shoddy in the comfortables it sold in Pennsylvania, and sued to enjoin enforcement of the law on the ground that it violated due process.

RULE OF LAW
A state law that prohibits the use of a certain fill material in bedding violates the Due Process Clause.

FACTS: Pennsylvania enacted a law that prohibited the use of shoddy, a mix of rags and debris, in making comfortables, a type of bedding. Palmer (P) made approximately 3 million comfortables a year, and about 750,000 of those were filled with shoddy. The shoddy could be sanitized at low cost, and there was no evidence that any sickness or disease was ever caused by the use of shoddy. Palmer (P), a Connecticut company that sold its comfortables in Pennsylvania, brought suit in federal district court to enjoin enforcement of the law. The district court granted the injunction, and the Supreme Court granted review.

ISSUE: Does a state law that prohibits the use of a certain fill material in bedding violate the Due Process Clause?

HOLDING AND DECISION: (Butler, J.) Yes. The prohibition on the use of shoddy is arbitrary and unreasonable because it does not protect public health. All dangers to health indisputably can be removed by sanitizing the shoddy at low cost. The evidence also shows that even in the absence of sterilization or disinfection there is little danger to the health of users of shoddy-filled comfortables.

DISSENT: (Holmes, J.) The Pennsylvania legislature should be given deference in its determinations that disease is likely to be spread by the use of unsterilized shoddy in comfortables. Therefore, if it regards the danger as a great one, without adequate remedies other than a ban, then, on the basis of preventing disease, the law is constitutional.

ANALYSIS

At the heart of the Court's invalidation of consumer protection laws, such as the one in *Weaver*, was the theory that the laws interfered with the freedom of contract of those who wished to buy and sell such products. As in *Weaver*,

the Court also narrowly defined the permissible scope of the government's police power in such cases.

Quicknotes

DUE PROCESS CLAUSE Clauses found in the Fifth and Fourteenth Amendments to the U.S. Constitution providing that no person shall be deprived of "life, liberty, or property, without due process of law."

FREEDOM OF CONTRACT A basic freedom guaranteed by Article I, section 10, clause 1, of the U.S. Constitution and which may not be denied by the state.

Nebbia v. New York

Grocery store proprietor (D) v. State (P)

291 U.S. 502 (1934).

NATURE OF CASE: Appeal from conviction for violation of an order of the Milk Board.

FACT SUMMARY: The State Milk Board fixed nine cents as the price to be charged for a quart of milk. Nebbia (D) sold two quarts of milk and a loaf of bread for eighteen cents.

🏛 RULE OF LAW
Upon proper occasion and by appropriate measures, a state may regulate a business in any of its aspects, including fixing prices.

FACTS: In 1933, the New York (P) legislature established a Milk Control Board. The Board was given the power to fix minimum and maximum retail prices to be charged by stores to consumers. The Board fixed the price of a quart of milk at nine cents. Nebbia (D), a grocery store proprietor, charged eighteen cents for two quarts of milk and a five-cent loaf of bread. The law establishing the Board was based on a legislative finding that, "Milk is an essential item of diet. Failure of producers to receive a reasonable return threatens a relaxation of vigilance against contamination. The production of milk is a paramount industry of the state, and largely affects the health and prosperity of its people."

ISSUE: Does the federal Constitution prohibit a state from fixing selling prices?

HOLDING AND DECISION: (Roberts, J.) No. Upon proper occasion and by appropriate measures, a state may regulate a business in any of its aspects, including fixing prices. The general rule is that both the use of property and the making of contracts shall be free from government interference. However, neither property rights nor contract rights are absolute. Equally fundamental with the private interest is the public's to regulate it in the common interest. The Fifth and Fourteenth Amendments do not prohibit governmental regulation for the public welfare. They merely guarantee that regulation shall be consistent with due process. The guarantee of due process demands only that the law shall not be unreasonable, arbitrary, or capricious and that the means selected shall have a real and substantial relation to the object sought to be attained. If an industry is subject to regulation in the public interest, its prices may be regulated. An industry that is "affected with a public industry" is one that is subject to police powers. A state is free to adopt whatever economic policy may be reasonably deemed to promote the public welfare. The courts are without authority to override such policies. If the laws passed have a rational relation to a legitimate purpose and are neither arbitrary nor discriminatory, the requirements of due process are satisfied. Price control may fulfill these requirements as well as any other type of regulation. The New York (P) law creating the Milk Board and giving it power to fix prices does not conflict with the due process guarantees and is constitutionally valid.

▶ ANALYSIS

The early attitude of the Court had been that the states could regulate selling prices only for industries affecting the public interest. Regulation of prices and rates charged by public utilities, dairies, grain elevators, etc., were upheld, but regulation of the prices of theater tickets or ice were not. *Nebbia* held that price control regulation was to be treated the same as other police powers and a rational relation to a legitimate goal was all that was necessary. The dissent, representing the court's earlier position, does not want to treat the legislation with the deference exercised by the majority. In its judgment, the method adopted by New York does not rationally relate to its goal. *Nebbia* represents the modern position of the Court, which is to presume the propriety of the legislation.

■═■

Quicknotes

DUE PROCESS CLAUSE Clauses found in the Fifth and Fourteenth Amendments to the U.S. Constitution providing that no person shall be deprived of "life, liberty, or property, without due process of law."

FREEDOM OF CONTRACT A basic freedom guaranteed by Article I, section 10, clause 1, of the U.S. Constitution and which may not be denied by the state.

■═■

West Coast Hotel Co. v. Parrish

Employer (D) v. Employee (P)

300 U.S. 379 (1937).

NATURE OF CASE: Appeal from money judgment favoring female employee (P) for the difference between wages paid to her by her employee (D) and minimum wages set by state law.

FACT SUMMARY: Washington state had a law that set the minimum wage for women. Parrish (P), a woman employed by West Coast Hotel Co. (D), brought suit to recover the difference between the wages paid to her and the minimum wages set by the state. West Coast Hotel Co. (D) challenged the minimum wage law as violating the Fourteenth Amendment's due process guarantees.

RULE OF LAW
A state minimum wage law for women does not violate the Fourteenth Amendment's due process guarantees.

FACTS: The state of Washington enacted a law entitled, "Minimum Wages for Women," that fixed minimum wages for women (and minors). West Coast Hotel Co. (D) was in the hotel business and employed Parrish (P), a woman, as a chambermaid. Parrish brought suit to recover the difference between the wages paid to her and the minimum wages set by the state. West Coast Hotel Co. (D) challenged the minimum wage law as violating the Fourteenth Amendment's due process guarantees. The Supreme Court of Washington, reversing the trial court, sustained the statute and directed judgment for Parrish (P). The Supreme Court granted review.

ISSUE: Does a state minimum wage law for women violate the Fourteenth Amendment's due process guarantees?

HOLDING AND DECISION: (Hughes, C. J.) No. It is alleged that the law works a deprivation of freedom of contract. However, "the Constitution does not speak of freedom of contract. It speaks of liberty and prohibits the deprivation of liberty without due process of law. . . . [R]egulation that is reasonable in its relation to its subject and is adopted in the interests of the community is due process." The freedom of contract may be restricted in the employment context for the protection of health and safety, and to ensure good work conditions and freedom from oppression. The safeguarding of women's health and their protection from unscrupulous employers is in the public interest. The state's legislature was entitled to consider the situation of women in employment—that they receive the least pay, they have weak bargaining power, and they are easily taken advantage of, or exploited at wages so low that they cannot meet the bare cost of living. The legislative response to these conditions is not arbitrary or capricious, and, therefore, the legislature's judgment must be deferred to. Moreover, the law reasonably furthers a legitimate public

purpose because "the denial of a living wage is not only detrimental to their health and well being, but casts a direct burden for their support upon the community."

ANALYSIS

This case expressly overruled *Adkins v. Children's Hospital*, 261 U.S. 525 (1923), which had held that a minimum wage law for women, much like the one in this case, was unconstitutional. *West Coast Hotel Co.* was one of the first cases that seemingly repudiated the entire principle of substantive due process and signaled an end to the *Lochner* era's laissez-faire doctrines. With *West Coast Hotel Co.*, the Court introduced a more relaxed and deferential standard of review to measure the connection between legislative means and ends.

Quicknotes

DUE PROCESS CLAUSE Clauses found in the Fifth and Fourteenth Amendments to the U.S. Constitution providing that no person shall be deprived of "life, liberty, or property, without due process of law."

FREEDOM OF CONTRACT A basic freedom guaranteed by Article I, section 10, clause 1, of the U.S. Constitution and which may not be denied by the state.

LIBERTY INTEREST A right conferred by the Due Process Clauses of the state and federal constitutions.

United States v. Carolene Products Co.

Federal government (P) v. Dairy company (D)

304 U.S. 144 (1938).

NATURE OF CASE: An appeal of a decision sustaining a demurrer to an indictment of the "Filled Milk Act."

FACT SUMMARY: Carolene Products (D) was attempting to have the "Filled Milk Act" declared unconstitutional.

🏛 RULE OF LAW
In cases challenging the constitutionality of legislation affecting ordinary commercial transactions, the Supreme Court will apply the rational basis test, which means that the person challenging the legislation has the burden of showing that a rational basis does not exist.

FACTS: Congress passed the "Filled Milk Act" which prohibited the shipment in interstate commerce of skimmed milk compounded with any fat or oil other than milk fat. Carolene Products Co. (D) was indicted for violating the Act. The trial court sustained a demurrer to the indictment by Carolene Products Co. (D) and the federal government (P) appealed to the Supreme Court. Carolene Products (D) claimed that the "Filled Milk Act" violated the Fifth Amendment because Congress had not attempted to regulate the interstate shipment of oleomargarine, which substituted vegetable fats for butter fat. It also claimed that the Act was void on its face because it lacked a rational basis.

ISSUE: In cases challenging the constitutionality of legislation affecting ordinary commercial transactions, will the Supreme Court apply the rational basis test?

HOLDING AND DECISION: (Stone, J.) Yes. In cases challenging the constitutionality of legislation affecting ordinary commercial transactions, the Supreme Court will apply the rational basis test. Legislation is not unconstitutional because it does not attempt to correct all similar evils at the same time. Congress could properly choose to control shipments of milk substitutes without regulating butter substitutes in the same manner. In cases challenging the constitutionality of legislation affecting ordinary commercial transactions, the Court will apply a rational basis test. Congress had held many hearings prior to passing the "Filled Milk Act" and the Court held that Congress could rationally believe that the Act was necessary for the protection of the general public. In dealing with legislation such as this, there is a presumption that it is constitutional and the Court stated that this presumption would be enough to sustain the Act. Carolene Products (D) had the burden to show that no rational basis existed for the "Filled Milk Act" and that burden had not been met. Therefore the trial court was wrong in sustaining the demurrer to the indictment.

▶ ANALYSIS

One of the most important steps in constitutional litigation is the determination by the Court of the approach they will use in deciding a case. If they decide to apply the rational basis test, the burden of showing that the legislation does not have a rational basis is on the person attacking it. It is almost impossible to show that facts do not exist which support the validity of the legislation or that Congress could not reasonably believe that they exist. When the Court feels that the legislation impinges on a fundamental right, the burden is on the government to show a compelling governmental interest that supports the legislation. This is also a difficult burden to prove. In most cases, the approach the Court decides to use determines the outcome of the case.

━━■

Quicknotes

DUE PROCESS CLAUSE Clauses found in the Fifth and Fourteenth Amendments to the U.S. Constitution providing that no person shall be deprived of "life, liberty, or property, without due process of law."

LIBERTY INTEREST A right conferred by the Due Process Clauses of the state and federal constitutions.

RATIONAL BASIS REVIEW A test employed by the court to determine the validity of a statute in equal protection actions, whereby the court determines whether the challenged statute is rationally related to the achievement of a legitimate state interest.

━━■

Williamson v. Lee Optical of Oklahoma, Inc.

State (P) v. Optical company (D)

348 U.S. 483 (1955).

NATURE OF CASE: Appeal from a district court's judgment holding unconstitutional three sections of a state ophthalmology law.

FACT SUMMARY: A state law prohibited any person from fitting or duplicating lenses without a prescription from an ophthalmologist or optometrist. It also prohibited soliciting the sale of frames and the renting of space in a retail store to any person purporting to do eye examination.

RULE OF LAW
The Due Process Clause will no longer be used to strike down state laws regulating business and industrial conditions because they may be unwise, improvident, or out of harmony with a particular school of thought.

FACTS: A state law prohibited any person who was not a licensed ophthalmologist or optometrist from fitting or duplicating lenses without a prescription from a licensed optometrist or ophthalmologist. Opticians are artisans qualified to grind lenses, fill prescriptions, and fit frames. The effect of the provision was to prevent opticians from fitting old glasses into new frames or duplicating a lost or broken lens without a prescription. Two other sections of the Act prohibited soliciting the sale of frames, mountings, or other optical appliances and the renting of space in a retail store to one purporting to do eye examinations.

ISSUE: Does a state law regulating the fitting and selling of eye lenses and frames conflict with the Due Process Clause?

HOLDING AND DECISION: (Douglas, J.) No. The Due Process Clause will no longer be used to strike down state laws, regulating business or industrial conditions, because they may be unwise, improvident, or out of harmony with a particular school of thought. For protection against abuses by the legislature, the people must resort to the polls, not the courts. The state law in question here may exact needless wasteful requirements in many cases. But it is for the legislatures, not the courts, to balance the advantages and disadvantages of the new requirement. The legislature may have concluded that the cases in which prescriptions are essential are frequent enough to justify requiring one in every case. Hence, it cannot be said that the regulation had no rational relation to legitimate objectives.

ANALYSIS

An example of the Court's deference to legislative judgments is *Ferguson v. Skrupa*, 372 (U.S. 726 [1963]), where the court reversed the invalidation of a state statute regulating the business of debt adjusting. The law prohibited that business except as an incident to the practice of law. The Supreme Court spoke of its abandonment of the use of the vague contours of the Due Process Clause to nullify laws that a majority of the Court believed to be economically unwise. "We refuse to sit as a super legislature to weigh the wisdom of legislation," the Court stated.

Quicknotes

DUE PROCESS CLAUSE Clauses found in the Fifth and Fourteenth Amendments to the U.S. Constitution providing that no person shall be deprived of "life, liberty, or property, without due process of law."

BMW of North America, Inc. v. Gore

Car distributor (D) v. Car purchaser (P)

517 U.S. 559 (1996).

NATURE OF CASE: Appeal from $2 million punitive damages award for injury involving only $4,000 actual damages, on the ground that it was excessive and violated the Fourteenth Amendment's due process guarantees.

FACT SUMMARY: Gore (P) purchased a "new" car from BMW of North America, Inc. (BMW) (D). The car had been repainted before being sold for the full price of a new car, but the repainting, which lowers the value of a car, was not disclosed to Gore (D). Gore (D) sued and won $2 million punitive damages on only $4,000 actual damages. BMW (D) appealed on the ground that the punitive damages award was constitutionally excessive.

🏛 RULE OF LAW
A $2 million punitive damages award for non-disclosure of presale repairs to a car is grossly excessive and violative of the Due Process Clause of the Fourteenth Amendment where actual damages were only $4,000.

FACTS: Gore (P) purchased a new car from BMW (D) in Alabama for about $41,000, only to discover several months after driving the car that it had been repainted before being sold to him. Such repainting lowered the value of a car by about ten percent. BMW (D) had a nationwide policy whereby new cars that sustained damage in manufacture or transport would be repaired without notice to dealers if the cost of the repair did not exceed 3 percent of the car's suggested retail price, and Gore's (P) car was repainted under this policy. BMW (D) had sold about 1,000 such repaired cars nationwide, with 14 having been sold in Alabama. Gore (P) sued for fraud, requesting $4,000 in actual damages and $4 million in punitive damages (representing $4,000 damages per car for each of the 1,000 similarly repaired cars). A jury awarded the requested relief, and BMW (D) challenged it as constitutionally excessive. The trial court held that the award was not grossly excessive, but on appeal, the Alabama Supreme Court reduced the punitive damages to $2 million on the ground that the jury had improperly multiplied Gore's (P) compensatory damages by the number of similar sales in all states, not just those in Alabama. BMW (D) appealed and the U.S. Supreme Court granted review.

ISSUE: Is a $2 million punitive damages award for nondisclosure of presale repairs to a car grossly excessive and violative of the Due Process Clause of the Fourteenth Amendment where actual damages were only $4,000?

HOLDING AND DECISION: (Stevens, J.) Yes. A punitive damages award that is "grossly excessive" in relation to a state's interests in punishing unlawful conduct violates the Due Process Clause of the Fourteenth Amendment. Also, state sovereignty and comity principles prohibit a state from imposing punitive damages on violators of its law with the intent of changing the tortfeasor's lawful conduct in other states. Here, Alabama does not have the power to award punitive damages based on BMW's (D) nationwide conduct because other states do not make such conduct unlawful and such an award would infringe on the other states' policy choices. There are three criteria to determine if a punitive award is grossly excessive. These are (1) the degree of reprehensibility of the defendant's conduct; (2) the ratio of the actual harm to the award; and (3) other available civil or criminal sanctions for similar misconduct. Here, BMW's (D) conduct was not reprehensible because its harm was purely economic and evidenced none of the aggravating factors for intentional or reckless misconduct. The 500 to 1 ratio of the award to actual damages was "breathtaking," especially given that no purchaser was threatened with any other potential harm, and penalties for similar deceptive trade practices in Alabama would not exceed $2,000, and would not exceed $10,000 in other states. Accordingly, the award is grossly excessive and exceeds constitutional limits.

DISSENT: (Scalia, J.) Punitive damages are not the Court's business under the Constitution, and the majority is therefore making an unjustified incursion into an area that is the exclusive province of the states. A state trial procedure that allows a jury to decide whether to impose punitive damages, which is subject to judicial review for reasonableness, is all the process that is "due" to a defendant. The Fourteenth Amendment does not guarantee the substantive fairness of such an award, but only guarantees procedurally that a defendant will be able to challenge the reasonableness of the award in state court. Taking the majority's holding to its logical conclusion would make unconstitutional every unreasonably imposed award, e.g., because not supported by the evidence.

▶ ANALYSIS

This case is important because it is the first time that a punitive damages award has been found excessive by the Supreme Court. It is also the first time since 1937 that the Court has engaged in economic substantive due process analysis to declare government action—here, by a state court—as violating due process guarantees.

■▬■

Continued on next page.

Quicknotes

DUE PROCESS CLAUSE Clauses found in the Fifth and Fourteenth Amendments to the U.S. Constitution providing that no person shall be deprived of "life, liberty, or property, without due process of law."

PUNITIVE DAMAGES Damages exceeding the actual injury suffered for the purposes of punishment of the defendant, deterrence of the wrongful behavior or comfort to the plaintiff.

SUBSTANTIVE DUE PROCESS A constitutional safeguard limiting the power of the state, irrespective of how fair its procedures may be; substantive limits placed on the power of the state.

State Farm Mutual Automobile Insurance Co. v. Campbell

Insurance provider (D) v. Insured (P)

538 U.S. 408 (2003).

NATURE OF CASE: Suit for bad faith, fraud, and intentional infliction of emotional distress filed by an insured against his insurance provider.

FACT SUMMARY: Campbell (P) sued his insurance provider, State Farm (D), in a Utah state trial court for its conduct during a wrongful death and tort action following a highway accident caused by Campbell (P). The jury awarded Campbell (P) $2.6 million in compensatory damages and $145 million in punitive damages, awards that the trial judge reduced to $1 million and $25 million, respectively. On appeal, the Utah Supreme Court reinstated the jury's punitive damages award of $145 million.

🏛 **RULE OF LAW**
A punitive damages award 145 times greater than the supporting compensatory damages award violates the Due Process Clause of the Fourteenth Amendment.

FACTS: Campbell's (P) driving caused a highway accident in Utah that resulted in one person's death and another person's permanent disability. Despite strong evidence that Campbell (P) was solely responsible for the accident, his insurance provider, State Farm (D), refused a settlement offer of $50,000, which represented Campbell's (P) policy limit of $25,000 for each of the two opposing parties. State Farm (D), ignoring the available evidence and the advice of its own investigators, contested liability at trial, assuring Campbell (P) that he was not liable and that his assets were safe. After the jury found Campbell (P) 100 percent liable for the accident and the trial court entered judgment against him for more than $185,000, State Farm (D) suggested that it would cover only $50,000 of the judgment for Campbell (P). On appeal, Campbell (P) retained his own counsel and agreed with his opponents to drop the appeal and instead sue State Farm (D) for its conduct during the wrongful death and tort action. Campbell (P) filed suit against State Farm (D) in a Utah state trial court, alleging bad faith, fraud, and intentional infliction of emotional distress. The jury awarded Campbell (P) $2.6 million in compensatory damages and $145 million damages in punitive damages, which the trial judge reduced to $1 million and $25 million, respectively. On appeal, the Utah Supreme Court left the compensatory-damages award at $1 million but reinstated the jury's punitive-damages award of $145 million.

ISSUE: Does a punitive-damages award 145 times greater than the supporting compensatory-damages award violate the Due Process Clause of the Fourteenth Amendment?

HOLDING AND DECISION: (Kennedy, J.) Yes. A punitive-damages award 145 times greater than the supporting compensatory-damages award violates the Due Process Clause of the Fourteenth Amendment. This is an easy case in light of the analytical framework and holding announced in *BMW v. Gore*, 517 U.S. 559 (1996). First, although State Farm's (D) conduct in the underlying wrongful death and tort action deserves censure, a more modest award of punitive damages would advance Utah's legitimate interest in deterring similar conduct in the future. Further undermining the rationale for so large an award of punitive damages is the Utah courts' grounding of the award in conduct allegedly engaged in by State Farm (D) in other cases. Punitive damages must punish conduct in this case, not in cases that are not before the court. Second, a ratio of 145-to-1 between punitive and compensatory damages dwarfs the generally acceptable single-digit ratio between such awards. Finally, the disparity between the punitive damages awarded here and Utah's largest possible criminal sanction for State Farm's (D) conduct ($10,000), also argues heavily against the punitive-damage award in this case. Accordingly, the Court concludes that the punitive-damages award against State Farm (D) was an unreasonable, irrational, arbitrary deprivation of property in contravention of the Fourteenth Amendment's Due Process Clause. Reversed.

DISSENT: (Scalia, J.) The Due Process Clause does not limit the size of punitive-damages awards. Moreover, the holding in *BMW v. Gore*, 517 U.S. 559 (1996), does not merit binding, stare decisis effect because it cannot be applied in a principled manner.

DISSENT: (Thomas, J.) Nothing in the Constitution limits the size of punitive-damages awards.

DISSENT: (Ginsburg, J.) Punitive damages belong under state supervision, and this case shows why. The Utah courts, as well as the Utah jury that found the facts in this case in the first instance, were in a better position than this Court to assess the reprehensibility of State Farm's (D) conduct. A finding of reprehensibility could legitimately have been based on much evidence omitted from the majority opinion; for example, testimony that State Farm (D) systematically underpaid claims, unjustifiably attacked witness credibility, and even deliberately falsified evidence. Such evidence shows why this Court has traditionally reviewed state-court judgments with great deference. The

Continued on next page.

numerical limits placed on state judgments in this case, which properly belong to legislative action, greatly exceed the bounds of judicial restraint.

▶ *ANALYSIS*

Justices of the Supreme Court frequently distinguish between judicial and legislative functions in their opinions, usually to portray an opinion with which the writing justice disagrees as being properly within the province of legislatures. See, e.g., *Troxel v. Granville*, 530 U.S. 57 (2000) (Scalia, J., dissenting). In another context, the Supreme Court has discussed the difference between legislation and adjudication in terms of legislation looking to the future and establishing policy, where adjudication looks to the past and establishes rights and liabilities in a particular case. See, e.g., *United States v. Florida East Coast Railway Co.*, 410 U.S. 224 (1973). Although as interpreter of the Constitution the Supreme Court clearly has a limited policy-making role in our government, the numerical specificity of the majority's rule in *State Farm v. Campbell*, as Justice Ginsburg notes in her dissent, goes well beyond the Court's limited but proper policy-making sphere of establishing constitutional principles.

■═■

Quicknotes

DUE PROCESS CLAUSE   Clauses found in the Fifth and Fourteenth Amendments to the U.S. Constitution providing that no person shall be deprived of "life, liberty, or property, without due process of law."

PUNITIVE DAMAGES   Damages exceeding the actual injury suffered for the purposes of punishment of the defendant, deterrence of the wrongful behavior or comfort to the plaintiff.

■═■

Philip Morris USA v. Williams

Cigarette maker (D) v. Widow of smoker (P)

127 S. Ct. 1057 (2007).

NATURE OF CASE: Review of a state supreme-court judgment.

FACT SUMMARY: A smoker's widow (P) sued cigarette manufacturer Philip Morris USA (D) for allegedly deceptive marketing campaigns, and the jury's punitive damages award was based in part on the desire to punish the company for its actions against smokers who were not parties to the lawsuit.

🏛 RULE OF LAW
The U.S. Constitution's Due Process Clause does not allow a jury to base a punitive damages award in part on its desire to punish a defendant for harming persons who are not before the court.

FACTS: Jesse Williams died of lung cancer at age 67 after smoking three packs of Marlboro cigarettes per day for most of his life. His widow (P) sued Phillip Morris USA (D), the maker of Marlboro cigarettes, arguing that the company had deliberately misled the public about the dangers of smoking. The jury found for Williams (P) and awarded her $821,485.50 in compensatory damages and $79.5 million in punitive damages. The trial judge found the punitive damages excessive and reduced them to $32 million. The Oregon Court of Appeals reinstated the $79.5 million award, holding that Phillip Morris's (D) conduct was reprehensible enough to warrant the large amount. The Oregon Supreme Court upheld the decision. Phillip Morris (D) appealed to the U.S. Supreme Court, arguing that the court had unreasonably exceeded federal guidelines on punitive damages. Phillip Morris (D) also argued that it was unfair to punish the company for its actions against smokers who were not parties to the suit.

ISSUE: Does the U.S. Constitution's Due Process Clause allow a jury to base a punitive damages award in part on its desire to punish a defendant for harming persons who are not before the court?

HOLDING AND DECISION: (Breyer, J.) No. The U.S. Constitution's Due Process Clause does not allow a jury to base a punitive damages award in part on its desire to punish a defendant for harming persons who are not before the court. Such an award would amount to a taking of property from the defendant without due process. It would be unfair to allow courts to award punitive damages for harm done to "strangers to the litigation," because defendants cannot defend themselves against such limitless and arbitrary charges. The "risk of harm to the general public" can be taken into account as a component of the reprehensibility of the defendant's actions, and highly reprehensible actions may warrant a larger award of punitive damages, but the award

cannot be increased as a direct result of harms inflicted on non-parties. Whether the $79.5 million award was excessive was not decided, and the case was remanded.

DISSENT: (Stevens, J.) Punitive damages, unlike compensatory damages, are punishment for the public harm the defendant's conduct has caused or threatened. There is little difference between criminal punishment, such as a prison sentence, and punitive damages. There is therefore no reason why a jury's interest in punishing a wrongdoer for harming persons not before the court should not be taken into consideration when decided on the amount of punitive damages.

DISSENT: (Thomas, J.) The Constitution does not limit the amount of punitive-damages awards.

DISSENT: (Ginsburg, J.) The purpose of punitive damages is to punish, and the punishment is for the reprehensibility of the defendant's conduct, which is directly related to how many the conduct may harm. If a jury properly considers the extent of harm suffered by others as a measure of reprehensibility, it follows that the amount associated with punishment can be based on the possibility of harm to others.

▶ ANALYSIS

The Court made a binding constitutional rule: that a punitive damage award violates due process if it is based in part on a jury's desire to punish a wrongdoer for harming "non-parties." The state supreme court was instructed to apply the standard set forth by the Court, and subsequently upheld the $79.5 million verdict.

■==■

Quicknotes

DUE PROCESS CLAUSE Clauses found in the Fifth and Fourteenth Amendments to the U.S. Constitution providing that no person shall be deprived of "life, liberty, or property, without due process of law."

PUNITIVE DAMAGES Damages exceeding the actual injury suffered for the purposes of punishment of the defendant, deterrence of the wrongful behavior or comfort to the plaintiff.

TAKING A governmental action that substantially deprives an owner of the use and enjoyment of his property, requiring compensation.

■==■

Home Building & Loan Assn. v. Blaisdell

Mortgagor (D) v. Mortgagee (P)

290 U.S. 398 (1934).

NATURE OF CASE: Action to secure an order extending the period of redemption from a foreclosure and sale of real property.

FACT SUMMARY: During the "Great Depression," Minnesota authorized county courts to extend the redemption period from foreclosure sales.

🏛 RULE OF LAW
The reservation of the reasonable exercise of the state's protective power is read into all contracts. A state may affect the obligations between two contracting parties so long as: (1) an emergency exists; (2) the legislation is addressed to a legitimate end; (3) the relief afforded and justified by the emergency could only be of a character appropriate to that emergency; (4) the conditions upon which relief is granted do not appear to be unreasonable; and (5) the legislation is temporary in operation.

FACTS: In 1933, Minnesota enacted a statute authorizing country courts to extend the period of redemption from foreclosure sales "for such additional time as the court may deem just and equitable (but not extending beyond May 1, 1975)." The Blaisdells (P) applied for a judicial extension, and the court granted the extension but also ordered the Blaisdells (P) to pay Home Building and Loan Association (D), the mortgagor of their home, $40 a month through the extended period. Home (D) appealed on the ground that the Minnesota Act violated Article I, § 10 of the U.S. Constitution ("No State shall . . . pass any . . . law impairing the obligation of Contracts"). The state supreme court upheld the Act's constitutionality.

ISSUE: May a state change the existing contractual obligations between two private parties?

HOLDING AND DECISION: (Hughes, C.J.) Yes. The reservation of the reasonable exercise of the state's protective power is read into all contracts. A state may affect the obligations between two contracting parties so long as: (1) an emergency exists; (2) the legislation is addressed to a legitimate end; (3) the relief afforded and justified by the emergency could only be of a character appropriate to that emergency; (4) the conditions upon which relief is granted do not appear to be unreasonable; and (5) the legislation is temporary in operation. The prohibition embodied in the Contracts Clause is not an absolute one. The state continues to possess authority to safeguard the vital interests of its people. The protection of contracts presupposes a government that views contractual obligations as worthwhile. A rational compromise must be found between public need and private rights, especially when an emergency is found to

exist upon judicial review. Provisions of the Constitution must yield to interpretations that respond to current problems not envisioned by the original Framers. The Contracts Clause should not be used to frustrate the states in advancing their fundamental interests. Here, the Act was an appropriate response because: (1) a true emergency in Minnesota existed; (2) the legislation was for the protection of a basic interest of society rather than the advantage of a few individuals; (3) the relief afforded was geared to the emergency (mass foreclosures); (4) the mortgagor's interests (no impairment of the indebtedness, the running of interest, validity of the sale, etc.) are not impaired; and (5) the legislation does not outlast the emergency, being temporary in duration.

▶ ANALYSIS

Despite the sweeping language of this opinion, the Court struck down only those state acts impairing contractual obligations in the following instances: exemption of payments on life insurance policies from garnishment (no time limitation, no limitation of amount to necessities); repeal of law protecting purchasers at state-conducted tax sales from attempts by the state to invalidate the transaction because of irregularities (purchaser had right to rely on earlier law so as to make land marketable); change of procedures for enforcement of payment of benefit assessments pledged as security for municipal improvement district bonds. Nonetheless, the *Blaisdell* decision sounded the deathknell of the Contracts Clause's viability as a means to assail the validity of state laws.

■═■

Quicknotes

CONTRACTS CLAUSE Article 1, section 10 of the U.S. Constitution prohibiting states from passing any "law impairing the Obligation of Contracts."

■═■

Energy Reserves Group, Inc. v. Kansas Power & Light Co.

Energy supplier (P) v. Public utility (D)

459 U.S. 400 (1983).

NATURE OF CASE: Appeal from dismissal of action to enforce natural gas contracts between an energy supplier (P) and a public utility (D).

FACT SUMMARY: Kansas Power & Light Co. (Kansas Power) (D) entered into a contract for natural gas with Energy Reserves Group, Inc. (ERG) (P) that provided that the price to be paid would be increased if governmental regulators fixed a price higher than the price specified in the contract. Kansas enacted a law that barred such price increases, and ERG (P) challenged the Kansas law as an unconstitutional impairment of the contract.

🏛 RULE OF LAW
A state law that interferes with an existing contract does not violate the Contracts Clause where the law does not substantially impair a party's contractual rights, the state's interests are significant and legitimate, and the law is reasonably related to achieving its goals.

FACTS: Kansas Power (D) entered into an intrastate contract with ERG (P) to purchase wellhead gas. The contract contained a "governmental price escalator clause," which provided that if any governmental authority fixed a price for any natural gas that was higher than the contract price, the contract price would be increased to that level. The federal government raised the ceiling on the price of certain types of gas, and ERG (P) sought to raise the price of its gas under its contract with Kansas Power (D) to the new federal levels. In the meantime, Kansas had passed a law that provided that the price to be paid for natural gas under an existing contract could not be increased because of prices set by federal authorities, and Kansas Power (D) cited this law in refusing to pay ERG's (P) demand for a higher price. ERG (P) sued to enforce the contract. A state trial court dismissed, holding, inter alia, that the Kansas law did not violate the Contracts Clause. The Kansas Supreme Court affirmed and the U.S. Supreme Court granted review.

ISSUE: Does a state law that interferes with an existing contract violate the Contracts Clause where the law does not substantially impair a party's contractual rights, the state's interests are significant and legitimate, and the law is reasonably related to achieving its goals?

HOLDING AND DECISION: (Blackmun, J.) No. The threshold inquiry is whether the state law has, in fact, substantially impaired the contractual relationship. Next, if substantial impairment has occurred, the inquiry is whether the state can justify the impairment with a significant and legitimate public purpose. If the state has a legitimate purpose, the final inquiry is whether the state's impairment of the contract is appropriate to achieving the state's purpose. Applying these

criteria here, the Kansas law has not impaired substantially plaintiff's contractual rights. The parties are operating in a heavily regulated industry, and the statement of intent in their contracts made clear that the escalator clauses were designed to guarantee price increases consistent with anticipated regulated increases in the value of ERG's gas, not that ERG (P) expected to receive deregulated prices. Moreover, the contract provision making any contractual term subject to relevant present and future state and federal law suggests that ERG (P) knew its contractual rights were subject to alteration by state price regulation. Second, to the extent, if any, the Kansas law impairs ERG's contractual interests, it rests on significant state interests in protecting consumers from the escalation of natural gas prices caused by deregulation and in correcting the imbalance between the interstate and intrastate markets by permitting the intrastate prices to rise only to a certain level. Nor are the means chosen to implement these purposes deficient, particularly in light of the deference to which the Kansas legislature's judgment is entitled.

▶ ANALYSIS

The three-part test articulated in this case sets forth the doctrinal test currently used by the Court to assess whether government interference with private contracts violates the Contracts Clause.

■■■■

Quicknotes

CONTRACTS CLAUSE Article 1, section 10 of the U.S. Constitution prohibiting states from passing any "law impairing the Obligation of Contracts."

■■■■

Allied Structural Steel Co. v. Spannaus

Steel company (P) v. State (D)

438 U.S. 234 (1978).

NATURE OF CASE: Appeal from an action for declaratory and injunctive relief.

FACT SUMMARY: Allied Structural Steel Co. (P) brought suit seeking declaratory and injunctive relief and claiming that the Minnesota Private Pension Act unconstitutionally impaired its contractual obligations to its employees under its pension agreement.

🏛 **RULE OF LAW**
If the Contracts Clause is to retain any meaning at all it must be understood to impose some limits upon the power of the states to abridge existing contractual relationships, even in the exercise of its otherwise legitimate police power.

FACTS: Allied Structural Steel Co. (P), a corporation with its principal place of business in Illinois, maintained an office in Minnesota with 30 employees. Under Allied's (P) general pension plan adopted in 1963 and qualified under § 401 of the I.R.C., it was the sole contributor to the pension trust fund. Although those contributions once made were irrevocable, the plan neither required Allied (P) to make specific contributions nor imposed any sanction on it for failing to contribute adequately to the fund. Allied (P) not only retained an unrestricted right to amend the plan, but was also free to terminate the plan and distribute the trust assets at any time for any reason. In sum, an employee who did not die, did not quit, and was not discharged before meeting the requirements of the plan would receive a fixed pension at age 65 if Allied (P) remained in business and elected to continue the pension plan. In 1974, Minnesota enacted the Private Pension Act. Under the Act, a private employer of 100 employees or more who provided benefits under a plan meeting the qualification of § 401 of the I.R.C. was subject to a pension funding charge if he either terminated the plan or closed a Minnesota office. The charge was assessed if the pension funds were not sufficient to cover full pensions for all employees who had worked at least 10 years. During 1974, Allied (P) began closing its Minnesota office. Thereafter, Minnesota notified Allied (P) that it owed a pension funding charge. Allied (P) brought this suit in a federal district court asking for declaratory and injunctive relief. Allied (P) claimed that the Pension Act unconstitutionally impaired its contractual obligations to its employees under its pension agreement. The court upheld the validity of the Act as applied to Allied (P). An appeal was made to the Supreme Court.

ISSUE: Is the Contracts Clause to be understood to impose some limits upon the power of the states to abridge

existing contractual relationships, even in the exercise of otherwise legitimate police power?

HOLDING AND DECISION: (Stewart, J.) Yes. If the Contracts Clause is to retain any meaning at all, it must be understood to impose some limits upon the power of a state to abridge existing contractual relationships, even in the exercise of its otherwise legitimate police power. In the present case, the first inquiry must be whether the state law has, in fact, operated as a substantial impairment of a contractual relationship. The severity of the impairment measures the height of the hurdle the state legislation must clear. Here, not only did Minnesota's Private Pension Act retroactively modify the compensation that the company had agreed to pay its employees from 1963 to 1974, but it did so by changing the company's obligations in an area where the element of reliance was vital—the funding of a pension plan. Thus, the statute nullifies express terms of the company's contractual obligations and imposes a completely unexpected liability in potentially disabling amounts. Yet there is no showing that this was necessary to meet an important general social problem. It did not operate in an area already subject to state regulation at the time Allied's (P) contractual obligations were originally undertaken. Also, its narrow aim was leveled not at every Minnesota employer, but only at those who had in the past been sufficiently enlightened as to voluntarily agree to establish pension plans for their employees.

DISSENT: (Brennan, J.) Today's decision greatly expands the Contracts Clause. The Minnesota Act does not abrogate or dilute any obligation due a party to a private contract; rather, like all positive social legislation, the act imposes new obligations on a particular class of persons. Any constitutional infirmity in the law must therefore derive, not from the Contracts Clause, but from the Due Process Clause of the Fourteenth Amendment.

▌ *ANALYSIS*

In *Home Building & Loan Assn. v. Blaisdell*, 290 U.S. 398 (1934), the Supreme Court upheld against a Contracts Clause attack a mortgage moratorium law that Minnesota had enacted to provide relief for homeowners threatened with foreclosure. Although the legislation conflicted directly with lenders' contractual foreclosure rights, the Court there acknowledged that, despite the Contracts Clause, the states retain residual authority to enact laws to safeguard the vital interests of their people. The Court found five factors significant. First, there existed an emergency need for the

Continued on next page.

protection of homeowners. Second, the law protected a basic societal interest. Third, the relief was tailored to the emergency. Fourth, the imposed conditions were reasonable. Finally, the legislation was limited to the duration of the emergency.

■■■

Quicknotes

CONTRACTS CLAUSE   Article 1, section 10 of the U.S. Constitution prohibiting states from passing any "law impairing the Obligation of Contracts."

■■■

United States Trust Co. v. New Jersey

Bondholders (P) v. States (D)

431 U.S. 1 (1977).

NATURE OF CASE: Action challenging the repeal of state covenants on the basis it violated the Contracts Clause.

FACT SUMMARY: New York (D) and New Jersey (D) enacted covenants to protect the interests of its bondholders.

🏛 RULE OF LAW
A state cannot refuse to meet its obligations merely because it would rather spend its funds on more important programs.

FACTS: New York (D) and New Jersey (D) formed a joint Port Authority. Bonds were sold to support the independent authority. Bridge and tunnel tolls were pledged to protect the bondholders. In 1960, the Authority took over a financially troubled, privately owned commuter train. In 1962, New York (D) and New Jersey (D) enacted covenants not to finance railroad deficits with revenue pledged to make bond payments. In 1974, both states retroactively repealed these covenants in order to permit greater use of tolls to subsidize mass transit. The United States Trust Co. of New York (P) and various bondholders (P) brought suit alleging that the repeal violated the Contracts Clause in that it impaired their rights to payment on the bonds. The court held the repeal as a valid exercise of the police powers and dismissed the action. It held that the states (D) could validly decide that the funds were better used for mass transit purposes.

ISSUE: May a state decide that its funds are more needed for other purposes than to pay its obligations?

HOLDING AND DECISION: (Blackmun, J.) No. A state may not decide that its funds are more needed for other purposes than to pay its obligations. The Contracts Clause does not prevent a state from enacting legislation that may affect existing contracts so long as reasonable conditions and public interests justify its enactment. When a state impairs its own contracts, the nature of the contract must be examined. If the authority/power that is contracted away has not been reserved to the state, e.g., police powers and eminent domain, it will normally be bound by its debts. Only where the promise is not purely financial may the state impair its own debts. Here, the reservation of tolls was purely financial. The states (D) may not impair their debts merely because they would prefer to spend the money in a different manner. Also, less restrictive means might have been adopted than the total repeal of the 1962 covenant.

DISSENT: (Brennan, J.) Lawful exercises of the states' police powers take precedence over private rights. The states were faced with overall environmental and energy problems that urgently needed a solution. Creditors cannot be disadvantaged without proper justification. I find such justification herein.

▶ ANALYSIS

If the debt itself is not compromised, but merely a security provision, no violation of the Contracts Clause occurs. Therefore, where a state guarantees to continue the operation of a plant, the guarantee is not for perpetuity. If the health or safety of the community demands it, the operation may be ceased without the impairment of contract. The value of the bonds themselves does not have to be destroyed before an impairment of contract rights may be found. *W. B. Worthen Co. v. Kavanaugh*, 295 U.S. 56 (1935).

■=■

Quicknotes

CONTRACTS CLAUSE Article 1, section 10 of the U.S. Constitution prohibiting states from passing any "law impairing the Obligation of Contracts."

POLICE POWER The power of a government to impose restrictions on the rights of private persons, so long as those restrictions are reasonably related to the promotion and protection of public health, safety, morals and the general welfare.

■=■

Loretto v. Teleprompter Manhattan CATV Corp.

Landlord (P) v. Cable TV company (D)

458 U.S. 419 (1982).

NATURE OF CASE: Appeal from dismissal of class action to enjoin state law that required a landlord (P) to permit cable television (CATV) (D) companies to install their facilities on the landlord's property for a nominal fee.

FACT SUMMARY: New York law provided that landlords had to permit cable television operators (D) to install cable facilities on their property. Loretto (P), a landlord whose apartment building was burdened by a forced cable installation, sued on the ground that the installation was an uncompensated taking of her property.

RULE OF LAW

A permanent physical occupation of private property authorized by the government constitutes a taking of property for which just compensation is due under the Fifth and Fourteenth Amendments.

FACTS: New York law provided that landlords had to permit cable television operators (D) to install cable facilities on their property and, by regulation, fixed $1 as reasonable compensation for such forced installations. Loretto (P), a landlord whose apartment building was burdened by Teleprompter's (D) cable installation, filed a class action for damages and injunctive relief on behalf of all landlords similarly burdened by forced cable installations on the ground that the installations pursuant to New York law were uncompensated takings of the landlords' property. A New York trial court dismissed the action, and New York's Court of Appeals (highest appellate court) affirmed. The Supreme Court granted review.

ISSUE: Does a permanent physical occupation of private property authorized by the government constitute a taking of property for which just compensation is due under the Fifth and Fourteenth Amendments?

HOLDING AND DECISION: (Marshall, J.) Yes. A permanent physical occupation authorized by government is a taking without regard to the public interests that it may serve. A summary of the case law reveals that a case for compensation occurs when the government deliberately occupies, or allows it agents to occupy, private property by a permanent physical occupation, regardless of the interests served or even if the occupation has only a minimal economic impact on the owner. The extent of the occupation is only a relevant factor in determining how much compensation is due, not whether a taking has occurred. Here, Teleprompter's (D) cable installation on Loretto's (P) building, involving hardware that physically attached to the roof and the exterior walls, was a taking under the traditional test.

DISSENT: (Blackmun, J.) As the majority indicated, there is no clear line between where regulation ends and taking begins. Nonetheless, the majority has created just such a bright-line test. The majority engages in an untenable distinction between "temporary" invasions, which are subject to a balancing test, and permanent physical occupations, which are takings without regard to other factors that a court might ordinarily examine. This is an unsound approach because it undercuts the legislative judgment.

▶ ANALYSIS

Permanent physical occupations trigger a per se takings rule. As in *Loretto*, which involved an occupation of about a cubic foot in size, the size of the physical occupation relates only to compensation, and is not determinative of whether a taking has occurred. A difficult issue with the per se rule is whether there is a permanent physical occupation of property when the government requires public access on the property.

■■■

Quicknotes

TAKINGS CLAUSE Provision of the Fifth Amendment to the U.S. Constitution prohibiting the government from taking private property for public use without providing just compensation therefor.

■■■

Pennsylvania Coal Co. v. Mahon

Coal mining company (D) v. Landowner (P)

260 U.S. 393 (1922).

NATURE OF CASE: Action by property owner to enjoin certain operations on adjacent property.

FACT SUMMARY: A Pennsylvania statute forbade the mining of coal in such fashion as to cause the subsidence of any structure used as a human habitation.

🏛 RULE OF LAW
While private property may be regulated to a certain degree, a taking under the Fifth Amendment will be found if the regulation results in a severe diminution of value. At a certain magnitude, there must be an exercise of eminent domain and compensation to sustain the regulatory act. While considerable deference is to be given the legislature's judgment, each case will turn upon its particular facts.

FACTS: In 1878, the Pennsylvania Coal Co. (D) conveyed some land but reserved in the deed the right to remove all coal under the land. The grantee agreed to assume any resulting damage. Mahon (P), who later acquired the land, was bound by the deed. Mahon (P), wanting to prevent further mining under the land, claimed that a 1922 state law changed the coal company's (D) rights. The act forbade the mining of coal in such manner as to cause the subsidence of any structure used as a human habitation with certain exceptions. Mahon's (P) injunction was denied, the trial court maintaining that the Act would be unconstitutional if applied to the present case. On appeal, the state supreme court reversed, holding that the statute was a legitimate exercise of the police power.

ISSUE: Must a state which, through legislation, destroys previously existing contractual and property rights between private parties to the extent of severe diminution of property value give compensation to the affected party?

HOLDING AND DECISION: (Holmes, J.) Yes. While private property may be regulated to a certain degree, a taking under the Fifth Amendment will be found if the regulation results in a severe diminution of value. At a certain magnitude, there must be an exercise of eminent domain and compensation to sustain the regulatory act. While considerable deference is to be given the legislature's judgment, each case will turn upon its particular facts. Where damage is inflicted on a single private house, even if similar damage is inflicted on others in different places, there is no public interest. On the other hand, the damage to the coal company's (D) contractual and property rights is considerable. The act cannot be sustained where, as an exercise of the police power, it affects reserved rights. To make coal mining commercially unprofitable is, in effect, to

destroy it. The rights of the public in a street purchased by eminent domain are those it has paid for. A strong public desire to improve the public condition is not enough to justify achieving it by a shorter cut than the constitutional way of paying for the charge. This is a question of degree and cannot be disposed of by general propositions. So long as private individuals or communities take the risk of contracting for or purchasing only surface rights, they must bear the loss.

DISSENT: (Brandeis, J.) Every restriction on the use of property is an abridgment by the state of rights in property without making compensation. Here, the restriction was only against a noxious use of property that remains in the Coal Company's (D) possession. The Company (D), once it discontinues its noxious use, is free to enjoy its property as before. A restriction does not cease to be public simply because some individuals may be benefited.

▶ ANALYSIS

Eventually, the same analysis of the "taking" issue was used in *United States v. Causby*, 328 U.S. 265 (1946). There, a group of chicken farmers who owned land adjacent to a military airport claimed that, as a result of the noise of planes flying over their property, their chickens were frightened literally to death and egg production fell off. Rejecting the government's argument that any damage was merely consequential of the public's right of freedom of transit, Justice Douglas, writing for the majority, stated, "It is the owner's loss, not the taker's gain, which is the measure of the value of the property taken. . . . The owner's right to possess and exploit the land—that is to say, his beneficial ownership of it—would be destroyed. . . . It would not be a case of incidental damages arising from a legalized nuisance." In dissent, Justice Black warned that "the effect of the court's decision is to limit, by the imposition of relatively absolute constitutional barriers, possible future adjustments through legislation and regulation which might become necessary with the growth of air transportation, and [because] the Constitution does not contain such barriers."

■■■

Quicknotes

POLICE POWER The power of a government to impose restrictions on the rights of private persons, so long as those restrictions are reasonably related to the promotion and protection of public health, safety, morals and the general welfare.

Continued on next page.

TAKINGS CLAUSE Provision of the Fifth Amendment to the U.S. Constitution prohibiting the government from taking private property for public use without providing just compensation therefor.

Miller v. Schoene

Tree owners (P) v. State official (D)

276 U.S. 272 (1928).

NATURE OF CASE: Appeal by property owners from state order to cut down certain trees on their property without compensation to prevent the spread of a tree disease.

FACT SUMMARY: Virginia mandated the uncompensated destruction of red cedar trees to prevent the spread of a tree disease. Tree owners (P) who were ordered to cut down their red cedars claimed the order was an uncompensated taking.

🏛 RULE OF LAW
The government does not effect a taking when it decides to destroy one class of property in order to preserve another class of property that it deems of greater value to the public.

FACTS: Acting under the Cedar Rust Act of Virginia, Schoene (D), the state's entomologist, ordered Miller (P) and other property owners to cut down red cedar trees infected with cedar rust that were on their property. Cedar rust is a highly infectious plant disease that does not directly affect the red cedar, but does destroy the fruit and leaves of the apple. It is communicable by spores that travel up to two miles, and the only way to protect the apple is to destroy the red cedar. Apple growing was one of Virginia's principal multimillion dollar agricultural businesses that was important economically to the state, and the Act was intended to protect apple orchards in the state. The destruction of the red cedars was uncompensated, and the property owners (P) challenged the order as an uncompensated taking. The state courts affirmed the order, and the Supreme Court granted review.

ISSUE: Does the government effect a taking when it decides to destroy one class of property in order to preserve another class of property that it deems of greater value to the public?

HOLDING AND DECISION: (Stone, J.) No. Virginia had to make a choice between the preservation of one class of property and that of the other wherever they were in relatively close proximity to each other. "When forced to such a choice the state does not exceed its constitutional powers by deciding upon the destruction of one class of property in order to save another which, in the judgment of the legislature, is of greater value to the public." This is not just a choice between two private interests, where the burdens of one are being shifted to the other. Here, there is also a significant public interest in preferring one of those private interests over the other, even to the point of its destruction. Thus, as here, where the choice between two

interests is unavoidable, and the public policy goals are not unreasonable, the state's exercise of its police power is not an unconstitutional taking.

▶ ANALYSIS

It is not a taking when government regulates property to prohibit nuisances. Although the Court did not reach the issue of whether the red cedar trees were a public nuisance, it deferred to Virginia's legislative declaration that any such trees that harbored cedar rust, were, in effect, a public nuisance. The Court also hinted that if Virginia had taken no action and had not enacted the Cedar Rust Act, its inaction could also be considered a form of regulation. The Court said that "It would have been none the less a choice if, instead of enacting the present statute, the state, by doing nothing, had permitted serious injury to the apple orchards within its borders to go on unchecked." Taking this dicta to its logical conclusion could lead to takings claims for any government inaction that leads to reduction in value or destruction of property, and would render incoherent the traditional notions of private property.

■=■

Quicknotes

POLICE POWER The power of a government to impose restrictions on the rights of private persons, so long as those restrictions are reasonably related to the promotion and protection of public health, safety, morals and the general welfare.

TAKINGS CLAUSE Provision of the Fifth Amendment to the U.S. Constitution prohibiting the government from taking private property for public use without providing just compensation therefor.

■=■

Penn Central Transportation Co. v. New York City

Property owner (P) v. Municipality (D)

438 U.S. 104 (1978).

NATURE OF CASE: Appeal of action challenging application of municipal landmark preservation law.

FACT SUMMARY: Penn Central (P) was denied a permit to erect a skyscraper over Grand Central Station, a designated landmark.

🏛 RULE OF LAW
A city may, as part of a comprehensive landmark preservation scheme, place restrictions on development affecting the landmark without paying "just compensation."

FACTS: New York (D) enacted a comprehensive landmark preservation ordinance requiring Commission approval prior to development affecting a designated landmark. In exchange for losing development rights, the owners of designated property were permitted to transfer development rights to other property. Grand Central Station, belonging to Penn Central (P), was designated a landmark. The Landmark Commission denied an application for the erection of a skyscraper over the station. Penn Central (P) filed suit, claiming that the ordinance constituted a "taking" in the Fifth Amendment sense. Penn Central (P) did not argue that Grand Central Station was profitable. The New York Court of Appeals held for New York City (D), and Penn Central (P) appealed.

ISSUE: May a city, as part of a comprehensive landmark preservation scheme, place restrictions on development affecting the landmark without paying "just compensation?"

HOLDING AND DECISION: (Brennan, J.) Yes. A city may, as part of a comprehensive landmark preservation scheme, place restrictions on development affecting the landmark without paying "just compensation." No precise rule exists for determining when regulation of private property becomes a taking in the Constitutional sense. Some factors include whether a physical invasion occurred, whether the interference is arbitrary or part of a common plan, and whether any reasonable return is left on the property. An analysis of these factors leads to the conclusion that no taking occurred. There was no invasion. The regulation was part of a comprehensive plan. Analysis also reveals that a reasonable return on the property still remains. This is especially true in light of the fact that Penn Central (P) is the beneficiary of transferred development rights. It is settled that a government may deny an owner the most profitable use of his property without a taking occurring, and this rule applies here.

DISSENT: (Rehnquist, J.) The City's law on preserving landmarks constitutes a taking that requires just compensation for the transportation company. Where the private landowner must bear substantial costs to comply with a law enacted for the public good, while realizing only the hollow benefit of honor for helping to promote the public good, a taking of private property has occurred. A city's difficult financial condition does not justify circumventing the constitutionally required payment for the taking.

▶ ANALYSIS

The Court has been highly deferential to state authority in this area of the law. While examples of holdings in favor of owners do exist (e.g., *Pennsylvania Coal Co. v. Mahon*, 260 U.S. 393 (1922)), it is difficult for an owner to prevail. Generally speaking, in the absence of an invasion or outright destruction, the regulation will not be held to constitute a taking.

■=■

Quicknotes

TAKINGS CLAUSE Provision of the Fifth Amendment to the U.S. Constitution prohibiting the government from taking private property for public use without providing just compensation therefor.

■=■

Lucas v. South Carolina Coastal Council

Real estate developer (P) v. State (D)

505 U.S. 1003 (1992).

NATURE OF CASE: Appeal of reversal of compensation award for a government "taking."

FACT SUMMARY: The Coastal Council (D) prevented Lucas (P) from building homes on his beachfront property.

🏛 RULE OF LAW
Where regulation prohibits all economically beneficial use of land, and the proscribed use could not have been prohibited under state nuisance law, the regulation is a "taking" that requires "just compensation" to be paid to the landowner.

FACTS: In 1986, Lucas (P) purchased two vacant beachfront lots in a residential area. In 1988, South Carolina passed a law creating a coastal zone in which no habitable improvements could be built. The law's stated purpose was to protect property from storms, tides, and beach erosion, and as an environmental protection. The law prevented Lucas (P) from constructing two homes he had planned. In suing the Coastal Council (D), Lucas (P) did not challenge the state's right to pass the law or its justifications for doing so. He simply claimed the law rendered his property valueless, which amounted to a "taking" under the Fifth Amendment, entitling him to just compensation. The trial court agreed, the South Carolina Supreme Court reversed, and Lucas (P) appealed.

ISSUE: Where regulation prohibits all economically beneficial use of land, and the proscribed use could not have been prohibited under state nuisance law, is the regulation a "taking" that requires "just compensation" to be paid to the landowner?

HOLDING AND DECISION: (Scalia, J.) Yes. Where regulation prohibits all economically beneficial use of land, and the proscribed use could not have been prohibited under state nuisance law, the regulation is a "taking" that requires that "just compensation" be paid to the landowner. Mandated preservation of private land looks like a conversion of private property to public, a classic "taking." Government cannot be permitted to regulate in this manner without compensation simply by reciting some police power or "prevention of harmful use" rationale. Such regulations must account for owners' traditional understandings as to the state's power over their property rights. The source of these understandings is state public and private nuisance law. Thus, the owner of a lake bed always is aware he may be stopped by law from flooding adjacent property to create a landfill. If the state restricts this use, even to deprive him of all economic benefit, he is not entitled to compensation. Here, however, South Carolina common-law principles probably would not prevent Lucas (P) from building homes on his land. If the state court determines they would not, Lucas (P) is entitled to just compensation.

DISSENT: (Blackmun, J.) This Court has long held that regulation preventing property use that the state finds harmful to citizens is not a taking. History indicates no common-law limit on state power to regulate harmful uses, even to the point of destroying all economic value. The health and safety justifications for the South Carolina law have not been questioned.

▶ ANALYSIS

Traditionally, "takings" were limited to direct appropriation of property by the government. Since this view was rejected in *Pennsylvania Coal Co. v. Mahon*, 260 U.S. 393 (1922), the Court has engaged in a case-by-case, ad hoc determination of when regulation becomes a "taking." The *Lucas* majority identified two categories of regulations that constitute takings regardless of the public interest in the regulation. One category is defined in the holding. The other is where the government physically invades the owner's property (e.g., where a city law requires landlords to place cable television facilities in their buildings).

■=■

Quicknotes

POLICE POWER The power of a government to impose restrictions on the rights of private persons, so long as those restrictions are reasonably related to the promotion and protection of public health, safety, morals and the general welfare.

TAKINGS CLAUSE Provision of the Fifth Amendment to the U.S. Constitution prohibiting the government from taking private property for public use without providing just compensation therefor.

■=■

Dolan v. City of Tigard

Store owner (P) v. Municipality (D)

512 U.S. 374 (1994).

NATURE OF CASE: Appeal from judgment affirming municipality's permit conditions in regulatory takings action.

FACT SUMMARY: The City of Tigard (D) granted Dolan's (P) permit to expand her store, conditioned on her dedicating a portion of her property to provide a flood plain and a bike path.

🏛 RULE OF LAW
Exactions imposed by a municipality's permit conditions must be roughly proportionate to the impact of the proposed development.

FACTS: Dolan (P) planned to double the size of her plumbing supply store located in the City of Tigard (D). In order to comply with open space and drainage requirements, Tigard (D) required that Dolan (P) dedicate a portion of her property to Tigard (D) for improvement of a storm drainage system and construction of a bike path. The Planning Commission (D) denied Dolan's (P) request for a variance, finding that the required flood plain and bike path were reasonably related to Dolan's (P) intensified development and to Tigard's (P) need for flood control and traffic reduction. The state supreme court affirmed, and Dolan (P) appealed, contending that the easement conditions violated her Fifth Amendment right to just compensation. The U.S. Supreme Court granted review.

ISSUE: Must exactions imposed by a municipality's permit conditions be roughly proportionate to the impact of the proposed development?

HOLDING AND DECISION: (Rehnquist, C.J.) Yes. Exactions imposed by a municipality's permit conditions must be roughly proportionate to the impact of the proposed development. The Court must first determine whether the "essential nexus" exists between the legitimate state interest and the permit conditions exacted by the city. The requisite nexus clearly exists between preventing flooding and limiting development in a flood plain, and between traffic reduction and providing alternative means of transportation. The second part of the analysis asks whether the degree of the exactions imposed by the city bears the required relationship of "rough proportionality" to the projected impact of Dolan's (P) development. In this case, the City of Tigard (D) wanted not only to prevent Dolan (P) from building in the flood plain but also to require her to dedicate that portion of her property to the public. [Because the record does not reflect evidence required under the new standard of "rough proportionality," the Court remanded the case for further proceedings consistent with this new standard.] Reversed and remanded.

DISSENT: (Stevens, J.) If a municipality can demonstrate that the conditions it has imposed in a land-use permit are rational, impartial and conducive to fulfilling the aims of a valid land-use plan, as Tigard (D) has done in this case, a strong presumption of validity should attach to those conditions.

▶ ANALYSIS

The majority's primary concern was with the loss of Dolan's (P) ability to exclude others—"one of the most essential sticks in the bundle of rights that are commonly characterized as property." Although that intangible interest is undoubtedly worthy of constitutional protection, as J. Stevens noted in his dissent, it is one that is already protected from arbitrary state action by the Due Process Clause. The majority's imposition of a novel, heightened burden of proof on a city overturns the property owner's traditional burden of demonstrating that permit conditions have unreasonably impaired the economic value of the proposed improvement.

■═■

Quicknotes

TAKINGS CLAUSE Provision of the Fifth Amendment to the U.S. Constitution prohibiting the government from taking private property for public use without providing just compensation therefor.

■═■

Palazzolo v. Rhode Island

Landowner (P) v. State (D)

533 U.S. 606 (2001).

NATURE OF CASE: Suit by landowner against state to permit development of coastal property.

FACT SUMMARY: Palazzolo (P) petitioned the Coastal Management Resources Council of Rhode Island (D) several times for permission to develop his coastline property. The Council denied his request each time. After the final denial, Palazzolo (P) sued Rhode Island (D), arguing that the Council's action denied him all use of his property, without just compensation, in violation of the Takings Clause.

🏛 RULE OF LAW
(1) A property owner who takes title after a government regulation restricts the property's use can assert a takings claim for the property.
(2) A regulatory restriction that allows a property to retain 6 percent of its total development value, where the permitted use is a substantial residence, does not constitute a total taking of the property.

FACTS: Palazzolo (P) and some of his associates formed a corporation and invested in coastal property in Rhode Island (D) in 1959. Palazzolo (P) bought out his associates and, now the sole shareholder in the corporation, petitioned a Rhode Island (D) agency to develop the property in 1962. That request was denied, as were similar requests in 1963 and 1966. In 1971, Rhode Island (D) created the Rhode Island Coastal Management Council, which promulgated regulations that designated waterfront property such as Palazzolo's (P) as "coastal wetlands." Palazzolo (P) personally took title to the property in 1978 when title passed directly to him following the revocation of his corporation's charter. He sought to develop the property again in 1983 and 1985, but the Council rejected his proposals both times; in 1983, the Council found that the proposed development would conflict with the Council's management plan for the area. Palazzolo (P) challenged the 1985 decision in court, suing the state for a total taking of his property, which his proof showed as having a development value of $3.15 million. Even with the Council's rejection of his proposal, however, Palazzolo's (P) property included an upland parcel that had development value of $200,000. The trial court ruled against Palazzolo (P), and so did the Rhode Island Supreme Court. The state supreme court specifically decided that Palazzolo (P) could not assert a takings claim because he took title to the property after the Council's regulatory restrictions took effect, and that the Council's denial could not be a total taking because a portion of the property retained a substantial development value. Palazzolo (P) petitioned the U.S. Supreme Court for certiorari.

ISSUE:
(1) Can a property owner who takes title after a government regulation restricts the property's use assert a takings claim for the property?
(2) Does a regulatory restriction that allows a property to retain 6 percent of its total development value, where the permitted use is a substantial residence, constitute a total taking of the property?

HOLDING AND DECISION: (Kennedy, J.)
(1) Yes. A property owner who takes title after a government regulation restricts the property's use can assert a takings claim for the property. The Takings Clause permits landowners to claim that certain government regulations are so unreasonable or burdensome that they are actually takings of property requiring just compensation by the government. Time does not lessen the burden of an unreasonable regulation, and future generations, too, therefore can assert takings claims in such circumstances, as Palazzolo (P) as done here.
(2) No. A regulatory restriction that allows a property to retain 6 percent of its total development value, where the permitted use is a substantial residence, does not constitute a total taking of the property. Government regulations must allow a landowner more than a token use of an affected property. Rhode Island (D) has satisfied that requirement here because Palazzolo (P) still can use his property by building a substantial residence on the upland parcel. Affirmed in part and reversed in part.

CONCURRENCE: (O'Connor, J.) Even under this case's holding on restrictions imposed before a landowner takes title to a property, *Penn Central Transportation Co. v. New York City*, 438 U.S. 104 (1978), still provides the framework for analyzing partial regulatory takings.

CONCURRENCE: (Scalia, J.) That a restriction on property was adopted before a landowner takes title is irrelevant to deciding whether the restriction constitutes a compensable taking.

CONCURRENCE AND DISSENT: (Stevens, J.) A landowner may challenge improperly enacted restrictions as takings at any time. For properly enacted restrictions, however, only the owner who held title at the time of the taking—that is, when the restriction was imposed on the property—may recover for a taking.

DISSENT: (Breyer, J.) Government regulations do not amount to a taking, even if they significantly reduce a given

Continued on next page.

property's value, if they are generally applicable and designed to prevent substantial public harm. Rhode Island's coastal wetlands regulation probably satisfies that standard.

▶ *ANALYSIS*

Justice Kennedy's majority opinion indirectly includes an important practice tip at the end of his majority opinion. That tip: Always raise available meritorious arguments at the earliest opportunity. Palazzolo (P) failed to argue in the state courts for a partial regulatory taking. Instead, he argued for a total-deprivation taking, a claim easily rejected because of the $200,000 development value of the upland parcel on his property. Palazzolo's (P) failure to raise the more nuanced partial-takings argument in a timely manner very likely cost him some amount of recovery because the Court refused to hear the untimely argument at all.

■■■

Quicknotes

TAKINGS CLAUSE Provision of the Fifth Amendment to the U.S. Constitution prohibiting the government from taking private property for public use without providing just compensation therefor.

■■■

Tahoe-Sierra Preservation Council, Inc. v.
Tahoe Regional Planning Agency

Landowners (P) v. Regional planning agency (D)

535 U.S. 302 (2002).

NATURE OF CASE: Appeal from decision that a moratorium on development imposed during the process of devising a comprehensive land-use plan does not constitute a per se taking of property requiring compensation under the Takings Clause.

FACT SUMMARY: Tahoe Regional Planning Agency (TRPA)(D), established to preserve Lake Tahoe, imposed a 32-month moratorium on development in the Lake Tahoe area while formulating a comprehensive land-use plan for the area. Once TRPA devised such a plan, California challenged it, and enjoined development for another three years. Landowners (P) affected by the moratorium filed suit, claiming that TRPA's (D) actions constituted a taking of their property without just compensation in violation of the Takings Clause.

RULE OF LAW

A moratorium on development imposed during the process of devising a comprehensive land-use plan does not constitute a per se taking of property requiring compensation under the Takings Clause.

FACTS: Tahoe Regional Planning Agency (TRPA)(D), established to preserve Lake Tahoe—which had an algae problem that was exacerbated by development—imposed a 32-month moratorium on development in the Lake Tahoe area while formulating a comprehensive land-use plan of environmentally sound growth for the area. During the moratorium, virtually all development was prohibited. Once TRPA devised such a plan, California challenged it, and enjoined development for another three years. Landowners (P) affected by the moratorium filed suit, claiming that TRPA's (D) actions constituted a taking of their property without just compensation in violation of the Takings Clause. The district court found a taking, but the court of appeals reversed. The Supreme Court granted review.

ISSUE: Does a moratorium on development imposed during the process of devising a comprehensive land-use plan constitute a per se taking of property requiring compensation under the Takings Clause?

HOLDING AND DECISION: (Stevens, J.) No. The issue here is whether a 32-month moratorium is equivalent to an "obliteration of the value" of a fee simple interest in property. The landowners (P) contend under *Lucas v. South Carolina Coastal Council*, 505 U.S. 1003 (1992), that the mere enactment of a temporary regulation that, while in effect, denies a property owner of all viable economic use of her or his property, gives rise to an unqualified constitutional obligation to compensate for

the value of the property's use during that period; they want to sever the 32-month period from the rest of the fee simple estate. However, defining the property interest taken in terms of the regulation being challenged is circular. Using that logic, every normal permit process would become a categorical taking. The landowners' "conceptual severance" argument is unavailing under *Penn Central Transportation Co. v. New York City*, 438 U.S. 104 (1978), which requires looking at "the parcel as a whole" in regulatory takings cases. Therefore, disaggregating property into temporal segments, as the district court did, is erroneous, and the Court has consistently rejected such an approach to the "denominator" question. Whereas a permanent deprivation of an owner's use of the entire property is a taking of "the parcel as a whole," a temporary restriction that merely causes a diminution in value is not; a fee simple cannot be rendered valueless by a temporary restriction because its value will recover when the restriction is lifted. *Lucas* was carved out for the "extraordinary case" in which a regulation permanently deprives property of all use; the default rule remains that a fact-specific inquiry is required in the regulatory taking context. Nevertheless, the Court will consider the landowners' (P) argument that the interest in protecting property owners from bearing public burdens "which, in all fairness and justice, should be borne by the public as a whole," justifies creating a new categorical rule. "Fairness and justice" will not be better served by a categorical rule that any deprivation of all economic use, no matter how brief, constitutes a compensable taking. That rule would apply to numerous normal delays in obtaining, e.g., building permits, and would require changes in practices that have long been considered permissible exercises of the police power. Such an important change in the law should be the product of legislative rulemaking, not adjudication. It may be true that a moratorium lasting more than one year should be viewed with special skepticism, but the district court found that the instant delay was not unreasonable. The restriction's duration is one factor for a court to consider in appraising regulatory takings claims, but with respect to that factor, the temptation to adopt per se rules in either direction must be resisted. The interest in "fairness and justice" will be better served in cases such as this one by using the *Penn Central* approach rather than by announcing a new categorical rule.

DISSENT: (Rehnquist, C.J.) Here, the ban on development lasting almost six years does not resemble any traditional land-use planning device. The majority is concerned that applying

Continued on next page.

Lucas here would compel a finding that many traditional, short-term, land-use planning devices are takings. However, the Court has recognized that property rights are enjoyed under an implied limitation. When a regulation merely delays a final land-use decision, there are other background principles of state property law that prevent the delay from being deemed a taking, as in the case of normal delays in obtaining building permits, changes in zoning ordinances, variances, and the like. However, a moratorium prohibiting all economic use for a period of six years is not one of the longstanding, implied limitations of state property law. Unlike a permit system in which it is expected that once conditions are met, a project will be approved, a moratorium that prohibits all uses is by definition contemplating a new land-use plan that would prohibit all uses.

▶ ANALYSIS

In a separate dissent, Justice Thomas called into question the majority's use of *Penn Central*'s "parcel as a whole" standard. He argued that if TRPA had enacted a permanent ban on development that was repealed after 32 months, there would have been a compensable taking under *Lucas* and that the timing of the repeal would have only been relevant to the issue of compensation, not to whether a taking had occurred. Under this approach, determining the "denominator" (the total property interest relevant to the claim) is arbitrary, because regulations prohibiting all productive uses of property are subject to *Lucas*'s per se rule regardless of whether the property retains theoretical useful life and value, if and when the "temporary" moratorium is lifted.

Quicknotes

POLICE POWER The power of a government to impose restrictions on the rights of private persons, so long as those restrictions are reasonably related to the promotion and protection of public health, safety, morals and the general welfare.

TAKINGS CLAUSE Provision of the Fifth Amendment to the U.S. Constitution prohibiting the government from taking private property for public use without providing just compensation therefor.

Hawaii Housing Authority v. Midkiff

State agency (D) v. Landlords (P)

467 U.S. 229 (1984).

NATURE OF CASE: Appeal from decision that legislation designed to break the oligopoly of land ownership in a state through the forced transfer of title from landlords to tenants violated the Public Use requirement of the Fifth Amendment.

FACT SUMMARY: Hawaii enacted legislation that was designed to break the oligopoly of land ownership in that state by creating a Housing Authority and empowering it to effectively transfer title from landlords to tenants. Landlords (P) challenged the law on the ground that it violated the Fifth Amendment's Public Use requirement.

🏛 RULE OF LAW
The forced, compensated transfer by a state of title to land from landlords to tenants to reduce the concentration of fee ownership in the state is a taking related to a public use.

FACTS: A historical development of the settlement of the Hawaiian Islands was that the state and federal governments owned about half of the total land on the islands, and that the rest was owned by very few landholders—resulting in an oligopoly. Concluding that this concentrated landownership was responsible for inflating land prices and injuring the public tranquility and welfare, the Hawaii Legislature enacted the Land Reform Act. This Act created the Hawaii Housing Authority (HHA) (D), which was empowered to seize the fee titles when enough tenants in any given "development tract" asked it to do so. After the fee titles were taken and paid for, the HHA (D) was authorized to sell the titles to the tenants and to lend the tenants up to 90 percent of the purchase price, effectively using the state's sovereign power to transfer ownership of land from landlords to tenants. Landlords (P) challenged the Act in district court on the ground that it violated the Public Use Clause of the Fifth Amendment. The district court held that the Act was constitutional, but the Court of Appeals reversed. The Supreme Court granted review.

ISSUE: Is the forced, compensated transfer by a state of title to land from landlords to tenants to reduce the concentration of fee ownership in the state a taking related to a public use?

HOLDING AND DECISION: (O'Connor, J.) Yes. The "public use" requirement is coterminous with the police power, even in the context of eminent domain. Where the exercise of the eminent domain power is rationally related to a conceivable public purpose, a compensated taking is not proscribed by the Public Use Clause. Therefore, here, the Act is constitutional because it is an effort to reduce the social and economic evils of a land oligopoly. Regulating oligopoly and its attendant evils is an exercise of the police power. Thus, no purely private taking is involved here. Attacking the evils of concentrated land ownership is a legitimate public purpose, and the condemnation power to achieve this purpose is not irrational. Therefore, the Public Use requirements of the Fifth and Fourteenth Amendments are satisfied.

▶ ANALYSIS

As this case illustrates, the Court's definition of "public use" is so expansive that almost any taking will meet the public use requirement; the Court is extremely deferential to the legislature about what constitutes a public use. As the language in this case shows, so long as the taking is rationally related to any "conceivable" public purpose, the public use requirement is satisfied.

■■■

Quicknotes

POLICE POWER The power of a government to impose restrictions on the rights of private persons, so long as those restrictions are reasonably related to the promotion and protection of public health, safety, morals and the general welfare.

PUBLIC USE Basis for governmental taking of property pursuant to its power of eminent domain so that property taken may be utilized for the benefit of the public at large.

TAKINGS CLAUSE Provision of the Fifth Amendment to the U.S. Constitution prohibiting the government from taking private property for public use without providing just compensation therefor.

■■■

Kelo v. City of New London

Homeowner (P) v. City (D)

545 U.S. 469 (2005).

NATURE OF CASE: Appeal from judgment for defendant city in condemnation suit.

FACT SUMMARY: New London, Connecticut (D), condemned the private residences of Kelo (P) and others in order to use their property as part of a planned economic development.

🏛 RULE OF LAW
Governmental economic development constitutes a "public use" under the Fifth Amendment's eminent domain.

FACTS: New London, Connecticut (D), revitalized the New London Development Corp. (NLDC) to propose plans for economic development after decades of decline. Pfizer, a pharmaceutical company, also announced plans to build a $300 million facility next to Fort Trumball in the New London (D) area. The NLDC operated as a private entity, but its plans intended to benefit the city's growth. New London (D) authorized NLDC to purchase or condemn property in its name for the purpose of its approved development plan. Kelo (P) owned property in the Fort Trumball development area and refused to sell. New London (D) initiated condemnation proceedings although Kelo's (P) property was not blighted or otherwise deteriorating. Kelo (P) filed suit in state court against New London (D) claiming that the condemnation violated the taking clause's "public use" restriction. The Connecticut Supreme Court held for the defendant city and Kelo (P) appealed to the U.S. Supreme Court.

ISSUE: Does governmental economic development constitute a "public use" under the Fifth Amendment's eminent domain?

HOLDING AND DECISION: (Stevens, J.) Yes. Governmental economic development constitutes a "public use" under the Fifth Amendment's eminent domain. The government cannot transfer private property from one private entity to another even if the first is adequately compensated. The government can, however, take private property from one private entity with just compensation for "public use." This particular case does not fit in either scenario. New London (D) cannot offer a pretextual "public use" if the true benefit is to a definable class of private individuals, but no such class can be identified here. It is true that the planned development will not be completely open to the public and the stores will not act as common carriers to the public, but such a literal definition of "public use" is not required. The precedent in *Berman*, 348 U.S. 26 (1954), and *Midkiff*, 467 U.S. 229 (1984), supports a broad interpretation of "public use." Kelo (P) requests a bright-line rule for "public use" that would not include

economic development. It is longstanding tradition of government to promote economic development and that development may be better served by using a private entity rather than government agencies. A bright-line rule cannot issue because legislatures need flexibility when determining appropriate action for the economic development of its cities. States are free to further restrict "public use" requirements beyond those of the federal government and many have already done so. Affirmed.

CONCURRENCE: (Kennedy, J.) A party may make a claim of pretextual "public use" taking that actually benefits a private entity. A presumption exists that the government acted reasonably in its taking, but courts should review all claims to the contrary by looking closely at the facts of the case. A city may take property with the public only incidentally benefiting. Here, no facts existed to show that Pfizer alone would benefit from New London (D) condemning Kelo's (P) property.

DISSENT: (O'Connor, J.) The Court's decision eliminates "for public use" from the takings clause because it allows for incidental public benefit from ordinary private use of property. The government simply cannot condemn private property when the condemnation is to benefit another private person or entity. The Court's reliance on *Berman* and *Midkiff* is misplaced because those cases actually underscore the public use versus private benefit. Both cases involved takings that directly benefited the public. Those properties were blighted and causing harm to the public in their current use. When private property is being used in its ordinary, non-harmful fashion, it cannot be taken to benefit another private user. It is nearly impossible to isolate the true motives behind a governmental taking, so the government can now condemn with near impunity. The government can also always seek to improve a property's use if the private owner is not making the most productive or attractive use of it. The facts of today's case do not justify the holding.

DISSENT: (Thomas, J.) The Court adopts the overly broad "public use" definitions of *Berman* and *Midkiff* without reasoned analysis. A legislature's determination of what constitutes "public use" is not entitled to such blind deference. The original intent of the Public Use Clause was to provide full legal rights to the public for the use of any condemned property. The Court should return to the original intent. Further, the property most likely to be taken under this new definition will be that of poor communities lacking political power and likely using their property at less than

Continued on next page.

its most productive use. These communities should be protected rather than exploited.

▶ *ANALYSIS*

This case caused a firestorm of fury throughout the United States. Multiple states quickly passed legislation tightening the state eminent domain laws to restrict the ability of governmental entities to take private property for anything less than blatantly public purposes. A small but vocal group of citizens began a petition to condemn Judge Breyer's private vacation residence so that the property may be put to a "better" use for the public.

■■■

Quicknotes

CONDEMNATION The taking of private property for public use so long as just compensation is paid therefor.

EMINENT DOMAIN The governmental power to take private property for public use so long as just compensation is paid therefor.

PUBLIC USE Basis for governmental taking of property pursuant to its power of eminent domain so that property taken may be utilized for the benefit of the public at large.

TAKINGS CLAUSE Provision of the Fifth Amendment to the U.S. Constitution prohibiting the government from taking private property for public use without providing just compensation therefor.

■■■

Brown v. Legal Foundation of Washington

Attorney's client (P) v. State fund for indigent litigants (D)

538 U.S. 216 (2003).

NATURE OF CASE: Suit by an attorney's client against a state fund for indigent litigants to recover interest earned on the client's funds while they were held in the attorney's trust account.

FACT SUMMARY: An attorney deposited Brown's (P) funds into a lawyer trust account. All interest on client funds in the account automatically became the property of the Legal Foundation of Washington (LFW) (D) because the account was required to participate in the state supreme court's Interest on Lawyer Trust Accounts (IOLTA) program. Brown (P) sued the LFW (D) to recover the interest earned on his funds.

🏛 **RULE OF LAW**
An attorney's client is not entitled to just compensation when a state appropriates interest earned on funds of the client's that the attorney deposits into an IOLTA account.

FACTS: The Washington State Supreme Court requires that client funds held by an attorney be deposited into an IOLTA account if the funds cannot earn net interest for the client. Washington's IOLTA program further requires attorneys to have their banks pay any interest earned on their IOLTA accounts to the LFW (D). The LFW (D) must use the funds for law-related charitable and educational purposes. As required the Washington Supreme Court, Brown's (P) attorney deposited Brown's (P) funds into the attorney's IOLTA account, and the LFW (D) collected the interest earned on Brown's (P) funds. Brown (P) sued the LFW (D) in federal court, alleging that the LFW's (D) appropriation of interest on his funds violated the Takings Clause. The Ninth Circuit Court of Appeals held that the appropriation of interest by the LFW (D) was not a taking and that, even if it were a taking, Brown (P) was entitled to no compensation. Brown petitioned for certiorari.

ISSUE: Is an attorney's client entitled to just compensation when a state appropriates interest earned on funds of the client's that the attorney deposits into an IOLTA account?

HOLDING AND DECISION: (Stevens, J.) No. An attorney's client is not entitled to just compensation when a state appropriates interest earned on funds of the client's that the attorney deposits into an IOLTA account. Although the LFW's (D) appropriation of the interest earned on Brown's (P) funds could be a taking, Brown's just compensation for the taking is zero. Just compensation is measured by how much property the owner loses, not by how much the government gains. Brown (P) has lost nothing because, for his funds to be in the IOLTA account at all, the Washington State Supreme Court's rules required that the funds be incapable of

earning net interest for Brown (P) in a non-IOLTA account. Accordingly, Washington State's IOLTA program does not violate the just-compensation component of the Takings Clause of the Fifth Amendment.

DISSENT: (Scalia, J.) Takings jurisprudence has long recognized that fair market value is the proper measure of just compensation. The majority, however, makes no effort to determine fair market value in this case. Instead, it relies on hypothetical arithmetic to ignore that interest earned on Brown's (P) funds clearly does have value—otherwise, the LFW (D) would have nothing to take from the IOLTA account. The majority fares no better by concluding that transaction costs and bank fees on the IOLTA account would necessarily offset the interest actually earned on the Brown's (P) funds. This Court's just-compensation cases provide no basis for depriving Brown (P) of the fair market value of the interest that he did, in fact, lose.

▶ **ANALYSIS**

The most common use of funds derived from IOLTA accounts—giving more people meaningful access to court—is obviously public and obviously beneficial. At the same time, the majority in *Brown* fails to refute Justice Scalia's central thesis that a government appropriating private property through an IOLTA account has just as obviously taken something of value from the owner without any compensation for the taking.

■══■

Quicknotes

TAKINGS CLAUSE Provision of the Fifth Amendment to the U.S. Constitution prohibiting the government from taking private property for public use without providing just compensation therefor.

■══■

Equal Protection

Quick Reference Rules of Law

Romer v. Evans

Parties not identified.

517 U.S. 620 (1996).

NATURE OF CASE: Appeal of order enjoining enactment of an amendment to a state constitution.

FACT SUMMARY: A Colorado (D) constitutional amendment, Amendment 2, which struck down local antidiscrimination laws based on sexual orientation, was challenged for being violative of the Equal Protection Clause.

🏛 RULE OF LAW
Colorado's Amendment 2 violates the Equal Protection Clause because it singles out a class of citizens, homosexuals, for disfavored legal status.

FACTS: In 1992, Colorado (D) amended its state constitution by a statewide referendum. Amendment 2, as it was designated, provided that the state and local branches of government were forbidden from enacting any laws or regulations that would protect homosexuals from discrimination. Amendment 2 was challenged in court as unconstitutional for violating the Equal Protection Clause. Colorado (D) responded that Amendment 2 simply denied homosexuals any special rights given to protected classes, such as minorities. The trial court enjoined enactment of Amendment 2, the Colorado Supreme Court affirmed, and the U.S. Supreme Court granted certiorari to decide the issue.

ISSUE: Does Colorado's Amendment 2 violate the Equal Protection Clause because it singles out a class of citizens, homosexuals, for disfavored legal status?

HOLDING AND DECISION: (Kennedy, J.) Yes. Colorado's Amendment 2 violates the Equal Protection Clause because it singles out a class of citizens, homosexuals, for disfavored legal status. The Colorado Supreme Court construction of Amendment 2 found that its objective was to repeal existing antidiscrimination ordinances. Thus, Amendment 2 is far reaching in that it places homosexuals in a solitary class, withdrawing legal protection against discrimination and forbidding reinstatement of these policies except by constitutional amendment. Thus, it imposes a special disability on homosexuals, who can now change the law only by amending the state constitution, no matter how local the harm. Generally, legislative classifications are constitutional if they bear a rational relation to a legitimate end. However, Amendment 2 identifies persons by a single trait and denies them protection across the board. Therefore, it violates the principle that the government remain open on impartial terms to all who seek its assistance. Finally, equal protection means that the desire to harm a politically unpopular group is not a legitimate government interest. Amendment 2 is extraordinary and explainable only by animus toward homosexuals. Accordingly, Amendment 2 violates the Equal Protection Clause and is unconstitutional.

DISSENT: (Scalia, J.) Amendment 2 does not violate the Equal Protection Clause. It merely provides that homosexuals in Colorado may not receive preferential treatment unless they first amend the state constitution. The goal of this amendment was not a "bare . . . desire to harm," as the majority concludes, but rather the perfectly legitimate interest of prohibiting special preferences for homosexuals, a group whose behavior has been condemned by governments in this country since the founding until only very recently. The Court has acted politically, not judicially, by concluding otherwise.

▶ ANALYSIS

Justice Scalia's dissenting opinion is astonishing for its not-at-all disguised animosity toward homosexuals, who will no doubt be surprised to find that they are politically powerful. The dissent is also remarkable for its tone of disgust toward the majority. At the heart of the majority decision is the recognition that homosexuality is more of a status (like sex, race, or ethnicity) than a conduct or lifestyle.

■■■

Quicknotes

EQUAL PROTECTION CLAUSE A constitutional provision that each person be guaranteed the same protection of the laws enjoyed by other persons in like circumstances.

■■■

United States Railroad Retirement Board v. Fritz
Federal agency (D) v. Restored railroad employees (P)

449 U.S. 166 (1980).

NATURE OF CASE: Appeal from finding of unconstitutionality of Railroad Retirement Act of 1974.

FACT SUMMARY: Fritz (P) and other active and retired railroad workers alleged that the portions of the Railroad Retirement Act of 1974, which denied them retirement benefits, violated equal protection standards.

🏛 RULE OF LAW
Social and economic legislation enacted by Congress will be upheld under the Equal Protection Clause if it is rationally related to a permissible government objective.

FACTS: Congress enacted the Railroad Retirement Act of 1974 to place that industry's retirement system on a sound financial basis. Under the former system, a person who worked for both railroad and nonrailroad employers received both railroad retirement benefits and Social Security retirement benefits. Under the 1974 act, railroad employees who had qualified for both sets of benefits as of the effective date of the legislation, but who had not yet actually retired, were entitled to receive benefits under both retirement schemes if they had either performed some railroad service during 1974 or as of December 31, 1974, had been employed by the railroad industry for 12 of the preceding 30 calendar months or had completed 25 years of railroad service as of December 31, 1974. Fritz (P) claimed that the distinctions used to determine eligibility for both sets of benefits violated equal protection standards. The lower court agreed, and the Board (D) appealed.

ISSUE: Will social and economic legislation enacted by Congress be upheld under equal protection provisions if it is rationally related to a permissible government objective?

HOLDING AND DECISION: (Rehnquist, J.) Yes. In the field of economic and social welfare, a legislative classification complies with equal protection standards if it has a reasonable basis. A classification is not unconstitutional merely because it results in some inequality. Here, because Congress could have eliminated dual benefits for all classes of employees, it was permissible for Congress to draw lines between groups of employees for the purpose of phasing out those benefits. The test used to determine benefits is not a patently arbitrary method of accomplishing the congressional objective.

DISSENT: (Brennan, J.) A legislative classification may be upheld only if it bears a rational relationship to a legitimate state purpose. Congress has stated that a principal purpose of the act was to preserve the vested, earned benefits of retirees who had already qualified for them. Because the statutory classification here deprives some retirees of vested dual benefits, it is not rationally related to Congress' stated purpose and therefore violates equal protection standards.

▌ ANALYSIS

The Supreme Court has used a reasonableness standard when reviewing legislative and administrative classifications contained in socioeconomic legislation. To be reasonable, a law or regulation must have a legitimate public purpose based upon some conception of the public good. However, the Court has traditionally given great deference to congressional determinations of the nature of public good.

▬═▬

Quicknotes

EQUAL PROTECTION CLAUSE A constitutional provision that each person be guaranteed the same protection of the laws enjoyed by other persons in like circumstances.

▬═▬

Railway Express Agency, Inc. v. New York

Trucking company (D) v. City (P)

336 U.S. 106 (1949).

NATURE OF CASE: Appeal from conviction for violation of a state advertising statute.

FACT SUMMARY: New York (P) had a regulation that prohibited advertising on vehicles but allowed advertising on business vehicles so long as the vehicles are engaged in their owner's usual work and are not used mainly for advertising.

🏛 RULE OF LAW
The Equal Protection Clause does not require that a statute eradicate all evils of the same type or none at all.

FACTS: A New York City (P) regulation prohibited advertising on vehicles. The statute did not prohibit, however, advertising on business vehicles so long as the vehicles are engaged in their owner's usual work and are not used merely or mainly for advertising. Railway (D) is engaged in a nationwide express business. It operated 1900 trucks in New York City (P). It sold space on the exterior of its trucks for advertising. Such advertising was generally unconnected with its business.

ISSUE: Does a regulation that prohibits general advertisements on vehicles while allowing advertisement of products sold by vehicle owners violate equal protection?

HOLDING AND DECISION: (Douglas, J.) No. The Equal Protection Clause does not require that a statute eradicate all evils of the same type or none at all. The court of special sessions concluded that advertising on vehicles using the streets of New York City (P) constituted a distraction to vehicle drivers and pedestrians, therefore affecting the public's safety in the use of the streets. The local authorities may well have concluded that those who advertise their own products on their trucks do not present the same traffic problem in view of the nature and extent of their advertising. The Court cannot say that such a judgment is not an allowable one. The classification has relation to the purpose for which it is made and does not contain the kind of discrimination against which the Equal Protection Clause protects. The fact that New York City (P) does not eliminate all distractions from its streets is immaterial. It is no requirement of equal protection that all evils of the same genus be eradicated or none at all.

CONCURRENCE: (Jackson, J.) Laws must not discriminate between people except upon some reasonable differentiation fairly related to the object of regulation. There is a real difference between doing in self-interest and doing for hire so that it is one thing to tolerate an action done in self-interest and another thing to permit the same action to be done for hire.

▶ ANALYSIS

Traditionally, the Equal Protection Clause supported only minimal judicial intervention. During the late sixties, however, it became the favorite and most far-reaching tool for judicial protection of fundamental rights not specified in the Constitution. For many years, the impact of the Equal Protection Clause was a very limited one. During the decades of extensive court intervention with state economic legislation, substantive due process, not equal protection, provided the touchstone to determine a statute's constitutionality. Also, as the concurring opinion points out, equal protection demanded only a "reasonable differentiation fairly related to the object of regulation." As demonstrated by this case, the rational classification requirement could be satisfied fairly easily, as the courts were extremely deferential to legislative judgment and easily convinced that the means used might relate rationally to a plausible end.

Quicknotes

EQUAL PROTECTION CLAUSE A constitutional provision that each person be guaranteed the same protection of the laws enjoyed by other persons in like circumstances.

RATIONAL BASIS REVIEW A test employed by the court to determine the validity of a statute in equal protection actions, whereby the court determines whether the challenged statute is rationally related to the achievement of a legitimate state interest.

New York City Transit Authority v. Beazer

Municipal agency (D) v. Methadone users (P)

440 U.S. 568 (1979).

NATURE OF CASE: Appeal from decision holding that a transit authority's policy of excluding all methadone users from employment violated the Equal Protection Clause.

FACT SUMMARY: The New York City Transit Authority (TA) (D) had a policy of excluding all methadone users from employment. Current and prospective TA employees who were methadone users (P) challenged the policy on the ground that it violated the Equal Protection Clause.

RULE OF LAW
A transit authority's policy of excluding all methadone users from employment does not violate the Equal Protection Clause.

FACTS: The TA (D) refused to employ all methadone users (P). Methadone is a drug that is used to cure the physical aspects of heroin addiction. The majority of those on methadone maintenance for over a year are free from illicit drug use, but up to 25 percent may go back to drug and alcohol abuse. Methadone users (P) who had been dismissed from, or were seeking employment with, the TA (D) brought suit in district court challenging the policy on the ground that it violated the Equal Protection Clause. The district court found the policy unconstitutional and the court of appeals affirmed. The Supreme Court granted review.

ISSUE: Does a transit authority's policy of excluding all methadone users from employment violate the Equal Protection Clause?

HOLDING AND DECISION: (Stevens, J.) No. The methadone users do not challenge the TA's rule as it is applied to the class of all regular users of narcotic drugs, but are claiming that methadone users should not be part of that class. However, the evidence shows that there is a relevant difference between those who use methadone and those who use no narcotics of any kind. In addition, a substantial percentage of methadone users do not complete the program. The methadone users would not object to a special rule barring employment for those methadone users who have been in the program less than a year, or a special rule that would keep any methadone users from the most risky jobs. However, because there is no bright line as to when a methadone user is totally rehabilitated, any rule short of total exclusion is less precise and more costly than the total exclusion rule. Therefore, the policy, which postpones eligibility for employment until the treatment program has been completed, is rational. Even though factually the TA's rule is broader than necessary to exclude only unemployable methadone users, this is a personnel matter that is not protected by the Equal Protection Clause. It is a legislative policy choice aimed at safety and efficiency, and as such, it is not constitutionally significant that the degree of rationality is not as great with respect to methadone users (an ill-defined subpart of the class) as it is with respect to narcotic users (the class as a whole).

DISSENT: (White, J.) The TA's policy excludes from employment all successful methadone users: those free from drug and alcohol use; successful methadone maintenance is not a good predictor of job performance; the TA (D) can use its regular employee screening methods to determine who are the successful and unsuccessful methadone users; and most methadone users who have been on program for a year or more are just as employable as applicants from the general population. Given these facts, the policy is not rational and is arbitrary. Many other groups, e.g., ex-offenders, former alcoholics, mental patients, diabetics, etc., are just as likely as the methadone users to have members that are unemployable. Therefore, the policy singles out the methadone users "for sacrifice to this at best ethereal and likely nonexistent risk of increased unemployability." Such an arbitrary assignment of burdens among classes that are similarly situated with respect to employability violates the Equal Protection Clause.

ANALYSIS

The no-drugs policy in this case was acknowledged to be overinclusive, but such overinclusiveness is tolerated under rational basis review. As the majority, applying minimal scrutiny, said, the policy is "supported by the legitimate inference that as long as a treatment program (or other drug use) continues, a degree of uncertainty persists." As the dissent pointed out, the policy was also underinclusive to the degree that it allowed employment of non-methadone users who might be a safety threat.

Quicknotes

EQUAL PROTECTION CLAUSE A constitutional provision that each person be guaranteed the same protection of the laws enjoyed by other persons in like circumstances.

RATIONAL BASIS REVIEW A test employed by the court to determine the validity of a statute in equal protection actions, whereby the court determines whether the challenged statute is rationally related to the achievement of a legitimate state interest.

U.S. Dept. of Agriculture v. Moreno
Federal agency (D) v. Low-income individuals (P)

413 U.S. 528 (1973).

NATURE OF CASE: Appeal from decision holding that a federal law that denies food stamps to any household containing an individual unrelated to any other member of the household violates the Equal Protection Clause.

FACT SUMMARY: Federal law denied food stamps to any household containing an individual unrelated to any other member of the household. Low-income individuals (P) who were members of households where not all members were related to each other challenged the law as violating the Equal Protection Clause.

RULE OF LAW
A federal law that denies food stamps to any household containing an individual unrelated to any other member of the household violates the Equal Protection Clause.

FACTS: The Food Stamp Act of 1964 denied food stamps to any household containing an individual unrelated to any other member of the household. The stated purpose of the Act was to raise the nutrition levels of poor people and to strengthen the agricultural economy. The legislative history of the Act showed that it was intended to prevent "hippies" and "hippie communes" from participating in the food stamps program. Low-income individuals (P) who were members of households where not all members were related to each other challenged the law as violating the Equal Protection Clause. The district court found that the law did violate the Equal Protection Clause, and the Supreme Court granted review.

ISSUE: Does a federal law that denies food stamps to any household containing an individual unrelated to any other member of the household violate the Equal Protection Clause?

HOLDING AND DECISION: (Brennan, J.) Yes. The challenged classification (households of related persons versus households with one or more unrelated persons) is irrelevant to the stated purpose of the Act; it does nothing to promote good nutrition or stimulate the agricultural economy. Therefore, to be sustained, the Act must rationally further some other legitimate purpose. The only other purpose—to prevent "hippies" and their communes from participating in the food stamps program—is not a legitimate purpose. This is because a bare congressional desire to harm a politically unpopular group (hippies) cannot be a legitimate government interest. The "unrelated persons" classification is also not rationally related to preventing fraud in the food stamps program. The government's assumptions about the differences between "related" and "unrelated" households as they pertain to fraud are unsubstantiated, and other provisions of the Act already deal with fraud. Thus, the classification here is not only imprecise, it is wholly without any rational basis.

DISSENT: (Rehnquist, J.) Although it may be that the Act's purposes will not be significantly furthered by the "unrelated persons" classification, it is not the Court's job to question the effects of the classification but to determine whether there is any rational basis for it. There is a rational basis in that the classification could conceivably deny food stamps to members of households that have been formed solely for the purpose of taking advantage of the food stamps program. The fact that the Act may have unfortunate or unintended consequences does not make it unconstitutional.

ANALYSIS
This case illustrates the principle that even under rational basis minimal scrutiny, judicial deference to legislative objectives, whether stated or inferred, is not complete, as where the objectives themselves are not legitimate.

Quicknotes
EQUAL PROTECTION CLAUSE A constitutional provision that each person be guaranteed the same protection of the laws enjoyed by other persons in like circumstances.

RATIONAL BASIS REVIEW A test employed by the court to determine the validity of a statute in equal protection actions, whereby the court determines whether the challenged statute is rationally related to the achievement of a legitimate state interest.

City of Cleburne, Texas v. Cleburne Living Center, Inc.

Municipality (D) v. Zoning permit applicant (P)

473 U.S. 432 (1985).

NATURE OF CASE: Appeal of order voiding municipal special use permit ordinance.

FACT SUMMARY: Cleburne Living Center, Inc. (P) contended that laws impacting the mentally retarded should be given heightened constitutional scrutiny.

🏛 **RULE OF LAW**
Laws impacting the mentally retarded are not to be given heightened constitutional scrutiny.

FACTS: The City of Cleburne, Texas, (D) had zoned multiple-residence dwellings as R-3. Most R-3 structures required no permit; however, any proposed home for the mentally retarded did. The Cleburne Living Center, Inc. (P) applied for such a permit. Responding to objections from nearby residents, the city council refused the application. The Center (P) challenged the ordinance as a denial of equal protection. The Fifth Circuit, applying a heightened level of scrutiny towards the mentally retarded, voided the ordinance. The Supreme Court granted review.

ISSUE: Are laws impacting the mentally retarded to be given heightened constitutional scrutiny?

HOLDING AND DECISION: (White, J.) No. Laws impacting the mentally retarded are not to be given heightened judicial scrutiny. Several factors support this conclusion. First, the great variation in treatment required for mentally retarded persons argues against divesting legislatures of authority in this area in order to vest greater oversight in the judiciary. Second, increased judicial scrutiny might discourage legislatures from passing laws regarding retarded persons. Third, the strength of the current legislative commitment to the mentally retarded amply proves that they are not politically powerless and that lawmakers are responsive to retarded people's needs. Finally, if a large and amorphous class such as the mentally retarded were to be given special protection under the Fourteenth Amendment, it is hard to see where the special treatment would stop. The Court therefore concludes that the mentally retarded are not entitled to heightened scrutiny. [The Court went on to hold that, even under the applicable rational-basis review, the ordinance failed to pass constitutional muster because it represented only "an irrational prejudice against the mentally retarded."]

▶ **ANALYSIS**

The Court's Equal Protection Clause analysis continues to evolve. As of the time of this case, three levels of scrutiny existed: rational basis, heightened, and strict. In years past, strict scrutiny automatically led to invalidation, rational basis to approval. As this case shows, this is no longer true.

Quicknotes

EQUAL PROTECTION CLAUSE A constitutional provision that each person be guaranteed the same protection of the laws enjoyed by other persons in like circumstances.

HEIGHTENED SCRUTINY A purposefully vague judicial description of all levels of scrutiny more exacting than minimal scrutiny.

RATIONAL BASIS REVIEW A test employed by the court to determine the validity of a statute in equal protection actions, whereby the court determines whether the challenged statute is rationally related to the achievement of a legitimate state interest.

■■■

Dred Scott v. Sanford

Former slave (D) v. Administrator (P)

60 U.S. (19 How.) 393 (1857).

NATURE OF CASE: Action in trespass.

FACT SUMMARY: Dred Scott (P) claimed to have been freed from his slave status by his travels to free states with his master, but Sanford (D) insisted Scott (P) could not bring a federal court action pressing the point because former slaves and their descendents are not "citizens."

🏛 RULE OF LAW
Since they are not "citizens" in the sense in which that word is used in the Constitution, Negroes who were slaves in this country, or who are the descendents of such slaves, cannot bring suit in federal court.

FACTS: Dred Scott (P), a slave, was taken along on his master's sojourns to the free state of Illinois and the free part of the Missouri Territory (according to the Missouri Compromise). It was after they returned to the slave state of Missouri that the master died, and Sanford (D) became the administrator of his estate. Scott (P) attempted to bring a diversity action in federal court based on his claim that his "residence" in the aforementioned free jurisdictions had liberated him from his status as a slave. He was, he insisted, thus properly considered a "citizen" of Missouri and was therefore entitled to bring suit in federal court against Sanford (D), who was a citizen of another state (New York). Sanford (D) argued that a former slave could not be considered a citizen of the United States or of Missouri. The lower court agreed with him. Scott (P) appealed.

ISSUE: Can a former slave be a "citizen" so as to qualify to bring an action in federal court?

HOLDING AND DECISION: (Taney, C.J.) No. Negroes who were slaves in this country, or who are the descendents of such slaves are, not "citizens" in the sense in which that word is used in the Constitution and are thus not entitled to maintain an action in federal court. A review of history reveals quite readily that neither that class of persons who had been imported as slaves nor their descendents, whether they had become free or not, were acknowledged as part of the "people" but were rather considered as mere property. They simply were not among those who were "citizens" of the several states when the Constitution was adopted, and that is the time frame that must be utilized in determining who was included as a "citizen" in the Constitution. Because he is not a "citizen," Scott (P) cannot maintain this action.

▶ ANALYSIS

The justices all knew this was a historically important case; each one took the time to write an opinion. Besides the primary opinion by Chief Justice Taney, there were six concurring and two dissenting opinions. No longer doctrinally important because of subsequent amendments to the Constitution resolving of the slavery issues, this case still serves as a prime example of the view that the Constitution, as Chief Justice Taney put it, forever speaks "not only in the same words, but with the same meaning and intent with which it spoke when it came from the hands of the Framers." It is a view that has been roundly criticized as too rigid and formalistic an approach to take toward a document that must be flexible enough to provide effective and operable guidelines and governing principles for an ever-evolving society.

Quicknotes

ACTION OF TRESPASS An action to recover damages resulting from the wrongful interference with a party's person, property or rights.

DIVERSITY ACTION An action commenced by a citizen of one state against a citizen of another state or against an alien, involving an amount in controversy set by statute, over which the federal court has jurisdiction.

Korematsu v. United States

Citizen of Japanese descent (D) v. Federal government (P)

323 U.S. 214 (1944).

NATURE OF CASE: Appeal from a conviction for violation of exclusion order No. 34.

FACT SUMMARY: Korematsu (D), an American citizen of Japanese ancestry, was convicted of violating exclusion order No. 34, a World War II decree that ordered all persons of Japanese ancestry to leave the military area of the Western United States.

RULE OF LAW
Apprehension by the proper military authorities of the gravest imminent danger to the public safety can justify the curtailment of the civil rights of a single racial group.

FACTS: Korematsu (D), an American citizen of Japanese ancestry, was convicted in federal district court for remaining in San Leandro, California, a "military area," contrary to civilian exclusion order No. 34 of the commanding general of the western command. The order directed that after May 9, 1942, all persons of Japanese ancestry should be excluded from the area in order to protect against acts of sabotage and espionage during World War II. Those of Japanese ancestry were to report to and temporarily remain in an assembly center and go under military control to a relocation center for an indeterminate period. Korematsu (P) appealed on grounds that the order denied equal protection.

ISSUE: Can apprehension by the proper military authorities of the gravest imminent danger to the public safety justify the curtailment of the civil rights of a single racial group?

HOLDING AND DECISION: (Black, J.) Yes. Apprehension by the proper military authorities of the gravest imminent danger to the public safety can justify the curtailment of the civil rights of a single racial group. While such a classification is immediately suspect and is subject to the most rigid scrutiny, pressing public necessity can sometimes justify such exclusions. When under conditions of modern warfare the country is threatened, "the power to protect must be commensurate with the threatened danger." Korematsu (D) was excluded because the United States was at war with the Empire of Japan, because the proper military authorities feared invasion of the west coast and believed security required exclusion, and because Congress, placing its confidence in the military, determined that the military should have that power.

DISSENT: (Murphy, J.) The exclusion of all persons of Japanese ancestry from the Pacific Coast area is racist. Although the military must be given great deference in times of war, there are limits on military discretion,

especially where martial law has not been declared, and military claims must be judicially scrutinized for their reasonableness. The judicial test of whether the government, on a plea of military necessity, can validly deprive an individual of any of his constitutional rights is whether the deprivation is reasonably related to a public danger that is "immediate, imminent, and impending." Here, the Civilian Exclusion Order does not meet this test. The Order violates the Equal Protection Clause, the right to live and work where one chooses, and due process, but is not reasonably related to any immediate, imminent, and impending public danger. It is "one of the most sweeping and complete deprivations of constitutional rights in the history of this nation." The evidence does not support the assumption underlying the Order that all persons of Japanese descent are potential enemies or are disloyal. Instead, the Order is based on racist half-truths and misinformation. A military judgment based on such racial and sociological considerations is not entitled to great weight. The Order is based on intimations that a few Japanese Americans aided the enemy and the inference from those intimations that the entire group is therefore suspect. Inferences like these are just like the ones that have been used in support of abhorrent and despicable treatment of minorities by the enemy that we are fighting. Moreover, there was no adequate reason for not treating Japanese Americans on an individual basis (the way Germans and Italians were treated) through loyalty hearings and investigations. Any inconvenience from such attempts at due process would not justify constitutional violations. "Racial discrimination . . . is utterly revolting among a free people. . . . "

DISSENT: (Jackson, J.) A civil court should not be made to enforce an order that violates constitutional limitations even if it is a reasonable exercise of military authority.

▶ ANALYSIS

This case has received severe and growing criticism over the years. However, C.J. Warren expressed the view that in some circumstances the court will simply not be in a position to reject descriptions by the executive of the degree of military necessity. Where time is of the essence, the Court could reject the necessity not on grounds of factual unassailability, but only for insufficiency. J. Douglas, 30 years later, wrote, "the decisions were extreme and went to the verge of wartime power. . . . It is easy in retrospect to denounce what was done, as there actually was no attempted Japanese invasion of our country . . . but those making plans for the defense of

Continued on next page.

the nation had no such knowledge and were planning for the worst." *De Funis v. Odegaard*, 416 U.S. 312 (1974).

■══■

Quicknotes

EQUAL PROTECTION CLAUSE A constitutional provision that each person be guaranteed the same protection of the laws enjoyed by other persons in like circumstances.

■══■

Loving v. Virginia

Interracial couple (D) v. State (P)

388 U.S. 1 (1967).

NATURE OF CASE: Appeal after conviction for violation of state law barring interracial marriage.

FACT SUMMARY: Loving (D), a white man, and Jeter (D), a black woman, both Virginia residents, were married in the District of Columbia. When they returned to Virginia, they were indicted for violating the state's ban on interracial marriage.

🏛 RULE OF LAW
A state law restricting the freedom to marry solely because of racial classification violates the Equal Protection Clause.

FACTS: In June 1958, Loving (D) a white man, and Jeter (D), a black woman, both Virginia residents, were married in the District of Columbia, pursuant to its laws. Shortly after their marriage, the Lovings (D) returned to Virginia and were indicted for violating the state's law barring interracial marriage. They pleaded guilty and were sentenced to one year in jail. The trial judge suspended the sentence for 25 years on the condition that the Lovings (D) leave the state and not return for 25 years. In 1963, they filed a motion to have the judgment vacated and set aside.

ISSUE: Does a state law restricting the freedom to marry solely because of racial classifications violate the Equal Protection Clause?

HOLDING AND DECISION: (Warren, C. J.) Yes. A state law restricting the freedom to marry solely because of racial classification violates the Equal Protection Clause. At the very least, the Equal Protection Clause demands that racial classifications, especially suspect in criminal statutes, be subjected to the most rigid scrutiny. If they are ever to be upheld, they must be shown to be necessary to the accomplishment of some legitimate state objective. Here, there is no question that Virginia's miscegenation statutes rest solely upon distinctions drawn according to race. The statutes proscribe generally accepted conduct if engaged in by members of different races. The fact that the statute prohibits only interracial marriages involving white persons indicates that its aim is to maintain white supremacy. There is patently no legitimate overriding purpose independent of invidious discrimination that justifies the classification. A statute restricting marriage solely because of race violates the Equal Protection Clause. These statutes also deprive the Lovings (D) of liberty without due process. Since marriage is a basic human civil right, to deny this freedom on so insupportable a basis as racial classifications deprives all the state's citizens of liberty without due process of the law.

▶ ANALYSIS

In *McLaughlin v. Florida*, 379 U.S. 184 (1964), a state law banning habitual nighttime cohabitation between whites and blacks not married to each other was held to violate the Equal Protection Clause, since other nonmarried couples were not subject to prosecution for the same acts. Ordinances establishing ghettos in which blacks must reside were found to violate the clause (*Buchanan v. Warley*, 245 U.S. 60 [1917]), as was judicial enforcement of covenants restricting ownership land to whites (*Shelley v. Kraemer*, 334 U.S. 1 [1948]); racial discrimination in the selection of jurors (*Patton v. Mississippi*, 332 U.S. 463 [1947]); hiring blacks for certain occupations; and establishing racial qualifications for public offices (*Anderson v. Martin*, 375 U.S. 399 [1964]).

Quicknotes

EQUAL PROTECTION CLAUSE A constitutional provision that each person be guaranteed the same protection of the laws enjoyed by other persons in like circumstances.

STRICT SCRUTINY Method by which courts determine the constitutionality of a law, when a law affects a fundamental right. Under the test, the legislature must have had a compelling interest to enact the law and measures prescribed by the law must be the least restrictive means possible to accomplish its goal.

Palmore v. Sidoti

Parent (D) v. Parent (P)

466 U.S. 429 (1984).

NATURE OF CASE: Appeal from order divesting natural mother of child custody.

FACT SUMMARY: The trial court divested Palmore (D) of custody of her child due to her marriage to a man of a different race.

🏛 **RULE OF LAW**
Custody cannot be denied based solely on racial considerations.

FACTS: Anthony Sidoti (P) petitioned the court for custody of his daughter based on his ex-wife's remarriage to Palmore, who was black. The court divested Linda Palmore (D) of custody, holding that the social stigma of a racially mixed marriage would subject the child to public ridicule, and therefore custody in Sidoti (P) was in the best interest of the child, even though both parents were unquestionably fit to raise the child. Linda Palmore (D) appealed.

ISSUE: Can custody be denied based solely on racial considerations?

HOLDING AND DECISION: (Burger, C.J.) No. Custody cannot be denied based solely on racial considerations. Private biases cannot be allowed to dictate the disposition of judicial decisions. Discrimination based on race is wholly contrary to public policy and cannot be used as a basis for denying custody. In this case, the court found Linda Palmore (D) a fit parent. Therefore, the sole ground for divesting her of custody was her mixed marriage. As a result, the order granting Sidoti (P) custody was erroneous.

▶ *ANALYSIS*

This case illustrates the strength of the judicially recognized public policy against racial discrimination. The perpetuation of prejudice by affording it recognition as the trial court did in this case was found by the court to be as destructive as the prejudice itself. Only through strong adherence to the sound dictates of expressed public policy can the judiciary extinguish improper discrimination. Race is one of the suspect classifications that triggers the use of strict scrutiny in determining whether a classification based on it is constitutional. This high burden extends to cases of family disputes as well.

■■■

Quicknotes

STRICT SCRUTINY Method by which courts determine the constitutionality of a law, when a law affects a fundamental right. Under the test, the legislature must have had a compelling interest to enact the law and measures prescribed by the law must be the least restrictive means possible to accomplish its goal.

■■■

Plessy v. Ferguson

Railroad passenger (D) v. State (P)

163 U.S. 537 (1896).

NATURE OF CASE: Appeal from criminal prosecution for violating a state railway accommodation segregation law.

FACT SUMMARY: Plessy (D) was arrested for trying to sit in a railroad car that was designated "for whites only."

🏛 RULE OF LAW
Segregation of the races is reasonable if based upon the established custom, usage, and traditions of the people in the state.

FACTS: Plessy (D), who was seven-eighths white and whose skin color was white, was denied a seat in an all white railroad car. When he (D) resisted, he was arrested for violating a state law that provided for segregated "separate but equal" railroad accommodations. Plessy (D) appealed the conviction on the basis that separation of the races stigmatized blacks and stamped them with the badge of inferiority. Plessy (D) claimed that segregation violated the Thirteenth and Fourteenth Amendments. The trial court found Plessy (D) guilty on the basis that the law was a reasonable exercise of the state's police powers based upon custom, usage, and tradition in the state.

ISSUE: May the state segregate the races in "separate but equal" facilities or accommodations?

HOLDING AND DECISION: (Brown, J.) Yes. The state may segregate the races in "separate but equal" facilities or accommodations. This is a valid exercise of the state's police power. Where this has been the established custom, usage or tradition in the state, it may continue to require such segregation as is reasonable to preserve order and the public peace. Such decisions have been continuously upheld. This is not a badge of "slavery" under the Thirteenth Amendment and it violates no provision of the Fourteenth Amendment. The enforced separation of the races is not a badge of servitude or inferiority regardless of how Plessy (D) and other blacks deem to treat it. The conviction is sustained.

DISSENT: (Harlan, J.) The statute interferes with the personal freedom of individuals to freely associate with others. The Constitution is color-blind. All citizens should and must be treated alike. Blacks are not subordinate or inferior things. They are citizens and are entitled to all of the privileges that this entails. Enforced separation is an impermissible burden on these privileges and freedoms. The conviction should be overturned.

▶ ANALYSIS

Plessy is of importance only for its historical perspective. Later cases borrowed the "separate but equal" phraseology

and turned it around 180 degrees. In *Brown v. Board of Education*, 347 U.S. 483 (1954), the Court, 58 years after *Plessy*, held that separate could never be considered equal. It thus expressly overruled *Plessy*.

■═■

Quicknotes

POLICE POWER The power of a government to impose restrictions on the rights of private persons, so long as those restrictions are reasonably related to the promotion and protection of public health, safety, morals and the general welfare.

■═■

Brown v. Board of Education

Students (P) v. School board (D)

347 U.S. 483 (1954).

NATURE OF CASE: Black minors sought the court's aid in obtaining admission to the public schools of their community on a nonsegregated basis.

FACT SUMMARY: Black children were denied admission to public schools attended by white children.

RULE OF LAW

The "separate but equal" doctrine has no application in the field of education, and the segregation of children in public schools based solely on their race violates the Equal Protection Clause.

FACTS: Black children had been denied admission to public schools attended by white children under laws requiring or permitting segregation according to race. It was found that the black children's schools and the white children's schools had been or were being equalized with respect to buildings, curricula, qualifications, and salaries of teachers.

ISSUE: Does segregation of children in public schools solely on the basis of race, even though the physical facilities are equal, deprive the children of the minority group of equal protection of the law?

HOLDING AND DECISION: (Warren, C.J.) Yes. The "separate but equal" doctrine has no application in the field of education, and the segregation of children in public schools based solely on their race violates the Equal Protection Clause. First, intangible as well as tangible factors may be considered. Hence, the fact that the facilities and other tangible factors in the schools have been equalized is not controlling. Segregation of white and black children in public schools has a detrimental effect on the black children because the policy of separating the races is usually interpreted as denoting the inferiority of the black children. A sense of inferiority affects children's motivation to learn. Segregation tends to deprive black children of some of the benefits they would receive in an integrated school. Any language in *Plessy v. Ferguson*, 163 U.S. 537 (1896), contrary to this is rejected. The "separate but equal" doctrine has no place in the field of education. Separate facilities are inherently unequal. Such facilities deprive black children of their right to equal protection of the laws.

ANALYSIS

In *Plessy v. Ferguson*, 163 U.S. 537 (1896), the court sustained a Louisiana statute requiring "equal, but separate accommodations" for black and white railway passengers. The separate but equal doctrine was born and under it a long line of statutes providing separate but equal facilities were upheld. Justice Harlan was the only dissenter in *Plessy*. He stated, "The arbitrary separation of citizens, on the basis of race, while they are on a public highway . . . cannot be justified upon any legal grounds. The thin disguise of equal accommodations for passengers in railway cars will not mislead anyone, nor atone for the wrong done this day." After the 1954 decision in *Brown*, the court found segregation unconstitutional in other public facilities as well. Despite the emphasis on the school context in *Brown*, the later cases resulted in per curiam orders simply citing *Brown*. Facilities that were desegregated included beaches, buses, golf courses, and parks.

Quicknotes

EQUAL PROTECTION CLAUSE A constitutional provision that each person be guaranteed the same protection of the laws enjoyed by other persons in like circumstances.

Johnson v. California

Prisoner (P) v. Prison system (D)

543 U.S. 499 (2005).

NATURE OF CASE: Review of federal court judgment.

FACT SUMMARY: California prisoner Garrison Johnson (P) alleged in federal district court that the California Department of Corrections (D) used race to assign temporary cell mates for new prisoners, a practice Johnson (P) said violated the U.S. Constitution's Equal Protection Clause.

RULE OF LAW

Strict scrutiny is the proper standard of review for an equal protection challenge to a department of corrections unwritten policy of racially segregating prisoners in double cells in reception centers for up to 60 days each time they enter a new correctional facility.

FACTS: California prisoner Garrison Johnson (P) alleged in federal district court that the California Department of Corrections (D) used race to assign temporary cell mates for new prisoners, a practice Johnson (P) said violated the U.S. Constitution's Equal Protection Clause. New inmates are held in reception centers for up to 60 days upon their arrival, and during that time are evaluated by prison officials to determine ultimate placement. The rest of the prison facilities, including permanent cells, are fully integrated. The prison's (D) rationale for the policy is that it is necessary to prevent violence caused by racial gangs.

ISSUE: Is strict scrutiny the proper standard of review for an equal protection challenge to a department of corrections unwritten policy of racially segregating prisoners in double cells in reception centers for up to 60 days each time they enter a new correctional facility?

HOLDING AND DECISION: (O'Connor, J.) Yes. Strict scrutiny is the proper standard of review for an equal protection challenge to a department of corrections unwritten policy of racially segregating prisoners in double cells in reception centers for up to 60 days each time they enter a new correctional facility. The fact that the policy was neutral in the sense that all prisoners were equally segregated does not allow the policy to escape strict scrutiny. Racial classifications must receive strict scrutiny even when they may be said to affect the races equally. In addition, the fact that the policy applies only in the prison context does not entitle it to a deferential standard of review. The case is remanded to the Court of Appeals for the Ninth Circuit, or the district court, to apply strict scrutiny and decide whether the policy violates the Equal Protection Clause.

DISSENT: (Stevens, J.) The state policy of segregation in prisons violates the Equal Protection Clause of the Fourteenth Amendment. The prison system (D) has failed to justify its policy under strict scrutiny or a more deferential standard. Segregation is inherently wrong, and the system (D) failed to explain why it could not rely on individual assessment of the prisoners' risk of violence as an alternative to automatic segregation.

DISSENT: (Thomas, J.) This case requires the reconciliation of two conflicting lines of precedent. On the one hand *Gratz v. Bollinger*, [539 U.S. 244 [2003]) holds that all racial classifications reviewable under the Equal Protection Clause must be strictly scrutinized. But the Court also held in *Turner v. Safley*, [482 U.S. 78 (1987)], that the relaxed standard of review applies to all circumstances in which the needs of prison administration affect constitutional rights. The majority followed the former line of cases to its conclusion that strict scrutiny was appropriate. But the Constitution demands less inside prison walls. The deferential standard set forth in *Turner* is more appropriate.

ANALYSIS

The *Johnson* case stands in contrast with a long line of cases, beginning with *Brown v. Board of Education*, 347 U.S. 483 (1954), that hold that because racial segregation is inherently unequal, it violates of the Fourteenth Amendment. *Johnson* holds that racial segregation is now to be treated like any other racial classification, and the court does not limit its decision to the prison context.

Quicknotes

EQUAL PROTECTION CLAUSE A constitutional provision that each person be guaranteed the same protection of the laws enjoyed by other persons in like circumstances.

FOURTEENTH AMENDMENT Declares that no state shall make or enforce any law that shall abridge the privileges or immunities of citizens of the United States. No state shall deny to any person within its jurisdiction the equal protection of the laws.

STRICT SCRUTINY Method by which courts determine the constitutionality of a law, when a law affects a fundamental right. Under the test, the legislature must have had a compelling interest to enact the law and measures prescribed by the law must be the least restrictive means possible to accomplish its goal.

Washington v. Davis

Federal agency (D) v. Civil service applicants (P)

426 U.S. 229 (1976).

NATURE OF CASE: Action for a declaratory judgment.

FACT SUMMARY: A qualifying test for positions as police officers in the District of Columbia was failed by a disproportionately high number of Negro applicants (P).

🏛 RULE OF LAW
A law or official governmental practice must have a "discriminatory purpose," not merely a disproportionate effect on one race, in order to constitute "invidious discrimination" under the Fifth Amendment Due Process Clause or the Fourteenth Amendment Equal Protection Clause.

FACTS: In order to be accepted in the District of Columbia Metropolitan Police Department, all applicants must receive a grade of at least 40 on "Test 21." This test was developed by the Civil Service Commission for use throughout the federal service to test "verbal ability, vocabulary, reading and comprehension." After failing this test, several Negro applicants (P) brought an action against the Commissioners of the United States Civil Service Commission (D) for a declaratory judgment that "Test 21" was unconstitutional. In this action, the Negro applicants (P) claimed that "Test 21" was unlawfully discriminatory against Negroes and, therefore, was in violation of the Fifth Amendment Due Process Clause. After the test was invalidated by the court of appeals, the Commissioners (D) appealed to this court.

ISSUE: Does a law or official governmental practice constitute "invidious discrimination" merely because it affects a greater proportion of one race than another?

HOLDING AND DECISION: (White, J.) No. A law or official governmental practice must have a "discriminatory purpose," not merely a disproportionate effect on one race, in order to constitute "invidious discrimination" under the Fifth Amendment Due Process Clause or the Fourteenth Amendment Equal Protection Clause. Of course, a disproportionate impact may be relevant as "evidence" of a "discriminatory purpose." However, such impact "is not the sole touchstone of invidious racial discrimination forbidden by the constitution," and, standing alone, "it does not trigger the rule that racial classifications are to be subjected to the strictest scrutiny." Here, "Test 21" is racially "neutral" on its face (i.e., it is designed to disqualify anyone who cannot meet the requirements of the police training program). As such, it is valid even though it has a disproportionate effect on Negroes.

DISSENT: (Brennan, J.) At a minimum, the police department should have been required to prove that Test 21

either measured job-related skills or predicted job performance. Otherwise, where written qualification examinations are validated through a correlation with written examinations in a training course, there is the risk that people with good verbal skills will do well on both types of exams as the result of their good verbal skills and not as a result of "job-specific ability." Where both such examinations are given, with the one validating the other, it is erroneous—and the majority is wrong—that the qualification examination is job related.

▌ ANALYSIS

In general, classifications based upon race are considered "suspect" and, therefore, subjected to "strict scrutiny" under the Equal Protection Clause or the Due Process Clause (i.e., such classifications must be justified by a "compelling state interest"). However, as this case illustrates, such "strict scrutiny" is applied only when there is "purposeful discrimination." As such, the court (as here) can avoid applying "strict scrutiny" by finding that any discriminatory impact is merely incidental. Note that here the Court also avoided applying the strict standard in Title VII of the Civil Rights Act of 1964 (by saying that only the constitutional issue was raised). Under Title VII, whenever hiring and promotion practices disqualify disproportionate numbers of blacks, they must be justified by more than a rational basis (i.e., must be validated in terms of job performance) even if no discriminatory purpose is shown.

■=■

Quicknotes

DISCRIMINATORY IMPACT The effect of an action that affects one group of persons more significantly than another; insufficient to prove discriminatory intent on its own.

DISCRIMINATORY PURPOSE Intent to discriminate; must be shown to establish an Equal Protection violation.

DUE PROCESS CLAUSE Clauses found in the Fifth and Fourteenth Amendments to the United States Constitution providing that no person shall be deprived of "life, liberty, or property, without due process of law."

EQUAL PROTECTION CLAUSE A constitutional provision that each person be guaranteed the same protection of the laws enjoyed by other persons in like circumstances.

STRICT SCRUTINY Method by which courts determine the constitutionality of a law, when a law affects a fundamental right. Under the test, the legislature must have had a compelling interest to enact the law and measures prescribed by the law must be the least restrictive means possible to accomplish its goal.

■=■

McCleskey v. Kemp

Inmate (D) v. State (P)

481 U.S. 279 (1987).

NATURE OF CASE: Appeal from denial of writ of habeas corpus.

FACT SUMMARY: McCleskey (D) contended he was denied equal protection when sentenced to death because blacks were statistically more likely to be so sentenced, and such was racially based.

🏛 RULE OF LAW
Capital cases require an evaluation of the motivations of individual jurors in sentencing; thus raw abstract statistical data are not dispositive of a lack of equal protection.

FACTS: McCleskey (D), a black man, was sentenced to death for killing a white. He petitioned for a writ of habeas corpus presenting a statistical study indicating blacks were more likely to be sentenced to death, and that such was racially motivated. The district court and the court of appeals rejected the statistical data as irrelevant to the disposition, and the Supreme Court granted certiorari.

ISSUE: May statistical data be used in a capital case to determine an absence of equal protection?

HOLDING AND DECISION: (Powell, J.) No. Capital cases require an evaluation of the motivations of individual jurors in sentencing; thus raw abstract statistical studies are irrelevant and not dispositive of a lack of equal protection. Each jury is unique in its composition, rendering statistical studies useless. Each case must be evaluated on its own merits. Thus, these data were properly excluded.

DISSENT: (Brennan, J.) The statistical evidence is great that black defendants charged with killing white victims in Georgia have a much greater chance of being sentenced to death. This holds true throughout the sentencing system, even in cases where the jury exercises little discretion. For example, the rate of capital sentencing in a white-victim case is 120 percent greater than in a black-victim case. Other evidence "relentlessly documents" that capital sentencing is racially influenced. Moreover, history and experience support the statistical evidence, given Georgia's history of racism and its former dual criminal justice system. Still yet, the Georgia capital-sentencing system itself provides opportunities for racial considerations in sentencing—juries are not provided with lists of aggravating and mitigating factors, and once a jury identifies one aggravating factor, it has complete discretion in choosing life or death without having to articulate a basis for its choice. The "reverberations of injustice" are not easily confined, and by failing to heed McCleskey's evidence, the majority is continuing injustice.

▶ ANALYSIS

The Court appeared reluctant to rely upon statistical data in overturning a jury verdict. The statistical manipulations and fact-gathering methodology in such studies may give a false conclusion regarding the result. Extrapolation and mathematical interpretation was felt to unreasonably influence the ultimate conclusion. Any individual jury, after voir dire, can be as independent as necessary, according to the Court, and thus such statistics merely cloud the issue.

Quicknotes

EQUAL PROTECTION CLAUSE A constitutional provision that each person be guaranteed the same protection of the laws enjoyed by other persons in like circumstances.

City of Mobile v. Bolden

Municipality (D) v. African American voters (P)

446 U.S. 55 (1980).

NATURE OF CASE: Appeal from class action on behalf of African American voters (P) alleging that a city's (D) at-large electoral system violated the Fourteenth and Fifteenth Amendments because it had discriminatory effect.

FACT SUMMARY: The City of Mobile (D) had an at-large system of municipal elections. Because Mobile was predominantly white, this meant, as a practical matter, that only whites were elected. Representing a sizable part of the Mobile community, Negro voters (P) challenged the electoral system on the ground that it violated the Fourteenth and Fifteenth Amendments.

🏛 RULE OF LAW
A municipal at-large electoral system that has discriminatory effect but does not have discriminatory purpose does not violate the Fourteenth and Fifteenth Amendments.

FACTS: The City of Mobile, since 1911, had an at-large system of elections for electing City Commissioners. Because Mobile was predominantly white, no Negro was ever elected to the City Commission. Negro voters (P) brought a class action on behalf of all black voters in the city, arguing that the discriminatory effect of the at-large electoral system violated the Equal Protection Clause and the Fifteenth Amendment. The district court found invidious discrimination, and the court of appeals affirmed. The Supreme Court granted review.

ISSUE: Does a municipal at-large electoral system that has discriminatory effect but does not have discriminatory purpose violate the Fourteenth and Fifteenth Amendments?

HOLDING AND DECISION: (Stewart, J.) No. State action that is racially neutral on its face violates the Fifteenth Amendment only if it is motivated by discriminatory purpose. Similarly, multi-member legislative districts are unconstitutional only if their purpose is to minimize the voting power of racial minorities; it is not enough to show that the minority groups have not elected representatives in proportion to their number. In Mobile, the Negro voters (P) register and vote without hindrance, and there is no obstacle to Negro candidates running for office. Additionally, past discrimination, such as that throughout Alabama's history, does not by itself render unconstitutional otherwise lawful state action. Thus, here there is no proof of discriminatory intent. Reversed and remanded.

DISSENT: (White, J.) As the trial court found, a discriminatory purpose can be inferred from the totality of the facts. Trial courts are in a special position to make such inferences. Here, the district court made detailed factual inquiry into the openness of the candidate selection process to blacks, and found overwhelming evidence that "the structure of the at-large election of city commissioners combined with strong racial polarization of Mobile's electorate continues to effectively discourage qualified black citizens from seeking office or being elected, thereby denying blacks equal access to the slating or candidate selection process." These findings support the inference of purposeful discrimination in violation of the Fourteenth and Fifteenth Amendments.

▶ ANALYSIS

In response to the Court's holding in *City of Mobile*, Congress passed the 1982 Amendments to the Voting Rights Act of 1965. The amendment prohibits electoral systems that dilute the voting power of a racial minority, essentially eliminating the need for proving discriminatory intent that was determinative in this decision.

Quicknotes

DISCRIMINATORY IMPACT The effect of an action that affects one group of persons more significantly than another; insufficient to prove discriminatory intent on its own.

DISCRIMINATORY PURPOSE Intent to discriminate; must be shown to establish an Equal Protection violation.

FIFTEENTH AMENDMENT The right of citizens of the United States to vote shall not be denied on account of race, color, or previous condition of servitude.

INVIDIOUS DISCRIMINATION Unequal treatment of a class of persons that is particularly malicious or hostile.

Palmer v. Thompson

African American citizens (P) v. City official (D)

403 U.S. 217 (1971).

NATURE OF CASE: Appeal from decision that city's decision not to operate swimming pools on an integrated basis does not violate the Equal Protection Clause.

FACT SUMMARY: Jackson, Mississippi, closed its swimming pools after a federal court ordered them to be desegregated. Negro citizens (P) of Jackson challenged the closings as a violation of the Equal Protection Clause.

🏛 RULE OF LAW
A city's facially neutral decision to not operate desegregated facilities does not violate the Equal Protection Clause.

FACTS: Following the court of appeals's affirmance of a district court judgment invalidating enforced segregation on equal protection grounds, the city council of Jackson, Mississippi, desegregated its public recreational facilities, including its five public parks, except for their swimming pools. Stating that the pools could not be operated safely and economically on an integrated basis, the council closed four city-owned pools. Negro citizens (P) of Jackson then sued on equal protection grounds, to force the city to reopen and operate the pools on a desegregated basis. The district court held there was no denial of equal protection. The court of appeals affirmed, and the Supreme Court granted review.

ISSUE: Does a city's facially neutral decision to not operate desegregated facilities violate the Equal Protection Clause?

HOLDING AND DECISION: (Black, J.) No. The state does not have a duty to operate swimming pools. Here, the closure affected all races equally. It is extremely difficult for a court to determine the true or dominant motivation of legislators, and "no case in this Court has held that a legislative act may violate equal protection solely because of the motivations of the men who voted for it." Although it may be true, as the black citizens (P) claim, that the legislators who voted for the closure were motivated by an ideological opposition to racial integration, here, substantial evidence supported the city's reason for closing the pools— that they could not be operated safely and economically on an integrated basis. Had Jackson denied the use of the pools to one group but not another, relief would be available, but that is not the case here.

DISSENT: (Douglas, J.) A state has the right to discontinue any of its municipal services—including schools, parks, pools, etc.—but may not do so for the purpose of perpetuating segregation. If the closure is racially motivated, then the closure becomes a device for perpetuating segregation, and that is constitutionally impermissible.

▶ ANALYSIS

Palmer suggests that discriminatory motivation alone is not enough to prove that a facially neutral decision or law constitutes a racially based classification. Sufficient proof is comprised of both a discriminatory impact and a discriminatory motivation behind it.

Quicknotes

DISCRIMINATORY IMPACT The effect of an action that affects one group of persons more significantly than another; insufficient to prove discriminatory intent on its own.

DISCRIMINATORY PURPOSE Intent to discriminate; must be shown to establish an Equal Protection violation.

EQUAL PROTECTION CLAUSE A constitutional provision that each person be guaranteed the same protection of the laws enjoyed by other persons in like circumstances.

Personnel Administrator of Massachusetts v. Feeney

State official (D) v. Female state employee (P)

442 U.S. 256 (1979).

NATURE OF CASE: Appeal from decision that a state's absolute employment preference for veterans discriminates against women in violation of the Equal Protection Clause.

FACT SUMMARY: Massachusetts provided that veterans were to be preferred for civil service jobs over other similarly qualified applicants. Feeney (P), a female state employee, challenged the preference on equal protection grounds, asserting that the preference discriminated against women because most veterans are men.

🏛 RULE OF LAW
A state's absolute employment preference for veterans does not discriminate against women in violation of the Equal Protection Clause.

FACTS: Massachusetts provided that all veterans who qualify for state civil service positions must be considered for appointment ahead of any qualifying nonveterans. Feeney (P), a female civil servant denied advancement pursuant to the veterans preference, challenged the law as discriminating against women in violation of the Equal Protection Clause. In fact, the preference did operate overwhelmingly to the advantage of males because 98 percent of veterans are male. The district court struck down the preference, finding that the state could promote the legitimate goal of supporting veterans through means that were less exclusionary to women. The Supreme Court granted review.

ISSUE: Does a state's absolute employment preference for veterans discriminate against women in violation of the Equal Protection Clause?

HOLDING AND DECISION: (Stewart, J.) No. Although the preference does favor males, it does not entirely exclude females, and Feeney (P) has not shown that a gender-based discriminatory purpose is behind the preference. Feeney's (P) argument rests on the presumption that a person intends the natural and foreseeable consequences of his voluntary actions. Here, the decision to grant the preference to veterans was "intentional" and the legislators, in passing the preference, could not have been unaware that most veterans are men. Thus, the adverse consequences of the preference for women was foreseeable. Taking this reasoning to its logical conclusion, the legislature intended the adverse consequences to women. Nevertheless, discriminatory purpose implies more than intent as volition or awareness of consequences. Instead, it implies that the decisionmaker chose a particular course of action "because of," not merely "in spite of," its adverse effects upon an identifiable group. Here, there was no evidence that the preference for veterans was enacted "because of" its collateral adverse impact on women. The law was what it purported to be: a preference for veterans of either sex over nonveterans of either sex.

▶ ANALYSIS

In this case, the Court's definition of intent was narrow, essentially rejecting the tort-law definition of intent as acting with knowledge of foreseeable consequences. Instead, the Court adopted a criminal-law definition of intent as the desire to cause a certain result. This places a greater burden of proof on those claiming that a facially neutral measure has a discriminatory purpose. Some have argued that a showing of disproportionate disadvantage to an already disadvantaged group should shift the burden to the government, which should be required to show that the measure was taken apart from prejudice. The Court has not taken this approach.

■=■

Quicknotes

DISCRIMINATORY IMPACT The effect of an action that affects one group of persons more significantly than another; insufficient to prove discriminatory intent on its own.

DISCRIMINATORY PURPOSE Intent to discriminate; must be shown to establish an Equal Protection violation.

EQUAL PROTECTION CLAUSE A constitutional provision that each person be guaranteed the same protection of the laws enjoyed by other persons in like circumstances.

■=■

Village of Arlington Heights v. Metropolitan Housing Development Corp.

Municipality (D) v. Developer of low-income housing (P)

429 U.S. 252 (1977).

NATURE OF CASE: Appeal from decision declaring a denial of a zoning request for the purpose of building low-income housing as violating the Equal Protection Clause.

FACT SUMMARY: Metropolitan Housing Development Corp. (MHDC) (P) applied to the Village of Arlington Heights (the Village) (D) for a rezoning of land from single-family to multi-family to permit construction of low-income housing. The Village (D) refused and MHDC (P) sued, charging that the refusal was racially discriminatory in violation of the Equal Protection Clause.

RULE OF LAW
A denial of a rezoning request does not violate the Equal Protection Clause where there is no proof that the denial was motivated by a discriminatory purpose.

FACTS: Metropolitan Housing Development Corp. (MHDC) (P) applied to the Village of Arlington Heights (the Village) (D) for a rezoning of land from single-family to multiple-family classification to permit construction of low-income housing. The Village (D) refused, and MHDC (P) sued, charging that the refusal was racially discriminatory in violation of the Equal Protection Clause. The district court found no racial discrimination, but the court of appeals reversed, finding that the "ultimate effect" of the rezoning denial was racially discriminatory. The Supreme Court granted review.

ISSUE: Does a denial of a rezoning request violate the Equal Protection Clause where there is no proof that the denial was motivated by a discriminatory purpose?

HOLDING AND DECISION: (Powell, J.) No. Government action is not unconstitutional merely because it results in a racially disproportionate impact. Proof of a racially discriminatory intent or purpose is required to show a violation of the Equal Protection Clause. When there is proof that a discriminatory purpose has been a motivating factor in the legislature's decision, judicial deference to the legislature is no longer justified. The issue then becomes what is sufficient to prove discriminatory purpose. Disparate impact is a starting point, but is by itself rarely enough. The historical background of the decision is another evidentiary source, particularly when there is a history of past intentional racial discrimination. Departures from normal procedures also might provide proof of improper purpose, as might the specific sequence of events leading up to the decision. Substantive departures may also be probative, and legislative or administrative history may

be highly relevant. Taking these evidentiary sources into account, here, the impact of the Village's decision does bear more heavily on racial minorities, but there is little suspicious about the sequence of events leading up to the denial. The rezoning request progressed according to the usual procedures, and the land at issue had been zoned for single-family use since the Village (D) adopted zoning. In sum, MHDC (P) failed to carry its evidentiary burden of proving that the denial was motivated by discriminatory purpose.

ANALYSIS

Village of Arlington Heights is significant mostly for its enumeration of evidentiary tools that can be used to prove discriminatory intent.

Quicknotes

DISCRIMINATORY IMPACT The effect of an action that affects one group of persons more significantly than another; insufficient to prove discriminatory intent on its own.

DISCRIMINATORY PURPOSE Intent to discriminate; must be shown to establish an Equal Protection violation.

EQUAL PROTECTION CLAUSE A constitutional provision that each person be guaranteed the same protection of the laws enjoyed by other persons in like circumstances.

Brown v. Board of Education

Students (P) v. School board (D)

349 U.S. 294 (1955).

NATURE OF CASE: Decision to determine the manner in which relief from segregation in public schools is to be accorded.

FACT SUMMARY: In May 1954, the court decided that racial discrimination in public education is unconstitutional. It requested further arguments on the question of relief.

🏛 RULE OF LAW
School authorities have the primary responsibility for assessing and solving the problem of achieving racial integration in the public schools.

FACTS: These cases were decided in May 1954. The opinions declared that racial discrimination in public education is unconstitutional. They are incorporated here. Because the cases arose under various local conditions and their disposition would involve a variety of local problems, the court requested additional arguments on the question of relief. All provisions of federal, state, and local laws that permit segregation in public schools must be modified.

ISSUE: Do school authorities have the primary responsibility for assessing and solving the problem of achieving racial integration in the public schools?

HOLDING AND DECISION: (Warren, C.J.) Yes. School authorities have the primary responsibility for assessing and solving the problem of achieving racial integration in the public schools. It will be for courts to consider whether the school authorities' actions are good faith implementation of the governing constitutional principles. Because of their proximity to local conditions and the possible need for further hearings, the courts that originally heard these cases can best perform this judicial appraisal. In doing so, the courts will be guided by the equitable principles of practical flexibility in shaping remedies and the facility for adjusting and reconciling public and private needs. The courts will require that the defendants make a prompt and reasonable start toward full racial integration in the public schools. Once such a start is made, the courts may determine that additional time is required to carry out the May 1954 ruling. However, the burden rests upon the defendant to determine that such time is necessary and consistent with good faith compliance with the Constitution. The courts may consider problems related to administration, the facilities, school transportation systems, and revision of school districts and local laws. They will also consider the adequacy of any plans proposed by the defendants and will retain jurisdiction during the transition period. The cases are remanded to the lower courts to enter orders consistent with this opinion as necessary to insure that the parties to these cases are admitted to public schools on a racially nondiscriminatory basis with all deliberate speed.

▶ ANALYSIS

After its promulgation of general guidelines in *Brown II* in 1955, the court maintained silence about implementation for several years. Enforcement of the desegregation requirement was left largely to lower court litigation. In 1958, the court broke its silence in *Cooper v. Aaron*, 358 U.S. 1, where it reaffirmed the *Brown* principles in the face of official resistance in Little Rock, Arkansas. It was not until the early sixties, however, that the court began to consider the details of desegregation plans. During the late sixties, court rulings on implementation came with greater frequency, specificity, and urgency. Finally, in *Alexander v. Holmes County Board of Education*, 369 U.S. 19 (1969), the court called for an immediate end to dual school systems.

■■■

Swann v. Charlotte-Mecklenburg Board of Education

Federal district court (P) v. School board (D)

402 U.S. 1 (1971).

NATURE OF CASE: Certiorari to review a district court school desegregation order.

FACT SUMMARY: When the Charlotte-Mecklenburg Board of Education (D) refused to adopt a reasonable plan for desegregation of its school system, a federal district court ordered imposition of its own desegregation plan.

🏛 RULE OF LAW
When school authorities deliberately maintain a racially segregated school system, the federal district courts have broad equitable powers to use any remedies that are reasonably necessary to desegregate that school system.

FACTS: For many years, the Charlotte-Mecklenburg Board of Education (D) engaged in actions that resulted in a racially segregated school system. In 1968, Swann (P) initiated an action against the Board (D) to obtain an order for desegregation of the school system. In response, the district court for North Carolina ordered the Board (D) to come forward with a plan for both faculty and student desegregation. In December 1969, the Board (D) submitted such a plan, but the district court held that the plan was unacceptable. Thereafter, the district court appointed an expert in education administration, Dr. John Finger, to prepare a school desegregation plan for the Charlotte-Mecklenburg school system. Subsequently, the district court adopted Dr. Finger's plan, which provided for the pairing and grouping of noncontiguous school zones, busing of students, etc. Thereafter, the district court ordered that the Charlotte-Mecklenburg Board (D) implement this plan, and the Supreme Court granted certiorari to review such order.

ISSUE: Can federal district courts impose their own desegregation plan on a school system which school authorities have deliberately maintained as racially segregated?

HOLDING AND DECISION: (Burger, C.J.) Yes. When school authorities deliberately maintain a racially segregated school system, the federal district courts have broad equitable powers to use any remedies that are reasonably necessary to desegregate that school system. Furthermore, the district courts may reasonably conclude in certain circumstances that it is necessary to employ any or all of the following remedies to promote desegregation. First, the district courts may use mathematical ratios as a "starting point" in the process of shaping a remedy for segregation (not as an "inflexible requirement"). Second, the district courts may require that "every all-Negro and all-white school" be eliminated unless the school authori-

ties can show that such school assignments are "genuinely nondiscriminatory." That is, school authorities should have the burden of showing that such schools are not a result of present or past discriminatory action on their parts. Third, the district courts may pair and group school districts and attendance zones on the basis of race in order to correct a racially dual school system, even if the new districts and zones will not be contiguous. Fourth, the district courts can require reasonable busing of students to schools beyond their immediate area. Here, the record supports the need for all of these four remedies. The Charlotte-Mecklenburg Board of Education (D) has deliberately maintained a racially segregated school system in violation of the Equal Protection Clause of the Constitution. As such, the district court's remedial plan was validly imposed. Affirmed.

▶ ANALYSIS

This case illustrates an attempt by the Supreme Court and by federal district courts to implement those principles first announced in *Brown v. Board of Education*, 347 U.S. 483 (1954). The Supreme Court in *Brown* held that "separate" public educational facilities based on race were "inherently unequal" (i.e., in violation of the Equal Protection Clause). Following *Brown*, the Supreme Court, at first, required that school boards use "all deliberate speed" to desegregate schools (*Watson v. Memphis*, 373 U.S. 526). Later, though, the court required that all school boards take affirmative action "at once" (i.e., immediately) to desegregate schools (*Green v. New Kent County School Board*, 391 U.S. 430 [1968]). Note, however, that the remedies for segregation accepted in *Swann* were only applied to "de jure" segregation (i.e., segregation resulting from purposeful action by school authorities). Today it is still unsettled as to whether all of such remedies can be applied to eliminate "de facto" segregation (i.e., segregation resulting from segregated residential neighborhoods, etc., but not from the purposeful activities of school authorities).

■=■

Quicknotes

DISCRIMINATORY IMPACT The effect of an action that affects one group of persons more significantly than another; insufficient to prove discriminatory intent on its own.

DISCRIMINATORY PURPOSE Intent to discriminate; must be shown to establish an Equal Protection violation.

EQUAL PROTECTION CLAUSE A constitutional provision that each person be guaranteed the same protection of the laws enjoyed by other persons in like circumstances.

■=■

Milliken v. Bradley

Student (P) v. School board (D)

418 U.S. 717 (1974).

NATURE OF CASE: Review of school desegregation decree.

FACT SUMMARY: The district court found de jure segregation in the city of Detroit's public schools and ordered an inter-district remedy.

🏛 RULE OF LAW
Before the boundaries of separate and autonomous school districts may be set aside for remedial purposes, it must first be shown that racially discriminatory acts of the state or local school districts have been a substantial cause of inter-district segregation.

FACTS: Milliken (P) alleged there was de jure school segregation in Detroit city schools. The district court agreed, and entered a decree that included 53 surrounding school districts. Bradley (D) appealed, alleging that there was no evidence of deliberate racially discriminatory action by the school districts.

ISSUE: Before the boundaries of separate and autonomous school districts may be set aside for remedial purposes, must it first be shown that racially discriminatory acts of the state or local school districts have been a substantial cause of inter-district segregation?

HOLDING AND DECISION: (Burger, C.J.) Yes. Before the boundaries of separate and autonomous school districts may be set aside for remedial purposes, it must first be shown that racially discriminatory acts of the state or local school districts have been a substantial cause of inter-district segregation. The remedy ordered by the court would impose on the outlying districts, not shown to have committed any constitutional violation, a wholly impermissible remedy not hinted at by other past decisions of this court.

DISSENT: (White, J.) The legal reality is that the constitutional violations, even if occurring locally, were committed by governmental entities for which the state is responsible and the state must respond to the command of the Fourteenth Amendment.

▶ ANALYSIS

This was the first case overturning a desegregation decree ordered by a district court because it went too far. The city was predominantly black and the outlying suburbs predominantly white. The Court responded to concerns voiced by advocates for local control of school districts.

Quicknotes

REMEDY Compensation for violation of a right or for injuries sustained.

Board of Education of Oklahoma City Public Schools v. Dowell

Board of education (D) v. Parents of black students (P)

498 U.S. 237 (1991).

NATURE OF CASE: Appeal from decision that a federal desegregation decree remains in effect beyond achievement of unitary status and good faith compliance with the decree.

FACT SUMMARY: A federal district court had ordered school desegregation in Oklahoma City. After it was satisfied that the order had been complied with and that unitary status had been achieved, the district court terminated the case. Subsequently, as the result of actions taken by the city's Board of Education (D), parents of black students (P) moved to reopen the case, but the district court denied their motion.

RULE OF LAW

A federal school desegregation order can be terminated without offending the Equal Protection Clause when the order had been complied with in good faith and the vestiges of past discrimination have been eliminated to the extent practicable.

FACTS: In 1972, finding that previous efforts had not been successful at eliminating de jure segregation, a federal district court entered a decree imposing a school desegregation plan on Oklahoma City Board of Education (Board) (D). In 1977, finding that the school district had achieved "unitary" status, the court issued an order terminating the case, which black students and their parents (P) did not appeal. In 1984, the Board adopted its Student Reassignment Plan (SRP), under which a number of previously desegregated schools would return to primarily one-race status for the asserted purpose of alleviating greater busing burdens on young black children caused by demographic changes. The district court thereafter denied the black students and parents' motion to reopen the terminated case. The court of appeals reversed, holding that a desegregation decree remains in effect until a school district can show "grievous wrong evoked by new and unforeseen conditions," and that circumstances had not changed enough to justify modification of the 1972 decree. The Supreme Court granted review.

ISSUE: Can a federal school desegregation order be terminated without offending the Equal Protection Clause when the order had been complied with in good faith and the vestiges of past discrimination have been eliminated to the extent practicable?

HOLDING AND DECISION: (Rehnquist, C. J.) Yes. The legal justification for a federal school desegregation order is that local authorities have violated the Constitution. Dissolving such an order after the local authorities have complied with it for a reasonable period of time recognizes the importance of local control over public

school systems and recognizes that the order should not extend beyond the time it takes to remedy the effects of past intentional discrimination. The criteria to be used in determining if dissolution of such an order is proper are (1) whether the Board (D) complied in good faith with the desegregation decree since it was entered, and (2) whether the vestiges of past discrimination have been eliminated to the extent practicable.

DISSENT: (Marshall, J.) The majority fails to expressly recognize the threat of a return to one-race schools as a relevant "vestige" of de jure segregation. A desegregation decree should not be lifted as long as such vestiges persist and there are feasible methods for removing them. Because the record shows that feasible steps can be taken to eliminate one-race schools, it is clear that the purpose of the decree has not yet been achieved. Evidence shows that already over one-half of the Oklahoma City schools are segregated. Therefore, lifting the decree is premature, and it should be reinstated.

► ANALYSIS

The Court's decision reinforces the notion that federal court oversight of school boards for desegregation purposes was intended to be temporary and not in perpetuity. Also, because the desegregation decree is a form of injunction, principles of injunction apply to the decrees. One of these principles is that an injunction may be modified or terminated upon compliance with the injunction.

◼══◼

Quicknotes

EQUAL PROTECTION CLAUSE A constitutional provision that each person be guaranteed the same protection of the laws enjoyed by other persons in like circumstances.

REMEDY Compensation for violation of a right or for injuries sustained.

◼══◼

Parents Involved in Community Schools v. Seattle School Dist. No.1

Parents of unadmitted students (P) v. Public school district (D)

127 S. Ct. 2738 (2007).

NATURE OF CASE: Suits challenging school-assignment plans under the Equal Protection Clause.

FACT SUMMARY: Two metropolitan school districts sought to assign students to schools to achieve racial balance.

🏛 RULE OF LAW
Racial balance between local high-school districts is not a compelling government interest under the Equal Protection Clause.

FACTS: The Seattle School District (Seattle) (D) implemented a student assignment plan designed to achieve numerically defined racial balance between Seattle's (D) ten public high schools. Seattle (D), however, had never been found to run racially segregated schools. The Jefferson County Public Schools in Louisville, Kentucky (Louisville) was under a desegregation order from 1975 to 2000; the order was dissolved in 2001 when a federal court ruled that Louisville (D) had reached unitary status by largely eliminating the district's earlier racial segregation. After the decree was dissolved, Louisville (D) voluntarily adopted a student-assignment plan that required specific minimum and maximum enrollment percentages for black students. Parents (P) of students who were denied admission in each school district sued their respective district, alleging, in part, violations of the Equal Protection Clause. After the intermediate appellate courts in both cases upheld the assignment plans, the parents (P) petitioned the Supreme Court for further review.

ISSUE: Is racial balance between local high-school districts a compelling government interest under the Equal Protection Clause?

HOLDING AND DECISION: (Roberts, C.J.) No. Racial balance between local high-school districts is not a compelling government interest under the Equal Protection Clause. Because both school districts (D) have apportioned government benefits on the basis of race, the applicable standard of review in these cases is strict scrutiny: Seattle (D) and Louisville (D) must show that their race-based discrimination (1) advances a compelling government interest through (2) means that are narrowly tailored to achieve the intended purpose. The asserted interests in both Seattle (D) and Louisville (D) reduce to nothing more than the goal of numerical racial balance between each district's (D) schools. This Court has consistently found such a purpose illegitimate. *Grutter v. Bollinger*, 539 U.S. 306 (2003), does not control here because *Grutter* involved the specific interests of higher education; it is also

instructive, though, that *Grutter* upheld the law-school admission policy there because racial diversity was only one of a mix of admissions criteria. Here, on the other hand, pure numerical racial balance, by itself, is the government interest, and that interest has never been recognized as valid. The plans at issue here also fail because the school districts (D) have failed to show that they seriously considered other means besides explicit racial classifications. Reversed.

CONCURRENCE: (Thomas, J.) Racial imbalance and racial segregation are not synonymous; it is possible to have racial imbalance through no conscious decision to segregate. Further, forced racial mixing of students may or may not provide educational benefits in general or higher achievement for black students in particular. The color-blind Constitution, then, requires that these student assignment plans be struck down.

CONCURRENCE: (Kennedy, J.) Contrary to the Chief Justice's plurality opinion, race can be considered as one among several factors in examining school enrollments. General, indirect solutions to problems of racial composition of schools are much better than the crude plans in these cases as ways to address those problems. The United States has special obligations to ensure equal opportunity for all children, and government should be permitted to consider race in its attempts to fulfill that mission. As the plurality correctly notes, though, government may not classify students based solely on race without first making a showing that such a step is necessary.

DISSENT: (Stevens, J.) In his demand of strict equality under the Constitution, the Chief Justice forgets that, before *Brown*, only black students were told where they could and could not go to school. Today's plurality decision rewrites the history of our landmark school-desegregation decision.

DISSENT: (Breyer, J.) These voluntary plans bear striking resemblances to plans that this Court has long required, permitted, and encouraged local school districts to formulate and use. Every branch of government has acknowledged that government may voluntarily use race-conscious plans to address race-based problems even when such plans are not constitutionally obligatory. The plurality overlooks the fact that no case has ever decided that all racial classifications should receive precisely the same scrutiny. Actually, our decisions have applied different standards to assess

Continued on next page.

racial classifications depending on whether the government's purpose was to exclude persons from, or to include persons in, government programs. The plurality's interpretation of strict scrutiny, however, would automatically invalidate all race-conscious government action. The school districts' (D) interest here serves remedial, educational, and democratic purposes; such a multiplicity of concerns means that *Grutter*'s rationale controls here and requires upholding these assignment plans. Even under the strictest scrutiny, though, the plans here pass muster under the Equal Protection Clause because they are more narrowly tailored than the plan approved in *Grutter*. Accordingly, these plans are consistent with equal protection of the laws.

▶ ANALYSIS

Chief Justice Roberts's plurality opinion in *Parents Involved* focuses on the firm percentages used by Seattle (D) and Louisville (D) in making student-assignment decisions. Despite Justice Breyer's objections in dissent, it is difficult to see how such an overtly numerical approach differs from the quota-based systems that the Court consistently has struck down under the Equal Protection Clause. See, e.g., *Regents of the University of California v. Bakke,* 438 U.S. 265, 307 (1978): "If [the University's] purpose is to assure within its student body some specified percentage of a particular group merely because of its race or ethnic origin, such a preferential purpose must be rejected not as insubstantial but as facially invalid."

■=■

Quicknotes

EQUAL PROTECTION CLAUSE A constitutional provision that each person be guaranteed the same protection of the laws enjoyed by other persons in like circumstances.

STRICT SCRUTINY Method by which courts determine the constitutionality of a law, when a law affects a fundamental right. Under the test, the legislature must have had a compelling interest to enact the law and measures prescribed by the law must be the least restrictive means possible to accomplish its goal.

■=■

Richmond v. J.A. Croson Co.

Municipality (D) v. Construction company (P)

488 U.S. 469 (1989).

NATURE OF CASE: Appeal from decision under 42 U.S.C. § 1983 finding that a city's set-aside program whereby general contractors on city construction projects were required to subcontract at least 30 percent of the contract amount to minority-owned businesses did not violate the Equal Protection Clause.

FACT SUMMARY: The city of Richmond (D) passed a set-aside program whereby general contractors on city construction projects were required to subcontract at least 30 percent of the contract amount to minority-owned businesses. J.A. Croson Co. (P), the sole bidder on a city construction contract, was denied the contract on the basis of the program and sued, alleging that the program was unconstitutional under the Fourteenth Amendment's Equal Protection Clause.

RULE OF LAW

A program that requires general contractors on city construction projects to subcontract at least 30 percent of the contract amount to minority-owned businesses violates the Equal Protection Clause.

FACTS: Richmond, Virginia, (D) adopted a Minority Business Utilization Plan (Plan) requiring general contractors awarded city construction contracts to subcontract at least 30 percent of the dollar amount of each contract to one or more "Minority Business Enterprises" (MBEs), which the Plan defined to include a business from anywhere in the country at least 51 percent of which is owned and controlled by Black, Spanish-speaking, Oriental, Indian, Eskimo, or Aleut citizens. Although the Plan declared that it was "remedial" in nature, it was adopted after a public hearing at which no direct evidence was presented that the city had discriminated on the basis of race in awarding contracts or that its general contractors had discriminated against minority subcontractors. J.A. Croson Co. (P), the sole non-minority bidder on a city construction contract, was denied the contract on the basis of the program and sued under 42 U.S.C. § 1983, alleging that the program was unconstitutional under the Fourteenth Amendment's Equal Protection Clause. The district court upheld the program, and the court of appeals originally affirmed, but reversed on remand. The Supreme Court granted review.

ISSUE: Does a program that requires general contractors on city construction projects to subcontract at least 30 percent of the contract amount to minority-owned businesses violate the Equal Protection Clause?

HOLDING AND DECISION: (O'Connor, J.) Yes. Although Congress may remedy the effects of past or society-wide discrimination does not mean that states or local governments may do so. The state or local government is limited to redressing only discrimination that occurs in its jurisdiction and must identify such discrimination with specificity. Because the Plan's classifications were based solely on race, it is subject to strict scrutiny. Strict scrutiny is necessary to determine if such race-based measures are benign or remedial or motivated by improper purposes. Here, the Plan fails the strict scrutiny test for two reasons. First, there is inadequate proof that Richmond's (D) objective of overcoming past discrimination in the construction industry is "compelling," and, second, even assuming that this objective is compelling, the Plan was not narrowly tailored to accomplish that objective. None of the evidence presented pointed to any identified discrimination in the Richmond construction industry. "To accept Richmond's claim that past societal discrimination alone can serve as the basis for rigid racial preferences would be to open the door to competing claims for 'remedial relief' for every disadvantaged group. The dream of a Nation of equal citizens in a society where race is irrelevant to personal opportunity and achievement would be lost in a mosaic of shifting preferences based on inherently unmeasurable claims of past wrongs." Also, the Plan is grossly overinclusive if its goal is to remedy past discrimination against blacks, given that it works in favor of other minorities, some of whom may have not ever resided in Richmond. The plan is not narrowly tailored to accomplish its remedial goal because Richmond has available to it a variety of race-neutral means to spur the award of public contracts to racial minorities. The Plan seems to be narrowly tailored only to the goal of racial balancing. Thus, Richmond (or any locality) could act to rectify the effects of identified discrimination within its jurisdiction, so long as such discrimination is specifically identified and proven. Because here Richmond failed to identify the need for remedial action, the Plan violates the Equal Protection Clause.

CONCURRENCE: (Stevens, J.) A government decision that is based on a racial classification should be allowed if it prevents discrimination in the future, not only if it remedies past discrimination.

CONCURRENCE: (Scalia, J.) State and local governments may not discriminate on the basis of race to remedy past wrongs. Government discrimination regardless of its purpose is immoral and inherently wrong. The only circumstance where state and local governments may act on the basis of race is to undo their own existing racist practices—such as in the case of school segregation. States

Continued on next page.

have means other than distinctions made on the basis of race for remedying past discrimination.

DISSENT: (Marshall, J.) Richmond, contrary to the majority's conclusions, did provide sufficient evidence of widespread discrimination in its construction industry, and the type of evidence provided was just the kind that the Court has used to uphold race-based measures designed to remedy past discrimination. In fact, Richmond's Plan, and the evidence used to support it, are indistinguishable from a similar federal plan that the court upheld (*Fullilove v. Klutznick*, 448 U.S. 448 [1980]). By adopting strict scrutiny to review race-conscious remedial measures, the majority is taking a giant step backward in its affirmative-action juris-prudence. Strict scrutiny should be applied only to measures that are racist in nature, not those that remedy past discrimination. The majority's adoption of this level of review signals that it believes government no longer needs to rectify racial injustice, but the reality is that the country is not close to having eradicated racial discrimination or its vestiges.

▶ *ANALYSIS*

Strict scrutiny applies to all racial classifications used by government, whether it is federal, state, or local. This standard of review applies to affirmative action. Those who favor strict scrutiny for affirmative action programs argue that all racial classifications, whether invidious or benign, should be subject to this standard of review be-cause any kind of government-sponsored discrimination is noxious, regardless of what motivates it. Those who argue for a lower level of judicial scrutiny for affirmative action measures emphasize, as Justice Marshall does in his dis-sent, that achieving social equality requires affirmative action at this point in our history.

■═■

Quicknotes

EQUAL PROTECTION CLAUSE A constitutional provision that each person be guaranteed the same protection of the laws enjoyed by other persons in like circumstances.

STRICT SCRUTINY Method by which courts determine the constitutionality of a law, when a law affects a funda-mental right. Under the test, the legislature must have had a compelling interest to enact the law and measures prescribed by the law must be the least restrictive means possible to accomplish its goal.

■═■

Grutter v. Bollinger

Law school applicant (P) v. State university (D)

539 U.S. 306 (2003).

NATURE OF CASE: Suit by a wait-listed but ultimately rejected white law school applicant to invalidate a race-conscious admissions policy at a state law school.

FACT SUMMARY: Grutter (P), a white resident of Michigan, applied for admission to the law school at the University of Michigan (D). Under its race-conscious admissions policy, the law school provisionally admitted Grutter (P), placing her on a waiting list, but ultimately declined to admit her. Grutter (P) filed suit against the University (D) in federal court.

RULE OF LAW
Student-body diversity is a compelling state interest sufficient to justify using a race-conscious university admissions policy consistent with the Equal Protection Clause, and enrolling an unspecified critical mass of minority students under such a policy is a narrowly tailored way to advance that interest.

FACTS: The law school at the University of Michigan (D) drafted and applied an admissions policy that flexibly used race as one factor among many in the school's admissions decisions. A diverse student body was an articulated goal of the school. Racial and ethnic diversity was an important component, but only a component, of the school's definition of diversity. In its commitment to diversity, however, the school openly sought to enroll an unspecified "critical mass" of students from traditionally underrepresented minorities so long as, like any other students admitted to the school, such students were likely to meet the school's academic standards. Grutter (P), a white resident of Michigan, applied for admission to the law school while the race-conscious admissions policy was in force. The school put her on a waiting list but ultimately did not enroll her in the school. She filed suit against the University (D) in federal court.

ISSUE: Is student-body diversity a compelling state interest sufficient to justify using a race-conscious university admissions policy consistent with the Equal Protection Clause; and, if so, is enrolling an unspecified critical mass of minority students under that policy a narrowly tailored way to advance that interest?

HOLDING AND DECISION: (O'Connor, J.) Yes. Student-body diversity is a compelling state interest sufficient to justify using a race-conscious university admissions policy consistent with the Equal Protection Clause. The benefits of a genuinely diverse student body—to all members of the student body, to the legal profession, and to society at large—are substantial and well documented. Moreover, the law school's admission of an unspecified critical mass of minority students under that policy is a

narrowly tailored way to advance that interest. The law school's flexible goal of a critical mass of minority students is not a veiled version of the rigid quota system struck down in *University of California Regents v. Bakke*, 438 U.S. 265 (1978). Further underscoring the flexibility of the law school's admissions policy is that race is only one in a mix of pertinent factors in an admissions review tailored to an individualized assessment of each application. With distinct improvements in minority education on the rise in the twenty-five years since *Bakke*, affirmative action such as the law school's admission policy should become unnecessary in the next twenty-five years. Because the University of Michigan law school's admissions policy is a narrowly tailored way to advance the compelling state interest of diversity in education, the race-conscious admissions policy does not violate the Equal Protection Clause.

CONCURRENCE: (Ginsburg, J.) Although conscious and unconscious racial bias still plagues American education at all levels, one can realistically hope that affirmative action will become unnecessary during the next generation.

CONCURRENCE AND DISSENT: (Scalia, J.) If diversity is a compelling state interest in higher education, then surely it is equally compelling in every other walk of life, too. This case, along with *Gratz v. Bollinger*, 539 U.S. 244 (2003), seems destined to prolong the litigation of affirmative-action programs. Definitions and applications of the sham concept of critical mass, a given school's level of commitment to the supposed educational benefits of diversity: all the highlights of the majority opinion will be litigated in the years to come. The better judicial course would have been a ruling unequivocally invalidating racial preferences in public universities or even a clear (albeit dead-wrong) holding that racial preferences are acceptable. Instead, the jurisprudential mish-mash in this case and *Gratz* will only extend the problems these cases presented.

CONCURRENCE AND DISSENT: (Thomas, J.) Under the Constitution, a public university may not set high standards for admission while exempting members of favored races from those standards, yet that is the goal of the law school's admissions policy. The law school's goal of a critical mass of minority students is little more than a devotion to classroom aesthetics. The school has therefore failed to show a compelling state interest, especially since the school's devotion to aesthetics translates into an interest no more compelling than maintaining an elite, exclusive state law school. With the Court's failure to articulate a cogent

Continued on next page.

legal principle for its compelling-state-interest holding, an implicit rationale therefore seems likely: the majority apparently grants deference to a policy of racial preference because the policy's discrimination purports to be benign. It is not benign, though, when the school admits underqualified students who can only flounder, nor when the stigma created by the policy attaches to all black students enrolled in the school. The majority is correct, however, that racial preferences among and between different racial minorities still violates equal protection, and that the law school's admissions policy will be illegal in twenty-five years. Because the policy is just as illegal today as it will be in twenty-five years, the majority opinion itself contradicts the Equal Protection Clause.

DISSENT: (Rehnquist, C.J.) The law school's admissions policy is not narrowly tailored to advance the school's asserted interest. Strict scrutiny demands a perfect fit between means and interest. The law school's policy, however, discriminates between minority groups by admitting substantially more African-Americans than Hispanics or Native Americans. The very means used to advance the law school's asserted interest thus actually violate the Equal Protection Clause themselves.

DISSENT: (Kennedy, J.) Under the guise of strict scrutiny, the Court has failed to scrutinize the admissions policy in a truly strict manner. Indeed, the review is the antithesis of strict, being merely deferential. Race is one constitutionally acceptable factor in a public university's admissions decisions, but the law school has failed to show that its goal of a critical mass of minority students is anything besides a forbidden quota.

▶ *ANALYSIS*

The justice writing for the majority in *Grutter*, Justice O'Connor, also wrote for the majority in *Adarand Constuctors v. Pena*, 515 U.S. 200 (1995), which held that all governmentally imposed racial classifications are subject to strict scrutiny. The majority opinion in *Adarand* made a special effort to "dispel the notion that strict scrutiny is 'strict in theory but fatal in fact,'" (p. 227), and *Grutter* proves that a government can win when courts strictly scrutinize its racially discriminatory policies. Whether scrutiny is strict or relatively deferential, of course, will vary from one judge to the next as they apply both the pertinent constitutional text and the case law interpreting it.

had a compelling interest to enact the law and measures prescribed by the law must be the least restrictive means possible to accomplish its goal.

■■■

Quicknotes

EQUAL PROTECTION CLAUSE A constitutional provision that each person be guaranteed the same protection of the laws enjoyed by other persons in like circumstances.

STRICT SCRUTINY Method by which courts determine the constitutionality of a law, when a law affects a fundamental right. Under the test, the legislature must have

Gratz v. Bollinger

Prospective undergraduate student (P) v. State university (D)

539 U.S. 244 (2003).

NATURE OF CASE: Suit by prospective undergraduate students who were denied admission by a state university that used a race-based admissions policy.

FACT SUMMARY: Gratz (P) and another high school student, both Caucasian, were denied admission to an undergraduate program at the University of Michigan (D). When Gratz (P) and the other student applied for admission, African-American, Hispanic, and Native American students were effectively guaranteed admission to the University.

🏛 RULE OF LAW

A public university's undergraduate admissions policy that automatically awards 20 percent of the minimum points required for admission to some students based solely on race violates the Equal Protection Clause.

FACTS: Gratz (P) and another high school student, both Michigan residents and both Caucasian, were qualified for, but were denied, admission to the University of Michigan (D). The University's (D) admissions policy allowed consideration of race, with almost every applicant who was African-American, Hispanic, or Native American admitted to undergraduate studies at the University (D). After several modifications of its admissions policy, the University now uses a "selection index" to assess undergraduate admissions applications. Part of the index automatically awards 20 percent of the minimum required number of points for admission to applicants who are African-American, Hispanic, or Native American. Gratz (P) and the other rejected applicant filed suit against the University (D) in federal court, alleging that the University's undergraduate admissions policy violates the Equal Protection Clause.

ISSUE: Does a public university's undergraduate admissions policy that automatically awards 20 percent of the minimum points required for admission to some students based solely on race violate the Equal Protection Clause?

HOLDING AND DECISION: (Rehnquist, C.J.) Yes. A public university's undergraduate admissions policy that automatically awards 20 percent of the minimum points required for admission to some students based solely on race violates the Equal Protection Clause. Though the interest in educational diversity is compelling, under strict scrutiny the University's (D) means of advancing that interest in this case are not narrowly tailored to the interest. Automatically awarding 20 percent of the required minimum number of points for admission—in effect, automatically awarding admission—based solely on an applicant's race does not provide the individualized assessment required under *Grutter v. Bollinger*, 539 U.S. 306 (2003). Accordingly, the University's (D) admissions policy violates the Equal Protection Clause. Reversed.

CONCURRENCE: (O'Connor, J.) The automatic award of points to applicants based on race prevents the individualized assessment that occurs under the admissions policy at the University of Michigan's law school.

DISSENT: (Ginsburg, J.) Benign racial discrimination by governments, undertaken for the purpose of including rather than excluding racial minorities, should be scrutinized with less than strict review. Under a proper level of review, one that extends a degree of deference to accommodate a purpose of inclusion, the University's (D) undergraduate admissions policy does not violate equal protection. No evidence shows that students who do not receive special consideration based on race are actually prejudiced by being denied admission to the University (D). This decision encourages schools to be dishonest instead of openly promoting racial minorities as the University (D) here has done.

▶ ANALYSIS

Gratz and *Grutter* were handed down as a pair, and they should be read the same way, each as a necessary complement to the other. *Grutter*'s holding that educational diversity is a compelling state interest relieved the Court from deciding that issue in *Gratz*. At the same time, *Gratz* provides a clear example of an admissions policy that does not pass muster under the narrow-tailoring prong of strict scrutiny following *Grutter*'s requirement of an individualized assessment of admissions applications.

◼═◼

Quicknotes

EQUAL PROTECTION CLAUSE A constitutional provision that each person be guaranteed the same protection of the laws enjoyed by other persons in like circumstances.

STRICT SCRUTINY Method by which courts determine the constitutionality of a law, when a law affects a fundamental right. Under the test, the legislature must have had a compelling interest to enact the law and measures prescribed by the law must be the least restrictive means possible to accomplish its goal.

◼═◼

Easley v. Cromartie

State (D) v. Redistricting challenger (P)

532 U.S. 234 (2001).

NATURE OF CASE: Suit to invalidate legislative redistricting for violation of the Equal Protection Clause.

FACT SUMMARY: [Facts not stated in casebook excerpt.]

🏛 RULE OF LAW
Evidence that fails to show alternative, more racially balanced boundaries for voting districts cannot support a finding that race motivated a legislative redistricting plan in violation of the Equal Protection Clause.

FACTS: [Facts not stated in casebook excerpt.]

ISSUE: Can evidence that fails to show alternative, more racially balanced boundaries for voting districts support a finding that race motivated a legislative redistricting plan in violation of the Equal Protection Clause?

HOLDING AND DECISION: (Breyer, J.) No. Evidence that fails to show alternative, more racially balanced boundaries for voting districts cannot support a finding that race motivated a legislative redistricting plan in violation of the Equal Protection Clause. The three-judge panel of the district court clearly erred by finding that race, not politics, motivated North Carolina's voting redistricting plan. As decided in earlier versions of this litigation, the high correlation between race and political affiliation in North Carolina means that neither the shape of the new districts nor the splitting of towns and counties nor the large number of African-American voters supports a finding of racial motivation for the redistricting plan. The same conclusion obtains this time, partly because evidence of voter registration does not demonstrate voting behavior. The party challenging a redistricting plan must show that alternative, more racially balanced plans exist. No such evidence is in this record, and the district court's findings, offered to support its conclusion that North Carolina violated the Equal Protection Clause, are therefore clearly erroneous. Reversed.

DISSENT: (Thomas, J.) This case is before the Court for deferential review of the record for clear error on a trial court's stated finding of fact. Such review does not permit this Court to substitute its view of the evidence for that of the trial-level finder of fact—but that is precisely what the majority has done. The majority's justification for retrying the case on appeal is not persuasive; the absence of intermediate appellate review of a three-day trial that included key expert testimony does not authorize this Court to retry a case on an appellate record. Record evidence supported the district court's finding that race, not politics, motivated the new redistricting plan. The trial court therefore did not commit clear error.

▶ ANALYSIS

Easley is an excellent study in appellate adjudication. Justice Breyer's majority opinion cites the right rules for the applicable "clearly erroneous" review but explains them away for purposes of deciding this case. On the other hand, Justice Thomas, in dissent, cites the same rules but overlooks the need for review of "the entire evidence" that is stated in the case upon which he relies in discussing clear error, *Anderson v. Bessemer City*, 470 U.S. 564 (1985). As so often happens in constitutional law, in *Easley* the case thus turns upon how the justices view an issue that the non-lawyer general public would call "just a technicality." *Easley*'s debate over the appropriate appellate standard of review is worth remembering while reading, for example, an opinion such as *Adarand Constructors v. Pena*, 515 U.S. 200 (1995), where the appropriate standard for judicial review of racial classifications is the substantive issue in the opinion.

■═■

Quicknotes

EQUAL PROTECTION CLAUSE A constitutional provision that each person be guaranteed the same protection of the laws enjoyed by other persons in like circumstances.

■═■

Frontiero v. Richardson

Servicewoman (P) v. Court (D)

411 U.S. 677 (1973).

NATURE OF CASE: Suit challenging the constitutionality of a statute.

FACT SUMMARY: A statute provides that servicemen's wives are automatically eligible for benefits as dependents while servicewomen must demonstrate that their husbands are dependent on them before they are eligible for the benefits.

🏛 RULE OF LAW
By according differential treatment to male and female members of the uniformed services for the sole purpose of achieving administrative convenience, the statutes are unconstitutionally discriminatory and violate the Due Process Clause of the Fifth Amendment.

FACTS: A servicewoman's request for increased benefits for her dependent husband was denied because she failed to affirmatively demonstrate that her husband was dependent on her for over one-half of his support. The controlling statute provided that a serviceman may claim his wife as a dependent without regard to whether she is actually dependent on him. A servicewoman can claim her husband as a dependent only if she demonstrates that he is actually dependent on her for over one-half of his support.

ISSUE: Are statutes providing stricter requirements for servicewomen's husbands claiming dependency benefits than for servicemen's wives claiming such benefits unconstitutionally discriminatory?

HOLDING AND DECISION: (Brennan, J.) Yes. Classifications based upon sex, like those based upon race, alienage, or national origin are inherently suspect and must be subjected to strict scrutiny. The U.S. has had a long and unfortunate history of sex discrimination. During the nineteenth century, the position of women was in many ways similar to that of blacks before the Civil War. Neither could hold office, serve on juries, or bring suit, and although black men were given the right to vote in 1870, women did not gain suffrage until 50 years later. Women (like blacks) still face pervasive, although at times more subtle, discrimination in education, employment, and especially in politics. Sex, like race, is an immutable characteristic, determined solely by birth and which bears no relation to ability to perform in society. Hence, statutory distinctions between the sexes often have the effect of invidiously regulating an entire class to an inferior legal status. Hence, a compelling state interest must be demonstrated if such distinctions are to be upheld. Here, it is argued that Congress might have reasonably concluded that it would be cheaper and easier to presume that wives were dependent on their husbands while presuming that husbands are not dependent on their wives. However, to withstand scrutiny, it must be shown that this practice is actually

cheaper, which was not done here. In fact, there was evidence that many servicemen's wives are not dependent on their husbands for over one-half of their support. Insofar as the statute requires female members to prove their husband's dependency while not so requiring male members, it violates the Due Process Clause of the Fifth Amendment.

CONCURRENCE: (Stewart, J.) The statutes work an unconstitutional discrimination and should be struck down.

CONCURRENCE: (Powell, J.) Although the statutes here discriminate against servicewomen in violation of the Fifth Amendment's Due Process Clause, it is not necessary to hold that sex-based classifications merit strict scrutiny. The Court can, and therefore should, decide this case under the reasoning of *Reed v. Reed*, 404 U.S. 71 (1971) [i.e., under rational-basis review, invalidating a statutory preference of men over women in appointing estate administrators].

▶ ANALYSIS

Despite the holding of the plurality opinion, the majority has consistently failed to adopt the view that sex classifications are inherently suspect. This has led to widely varying results when challenges to statutes on the basis of sex discrimination are brought before the Court. The Court has sustained an attack on the Social Security System, which provided survivor's benefits to a minor child and widow but not to a widower, because it discriminated against women wage earners by affording them less protection for their survivors. A Utah court's finding—that support payments ended at 18 for a daughter and 21 for a son—was struck down as discriminatory. But in a California case, the Court upheld a provision in the state's disability insurance program that excluded coverage for a woman undergoing a normal pregnancy. Also upheld was a Florida statute that provided property tax exemptions for widows but not for widowers. And a naval regulation allowing women officers a longer tenure before discharge due to lack of promotion was approved. The proposed Twenty-Seventh Amendment to the Constitution provides that "equality of rights under the law shall not be denied or abridged by the United States or by any state on account of sex."

■■■

Quicknotes

DUE PROCESS CLAUSE Clauses found in the Fifth and Fourteenth Amendments to the U.S. Constitution providing that no person shall be deprived of "life, liberty, or property, without due process of law."

Continued on next page.

INTERMEDIATE SCRUTINY A standard of reviewing the propriety of classifications pertaining to gender or legitimacy under the Equal Protection Clause of the U.S. Constitution which requires a court to ascertain whether the classification furthers an important state interest and is substantially related to the attainment of that interest.

STRICT SCRUTINY Method by which courts determine the constitutionality of a law, when a law affects a fundamental right. Under the test, the legislature must have had a compelling interest to enact the law and measures prescribed by the law must be the least restrictive means possible to accomplish its goal.

SUSPECT CLASSIFICATION A class of persons that have historically been subject to discriminatory treatment; statutes drawing a distinction between persons based on a suspect classification, i.e., race, nationality or alienage, are subject to a strict scrutiny standard of review.

Craig v. Boren

Males 18-20 years of age (P) v. State (D)

429 U.S. 190 (1976).

NATURE OF CASE: Appeal from an action to have an Oklahoma statute declared unconstitutional.

FACT SUMMARY: Craig (P) appealed after a federal district court upheld two sections of an Oklahoma statute prohibiting the sale of "nonintoxicating" 3.2 percent beer to males under the age of 21 and to females under the age of 18 on the ground that such a gender-based differential did not constitute a denial to males 18–20 years of age equal protection of the laws.

🏛 RULE OF LAW
Laws that establish classifications by gender must serve important governmental objectives and must be substantially related to achievement of those objectives to be constitutionally in line with the Equal Protection Clause.

FACTS: Craig (P) brought suit to have two sections of an Oklahoma statute, which prohibits the sale of "nonintoxicating" 3.2 percent beer to males under the age of 21 and to females under the age of 18, declared unconstitutional. Craig (P) contended that such a gender-based differential constituted a denial to males 18–20 years of age of the equal protection of the laws in violation of the Fourteenth Amendment. Boren (D), representing the state of Oklahoma, argued that this law was enacted as a traffic safety measure and that the protection of public health and safety was an important function of state and local governments. Boren (D) introduced statistical data demonstrating that 18–20-year-old male arrests for "driving under the influence" and "drunkenness" substantially exceeded female arrests for the same age period. The district court upheld the ordinance on the ground that it served the important governmental objective of traffic safety. Craig (P) appealed.

ISSUE: Are laws that establish classifications by gender constitutional if they do not serve important governmental objectives and are not substantially related to achievement of those objectives?

HOLDING AND DECISION: (Brennan, J.) No. Laws that establish classifications by gender must serve important governmental objectives and must be substantially related to achievement of those objectives to be constitutionally in line with the Equal Protection Clause. It appears that the objective underlying the statute in controversy is the enhancement of traffic safety. Clearly, the protection of public health and safety represents an important function of state and local governments. However, the statistics presented by Boren (D) in this court's view cannot support the conclusion that the gender-based distinction closely serves to achieve the objective. The most relevant of the statistical surveys presented as evidence by Boren (D) in support of the statute, arrests of 18–20-year-olds for alcohol related driving offenses, establish 2 percent more males than females are arrested for that offense. Such a disparity can hardly form the basis for employment of a gender line as a classifying device. Certainly, if maleness is to serve as a proxy for drinking and driving, a correlation of 2 percent must be considered unduly tenuous. Indeed, prior cases have consistently rejected the use of sex as a decision-making factor. Therefore, since the gender-based differential does not serve an important governmental objective, the Oklahoma statute constitutes a denial of the equal protection of the laws to males aged 18–20 and is unconstitutional.

DISSENT: (Rehnquist, J.) The court's disposition of this case is objectionable on two grounds. First is its conclusion that men challenging a gender-based statute which treats them less favorably than women may invoke a more stringent standard of judicial review than pertains to most other types of classifications. Second is the court's enunciation of this standard, without citation to any source, as being that "classifications by gender must serve important governmental objectives and must be substantially related to achievement of those objectives." The Equal Protection Clause contains no such language, and none of our previous cases adopt that standard. The challenged statute need only pass the rational basis test. Under that analysis, the statute is constitutional.

▶ ANALYSIS

Cases that consider at what age males and females should be considered to attain a majority age have met with some stiff opposition. In *Stanton v. Stanton*, a Utah justice observed: "Regardless of what a judge may think about equality, his thinking cannot change the facts of life. To judicially hold that males and females attain their maturity at the same age is to be blind to the biological facts of life."

■■■

Quicknotes

EQUAL PROTECTION CLAUSE A constitutional provision that each person be guaranteed the same protection of the laws enjoyed by other persons in like circumstances.

■■■

United States v. Virginia

Federal government (P) v. State (D)

518 U.S. 515 (1996).

NATURE OF CASE: Appeal from final judgment upholding a college's male-only admission policy.

FACT SUMMARY: Virginia Military Institute (VMI) (D), a state-sponsored university, had a policy of excluding women from attending.

 RULE OF LAW
Public schools may not exclude women.

FACTS: Since 1839, VMI (D), a Virginia (D) public institution, had been a male-only college that sought to train "citizen-soldiers." In 1990, the Attorney General (P) sued VMI (D) and Virginia (D), claiming that the admission policy violated the Equal Protection Clause. Virginia (D) eventually proposed a remedial plan under which a parallel program would be developed for women. The Virginia Women's Institute for Leadership (VWIL) would be created at Mary Baldwin College. The trial court and an appellate court upheld this remedial plan, but the Attorney General (P) appealed and the Supreme Court granted a writ of certiorari.

ISSUE: May public schools exclude women?

HOLDING AND DECISION: (Ginsburg, J.) No. Public schools may not exclude women. States must show that a sex-based government action serves important governmental objectives and that the discriminatory means employed are substantially related to the achievement of those objectives. There must an exceedingly persuasive justification for the action. This heightened review standard prevents classifications that perpetuate the legal, social, and economic inferiority of women. While single-sex education may provide benefits to some students, Virginia (D) has not shown that it pursued this option as a means to providing a diversity of educational opportunities. On the other hand, the historical record shows that Virginia (D) has systematically prevented women from obtaining higher education until relatively recently. The fact that women have been successfully integrated into the armed forces and service academies demonstrates that VMI's (D) stature will not be downgraded by admitting women. The proposed VWIL does not qualify as VMI's (D) equal in terms of faculty, facilities, course offerings, and its reputation. Accordingly, since Virginia (D) is unable to provide substantial equal opportunities for women who desire to attend VMI (D), the male-only admission policy is unconstitutional.

DISSENT: (Scalia, J.) The majority sweeps away an institution that has thrived for 150 years and the precedents of this Court to embark on a course of proscribing its own elite opinions on society. Virginia (D) has an important interest in providing education, and single-sex instruction is an approach substantially related to this goal.

ANALYSIS

Justice Scalia's dissent carries a tone of disgust for the majority opinion. As he did in *Romer v. Evans*, 116 S. Ct. 1620 (1996), Scalia states that the majority seeks to satisfy some unidentified group of antimajoritarian elites. This attitude is unusual for a member of the Supreme Court since dissents are usually restricted to attacks on the majority's legal reasoning.

Quicknotes

HEIGHTENED SCRUTINY A purposefully vague judicial description of all levels of scrutiny more exacting than minimal scrutiny.

INTERMEDIATE SCRUTINY A standard of reviewing the propriety of classifications pertaining to gender or legitimacy under the Equal Protection Clause of the U.S. Constitution which requires a court to ascertain whether the classification furthers an important state interest and is substantially related to the attainment of that interest.

Geduldig v. Aiello

State official (D) v. Women with pregnancy-related disabilities (P)

417 U.S. 484 (1974).

NATURE OF CASE: Appeal from decision that a state disability insurance system's exclusion of pregnancy-related disabilities violates the Equal Protection Clause.

FACT SUMMARY: California's disability insurance system excluded disabilities resulting from normal pregnancies and birth. Women with pregnancy-related disabilities (P) challenged the exclusion as violating the Equal Protection Clause.

🏛 RULE OF LAW
A state disability insurance system's exclusion of pregnancy-related disabilities does not violate the Equal Protection Clause.

FACTS: For 30 years, California administered a disability insurance system that paid the benefits to persons in private employment who were temporarily unable to work because of disability not covered by workmen's compensation. Under the entirely self-supporting program, an employee paid one percent of his income to the disability fund. In return for this contribution, employees were insured against the risk of disability stemming from a substantial number of mental and physical injuries and illnesses. A provision of the program defined "disability" to exclude from coverage certain disabilities resulting from pregnancy. Women otherwise qualified under the program who had pregnancy-related disabilities (P) challenged the exclusion as violating the Equal Protection Clause. The district court found gender-based discrimination, and the Supreme Court granted review.

ISSUE: Does a state disability insurance system's exclusion of pregnancy-related disabilities violate the Equal Protection Clause?

HOLDING AND DECISION: (Stewart, J.) No. Not every disabling condition is covered under the program, and the program is intended to function like regular insurance. Coverage for the excluded pregnancy-related disabilities would be so expensive that the program could not be maintained only by employee contributions. California does not on the face of the program discriminate with respect to the persons or groups eligible under the program—it has merely chosen not to insure certain risks—and this decision is reflected in the level of annual contributions exacted from employees. Especially with respect to social welfare programs such as this one, the state's choice need only be rationally supportable. To have a program that covered all disabilities would require state subsidy, higher contributions, and possibly lower benefits. The Constitution does not require that a state have a more comprehensive social welfare program than it already has. California's interest in maintaining a self-supporting insurance program is a thus a legitimate one, and

provides a completely noninvidious basis for the state's decision not to create a more comprehensive program. Moreover, the exclusion's distinction is not based on sex but on pregnancy (those who don't have pregnancy-related disabilities are both men and women). Therefore, the exclusion of these disabilities is not invidious discrimination.

DISSENT: (Brennan, J.) Disabilities caused by pregnancy require the same kind of treatments and procedures, and have the same kind of economic impact, as other disabilities covered by the program. By not covering a gender-linked disability peculiar to women, the state creates a double-standard for disability compensation: women do not receive full coverage for female-specific disabilities, whereas men receive full coverage for male-specific disabilities. Such disparate treatment based on sex is gender-based discrimination.

▶ ANALYSIS

The Court's reasoning, at least to the extent it was saying pregnancy is not a sex-based characteristic, can be criticized, as the dissent seems to do. The entire burden from the exclusion of pregnancy is carried by women—those who are already pregnant and those who could become pregnant. Congress effectively overruled *Geduldig* on this basis when it enacted the Pregnancy Discrimination Act (1978), which defines sex discrimination to include pregnancy discrimination and prohibits discrimination on that basis. Far more plausible was the Court's rational-basis reasoning—that a state can choose the health risks it wishes to insure against and that exclusion of certain disabilities is rationally related to that objective.

■=■

Quicknotes

EQUAL PROTECTION CLAUSE A constitutional provision that each person be guaranteed the same protection of the laws enjoyed by other persons in like circumstances.

INVIDIOUS DISCRIMINATION Unequal treatment of a class of persons that is particularly malicious or hostile.

■=■

Orr v. Orr

Husband (P) v. Wife (D)

440 U.S. 268 (1979).

NATURE OF CASE: Appeal from ruling that a state statute that provides only husbands may be required to pay alimony does not violate the Equal Protection Clause.

FACT SUMMARY: Alabama required only husbands to pay alimony upon divorce. A divorcing husband (P) challenged the requirement on the ground that it violated the Equal Protection Clause.

🏛 RULE OF LAW
A requirement that only husbands pay alimony violates the Equal Protection Clause.

FACTS: An Alabama statute required only husbands to pay alimony upon divorce. This requirement was designed to help the wife of a broken marriage who needs financial assistance (and was thus based on the stereotype of the wife as dependent on the husband during marriage). A divorcing husband (P) who was required to pay alimony under the statute challenged the statute on the ground that it violated the Equal Protection Clause. Alabama's courts upheld the statute, and the Supreme Court granted review.

ISSUE: Does a requirement that only husbands pay alimony violate the Equal Protection Clause?

HOLDING AND DECISION: (Brennan, J.) Yes. The requirement that only husbands pay alimony discriminates on the basis of sex and therefore must serve important governmental objectives and must be substantially related to achieving those objectives. Here, Alabama's objectives are to provide help for needy spouses, using sex as a proxy for need, or to compensate women for past discrimination during marriage, which leaves them unprepared to enter the working world. These are legitimate goals, but the law is insubstantially related to those objectives because Alabama already requires individualized hearings at which it would be easy to determine which spouse was in fact needy and which had in fact been discriminated against during the marriage. Needy male spouses could also be helped. Thus, there is no reason to use sex as a proxy for need, and the state's objectives would be served just as well, and at no additional cost, with a gender-neutral rule that does not carry with it "the baggage of sexual stereotypes." Reversed and remanded.

▶ ANALYSIS

As in *Orr*, the Court has frequently invalidated laws that benefit women and disadvantage men when the Court perceives the law as being based on "the baggage of sexual stereotypes" of women being economically dependent on their husbands, but men being economically

independent of their wives. By doing so, the Court affords equal protection to spouses of each gender.

■═■

Quicknotes

EQUAL PROTECTION CLAUSE A constitutional provision that each person be guaranteed the same protection of the laws enjoyed by other persons in like circumstances.

GENDER DISCRIMINATION Unequal treatment of individuals without justification on the basis of their sex.

■═■

Mississippi University for Women v. Hogan

University (D) v. Applicant (P)

458 U.S. 718 (1982).

NATURE OF CASE: Action to declare unconstitutional a gender-based statute.

FACT SUMMARY: Hogan (P) sought to strike down a Mississippi statute that excluded males from enrolling in a state-supported nursing school.

🏛 RULE OF LAW
A statute that discriminates against men must meet the same "heightened scrutiny" equal protection analysis as statutes that discriminate against women.

FACTS: The Mississippi University for Women (D), created by the Mississippi legislature in 1884, has traditionally barred males from enrolling. In 1971, the University (D) established a school of nursing. Hogan (P) applied to the nursing school and was turned down solely by virtue of his gender. He was told that he could audit any courses in which he was interested, but that he could not enroll for credit. He brought a suit in district court, contending that the female-only policy of the state-run institution violated his guarantee of equal protection under the Fourteenth Amendment. The district court denied the requested relief. On appeal, the Fifth Circuit reversed, holding that the lower court erred in using "rational basis" analysis, rather than the "heightened scrutiny" required in gender-based discrimination cases. The University (D) appealed.

ISSUE: Must a court examine with "heightened scrutiny" a statute that discriminates against men?

HOLDING AND DECISION: (O'Connor, J.) Yes. The test that must be applied when a statute involves gender-based discrimination is whether the discriminatory classification serves important governmental objectives and whether the means employed are substantially related to the achievement of those objectives. Thus, the standard is more heightened than the mere "rational basis" standard generally employed in equal protection cases but slightly lower than the "strict scrutiny" applied in cases involving suspect classes or fundamental rights. The fact that the statute discriminates against males rather than females does not lower the standard of judicial review. In the instant case, the University (D) failed to meet either requirement of the heightened scrutiny test. It contended that the all-female requirement was necessary to compensate for past discriminatory practices against women. Yet, the statistics show that over 90 percent of the members of the nursing profession are women. Clearly, compensation is not necessary in this area. Similarly, the University's (D) second contention, that admitting men would tend to adversely affect the women at the school, is undermined by the practice of allowing men to audit the classes. As the University (D) has not met its burden of showing that an important governmental objective necessitates the statute in question, the statute must fall.

DISSENT: (Powell, J.) This is not the type of case in which the Equal Protection Clause was meant to be applied. There is no discrimination involved. Both men and women in Mississippi are provided with a choice regarding the institution of higher learning that they wish to attend. The Court's decision today merely means that one such choice—an all female college—will no longer be available to women.

▶ ANALYSIS

See also *Caban v. Mohammed*, 441 U.S. 380 (1979), where a section of the New York Domestic Relations Law, which permitted an unwed mother, but not an unwed father, to prevent the adoption of their child simply by withholding consent, was challenged under the Equal Protection Clause. The Court found that the state had been unable to advance any important interests justifying the gender-based discrimination and, thus, ruled the statute unconstitutional.

■==■

Quicknotes

EQUAL PROTECTION CLAUSE A constitutional provision that each person be guaranteed the same protection of the laws enjoyed by other persons in like circumstances.

GENDER DISCRIMINATION Unequal treatment of individuals without justification on the basis of their sex.

HEIGHTENED SCRUTINY A purposefully vague judicial description of all levels of scrutiny more exacting than minimal scrutiny.

■==■

Michael M. v. Superior Court of Sonoma County

Minor male (P) v. Court (D)

450 U.S. 464 (1981).

NATURE OF CASE: Appeal from refusal to set aside complaint for statutory rape.

FACT SUMMARY: Michael (P), 17½ years old, engaged in sex with a female under the age of 18 and sought to set aside a criminal complaint brought under a California statute that imposes criminal liability for sex with underage females but not with underage males.

🏛 RULE OF LAW
A state may enact a criminal statute prohibiting sex with females under the age of 18 without violating the Equal Protection Clause by not similarly prohibiting such acts with males under the age of 18.

FACTS: Michael (P) was a 17-year-old male who engaged in sexual intercourse with a female under age 18. A criminal complaint was drawn against him under § 261.5 of the California Penal Code. This section prohibits sex with a female under the age of 18, but does not prohibit sex with males under 18. Michael (P) sought to have the complaint set aside on the ground that the exclusion of males from the protection of the statute violated the Equal Protection Clause. The trial court, court of appeals, and the California Supreme Court all denied the request, and Michael (P) appealed.

ISSUE: May a state enact a criminal statute prohibiting sex with females under the age of 18 without violating the Equal Protection Clause by not similarly prohibiting such acts with males under the age of 18?

HOLDING AND DECISION: (Rehnquist, J.) Yes. The legislative purpose for the statute found by the California Supreme Court was to prevent teenage pregnancies. This legislative concern is entitled to great deference on our part. The state has a strong interest in preventing such pregnancies because most end in abortion and those resulting in birth make the children so born likely candidates to be wards of the state. Young men and young women are not similarly situated with respect to the problems inherent in sexual intercourse. Women can become pregnant and suffer disproportionately the profound physical, psychological, and emotional consequences of sex. Thus, a state may enact a criminal statute prohibiting sex with females under the age of 18 without violating the Equal Protection Clause by not similarly prohibiting such acts with males under the age of 18. Affirmed.

DISSENT: (Brennan, J.) The question is whether a concededly gender-biased classification survives the "middle-level" scrutiny applicable to such cases. There is no reason why a gender-neutral law would not serve whatever objectives are served by the present law. In fact, a gender-neutral law would be a greater deterrent of sexual activity as both males and females could be subjected to criminal liability for illicit sex. Thus, there has been no showing that the gender-based law is more effective than a gender-neutral one and the burden of the state has not been met. Section 261.5 violates the Equal Protection Clause.

DISSENT: (Stevens, J.) It is local custom and belief rather than laws that will determine the volume of sexual activity among unmarried teenagers. The question, once it is admitted that some law is necessary, is whether the difference between males and females justifies the statutory discrimination between them. The fact that a female confronts a greater risk from sex than a male is a reason to apply the prohibition against her, not to allow her to use her judgment where the law presumes she has not the ability to use it wisely. This law presumes that the male is the more guilty party, perhaps because the decision to engage in sex is his rather than the female's. But this is not supported by the record here or by the legislative history of the law. Thus, this law punishes one of two equally guilty parties and violates the Equal Protection Clause.

▌ ANALYSIS

This case represents a social welfare concern serving to uphold an underinclusive law. The logic, in view of modern times, of punishing only males is questionable and can be argued ad infinitum, as is painfully obvious from the number of opinions from the Court. Nonetheless, not all discrimination on the basis of sex is unwarranted and, in fact, gender is not regarded as a suspect classification for constitutional law purposes.

Quicknotes

EQUAL PROTECTION CLAUSE A constitutional provision that each person be guaranteed the same protection of the laws enjoyed by other persons in like circumstances.

Rostker v. Goldberg

Selective service claimant (P) v. Solicitor general (D)

453 U.S. 57 (1981).

NATURE OF CASE: Challenge to congressional legislation.

FACT SUMMARY: The Military Selective Service Act was challenged as unconstitutional because it only applied to males.

 RULE OF LAW
Congress may limit draft registration to males.

FACTS: Section 3 of the Military Selective Service Act (MSSA) empowered the president to proclaim a draft. The MSSA, by its terms, only applied to males. The MSSA was challenged as violative of the Equal Protection Clause of the Constitution. The challenge was rejected in the lower courts, and the Supreme Court granted review.

ISSUE: May Congress limit draft registration to males?

HOLDING AND DECISION: (Rehnquist, J.) Yes. Congress may limit draft registration to males. Gender discrimination in a law triggers heightened scrutiny: the gender discrimination must substantially advance an important governmental interest. Here, men, not women, are potentially affected by a draft if one is called. However, it must be remembered that only men are eligible for combat; women do not engage in combat. This difference in the Court's opinion indicates a legitimate basis for differential treatment, and therefore no constitutional violation is created by the law.

DISSENT: (White, J.) Limiting draft registration to men violates the equal-protection component of the Fifth Amendment's Due Process Clause. Not every position in the military requires a combat-ready man; defense officials estimate that approximately 80,000 drafted women could be used by the military in the first six months of a major mobilization of troops. Without any evidence that Congress concluded that a combat-ready man must fill every position in the military, there is no adequate rationale in this record to justify the sex-based discrimination in the Military Selective Service Act.

▶ *ANALYSIS*

The Court has generally shown great deference to Congress and the president in matters of national security. As the draft is inextricably linked to military power, the Court's result here is not surprising.

Quicknotes

EQUAL PROTECTION CLAUSE A constitutional provision that each person be guaranteed the same protection of the laws enjoyed by other persons in like circumstances.

HEIGHTENED SCRUTINY A purposefully vague judicial description of all levels of scrutiny more exacting than minimal scrutiny.

Califano v. Webster

Parties not identified.

430 U.S. 313 (1977).

NATURE OF CASE: Appeal from an action to have § 215 of the Social Security Act declared unconstitutional.

FACT SUMMARY: A district court held that § 215 of the Social Security Act, which allows women to eliminate additional low-earning years from the calculation of their retirement benefits, was violative of the equal protection component of the Due Process Clause of the Fifth Amendment.

🏛 RULE OF LAW
Section 215 of the Social Security Act, which allows women to eliminate additional low-earning years from the calculation of their retirement benefits, does not violate the Fifth Amendment because it works directly to remedy past discrimination.

FACTS: This suit was brought to challenge the constitutionality of § 215 of the Social Security Act, which allows women to eliminate additional low-earning years from the calculation of their retirement benefits. The district court held that, on two grounds, the statutory scheme violated the equal protection component of the Due Process Clause of the Fifth Amendment: (1) that to give women who reached age 62 before 1975 greater benefits than men of the same age and earnings record was irrational, and (2) that the 1972 amendment, under which elapsed years for calculation of retirement benefits no longer depended on sex, was to be construed to apply retroactively, because construing the amendment to give men who reach age 62 in 1975 or later its benefit but denying to older men the same benefit is irrational and therefore unconstitutional.

ISSUE: Does § 215 which allows women to eliminate additional low-earning years from the calculation of their retirement benefits violate the Fifth Amendment?

HOLDING AND DECISION: (Per curiam) No. To withstand scrutiny under the equal protection component of the Fifth Amendment's Due Process Clause, classifications by gender must serve important governmental objectives and must be substantially related to achievement of those objectives. Reduction of the disparity in economic condition between men and women has been recognized as an important governmental objective. However, the Court must also inquire into the legislative purposes behind such benign gender-based classifications. The only discernible purpose of § 215's more favorable treatment of women is the permissible one of redressing our society's longstanding disparate treatment of women.

▶ ANALYSIS

In Title VII sex discrimination cases, the standard of proof is not the showing of a motive of purposeful discrimination. Rather, "to establish a prima facie case of discrimination, a plaintiff need only show that facially neutral standards in question select applicants for hire in a significantly discriminatory pattern. Once it is shown that employment standards are discriminatory in effect," the employer must meet the burden of showing that the requirements are manifestly related to the employment (*Dothard v. Rawlinson*, 433 U.S. 321, 1977).

Quicknotes

DUE PROCESS CLAUSE Clauses found in the Fifth and Fourteenth Amendments to the U.S. Constitution providing that no person shall be deprived of "life, liberty, or property, without due process of law."

Nguyen v. Immigration & Naturalization Service

Foreign citizen (D) v. Federal agency (P)

533 U.S. 53 (2001).

NATURE OF CASE: Deportation proceedings for a foreign-born person with one U.S. citizen biological parent.

FACT SUMMARY: The Immigration & Naturalization Service (INS) (P) initiated deportation proceedings against the foreign-born Nguyen (D), son of an unwed U.S. citizen father and a Vietnamese mother, after he pled guilty to two counts of sexual assault and was sentenced to eight years on each count. Nguyen (D) was ruled deportable despite a belated court order establishing that the U.S. citizen was Nguyen's (D) biological father.

RULE OF LAW

Citizenship requirements for foreign-born persons with one unwed U.S. citizen biological parent do not violate the Equal Protection Clause where the requirements place more burdens upon children of unwed U.S. citizen fathers than upon children of unwed U.S. citizen mothers.

FACTS: Nguyen (D) was born in Vietnam. His father was a U.S. citizen and his mother a Vietnamese citizen, but the two were not married when Nguyen (D) was born. Nguyen (D) came to America to live with his father at the age of six, and he lived with his father in Texas as a lawful permanent resident. Sixteen years after he came to America, Nguyen (D) pled guilty to two counts of sexual assault and was sentenced to eight years in prison on each count. Three years later, the INS (P) initiated deportation proceedings against him based on the criminal convictions entered against him in Texas. In those proceedings, Nguyen (D) claimed to be a Vietnamese citizen. The judge ruled that he was deportable. Nguyen (D) appealed. His U.S. citizen father then obtained DNA evidence, and a court order, showing that he was Nguyen's (D) biological father. The administrative appellate tribunal dismissed the appeal because Nguyen (D) had failed to comply with the federal statute for establishing U.S. citizenship. To establish U.S. citizenship, the pertinent statute required one of three affirmative steps for children born of an unwed U.S. citizen father that were not required for children born of an unwed U.S. citizen mother: legitimization, a declaration of paternity, or a court order establishing paternity. Nguyen's (D) father complied with none of those alternatives until Nguyen (D) had appealed his deportation order. Nguyen (D) appealed to the Court of Appeals for the Fifth Circuit, which affirmed the administrative rulings against him.

ISSUE: Do citizenship requirements for foreign-born persons with one U.S. citizen biological parent violate the Equal Protection Clause where the requirements place more burdens upon children of unwed U.S. citizen fathers than upon children of unwed U.S. citizen mothers?

HOLDING AND DECISION: (Kennedy, J.) No. Citizenship requirements for foreign-born children with one unwed U.S. citizen biological parent do not violate the Equal Protection Clause where the requirements place more burdens upon children of unwed U.S. citizen fathers than upon children of unwed U.S. citizen mothers. Gender-based classifications require intermediate scrutiny under the Equal Protection Clause. Such classifications must advance important governmental objectives, and the means used to advance those objectives must be substantially related to them. The federal statute on establishing U.S. citizenship for foreign-born children of one unwed U.S. citizen parent meets this standard. One important objective is assuring the father's status as a biological parent. Another is ensuring that the father and child have an opportunity to develop a real relationship. Not placing such burdens upon children born of unwed U.S. citizen mothers is not the result of mere stereotype. The fact of motherhood, with the actual biological mother unmistakably present at the child's birth, supports the distinction between U.S. citizen fathers and mothers in the statute. Affirmed.

DISSENT: (O'Connor, J.) The Court misapplies the heightened scrutiny that should govern this case. One problem lies in the statute's loose fit between means and objective. Further, the INS (P) itself has not urged the majority's first identified important objective (establishing paternity), and the asserted goal of developing a genuine parent-child relationship is far too hypothetical for heightened scrutiny. Mere stereotype supports the majority's opinion.

ANALYSIS

Unlike the alimony statutes at issue in *Orr v. Orr*, 440 U.S. 268 (1979), which provided that men could be required to pay alimony while exempting wives from the same burden, the citizenship statute at issue in *Nguyen* is much less easily portrayed as merely stereotypical. A woman's parentage is, after all, an easily discernible biological fact at the moment of birth, whereas the father's just as clearly is not. At the same time, as noted by Justice O'Connor in her dissent, the majority's reasoning in *Nguyen* leaves much to be desired, since the Court grounded its decision on a governmental objective that the parties apparently did not brief and scrutinized the objective that the INS (P) did brief with relatively deferential review.

Continued on next page.

Quicknotes

EQUAL PROTECTION CLAUSE A constitutional provision that each person be guaranteed the same protection of the laws enjoyed by other persons in like circumstances.

HEIGHTENED SCRUTINY A purposefully vague judicial description of all levels of scrutiny more exacting than minimal scrutiny.

Graham v. Richardson

Parties not identified.

403 U.S. 365 (1971).

NATURE OF CASE: Action to test the constitutionality of two welfare statutes.

FACT SUMMARY: In two cases consolidated here for appeal, resident aliens (P) were denied welfare benefits under state statutes restricting such benefits to United States citizens or longtime resident aliens.

🏛 RULE OF LAW
The Equal Protection Clause of the Fourteenth Amendment applies to resident aliens as well as United States citizens, and any state law that discriminates against resident aliens violates the Equal Protection Clause unless it is justified by a "compelling" state interest.

FACTS: Two cases involving welfare benefits for resident aliens were consolidated for this appeal. First, Richardson (P), a resident alien for 13 years, was denied welfare disability benefits under an Arizona statute. This statute restricts such benefits to United States citizens and aliens who have resided in the United States for 15 years. Second, Mary Leger (P), a resident alien, was denied welfare benefits under a Pennsylvania statute. This statute restricts such benefits to United States citizens. After denial of welfare benefits, Richardson (P) and Leger (P) brought actions to recover such benefits. In each case, a court ruled that the questioned statute violated the Equal Protection Clause of the Fourteenth Amendment.

ISSUE: Can a state condition welfare benefits upon United States citizenship or, if the beneficiary is an alien, upon United States residency for a specific period?

HOLDING AND DECISION: (Blackmun, J.) No. The Equal Protection Clause of the Fourteenth Amendment applies to resident aliens as well as United States citizens, and any state law that discriminates against resident aliens violates the Equal Protection Clause unless it is justified by a "compelling" state interest. Of course, there is no such "compelling" state interest to justify discrimination against resident aliens in the area of welfare benefits. A state's desire to preserve limited welfare benefits for its own citizens is unreasonable as well as inadequate, since resident aliens also contribute to state revenues.

▶ ANALYSIS

This case illustrates the "strict scrutiny" equal-protection test applied to state laws that discriminate on the basis of alienage. Under this test, though, a few such classifications have been upheld. For example, although the court has held that resident aliens cannot be excluded from "all" civil service jobs, it has upheld their exclusion from the right to vote and from holding "high public office" (*Sugarman v. Dougall*, 413 U.S. 634 [1973]). Note, in conclusion, that classifications based upon alienage can be attacked (as in *Graham*) on the basis that they interfere with exclusive federal power over admission and residence of aliens.

Quicknotes

ALIENAGE The condition of being an individual who is a citizen of a foreign country.

EQUAL PROTECTION CLAUSE A constitutional provision that each person be guaranteed the same protection of the laws enjoyed by other persons in like circumstances.

FOURTEENTH AMENDMENT Declares that no state shall make or enforce any law that shall abridge the privileges or immunities of citizens of the United States. No state shall deny to any person within its jurisdiction the equal protection of the laws.

STRICT SCRUTINY Method by which courts determine the constitutionality of a law, when a law affects a fundamental right. Under the test, the legislature must have had a compelling interest to enact the law and measures prescribed by the law must be the least restrictive means possible to accomplish its goal.

Foley v. Connelie

Alien (P) v. State official (D)

435 U.S. 291 (1978).

NATURE OF CASE: Appeal from decision that a state law that requires police officers to be American citizens does not violate the Equal Protection Clause.

FACT SUMMARY: New York State required police officers to be American citizens. Pursuant to this rule, Foley (P), a noncitizen alien, was denied the opportunity to take an examination to become a state trooper. He challenged the rule as a violation of the Equal Protection Clause.

RULE OF LAW
A state law that requires police officers to be American citizens does not violate the Equal Protection Clause.

FACTS: A New York statute required that police officers be American citizens. Foley (P), a noncitizen alien, applied to take the state trooper examination, but was refused under the statute. He brought a class action on behalf of aliens wanting to become police officers, claiming that the statute violated the Equal Protection Clause. A district court held that the statute was constitutional. The Supreme Court granted review.

ISSUE: Does a state law that requires police officers to be American citizens violate the Equal Protection Clause?

HOLDING AND DECISION: (Burger, C. J.) No. Restrains imposed by states on aliens are not inherently invalid or suspect. However, such restraints also do not have to clear strict scrutiny review because to do so would depreciate the value of citizenship. This is in keeping with the recognition that states have the power to exclude aliens from participating in its political institutions. Here, therefore, rational-basis review is enough. The police function is a basic function of government and fulfills "a most fundamental obligation of government to its constituency." Because police officers participate in executing policy and enforcing laws, and are invested with substantial discretionary powers, the police function is one where citizenship bears a rational relationship to the unique position of police officers in our democracy.

DISSENT: (Marshall, J.). Contrary to the majority's view, police officers do not perform functions that place them within the narrow exception to the rule that discrimination against aliens is presumptively unconstitutional. Police officers execute policy to the same extent that other public employees—such as sanitation workers or firefighters—execute public policy. Therefore, the exception, based on "execution of broad public policy," cannot mean simply carrying out government programs, but must mean setting government policy pursuant to legislatively

delegated authority. Police officers do not execute public policy in this sense, and therefore should not come under the exception. Moreover, the Court should identify the group characteristic of aliens that justifies discrimination against them to be able to determine if such characteristic adequately explains the discrimination or if the discrimination is without justification.

▶ ANALYSIS

Foley illustrates the application of the political-function exception to strict scrutiny review for discrimination against aliens. That exception suggests that a state can legitimately deny aliens public employment in positions that involve the discharge of a political function. When the alienage classification relates to self-government and the democratic process, a rational-basis test is used, and, instead of requiring a compelling state interest, there need be only a rational relationship between the interest to be protected and the limiting classification.

■=■

Quicknotes

ALIENAGE The condition of being an individual who is a citizen of a foreign country.

EQUAL PROTECTION CLAUSE A constitutional provision that each person be guaranteed the same protection of the laws enjoyed by other persons in like circumstances.

RATIONAL BASIS REVIEW A test employed by the court to determine the validity of a statute in equal protection actions, whereby the court determines whether the challenged statute is rationally related to the achievement of a legitimate state interest.

STRICT SCRUTINY Method by which courts determine the constitutionality of a law, when a law affects a fundamental right. Under the test, the legislature must have had a compelling interest to enact the law and measures prescribed by the law must be the least restrictive means possible to accomplish its goal.

■=■

Ambach v. Norwick

State (D) v. Aliens (P)

441 U.S. 68 (1979).

NATURE OF CASE: Review of refusal to hire aliens as elementary and secondary schoolteachers.

FACT SUMMARY: The State of New York refused to employ aliens, though eligible for citizenship and otherwise qualified, as elementary and secondary public school teachers.

🏛 **RULE OF LAW**
Teaching in a public school constitutes a governmental function from which a state may bar aliens without violating the Fourteenth Amendment.

FACTS: The State of New York maintained a policy of refusing employment as elementary and secondary public school teachers to aliens. Aliens were excluded even if they were eligible for citizenship but did not obtain it and even if they were otherwise qualified for teaching positions.

ISSUE: Does teaching in a public school constitute a governmental function from which a state may bar aliens without violating the Fourteenth Amendment?

HOLDING AND DECISION: (Powell, J.) Yes. Some state functions are so bound up with the operation of the state as a governmental entity as to permit the exclusion from those functions of all persons who have not become part of the process of self-government. The Court recently held that New York could exclude aliens from the ranks of its police force because such a job cloaked with substantial discretionary powers can be appropriately restricted to citizens. Though alienage is a "suspect classification," the standard usually applicable to justify an exclusion of aliens is lessened when a governmental function is involved. In such a case, like this one, a showing of some rational relationship between the interest to be protected and the limiting classification is sufficient to justify the exclusion. Public education, like the police function, fulfills a fundamental obligation of the government, and is thus properly regarded as a governmental function. Teachers have an obligation to promote civic virtue and serve as an example to students, and the state has an interest in furthering these goals. Teaching in a public school, therefore, constitutes a governmental function from which a state may bar aliens without violating the Fourteenth Amendment. There is a rational relationship between the state's educational goals and the barring of aliens from teaching.

DISSENT: (Blackmun, J.) The statutes of New York imposing a requirement of citizenship for certain occupations hail from a time when fear of the foreigner was the order of the day. Classifications based on alienage are inherently "suspect and subject to close judicial scrutiny" under our previous decisions. Furthermore, the restriction is not logically related to all the objectives of New York as to its schools. It is absurd that a Frenchman may not teach French or an Englishwoman may not teach English grammar. It is nonsensical to hire a poor citizen teacher rather than an excellent resident alien teacher.

▶ **ANALYSIS**

Citizenship may not be a precondition to employment in any position in the competitive class of the civil service system: *Sugarman v. Dougall*, 413 U.S. 634 (1973); nor can citizenship be required for admission to the bar: *In re Griffiths*, 413 U.S. 717 (1973). In a footnote to the majority opinion in *Ambach*, these cases are distinguished on the curious ground that the New York statute barring aliens from teaching excludes only those employees (public school teachers) "employed by and acting as agents of the state."

■=■

Quicknotes

ALIENAGE The condition of being an individual who is a citizen of a foreign country.

EQUAL PROTECTION CLAUSE A constitutional provision that each person be guaranteed the same protection of the laws enjoyed by other persons in like circumstances.

RATIONAL BASIS REVIEW A test employed by the court to determine the validity of a statute in equal protection actions, whereby the court determines whether the challenged statute is rationally related to the achievement of a legitimate state interest.

STRICT SCRUTINY Method by which courts determine the constitutionality of a law, when a law affects a fundamental right. Under the test, the legislature must have had a compelling interest to enact the law and measures prescribed by the law must be the least restrictive means possible to accomplish its goal.

SUSPECT CLASSIFICATION A class of persons that have historically been subject to discriminatory treatment; statutes drawing a distinction between persons based on a suspect classification, i.e., race, nationality or alienage, are subject to a strict scrutiny standard of review.

■=■

Plyler v. Doe

State (D) v. Children of undocumented aliens (P)

457 U.S. 202 (1982).

NATURE OF CASE: Constitutional challenge to a state educational restriction statute.

FACT SUMMARY: A class action suit challenged a Texas law that prohibited the use of state funds to educate the children of undocumented aliens.

🏛 RULE OF LAW
Absent a showing that such a policy furthers a substantial state interest, a state may not deny a public education to the children of undocumented aliens.

FACTS: In a class action suit, a Texas statute (Tex. Educ. Code Ann. § 21.031 [1981]) was sought to be invalidated on the ground that it unconstitutionally denied equal protection to the children of undocumented aliens. The statute prohibited the use of state funds for the education of any children not legally admitted to the United States. Both the district court and the Fifth Circuit Court of Appeals held that § 21.031 violated the Equal Protection Clause of the Fourteenth Amendment. Texas (D) appealed, contending that the statute was not unduly discriminatory and was, in fact, justified for three reasons: (1) it was designed to protect the state from an influx of illegal immigrants; (2) it would relieve some of the special burdens which educating undocumented aliens imposes on the educational system; and (3) it would relieve the state of the burden of educating children who are less likely to remain in the state and contribute than other children.

ISSUE: May a state deny a public education to the children of undocumented aliens, absent a showing that such a policy is justified by a substantial state interest?

HOLDING AND DECISION: (Brennan, J.) No. To begin with, the proper standard of judicial scrutiny must be identified. As the people involved (undocumented aliens) are not members of a suspect class and as the right to an education, although clearly important, has not been held to constitute a fundamental constitutional right, the statute in question will be upheld if it is found to be rationally related to a substantial state interest. Upon examination, however, none of the three state interests advanced by Texas (D)—protection from an influx of illegal immigrants; relief from special burdens on the educational system; or relief from the burdens of educating children who will be more likely to leave the state—justifies the statute in question. The legislative scheme found in § 21.031 cannot in any way be deemed as advancing the interests asserted by the state (even assuming that these interests are "substantial state interests"). Denying children who are not responsible for their status a public education will stigmatize them with the heavy burden of illiteracy for the rest of their lives. They will be unable to participate in our civic institutions. The cost to the nation over their life spans will be greater than the cost of providing them an education now. As such, the statute must fall, as it is in violation of the Equal Protection Clause.

DISSENT: (Burger, C.J.) The Court oversteps its bounds in striking down the Texas statute. Once it is conceded that neither a suspect class or fundamental right is involved, only a rational relationship to a legitimate state interest need be found to uphold the law. Despite the fact that it may not be the same course the members of the Court would take if they were legislating, it cannot be said that the Texas law is irrational. As such, it is a valid law.

▶ ANALYSIS

As Justice Marshall mentioned in his concurrence in this case, the Court seems to be taking one step closer to the "sliding scale" approach of equal protection analysis that has been advocated by certain legal theorists for a long time. Under this approach, a court would have greater flexibility than merely identifying the analysis required as being either "strict scrutiny" or "rational basis" and, as such, could better tailor the legal analysis to the facts of the case and the interests involved.

▪■▪

Quicknotes

ALIENAGE The condition of being an individual who is a citizen of a foreign country.

EQUAL PROTECTION CLAUSE A constitutional provision that each person be guaranteed the same protection of the laws enjoyed by other persons in like circumstances.

RATIONAL BASIS REVIEW A test employed by the court to determine the validity of a statute in equal protection actions, whereby the court determines whether the challenged statute is rationally related to the achievement of a legitimate state interest.

SUSPECT CLASSIFICATION A class of persons that have historically been subject to discriminatory treatment; statutes drawing a distinction between persons based on a suspect classification, i.e., race, nationality or alienage, are subject to a strict scrutiny standard of review.

▪■▪

Massachusetts Board of Retirement v. Murgia

State agency (D) v. Older state employee (P)

427 U.S. 307 (1976).

NATURE OF CASE: Appeal from decision that law requiring police officer to retire at age 50 violates the Equal Protection Clause.

FACT SUMMARY: Massachusetts required police officers to retire at age 50. Murgia (P), a police officer who turned 50, challenged the law as a violation of the Equal Protection Clause.

🏛 RULE OF LAW

A state law requiring police officers to retire at age 50 does not violate the Equal Protection Clause.

FACTS: Massachusetts required that a uniformed state police officer who turned 50 had to be retired. Murgia (P), a state police officer who turned 50 and was automatically retired pursuant to the law, challenged the law as a violation of the Equal Protection Clause. The district court held that the law was unconstitutional, and the Supreme Court granted review.

ISSUE: Does a state law requiring police officers to retire at age 50 violate the Equal Protection Clause?

HOLDING AND DECISION: (Per curiam) No. Strict scrutiny is not required here because strict scrutiny in equal protection analysis is required only when the classification interferes with a fundamental right or disadvantages a suspect class. Neither of these situations is involved here. First, government employment is not a fundamental right. Second, a classification based on age is not a suspect classification. Although there is some discrimination against the aged, there is not the history of purposeful unequal treatment of age such as there has been with race or national origin. Also, the aged are not an insular or discrete group, because all of us have the potential of joining that group. Here, under the rational-basis standard, the goal of ensuring a physically fit police force is a legitimate purpose. Because physical ability generally declines with age, the law requiring mandatory retirement is rationally related to the state's goal.

DISSENT: (Marshall, J.) The right to work is a core freedom protected by the Fourteenth Amendment and to deny that right to members of the police force who have shown that they are medically fit is unconstitutional. Depriving older workers of employment is especially burdensome to them because it is more difficult at their age to find work. Whether the classification of older workers is a suspect classification or not, it is undisputable that they constitute a class that is subject to repeated and arbitrary discrimination. Here, the state's purpose is compelling, but the means—the mandatory retirement law—is overinclusive, because the state can test individual police officers to determine if they are fit or not. To automatically terminate fit officers is irrational.

▶ ANALYSIS

As the dissent intimates, this case stands for the principle that in Equal Protection Clause cases, rational overinclusiveness is permissible. Although many of the factors that justify heightened scrutiny for race, national origin, gender, alienage, and legitimacy classifications exist with regard to age classifications, the Court has expressly held that only rational basis review should be used when age discrimination is claimed. This case provides some of the Court's reasons for this distinction.

■══■

Quicknotes

EQUAL PROTECTION CLAUSE A constitutional provision that each person be guaranteed the same protection of the laws enjoyed by other persons in like circumstances.

RATIONAL BASIS REVIEW A test employed by the court to determine the validity of a statute in equal protection actions, whereby the court determines whether the challenged statute is rationally related to the achievement of a legitimate state interest.

SUSPECT CLASSIFICATION A class of persons that have historically been subject to discriminatory treatment; statutes drawing a distinction between persons based on a suspect classification, i.e., race, nationality or alienage, are subject to a strict scrutiny standard of review.

■══■

Fundamental Rights Under Due Process and Equal Protection

Quick Reference Rules of Law

Zablocki v. Redhail

County clerk (D) v. Applicant (P)

434 U.S. 378 (1978).

NATURE OF CASE: Appeal from an action seeking declaratory and injunctive relief.

FACT SUMMARY: Redhail (P) brought this action challenging the constitutional validity of a Wisconsin statute that provides that members of a certain class of Wisconsin residents may not marry without first obtaining a court order granting permission to marry.

🏛 RULE OF LAW

When a statutory classification significantly interferes with the exercise of a fundamental right, it cannot be upheld unless it is supported by sufficiently important state interests and is closely tailored to effectuate only those interests.

FACTS: A Wisconsin statute provides that members of a certain class of Wisconsin residents may not marry, within the state or elsewhere, without first obtaining a court order granting permission to marry. The class is defined by the statute to include any Wisconsin resident having minor issue not in his custody and that he is under an obligation to support by any court order or judgment. Redhail (P) is a Wisconsin resident who, under the terms of the statute, is unable to enter into a lawful marriage because he has not satisfied his support obligations to his illegitimate child. After Zablocki (D), the County Clerk of Milwaukee County, denied Redhail's (P) marriage application on the ground that he had not received court permission to marry, Redhail (P) brought this class action seeking declaratory and injunctive relief. Redhail (P) contended that the statute violates the Equal Protection Clause of the Fourteenth Amendment. A three-judge federal district court concluded that strict scrutiny was required because the classification created by the statute infringed upon the fundamental right to marry. The court then held the statute invalid and enjoined the county clerks from enforcing it. An appeal was made to the Supreme Court.

ISSUE: Can a statutory classification that significantly interferes with a fundamental right be upheld if it is unsupported by sufficiently important state interests and closely tailored to effectuate only those interests?

HOLDING AND DECISION: (Marshall, J.) No. When a statutory classification significantly interferes with the exercise of a fundamental right, such as the right to marry, it cannot be upheld unless it is supported by sufficiently important state interests and is closely tailored to effectuate only those interests. Zablocki (D) asserts that two interests are served by the challenged statute: the permission-to-marry proceeding furnishes an opportunity to counsel

the applicant as to the necessity of fulfilling his prior support obligations; and the welfare of the out-of-custody children is protected. The Court may accept that these are legitimate and substantial interests but, since the means selected by the state for achieving these interests unnecessarily impinge on the right to marry, the statute cannot be sustained. First, the statute merely prevents the applicant from getting married without any provision for counseling, without delivering any money into the hands of the children. More importantly, the state already has numerous other means for exacting compliance with support obligations and yet which do not impinge upon the right to marry.

CONCURRENCE: (Stewart, J.) The Equal Protection Clause deals not with substantive rights, such as the right to marry, but with invidiously discriminatory classifications. Furthermore, there is no right to marry in the constitutional sense.

DISSENT: (Rehnquist, J.) Under the Equal Protection Clause, the statute need pass only the rational basis test, and under the Due Process Clause, it need be shown to bear only a rational relation to a constitutionally permissible objection. The statute so viewed is a permissible exercise of the state's power to regulate family life.

▶ ANALYSIS

In *Loving v. Virginia*, 388 U.S. 1 (1967), the Supreme Court held that the freedom to marry has long been recognized as one of the vital personal rights essential to the orderly pursuit of happiness by free men. More recent decisions have established that the right to marry is part of the fundamental rights of privacy implicit in the Fourteenth Amendment's Due Process Clause. However, the Court reiterates in the *Redhail* decision that, by reaffirming the fundamental character of the right to marry, it does not mean to suggest that every state regulation that relates in any way to the incidents of, or prerequisites for, marriage must be subjected to rigorous scrutiny.

■=■

Quicknotes

EQUAL PROTECTION CLAUSE A constitutional provision that each person be guaranteed the same protection of the laws enjoyed by other persons in like circumstances.

FUNDAMENTAL RIGHT A liberty that is either expressly or impliedly provided for in the United States Constitution,

Continued on next page.

the deprivation or burdening of which is subject to a heightened standard of review.

RATIONAL BASIS REVIEW A test employed by the court to determine the validity of a statute in equal protection actions, whereby the court determines whether the challenged statute is rationally related to the achievement of a legitimate state interest.

Michael H. v. Gerald D.

Father (P) v. Husband (D)

491 U.S. 110 (1989).

NATURE OF CASE: Review of a state evidentiary presumption regarding fatherhood.

FACT SUMMARY: Michael H. (P) challenged California's irrebuttable presumption that a child born into a family unit is the product of the husband.

🏛 RULE OF LAW
A state may create an irrebuttable presumption that a child born into a family unit is the product of the husband.

FACTS: Carole D. was wife to Gerald D. (D). Gerald (D) and Carole separated for a period of time, and she had an affair with Michael H. (P). A child, Victoria (P), was born to Carole. Blood tests proved that there was a 98 percent chance that Gerald (D) was not the father. Gerald (D) and Carole later reconciled, and Gerald (D) exercised parental rights over Victoria (P), to the exclusion of Michael (P). Michael (P) brought an action seeking certain parental rights. Victoria (P), through a guardian ad litem, joined. The trial court, citing a state evidentiary presumption that a child born into a family where the husband was not sterile or impotent was the issue of the husband, dismissed the suit. The state court of appeal affirmed, and the state supreme court denied review. The U.S. Supreme Court granted review.

ISSUE: May a state create an irrebuttable presumption that a child born into a family unit is the product of the husband?

HOLDING AND DECISION: (Scalia, J.) Yes. A state may create an irrebuttable presumption that a child born into a family unit is the product of the husband. Such a presumption, although procedural in form, actually is the product of a substantive decision that, as a matter of social policy, given the relationship between man and wife, the husband should be held responsible for the child and the integrity of the family unit maintained. When this Court has struck down irrebuttable presumptions, it has been because they did not rationally advance their purported goals. Such is not the case here. As far as substantive due process is concerned, the Clause only protects those interests found to be fundamental rights. This Court does not accept that to exercise parental rights over a child born into another family is a fundamental right sufficient to override a state's conclusion that the integrity of the family should be maintained. For these reasons, the evidentiary presumption is valid.

DISSENT: (Brennan, J.) The Court seems to limit that which may be a fundamental right protected in a substantive sense by the Due Process Clause to certain traditional liberties. However, as society evolves, nontraditional rights may become fundamental. Such a right is that involved here.

▶ ANALYSIS

Only four justices joined the main opinion. Three justices joined Justice Brennan's contention that a fundamental right was at stake here. Justice Stevens appears to waffle on this issue, causing this to be an inconclusive case in terms of precedent.

Quicknotes

EQUAL PROTECTION CLAUSE A constitutional provision that each person be guaranteed the same protection of the laws enjoyed by other persons in like circumstances.

FUNDAMENTAL RIGHT A liberty that is either expressly or impliedly provided for in the United States Constitution, the deprivation or burdening of which is subject to a heightened standard of review.

IRREBUTTABLE PRESUMPTION A rule of law, inferred from the existence of a particular set of facts, that is not subject to dispute.

RATIONAL BASIS REVIEW A test employed by the court to determine the validity of a statute in equal protection actions, whereby the court determines whether the challenged statute is rationally related to the achievement of a legitimate state interest.

SUBSTANTIVE DUE PROCESS A constitutional safeguard limiting the power of the state, irrespective of how fair its procedures may be; substantive limits placed on the power of the state.

Moore v. City of East Cleveland, Ohio

Grandmother (D) v. Municipality (P)

431 U.S. 494 (1977).

NATURE OF CASE: Constitutional challenge to zoning law.

FACT SUMMARY: East Cleveland's (P) zoning ordinance prohibited the cohabitation of nonfamily members, which included cousins and other members of the traditional "family."

🏛 RULE OF LAW
A zoning ordinance prohibiting or restricting members of the traditional "family" from living together is invalid.

FACTS: A zoning ordinance adopted by the City of East Cleveland (P) prohibited nonfamily members from residing together. "Family" was defined in such a manner as to exclude many relationships normally included in the traditional definition of "family." Moore (D) lived with her son and two grandsons (who were cousins). Moore (D) was informed that John, one of the grandsons, was an illegal occupant under the ordinance and had to move. Moore (D) refused and was jailed and fined. Moore (D) appealed, alleging that the ordinance violated the Due Process Clause of the Fourteenth Amendment.

ISSUE: May a zoning ordinance prohibit or restrict the rights of members of a traditional "family" unit from living together?

HOLDING AND DECISION: (Powell, J.) No. A zoning ordinance that attempts to prohibit or restrict the rights of members of the traditional "family" unit from residing together is invalid. Such an intrusive regulation of the "family" cannot be sustained. It serves no useful or proper governmental purpose; it is arbitrary and capricious; and it destroys important and historically protected rights. Our culture is not based on the concept of the nuclear family. We have a tradition filled with brothers, cousins, etc., all living in the same house. Substantive due process recognizes and protects such historical values. At best, the City's (D) goals of preventing overcrowding and traffic congestion have an attenuated relationship to the ordinance. While a city may validly restrict unrelated persons from residing together, it may not interfere with traditional family relationships. Reversed.

DISSENT: (Stewart, J.) The grandmother-grandson relationship does not transform the grandmother's (D) freedom-of-association or privacy claim into a constitutional violation by the City of East Cleveland (P). Similarly, her substantive due process claim fails the standards set in cases where laws regulated the choices whether to have children and how to raise them. Any definition of family would cause some hardships, but causing a few hardships, as all laws do, does not mean that a law violates the Constitution.

▶ ANALYSIS

Moore specifically modifies *Village of Belle Terre v. Boreas*, 416 U.S. 1 (1974). *Belle Terre* held that a government entity could impose valid restrictions on the rights of nonfamily members to reside together. Since limitations on congestion, traffic, etc. were deemed proper police power objectives, the ordinance was upheld under the rationale in *Euclid v. Amber Realty Co.*, 272 U.S. 365 (1926). *Moore* does no more than state that no proper police purpose is served by regulating the "traditional family."

Quicknotes

SUBSTANTIVE DUE PROCESS A constitutional safeguard limiting the power of the state, irrespective of how fair its procedures may be; substantive limits placed on the power of the state.

Meyer v. Nebraska

Teacher (D) v. State (P)

262 U.S. 390 (1923).

NATURE OF CASE: Appeal from conviction under statute making it a crime to teach any language other than English to children.

FACT SUMMARY: Meyer (D) was convicted under a Nebraska (P) statute that made it a crime to teach children any language other than English. Meyer challenged his conviction on due process grounds.

RULE OF LAW

A state statute that makes it a crime to teach children any language other than English violates the due process guarantees of the Fourteenth Amendment.

FACTS: Nebraska (P) made it a crime to teach any language other than English. Meyer (D), a teacher, was tried and convicted in a Nebraska trial court of teaching German to a ten-year-old child. The Nebraska Supreme Court affirmed the conviction, and the Supreme Court granted review.

ISSUE: Does a state statute that makes it a crime to teach children any language other than English violate the due process guarantees of the Fourteenth Amendment?

HOLDING AND DECISION: (McReynolds, J.) Yes. The liberty guaranteed by the Fourteenth Amendment includes not only economic rights, but the right to "acquire useful knowledge, to marry, establish a home and bring up children, to worship God according to the dictates of his own conscience, and generally to enjoy those privileges long recognized at common law as essential to the orderly pursuit of happiness by free men." The right of the teacher to teach German and the right of the parents to control the upbringing of their children are encompassed by this notion of liberty in the Fourteenth Amendment. The goal of having a homogeneous people prepared to understand discussions of civic matters is legitimate, but the means are overbroad and violate the liberty rights of the teacher.

ANALYSIS

Meyer was the first case to define the term liberty in the Due Process Clause to protect basic aspects of family autonomy. One can see in this case how modern substantive due process for noneconomic rights had its origins in the Court's economic substantive due process jurisprudence. The case affirms a parent's right to control the upbringing of his or her children.

Quicknotes

DUE PROCESS CLAUSE Clauses found in the Fifth and Fourteenth Amendments to the U.S. Constitution providing that no person shall be deprived of "life, liberty, or property, without due process of law."

LIBERTY INTEREST A right conferred by the Due Process Clauses of the state and federal constitutions.

SUBSTANTIVE DUE PROCESS A constitutional safeguard limiting the power of the state, irrespective of how fair its procedures may be; substantive limits placed on the power of the state.

Troxel v. Granville

Grandparents (P) v. Mother (D)

530 U.S. 57 (2000).

NATURE OF CASE: Petition seeking visitation rights.

FACT SUMMARY: The Troxels (P) petitioned a Washington Superior Court for the right to visit their grandchildren over the protest of the children's mother (D).

RULE OF LAW
A parent has a fundamental right in the care, custody and control of his or her child.

FACTS: Tommie Granville (D) and Brad Troxel had two daughters together but never married. The couple separated and Brad later committed suicide. Granville (D) notified the Troxels (P) that she wished to limit their visitation to one short visit per month and they brought suit seeking to obtain visitation rights. Their petition was based on Wash. Rev. Code § 26.10.160(3), which provides that "Any person may petition the court for visitation rights at any time, including, but not limited to, custody proceedings." The superior court entered a visitation decree ordering visitation for one weekend per month, one week during the summer and four hours on each of the grandparents' (P) birthdays. Granville (D) appealed and the case was remanded, during which time she married. Her husband later adopted the children. The court of appeals reversed the lower court's decision and dismissed the petition, holding that nonparents lack standing to seek visitation unless a custody action is pending. The Washington Supreme Court found that the Troxels (P) had standing to seek visitation under the statute, but concluded that they could not obtain visitation because § 26.10.160(3) unconstitutionally infringes on the fundamental rights of parents to rear their children. This Court granted certiorari.

ISSUE: Does a parent have a fundamental right in the care, custody and control of his or her child?

HOLDING AND DECISION: (O'Connor, J.) Yes. A parent has a fundamental right in the care, custody and control of his or her child. The Fourteenth Amendment prohibits states from "depriving any person of life, liberty or property, without due process of law." The clause also provides heightened protection against government interference with certain fundamental rights and liberty interests. The liberty interest at issue here is that of parents in the care, custody and control of their children. Section 26.10.160(3) here unconstitutionally infringes on Granville's (D) fundamental parental right. The statute is extremely broad, permitting any third party to subject any decision by a parent concerning visitation of the parent's children to state-court review placing the best interests determination exclusively in the hands of the judge. Several factors here

compel the conclusion that the section as applied violates due process. First, the Troxels (P) did not allege, nor did the court find, that Granville (D) was an unfit parent. There is a presumption that fit parents act in the best interests of their children. Where this is the case, there is usually no reason for the state to interject itself into the private realm of the family. The superior court's decision directly contravened this presumption and failed to provide any protection for Granville's fundamental constitutional right to make decisions regarding the rearing of her own daughters.

CONCURRENCE: (Souter, J.) I concur in the judgment affirming the decision of the Washington Supreme Court, whose facial invalidation of its own state statute is consistent with this Court's prior cases addressing the interests at stake.

CONCURRENCE: (Thomas, J.) Neither party has argued that our substantive due process cases were wrongly decided and that the original understanding of the Due Process Clause precludes judicial enforcement of unenumerated rights.

DISSENT: (Stevens, J.) The Court should not have accepted a case in which a state supreme court has merely required a state legislature to redraft a statute to comply with the federal Constitution. Having accepted the case, though, this Court should directly address the federal questions instead of holding the statute facially invalid on grounds that have no basis in this Court's jurisprudence.

DISSENT: (Scalia, J.) How to raise one's children was one of the "unalienable rights" implied by the Declaration of Independence, as well as one of the amorphous body of rights "retained by the people" in the Ninth Amendment. Nonetheless, that conclusion is only a personal view. As such, the matter appropriately belongs in a legislative debate, not in the judicial process of deciding cases under the Constitution. Reading this unenumerated right into the Constitution improperly creates a judicially imposed, federalized body of family law.

DISSENT: (Kennedy, J.) The Supreme Court of Washington State erred in concluding that nonparents who seek visitation with children must always prove that withholding the visitation would harm the children. That court's judgment thus should be vacated, and the case should be remanded to that court for further proceedings consistent with the appropriate federal constitutional standard. If the state court then should invalidate the statute for insufficiently protecting the parent's rights in this case,

Continued on next page.

or for permitting just anyone to have visitation rights with children, this Court then could address those or other properly framed federal questions at the proper time.

▶ ANALYSIS

In *V.C. v. M.J.B.*, 319 N.J. Super. 103 (1999), a New Jersey court held that a lesbian partner was entitled to visitation with the other partner's child. The court established a four-part test for determining whether a third party is entitled to visitation rights: (1) the biological parent consent to the establishment of a parent-like relationship with the child; (2) the party seeking visitation and the child lived together in the same home; (3) the party seeking visitation assumed parental obligations; and (4) the party seeking visitation had been in a parental role for sufficient amount of time to establish a parental relationship.

■═■

Quicknotes

DUE PROCESS CLAUSE Clauses found in the Fifth and Fourteenth Amendments to the U.S. Constitution providing that no person shall be deprived of "life, liberty, or property, without due process of law."

FUNDAMENTAL RIGHT A liberty that is either expressly or impliedly provided for in the U.S. Constitution, the deprivation or burdening of which is subject to a heightened standard of review.

LIBERTY INTEREST A right conferred by the Due Process Clauses of the state and federal constitutions.

■═■

Skinner v. Oklahoma

Habitual criminal (D) v. State (P)

316 U.S. 535 (1942).

NATURE OF CASE: Constitutional challenge to state law.

FACT SUMMARY: Skinner (D) was deemed to be a habitual criminal and was ordered sterilized under a State (P) statute.

🏛 RULE OF LAW
A statute that arbitrarily excludes a class from its purview violates the Equal Protection Clause of the Fourteenth Amendment where fundamental rights are involved.

FACTS: Skinner (D) was convicted of crimes on three separate occasions. Under an Oklahoma (P) statute he could be declared a habitual criminal and could be ordered to be sterilized to prevent the passing on of criminal genetic traits. The statute applied to those convicted of two or more crimes amounting to felonies involving moral turpitude. The attorney general could maintain a suit to have the convicted party sterilized. A full trial would be held. The issue was confined to whether the party was a habitual criminal and whether he should be sterilized. Offenses arising out of violations of prohibitory laws, revenue acts, embezzlement, or political offenses were not within the purview of the Act. Skinner (D) was adjudged a habitual criminal and was ordered sterilized. Skinner (D) challenged the constitutionality of the statute.

ISSUE: May a state arbitrarily discriminate between like classes where fundamental rights are involved?

HOLDING AND DECISION: (Douglas, J.) No. We do not pass on the constitutionality of sterilization of habitual criminals or the state's procedure. We do find that the State (P) statute is unconstitutional under the Equal Protection Clause of the Fourteenth Amendment. We are dealing herein with a fundamental right, i.e., the right to have children. Statutes dealing with such rights are closely scrutinized. While a state may treat classes unequally based on experience, it may not arbitrarily seek to add or exclude a particular group from treatment. There must be a rational basis for the distinction. The law treats the embezzler in the same manner as other criminals, e.g., those convicted of grand larceny. There is no viable difference between their offenses or gene traits. Failure to treat them equally under the sterilization statute cannot be supported and violates the Equal Protection Clause. The statute is unconstitutional on its face.

CONCURRENCE: (Stone, C.J.) The Oklahoma statute violates the federal Constitution, but the Equal Protection Clause does not provide the best basis for decision. The better theory resides in the Fourteenth Amendment's Due Process Clause: The unassailable deprivation of personal liberty is not the process to which the individual is due.

▶ *ANALYSIS*

A law that condemns, without hearing, all of the individuals of a class to a harsh measure merely because some or many are deserving of such treatment, lacks the basic attributes of due process. *Morrison v. California*, 291 U.S. 82 (1934). In *Skinner*, the Court expressly left the constitutional issue as to sterilization open even if the equal protection problem was solved. This is based on the Court's concern to decide all cases on the narrowest possible grounds.

Quicknotes

DUE PROCESS CLAUSE Clauses found in the Fifth and Fourteenth Amendments to the U.S. Constitution providing that no person shall be deprived of "life, liberty, or property, without due process of law."

EQUAL PROTECTION CLAUSE A constitutional provision that each person be guaranteed the same protection of the laws enjoyed by other persons in like circumstances.

FUNDAMENTAL RIGHT A liberty that is either expressly or impliedly provided for in the U.S. Constitution, the deprivation or burdening of which is subject to a heightened standard of review.

Griswold v. Connecticut

Doctor/director (D) v. State (P)

381 U.S. 479 (1965).

NATURE OF CASE: Appeal from conviction for violating state laws prohibiting the counseling of married persons to take contraceptives.

FACT SUMMARY: Doctor (D) and layman (D) were prosecuted for advising married persons on the means of preventing conception.

🏛 RULE OF LAW
The right to marital privacy, although not explicitly stated in the Bill of Rights, is a penumbra, formed by certain other explicit guarantees. As such, it is protected against state regulation that sweeps unnecessarily broad.

FACTS: Griswold (D), the Executive Director of the Planned Parenthood League of Connecticut, and Dr. Buxton (D) were convicted under a Connecticut law that made counseling of married persons to take contraceptives a criminal offense.

ISSUE: Is the right to privacy in the marital relationship protected by the Constitution despite the absence of specific language recognizing it?

HOLDING AND DECISION: (Douglas, J.) Yes. The various guarantees which create penumbras, or zones, of privacy include the First Amendment's right of association, the Third Amendment's prohibition against the peacetime quartering of soldiers, the Fourth Amendment's prohibition against unreasonable searches and seizures, the Fifth Amendment's Self-Incrimination Clause, and the Ninth Amendment's reservation to the people of unenumerated rights. The Connecticut law, by forbidding the use of contraceptives rather than regulating their manner or sale, seeks to achieve its goals by means having a maximum destructive impact upon a relationship that lies within the zone of privacy.

CONCURRENCE: (Goldberg, J.) The Ninth Amendment, while not constituting an independent source of rights, suggests that the list of rights in the first eight amendments is not exhaustive. This right is a "fundamental" one that cannot be infringed on the state's slender justification in protecting marital fidelity.

CONCURRENCE: (Harlan, J.) The court, instead of focusing on "specific provisions" of the Bill of Rights, should have instead relied on the Due Process Clause in finding this law violative of basic values "implicit in the concept of ordered liberty."

CONCURRENCE: (White, J.) The Due Process Clause should be the test in determining whether such laws are reasonably necessary for the effectuation of a legitimate and substantial state interest and are not arbitrary or capricious in application. Here, the causal connection between married persons engaging in extramarital sex and contraceptives is too tenuous.

DISSENT: (Black, J.) While the law is offensive, neither the Ninth Amendment nor the Due Process Clause invalidates it. Both lead the court into imposing its own notions as to what are wise or unwise laws. What constitutes "fundamental" values this court is incapable of determining. Keeping the Constitution "in tune with the times" is accomplished only through the amendment process. Similarly, the Due Process Clause is too imprecise and lends itself to subjective interpretation.

DISSENT: (Stewart, J.) This case requires the Court to decide whether Connecticut's uncommonly silly law violates the Constitution—not to read the judges' own personal views into the Constitution and thereby invalidate the law for violating what is actually only personal preference. The proper way to invalidate the statute is to return it to the people of Connecticut to give them an opportunity to repeal it through the legislative process.

▶ ANALYSIS

Although the theory of "substantive due process" has declined as a means to review state economic regulation—at least since 1937—the court, as here, has freely applied strict scrutiny of state laws affecting social areas.

■■■

Quicknotes

DUE PROCESS CLAUSE Clauses found in the Fifth and Fourteenth Amendments to the U.S. Constitution providing that no person shall be deprived of "life, liberty, or property, without due process of law."

EQUAL PROTECTION CLAUSE A constitutional provision that each person be guaranteed the same protection of the laws enjoyed by other persons in like circumstances.

FUNDAMENTAL RIGHT A liberty that is either expressly or impliedly provided for in the U.S. Constitution, the deprivation or burdening of which is subject to a heightened standard of review.

Continued on next page.

LIBERTY INTEREST A right conferred by the Due Process Clauses of the state and federal constitutions.

PENUMBRA A doctrine whereby authority of the federal government is implied pursuant to the Necessary and Proper Clause; one implied power may be inferred from the conferring of another implied power.

SUBSTANTIVE DUE PROCESS A constitutional safeguard limiting the power of the state, irrespective of how fair its procedures may be; substantive limits placed on the power of the state.

Eisenstadt v. Baird

Sheriff (P) v. Abortion clinic director (D)

405 U.S. 438 (1972).

NATURE OF CASE: Appeal from vacatur of a dismissal of a writ of habeas corpus petition for conviction under a state statute making it a crime to give contraceptives to an unmarried person.

FACT SUMMARY: Massachusetts made it a crime to give contraceptives to an unmarried person. Baird (D) gave a contraceptive to a single person and was convicted under the Massachusetts law. Baird (D) challenged his conviction under the Equal Protection Clause.

RULE OF LAW
A state law that makes it a crime to give contraceptives to an unmarried person violates the Equal Protection Clause.

FACTS: At the end of his lecture on birth control, Baird (D), who was neither a physician nor a pharmacist, gave a single woman a package of vaginal foam. He was convicted under a Massachusetts statute that made it a crime to give contraceptives to an unmarried person. The statute permitted only physicians and pharmacists to dispense contraceptives, and then only to married persons. The state courts upheld the conviction, the district court dismissed his petition for a writ of habeas corpus, and the court of appeals vacated the dismissal. The Supreme Court granted review.

ISSUE: Does a state law that makes it a crime to give contraceptives to an unmarried person violate the Equal Protection Clause?

HOLDING AND DECISION: (Brennan, J.) Yes. There is no rational basis for treating married persons and unmarried persons differently. Even if the state's goal is to limit fornication, the ban on distributing contraceptives to unmarried persons has a tenuous relation to achieving that goal—it is unreasonable to think that pregnancy and childbirth are the punishment the state wants to inflict on those who fornicate. Therefore, the law cannot be upheld as either a health measure or as a deterrent to fornication. Regardless of what the law's purpose is, the rights of access to contraceptives must be the same for the unmarried as they are for the married. "If the right of privacy means anything, it is the right of the individual, married or single, to be free from unwarranted governmental intrusion into matters so fundamentally affecting a person as the decision whether to bear or beget a child."

DISSENT: (Burger, C.J.) Baird (P) was properly convicted for dispensing medicine without a license. Nothing in the Constitution requires that contraceptives be available to everyone. Here, limiting the class of distributors of contraceptives will not impair the right (affirmed in *Griswold v. Connecticut*, 381 U.S. 479 [1965]) to use contraceptives.

ANALYSIS

Eisenstadt recognized the right to control reproduction as a fundamental right of both single and married persons, as well as the right to distribute and use contraceptives. In doing so, the Court continued its revival of the use of substantive due process that it had started in *Griswold*. Justice Brennan's dictum, quoted above, was influential in subsequent cases in this area.

Quicknotes

DUE PROCESS CLAUSE Clauses found in the Fifth and Fourteenth Amendments to the U.S. Constitution providing that no person shall be deprived of "life, liberty, or property, without due process of law."

EQUAL PROTECTION CLAUSE A constitutional provision that each person be guaranteed the same protection of the laws enjoyed by other persons in like circumstances.

FUNDAMENTAL RIGHT A liberty that is either expressly or impliedly provided for in the U.S. Constitution, the deprivation or burdening of which is subject to a heightened standard of review.

Roe v. Wade

Single pregnant woman (P) v. State (D)

410 U.S. 113 (1973).

NATURE OF CASE: Challenge to state laws making it a crime to procure an abortion except by medical advice to save the life of the mother.

FACT SUMMARY: Roe (P), a single woman, wished to have her pregnancy terminated by an abortion.

🏛 RULE OF LAW
The right of privacy found in the Fourteenth Amendment's concept of personal liberty and restrictions upon state action is broad enough to encompass a woman's decision whether or not to terminate her pregnancy.

FACTS: The Texas abortion laws challenged here were typical of those adopted by most states. The challengers were Roe (P), a single pregnant woman, a childless couple with the wife not pregnant (J and M Doe), and a licensed physician with two criminal charges pending (Halford). Only Roe (P) was found to be entitled to maintain the action. Although her 1970 pregnancy had been terminated, her case was not found moot since pregnancy "truly could be capable of repetition, yet evading review."

ISSUE: Does the constitutional right of privacy include a woman's right to choose to terminate her pregnancy?

HOLDING AND DECISION: (Blackmun, J.) Yes. While the Constitution does not explicitly mention any right of privacy, such a right has been recognized. This right of privacy, whether founded in the Fourteenth Amendment's concept of personal liberty and restrictions upon state action, as this court feels it is, or in the Ninth Amendment's reservation of rights to the people, is broad enough to encompass a woman's decision to terminate her pregnancy. A statute regulating a fundamental right, such as the right to privacy, may be justified only by a compelling state interest and such statutes must be narrowly drawn. Here, Texas (D) argued that the fetus is a person within the meaning of the Fourteenth Amendment whose right to life is guaranteed by that Amendment. However, there are no decisions indicating such a definition for "fetus." The unborn have never been recognized in the law as persons in the whole sense. Texas (D) may not, by adopting one theory of life, override the rights of the pregnant woman that are at stake. However, neither are the woman's rights to privacy absolute. The state does have a legitimate interest in preserving the health of the pregnant woman and in protecting the potentiality of life. Each of these interests grows in substantiality as the woman approaches term, and, at a point, each becomes compelling. During the first trimester, mortality in abortion is less than mortality in childbirth. After that point, in promoting its interest in the

mother's health, the state may regulate the abortion procedure in ways related to maternal health (i.e., licensing of physicians, facilities, etc.). Prior to viability, the physician, in consultation with the pregnant woman, is free to decide that a pregnancy should be terminated without interference by the state. Subsequent to viability, the state, in promoting its interest in the potentiality of life, may regulate, and even proscribe abortion, except where necessary to save the mother's life. Because the Texas (D) statute makes no distinction between abortions performed in early pregnancy and those performed later, it sweeps too broadly and is, therefore, invalid.

DISSENT: (Rehnquist, J.) The test to be applied is whether the abortion law has a rational relation to a valid state objective. Here, the court applies the compelling-state-interest test. The application of this test requires the court to examine the legislative policies and pass on the wisdom of those policies, tasks better left to the legislature.

▎ANALYSIS

Doe v. Bolton was the companion case to *Roe v. Wade*. The Georgia laws attacked in *Doe* were more modern than the Texas laws. They allowed a physician to perform an abortion when the mother's life was in danger or the fetus would likely be born with birth defects or the pregnancy had resulted from rape. The Court held that a physician could consider all attendant circumstances in deciding whether an abortion should be performed. No longer could only the three situations specified be considered. The Court also struck down the requirements of prior approval for an abortion by the hospital staff committee and of confirmation by two physicians. They concluded that the attending physician's judgment was sufficient. Lastly, the court struck down the requirement that the woman be a Georgia resident.

Quicknotes

FUNDAMENTAL RIGHT A liberty that is either expressly or impliedly provided for in the U.S. Constitution, the deprivation or burdening of which is subject to a heightened standard of review.

LIBERTY INTEREST A right conferred by the Due Process Clauses of the state and federal constitutions.

NINTH AMENDMENT The Ninth Amendment to the U.S. Constitution provides that the enumeration of any rights

Continued on next page.

contained therein is not to be construed as denying or disparaging other rights retained by the people.

RATIONAL BASIS REVIEW A test employed by the court to determine the validity of a statute in equal protection actions, whereby the court determines whether the challenged statute is rationally related to the achievement of a legitimate state interest.

■═■

Planned Parenthood v. Casey

Clinics/doctors (P) v. State (D)

505 U.S. 833 (1992).

NATURE OF CASE: Appeal of order upholding abortion statutes, except a husband-notification provision.

FACT SUMMARY: Planned Parenthood (P) facially challenged the constitutionality of Pennsylvania's (D) abortion law.

▥ RULE OF LAW

A law is unconstitutional as an undue burden on a woman's right to an abortion before fetal viability, if the law places a substantial obstacle in the path of a woman seeking to exercise her right.

FACTS: The Pennsylvania Abortion Control Act required (a) a doctor to provide a woman seeking an abortion with information designed to persuade her against abortion and imposed a waiting period of at least 24 hours between provision of the information and the abortion; (b) a minor to obtain consent of one parent or a judge's order before having an abortion; (c) a married woman to sign a statement averring that her husband had been notified, her husband was not the father, her husband forcibly had impregnated her, or that she would be physical harmed if she notified her husband; and (d) a public report on every abortion, detailing information on the facility, physician, patient, and steps taken to comply with the Act. The name of the patient was confidential. It provided the first three provisions would not apply in a "medical emergency," i.e., a condition a doctor determines to require immediate abortion to avert death or serious risk of substantial, irreversible impairment of a major bodily function. Five clinics (P), including Planned Parenthood (P), and five doctors (P) sued Pennsylvania (D), including Governor Casey (D), claiming the Act was unconstitutional on its face. The district court held the entire Act invalid under *Roe v. Wade*, 410 U.S. 113 (1973). The court of appeals reversed, upholding the entire Act except the husband-notification requirement. Planned Parenthood et al. (P) appealed.

ISSUE: Is a law unconstitutional as an undue burden on a woman's right to an abortion before fetal viability, if the law places a substantial obstacle in the path of a woman's exercise of her right?

HOLDING AND DECISION: (O'Connor, Kennedy, and Souter, JJ.) Yes. A law is unconstitutional as an undue burden on a woman's right to an abortion before fetal viability, if the law places a substantial obstacle in the path of a woman seeking to exercise her right. For two decades people have organized lives relying on the availability of abortion. The Court rarely resolves a controversy as intensely divisive as in *Roe*. Such a decision should be overturned only if it proves unworkable or if new informa-

tion arises which renders the decision unjustified in the present. *Roe* is neither unworkable nor based on outdated assumptions. Medical technology has altered the age of viability, but that does not affect the validity of viability as a dividing line. Viability is the point at which a fetus can be said to be an independent life, so that the state's interest in protecting it then outweighs the mother's decision-making interest. The Court and the nation would be seriously damaged if the Court were to overturn *Roe* simply on the basis of a philosophical disagreement with the 1973 Court, or as a surrender to political pressure. The liberty rights of women and the personal, intimate nature of childbearing sharply limit state power to insist a woman carry a child to term or accept the state's vision of her role in society. Thus, the integrity of the Court, stare decisis, and substantive due process require the central principle of *Roe* to be reaffirmed: a state may not prevent a woman from making the ultimate decision to terminate her pregnancy before viability. *Roe* also recognized the state interest in maternal health and in protecting potential life. Application of the rigid trimester framework often ignored state interests, leading to striking down abortion regulations that in no real sense deprived women of the ultimate decision. Therefore, the trimester framework must be rejected and undue burden analysis put in its place.

CONCURRENCE AND DISSENT: (Blackmun, J.) The Court correctly reaffirms a woman's right to abortion. However, that right should remain fundamental, and any state-imposed burden upon it should be subjected to the strictest judicial scrutiny. Categorizing a woman's right to abortion as merely a "liberty interest" is not sufficient. The trimester framework should be maintained. No other approach better protects a woman's fundamental right while accommodating legitimate state interests.

CONCURRENCE AND DISSENT: (Rehnquist, C.J.) *Roe* was wrongly decided and should be overturned. In viewing the right to terminate a pregnancy as fundamental, the Court in *Roe* read the earlier opinions upon which it based its decision too broadly. Unlike marriage, procreation, and contraception, abortion terminates potential life and must be analyzed differently. Historic traditions of the American people, critical to an understanding of fundamental rights, do not support a right to abortion.

CONCURRENCE AND DISSENT: (Scalia, J.) The limits on abortion should be decided democratically. The Constitution is silent on abortion, and American traditions

Continued on next page.

have allowed it to be proscribed. *Roe* did not resolve the deeply divisive issue of abortion. It made compromise impossible and elevated the issue to a national level where it has proven infinitely more difficult to resolve.

▶ *ANALYSIS*

The Court also affirmed *Roe*'s holding that after viability the state may regulate, or even proscribe, abortion, except where it is necessary to preserve the life or health of the mother. This is only the second time in modern Supreme Court jurisprudence that an opinion has been jointly authored. Justice Kennedy's portion of the opinion addresses the importance of public faith in and acceptance of the Court's work by opening with the statement: "Liberty finds no refuge in a jurisprudence of doubt." Justice O'Connor expounds on the essential nature of a woman's right to an abortion, while Justice Souter performs the stare decisis analysis, concluding that there is no reason to reverse the essential holding of *Roe*. It appears that the instant case marks the first time the Court has downgraded a fundamental right to a protected liberty and by so doing removed from the usual strict scrutiny standard of review.

■══■

Quicknotes

FUNDAMENTAL RIGHT A liberty that is either expressly or impliedly provided for in the U.S. Constitution, the deprivation or burdening of which is subject to a heightened standard of review.

LIBERTY INTEREST A right conferred by the Due Process Clauses of the state and federal constitutions.

STARE DECISIS Doctrine whereby courts follow legal precedent unless there is good cause for departure.

■══■

Gonzales v. Carhart

Attorney General (D) v. Abortion doctor (P)

127 S. Ct. 1610 (2007).

NATURE OF CASE: Facial due-process challenge to the federal Partial-Birth Abortion Ban Act.

FACT SUMMARY: Congress passed a statute that criminalized doctors' performance of partial-birth abortions.

🏛 RULE OF LAW

The Partial-Birth Abortion Ban Act does not place a substantial obstacle to late-term, but pre-viability, abortions.

FACTS: In 2003, Congress enacted the Partial-Birth Abortion Ban Act, which criminalized doctors' performance of partial-birth abortions. The Act explicitly and precisely defined "partial-birth abortion," in part as an abortion following the "deliver[y] [of] a living fetus." [Carhart (P), a doctor who performed partial-birth abortions, filed suit for injunctive relief to prohibit the Act from being applied against him. The trial court granted the injunction, and the intermediate appellate court affirmed.] The government (D) sought further review in the Supreme Court.

ISSUE: Does the Partial-Birth Abortion Ban Act place a substantial obstacle to late-term, but pre-viability, abortions?

HOLDING AND DECISION: (Kennedy, J.) No. The Partial-Birth Abortion Ban Act ("the Act") does not place a substantial obstacle to late-term, but pre-viability, abortions. The Act can be construed as not prohibiting the standard form of partial-birth abortion invalidated in *Stenberg v. Carhart*, 530 U.S. 914 (2000), and the Act therefore is not facially invalid on that basis. Further, instead of placing a substantial obstacle to a partial-birth abortion, the Act simply respects human life—an objective that lies within the legislative power. The Act advances that objective by ensuring that women will be fully informed about the methods of abortion to which they consent. Moreover, Congress can legitimately legislate even in the face of the medical uncertainty on whether such a prohibition on one form of abortion subjects women "to significant health risks." Such uncertainty does not support a facial challenge to the Act. The proper way to attack the Act would be through an as-applied challenge that would permit review of a more precise factual scenario. [Reversed.]

CONCURRENCE: (Thomas, J.) The Court correctly applies existing law, but the Constitution provides no basis at all for the Court's abortion jurisprudence.

DISSENT: (Ginsburg, J.) This decision mocks *Casey*, 505 U.S. 833 (1992), and *Stenberg*, and it flies in the face of medical approval of abortion procedures. The Act does subject women to significant health risks by forcing them to choose less safe methods of abortion, and, in the process,

the statute does not save even one fetus because the Act merely criminalizes a method of abortion, not abortion itself. As the Court suggests, the real basis for today's decision is "moral concerns" for what the majority sees as emotionally fragile women. This rationale circumvents the concerns for stare decisis that have supported our prior decisions in this area. Today's decision is actually only a veiled attempt to undermine, in a piecemeal fashion, a woman's established right to an abortion.

▶ ANALYSIS

The right to an abortion announced in *Roe v. Wade,* 410 U.S. 113 (1973), remains intact after *Gonzales v. Carhart.* That right is now more difficult to exercise, though, and, as Justice Ginsburg suggests in dissent, the federal statute's omission of safeguards for women's health is at best problematic under the Court's prior abortion decisions.

■══■

Quicknotes

DUE PROCESS The constitutional mandate requiring the courts to protect and enforce individuals' rights and liberties consistent with prevailing principles of fairness and justice and prohibiting the federal and state governments from such activities that deprive its citizens of life, liberty, or property interest.

INJUNCTION A court order requiring a person to do, or prohibiting that person from doing, a specific act.

INJUNCTIVE RELIEF A court order issued as a remedy, requiring a person to do, or prohibiting that person from doing, a specific act.

STARE DECISIS Doctrine whereby courts follow legal precedent unless there is good cause for departure.

■══■

Maher v. Roe

State (D) v. Indigent woman (P)

432 U.S. 464 (1977).

NATURE OF CASE: Appeal from an action seeking a declaratory judgment.

FACT SUMMARY: Poe (P) and Roe (P) brought this action seeking a declaratory judgment that a Connecticut statute which limited state Medicaid benefits for abortions to those that were medically necessary was unconstitutional.

🏛 RULE OF LAW
The Constitution does not require a state to pay for nontherapeutic abortions when it pays for childbirth.

FACTS: A regulation of the Connecticut Welfare Department limited state Medicaid benefits for first trimester abortions to those that were medically necessary. Connecticut enforced this limitation through a system of prior authorization from its Department of Social Services. This attack on the validity of the regulation was brought against Maher (D), the Commissioner of Social Services, by Roe (P) and Poe (P), two indigent women who were unable to obtain a physician's certificate of medical necessity. A three-judge district court invalidated the regulation, holding that the Equal Protection Clause forbids the exclusion of nontherapeutic abortions from a state welfare program that generally subsidizes the medical expenses incident to pregnancy and childbirth. Maher (D) appealed to the Supreme Court.

ISSUE: If a state subsidizes the medical expenses of childbirth, must it also pay for nontherapeutic abortions?

HOLDING AND DECISION: (Powell, J.) No. *Roe v. Wade* (410 U.S. 113 [1973]) did not declare an unqualified constitutional right to an abortion as the district court seemed to think. Rather, the right protects the woman from unduly burdensome interference with her freedom to decide whether to terminate her pregnancy. It implies no limitation on the authority of a state to make a value judgment favoring childbirth over abortion and to implement that judgment by the allocation of public funds. The Connecticut regulation places no obstacles in the pregnant woman's path to an abortion. An indigent woman continues as before to be dependent on private sources for the services she desires. The state unquestionably has a strong and legitimate interest in encouraging normal childbirth. Thus, this court holds the Connecticut funding scheme satisfies the equal protection test of rationality that applies in the absence of a suspect classification or the impingement of a fundamental right.

DISSENT: (Brennan, J.) The fact that the state will pay the medical expenses associated with childbirth, but not those associated with an abortion, operates to coerce indigent women to bear children they would not otherwise choose to have. This is an unconstitutional impingement upon their right of privacy derived from the Due Process Clause.

▶ ANALYSIS

In distinguishing between direct state interference with a protected activity and state encouragement of an alternative activity, the Supreme Court relied on *Meyer v. Nebraska*, 262 U.S. 390 (1923), and *Pierce v. Society of Sisters*, 268 U.S. 510 (1925). The Court concluded that while both decisions invalidated restrictions on constitutionally protected liberty interests, neither case denied to a state the policy choice of encouraging the preferred course of action such as favoring public rather than private schools.

■=■

Quicknotes

DUE PROCESS CLAUSE Clauses found in the Fifth and Fourteenth Amendments to the U.S. Constitution providing that no person shall be deprived of "life, liberty, or property, without due process of law."

EQUAL PROTECTION CLAUSE A constitutional provision that each person be guaranteed the same protection of the laws enjoyed by other persons in like circumstances.

FUNDAMENTAL RIGHT A liberty that is either expressly or impliedly provided for in the U.S. Constitution, the deprivation or burdening of which is subject to a heightened standard of review.

LIBERTY INTEREST A right conferred by the Due Process Clauses of the state and federal constitutions.

RATIONAL BASIS REVIEW A test employed by the court to determine the validity of a statute in equal protection actions, whereby the court determines whether the challenged statute is rationally related to the achievement of a legitimate state interest.

■=■

Planned Parenthood v. Casey

Abortion clinics (P) v. State governor (D)

505 U.S. 833 (1992).

NATURE OF CASE: Appeal from part of a decision holding that a state abortion law's husband-notification requirement violates due process and equal protection.

FACT SUMMARY: Pennsylvania's abortion law provided, with some exceptions, that a married woman must notify her husband of her decision to have an abortion. Abortion clinics challenged the requirement as a violation of due process and equal protection.

🏛 RULE OF LAW
A state abortion law's husband-notification requirement violates due process and equal protection.

FACTS: Section 3209 (one of several provisions) of Pennsylvania's abortion law provided, except in cases of medical emergency and a few other limited circumstances, e.g., a pregnancy that is the result of spousal rape, that no physician could perform an abortion on a married woman without a signed statement from her that she notified her husband of her intent to have an abortion. If the physician performed the abortion without the statement, the physician would be liable to the husband for damages and could have his license revoked. Abortion clinics (P) challenged the notification requirement as a violation of due process and equal protection. The district court struck down this requirement, along with all the other provisions of the abortion law, and the court of appeals affirmed as to the notification requirement, but upheld the other provisions. The Supreme Court granted review.

ISSUE: Does a state abortion law's husband-notification requirement violate due process and equal protection?

HOLDING AND DECISION: (O'Connor, J.) Yes. A state abortion law's husband-notification requirement violates due process and equal protection. The facts are that a vast majority of women notify their male partners of their decision to have an abortion. Otherwise, a married woman usually does not notify her husband of this decision because either the pregnancy is the result of an extramarital affair or the woman is afraid of physical or psychological abuse. There are millions of women in the country who fear such abuse. The spousal notification is thus an undue burden and will likely prevent a significant number of women from obtaining an abortion—as surely as if abortion were outlawed in all cases. The state's argument that this requirement is felt by only 1 percent of women who obtain abortions fails because the proper focus of the constitutional inquiry is the group—here, the 1 percent—for whom the law is a restriction, not the group for whom the law is irrelevant. Although the husband has

an interest in his wife's pregnancy, the wife's privacy interest—the right to be free from government intrusion into whether one will bear or beget a child—outweighs the husband's interest before birth. For those women who are victims of spousal abuse, the notification requirement gives the husband a veto over the wife's abortion decision. Such a veto is unconstitutional, as is the state's empowerment of the husband with the veto. Women do not lose their constitutional liberties when they marry, and are free from governmental abuse of power, even when that power is used to benefit their husbands.

DISSENT: (Rehnquist, C.J.) The state has a legitimate interest in protecting the husband's interest and in protecting the life of the fetus, and the husband-notification requirement is reasonably related to advancing these interests. If a wife discusses her desire for an abortion with the husband, the husband may participate in the decision and the pregnancy may not be terminated. The notice requirement is also a rational attempt to further the integrity of the marital relationship—a legitimate state interest—by promoting dialogue between husband and wife. Although in some cases the notice requirement will not have these effects, this does not make the requirement irrational, and, therefore, the legislature's determination must be deferred to.

▶ ANALYSIS

Casey announced an "undue burden" test for abortion regulations. The test says that states may regulate pre-viability abortions, but if the regulation places an undue burden on the woman's right to an abortion—the regulation has the purpose or effect of placing a substantial obstacle to getting an abortion—the regulation is invalid. In this part of the *Casey* opinion, the Court implied that an "undue burden" on the right to an abortion exists where a court determines that a regulation will prevent women from receiving an abortion.

■━■

Quicknotes

DUE PROCESS CLAUSE Clauses found in the Fifth and Fourteenth Amendments to the U.S. Constitution providing that no person shall be deprived of "life, liberty, or property, without due process of law."

EQUAL PROTECTION CLAUSE A constitutional provision that each person be guaranteed the same protection of the laws enjoyed by other persons in like circumstances.

Continued on next page.

RATIONAL BASIS REVIEW A test employed by the court to determine the validity of a statute in equal protection actions, whereby the court determines whether the challenged statute is rationally related to the achievement of a legitimate state interest.

UNDUE BURDEN A burden which is unlawfully oppressive or troublesome.

Bellotti v. Baird

State attorney general (D) v. Abortion clinic director (P)

443 U.S. 622 (1979).

NATURE OF CASE: Appeal from decision that a state statute requiring an unmarried minor seeking an abortion to obtain the consent of both parents or a court order violates due process and equal protection.

FACT SUMMARY: Massachusetts (D) required an unmarried minor seeking an abortion to obtain the consent of both parents or a court order. Baird (P), an abortion clinic director and others, including a pregnant unmarried minor, challenged the law as violating due process and equal protection.

🏛 RULE OF LAW
A state statute that requires an unmarried minor seeking an abortion to obtain the consent of both parents or a court order violates due process and equal protection.

FACTS: A Massachusetts statute requires parental consent before an abortion can be performed on an unmarried woman under the age of 18. If one or both parents refuse such consent, however, the abortion may be obtained by order of a judge of the superior court "for good cause shown." Physicians performing abortions in the absence of such consent or order are subject to criminal penalties. Baird (P), an abortion-clinic director, a physician who performed abortions, and others, including a pregnant unmarried minor, challenged the law as violating due process and equal protection. A district court held that the law was unconstitutional, and the Supreme Court granted review.

ISSUE: Does a state statute that requires an unmarried minor seeking an abortion to obtain the consent of both parents or a court order violate due process and equal protection?

HOLDING AND DECISION: (Powell, J.) Yes. The abortion decision differs in important ways from other decisions facing minors, and the state is required to act with particular sensitivity when it legislates to foster parental involvement in this matter. If a state decides to require a pregnant minor to obtain one or both parents' consent to an abortion, it also must provide an alternative procedure whereby authorization for the abortion can be obtained. A pregnant minor is entitled in such a proceeding to show either that she is mature enough and well enough informed to make her abortion decision, in consultation with her physician, independently of her parents' wishes, or that even if she is not able to make this decision independently, the desired abortion would be in her best interests. Such a procedure must ensure that the provision requiring parental consent does not in fact amount to an impermissible absolute, and possibly arbitrary, veto. Here, the Massachusetts statute unduly burdens the right to seek an abortion. The statute falls short of constitutional standards in two respects. First, it permits judicial authorization for an abortion to be withheld from a minor who is found by the superior court to be mature and fully competent to make this decision independently. Second, it requires parental consultation or notification in every instance, whether or not that is in the pregnant minor's best interests, without affording her an opportunity to receive an independent judicial determination that she is mature enough to consent or that an abortion would be in her best interests. Affirmed.

CONCURRENCE: (Stevens, J.) The Massachusetts statute is unconstitutional because under the statute, no minor, no matter how mature and capable of informed decision making, may receive an abortion without the consent of either both parents or a superior court judge, thus making the minor's abortion decision subject in every instance to an absolute third-party veto. Such a veto is fundamentally at odds with the minor's privacy rights.

▶ ANALYSIS

The judicial procedure that in this case was provided as an alternative to parental consent, also known as a judicial bypass, has been upheld where it comports with the requirements set forth in *Bellotti*. See *Planned Parenthood v. Ashcroft*, 462 U.S. 476 (1983).

Quicknotes

DUE PROCESS CLAUSE Clauses found in the Fifth and Fourteenth Amendments to the U.S. Constitution providing that no person shall be deprived of "life, liberty, or property, without due process of law."

EQUAL PROTECTION CLAUSE A constitutional provision that each person be guaranteed the same protection of the laws enjoyed by other persons in like circumstances.

UNDUE BURDEN A burden which is unlawfully oppressive or troublesome.

Cruzan v. Director, Missouri Dept. of Health

Individual on life support (P) v. State (D)

497 U.S. 261 (1990).

NATURE OF CASE: Review of challenge to state procedural requirement regarding termination of life support.

FACT SUMMARY: Missouri (D) required clear and convincing evidence of prior consent by an individual prior to the cessation of life support systems operating upon that individual.

🏛 RULE OF LAW
A state may require clear and convincing evidence of consent by an individual prior to the cessation of life support procedures upon that individual.

FACTS: Cruzan (P) was rendered comatose by an automobile accident, and remained in that state without any reasonable chance of recovery. When her next of kin requested that life support be terminated, the medical personnel caring for her refused to do so on the basis of state law, requiring clear and convincing evidence of an individual's prior consent in order for the cessation of life support procedures to be effected. An action was brought on behalf of Cruzan (P), alleging that the law violated her constitutional "right to die." This argument was rejected by the Missouri state courts, and the Supreme Court granted review.

ISSUE: May a state require clear and convincing evidence of consent by an individual prior to the cessation of life support procedures upon that individual?

HOLDING AND DECISION: (Rehnquist, C.J.) Yes. A state may require clear and convincing evidence of consent by an individual prior to the cessation of life support procedures upon that individual. For purposes of argument, this Court will assume that the right to refuse artificial hydration and feeding is a liberty interest protected by the Fourteenth Amendment. However, this liberty interest must be weighed against a state's interest in the challenged regulation. In the context of this case, the state's interest involved is the lives of its citizens, a highly compelling interest. A state is free to adopt procedures designed to ensure that, prior to the cessation of artificial life support, the individual undergoing such support had, when competent, desired that such support be withheld. Due to the highly compelling nature of the state's interest in this type of situation, a clear and convincing evidentiary standard does not run afoul of any right to terminate such treatment that may exist.

CONCURRENCE: (O'Connor, J.) A right to deny artificial life support should be clearly recognized. Also, this decision should not be read to apply to a situation involving a surrogate decisionmaker.

CONCURRENCE: (Scalia, J.) As with abortion, the federal courts do not belong in this field, and matters of this type should be left to the states for decision.

DISSENT: (Brennan, J.) An individual has a fundamental interest in avoiding unwanted medical treatment. A state may only effect procedures to determine the wishes of an incompetent individual with the aim of reflecting as accurately as possible those wishes. A clear and convincing evidentiary standard improperly amounts to a presumption against the cessation of treatment.

▶ ANALYSIS

This case is as important for what it does not say for what it does. The Court did not declare, as many expected, that a right to die does or does not exist. Consequently, the invitation for other cases presenting this issue appears to be open.

■═■

Quicknotes

COMPELLING STATE INTEREST Defense to an alleged Equal Protection Clause violation; that a state action was necessary in order to protect an interest the government is under a duty to protect.

LIBERTY INTEREST A right conferred by the Due Process Clauses of the state and federal constitutions.

■═■

Washington v. Glucksberg

State (D) v. Doctors (P)

521 U.S. 702 (1997).

NATURE OF CASE: Review of judgment declaring that a state law prohibiting assisted suicide was unconstitutional.

FACT SUMMARY: A group of Washington physicians (P) and a nonprofit organization (P) that counseled people considering physician-assisted suicide filed suit seeking a declaration that the state's assisted-suicide ban was facially unconstitutional.

🏛 RULE OF LAW
The right to assistance in committing suicide is not a fundamental liberty interest protected by the Due Process Clause.

FACTS: A Washington law stated that "a person is guilty of promoting a suicide attempt when he knowingly causes or aids another person to attempt suicide." Breaking the law was a felony punishable by up to five years' imprisonment and up to a $10,000 fine. Washington also had a Natural Death Act, which stated that withholding or withdrawal of life-sustaining treatment at a patient's discretion did not constitute a suicide. Physicians (P) practicing in Washington and Compassion in Dying (P), a nonprofit organization that counseled people considering physician-assisted suicide, filed suit seeking a declaration that the ban on assisted suicide was unconstitutional. The physicians (P), who treated many terminally ill, suffering patients, declared that they would have assisted some of these patients in ending their lives were it not for Washington's law. The district court found the statute invalid, and the court of appeals ultimately affirmed. The appellate court held that the Constitution encompasses a due process liberty interest in controlling the time and manner of one's death, and that the state's assisted-suicide ban was unconstitutional as applied to terminally ill competent adults who wish to hasten their deaths with medication prescribed by their physicians. The Supreme Court granted certiorari.

ISSUE: Is the right to assistance in committing suicide a fundamental liberty interest protected by the Due Process Clause?

HOLDING AND DECISION: (Rehnquist, C.J.) No. The right to assistance in committing suicide is not a fundamental liberty interest protected by the Due Process Clause. In almost every state and every western democracy, it is a crime to assist a suicide. These laws reflect a longstanding commitment to the protection and preservation of human life. In 1991, Washington voters rejected a ballot measure that would have permitted a form of physician-assisted suicide. The Court must exercise extreme prudence in expanding the Due Process Clause to include new

fundamental rights and liberties. In *Cruzan v. Director, Missouri Dept. of Health*, 497 U.S. 261 (1990), the Court suggested that the Due Process Clause protects the right to refuse unwanted lifesaving medical treatment. The physicians' (P) reliance on *Cruzan* is misplaced. At common law, forced medication was a battery; however, the decision to commit suicide has never been afforded similar legal protection. Washington (D) also has a fundamental interest in protecting the integrity of the medical profession, and the American Medical Association has concluded that physician-assisted suicide is fundamentally incompatible with the physician's role as a healer. Finally, the state has an interest in protecting vulnerable groups from abuse, neglect, and mistakes. There is a very real risk of subtle coercion and undue influence in end-of-life situations that legalized physician-assisted suicide would likely exacerbate. Therefore, the statute does not violate the Fourteenth Amendment either on its face or as applied. Reversed.

CONCURRENCE: (O'Connor, J.) While the majority correctly holds that there is no generalized "right" to commit suicide, the question of whether a mentally competent person experiencing great suffering has a constitutional right to control the circumstances of his or her imminent death should not be precluded by this decision.

CONCURRENCE: (Stevens, J.) The Court's holding that Washington's statute is not invalid on its face does not foreclose the possibility that some applications of the statute might well be invalid. The state's interest in supporting a general rule banning the practice of physician-assisted suicide does not have the same force in all cases.

CONCURRENCE: (Breyer, J.) The Court has misstated the claimed liberty interest. A more accurate formulation would use words like a "right to die with dignity" and would be closely linked with a right to avoid severe physical pain connected with death. Nevertheless, given the facts at hand, the Court need not decide now whether or not such a right is "fundamental."

▶ ANALYSIS

The four concurring justices all left the door wide open for the Court to revisit this decision given a more fact-specific case. While they all strongly suggested that an individual under certain, limited circumstances may have a constitutionally protected right to assisted suicide, they were cautious in taking that leap given the specific question at issue here. While several states, including Washington and

Continued on next page.

California, have voted down statutes permitting physician-assisted suicide, it is likely that one will eventually pass, and the Court will again be presented with these issues.

■══■

Quicknotes

DUE PROCESS CLAUSE Clauses found in the Fifth and Fourteenth Amendments to the U.S. Constitution providing that no person shall be deprived of "life, liberty, or property, without due process of law."

FUNDAMENTAL RIGHT A liberty that is either expressly or impliedly provided for in the U.S. Constitution, the deprivation or burdening of which is subject to a heightened standard of review.

LIBERTY INTEREST A right conferred by the Due Process Clauses of the state and federal constitutions.

■══■

Lawrence v. Texas

Convicted criminal (D) v. State (P)

539 U.S. 558 (2003).

NATURE OF CASE: Appeal from a conviction for deviate sexual intercourse with a person of the same sex.

FACT SUMMARY: Police officers saw Lawrence (D), a man, having anal sex with another man inside an apartment. The two men were charged with, and convicted of, the Texas crime of deviate sexual intercourse with a member of the same sex.

🏛 RULE OF LAW
A state cannot criminalize intimate sexual conduct between two persons of the same sex consistent with the substantive protections of the Due Process Clause of the Fourteenth Amendment.

FACTS: Responding to a reported weapons disturbance, police officers arrived at an apartment and found Lawrence (D), a man, having anal sex with another man inside the apartment. The officers arrested both men, who were charged with violating Texas criminal statutes that explicitly prohibited deviate sexual intercourse between persons of the same sex. Texas defined "deviate sexual intercourse" as "any contact between any part of the genitals of one person and the mouth or anus of another person." Lawrence (D) and the other man were convicted by a justice of the peace. They appealed.

ISSUE: Can a state criminalize intimate sexual conduct between two persons of the same sex consistent with the substantive protections of the Due Process Clause of the Fourteenth Amendment?

HOLDING AND DECISION: (Kennedy, J.) No. A state cannot criminalize intimate sexual conduct between two persons of the same sex consistent with the substantive protections of the Due Process Clause of the Fourteenth Amendment. Properly framed, the issue is whether the Texas statutes violate the substantive right to privacy protected by the Due Process Clause. In *Bowers v. Hardwick*, 478 U.S. 186 (1986), which upheld a Georgia law that criminalized sodomy, the Court framed the issue too narrowly, as whether the Constitution contains a fundamental right for homosexuals to commit sodomy. Because the historical reasoning of *Bowers* was overstated, if not simply wrong, *Bowers* is now overruled. The behavior proscribed by Texas's statutes criminalizing deviate sexual intercourse with a person of the same sex falls within the privacy right contained in the Due Process Clause. Such a law advances no legitimate state interest. Accordingly, the statute violates due process.

CONCURRENCE: (O'Connor, J.) *Bowers* need not be overruled. The better basis for decision in this case is equal protection. As the Court held in *Romer v. Evans*, 517 U.S. 620 (1996), "a bare . . . desire to harm" homosexuals is not a legitimate state interest under rational-basis review. Contrary to Texas's arguments in this case, moral disapproval alone is not a legitimate state interest. The Texas law targets homosexuality, not merely homosexual conduct, which, as with the state constitutional amendment in *Romer v. Evans*, amounts to a bare desire to harm an unpopular group.

DISSENT: (Scalia, J.) The Court fails to declare that homosexual sodomy is a fundamental right under the Constitution, and it fails to apply the standard of review reserved for analysis of fundamental rights, strict scrutiny. Instead, this decision rests on an utterly novel form of rational-basis review, which flatly contradicts the law of substantive due process. *Bowers*'s historical underpinnings were and are correct, despite the majority's eagerness to do away with *Bowers* just seventeen years after it was handed down. Justice O'Connor's equal-protection analysis, furthermore, cannot be sound because the law here proscribes same-sex interaction precisely as marriage laws do. In sum, this entire matter would be much more appropriately addressed through the democratic process of legislation than by a panel of judges.

DISSENT: (Thomas, J.) Nothing in the Constitution protects a right to privacy within the liberty interest that is secured by the Due Process Clause of the Fourteenth Amendment.

▶ ANALYSIS

As Justice Scalia notes, substantive due process requires strict judicial scrutiny of the challenged government action. The majority, however, unmistakably applies rational-basis review to what it frames as a manifestation of the privacy right that has been held to reside in the liberty interest enumerated in the Due Process under *Griswold v. Connecticut*, 381 U.S. 479 (1965), and its progeny. If the majority insisted on rational-basis review, and if the majority had followed the principle that courts should decide cases in ways that disturb existing law as little as possible, then Justice O'Conner's concurrence states the better basis of decision: *Romer v. Evans*, 517 U.S. 620 (1996), would have easily invalidated the Texas statute on equal-protection grounds, without having the Court cause the major disturbance of overruling relatively recent precedent.

■■■

Quicknotes

DUE PROCESS CLAUSE Clauses found in the Fifth and Fourteenth Amendments to the U.S. Constitution providing that

Continued on next page.

no person shall be deprived of "life, liberty, or property, without due process of law."

EQUAL PROTECTION CLAUSE A constitutional provision that each person be guaranteed the same protection of the laws enjoyed by other persons in like circumstances.

FUNDAMENTAL RIGHT A liberty that is either expressly or impliedly provided for in the U.S. Constitution, the deprivation or burdening of which is subject to a heightened standard of review.

LIBERTY INTEREST A right conferred by the Due Process Clauses of the state and federal constitutions.

RATIONAL BASIS REVIEW A test employed by the court to determine the validity of a statute in equal protection actions, whereby the court determines whether the challenged statute is rationally related to the achievement of a legitimate state interest.

SUBSTANTIVE DUE PROCESS A constitutional safeguard limiting the power of the state, irrespective of how fair its procedures may be; substantive limits placed on the power of the state.

Whalen v. Roe

State official (D) v. Medical patient (P)

429 U.S. 589 (1977).

NATURE OF CASE: Appeal from order enjoining enforcement of a state law that required storage of the private information of medical patients (P) who received prescriptions for drugs susceptible to illegal abuse.

FACT SUMMARY: New York required storage of the private information of medical patients (P) who received prescriptions for drugs susceptible to illegal abuse. Medical patients (P) challenged the law as a violation of their constitutionally protected right to privacy.

🏛 RULE OF LAW
A state law that requires storage of the private information of medical patients who received prescriptions for drugs susceptible to illegal abuse does not violate the patients' constitutionally protected privacy right.

FACTS: A New York law required that physicians provide reports identifying patients receiving prescription drugs that have a potential for abuse. The state maintained a centralized computer file that listed the names and addresses of the patients. The reports and the computer files were kept under tight security, and disclosing the information to the public was a crime. Medical patients (P) challenged the law, arguing that the database infringed their constitutionally protected right to privacy. The district court found the law was unconstitutional, and the Supreme Court granted review.

ISSUE: Does a state law that requires storage of the private information of medical patients who received prescriptions for drugs susceptible to illegal abuse violate the patients' constitutionally protected privacy right?

HOLDING AND DECISION: (Stevens, J.) No. The law was passed in response to a legislative concern that the drugs for which reports were required were being diverted for illegal use—a problem of vital local concern. States have wide latitude in experimenting with possible solutions to such problems, and here, the reporting system is a "considered" and reasonable attempt to address the problem. Cases dealing with the right to privacy involve two kinds of interest: (1) the right to avoid disclosure of personal matters, and (2) the right to independence in making certain kinds of important decisions. The New York law does not on its face pose a sufficient threat to either of these privacy interests for constitutional purposes. Given the law's security provisions, it is unlikely that there will be an unwarranted disclosure of private information to the public, and even the remote possibility that this information might be disclosed in a judicial proceeding is not enough to invalidate the entire patient-identification program. And, any disclosures made to state officials who are part of the program are no more invasive than other revelations necessary for health care—such as those made to providers, insurance companies, hospitals, etc. Such disclosures are a necessary part of health care, even when they may reflect unfavorably on the character of the patient. Requiring such disclosures to state health officials charged with maintaining the health of the community is not an impermissible invasion of privacy under the Fourteenth Amendment because there is no immediate or threatened impact on the reputation or independence of the patients.

▶ ANALYSIS

Consistent with *Whalen*, the Court has not yet recognized a broad right of data privacy. The majority in *Whalen* did keep open the possibility that such a right to privacy might be recognized in the future, given "the threat to privacy implicit in the accumulation of vast amounts of personal information in computerized data banks or other massive government files." In an era where private information is increasingly stored in electronic format and can readily be broadcast to a vast public audience through networks such as the Internet, it is possible the Court may directly face this issue in the near future.

■≡■

Quicknotes

PRIVACY RIGHT Those personal liberties or relationships that are protected against unwarranted governmental interference.

■≡■

Saenz v. Roe

New state resident (P) v. State government (D)

526 U.S. 489 (1999).

NATURE OF CASE: Appeal from an order enjoining implementation of a state statute.

FACT SUMMARY: When California (D) discriminated against citizens who had resided in the state for less then one year in distributing welfare benefits, the state statute was challenged and held to be unconstitutional.

🏛 RULE OF LAW
Durational residency requirements violate the fundamental right to travel by denying a newly arrived citizen the same privileges and immunities enjoyed by other citizens in the same state, and are therefore subject to strict scrutiny.

FACTS: In 1992, California (D) enacted a statute limiting the maximum first-year welfare benefits available to newly arrived residents to the amount they would have received in the state of their prior residence. Saenz (P) and other California residents who were eligible for such benefits challenged the constitutionality of the durational residency requirement, alleging their right to travel was violated. The district court preliminarily enjoined implementation of the statute and the court of appeals affirmed. Congress enacted the Personal Responsibility and Work Opportunity Reconciliation Act of 1996, which expressly authorized states to apply the rules (including benefit amounts) of another state if the family has resided in the state for less than twelve months. California (D) appealed, alleging that the statute should be upheld if it has a rational basis, and that the state's (D) legitimate interest in saving over $10 million a year satisfied that test.

ISSUE: Do durational residency requirements violate the fundamental right to travel by denying a newly arrived citizen the same privileges and immunities enjoyed by other citizens in the same state, and are they thus subject to strict scrutiny?

HOLDING AND DECISION: (Stevens, J.) Yes. Durational residency requirements violate the fundamental right to travel by denying a newly arrived citizen the same privileges and immunities enjoyed by other citizens in the same state, and are therefore subject to strict scrutiny. The first sentence of Article IV, § 2, provides that the citizens of each state shall be entitled to all privileges and immunities of citizens in the several states. The right of a newly-arrived citizen to the same privileges and immunities enjoyed by other citizens of the same state is protected not only by the new arrival's status as a state citizen, but also by her status as a citizen of the United States. The Citizenship Clause of the Fourteenth Amendment protects all citizens' right to choose

to be citizens of the state wherein they reside. Neither mere rationality nor some intermediate standard of review should be used to judge the constitutionality of a state rule that discriminates against some of its citizens because they have been domiciled in the state for less than a year. The state's legitimate interest in saving money provides no justification for its decision to discriminate among equally eligible citizens.

DISSENT: (Rehnquist, C.J.) The right to travel and the right to become a citizen are distinct, and one is not a "component" of the other. If states can require an individual to reside in-state for a year before exercising the right to educational benefits, the right to terminate a marriage, or the right to vote in primary elections that all other state citizens enjoy, then it may surely do the same for welfare benefits. California has reasonably exercised its power to protect state resources through an objective, narrowly tailored residence requirement. There is nothing in the Constitution that should prevent the enforcement of that requirement.

▌ ANALYSIS

The Court in this case found that a state violated the Privileges and Immunities Clause when it discriminated against citizens who had been residents for less than one year. In his dissent, Justice Thomas alleged that this was contrary to the original understanding at the time the Fourteenth Amendment was enacted. In his dissent, Chief Justice Rehnquist went on to point out that a welfare subsidy is as much an investment in human capital as is a tuition subsidy and their attendant benefits are just as portable.

■=■

Quicknotes

FUNDAMENTAL RIGHT A liberty that is either expressly or impliedly provided for in the U.S. Constitution, the deprivation or burdening of which is subject to a heightened standard of review.

PRIVILEGES AND IMMUNITIES CLAUSE Article IV, section 2, clause 1 of the U.S. Constitution, which states that a state cannot favor its own citizens by discriminating against other states' citizens who may come within its borders.

STRICT SCRUTINY Method by which courts determine the constitutionality of a law, when a law affects a fundamental right. Under the test, the legislature must have had a compelling interest to enact the law and measures prescribed by the law must be the least restrictive means possible to accomplish its goal.

■=■

Harper v. Virginia State Board of Elections

Residents (P) v. State (D)

383 U.S. 663 (1966).

NATURE OF CASE: Suits challenging the constitutionality of Virginia's poll tax.

FACT SUMMARY: Harper (P) and other Virginia residents brought this suit to have Virginia's (D) poll tax declared unconstitutional.

🏛 RULE OF LAW
The right to vote is a fundamental and basic right, and where such rights are asserted under the Equal Protection Clause, classifications that might restrain those rights must be closely scrutinized and carefully confined. Lines drawn on the basis of wealth or property, like those of race, are traditionally disfavored.

FACTS: Harper (P) and other Virginia residents brought these suits to have Virginia's (D) poll tax declared unconstitutional. The three-judge district court, feeling bound by the court's decision in *Breedlove v. Suttles*, 302 U.S. 277 (1937), dismissed the complaint. Harper (P) appealed. The law at issue conditions the right to vote in state elections upon the payment of a poll tax.

ISSUE: Is a poll tax, the payment of which is a required prerequisite for voting, constitutional?

HOLDING AND DECISION: (Douglas, J.) No. A state violates the Equal Protection Clause whenever it makes the affluence of the voter or the payment of a fee an electoral standard. The right to vote is a basic and fundamental one, especially since it preserves other rights. Any alleged infringement on the right to vote must be carefully scrutinized. A state's interest, when it comes to voting, is limited to the power to fix qualifications. Wealth, like race or creed or color, is irrelevant to one's ability to participate intelligently in the electoral process. Further lines drawn on the basis of wealth or property, like those of race, are traditionally disfavored. The requirement of the payment of a fee as a condition of obtaining a ballot causes invidious discrimination. *Breedlove* sanctioned this use of the poll tax, and to that extent it is overruled.

▶ ANALYSIS

If, as the dissenters in *Harper* argue, the poll tax classification is not wholly "irrational," the case represents a greater intervention than the courts undertook under old equal protection. There is some question as to whether this greater scrutiny was because the "fundamental rights" of voting are affected or because "lines drawn on the basis of wealth" are traditionally disfavored. In *McDonald v. Board of Election Commissioners*, 394 U.S. 802 (1969), the Court sees wealth as an independent ground (apart from impact on fundamental rights) for strict scrutiny. There is a series of cases preceding and following *Harper* (among them *Reynolds v. Sims*, 377 U.S. 533 (1964)) that support the invoking of strict scrutiny when voting rights are affected.

■══■

Quicknotes

EQUAL PROTECTION CLAUSE A constitutional provision that each person be guaranteed the same protection of the laws enjoyed by other persons in like circumstances.

FUNDAMENTAL RIGHT A liberty that is either expressly or impliedly provided for in the U.S. Constitution, the deprivation or burdening of which is subject to a heightened standard of review.

STRICT SCRUTINY Method by which courts determine the constitutionality of a law, when a law affects a fundamental right. Under the test, the legislature must have had a compelling interest to enact the law and measures prescribed by the law must be the least restrictive means possible to accomplish its goal.

■══■

Kramer v. Union Free School District

Single man (P) v. School district (D)

395 U.S. 621 (1969).

NATURE OF CASE: Action challenging the constitutionality of a state law.

FACT SUMMARY: A New York law provides that residents who are otherwise eligible to vote in state and federal elections may vote in the school district election only if they own or lease taxable property in the district or have custody of children enrolled in local public schools.

RULE OF LAW
A statute that grants the right to vote to some residents of requisite age and citizenship and denies this right to others must be subjected to strict scrutiny by the court.

FACTS: A New York law provides that in certain school districts, residents who are otherwise eligible to vote in state and federal elections may vote in the school district elections only if they own or lease taxable property within the district or have custody of children enrolled in local public schools. Kramer (P) was a bachelor who neither owned nor leased taxable property. He claimed the law violated equal protection.

ISSUE: Will a law that denies some residents the right to vote be subjected to strict scrutiny by the court?

HOLDING AND DECISION: (Warren, C.J.) Yes. A statute that grants the right to vote to some residents of requisite age and citizenship and denies this right to others must be subjected to strict scrutiny by the court. The right to vote in a free and unimpaired manner is preservative of other basic and civil rights. Any unjustified discrimination in determining who may vote undermines the legitimacy of representative government. Hence, a statute that grants the right to vote to some residents of requisite age and citizenship while denying it to others must be subjected to strict scrutiny by the court. Such statutes are not granted the presumption of constitutionality given other state laws, and they must be supported by a compelling state interest rather than merely a rational basis. Here, assuming arguendo that, as New York argues, a state can limit the right to vote to those primarily interested, close scrutiny demonstrates that this law does not accomplish this purpose with sufficient precision since it denies the right to many who might be so interested (such as parents of preschool children who neither own nor lease property).

DISSENT: (Stewart, J.) This law has a rational basis. A stricter standard is not applicable because neither a racial classification nor any constitutionally protected right is involved. (The Constitution does not confer the right of suffrage upon anyone.)

ANALYSIS

In *Cipriano v. City of Houma*, 395 U.S. 701 (1969), decided the same day as *Kramer*, the Court was unanimous in invalidating a law granting only property taxpayers the right to vote on the approval of the issuance of revenue bonds by a municipal utility. The Court noted that the revenue bonds would be financed from the operation of the utilities, not from property taxes. In a concurring notation, Justices Black and Stewart stated that this case, unlike *Kramer*, involved a voting classification wholly irrelevant to the achievement of the state's objective.

Quicknotes

COMPELLING STATE INTEREST Defense to an alleged Equal Protection Clause violation; that a state action was necessary in order to protect an interest the government is under a duty to protect.

EQUAL PROTECTION CLAUSE A constitutional provision that each person be guaranteed the same protection of the laws enjoyed by other persons in like circumstances.

FUNDAMENTAL RIGHT A liberty that is either expressly or impliedly provided for in the U.S. Constitution, the deprivation or burdening of which is subject to a heightened standard of review.

RATIONAL BASIS REVIEW A test employed by the court to determine the validity of a statute in equal protection actions, whereby the court determines whether the challenged statute is rationally related to the achievement of a legitimate state interest.

STRICT SCRUTINY Method by which courts determine the constitutionality of a law, when a law affects a fundamental right. Under the test, the legislature must have had a compelling interest to enact the law and measures prescribed by the law must be the least restrictive means possible to accomplish its goal.

Ball v. James

State official (D) v. Voters with little or no land (P)

451 U.S. 355 (1981).

NATURE OF CASE: Appeal from decision that a one-acre, one-vote voting scheme for electing the directors of a water storage district violates the Equal Protection Clause.

FACT SUMMARY: An Arizona water storage district's directors were elected only by landowners with an acre or more of property. Registered voters (P) who lived in the district, but owned no land or less than an acre, challenged the voting scheme as a violation of the Equal Protection Clause.

🏛 RULE OF LAW
A one-acre, one-vote voting scheme for electing the directors of a water storage district does not violate the Equal Protection Clause.

FACTS: The Salt River Project Agricultural Improvement and Power District (District), a governmental entity, stored and delivered untreated water to the owners of 236,000 acres of land in central Arizona, and, to subsidize its water operations, sold electricity to hundreds of thousands of people in an area including a large part of metropolitan Phoenix. Under Arizona law, the system for electing the District's directors limited voting eligibility to landowners and apportions voting power according to the number of acres owned. A class of registered voters (P) living within the District but owning either no land or less than an acre of land there filed suit, claiming that the election scheme violated the Equal Protection Clause of the Fourteenth Amendment. They alleged that because the District had such governmental powers as the authority to condemn land and sell tax-exempt bonds, and because it sold electricity to virtually half the state's population and exercised significant influence on flood control and environmental management, its policies and actions substantially affected all District residents, regardless of property ownership. The district court upheld the constitutionality of the voting scheme, but the court of appeals reversed. It held that the case was governed by the one-person, one-vote principle. The Supreme Court granted review.

ISSUE: Does a one-acre, one-vote voting scheme for electing the directors of a water storage district violate the Equal Protection Clause?

HOLDING AND DECISION: (Stewart, J.) No. Despite its impacts, the District does not have the kind of governmental power that would require a one-person, one-vote voting scheme. It cannot impose property or sales taxes, control the conduct of citizens, or administer normal government functions such as the operation of schools or maintenance of streets. Even with regard to water, the District only stores it and delivers it, but does not own or sell the water. This narrow function of the District justifies the voting

scheme it uses because it disproportionately affects those eligible to vote. The voting landowners are the only ones subject to the District's liens and acreage-based taxes, or who have committed capital to the District. The voting scheme is constitutional because it bears a reasonable relationship to its statutory goals—the District may have not come about if landowners had not been assured a voice in the conduct of the District's business. Thus, the limiting the vote to landowners is rational, as is making the weight of the vote dependent on acreage, since that number reasonably reflects the relative risks they incurred as landowners and the distribution of the benefits and burdens of the District's operations.

DISSENT: (White, J.) The District's function is not a narrow one, given its provision of water and electricity to several hundred thousand people. Here, the District exercises substantial governmental powers. It is a political subdivision of the state and enjoys the same status as any other municipality. It has attributes associated with municipalities and has broad authority over energy generated by the District. It affects the daily lives of thousands of people who have no meaningful way to participate in the District's operations, and, therefore, its function cannot be viewed as too private to warrant Fourteenth Amendment safeguards.

▶ ANALYSIS

Ball, along with *Salyer Land Co. v. Tulare Lake Basin Water Storage District*, 410 U.S. 719 (1973), which also upheld a one-acre, one-vote voting scheme for a water storage district, seem to establish that the Court will uphold the validity of property qualifications for voting only where there are special purpose elections for limited-purpose governmental units whose functions primarily (though not exclusively) affect the property-qualified voters. Otherwise, the Court will adhere to the one-person, one-vote principle.

■=■

Quicknotes

EQUAL PROTECTION CLAUSE A constitutional provision that each person be guaranteed the same protection of the laws enjoyed by other persons in like circumstances.

■=■

Crawford v. Marion County Election Board

Voters (P) v. State (D)

128 S. Ct. 1610 (2008).

NATURE OF CASE: Review of federal appeals court judgment.

FACT SUMMARY: The state of Indiana (D) required voters to present federal or state issued identification in order to vote. Citizens (P) challenged the law.

🏛 RULE OF LAW
A law that requires voters to present photo identification issued by the federal or state government does not unduly burden citizens' right to vote.

FACTS: A law was passed by the Indiana legislature that required all voters who voted in person to present a photo identification issued by the United States or the state (D). The local Democratic Party (P) and interest groups representing minority and elderly citizens (P) argued that the law constituted an undue burden on the right to vote.

ISSUE: Does a law that requires voters to present photo identification issued by the federal or state government unduly burden citizens' right to vote?

HOLDING AND DECISION: (Stevens, J.) No. A law that requires voters to present photo identification issued by the federal or state government does not unduly burden citizens' right to vote. For the law to be constitutional, the state (D) must show that it supports state interests that justify the burden imposed by its rule. The state (D) has a legitimate interest in counting only the votes of eligible voters, which is to prevent voter fraud and protect the integrity of the election process, and the photo identification requirement is closely related to Indiana's (D) legitimate state interests in preventing voter fraud. The burdens on the voters (P) in Indiana (D) is slight, because the state (D) provides free voter registration cards to the relatively few who do not have a driver's license or other photo identification. The slight burden the law imposes on voters' (P) rights does not outweigh the state's (D) interests, which are "neutral and nondiscriminatory."

CONCURRENCE: (Scalia, J.) The case was decided on the grounds that the voters (P) have not shown that the special burden placed on them is severe enough to warrant strict scrutiny, and that the state (D) therefore only had to have a legitimate state interest that justified the relatively slight burden placed on voters (P). True enough, but the case should be decided on the grounds that the voters' (P) premise—that the voter-identification law may have imposed a special burden on some voters—is irrelevant, and the burden at issue is minimal and justified.

DISSENT: (Souter, J.) The burden placed on voters (P) by the state (D) is nontrivial and affects tens of thousands of citizens, a significant number of which will be deterred from voting. The statute is unconstitutional, because a state may not burden the right to vote merely by invoking abstract interests, even if legitimate or compelling, but must make particular, factual showing that threats to its interests outweigh the particular impediments it has imposed. Indiana (D) failed to make that showing.

▶ ANALYSIS

Though Justice Stevens wrote the lead opinion, there was no majority opinion, because there was a 3-3-3 split among the justices. The Indiana voter ID case is the most important voting rights case since *Bush v. Gore*. Critics have argued that the Indiana law is the most restrictive ID law in America and will exclude many eligible voters from participating in our democratic process.

■=■

Quicknotes

LEGITIMATE STATE INTEREST Under a rational basis standard of review, a court will not strike down a statute as unconstitutional if it bears a reasonable relationship to the furtherance of a legitimate governmental objective.

■=■

Reynolds v. Sims

Parties not identified.

377 U.S. 533 (1964).

NATURE OF CASE: Appeal from a decision of a federal district court holding invalid the existing and two proposed plans for apportionment.

FACT SUMMARY: The federal district court held that the existing and two proposed plans for apportionment of seats in the Alabama legislature violated the Equal Protection Clause.

🏛 RULE OF LAW
The Equal Protection Clause guarantees the opportunity for equal protection by all voters in the election of state legislators and requires that the seats in both houses of a bicameral state legislature be apportioned on a population basis.

FACTS: The federal district court for the Middle District of Alabama held that the existing and two legislatively proposed plans for the apportionment of seats in the two houses of the Alabama legislature violated the Equal Protection Clause. The court ordered into effect a temporary reapportionment plan comprised of part of the proposed plans.

ISSUE: Does the Equal Protection Clause require that seats in both houses of a bicameral state legislature be apportioned on a population basis?

HOLDING AND DECISION: [Judge not stated in casebook excerpt.] Yes. Concededly, the basic aim of legislative apportionment is the achieving of fair and effective representation for all citizens. The Equal Protection Clause guarantees the opportunity for equal participation by all voters in the election of state legislators. Overweighting and overvaluation of the votes of persons living in one area has the effect of dilution and undervaluation of those living in another area. Diluting the weight of votes because of place of residence impairs basic constitutional rights under the Fourteenth Amendment, just as much as invidious discrimination based upon race. It is argued that the apportionment issue is a political one that the court should leave alone. However, a denial of constitutionally protected rights demands judicial protection. The weight of a citizen's vote cannot be made to depend on where he lives. The Equal Protection Clause requires that the seats in both houses of a bicameral state legislature must be apportioned on a population basis. Analogy to the federal system will not sustain a system not based on population. The federal system grew out of compromise and concession needed to band together states that formerly were independent. Political subdivisions of states (cities, counties) never were independent entities. The decision does not mean that the two bodies in a state legislature cannot consist of different constituencies, have different length terms, represent geographical districts of different sizes or be of different sizes. It does mean that in apportionment's overriding objective—whatever the method used—must be substantial equality of population among the various districts. Neither history, nor economics, nor other group interests, will justify disparity from population-based representation. One factor that could justify some deviation from such representation is political subdivisions. Decennial reapportionment would meet the requirement for reasonable currency. It will be for the federal courts to devise the particular remedies to be utilized in such cases.

DISSENT: (Harlan, J.) State legislative apportionments are wholly free of constitutional limitations save those imposed by the Republican Form of Government Clause (Article IV, § 4). This decision places basic aspects of state political systems under the overlordship of the federal judiciary, a move that is ill advised and constitutionally impermissible.

▶ ANALYSIS

For many years, the Court refused jurisdiction of cases challenging the fairness of the representation in state legislatures, on the ground that the issue involved was a "political question." The Court abandoned this position in *Baker v. Carr*, 369 U.S. 186 (1962), and ever since has held that the federal courts have the jurisdiction to determine the fairness and validity of state legislative apportionment plans. The result has been that a traditionally political question has become justiciable, and the courts have exerted what was traditionally deemed a legislative power in determining what is, and what is not, a fair plan of legislative apportionment.

■═■

Quicknotes

EQUAL PROTECTION CLAUSE A constitutional provision that each person be guaranteed the same protection of the laws enjoyed by other persons in like circumstances.

■═■

Bush v. Gore

Republican presidential candidate (D) v. Democratic presidential candidate (P)

531 U.S. 98 (2000).

NATURE OF CASE: Suit by presidential candidate contesting a state's certification of election results and requesting a recount of ballots.

FACT SUMMARY: In the 2000 presidential election, Gore (P) lost the popular vote in Florida to Bush (D) by less than one-half of one percent of the total votes cast. After some recounting of ballots over the next two weeks, Florida declared Bush (D) the winner in Florida. Gore (P) sued Bush (D) in state court to contest the election results and order a more extensive recount. The Florida Supreme Court eventually ordered a manual recount of ballots in all Florida counties in which undervotes had not been manually reviewed.

RULE OF LAW
The use of standardless manual recounts of ballots violates the Equal Protection Clause.

FACTS: On November 8, 2000, the day after the 2000 presidential election, results showed Bush (D) beating Gore (P) in Florida by less than one-half of 1 percent of all votes cast in Florida (a margin of 1,784 votes). A recount permitted by Florida law in such a close election reduced Bush's (D) margin of victory but still showed him carrying the state. Gore (P) requested manual recounts in four counties, and the Florida Supreme Court extended the deadline for those recounts to November 26, 2000. On that date, Florida certified the election results and declared Bush the winner of the state's twenty-five electoral votes. Gore (P) sued Bush (D) in state court, basing his complaint on the recounts. The trial court denied relief. On expedited review, the Florida Supreme Court held that Gore (P) failed to meet his burden of proof as to recounts in two counties, but that he had carried his burden with respect to a county with 9,000 ballots that failed to show any vote for President. (Such ballots were called "undervotes.") Noting that Florida law permitted the courts to grant any appropriate relief in such cases, the Florida Supreme Court ordered a manual recount in all counties that had not manually reconsidered undervotes. The Florida Supreme Court, however, provided no guidance about how the ballots should be examined to determine voter intent. Bush (D) petitioned the U.S. Supreme Court to stay the mandated recount. The Court treated the petition as a petition for certiorari and granted the petition while also staying the Florida proceedings.

ISSUE: Does the use of standardless manual recounts of ballots violate the Equal Protection Clause?

HOLDING AND DECISION: (Per curiam) Yes. The use of standardless manual recounts of ballots violates

the Equal Protection Clause. The right to vote for President is fundamental when a state vests that right in its people, and each person's vote shall have equal weight. Consistent with the Equal Protection Clause, a state may not arbitrarily treat one person's vote as more important than another's. The absence of standards for the recounts in this case, though, would necessarily result in a purely arbitrary recount process from one county to the next and even from one ballot to the next. Indeed, some of the votes already required to be accepted by the Florida Supreme Court suffer from that infirmity. These inevitably arbitrary recounts contradict the "one person, one vote" requirement of the Equal Protection Clause. Further, the ordered inclusion of partial votes from one county necessarily results in an unequal valuing of votes. Because the recount cannot occur in compliance with both equal protection and the federal statutory deadline for certifying election results, the recount order of the Florida Supreme Court is reversed.

CONCURRENCE: (Rehnquist, C.J.) Most of the time, this Court should defer to a state supreme court on issues requiring interpretation of state law. This case presents a rare exception to that rule. Given the express command in Article 2, Section 1 of the federal Constitution—which commands state legislators to appoint electors for President—in this case this Court must also defer to and protect the Florida legislature by subjecting its statutes to further review. The Florida Supreme Court has failed in several ways to read Florida statutes to effectuate the intent of the Florida legislature. Perhaps the most telling misreading of Florida law by the Florida Supreme Court is its reading of the statute authorizing all appropriate relief in voting recounts. The Florida legislature surely intended that such relief would be appropriate partly by virtue of complying with the deadline explicitly required by federal statute. Accordingly, the ordered recount is not appropriate relief under Florida law, which constitutes a separate ground for reversing the state supreme court's recount order.

DISSENT: (Stevens, J.) This Court accepts as definitive the rulings of a state's highest court on interpretations of state law. This case provides no reason to depart from that settled practice. The Florida Supreme Court's failure to articulate precise standards for the recounts does not violate the Equal Protection Clause—or so no prior decision by this Court has held. Overvaluing finality, as the majority clearly does, effectively disenfranchises many Florida voters. Regrettably, this case also eviscerates the public's confidence in the impartiality of the judiciary.

Continued on next page.

DISSENT: (Souter, J.) This case presents three easy issues. The federal statutory issue means only that Florida would lose its safe harbor for failing to meet the federal deadline for certifying election results. Additionally, the Florida Supreme Court's interpretations of the state election laws pertinent to Article 2, Section 1 of the federal Constitution are not so unreasonable as to require this Court's intervention. And, third, on the only meritorious issue in the case, the equal-protection claim, the Court should remand the case to allow Florida to establish uniform standards for the recount. No justification supports the majority's decision not to remand.

DISSENT: (Ginsburg, J.) The Florida Supreme Court's judgment should be affirmed on federalism grounds alone. On the merits, Bush (D) has failed to raise a substantial equal-protection issue. Even if a meritorious equal-protection issue were before the Court, the recount should be allowed to proceed despite the flexible deadline imposed by the federal statutes.

DISSENT: (Breyer, J.) The Court should not have accepted this case. None of the three equal-protection problems identified by the majority justifies reversing the Florida Supreme Court's judgment. There is no evidence that either a manual recount of overvotes would add legal votes or that all ballots, but not undervotes, were counted in some counties but not in others. The third equal-protection issue, on the lack of uniform standards, does raise substantial questions of arbitrariness, but the issue could be resolved with the less drastic remedy of a remand to give Florida an opportunity to establish the requisite standards. The legally wrong decision to take this case at all—without any momentous legal issue in the case—is now unfortunate for the damage it has done and will continue to do to the credibility of this Court.

▶ ANALYSIS

One of the Rehnquist Court's chief legacies will be its championing of federalism, its concerted effort over more than two decades to return power to the states. In *Bush v. Gore*, however, the three staunchest supporters of states' rights on the Court—Chief Justice Rehnquist, Justice Scalia, and Justice Thomas—articulated a remarkably weak rationale for the Court's heavy-handed interference with state proceedings. As the majority correctly notes, seven justices saw a substantial equal-protection problem in the standardless manual recounts. Given the disfavor of arbitrary decision-making embodied by the Equal Protection Clause, the recounts, as ordered, do raise a substantial equal-protection question. The time constraints unnecessarily imposed by the Court, however, meant that those issues were not properly briefed by the parties or researched and considered by the Court. In addition to giving Florida time to comply with the Equal Protection Clause, Justice Souter's and Justice Breyer's suggested remand thus would have had the additional advantage of permitting the Court to decide the case in proper judicial repose instead of in haste.

■■■

Quicknotes

EQUAL PROTECTION CLAUSE A constitutional provision that each person be guaranteed the same protection of the laws enjoyed by other persons in like circumstances.

FEDERALISM A scheme of government whereby the power to govern is among a central and localized government.

FUNDAMENTAL RIGHT A liberty that is either expressly or impliedly provided for in the U.S. Constitution, the deprivation or burdening of which is subject to a heightened standard of review.

■■■

Boddie v. Connecticut

Indigent (P) v. State (D)

401 U.S. 371 (1971).

NATURE OF CASE: Constitutional challenge to imposition of a filing fee.

FACT SUMMARY: Boddie (P), an indigent seeking a divorce, brought a suit after unsuccessfully attempting to have the $45 filing fee and $15 fee for service of process waived.

🏛 RULE OF LAW
When the only method for obtaining a divorce in a state is through its courts, a refusal to waive for an indigent those fees required to bring a divorce case before the court constitutes a denial of due process.

FACTS: Connecticut (D) refused to waive the $45 filing fee and $15 fee for service of process to enable Boddie (P), an indigent, to commence divorce proceedings in its courts. Boddie (P) brought suit, claiming a denial of constitutional due process rights.

ISSUE: Is it a denial of due process to effectively deny an indigent access to the courts (to which he must resort to obtain a divorce) by refusing to waive those fees normally required to bring a divorce case before the court?

HOLDING AND DECISION: (Harlan, J.) Yes. There are no states in which parties may liberate themselves from their marriage, even if they both consent to a divorce, without invoking the state's judicial machinery. In such a case, a refusal to waive the normal fees so that an indigent may bring his divorce case before the courts is equivalent to denying that indigent an opportunity to be heard on his claimed right to a dissolution of his marriage. In the absence of a sufficient countervailing justification, this is a denial of due process. None of the justifications advanced by Connecticut (D) are sufficient to override the interest of indigents in having access to the only avenue open for dissolving their marriages. Reversed.

DISSENT: (Black, J.) The *Griffin* line of cases dealt with criminal cases. Our Constitution does not place civil cases on the same high level as it places criminal trials and punishment.

▶ *ANALYSIS*

Just two years later, the Supreme Court reversed a district court's decision that due process required the usual $50 fee required to file a bankruptcy petition to be waived for an indigent party who wished to file a bankruptcy petition. It also concluded that no denial of equal protection was involved. *United States v. Kras,* 409 U.S. 434 (1973). Where the legal process is not clearly necessary to the protection of a

"fundamental" constitutional right, filing fees need not be waived in order to comply with due process requirements.

■═■

Quicknotes

DUE PROCESS CLAUSE Clauses found in the Fifth and Fourteenth Amendments to the U.S. Constitution providing that no person shall be deprived of "life, liberty, or property, without due process of law."

■═■

United States v. Kras

Federal government (D) v. Indigent (P)

409 U.S. 434 (1973).

NATURE OF CASE: Appeal from decision that a bankruptcy filing fee for indigents violates the Fifth Amendment's due process and equal protection guarantees.

FACT SUMMARY: The federal Bankruptcy Act required payment of a fee to institute bankruptcy proceedings. Kras (P), an indigent, filed for bankruptcy, but challenged the fee as applied to him as a violation of the Fifth Amendment.

🏛 RULE OF LAW
A bankruptcy filing fee for indigents does not violate the Fifth Amendment's due process and equal protection guarantees.

FACTS: Kras (P), an indigent, made a voluntary petition in bankruptcy in federal district court, but moved to proceed without paying the $50 fee imposed by the Bankruptcy Act for instituting bankruptcy proceedings. Kras (P) claimed that the fee violated the Fifth Amendment and fell within *Boddie v. Connecticut*, 401 U.S. 371 (1971), which held that indigents do not have to pay a fee to commence divorce proceedings. The district court held that the bankruptcy fee as applied to an indigent violated the Fifth Amendment, and the Supreme Court granted review.

ISSUE: Does a bankruptcy filing fee for indigents violate the Fifth Amendment's due process and equal protection guarantees?

HOLDING AND DECISION: (Blackmun, J.) No. *Boddie* is not controlling here. First, divorce relates to a fundamental constitutional right to marry. A person cannot remarry, and exercise that right, unless they get a divorce from their current spouse. However, the right to have one's debts discharged in bankruptcy is not a fundamental right, and by not getting a bankruptcy discharge, Kras (P) will not be affected with respect to basic necessities. Second, the state has a monopoly in granting divorces; a person can get a divorce only through the courts. "In contrast with divorce, bankruptcy is not the only method available to a debtor for the adjustment" of his debts. A debtor has the option of negotiating with his creditors to adjust his debts. Because there is no constitutional right to bankruptcy, there is a rational basis for the filing fee requirement, given Congress's plenary power over bankruptcy. Still yet, as applied to Kras (P), the filing fee does not seem so onerous because the $50 fee can be paid in installments over nine months—about $1.28 per week. This sum is less than the cost of a movie, a couple packs of cigarettes, etc.—he should be able to come up with this relatively small amount of money.

DISSENT: (Stewart, J.) This case cannot be distinguished from *Boddie*. As was true in *Boddie*, the indigent's income barely suffices to meet the costs of daily living, with no extra for gaining access to the courts. Like a married person seeking a divorce, the debtor originally entered into his contracts voluntarily, but it is the government's legal system that continues to enforce the obligations under those contracts. In the case of the indigent bankrupt, it is also the government that provides the only effective means to being free from these government-imposed obligations. Contrary to the majority's assertions, there is no alternative for an indigent, because the indigent has no money to offer his creditors, so negotiation is not an option.

DISSENT: (Marshall, J.) The majority's assumptions about how poor people live are unfounded. It really is not within the poor person's reach to come up with even very small amounts of money such as the installment payments permitted for the filing fee. Contrary to what the majority believes, poor people rarely can afford to go to a movie (which the majority believes is a weekly activity), or buy cigarettes, which for them are a luxury. "It is perfectly proper for judges to disagree about what the Constitution requires. But it is disgraceful for an interpretation of the Constitution to be premised upon unfounded assumptions about how people live."

▶ ANALYSIS

Generally, the Court has refused to find that filing fees for access to the civil judicial system impermissibly violate equal protection or due process. As in *Boddie*, the Court has found fees unconstitutional only when it has determined that a fundamental constitutional right, other than the right to access the courts, is implicated.

■=■

Quicknotes

DUE PROCESS CLAUSE Clauses found in the Fifth and Fourteenth Amendments to the U.S. Constitution providing that no person shall be deprived of "life, liberty, or property, without due process of law."

EQUAL PROTECTION CLAUSE A constitutional provision that each person be guaranteed the same protection of the laws enjoyed by other persons in like circumstances.

Continued on next page.

FUNDAMENTAL RIGHT A liberty that is either expressly or impliedly provided for in the U.S. Constitution, the deprivation or burdening of which is subject to a heightened standard of review.

RATIONAL BASIS REVIEW A test employed by the court to determine the validity of a statute in equal protection actions, whereby the court determines whether the challenged statute is rationally related to the achievement of a legitimate state interest.

■══■

M.L.B v. S.L.J.

Parent (P) v. Party not Identified (D)

519 U.S. 102 (1996).

NATURE OF CASE: Appeal from decree terminating parental rights.

FACT SUMMARY: A Mississippi court dismissed M.L.B.'s (P) appeal of the termination of her parental rights to her two minor children when she was unable to pay the required record-preparation fees.

🏛 RULE OF LAW
A state may not condition appeals from trial court decrees terminating parental rights on the affected parent's ability to pay record-preparation fees.

FACTS: A Mississippi court ordered M.L.B.'s (P) parental rights to her two minor children terminated. M.L.B. (P) sought to appeal the termination decree, but the state required that she pay in advance over $2,000 in record-preparation fees. Because M.L.B. (P) did not have the money to pay the fees, her appeal was dismissed. The Supreme Court granted certiorari to determine whether the Due Process and Equal Protection Clauses of the Fourteenth Amendment permitted such appeals to be conditioned on the ability to pay certain fees.

ISSUE: May a state condition appeals from trial court decrees terminating parental rights on the affected parent's ability to pay record-preparation fees?

HOLDING AND DECISION: (Ginsburg, J.) No. A state may not condition appeals from trial court decrees terminating parental rights on the affected parent's ability to pay record-preparation fees. Fee requirements are generally examined only for their rationality. While the Court has not prohibited state controls on every type of civil action, it has consistently distinguished those involving intrusions on family relationships. However, the stakes for M.L.B. (P), i.e., the forced dissolution of her parental rights, are far greater than any monetary loss. Mississippi's interest, on the other hand, in offsetting the costs on its court system, is purely financial. Decrees forever terminating parental rights fit in the category of cases in which a state may not "bolt the door to equal justice."

DISSENT: (Thomas, J.) The majority's newfound constitutional right to free transcripts in civil appeals cannot be effectively restricted to this case. M.L.B. (P) requested relief under both the Due Process and Equal Protection Clauses, yet the majority does not specify the source of the relief it has granted. Mississippi's transcript rule cannot be said to violate due process because due process typically requires no additional process beyond an adequate hearing. Where the Constitution requires additional process, it does so under the Equal Protection Clause, as in *Griffin v.*

Illinois, 351 U.S. 12 (1956). The criminal context of *Griffin*, however, makes it inapplicable in the civil setting of a parental-rights termination proceeding.

▶ ANALYSIS

While the majority's rationale in granting M.L.B. (P) relief may have been vaguely articulated, as the dissent has alleged, it would seem that the issues at stake here go beyond simple textual analysis. It is not merely M.L.B.'s (P) rights that must be considered, but the impact that the termination of those rights will have on her two minor children. It will likely not be as great of a problem as the dissent suggests to limit the application of this holding to similarly situated parents.

■==■

Quicknotes

DUE PROCESS CLAUSE Clauses found in the Fifth and Fourteenth Amendments to the U.S. Constitution providing that no person shall be deprived of "life, liberty, or property, without due process of law."

EQUAL PROTECTION CLAUSE A constitutional provision that each person be guaranteed the same protection of the laws enjoyed by other persons in like circumstances.

■==■

Lewis v. Casey

Prison officials (D) v. Inmates (P)

518 U.S. 343 (1996).

NATURE OF CASE: Appeal from decision that a prison's inadequate legal research facilities and inadequate legal assistance violate prisoners' rights to access to the courts.

FACT SUMMARY: Inmates (P) filed a class action claiming that prison officials (D) maintained inadequate legal research facilities and provided inadequate legal assistance to prisoners in violation of their First, Sixth, and Fourteenth Amendment rights.

🏛 RULE OF LAW
A prison's inadequate legal research facilities and legal assistance, without a showing that these have caused widespread actual injury to prisoners, do not violate prisoners' constitutional right to access to the courts.

FACTS: Inmates (P) of various prisons operated by the Arizona Department of Corrections (ADOC) brought a class action against ADOC officials (D), alleging that the prison officials were furnishing them with inadequate legal research facilities and thereby depriving them of their right of access to the courts, in violation of *Bounds v. Smith*, 430 U.S. 617 (1977). The district court found petitioners to be in violation of *Bounds* and issued an injunction mandating detailed, system-wide changes in ADOC's prison law libraries and in its legal assistance programs. The court of appeals affirmed both the finding of a *Bounds* violation and the injunction's major terms. The Supreme Court granted review.

ISSUE: Do a prison's inadequate legal research facilities and legal assistance, without a showing that these have caused widespread actual injury to prisoners, violate prisoners' constitutional right to access to the courts?

HOLDING AND DECISION: (Scalia, J.) No. A prisoner alleging a violation under *Bounds*, which held that prisons must provide prisoners with adequate law libraries and adequate legal assistance, must show actual injury, which is a standing requirement. Prison law libraries and legal assistance programs are not ends in themselves. They are a means to ensuring that constitutional violations of prisoners' rights get presented in court. "Because *Bounds* did not create an abstract, freestanding right to a law library or legal assistance, an inmate cannot establish relevant actual injury simply by establishing that his prison's law library or legal assistance program is sub par in some theoretical sense." The prisoner must show that these shortcomings actually hindered his efforts to pursue a legal claim. *Bounds* itself did not require a showing of actual injury, but this requirement is a constitutional

prerequisite in access-to-court cases. Also, *Bounds* went too far when it said that the state must enable prisoners to discover grievances and to litigate effectively in court, and, therefore, these elaborations on the right of access to the courts are expressly disclaimed. Moreover, the actual-injury requirement is not satisfied by showing that any legal claim was frustrated; the frustrated claims must be related to the inmates' incarceration, such as claims attacking their sentence or challenging the conditions of their confinement. Finally, a claim that a prisoner's right of access to the courts has been violated is subject to rational-basis review.

CONCURRENCE: (Thomas, J.) The district court's extremely detailed injunction was tantamount to having federal judges running a state prison. Such gross overreaching by a federal district court cannot be tolerated in our federal system, which requires that state prisons should be run by the state and its officials. Also, there is no requirement in the Constitution that the state should pay for law libraries or legal assistance programs in prisons.

DISSENT: (Stevens, J.) Even prisoners do not lose all their liberty rights. The right of access to the courts is one of those liberties, and the state must affirmatively protect it. The majority's view of the actual-injury (standing) requirements is too strict. If a prisoner alleges that he has been denied the right to effective access to the courts, that itself suffices to confer standing.

▶ ANALYSIS

Lewis dramatically limited *Bounds* and gains that prisoners had made in securing their right to access to the courts. It is consistent with the current Court's hostility to prisoners' claims. After *Lewis*, prisoners still have the right to use the courts to remedy their grievances and challenge their convictions and sentences, but the right is protected only minimally by rational-basis review. The inmate will need to demonstrate that the barrier to access directly prevented adequate relief for such claims. The practical effect of *Lewis* most likely is that it will leave many prisoners without meaningful access to the courts. The Court's focus on standing means that in order for an inmate to sue, they will have to meet an extremely heavy burden of showing they would have won in court if only better legal research facilities or legal assistance programs had been available to them.

■=■

Continued on next page.

Quicknotes

RATIONAL BASIS REVIEW A test employed by the court to determine the validity of a statute in equal protection actions, whereby the court determines whether the challenged statute is rationally related to the achievement of a legitimate state interest.

STANDING The right to commence suit against another party because of a personal stake in the resolution of the controversy.

San Antonio Independent School District v. Rodriguez

School district (D) v. School children (P)

411 U.S. 1 (1973).

NATURE OF CASE: Appeal from a finding that a school tax finance plan denies equal protection.

FACT SUMMARY: Rodriguez (P) argued that the Texas Public School finance system denied equal protection because students who lived in districts with a low property tax base received lower quality education than students who lived in high property tax base districts.

🏛 RULE OF LAW
School finance systems based upon differing property tax rates in different school districts do not violate equal protection.

FACTS: Rodriguez (P) brought this class action suit on behalf of school children throughout Texas who are members of minority groups or who are poor and reside in school districts having a low property tax base. Texas finances its public schools through a system of state and local funding. The local funds are apportioned to reflect each district's relative taxpaying ability. Rodriguez (P) resides in Edgewood, one of seven school districts in the San Antonio metropolitan area. Edgewood has the lowest property value and highest tax rate of the seven districts and spends $356 per pupil. Alamo Heights, the most affluent of the seven, has the highest property value and the lowest tax rate and spends $594 per pupil. The district court found wealth to be a suspect classification and education to be a fundamental interest and held that the Texas system discriminates on the basis of wealth in the way education is provided. San Antonio (D) appealed.

ISSUE: Do school finance systems based upon differing property tax rates in different school districts violate equal protection?

HOLDING AND DECISION: (Powell, J.) No. School finance systems based upon differing property tax rates in different school districts do not violate equal protection. There is no suspect class in this case because the alleged discriminatory system has none of the traditional characteristics of suspectness, and the Texas system therefore does not operate to the peculiar disadvantage of any suspect class. As for a fundamental interest, the determination of whether education is fundamental lies in assessing whether there is a right to education explicitly or implicitly guaranteed by the Constitution. Education is not explicitly guaranteed, and no basis exists for finding it to be implicitly guaranteed. Accordingly, Texas need show only that the challenged program rationally advances a legitimate state purpose. This case is a direct attack on Texas's method of raising and disbursing tax revenues, and the Court has

traditionally disliked interfering with a state's fiscal policies under the Equal Protection Clause. Further, no scheme of taxation has ever been devised completely free of some discriminatory impact. Moreover, this case raises important questions of educational policy that the Court is not equipped to address, and of federalism that the Court is loath to disturb. The Court declines the invitation to undermine programs for financing public education that exist in almost every state. Reversed.

DISSENT: (Brennan, J.) The majority is wrong in its assertion that for the purpose of equal protection analysis a right is "fundamental" only if it is explicitly or implicitly guaranteed by the Constitution. Instead, a right is fundamental if it is important in effectuating constitutionally guaranteed rights. Education is a fundamental right because it has a very close nexus with the right to vote and the rights of free speech and association. Therefore, any classification affecting education must be subjected to strict scrutiny. Here, it is acknowledged that the state's school financing scheme cannot pass such scrutiny, and, therefore, it is constitutionally invalid.

DISSENT: (Marshall, J.) The great inequality in financing for public education between school districts in Texas violates equal protection. The fundamental equality shared by all Americans is too important to allow a state's discriminatory school-financing program to undermine it. Education does qualify as a fundamental right in this country—as this Court's decisions attest, as the special place of public education in our society shows, and as the vital connection between education and First Amendment and political freedoms strongly suggests. With such an important right at stake, the Court has an obligation to subject the challenged program to a searching review instead of entrusting the problem to legislative resolution.

⧫ ANALYSIS

In applying "traditional equal protection analysis," the Court, per Justice Brennan, held that a food-stamp act provision that prevented a person from obtaining food stamps if he lived in a household containing an individual unrelated to any other household member was lacking any rational basis, *U.S. Dept. of Agriculture v. Moreno*, 413 U.S. 528 (1973). In another equal protection case, the Court, per Justice Douglas, upheld a zoning ordinance that defined a "family" as persons related by blood, adoption, or marriage, or no more than two unrelated persons living together. This was rational, *Village of Belle Terre v. Boraas*, 416 U.S. 1 (1974). The cases reached

Continued on next page.

opposite conclusions as to rationality without broadening the scope of fundamental rights.

■═■

Quicknotes

EQUAL PROTECTION CLAUSE A constitutional provision that each person be guaranteed the same protection of the laws enjoyed by other persons in like circumstances.

FUNDAMENTAL RIGHT A liberty that is either expressly or impliedly provided for in the U.S. Constitution, the deprivation or burdening of which is subject to a heightened standard of review.

RATIONAL BASIS REVIEW A test employed by the court to determine the validity of a statute in equal protection actions, whereby the court determines whether the challenged statute is rationally related to the achievement of a legitimate state interest.

STRICT SCRUTINY Method by which courts determine the constitutionality of a law, when a law affects a fundamental right. Under the test, the legislature must have had a compelling interest to enact the law and measures prescribed by the law must be the least restrictive means possible to accomplish its goal.

■═■

Daniels v. Williams

Inmate (P) v. Prison official (D)

474 U.S. 327 (1986).

NATURE OF CASE: Appeal from dismissal of federal action based on due process.

FACT SUMMARY: Daniels (P), an inmate who was injured due to the negligence of a prison official, argued that his due process rights were violated thereby.

🏛 RULE OF LAW
Negligent acts by state officials do not constitute due process violations.

FACTS: Daniels (P) was injured due to a negligent act of a prison official. Daniels (P) brought a federal action, arguing that the official's conduct deprived him of a liberty interest in freedom from injury, in violation of due process. The district court and court of appeals rejected this, and Daniels (P) appealed.

ISSUE: Do negligent acts by state officials constitute due process violations?

HOLDING AND DECISION: (Rehnquist, J.) No. Negligent acts by state officials do not constitute due process violations. The guarantee of due process historically was to shield an individual from deliberate governmental actions. It was designed to protect against abuses of power. To apply it to acts of negligence would be to commingle the Fourteenth Amendment into existing tort systems, which would be an improper interference with state law. Tort and constitutional law do not address the same concerns.

▌ ANALYSIS

The view of the Court here would seem to have ample foundation. Virtually all protections of a constitutional dimension arose historically out of fears of abuse of power. Significantly, this fear, abuse of power, was the basis for the Magna Carta, which limited the power of the Crown.

■══■

Quicknotes

NEGLIGENCE Conduct falling below the standard of care that a reasonable person would demonstrate under similar conditions.

PROCEDURAL DUE PROCESS The constitutional mandate that if the state or federal government acts so as to deny a citizen of a life, liberty or property interest the individual is first entitled to notice and the right to be heard.

■══■

County of Sacramento v. Lewis

County (D) v. Relative of decedent (P)

523 U.S. 833 (1998).

NATURE OF THE CASE: Appeal from a judgment holding that a high-speed pursuit of a suspect by a police officer that results in death violates the Fourteenth Amendment.

FACT SUMMARY: Defendant contends that pursuing a suspect in a high-speed chase is not so shocking and arbitrary as to label it a violation of substantive due process.

🏛 RULE OF LAW
In cases of official misconduct, *Rochin v. California*, 342 U.S. 165 (1952), holds that in order to constitute a violation of substantive due process, the alleged misconduct must rise to a level that "shocks the conscience" or is beyond the bounds of decency.

FACTS: A sheriff's deputy and another officer (D) were returning to their patrol cars after responding to a call to break up a fight. The officers observed a motorcycle approaching at high speed. It was operated by 18-year-old Brian Willard, and 16-year-old Philip Lewis was a passenger. One of the officers turned on his overhead lights and yelled for the motorcycle to stop, and pulled his car closer to the other in an attempt to make them stop. Instead of obeying the officers, the motorcycle maneuvered between the cars and sped off. The sheriff's deputy turned on his emergency lights and siren and pursued the motorcycle at high speed. Both the motorcycle and the deputy's car were traveling approximately 100 miles per hour. The motorcycle tipped over when the operator tried to make a sharp turn. Although the deputy attempted to stop, his car collided with Lewis, who was pronounced dead at the scene.

ISSUE: Was the high-speed pursuit of the teens so shocking and reckless that it violates due process?

HOLDING AND DECISION: (Souter, J.) No. In order to prove a violation of due process in a case such as this, the alleged misconduct must not be related to the legitimate goal of arrest and the conduct must be done with the purpose to cause harm. The teens chose to disobey the officers and were ultimately responsible for the chase. Very often, law enforcement officers are forced to make quick decisions and to act on instinct. There was no time for prior deliberation on the part of the officers, and they did not chase for the purpose of harming the suspects. Since the officers acted in order to make an arrest and did not act with the intention of causing harm, their behavior did not rise to the level of indecency as to find a due process violation.

▶ ANALYSIS

This case makes reference to prison officials and the standard of behavior necessary to find a due process

violation when a prison inmate is harmed. A prison guard may be held to a different standard because the guard may be allowed some time to deliberate prior to acting. In this case, however, when a suspect flees, the officer has no time for deliberation and must respond immediately.

■=■

Quicknotes

DUE PROCESS The constitutional mandate requiring the courts to protect and enforce individuals' rights and liberties consistent with prevailing principles of fairness and justice and prohibiting the federal and state governments from such activities that deprive its citizens of life, liberty, or property interest.

■=■

DeShaney v. Winnebago County Dept. of Social Services

Child (P) v. State (D)

489 U.S. 189 (1989).

NATURE OF CASE: Appeal from denial of damages for substantive due process violation.

FACT SUMMARY: After investigating claims of child abuse concerning Joshua DeShaney (P), the DSS (D) concluded there was insufficient evidence to establish a case against Joshua's (P) father, Randy, who subsequently beat Joshua (P) severely enough to cause him permanent brain damage.

🏛 RULE OF LAW
The language of the Fourteenth Amendment Due Process Clause does not require the state to protect the life, liberty, and property of its citizens against invasion by private actors.

FACTS: After his parents were divorced, Joshua DeShaney (P) was placed in his father's custody. Joshua's (P) father, Randy, remarried, and when Joshua's (P) stepmother later sought a divorce, she notified the Winnebago County Department of Social Services (D) (DSS) that Joshua's (P) father had abused him. Randy denied the accusations when interviewed by DSS (D). Over the next few months, Joshua (P) was admitted to the hospital several times with multiple bruises and a number of suspicious injuries on his head. He was placed in the temporary custody of the hospital, at the recommendation of the DSS (D). However, a "child protection team" determined there was insufficient evidence to retain custody, and Joshua (P) was returned to his father. Although a DSS (D) caseworker continued to suspect that Joshua (P) was being abused by someone in his household, the DSS (D) took no action. Finally, in March 1984, Randy DeShaney beat Joshua (P) so severely that he lapsed into a life-threatening coma. He suffered such severe brain damage that he was expected to be confined to an institution for the severely retarded for the remainder of his life. Through his mother, Joshua (P) filed suit for damages, claiming that the DSS (D) deprived him of his Fourteenth Amendment rights to liberty when it failed to protect him "against a risk of violence at his father's hands of which they knew or should have known."

ISSUE: Does the language of the Fourteenth Amendment Due Process Clause require the state to protect the life, liberty, and property of its citizens against invasion by private actors?

HOLDING AND DECISION: (Rehnquist, C.J.) No. The language of the Fourteenth Amendment Due Process Clause does not require the state to protect the life, liberty, and property of its citizens against invasion by private actors. The claim is one invoking the substantive rather than procedural component of the Due Process Clause. The purpose of

the Clause was to protect the people from the state, not to ensure that the state protected them from each other. Thus, this Court has recognized that the Due Process Clause generally confers no affirmative right to governmental aid, even where such aid may be necessary to secure life, liberty, or property interests of which the government itself may not deprive the individual. If the Due Process Clause does not require the state to provide its citizens with particular protective services, it follows that the state cannot be held liable under the Clause for injuries that could have been averted had it chosen to provide them. Thus, a state's failure to protect an individual against private violence simply does not constitute a violation of the Due Process Clause. That DSS (D) once took temporary custody of Joshua (P) does not alter the analysis, for when it returned him to his father's custody, it placed him in no worse position than that in which he would have been had it not acted at all; the state does not become the permanent guarantor of an individual's safety by having once offered him shelter. Under these circumstances, DSS (D) had no constitutional duty to protect Joshua (P).

DISSENT: (Brennan, J.) Contrary to the majority opinion, this Court's cases stand for the much more generous proposition that, if a state cuts off private sources of aid and then refuses aid itself, it cannot wash its hands of the harm that results from its inaction. Through its child-protection program, the state actively intervened in Joshua's (P) life, and, by virtue of this intervention, relieved ordinary citizens and other governmental bodies of any sense of obligation to do anything more than report their suspicions of child abuse to DSS (D). This opinion construes the Due Process Clause to permit a state to displace private sources of protection and then to shrug its shoulders and turn away from the harm that it has promised to try to prevent.

DISSENT: (Blackmun, J.) The question presented by this case is an open one, and Fourteenth Amendment precedents may be read more broadly or narrowly depending upon how one chooses to read them. Faced with a choice, a sympathetic reading, one that comports with dictates of fundamental justice and recognizes that compassion need not be exiled from the province of judging, is preferable.

▸ ANALYSIS

Citing its prior rulings, the Court asserted that a state's affirmative duty to protect arises not from the state's knowledge of an individual's predicament or from its

Continued on next page.

expressions of intent to help him, but from the limitation that it has imposed on his freedom to act on his own behalf. Thus, in the substantive due process analysis, it is a state's affirmative act of restraining an individual's freedom to act on his own behalf—through incarceration, institutionalization, or other similar restraint of personal liberty—that triggers the protection of the Due Process Clause, not its failure to act to protect his liberty interests against harms inflicted by other means.

■══■

Quicknotes

DUE PROCESS CLAUSE Clauses found in the Fifth and Fourteenth Amendments to the U.S. Constitution providing that no person shall be deprived of "life, liberty, or property, without due process of law."

LIBERTY INTEREST A right conferred by the Due Process Clauses of the state and federal constitutions.

SUBSTANTIVE DUE PROCESS A constitutional safeguard limiting the power of the state, irrespective of how fair its procedures may be; substantive limits placed on the power of the state.

■══■

Town of Castle Rock v. Gonzales

Local government (D) v. Citizen (P)

545 U.S. 748 (2005).

NATURE OF CASE: Review of federal appeals court judgment.

FACT SUMMARY: Jessica Gonzales (P) sued the City of Castle Rock, Colorado (D), and several individual police officers (D) on behalf of herself and her deceased minor children. Gonzales (P) alleged that their substantive and procedural due process rights were violated when the police officers failed to enforce a restraining order against her estranged husband after he abducted their three daughters.

🏛 RULE OF LAW
The holder of a restraining order cannot bring a procedural due process claim under the Fourteenth Amendment of the U.S. Constitution against a local government for its failure to actively enforce the order and protect the holder from violence.

FACTS: A state trial court issued a restraining order at the request of Jessica Gonzales (P) against her estranged husband. The order prohibited the husband from seeing Gonzales (P) or their three daughters except during pre-arranged visits. Approximately one month later, Gonzales's (P) husband abducted the three children. Gonzales repeatedly called the police (D) and urged them to search for and arrest her husband, but they told her to wait to see if her husband brought the children back. Approximately six hours after Gonzales (P) made her first call, her husband opened fire inside the police station and was killed when police (D) returned fire. Police (D) discovered that some time during the night, Gonzales's husband murdered all three children. Gonzales (P) filed suit in federal district court, charging that the Castle Rock police (D) had violated her rights under the Due Process Clause of the Constitution by willfully or negligently refusing to enforce her restraining order. The district court dismissed the complaint, ruling that no principle of substantive or procedural due process allowed Gonzales (P) to sue a local government (D) for its failure to enforce a restraining order. On appeal, the Court of Appeals for the Tenth Circuit affirmed that Gonzales had no substantive due process claim, but reversed with regard to the procedural due process claim. The court found that mandatory language in the Colorado statute regarding restraining orders created an entitlement for Gonzales (P) to receive protective services from the police (D), and that she stated a claim for deprivation of procedural due process because of the failure of the police officers (D) to arrest, or even to attempt to arrest, her husband pursuant to the order. After a rehearing en banc, a closely divided court affirmed the opinion of the first panel.

ISSUE: Can the holder of a restraining order bring a procedural due process claim under the Fourteenth Amendment of the U.S. Constitution against a local government for its failure to actively enforce the order and protect the holder from violence?

HOLDING AND DECISION: (Scalia, J.) No. The holder of a restraining order cannot bring a procedural due process claim under the Fourteenth Amendment of the U.S. Constitution against a local government for its failure to actively enforce the order and protect the holder from violence. Gonzales (P) had no constitutionally protected property interest in the enforcement of the restraining order, and therefore could not claim that the police had violated her right to due process. The state law did not entitle the holder of a restraining order to any specific mandatory action by the police (D). Instead, restraining orders only provide grounds for arresting the subject of the order, but police (D) have discretion to determine the specific action they take with respect to the order. This is not the sort of "entitlement" out of which a property interest is created. Since Colorado has not created such an entitlement, Gonzales (P) had no property interest and the Due Process Clause was therefore inapplicable.

DISSENT: (Stevens, J.) The restraining order entered by the Colorado trial court created a "property" interest that is protected from arbitrary deprivation by the Due Process Clause. But the question must be decided as a matter of Colorado law, and the question should be certified to the Colorado Supreme Court. It is unwise to decide to answer a state law question de novo. But in any event, the correct result is that the law created a statutory guarantee of enforcement, which is an individual benefit and constitutes a protected property interest.

▶ ANALYSIS

Some critics of this case saw it as a major defeat for activists dedicated to ending violence against women. They saw the result as proof that restraining orders are ineffective to protect victims of domestic violence and as conferring freedom to abuse on predators.

■=■

Quicknotes

PROCEDURAL DUE PROCESS The constitutional mandate that if the state or federal government acts so as to

Continued on next page.

deny a citizen of a life, liberty or property interest the individual is first entitled to notice and the right to be heard.

SUBSTANTIVE DUE PROCESS A constitutional safeguard limiting the power of the state, irrespective of how fair its procedures may be; substantive limits placed on the power of the state.

■≡■

Goldberg v. Kelly

State (D) v. Welfare recipients (P)

397 U.S. 254 (1970).

NATURE OF CASE: Appeal from order requiring hearing prior to termination of welfare benefits.

FACT SUMMARY: Kelly (P) and other residents of New York City who had been receiving aid pursuant to a state welfare scheme, brought this action alleging that benefits had been terminated without prior notice and hearing.

🏛 RULE OF LAW
A state that terminates public assistance payments to a recipient without affording him the opportunity for an evidentiary hearing prior to termination denies the recipient procedural due process.

FACTS: Kelly (P) and other residents of New York City who had been receiving aid pursuant to a state welfare scheme, brought this action alleging that welfare benefits had been or would be terminated, under New York law, without prior notice and hearing in violation of the Due Process Clause. The state contended that its post-termination notice and hearing procedure was constitutionally sufficient. Under the procedure a caseworker with doubts about a recipient's continued eligibility would first discuss the matter with the recipient, and then recommend termination of benefits if the recipient was still considered ineligible. Notification of termination was then sent in writing to the recipient together with information about the availability of a post-termination hearing. If the recipient prevailed he would be paid all funds erroneously held. The district court held that only a pre-termination evidentiary hearing would satisfy the Due Process Clause. Goldberg (D), as Commissioner of Social Services, appealed.

ISSUE: Does a state that terminates public assistance payments to a recipient without affording him the opportunity for an evidentiary hearing prior to termination deny the recipient procedural due process?

HOLDING AND DECISION: (Brennan, J.) Yes. A state that terminates public assistance payments to a recipient without affording him the opportunity for an evidentiary hearing before the termination denies the recipient procedural due process. The extent to which procedural due process must be afforded the recipient is influenced by the extent to which he may be condemned to suffer grievous loss, and depends upon whether the recipient's interest in avoiding that loss outweighs the governmental interest in summary adjudication. It is true, of course, that some governmental benefits may be administratively terminated without affording the recipient a pre-termination evidentiary hearing. When welfare is discontinued, however, so is the means to obtain essential food, clothing, housing, and medical care. Termina-tion of aid pending resolution of a controversy over eligibility thus might deprive an eligible recipient of the very means by which he lives. Moreover, important governmental interests are promoted by affording recipients a pre-termination evidentiary hearing. This hearing, though, need not be a judicial or even quasi-judicial undertaking. The hearing's only purpose is to provide initial protection to recipients before they lose their benefits. To accomplish that goal, neither the record nor the government's stated opinion need be comprehensive. Rudimentary due process will suffice: timely and adequate notice of the proposed reasons for termination, and an opportunity to be heard that includes confrontation of opposing witnesses and to present oral evidence and argument.

DISSENT: (Black, J.) Our contemporary welfare state consists of millions of people who regularly receive gratuities from the government. The administrative burdens of welfare programs were already great before this decision, often too great to ensure an accurate disbursement of the gratuities to recipients; many recipients dishonestly or at least mistakenly collect their government allowances. No provision in the Constitution requires the government to provide a hearing before terminating benefits that frequently are inaccurately awarded anyway. The extra burdens placed on the government by this decision will have the opposite effect of that intended by the majority. Because the government will now exhaustively investigate applicants for welfare recipients, many people who probably would have received welfare under the former procedural requirements now will not receive benefits at all.

▌ ANALYSIS

The Court points out in *Goldberg* that the pre-termination hearing need not take the form of a judicial or quasi-judicial trial. It must be born in mind that the statutory fair hearing will provide the recipient with a full adminis-trative review. Accordingly, the pre-termination hearing has one function only: to produce an initial determination of the validity of the welfare department's grounds for discontinuance of payments in order to protect a recipient against an erroneous termination of benefits.

■=■

Quicknotes

PROCEDURAL DUE PROCESS The constitutional mandate that if the state or federal government acts so as to deny a citizen of a life, liberty or property interest the individual is first entitled to notice and the right to be heard.

■=■

Board of Regents v. Roth

University (D) v. Roth (P)

408 U.S. 564 (1972).

NATURE OF CASE: Appeal from summary judgment order of right to hearing.

FACT SUMMARY: Roth (P), a nontenured Wisconsin State University instructor, was not rehired after a year of teaching after making certain anti-University statements, and alleged, that he was deprived of a property right in his job and a liberty interest to make the statements.

🏛 RULE OF LAW
An employee of a state-operated facility has no property interest in future employment guaranteed by the Constitution beyond those granted in his employment contract.

FACTS: Roth (P) was a nontenured instructor at Wisconsin State University. After a year of teaching, Roth (P) was not rehired. His contract of employment with the University secured him no rights to employment after its expiration at the time of Roth's (P) termination. Roth (P) brought this action against the University Board (D), alleging insufficient notice and hearing and a deprivation of a property right in his job along with a deprivation of a liberty interest to make statements against the University, which he alleged led to his dismissal. The district court granted Roth's (P) motion for summary judgment against the Board (D) and the court of appeals affirmed. The Supreme Court granted certiorari.

ISSUE: Has an employee of a state-operated facility a property interest in future employment guaranteed by the Constitution beyond those granted in his employment contract?

HOLDING AND DECISION: (Stewart, J.) No. Not all interests are protected by the Fourteenth Amendment so as to require procedural due process in the form of a prior hearing before the interest is lost. Roth (P) was hired by his contract for one year and no more, and he is not deprived of a right because he was not offered another contract. Any property right he may have had was completely set forth in his contract, and no liberty right deprivation has been shown. An employee of a state-operated facility has no property interest in future employment guaranteed by the Constitution beyond those granted in his employment contract. Under these circumstances, no hearing or notice beyond what was given was required.

DISSENT: (Marshall, J.) The University (D) deprived the assistant professor, Roth (P), of a property right when it failed to re-hire him for the following term and failed to offer a statement for the reason. A government employer may not act unreasonably or capriciously with respect to employment practices. Just because a government employee does not have a contract guaranteeing continued employment does not mean that he may be discharged for any reason or even no reason at all. The property right guaranteed in the Fourteenth Amendment includes government jobs. Every applicant who applies for a government job is entitled to it unless the government can offer a reason for denial of the job. Furthermore, it would not be burdensome to give a short statement of reasons when an employee or applicant is refused employment or discharged.

▶ ANALYSIS

The broad protection of the Fourteenth Amendment in this area envisioned by Justice Powell finds little support in the cases that followed except where the deprivation or refusal to rehire forecloses a wide range of employment opportunities for the employee. If the foreclosure encompasses both the public and private sectors, a fair hearing will be required.

■■■■

Quicknotes

DUE PROCESS CLAUSE Clauses found in the Fifth and Fourteenth Amendments to the U.S. Constitution providing that no person shall be deprived of "life, liberty, or property, without due process of law."

LIBERTY INTEREST A right conferred by the Due Process Clauses of the state and federal constitutions.

PROCEDURAL DUE PROCESS The constitutional mandate that if the state or federal government acts so as to deny a citizen of a life, liberty or property interest the individual is first entitled to notice and the right to be heard.

PROPERTY RIGHTS A legal right in specified personal or real property.

■■■■

Goss v. Lopez

Ohio public school (D) v. High school students (P)

419 U.S. 565 (1975).

NATURE OF THE CASE: Appeal from a judgment concerning due process rights.

FACT SUMMARY: The school administrators of the Ohio School System (P) claim that there is no constitutional right to a public education; therefore, the Due Process Clause does not protect against expulsions.

🏛 RULE OF LAW
A student's entitlement to a public education is a property right, and such right is protected by the Due Process Clause.

FACTS: An Ohio statute allows a school to suspend or expel a student for misconduct. In either case, the student's parents must be notified within 24 hours and be notified of the reasons. In the case of expulsion, the student or parents may appeal the decision to the Board of Education to have the student reinstated. Although there is no similar provision for suspended students, there is offered a description of behavior for which a student may be suspended. Nine students (P) claim that they were suspended up to ten days without a hearing.

ISSUE: Is there a property right to a public education that is protected by the Due Process Clause?

HOLDING AND DECISION: (White, J.) Yes. There a property right to a public education that is protected by the Due Process Clause. The suspended students (P) were legitimately entitled to a public education. These rights were evidenced by the Ohio statutes providing an education to students between the ages of 5 and 21, as well as the mandatory attendance law requiring attendance of no less than 32 weeks a year. Each school has its own rules governing grounds for suspension or expulsion. However, in the interest of fundamental fairness, there need to be procedures to determine whether or not such specific misconduct occurred. Because the right to a public education is a property right, it cannot be arbitrarily taken away. The students' (P) liberty interest was also at issue because their good name, reputation or integrity was at stake. When the students (P) were suspended, it was recorded in their records, which, if the charges were sustained, could affect their standing with teachers and fellow students, as well as their opportunities for higher education or employment. The state cannot unilaterally and without process decide that misconduct occurred. According to *Brown v. Board of Education*, 328 U.S. 294 (1955), education is a serious function of government and to force a student to be excluded from it is a serious event. The school authorities need to be bound by the notice and hearing requirements.

The notice can be written or oral. If the student denies the charges, he may present his or her side. He must also be notified of the school's evidence in support of the disciplinary action against him. This is necessary to avoid unfair suspensions.

DISSENT: (Powell, J.) Suspension of a student does not infringe upon his or her due process rights. Education officials and the legislature should be deciding the issue. In allowing this court to decide, they have identified a new constitutional right—the right not to be suspended without notice and due process hearing.

▶ ANALYSIS

Two important points can be taken from this case. First, the Supreme Court suggested that a person has a liberty interest in his or her reputation. Second, the Supreme Court found that students have a property right in attending school.

■■■

Quicknotes

DUE PROCESS CLAUSE Clauses found in the Fifth and Fourteenth Amendments to the U.S. Constitution providing that no person shall be deprived of "life, liberty, or property, without due process of law."

LIBERTY INTEREST A right conferred by the Due Process Clauses of the state and federal constitutions.

PROCEDURAL DUE PROCESS The constitutional mandate that if the state or federal government acts so as to deny a citizen of a life, liberty or property interest the individual is first entitled to notice and the right to be heard.

PROPERTY RIGHTS A legal right in specified personal or real property.

■■■

Paul v. Davis

Police chief (D) v. Alleged shoplifter (P)

424 U.S. 693 (1976).

NATURE OF THE CASE: Appeal from a judgment concerning a violation of a liberty interest protected by the Due Process Clause.

FACT SUMMARY: Police officers (D) claim that labeling Davis (P) as an "active shoplifter" without a conviction does not violate Davis's (P) property interest protected by the Due Process Clause.

RULE OF LAW
Reputation alone is not a property or liberty right protected by the Due Process Clause.

FACTS: Paul (D) and McDaniel decided that during the Christmas season of 1972 they would warn local merchants, through the use of flyers, of possible shoplifters in the area. The flyer contained the names and photos of individuals either convicted of shoplifting or involved in other criminal activities in shopping areas during 1971 and 1972. Davis, (P) one of the individuals featured in the flyer, pleaded not guilty to a shoplifting charge in 1971, but the charge was left outstanding. As the flyer was being circulated, Davis's (P) guilt or innocence had not been proven, and, shortly after circulation, the shoplifting charges were dismissed. Davis (P) claimed that being labeled an active shoplifter violated his liberty interest under the Fourteenth Amendment because the label inhibited him from entering certain establishments for fear he would be suspected of shoplifting. He also claimed that the label would negatively affect any future opportunities including possible employment.

ISSUE: Is reputation alone a property or liberty right protected by the Due Process Clause?

HOLDING AND DECISION: (Rehnquist, J.) No. Reputation alone is not a liberty or property right protected by the Due Process Clause. This case differs from *Goss v. Lopez*, 419 U.S. 565 (1975), in that in *Lopez* the state enacted a statute entitling students to an education. Here, the state of Kentucky did not enact a statute entitling its citizens to a favorable reputation. If the state chooses to protect one's right to a favorable reputation, it should do so through tort law, and any violations would then be addressed in damage proceedings in state court. Regardless of the harm caused, there was no entitlement given by the state, and therefore no deprivation of a liberty or property interest protected by the Due Process Clause.

DISSENT: (Brennan, J.) The label of a criminal carries a serious stigma, and that label should not be freely given by police officers without a trial. The constitutional safe-guards given to an accused during a criminal trial should be applied in this case. A police officer's duty is to be fair in his enforcement of the law, and without that protection, no individual would be safe from being labeled arbitrarily as a criminal and receiving ex parte punishment. A finding that reputation is not a protected interest would unduly restrict the construction of the Bill of Rights and be contrary to case law.

ANALYSIS

Contrast this case with *Lopez*, where the Court found that suspension from public school without a hearing was a deprivation of a property interest, and the loss of reputation resulting from the suspension was a deprivation of a liberty interest. The reason the *Lopez* court found a property deprivation was due to a state statute entitling students to a public education up to age 21, along with mandatory attendance guidelines. Although *Lopez* also found a deprivation of liberty in loss of reputation due to suspension, the majority of the *Lopez* court's reasoning focused on the property interest in attending school. It then remains unclear whether the *Lopez* court would have found a deprivation of due process if the issue was a loss of reputation alone.

Quicknotes

DUE PROCESS CLAUSE Clauses found in the Fifth and Fourteenth Amendments to the U.S. Constitution providing that no person shall be deprived of "life, liberty, or property, without due process of law."

LIBERTY INTEREST A right conferred by the Due Process Clauses of the state and federal constitutions.

PROPERTY RIGHTS A legal right in specified personal or real property.

Mathews v. Eldridge

Payment recipient (P) v. Federal agency (D)

424 U.S. 319 (1976).

NATURE OF CASE: Action seeking disability payment termination hearing.

FACT SUMMARY: A recipient of Social Security disability benefits claimed that he could not be deprived of those benefits until after an evidentiary hearing.

🏛 RULE OF LAW
The Due Process Clause of the Fifth Amendment does not require that prior to the termination of Social Security disability benefit payments the recipient be afforded an opportunity for an evidentiary hearing.

FACTS: After receiving Social Security disability benefits for almost four years, Eldridge (P) answered a questionnaire about his medical condition for a state agency monitoring his case for the federal Social Security Administration (SSA). Eldridge (P) answered that his disability persisted and listed physicians who had recently treated him. Reports obtained by the agency from Eldridge's (P) physician and a psychiatric consultant led the state agency to tentatively recommend terminating Eldridge's (P) disability benefits; the medical reports indicated that his disability had ended. By letter, the agency notified Eldridge (P) of its tentative determination and also told him why the agency proposed to terminate his benefits. Eldridge (P) responded, also in writing, challenging one part of the medical assessment considered by the agency. The SSA accepted the state agency's recommendation. Four months after Eldridge (P) answered the questionnaire, the SSA informed him, in writing, that his disability benefits would end in one month. Eldridge (P) filed suit. The trial court and court of appeals both agreed with him that due process required an evidentiary hearing before the termination of his disability benefits.

ISSUE: Does the Due Process Clause of the Fifth Amendment require that prior to termination of Social Security disability payments the recipient be afforded an opportunity for an evidentiary hearing?

HOLDING AND DECISION: (Powell, J.) No. The Due Process Clause does not require an evidentiary hearing before the termination of Social Security disability benefits. An assessment of the process that is due before a person can be deprived of a property interest depends on three factors: (1) the private interest of the individual, (2) the danger of mistakenly depriving the individual of his property and the value of any additional procedural safeguards, and (3) the government or public interest. In this case, a recipient of disability benefits is given a hearing after the termination of benefits and is awarded full retroactive relief if he ultimately prevails. Consequently, in this context

a recipient's sole property interest is in the uninterrupted receipt of this source of income pending a final administrative decision on his claim. Although Eldridge's (P) potential injury is similar to that of the welfare recipient in *Goldberg v. Kelly*, 397 U.S. 254 (1970), the *Goldberg* Court emphasized that the benefits there were awarded to persons on the margin of existence. Due process therefore requires an evidentiary hearing before the termination of a welfare recipient's benefits. In contrast, eligibility for disability benefits does not depend on financial need. Further, here there is relatively little risk of error in the determination because medical conditions can be assessed relatively accurately through written reports. Finally, the additional administrative and financial burdens that extra procedural safeguards would place on the government, and thus on the public, would be relatively great, especially where the government actors can make the necessary determination relatively accurately through written reports. Accordingly, due process does not require an evidentiary hearing before the termination of Social Security disability benefits.

DISSENT: (Brennan, J.) The possibility that a discontinuance of a worker's disability benefits will be only a temporary deprivation is speculation and nothing more. The fact that the legislature had allowed benefits without a determination of need presumes that need exists, a presumption this Court should not denigrate.

▶ ANALYSIS

In this case the Supreme Court outlined a three-factor test for determining the adequacy in due process terms of a particular procedure: the private interest affected, the risk of error in the challenged procedures, and the burden imposed on government by more demanding procedural requirements. Furthermore, it indicates a turning away from *Goldberg v. Kelly*, by a differently composed court.

■=■

Quicknotes

DUE PROCESS CLAUSE Clauses found in the Fifth and Fourteenth Amendments to the U.S. Constitution providing that no person shall be deprived of "life, liberty, or property, without due process of law."

PROCEDURAL DUE PROCESS The constitutional mandate that if the state or federal government acts so as to deny a citizen of a life, liberty or property interest the individual is first entitled to notice and the right to be heard.

■=■

First Amendment: Freedom of Expression

Quick Reference Rules of Law

CHAPTER **9**

Turner Broadcasting System, Inc. v. Federal Communications Commn.

Cable television company (P) v. Federal regulatory agency (D)

512 U.S. 622 (1994).

NATURE OF CASE: Appeal from summary judgment upholding the Cable Television Consumer Protection and Competition Act of 1992 (CTCPCA).

FACT SUMMARY: Turner (P) challenged the CTCPCA's requirement that all cable television systems dedicate some of their channels to local broadcast television stations.

🏛 RULE OF LAW
The "must-carry" provisions of the CTCPCA do not violate the First Amendment, as they further important governmental interests and do not substantially burden speech more than necessary.

FACTS: In 1992, Congress enacted the Cable Television Consumer Protection and Competition Act, which required cable television stations to dedicate some of their channels to local broadcast stations. Turner (P) challenged the law, and the district court granted summary judgment to the FCC (D). On appeal, the Supreme Court agreed that the law was content neutral, but remanded to determine the importance of the state interest and whether the Act burdened speech more than necessary to further those interests. After many factual developments, the district court again granted the FCC (D) summary judgment and Turner (P) appealed.

ISSUE: Do the "must-carry" provisions of the CTCPCA violate the First Amendment?

HOLDING AND DECISION: (Kennedy, J.) No. The "must-carry" provisions of the CTCPCA do not violate the First Amendment. Although the Act regulates cable speech, it is content neutral because it regulates cable providers regardless of the basis of their views and expressed ideas. When speech content is not being regulated, intermediate scrutiny is all that is required. The burdens imposed on cable providers by this regulation, specifically reducing the number of controlled channels and increasing competition among the remaining channels, are minimal and unrelated to content.

CONCURRENCE AND DISSENT: (O'Connor, J.) Strict scrutiny is required when the government favors one form of speech to the detriment of another. Here, the Court gives a preference to broadcasters over cable programmers, and valuation of content can be the only justification. The government should not be determining which speech, whether localized because coming from a broadcaster or general because on cable, is more valuable and thus better deserving of First Amendment protections.

▶ ANALYSIS

The right of the press to publish and the extent to which the freedom of speech protects the press has long been debated. Pursuant to *Smith v. Daily Mail Publishing Co.*, 443 U.S. 97 (1979), truthful information that has been lawfully obtained concerning a matter of public significance can only be prohibited by a narrowly tailored statute serving a state interest of the highest order. However, due to the number of limited frequencies, radio and television broadcasting can be more restricted than the published press. See *Los Angeles v. Preferred Communications, Inc.*, 476 U.S. 488 (1986).

■═■

Quicknotes

INTERMEDIATE SCRUTINY A standard of reviewing the propriety of classifications pertaining to gender or legitimacy under the Equal Protection Clause of the U.S. Constitution which requires a court to ascertain whether the classification furthers an important state interest and is substantially related to the attainment of that interest.

STRICT SCRUTINY Method by which courts determine the constitutionality of a law, when a law affects a fundamental right. Under the test, the legislature must have had a compelling interest to enact the law and measures prescribed by the law must be the least restrictive means possible to accomplish its goal.

■═■

Boos v. Barry

Sign-carrying protesters (D) v. District government (P)

485 U.S. 312 (1988).

NATURE OF THE CASE: Appeal from a judgment holding a provision of the District of Columbia Code does not violate the First Amendment.

FACT SUMMARY: Three individuals (D) claim that a provision prohibiting the display of signs that may bring a government into "public disrepute" within 500 feet of a foreign embassy violates First Amendment protections.

🏛 RULE OF LAW
If a restriction on protected free speech is not content neutral, it must be narrowly tailored and necessary to achieve a compelling governmental interest.

FACTS: A section of the District of Columbia Code prohibits the display of a sign within 500 feet of a foreign embassy if the sign brings such foreign government into "public disrepute." Petitioners wished to display signs criticizing the Soviet and Nicaraguan governments in front of their respective embassies. Two protesters (D) wanted to display signs saying "FREE SAKHAROV" and "SOLIDARITY" within 500 feet of the Soviet embassy, and one defendant wanted to display the sign "STOP THE KILLING" within 500 feet of the Nicaraguan embassy.

ISSUE: If a statute restricting protected free speech is not content neutral, must it be narrowly tailored and necessary to achieve a compelling governmental interest?

HOLDING AND DECISION: (O'Connor, J.) Yes. The provision in the D.C. Code is not content neutral because it regulates speech according to its potential impact and states what types of speech are permitted within 500 feet of an embassy and what types of speech are not. Because it is not content neutral, in order to pass constitutional muster, it must be narrowly tailored and necessary to achieve a compelling state interest. In deciding whether protecting a foreign diplomat from possible insult is compelling, the Court finds that it is not. An important principle central to the First Amendment is open, uninhibited debate on public issues. During such debate, however, Americans generally must tolerate insulting and outrageous speech. Foreign diplomats should be treated no differently. Shielding foreign diplomats from insult is not a compelling interest sufficient to uphold a provision restricting free speech.

▌ *ANALYSIS*

Not all speech is treated equally. In deciding the constitutional protections, the determination must be made as to whether the speech is defamatory, obscene, or has the possibility of inciting illegal activity. The government does have a legitimate interest in regulating those types of speech, so

constitutionality of a regulation will be determined using a lesser standard. The government does not, however, have a legitimate interest in suppressing unpopular ideas. See *Turner Broadcasting System, Inc. v. Federal Communication Commission*, 512 U.S. 622 (1994).

▬▬■

Quicknotes

COMPELLING INTEREST TEST A standard employed by the court under strict scrutiny review to determine the constitutionality of a statute, whereby the proponent of the statute must demonstrate that classifications drawn therein serve a compelling interest and are necessary for the furtherance of a state objective.

▬▬■

Republican Party of Minnesota v. White

Parties not identified.

536 U.S. 765 (2002).

NATURE OF CASE: Appeal from summary judgment award.

FACT SUMMARY: The state of Minnesota prohibits judicial candidates from announcing views on disputed political or legal issues. One such candidate sought a declaratory judgment that the prohibition was unconstitutional.

RULE OF LAW
It is a violation of the First Amendment to prohibit judicial candidates from announcing views on disputed political or legal issues.

FACTS: Minnesota elects all judges for state judicial positions. A canon of the Minnesota Supreme Court on judicial conduct prohibits judicial candidates from announcing his or her position on disputed political or legal issues. One such candidate seeking office distributed literature taking a stance on several issues. The ethics board did not sanction the candidate, but he withdrew from the race. In a later election for a judicial position, the same candidate sought a declaratory judgment in federal district court that the prohibition was unconstitutional. The district court granted summary judgment to the defendants and plaintiff appealed. The court of appeals affirmed, and the U.S. Supreme Court granted certiorari.

ISSUE: Is it a violation of the First Amendment to prohibit judicial candidates from announcing views on disputed political or legal issues?

HOLDING AND DECISION: (Scalia, J.) Yes. It is a violation of the First Amendment to prohibit judicial candidates from announcing views on disputed political or legal issues. Strict scrutiny is required here because the prohibition implicates the First Amendment. The prohibition must therefore be narrowly tailored to serve a compelling state interest. The argument for the prohibition is that it preserves the appearance and the actual fact of impartiality on the part of elected judges. Impartiality, however, is not a compelling state interest and this prohibition is too broad. Impartiality may be defined as "the equal application of the law," no preconceptions for or against a particular legal view, or open mindedness. Prohibiting opinions from being discussed during campaigns does not ensure any of the possible definitions of impartiality. Judges must apply the law in a constitutional manner, regardless of personal views. Any judicial candidate who is qualified will have, at one point or another in a written decision or in a public statement, conveyed an opinion. Judges utterly without opinion are likely unqualified. Voters are entitled to information on judicial candidates' views and the content-based restriction

of this judicial canon does not achieve its arguable purpose. Reversed and remanded.

CONCURRENCE: (O'Connor, J.) Judicial elections are cause for concern because judges may feel they have at least some personal stake in the outcome of cases, and feel the need to constantly campaign. Campaigns cost money, and eventually, only the wealthy will be contenders for judicial posts. Such a process necessarily involves risking judicial bias as outlined in today's opinion.

CONCURRENCE: (Kennedy, J.) Unless a content-based restriction falls into one of the clear exceptions, it should be invalidated without further inquiry. The voters should have the right to determine what speech is relevant when selecting a judicial candidate, and the state should not be involved in restricting such speech.

DISSENT: (Stevens, J.) The standards of political campaigns do not apply to judicial campaigns. A judicial candidate should not make issue statements because taking a stance on a particular issue could imply a closed mind on that issue. Judges do not serve a particular constituency and should not intimate that they do.

DISSENT: (Ginsburg, J.) The judiciary cannot act as politicians do because judges do not serve a particular constituency. Judges must behave with impartiality regardless of the means of their appointment. When judges are elected, rules such as those imposed by Minnesota are necessary to ensure the continued appearance of impartiality.

ANALYSIS

This decision could lead to the judiciary behaving as politicians, as expressed by the dissenting justices. Regardless of the campaign "promises" that judicial candidates would make, however, judges must abide by judicial codes of ethics requiring them to be impartial. The appearance of impartiality is important, but the actual fact of it should be the only true concern of the voting public.

Quicknotes

COMPELLING INTEREST TEST A standard employed by the court under strict scrutiny review to determine the constitutionality of a statute, whereby the proponent of the statute must demonstrate that classifications drawn therein serve a compelling interest and are necessary for the furtherance of a state objective.

Continued on next page.

STRICT SCRUTINY Method by which courts determine the constitutionality of a law, when a law affects a fundamental right. Under the test, the legislature must have had a compelling interest to enact the law and measures prescribed by the law must be the least restrictive means possible to accomplish its goal.

■━━■

City of Renton v. Playtime Theatres, Inc.

Municipality (D) v. Adult movie theaters (P)

475 U.S. 41 (1986).

NATURE OF CASE: Appeal from reversal of summary judgment in an obscenity action.

FACT SUMMARY: Renton (D) enacted an ordinance geographically limiting adult motion picture theaters.

RULE OF LAW
A municipality may enact zoning regulations limiting the area where adult motion picture theaters may operate.

FACTS: The City of Renton (D), concerned about the effect of adult movie houses on the surrounding areas, enacted a zoning ordinance proscribing the operation of such an establishment within 1,000 feet of certain public and private facilities and within a mile of a school. This effectively removed 95 percent of the City (D) from such enterprises. Playtime Theaters (P) brought an action, claiming the ordinance violated the free speech provisions of the First and Fourteenth Amendments. The district court granted summary judgment in favor of Renton (D), but the Ninth Circuit reversed. Renton (D) appealed.

ISSUE: May a municipality enact zoning regulations limiting the area where adult motion picture theaters may operate?

HOLDING AND DECISION: (Rehnquist, J.) Yes. A municipality may enact zoning regulations limiting the area where adult motion pictures theaters may operate. "Content-neutral" restrictions on speech are permissible so long as they serve a substantial interest and do not unreasonably limit alternative avenues of communication. Here, the regulations are content-neutral, as the purpose of the ordinance was to prevent the blight associated with adult theaters, not the content of the films. This is a substantial interest.

DISSENT: (Brennan, J.) The regulations are not content neutral, and the ordinance must be looked at much more critically.

▶ ANALYSIS

The Court often finds itself fashioning standards of review for an issue. Historically, the Court has employed either a rubber-stamp rationality test or a very-difficult-to-meet strict scrutiny standard. The standard enunciated here seems to fall in between the two.

Quicknotes

CONTENT BASED Refers to statutes that regulate speech based on its content.

CONTENT NEUTRAL Refers to statutes that regulate speech regardless of its content.

National Endowment for the Arts v. Finley

National arts funding agency (P) v. Artist (D)

524 U.S. 569 (1998).

NATURE OF CASE: Appeal of decision finding that a statute is discriminatory and void for vagueness.

FACT SUMMARY: Congress added an amendment that required the National Endowment for the Arts (P) to consider general standards of decency and respect for the diverse beliefs and values of the American public.

🏛 RULE OF LAW
Where a statute merely takes decency and respect into consideration, and it was aimed at reforming procedures rather than precluding speech, the legislation is not unconstitutional.

FACTS: Two provocative works of art sponsored by the National Endowment for the Arts (NEA) generated formal complaints about misapplied funds and abuse of the public's trust. In response, Congress amended the bipartisan National Foundation on the Arts and Humanities Act with the Williams/Coleman Amendment. Under this amendment, which eventually became 20 U.S.C. § 954(d)(1), the NEA was required to judge the artistic merit of grant applications to take into consideration general standards of decency and respect for the diverse beliefs and values of the American public. Finley and other respondents argued that this provision violated the First Amendment.

ISSUE: Is § 954(d)(1) unconstitutional?

HOLDING AND DECISION: (O'Connor, J.) No. Where a statute merely takes decency and respect into consideration, and it was aimed at reforming procedures rather than precluding speech, the legislation is not unconstitutional. Section 954(d)(1) does not preclude awards to projects that might be deemed "indecent" or "disrespectful," nor place conditions on grants, or even specify that those factors must be given any particular weight in reviewing an application. Given the different interpretations of the various criteria and the vague admonition to take decency and respect for diverse beliefs into consideration, this requirement seems unlikely to introduce any greater element of selectivity than other criteria, such as "artistic excellence."

DISSENT: (Souter, J.) The decency and respect criteria forces viewpoint-based decisions in the disbursement of government subsidies. This sort of viewpoint discrimination by a public authority violates the First Amendment and there is no reason for exemption.

▶ ANALYSIS

Although artists are still free to create offensive works on their own, without funding they may not be able to afford to do so. Therefore, Congress is restricting speech by pulling the purse strings. On the other hand, the NEA should consider the possible popularity of proposed works since they would not want to fund a project that few people would ever appreciate.

◼═◼

Quicknotes

FIRST AMENDMENT Prohibits Congress from enacting any law respecting an establishment of religion, prohibiting the free exercise of religion, abridging freedom of speech or the press, the right of peaceful assembly and the right to petition for a redress of grievances.

◼═◼

United States v. American Library Assn., Inc.

Federal government (D) v. Organization of librarians (P)

539 U.S. 194 (2003).

NATURE OF CASE: Constitutional challenge to federal statute.

FACT SUMMARY: A federal statute prohibits federal assistance to libraries absent the library employing Internet filters to block pornographic sites. The organization of libraries challenged the constitutionality of the statute on its face.

🏛 RULE OF LAW
A public library's use of Internet-blocking software does not violate patrons' First Amendment rights, thus the Children's Internet Protection Act does not induce libraries to violate First Amendment rights and is an appropriate exercise of Congress's spending power.

FACTS: The Children's Internet Protection Act (CIPA) prohibited federal assistance to libraries refusing to implement Internet software to block pornographic materials. The American Library Association, Inc. (the Association) (P) challenged the facial constitutionality of the statute on the grounds that it induced libraries to violate patrons' First Amendment rights. The Association (P) also argued that the statute was an abuse of Congress's spending power because it tied federal funds to the implementation of the filtering software.

ISSUE: Does a public library's use of Internet blocking software violate patrons' First Amendment rights?

HOLDING AND DECISION: (Rehnquist, C.J.) No. A public library's use of Internet-blocking software does not violate patrons' First Amendment rights, thus the Children's Internet Protection Act does not induce libraries to violate First Amendment rights and is an appropriate exercise of Congress's spending power. Librarians make daily decisions on appropriate content to stock the library shelves, and the content from the Internet should be treated no differently. Adult patrons are entitled to request that the filtering software be disabled or that a particular site be unblocked. While this may prove embarrassing to some patrons, the Constitution does not guarantee embarrassment-free trips to the library. The protection of society's children from the effects of easily obtained pornography is of great import and the burden placed upon the library patrons is not overwhelming. Additionally, Congress has traditionally tied the availability of funds to a desired action on the part of the recipient of the funds. That is no different in this case and the congressional action is not an abuse of its spending power. The statute is constitutional.

CONCURRENCE: (Kennedy, J.) The challenge to the statute could be viewed as an unconstitutional "as-applied" challenge rather than a facial challenge if some

libraries demonstrate an inability or unwillingness to disable the filtering software. Here, the burden on patrons is minimal and the protection of minors from pornography is a legitimate state interest.

CONCURRENCE: (Breyer, J.) Heightened scrutiny is appropriate here because the statute involves the selection process for a library collection, but the statute survives even heightened scrutiny. The burden on the patron is comparatively small to the protection afforded minors.

DISSENT: (Stevens, J.) Local libraries should be able to make the decision to install filters based on local need rather than being forced to submit to a nationwide censorship ban of constitutionally protected materials. It is not unconstitutional for libraries to choose to install filters, but it is unconstitutional for the federal government to impose such requirements because of "overblocking" of protected, legitimate materials. Federal funds should not be tied to the enforcement of restrictions of First Amendment rights.

DISSENT: (Souter, J.) Libraries would be violating First Amendment rights if they took this action on their own, so the statute is unconstitutional in requiring them to take this action now. Alternatives to enforced filtration could include providing blocked terminals to children while leaving unblocked terminals for adults. Librarians should not be able to completely censor an adult patron's access to certain information. The unblocking ability is discretionary and if a librarian chooses not to unblock a site, that patron will not have access to the censored content. That is unconstitutional.

▌ANALYSIS

Critics of this decision argue that libraries on a local level had already handled the issue of pornographic content available over the Internet and did not require federal interference. Many libraries installed filters on computers specifically designated for children's use. With this opinion, adult patrons must explain his or her research purposes to the librarian and the librarian has the discretion to leave or remove the block. Free speech and anonymity advocates were not pleased with this opinion. The other side of the opinion, however, is the perceived benefit of protecting children from being inundated with unfiltered pornographic websites. With filters in place, librarians can spend less time playing discerning parent to children employing the Internet and more time being librarians.

■■■

Continued on next page.

Quicknotes

FIRST AMENDMENT RIGHTS Rights conferred by the First Amendment to the U.S. Constitution prohibiting Congress from enacting any law respecting an establishment of religion, prohibiting the free exercise of religion, abridging freedom of speech or the press, the right of peaceful assembly and the right to petition for a redress of grievances.

Near v. State of Minnesota ex rel. Olson

News publisher (D) v. State (P)

283 U.S. 697 (1931).

NATURE OF CASE: Suit for injunction to prevent further publication of a news periodical.

FACT SUMMARY: Near (D) published a news periodical that was found to have violated a statute prohibiting malicious, scandalous, and defamatory newspapers. His periodical was determined to be a public nuisance and an injunction was issued to prevent further publication.

RULE OF LAW
Freedom of the press is a fundamental right that forms a cornerstone of our Constitution, and prior restraint of that freedom will be tolerated only in the most exceptional circumstances involving direct threats to national security or a violent upset of an orderly government.

FACTS: Near (D) was the publisher of a news periodical that had made charges of extensive corruption and dereliction of duty against several city and county officials, including one member of the grand jury. According to a statute, any person who published or circulated a malicious, scandalous, and defamatory news periodical was guilty of a nuisance. The person found to be committing the nuisance could be enjoined perpetually from committing or maintaining the nuisance. The only defense that could be asserted was that the material was true and was published with good motives and justifiable ends. Near (D) and his periodical were charged under the statute and were adjudged a nuisance, and an injunction was issued restraining him from further violations of the statute.

ISSUE: Since some forms of expression have been found not to enjoy the absolute protection of the First Amendment (e.g., libel), may a state be allowed to impose an injunction, in the nature of a prior restraint on such expression?

HOLDING AND DECISION: (Hughes, C.J.) No. Blackstone noted that prior restraints on the right to publish would destroy freedom of the press. In his view, a person should be allowed to publish anything so long as he was prepared to respond in damages for that which was improper, mischievous, or illegal. Only under the most exceptional circumstances will prior restraint of expression be tolerated. Those circumstances are limited to direct threats to national security or in the incitement to acts of violence or overthrow by force of an orderly government. The criticism of public officials for which Near (D) was convicted was exactly the type of press activity that the First Amendment sought to protect. The statutory defense provided for those charged cannot salvage the unconstitutional invasion of basic rights.

Truth was not a requirement to qualify for the freedom of press guarantee. Further, truth alone would not even be a good defense, for the defendant must also show his proper motives and justifiable ends. The subjects of Near's (D) accusations have not been deprived of their private rights of action against him. The Minnesota statute operates as a prior restraint on the freedom of the press and cannot stand in the face of the strong fundamental guarantees of the First Amendment.

ANALYSIS

The Court's distaste for prior restraints on expression has remained unchanged, as was evidenced by the Daniel Ellsberg-Pentagon Papers case. Even more recently, the Berger court struck down a Tennessee statute that had prevented a presentation of the stage play *Hair*. In the principal case, the majority chose not to discuss another problem area presented by the Minnesota statute. The statute speaks in terms of malicious, scandalous, and defamatory publication. While the term defamatory may be sufficiently specific to afford a legal remedy, the other two terms would seem to be so vague as to thwart proper judicial application. In view of Justice Butler's view that libel laws in 1931 were inadequate to protect against defamations, one wonders what his reaction to the *Sullivan-Hill-Gertz* line of cases would have been.

Quicknotes

FREEDOM OF THE PRESS The right to publish and publicly disseminate one's views.

PRIOR RESTRAINT A restriction imposed on speech imposed prior to its communication.

New York Times Co. v. United States

Newspaper (D) v. Federal government (P)

403 U.S. 713 (1971).

NATURE OF CASE: Action seeking an injunction.

FACT SUMMARY: The federal government (P) sought to enjoin the New York Times (D) and the Washington Post (D) from publishing the Pentagon Papers.

🏛 RULE OF LAW
Any system of prior restraints of expression comes to the court bearing a heavy presumption against its constitutional validity.

FACTS: The federal government (P) sought to enjoin the New York Times (D) and the Washington Post (D) from publishing the contents of a classified study entitled, "History of U.S. Decision-Making Process on Viet Nam Policy" (The Pentagon Papers).

ISSUE: Must one seeking a prior restraint on expression meet a heavy burden of showing justification for imposition of the restraint?

HOLDING AND DECISION: (Per curiam) Yes. Any system of prior restraints of expression comes to the court bearing a heavy presumption against its constitutional validity. Here, the federal government (P) carried a heavy burden of showing justification for the enforcement of such a restraint. It did not meet that burden. The denial of injunctive relief is affirmed.

CONCURRENCE: (Black, J.) The cases should have been dismissed and relief denied when they were first presented to the court. Every moment's continuance of the injunctions against the newspapers amounts to a flagrant, indefensible violation of the First Amendment.

CONCURRENCE: (Douglas, J.) The First Amendment leaves no room for government restraint on the press. Its dominant purpose was to prohibit the widespread practice of governmental suppression of embarrassing information.

CONCURRENCE: (Brennan, J.) The error that has pervaded these cases was the granting of any injunctive relief whatsoever since the entire thrust of the federal government (P) claim was that publication of the material "could" or "might" or "may" prejudice the national interest. Only governmental allegation and proof that publication must inevitably, directly, and immediately cause the occurrence of an event kindred to imperiling the safety of a transport already at sea can support even the issuance of an interim restraining order.

CONCURRENCE: (Stewart, J.) Since it cannot be said that publication of this material will surely result in direct, immediate, and irreparable damage to the nation, the relief sought must be denied.

CONCURRENCE: (White, J.) Though publication will do substantial damage to public interests, the federal government (P) has not met its heavy burden to prove "direct, immediate, and irreparable damage to the nation."

CONCURRENCE: (Marshall, J.) It would be utterly inconsistent with the concept of separation of power for the Court to use its power of contempt to prevent behavior that Congress has specifically declined to prohibit. For an injunction to issue, it must be shown that such an injunction would enhance the already existing power of the federal government (P) to act. Equity will not be a useless thing, and the federal government (P) never even mentioned whether it believed probable cause that a crime was committed existed or whether a conspiracy to commit future crimes existed.

DISSENT: (Burger, C.J.) The First Amendment is not an absolute. The record here is not a complete enough one for the Court to act upon. Its incompleteness is due to the fact that these cases have been conducted in unseemly haste. The course followed by the New York Times (D) precluded any possibility of an orderly litigation of the issues.

DISSENT: (Harlan, J.) In the name of the presumption against prior restraints, the Court has been almost irresponsibly feverish in dealing with these cases. The doctrine of prior restraints does not prevent the courts from maintaining the status quo long enough to act responsibly.

DISSENT: (Blackmun, J.) The First Amendment is not absolute. Here, there is a danger that publication would result in the death of soldiers, the destruction of alliances, the greatly increased difficulty of negotiation with our enemies, the prolongation of the war, and further delay in the freeing of United States prisoners.

▌ ANALYSIS

On June 13, 1971, the New York Times began publishing parts of the Pentagon Papers. On June 18, the Washington Post also began publishing parts of the papers. The federal government (P) brought an action to restrain publication. Between June 15 and June 28, two district courts and two courts of appeal considered the case. On June 25, the Supreme Court granted certiorari. Restraining orders were continued in effect pending decision, which was

Continued on next page.

handed down on June 30. Four justices, Brennan, Marshall, Douglas, and Black, dissented from the grants of certiorari, urging summary action and stating that they would not continue the restraint on the newspapers.

■══■

Quicknotes

FREEDOM OF THE PRESS The right to publish and publicly disseminate one's views.

PRIOR RESTRAINT A restriction imposed on speech imposed prior to its communication.

■══■

Nebraska Press Assn. v. Stuart

Media association (P) v. Judge (D)

427 U.S. 539 (1976).

NATURE OF CASE: Appeal from order restraining press coverage of a criminal trial.

FACT SUMMARY: Simants's (D) criminal trial was not reported by the press due to a court order restraining such reporting on the basis it would deny him a fair trial.

🏛 RULE OF LAW
Prior restraint on freedom of the press may be used by courts only where less inhibiting measures to protect a right to a fair trial have been found to be unavailable.

FACTS: Simants (D) was arrested for the brutal murder of a Nebraska family. Due to the extensive news coverage, his attorney moved to preclude reporting on certain salient aspects of the trial. The district court issued the order, and the Nebraska Press Association (P) sought leave to intervene, contending the restrictions constituted prior restraint and were unconstitutional. The Nebraska Supreme Court upheld the order in a modified form, and the U.S. Supreme Court granted certiorari.

ISSUE: Is prior restraint available only in the absence of other less inhibiting methods of ensuring a fair trial?

HOLDING AND DECISION: (Burger, C.J.) Yes. Prior restraint on freedom of the press may be used only where less inhibiting measures to protect the right to a fair trial are unavailable. In this case no evidence appears in the record indicating that other measures were considered which may have been less inhibiting on freedom of the press. The trial judge had to review the pretrial news coverage, determine whether less restrictive means could address extensive pretrial coverage, and the potential effectiveness of a restraining order. The judge reviewed several newspapers evidencing the already extensive pretrial coverage, which supported the determination that the widespread publicity would continue. The trial court did not, however, make express findings as to the availability of less restrictive means than a restraining order. In the absence of finding on this issue, an order calling for prior restraint cannot stand.

▶ ANALYSIS

In *Bridges v. California*, 314 U.S. 252 (1941), the Court held that the power of courts to limit information is finite. Previously, state and federal courts imposed contempt orders on media that had acted to compromise a defendant's right to a fair trial.

Quicknotes

FREEDOM OF THE PRESS The right to publish and publicly disseminate one's views.

PRIOR RESTRAINT A restriction imposed on speech imposed prior to its communication.

■=■

Alexander v. United States

Owner of adult entertainment business (D) v. Federal government (P)

509 U.S. 544 (1993).

NATURE OF THE CASE: Action to determine whether forfeiture of assets pursuant to RICO violations based on obscenity convictions violates the First Amendment.

FACT SUMMARY: Owner of "adult entertainment" business claims that forfeiture of assets and ultimate loss of his entire business pursuant to Racketeer Influenced and Corrupt Organizations Act (RICO) constitutes a prior restraint on protected free speech.

🏛 RULE OF LAW
Forfeiture of materials and assets predicated upon previous obscenity violations does not operate as prior restraint on future presumptively protected expression in retaliation for prior unprotected speech.

FACTS: Alexander (D) was the owner of an "adult entertainment" business. He owned several retail stores that distributed various pornographic materials. Three videotapes and four magazines that Alexander (D) sold were found to be obscene, and he was later convicted of 17 counts of obscenity. In addition, Alexander (D) was also convicted of violating the RICO Act, to which the obscenity convictions served as predicates. Alexander (D) received a prison sentence, a fine, and was ordered to forfeit the assets related to his racketeering activities. He (D) was forced to forfeit his entire business, including all of the assets, which totaled approximately $9 million—the logic being that one should not be able to retain profits and assets related to illegal activity. When the federal government (P) took possession of the assets, it destroyed them instead of selling them. Alexander (D) claims that the forfeiture and destruction of his entire business acts as a prior restraint that prevents future protected speech in retaliation for prior unprotected speech.

ISSUE: Does the forfeiture of materials and assets predicated upon previous obscenity violations operate as prior restraint on future presumptively protected expression in retaliation for prior unprotected speech?

HOLDING AND DECISION: (Rehnquist, C.J.) No. This is a not a prior restraint, but a subsequent punishment. Alexander (D) had a full trial and was found guilty; this differs from a prior restraint, which forbids expression before it occurs. All of the assets were ordered forfeited because they were related to the RICO violations, not because they were pornographic. The forfeiture of the assets does not prohibit Alexander (D) from exercising his right to free speech, since he was not prohibited from re-entering the business of "adult entertainment." The Petitioner is free to return to the business of "adult entertainment" if he chooses, but he may not do so using any of the assets

involved in the RICO violations. Under RICO, any assets related to the racketeering are subject to forfeiture and they were forfeited after Alexander (D) was given a full trial as well as the constitutional safeguards that accompany it. Therefore, there was no error in ordering the forfeiture of Defendant's business and assets.

DISSENT: (Kennedy, J.) The Government's destruction of a business that included protected items undermines free speech principles. The Court's decision serves as an indirect threat to those in the business of "adult entertainment" because it makes presumptively protected materials equally subject to seizure. This amounts to suppression of free speech, which the court finds disfavorable, and is not a mere punishment.

▶ ANALYSIS

This was not a clear-cut RICO violation, because the RICO violation was based on the obscenity conviction. The entire business was not adjudged to be obscene, yet the Defendant's entire business was forfeited under the RICO statute. It does not seem unreasonable that the Court could have outlined a formula to determine the revenue and assets derived from only the obscene material. This option would have been consistent with the intent of the forfeiture provision in RICO, while reducing the threat of any further constitutional violations. Furthermore, the dissent mentions that there are no prior cases that allow for the destruction of materials not adjudged obscene. Therefore, the result in this case was the equivalent to having the entire business adjudged obscene.

■■■

Quicknotes

PRIOR RESTRAINT A restriction imposed on speech imposed prior to its communication.

■■■

Watchtower Bible and Tract Society of New York, Inc. v. Village of Stratton

Jehovah's Witnesses (P) v. Village government (D)

536 U.S. 150 (2002).

NATURE OF CASE: Constitutional challenge to validity of village ordinance.

FACT SUMMARY: The Village of Stratton (D) passed an ordinance requiring door-to-door canvassers to first obtain a permit from the mayor. The coordinating society of Jehovah's Witnesses (P) challenged the validity of the ordinance on First Amendment grounds.

🏛 RULE OF LAW
A permit requirement for door-to-door canvassing is an unreasonable restriction on speech and violates the First Amendment.

FACTS: The Village of Stratton (D) passed an ordinance requiring any person to first obtain a permit from the mayor's office prior to engaging in door-to-door canvassing. Those requiring permits included religious proselytizers, political campaigners, and salespersons. There was no charge for the permit, but the applicant had to complete a detailed registration form. Village residents could file a form with the mayor's office prohibiting solicitation on their private property and could post "No Solicitation" signs to prevent even those with permits from entering private property, but few residents actually did so. The Watchtower Bible and Tract Society of New York, Inc. (Watchtower) (P) oversees the evangelism of Jehovah's Witnesses, which includes door-to-door preaching. Watchtower (P) challenged the validity of the ordinance on First Amendment grounds.

ISSUE: Is a permit requirement for door-to-door canvassing an unreasonable restriction on speech and a violation of the First Amendment?

HOLDING AND DECISION: (Stevens, J.) Yes. A permit requirement for door-to-door canvassing is an unreasonable restriction on speech and violates the First Amendment. The United States has a history of encouraging and accepting door-to-door canvassing as a vital communication tool for persons with few financial resources. Door-to-door proselytizing is also an important part of several religions and is in fact a requirement of the faith for Jehovah's Witnesses. The Village of Stratton (D) argues that its ordinance protected its citizens' privacy and safety, and protected against fraud. Citizens can safeguard their own privacy, however, by filing the appropriate "No Solicitation" form with the mayor's office or by simply not answering the uninvited knock at the door. While protecting citizen safety is an important consideration, nothing indicates that criminals are less likely to approach a private residence because of the permit requirement. Criminals could assume the role of a census taker or a person in need of a telephone and not be in violation of the ordinance. It is also possible to apply for the permit without verifying one's identity, so a criminal could receive a permit under a false name. Finally, as to the fraud argument, the ordinance is not narrowly tailored to protect against fraud because it does not apply only to commercial solicitations or those seeking financial contributions. The ordinance is broad enough that it could operate to prevent one neighbor from encouraging another to vote against the mayor unless that neighbor first sought a permit from the mayor. Anonymity can be an important component to free speech and an applicant surrenders that anonymity when required to first complete an application identifying himself. This Court often struck down similar prohibitions during World War II. It is just as unreasonable today as it was then. The ordinance is constitutionally invalid.

DISSENT: (Rehnquist, C.J.) The ordinance at issue here does not prohibit door-to-door canvassing but merely requires a permit, which the mayor does not have the discretion to refuse. Anyone completing the application receives the permit, which is a requirement this Court has held to be constitutional until today. The majority incorrectly applies strict scrutiny when intermediate scrutiny was all that was necessary, and this ordinance withstands intermediate scrutiny. Even applying strict scrutiny, the majority should not have so blithely dismissed the argument about citizen safety. A recent murder of two citizens in another town by persons posing as door-to-door canvassers certainly lends credence to that argument and the law should not be required to be a complete barrier to crime to be constitutional.

▶ ANALYSIS

The Sixth Circuit initially upheld the validity of the ordinance on the grounds that the expressed governmental interests in protections against crime and fraud were important ones and that the ordinance applied to all canvassers, not just Jehovah's Witnesses. The Watchtower (P) has historically fought such ordinances and has usually won on arguments that the ordinances violate the First Amendment rights of free speech, free association, and anonymity. As the majority noted, it is offensive to the American public to be required to inform the government prior to speaking to a neighbor.

Continued on next page.

Quicknotes

PRIOR RESTRAINT A restriction imposed on speech imposed prior to its communication.

STRICT SCRUTINY Method by which courts determine the constitutionality of a law, when a law affects a fundamental right. Under the test, the legislature must have had a compelling interest to enact the law and measures prescribed by the law must be the least restrictive means possible to accomplish its goal.

■━━■

Thomas & Windy City Hemp Development Board v. Chicago Park District

Permit applicants (P) v. City parks department (D)

534 U.S. 316 (2002).

NATURE OF CASE: Constitutional challenge to municipal-parks ordinance.

FACT SUMMARY: The Chicago Park District (D) required events involving 50-plus persons to obtain a permit prior to gathering on parkland. Petitioners (P) filed various applications for rallies advocating the legalization of marijuana; some were granted and others were not. Plaintiff challenged the permit ordinance as unconstitutional.

🏛 RULE OF LAW
The First Amendment guarantee of freedom of speech does not require specific procedural safeguards in content-neutral licensing schemes.

FACTS: The Chicago Park District (D), charged with overseeing the Chicago municipal parks, passed an ordinance requiring permits for large-scale activities held on park property. Applicants must apply for a permit if 50 or more persons will be present at the activity. The permit application must be approved or denied within fourteen days, and denial may only be based on one of 13 specific criteria. Appeal processes were included in the ordinance in the case of a denial. Thomas and the Windy City Hemp Development Board (Thomas) (P) filed various permit applications for rallies encouraging the legalization of marijuana. Some applications were granted and some were denied, but Thomas (P) challenged the constitutionality of the ordinance on its face because it did not provide certain procedural safeguards, such as effective judicial review.

ISSUE: Does the First Amendment guarantee of freedom of speech require specific procedural safeguards in content-neutral licensing schemes?

HOLDING AND DECISION: (Scalia, J.) No. The First Amendment guarantee of freedom of speech does not require specific procedural safeguards in content-neutral licensing schemes. This ordinance does not censor the content of the permit applicant's activities or speech, but may merely restrict the activity based on one of 13 criteria. For example, if another group has booked the park on the same day at the same time, the permit may be denied to the later applicant. Another category for denial is if the applicant is untruthful on the application. The 13 criteria do not give the Chicago Park District (D) unfettered discretion to approve or deny permits based on content of the permit-seekers' speech. This is completely unlike the content-based restrictions in the licensing scheme of *Freedman v. Maryland*, 380 U.S. 51 (1965). This Court required specific and extensive procedural safeguards in that case because the censorship was blatantly content-based. Not so here. This ordinance actually protects free speech and expression because it organizes and regulates the use of parkland for the benefit of all citizens. If anyone could come at any time with innumerable participants, free speech could be stifled as groups compete for limited space and attention. An adequate appeals process for permit denials is in place with this ordinance and the Chicago Park District (D) may only deny a permit for one of the delineated reasons. The ordinance is constitutional.

▶ *ANALYSIS*

The justices had historically split on cases rejecting First Amendment freedom of speech claims, but this case was a unanimous decision affirming the Tenth Circuit's decision. The justices successfully avoided the issue of defining "prompt" judicial response to an appeal of a permit denial. That issue would not be addressed until the 2004 decision in *City of Littleton, Colorado v. Z.J. Gifts D-4, L.L.C.*, 514 U.S. 774.

■===■

Quicknotes

CONTENT BASED Refers to statutes that regulate speech based on its content.

CONTENT NEUTRAL Refers to statutes that regulate speech regardless of its content.

■===■

City of Littleton, Colorado v. Z.J. Gifts D-4, L.L.C.

City government (D) v. Provider of adult books (P)

514 U.S. 774 (2004).

NATURE OF CASE: Facial challenge to constitutionality of licensing ordinance.

FACT SUMMARY: Plaintiff challenged the constitutionality of the defendant city's licensing ordinance for adult businesses because the ordinance did not require a prompt judicial decision if the license was denied.

🏛 RULE OF LAW
An "adult business" licensing ordinance is constitutional although it does not guarantee a prompt judicial decision on an appeal to the denial of a license.

FACTS: Z.J. Gifts D-4, L.L.C. (ZJ) (P) began selling "adult" books in its store. The City of Littleton, Colorado (Littleton) (D) had required "adult businesses" to obtain a license. The license was denied if the applicant fell within one of eight objective categories. Upon denial, the First Amendment guarantees the applicant prompt judicial access based on the Supreme Court decision in *FW/PBS, Inc. v. Dallas*, 493 U.S. 215 (1990). Rather than applying for a license, however, ZJ (P) challenged the constitutionality of the ordinance because the ordinance did not explicitly provide for a prompt judicial determination of the appeal.

ISSUE: Is an "adult business" licensing ordinance constitutional although it does not guarantee a prompt judicial decision on an appeal to the denial of a license?

HOLDING AND DECISION: (Breyer, J.) Yes. An "adult business" licensing ordinance is constitutional although it does not guarantee a prompt judicial decision on an appeal to the denial of a license. This Court's decision in *FW/PBS* guaranteed prompt judicial access, which includes a prompt decision. The Colorado state courts will respond within an appropriate timeframe and can accelerate that time frame on a case-by-case basis. Unreasonable delays of license appeals result in First Amendment violations because free speech is unconstitutionally suppressed during the interim. The Colorado courts are aware of this danger and will act accordingly. Littleton's (D) ordinance does not result in complete censorship of "adult businesses" if a license is denied, so special rules need not be written to force acceleration of judicial decisions. The eight denial categories are objective categories, and the city has no discretion in granting or denying a license to an applicant falling within one of the categories. If one applicant does not meet the licensing criteria, another one will and the "adult business" niche will be filled. Special rules would only be necessary if license denial to any one applicant resulted in complete censorship of "adult" materials. Finally,

Littleton (D) does not have to include every judicial review safeguard in each ordinance. The safeguards inherent in this ordinance are sufficient and the ordinance is constitutional.

▶ ANALYSIS

The Tenth Circuit found the ordinance to be unconstitutional because the ordinance did not expressly require prompt judicial decisions when licenses were denied, which could result in unreasonable delays and First Amendment infringements on the free speech rights of the adult business owners. Although the Supreme Court disagreed, critics contend that the Court did not actually solve anything in determining that the ordinance did include a requirement for prompt judicial decisions. The question becomes, "How prompt is prompt?" If other court decisions take months, so could appeals to license denials, so advocates for adult businesses were not encouraged by this case.

▬■

Quicknotes

FIRST AMENDMENT RIGHTS Rights conferred by the First Amendment to the U.S. Constitution prohibiting Congress from enacting any law respecting an establishment of religion, prohibiting the free exercise of religion, abridging freedom of speech or the press, the right of peaceful assembly and the right to petition for a redress of grievances.

▬■

United States v. National Treasury Employees Union

Federal government (D) v. Union (P)

513 U.S. 454 (1995).

NATURE OF CASE: Appeal from a judgment granting plaintiff's motion for summary judgment in an action challenging the constitutionality of a federal law.

FACT SUMMARY: After Congress enacted a law broadly prohibiting federal employees from accepting any compensation for making speeches or writing articles in their spare time, the National Treasury Employees Union (P) and others filed suit, challenging the constitutionality of the honoraria ban.

🏛 RULE OF LAW
Congress may not prohibit federal civil servants from accepting pay for speeches and articles.

FACTS: In the Ethics Reform Act of 1989, Congress broadly prohibited federal employees from accepting any compensation or honorarium for making speeches or writing articles. The 1989 Act defined "honorarium" to encompass any compensation paid to a government employee for "an appearance, speech or article." The 1992 Appropriations Act amended that definition to exclude any series of appearances, speeches, or articles unrelated to the employee's official duties or status. The National Treasury Employees Union (P) and others filed suit, challenging the constitutionality of the honoraria ban. The district court granted the Union's (P) motion for summary judgment, holding the statute unconstitutional insofar as it applied to executive branch employees of the United States government (D) and enjoined the government (D) from enforcing the statute against any executive branch employee. The court of appeals affirmed. The government (D) appealed.

ISSUE: May Congress prohibit federal civil servants from accepting pay for speeches and articles?

HOLDING AND DECISION: (Stevens, J.) No. Congress may not prohibit federal civil servants from accepting pay for speeches and articles. Congress shall make no law abridging the freedom of speech. Even though members of the Union (P) work for the government (D), they have not relinquished the First Amendment rights they would otherwise enjoy as citizens to comment on matters of public interest. The Union (P) members' expressive activities in this case fall within the protected category of citizen comment on matters of public concern rather than employee comment on matters related to personal status in the workplace. High-ranking officials will not likely curtail speaking engagements simply because of a lack of compensation. However, the denial of compensation for lower paid employees will certainly diminish their creative output. This is an unnecessary loss. The ban on all honoraria is overinclusive. Therefore, the judgment

granting an injunction against enforcement of the ban as applied to the Union (P) is affirmed, but it is reversed as to relief granted to parties not before the Court.

DISSENT: (Rehnquist, C.J.) Because there is only a limited burden on the Union's (P) First Amendment rights, Congress reasonably could have determined that its paramount interests in preventing impropriety and the appearance of impropriety in its work force justified the honoraria ban. Thus, the court of appeals should be affirmed only insofar as its judgment affirmed the injunction against the enforcement of the statute as applied to executive branch employees below grade GS-16 who seek honoraria unrelated to their government employment.

▶ ANALYSIS

Congress may impose restraints on the job-related speech of public employees that would be plainly unconstitutional if applied to the public at large. However, when a court is required to determine the validity of such a restraint, it must arrive at a balance between the interests of the employee as a citizen in commenting upon matters of public concern and the interest of the state, as an employer, in promoting the efficiency of the public services it performs through its employees. The invalidation of the ethics law in *National Treasury* was one of four federal laws declared unconstitutional during the 1994-1995 term, a relatively high number in light of the fact that the Court has only invalidated 129 laws in its 205-year history.

■=■

Quicknotes

FIRST AMENDMENT RIGHTS Rights conferred by the First Amendment to the U.S. Constitution prohibiting Congress from enacting any law respecting an establishment of religion, prohibiting the free exercise of religion, abridging freedom of speech or the press, the right of peaceful assembly and the right to petition for a redress of grievances.

■=■

West Virginia State Board of Education v. Barnette

State (D) v. Expelled student (P)

319 U.S. 624 (1943).

NATURE OF CASE: Appeal from decision invalidating a state statute requiring a flag salute in the public schools.

FACT SUMMARY: After he was expelled from school for failing to salute the flag as mandated by state statute, Barnette (P) challenged the constitutionality of the statute.

🏛 RULE OF LAW
A state may not condition the right to public education on a compulsory flag salute and pledge of allegiance to the flag.

FACTS: Barnette (P), son of members of Jehovah's Witnesses, was expelled from school when he refused to salute the flag as mandated by a West Virginia statute. The Witnesses proffered a version of the required pledge acceptable to them, but the state rejected this version. The district court found for Barnette (P), and the West Virginia State Board of Education (D) appealed.

ISSUE: May a state condition the right to public education on a compulsory flag salute and pledge of allegiance to the flag?

HOLDING AND DECISION: (Jackson, J.) No. A state may not condition the right to public education on a compulsory flag salute and pledge of allegiance to the flag. There is no doubt that, in connection with the pledges, the flag salute is a form of utterance. Symbolism is a primitive but effective way of communicating ideas. It is now a commonplace that censorship or suppression of expression of opinion is tolerated by our Constitution only when the expression presents a clear and present danger of action of a kind the state is empowered to prevent and punish. But here the power of compulsion is invoked without any allegation that remaining passive during a flag salute ritual creates a clear and present danger that would justify an effort even to muffle expression. To sustain the compulsory flag salute would require this Court to say that a Bill of Rights that guards the individual's right to speak his own mind left it open to public authorities to compel him to utter what is not in his mind. The Fourteenth Amendment protects the citizen against the state itself and all of its creatures—boards of education not excepted. It is important to note that, while it is the Fourteenth Amendment that bears directly upon the state, it is the more specific limiting principles of the First Amendment that finally govern this case.

DISSENT: (Frankfurter, J.) A judge's own opinion about the wisdom or evil of a law should be excluded altogether when one is making decisions on the bench. The only opinion of our own that matters is a judge's opinion of whether legislators could with reason have enacted such a law. I cannot believe this Court has the authority to deny to the State of West Virginia a legitimate legislative end—the promotion of good citizenship.

▶ ANALYSIS

The Court declared that the freedom to differ would be a mere shadow of freedom, if it were limited to things that do not matter much. The test of the freedom's substance is the right to differ as to things that touch the heart of the existing order. Moreover, that states are educating the young for citizenship is reason for scrupulous protection of constitutional freedoms of the individual. Although this action was brought chiefly on religious grounds, the Court appeared to ground its decision on a broad reading of First Amendment rights of free speech and expression.

■=■

Quicknotes

FIRST AMENDMENT RIGHTS Rights conferred by the First Amendment to the U.S. Constitution prohibiting Congress from enacting any law respecting an establishment of religion, prohibiting the free exercise of religion, abridging freedom of speech or the press, the right of peaceful assembly and the right to petition for a redress of grievances.

RIGHT OF FREE SPEECH Right guaranteed by the First Amendment to the U.S. Constitution prohibiting Congress from enacting any law abridging freedom of speech or the press.

■=■

Rumsfeld v. Forum for Academic and Institutional Rights, Inc.

U.S. Secretary of Defense (D) v. Association of law schools (P)

547 U.S. 47 (2006).

NATURE OF CASE: Suit challenging a federal statute's ability to condition federal educational funds on U.S. military recruiters having equal access to educational institutions.

FACT SUMMARY: Law schools restricted access to military recruiters because of the military's policy of excluding openly homosexual persons from military service.

🏛 RULE OF LAW
The Solomon Amendment does not infringe on the freedoms of speech and association of U.S. law schools by conditioning the receipt of federal educational funds on the law schools' grant of equal access to military recruiters.

FACTS: An association of U.S. law schools, the Forum for Academic and Institutional Rights, Inc. (FAIR) (P), protested the U.S. military's policy of excluding openly homosexual persons by restricting military recruiters' access to the schools' facilities and students. Congress responded by enacting the Solomon Amendment, 10 U.S.C. § 983, which provided that an entire educational institution would lose federal funding if any part of the institution fails to provide access to military recruiters that is equal to the access enjoyed by all other recruiters. FAIR (P) sued, alleging that the Solomon Amendment violated the law schools' (P) rights to freedom of speech and association. The trial court ruled for the government (D), but the court of appeals reversed. The government (D) sought further review in the Supreme Court.

ISSUE: Does the Solomon Amendment infringe on the freedoms of speech and association of U.S. law schools by conditioning the receipt of federal educational funds on the law schools' grant of equal access to military recruiters?

HOLDING AND DECISION: (Roberts, C.J.) No. The Solomon Amendment does not infringe on the freedoms of speech and association of U.S. law schools by conditioning the receipt of federal educational funds on the law schools' grant of equal access to military recruiters. The Solomon Amendment requires the law schools (P) to permit military recruiters the same access to facilities and students that are granted to any other employers; if a law school (P) fails to permit such equal access, the entire institution will lose certain federal funds. Congress enacted the Solomon Amendment pursuant to the Constitution's Spending Clause, and not under Congress's military authority, but that choice does not affect the great judicial deference required for a statute that promotes military recruiting. The condition imposed on universities in this case clearly would satisfy the First Amendment even if it

the condition had been passed directly under Congress's military authority, and the condition, therefore, also satisfies the First Amendment if, as here, it was passed indirectly under the Spending Clause. The law schools (P) remain totally free to say whatever they please about military policies: the statute regulates conduct, not speech, toward the goal of ensuring equal access for military recruiters. This freedom exists even though the law schools (P) must provide notices to students about military recruiters, and even though the schools (P) must to some extent accommodate speech made by the military. These requirements are not tantamount to compelling the law schools (P) to express the military's message; unlike prior cases, the complaining party here does not have its own speech affected in any way by the speech that it must accommodate. Ultimately, a law school's (P) decision to permit access to a recruiter simply is not inherently expressive, as prior cases require. Moreover, the Solomon Amendment also fails to regulate conduct in violation of the First Amendment. The expressive purpose of a law school's (P) restriction on certain recruiters is not overwhelmingly apparent from the fact of the restriction itself, unlike, for example, the conduct involved in burning the American flag. Here, any understanding of a school's (P) expressive purpose arises solely from other speech by the law schools (P) that merely accompanies the regulated conduct. The Solomon Amendment also does not impose an improper incidental burden on speech because the statute promotes a substantial government interest that would not be achieved as effectively without the regulation. Finally, the Amendment also satisfies the freedom of association guaranteed by the First Amendment because the statute does not force law schools (P) to accept expressive members whom they do not want. Reversed.

▶ *ANALYSIS*

In this unanimous opinion, the Court holds that the Solomon Amendment does not violate FAIR's (P) First Amendment rights to freedom of speech and association. The great distance between the non-expressive speech compelled here and the strongly expressive speech compelled in, for example, *West Virginia Bd. of Educ. v. Barnette*, 319 U.S. 624 (1943), helped to fatally undermine the speech claims in this case. Similarly, the statute's failure to require FAIR (P) to admit military recruiters as expressive members of the law schools (P) greatly weakened FAIR's (P) freedom-of-association claim, as well.

■▬■

Continued on next page.

Quicknotes

FIRST AMENDMENT Prohibits Congress from enacting any law respecting an establishment of religion, prohibiting the free exercise of religion, abridging freedom of speech or the press, the right of peaceful assembly and the right to petition for a redress of grievances.

■━■

McIntyre v. Ohio Elections Commn.

Leaflet distributor (P) v. State agency (D)

514 U.S. 334 (1995).

NATURE OF CASE: Appeal from the reinstatement of a fine in an action charging violation of state election laws.

FACT SUMMARY: McIntyre (P) protested the imposition of a fine under Ohio (P) state law for her distribution of anonymous leaflets protesting a proposed school tax levy to be considered in an upcoming election.

🏛 RULE OF LAW
Individuals have a free-speech right to pass out anonymous leaflets on political topics.

FACTS: When the superintendent of schools planned to discuss an imminent referendum on a proposed school tax levy, McIntyre (P) distributed leaflets to persons attending the public school meeting, expressing her opposition to the levy. Some of her handbills identified her as the author, while others purported to express the views of "CONCERNED PARENTS AND TAXPAYERS." After the levy finally passed on the third try, a school official filed a complaint with the Ohio Elections Commission (D), charging that McIntyre's (P) distribution of unsigned leaflets violated § 3599.09(A) of the Ohio Code. The Commission (D) agreed, imposing a fine of $100. The court of common pleas reversed, finding that McIntyre (P) did not mislead the public or act in a surreptitious manner. The court concluded that the statute was unconstitutional as applied to her conduct. The court of appeals reinstated the fine, and the state supreme court affirmed. McIntyre (P) appealed.

ISSUE: Do individuals have a free-speech right to pass out anonymous leaflets on political topics?

HOLDING AND DECISION: (Stevens, J.) Yes. Individuals have a free-speech right to pass out anonymous leaflets on political topics. Where a law burdens core political speech, the restriction will be upheld only if it is narrowly tailored to serve an overriding state interest. An author generally is free to decide whether or not to disclose her true identity. The Ohio (D) statute contains no language limiting its application to fraudulent, false, or libelous statements. As the facts of this case demonstrate, the ordinance plainly applies even when there is no hint of falsity or libel. Section 3599.09(A) does not control the mechanics of the electoral process. It is a regulation of pure speech. Moreover, it is a direct regulation of the content of speech. The speech in which Mrs. McIntyre (P) engaged is the essence of First Amendment expression. Under the Constitution, anonymous pamphleteering is not a pernicious, fraudulent practice, but an honorable tradition of advocacy and of dissent. Anonymity is a shield from the tyranny of the majority.

CONCURRENCE: (Thomas, J.) Ohio's (D) election law is inconsistent with the First Amendment. However, instead of asking whether an honorable tradition of anonymous speech has existed throughout American history or what the value of anonymous speech might be, we should determine whether the phrase "freedom of speech, or of the press," as originally understood, protects anonymous political leafletting. It does.

DISSENT: (Scalia, J.) To prove that anonymous electioneering was used frequently is not to establish that it is a constitutional right. There is no reason why an anonymous leaflet is any more honorable than an anonymous phone call or an anonymous letter. It facilitates wrong by eliminating accountability, which is ordinarily the very purpose of the anonymity. Where anonymity is needed to avoid threats, harassment, or reprisals, the First Amendment will require an exemption from the Ohio (D) law. But it is not necessary to strike it down on the ground that all anonymous communication is in our society traditionally sacrosanct.

▶ ANALYSIS

As this case demonstrates, the absence of the author's name on a document does not necessarily protect either that person or a distributor of a forbidden document from being held responsible for compliance with the election code. The Court rejected Ohio's (D) reliance on the opinions in *First Nat. Bank of Boston v. Bellotti*, 435 U.S. 765 (1978), and *Buckley v. Valeo*, 424 U.S. 1 (1976). *Bellotti* concerned the scope of First Amendment protection afforded to corporations, while the relevant portion of *Buckley* concerned mandatory disclosure of campaign-related expenditures. Neither case involved a prohibition of anonymous campaign literature.

∎══∎

Quicknotes

FIRST AMENDMENT Prohibits Congress from enacting any law respecting an establishment of religion, prohibiting the free exercise of religion, abridging freedom of speech or the press, the right of peaceful assembly and the right to petition for a redress of grievances.

∎══∎

Rust v. Sullivan

Doctors/Grantees (P) v. Government agency (D)

500 U.S. 173 (1991).

NATURE OF CASE: Review of order dismissing challenge to Public Health Service Act regulations.

FACT SUMMARY: Rust (P) challenged government regulations promulgated under the Public Health Service Act, which prohibited grantees from offering or advocating abortion as a method of family planning.

🏛 RULE OF LAW
The government may prohibit grantees of funds given under the Public Health Service Act from offering or advocating abortion as a method of family planning.

FACTS: Title X of the Public Health Service Act, enacted in 1970, created a program wherein medical clinics could receive funds to be used for family planning services. In 1988, the Department of Health and Human Services (HHS) (D) promulgated clarifying regulations. The regulations provided that no grantee could use funds for performing abortions, promoting abortion, or giving abortion referrals in the context of family planning. These regulations were challenged as unconstitutional. The district and appellate courts ruled the regulations valid, and the Supreme Court granted review.

ISSUE: May the government prohibit grantees of funds given under the Public Health Service Act from offering or advocating abortion as a method of family planning?

HOLDING AND DECISION: (Rehnquist, C.J.) Yes. The government may prohibit grantees of funds given under the Public Health Service Act from offering or advocating abortion as a method of family planning. Congress has broad discretion under the Spending Clause to use federal funds to promote policy in areas where it cannot directly regulate. Congress is completely free to conclude that certain policies or practices are better than others and fund those policies of choice. The regulation prohibiting the giving of abortion counseling or referrals is not an infringement on First Amendment rights; it is the government's saying how its money is to be spent. Similarly, no woman's reproductive rights are being curtailed; the regulations merely require that one seeking to exercise such rights go somewhere other than a Title X medical facility. In short, the regulations here do not infringe on any constitutional rights but merely ensure that Congress's intent in acting under the Spending Clause is effected.

DISSENT: (Blackmun, J.) The Court has, in this case, upheld a viewpoint-based suppression of speech solely because it is imposed on those dependent upon the government for economic support. This raises serious constitutional concerns.

▶ ANALYSIS

The issue of federal spending on abortions has long been controversial. Not long after *Roe v. Wade*, 410 U.S. 113 (1973), was decided, Congress prohibited the use of Medicare funds for abortions. This was upheld, on reasoning similar to that used in the present action, in *Maher v. Roe*, 432 U.S. 464 (1977). The First Amendment implications arise in the broader free-speech context. The Court in *Rust* did not place distinct boundaries on the kinds of government-funded speech that could be limited. For example, if the government was hostile to a particular policy that might arise in a case where a Legal Services Corporation lawyer is representing an indigent client, it is unclear whether the LSC lawyer's case theory could be involuntarily altered so as not to offend government policy.

■=■

Quicknotes

SPENDING POWER The power delegated to Congress by the Constitution to spend money in providing for the nation's welfare.

■=■

Legal Services Corp. v. Velazquez

Federal legal aid funding organization (D) v. Lawyers for indigents (P)

531 U.S. 533 (2001).

NATURE OF CASE: Appeal from a decision that a Legal Services Corporation (LSC) program restriction violates the First Amendment.

FACT SUMMARY: Legal Services Corporation (LSC) (D) distributes funds appropriated by Congress to local grantee organizations providing free legal assistance to indigent clients. Congress prohibited LSC funding of any organization that represented clients in an effort to amend or otherwise challenge existing welfare law. Lawyers employed by LSC grantees (P) challenged the restriction as a violation of the First Amendment.

🏛 RULE OF LAW

A Legal Services Corporation (LSC) program restriction that prohibits federal LSC funding of any organization that represents indigent clients in an effort to amend or otherwise challenge existing welfare law violates the First Amendment.

FACTS: The Legal Services Corporation (LSC) (D) was established as a nonprofit corporation to distribute funds appropriated by Congress to local grantee organizations providing free legal assistance to indigent clients. Section 504(a)(16) of a 1996 appropriations act placed a condition on the use of LSC (D) funds that prohibited LSC funding of any organization that represented clients in an effort to amend or otherwise challenge existing welfare law. As interpreted by the government, the statute bars grantees from continuing representation in a welfare matter even where a constitutional or statutory validity challenge becomes apparent after representation is well under way. Also, the statute bars a lawyer from arguing to a court that a state law conflicts with federal law or that either a state or federal statute is unconstitutional. However, grantees may argue that an erroneous factual determination was made, or that a term in an existing welfare statute was misread or misapplied. Lawyers employed by LSC grantees (P) filed suit to declare, inter alia, the restriction invalid as a violation of the First Amendment. The district court denied them a preliminary injunction, but the Second Circuit reversed. The Supreme Court granted review.

ISSUE: Does a Legal Services Corporation (LSC) program restriction that prohibits federal LSC funding of any organization that represents indigent clients in an effort to amend or otherwise challenge existing welfare law violate the First Amendment?

HOLDING AND DECISION: (Kennedy, J.) Yes. A Legal Services Corporation (LSC) program restriction that prohibits federal LSC funding of any organization that represents indigent clients in an effort to amend or

otherwise challenge existing welfare law violates the First Amendment. LSC (D) claims that *Rust v. Sullivan*, 500 U.S. 173 (1991), in which the Court upheld a restriction prohibiting doctors employed by federally funded family planning clinics from discussing abortion with their patients, supports the restriction here. However, the Court has since explained that the *Rust* counseling activities amounted to governmental speech, and that viewpoint-based funding decisions will be sustained in instances in which the government is itself the speaker, or instances, like *Rust*, in which the government uses private speakers to transmit information pertaining to its own program. Although the government has the latitude to ensure that its own message is being delivered, neither that latitude nor its rationale applies to subsidies for private speech in every instance. The LSC program was designed to facilitate private speech, not to promote a governmental message. An LSC attorney speaks on behalf of a private, indigent client in a welfare benefits claim, whereas the government's message is delivered by the attorney defending the benefits decision. The attorney's advice to the client and advocacy to the courts cannot be classified as governmental speech even under a generous understanding of that concept. In this vital respect this suit is distinguishable from *Rust*. The private nature of the instant speech and the extent of LSC's regulation of private expression are indicated further by the circumstance that the government seeks to control an existing medium of expression in ways which distort its usual functioning. Cases involving a limited forum, though not controlling, provide instruction for evaluating restrictions in governmental subsidies. Here the program presumes that private, nongovernmental speech is necessary, and a substantial restriction is placed upon that speech. By providing subsidies to LSC, the government seeks to facilitate suits for benefits by using the state and federal courts and the independent bar on which they depend for the proper performance of their duties and responsibilities. Restricting LSC attorneys in advising their clients and in presenting arguments and analyses to the courts distorts the legal system by altering the attorneys' traditional role in much the same way broadcast systems or student publication networks were changed in limited forum cases. The government may not design a subsidy to effect such a serious and fundamental restriction on the advocacy of attorneys and the functioning of the judiciary. An informed, independent judiciary presumes an informed, independent bar. However, the instant restriction prevents LSC attorneys from advising the courts of serious

Continued on next page.

statutory validity questions. It also threatens severe impairment of the judicial function by sifting out cases presenting constitutional challenges in order to insulate the government's laws from judicial inquiry. The result of this restriction would be two tiers of cases. There would be lingering doubt whether an LSC attorney's truncated representation had resulted in complete analysis of the case, full advice to the client, and proper presentation to the court; and the courts and the public would come to question the adequacy and fairness of professional representations when the attorney avoided all reference to statutory validity and constitutional authority questions. A scheme so inconsistent with accepted separation-of-powers principles is an insufficient basis to sustain or uphold the restriction on speech. That LSC attorneys can withdraw does not make the restriction harmless, for the statute is an attempt to draw lines around the LSC program to exclude from litigation arguments and theories Congress finds unacceptable but which by their nature are within the courts' province to consider. The restriction is even more problematic because in cases where the attorney withdraws, the indigent client is unlikely to find other counsel. There may be no alternative source of vital information on the client's constitutional or statutory rights, in stark contrast to *Rust*, where a patient could receive both governmentally subsidized counseling and consultation with independent or affiliate organizations. Finally, the restriction insulates the government's interpretation of the Constitution from judicial challenge. The Constitution does not permit the government to confine litigants and their attorneys in this manner. When private speech is involved, even Congress's antecedent funding decision cannot be aimed at the suppression of ideas thought inimical to the government's own interests.

DISSENT: (Scalia, J.) The majority's distinguishing *Rust* on the basis that the program in Rust subsidized government speech, whereas the LSC funds private speech, is extremely unpersuasive. In *Rust*, the doctors' confidential advice could hardly be said to constitute government speech, and the doctors had a professional obligation to serve the interests of their patients, just as the lawyers here have a similar obligation to serve the interests of their clients. Furthermore, the majority's assertion that *Rust* is distinguishable because the welfare funding restriction "seeks to use an existing medium of expression and to control it . . . in ways which distort its usual functioning" is wrong on the law and the facts. It is wrong on the law because there is no precedent for the novel proposition that the First Amendment has anything to do with government funding that—though it does not actually abridge anyone's speech—"distorts an existing medium of expression." The only basis for distinguishing *Rust* is that in that case, even patients who wished to receive abortion counseling could receive nonabortion services offered by the federally funded clinic, whereas here, some potential LSC (D) clients may not get any representation where their case raises a welfare reform claim. This difference from *Rust*, however, has no

bearing on the First Amendment issue, which is whether the funding scheme has a coercive effect on those who do not hold the subsidized position. In sum, the LSC (D) subsidy does not prevent speech nor coerce anyone to change speech, and is distinguishable in all relevant respects from *Rust*.

▶ *ANALYSIS*

This case continues the inconsistent application of the unconstitutional conditions doctrine, as is made clear by the majority's and dissent's core disagreement over whether *Rust v. Sullivan* is distinguishable. Because the cases in this area are difficult, if not impossible, to reconcile, it has been suggested that they in fact cannot be reconciled and that they simply turn on whether the Court wishes to uphold or strike down a particular condition.

■═■

Quicknotes

FIRST AMENDMENT Prohibits Congress from enacting any law respecting an establishment of religion, prohibiting the free exercise of religion, abridging freedom of speech or the press, the right of peaceful assembly and the right to petition for a redress of grievances.

■═■

Schenck v. United States

Publisher (D) v. Federal government (P)

249 U.S. 47 (1919).

NATURE OF CASE: Appeal from conviction for conspiracy to violate the Espionage Act, conspiracy to use the mails for transmissions of non-mailable material, and unlawful use of the mails.

FACT SUMMARY: During a time of war, Schenck (D) mailed circulars to draftees that were calculated to cause insubordination in the armed services and to obstruct the U.S. recruiting and enlistment program in violation of military laws.

🏛 **RULE OF LAW**
The test to determine the constitutionality of a statute restricting free speech is whether, under the circumstances, the speech is of such a nature as to create a clear and present danger that it will bring about the substantive evils that Congress has a right to prevent.

FACTS: During a time of war, Schenck (D) mailed circulars to draftees. The circulars stated that the Conscription Act was unconstitutional and likened conscription to conviction. They intimated that conscription was a monstrous wrong against humanity in the interest of Wall Street's chosen few and described nonconscription arguments as coming from cunning politicians and a mercenary capitalist press. They urged: "Do not submit to intimidation," but advised only peaceful actions such as a petition to repeal the Conscription Act. Schenck (D) did not deny that the jury could find that the circulars could have no purpose except to influence draftees to obstruct the carrying out of the draft.

ISSUE: Does the right to freedom of speech depend upon the circumstances in which the speech is spoken?

HOLDING AND DECISION: (Holmes, J.) Yes. The character of every act depends on the circumstance in which it is done. The most stringent protection of free speech would not protect a person's falsely shouting fire in a theatre and causing a panic. "The question in every case is whether the words are used in such circumstances and are of such a nature as to create a clear and present danger that they will bring about the substantive evils that Congress has a right to prevent. It is a question of proximity and degree." During a war, things that could be said during peaceful times may be such a hindrance to the war effort that they will not be permitted.

▶ **ANALYSIS**

The Court's first significant encounter with the problem of articulating the scope of constitutionally protected speech came in a series of cases involving agitation against the draft and war during World War I [*Schenck; Frohwerk v. United States*, 249 U.S. 204 (1919); *Debs v. United States*, 249 U.S. 211 (1919)]. *Schenck* announces the "clear and present danger" test, the test for determining the validity of legislation regulating speech. In *Schenck*, Justice Holmes rejected perfect immunity for speech. But he also rejected a far more restrictive, far more widely supported, alternative test: that "any tendency in speech to produce bad acts, no matter how remote, would suffice to validate a repressive statute."

■═■

Quicknotes

CLEAR AND PRESENT DANGER TEST Doctrine that restraints on freedom of speech are permissible if the speech incites persons to engage in unlawful conduct.

■═■

Frohwerk v. United States

Conspirator (D) v. Federal government (P)

249 U.S. 204 (1919).

NATURE OF THE CASE: Appeal of a conviction under the Espionage Act of 1917.

FACT SUMMARY: United States (P) contends that during time of war, certain types of speech are not protected.

🏛 RULE OF LAW
During time of war, the "clear and present danger" test will determine whether speech is protected.

FACTS: Frohwerk (D) was indicted on 13 counts of conspiracy to violate the Espionage Act of 1917. Frohwerk (D) and one Carl Gleeser published and circulated the newspaper, the *Missouri Staats Zeitung*, that contained articles critical of the U.S. involvement in World War I, and even contained some words of warning to the U.S. The U.S. Government alleged that in his publication, Frohwerk (D) attempted to cause disloyalty and refusal of duty in the U.S. military. Frohwerk was convicted on all but one count.

ISSUE: During time of war, will the clear and present danger test determine whether speech is protected?

HOLDING AND DECISION: (Holmes, J.) Yes. There did not seem to be any special effort to reach or influence men subject to the draft. However, the Court is unable to determine the desired result of the various articles as well as whether the publishers had any idea that articles would influence masses of people.

▶ ANALYSIS

The Government has the right to restrict speech that presents a "clear and present danger." The test is whether the speech of a certain nature in a certain circumstance will bring about "the substantive evils that Congress has a right to prevent." See *Schenck v. United States*, 249 U.S. 47 (1919).

■═■

Quicknotes

CLEAR AND PRESENT DANGER TEST Doctrine that restraints on freedom of speech are permissible if the speech incites persons to engage in unlawful conduct.

■═■

Debs v. United States

Accused inciter (D) v. Federal government (P)

249 U.S. 211 (1919).

NATURE OF THE CASE: Appeal of a conviction of the Espionage Act of 1917.

FACT SUMMARY: United States (P) contends that during times of war, certain types of speech are not protected.

🏛 RULE OF LAW
During time of war, the "clear and present danger" test will determine whether speech is protected.

FACTS: Debs (D) was indicted pursuant to the Espionage Act of 1917. Prior to the indictment, he (D) delivered a speech where he encouraged the obstruction of the military recruitment services. Debs (D) was accused of causing, or attempting to cause, insubordination and refusal of duty in the U.S. military during a public speech. He was also accused of obstructing, or attempting to obstruct, recruitment and enlistment in the U.S. military during a public speech. Debs (D) was convicted.

ISSUE: During time of war, will the clear and present danger test determine whether speech is protected?

HOLDING AND DECISION: (Holmes, J.) Yes. The defendant did encourage the obstruction of military recruitment. In addition, he also encouraged insubordination because the jury was instructed that anyone enrolled under the Act of May 18, 1917, would be considered part of the U.S. military.

▶ ANALYSIS

Contrast this case and the *Frohwerk* case, 249 U.S. 204 (1919), with Justice Holmes's dissenting opinion in *Abrams v. United States*, 250 U.S. 616 (1919). That dissent seems to be contrary to Justice Holmes's earlier opinions, but the difference appears to be that in *Abrams*, Justice Holmes did not feel that the defendant's intent was to impede the U.S. war effort. Even if a defendant's expression of opinions is "fraught with death," Justice Holmes felt it should have some protection if it is not imminently threatening.

■══■

Quicknotes

CLEAR AND PRESENT DANGER TEST Doctrine that restraints on freedom of speech are permissible if the speech incites persons to engage in unlawful conduct.

■══■

Abrams v. United States

Russian immigrants (D) v. Federal government (P)

250 U.S. 616 (1919).

NATURE OF CASE: Appeal of convictions under the Espionage Act.

FACT SUMMARY: Russian immigrants (D) issued fliers that advocated a general strike in ammunition factories to prevent ammunition from being used against Russian revolutionaries.

🏛 RULE OF LAW
The United States may constitutionally restrict speech that has the intended effect of hindering the United States in a war effort by means of riots and sedition.

FACTS: During World War I, in 1918, the United States sent forces to Russia following the overthrow of the Czarist government as part of a strategic operation against Germany on the eastern front. Russian immigrants (D) to the U.S. circulated literature advocating a general strike in ammunition plants to hinder the U.S. effort, as they perceived it, to crush the revolutionary struggle in Russia. The Russian immigrants (D) were charged under the Espionage Act for inciting actions that hindered the U.S. war effort. Abrams (D) and others appealed.

ISSUE: Can the U.S. government properly restrict speech that has the intended effect of hindering the United States in a war effort by means of riots and sedition?

HOLDING AND DECISION: (Clarke, J.) Yes. The United States may constitutionally restrict speech that has the intended effect of hindering the United States in a war effort by means of riots and sedition. Individuals may be held accountable for the intended consequences of their actions. While speech is protected by the Constitution, it is not without limits. When speech is intended to incite riots and rebellion in such a critical time as that of war, it cannot be given the protection normally accorded to speech in the United States. Here, the Russian immigrants (D) hoped to generate a sympathetic revolution in the United States for the purpose of defeating military plans in Europe. Such a goal was so contrary to the concerns of the United States during time of war that it could not be permitted to proceed. Affirmed.

DISSENT: (Holmes, J.) This decision deeply undermines the liberties that the First Amendment was drafted to protect. Expression of dissenting opinions is the very foundation of freedom. It is only the present danger of immediate evil or an intent to bring it about that warrants Congress's setting a limit to expression of opinion. These convictions on the basis of two leaflets should not be sustained.

▶ ANALYSIS

Justice Holmes's famous dissent sounds as though the contentious words require a greater immediacy of threat than he indicated in his opinion in *Schenck v. United States*, 249 U.S. 47 (1919), which articulated the clear and present danger test. Commentators have found support for this interpretation in other writings of Justice Holmes. It appears that he realized the need to leave some element in place to protect speech, even while permitting some level of protection against dangerous speech.

■==■

Quicknotes

CLEAR AND PRESENT DANGER TEST Doctrine that restraints on freedom of speech are permissible if the speech incites persons to engage in unlawful conduct.

■==■

Gitlow v. New York

Publisher (D) v. State (P)

268 U.S. 652 (1925).

NATURE OF CASE: Appeal from a conviction for criminal anarchy.

FACT SUMMARY: Gitlow (D) printed and circulated literature advocating a Communist revolt against the U.S. government.

🏛 RULE OF LAW
Under its police powers, a state may validly forbid any speech or publication that has a tendency to produce action dangerous to public security, even where such speech or publication presents no clear and present danger to the security of the public.

FACTS: Gitlow (D) was a member of the Left Wing Section of the Socialist Party in New York, and he was responsible for printing the official organ of the left wing called the *Revolutionary Age*. In this paper, Gitlow (D) printed articles advocating the accomplishment of the Communist revolution through militant revolutionary socialism. Gitlow (D) further advocated a class struggle mobilization of the proletariat through mass industrial revolts and political strikes to conquer and destroy the U.S. government and replace it with a dictatorship of the proletariat. Although there was no evidence that these writings resulted in any such action, Gitlow (D) was arrested, tried, and convicted for advocating the overthrow of the government by force under a New York criminal anarchy act. At trial, Gitlow's (D) counsel urged that since there was no resulting action flowing from the publication of the Gitlow (D) "Manifesto," the statute penalized the mere utterance of doctrine having no propensity toward incitement of concrete action.

ISSUE: Is a state statute punishing the mere advocacy of overthrowing the government by force an unconstitutional denial of the freedom of speech and press as protected under the First Amendment and applied to the states by the Fourteenth Amendment?

HOLDING AND DECISION: (Sanford, J.) No. Under its police powers, a state may validly forbid both speech and publication if they have a tendency to result in action that is dangerous to public security, even though such utterances present no "clear and present danger." The New York criminal anarchy act did not punish the utterance of abstract doctrine, having no quality of incitement to action. It prohibits advocacy to overthrow organized government by unlawful means. These words imply advocacy of action. Clearly, Gitlow's (D) "Manifesto," which spoke in terms of "mass action" of the proletariat for the "Communist reconstruction of society—the struggle for these," is language of direct incitement. The means suggested imply force and violence and are inherently unlawful in a constitutional form of government based on law and order. Although freedom of speech and press are protected by the First and Fourteenth Amendments, it is fundamental that this freedom is not absolute. The police power extends to a state the right to punish those who abuse this freedom by advocating action inimical to the public welfare, tending to corrupt public morals, incite to crime, or to threaten the public security. The state need not wait for such dangers to arise. It may punish utterances likely to bring about such substantive evils. The "clear and present danger" test announced in the *Schenck* case, 249 U.S. 47 (1919), does not apply here since the legislature has previously determined the danger of the substantive evils that may arise from specified utterances. As long as the statute is constitutional and the use of the language sought to be penalized comes within the prohibition, the statute will be upheld. And it is not necessary that the defendant advocate some definite or immediate act of force or violence. It is sufficient if they were expressed in general terms.

DISSENT: (Holmes, J.) The "clear and present danger" test applies, and there was no clear and present danger here. The followers of Gitlow (D) were too few to present one. Every idea is an incitement. The only meaning of free speech is to allow everyone to have their say.

▶ ANALYSIS

The *Gitlow* case is an example of what has been termed the "bad tendency" test. This test punishes utterances whose meaning lies somewhere between "clear and present danger" and mere advocacy of abstract ideas. The key question here is whether the language "tends" to produce action resulting in a danger to public security. The holding of the Court in this case, while recognizing Gitlow's (D) constitutional rights of free speech and press, bypassed these rights by saying that the New York (P) statute did not unduly restrict such freedom. However, in light of the modern test of "clear and present danger," it seems that the "bad tendency" test is all but dead. The "clear and present danger" test requires language that results in imminent lawless action. Tendency is not enough. It is important to note that the "bad tendency" test has not been used by the Court since *Gitlow*.

■■■

Continued on next page.

Quicknotes

CLEAR AND PRESENT DANGER TEST Doctrine that restraints on freedom of speech are permissible if the speech incites persons to engage in unlawful conduct.

POLICE POWER The power of a government to impose restrictions on the rights of private persons, so long as those restrictions are reasonably related to the promotion and protection of public health, safety, morals and the general welfare.

Whitney v. California

Communist party member (D) v. State (P)

274 U.S. 357 (1927).

NATURE OF CASE: Appeal from conviction for violation of Criminal Syndicalism Act.

FACT SUMMARY: Whitney (D), organizer and member of the Communist Labor Party of California, was convicted of aiding in that organization's violation of the Criminal Syndicalism Act.

🏛 RULE OF LAW

A state may, in the exercise of its police power, punish abuses of freedom of speech where such utterances are inimical to the public welfare as tending to incite crime, disturb the peace, or endanger organized government through threats of violent overthrow.

FACTS: In 1919, Whitney (D) attended a convention of the Socialist Party. When the convention split into factions, Whitney (D) went with the radicals and helped form the Communist Labor Party (CLP). Later that year, Whitney (D) attended another convention to organize a new California unit of CLP. There, Whitney (D) supported a resolution that endorsed political action and urged workers to vote for CLP member-candidates at all elections. This resolution was defeated and a more extreme program of action was adopted, over Whitney's (D) protests. At trial, upon indictment for violation of the California Criminal Syndicalism Act, which held it unlawful to organize a group that advocated unlawful acts of violence as a means of effecting change in industrial ownership and in political change, Whitney (D) contended that she never intended the CLP to become a terrorist organization. Whitney (D) further contended that since she had no intent to aid the CLP in a policy of violent political reform, her mere presence at the convention was not a crime. Whitney (D) contends that the Act thus deprived her of her liberty without due process and freedom of speech, assembly, and association.

ISSUE: Is a state statute that punishes a person for becoming a knowing member of an organization that advocates use of unlawful means to effect its aims, a violation of due process and a restraint of freedom of speech, assembly, and association secured by the Constitution?

HOLDING AND DECISION: (Sanford, J.) No. Freedom of speech, secured by the Constitution, does not confer an absolute right to speak, without responsibility. A state may in the exercise of its police power, punish abuses of freedom of speech where such utterances are inimical to the public welfare as tending to incite crime, disturb the peace, or endanger organized government through violent overthrow. Here, the Syndicalism Act of California declared that to become a knowing member of or to assist in an organization

that advocates crimes involving danger to the public peace and security of the state was punishable in the exercise of the state's police powers. The essence of the offense was the combining with others to accomplish desired ends through advocacy and use of criminal means. This is in the nature of criminal conspiracy and involves an even greater danger to public security than individual acts. The Act is a reasonable exercise of the State's police power and does not violate freedom of speech.

CONCURRENCE: (Brandeis, J.) Whitney (D) is here punished for a step in the preparation of incitement that only threatens the public remotely. The Syndicalism Act of California aims at punishing those who propose to preach, not put into action, criminal syndicalism. The right of freedom of speech, assembly, and association, protected by the Due Process Clause of the Fourteenth Amendment and binding on the states, are restricted if they threaten political, moral, or economic injury to the state. However, such restriction does not exist unless speech would produce a clear and imminent danger of some substantive evil to the state. The Court has not yet fixed standards in determining when a danger shall be clear. But no danger flowing from speech can be deemed clear and present unless the threatened evil is so imminent that it may strike before opportunity for discussion on it. There must be, however, probability of serious injury to the state. As to review by this Court of an allegation of unconstitutionality of a criminal syndicalism act, whenever fundamental rights of free speech and assembly are alleged to have been invaded, the defendant must be allowed to present the issue of whether a clear and present danger was imminent by his actions. Here, mere advocacy of revolution by mass action at some future date was within the Fourteenth Amendment protection. But our power of review was lacking since there was evidence of a criminal conspiracy and such precludes review by this court of errors at a criminal trial absent a showing that constitutional rights were deprived.

▶ ANALYSIS

The *Whitney* case is important for having added to the *Schenck*, 249 U.S. 47 (1919), test of "clear and present danger" the further requirement that the danger must be "imminent." Justice Brandeis's opinion in the *Whitney* case should be viewed as a dissenting opinion. His addition of "imminent" flies directly in the face of the majority opinion that punished "mere advocacy" of threatened action against the state. The "mere advocacy" test has not survived. Today, through the Smith Act that continues to punish criminal

Continued on next page.

syndicalism, "mere advocacy" is not punishable. The urging of action for forcible overthrow is necessary before punishment will be imposed. Thus, the "urging of action" is the modern test of "clear and present imminent danger" espoused by Justie Brandeis in *Whitney*.

■━■

Quicknotes

CLEAR AND PRESENT DANGER TEST Doctrine that restraints on freedom of speech are permissible if the speech incites persons to engage in unlawful conduct.

DUE PROCESS CLAUSE Clauses found in the Fifth and Fourteenth Amendments to the U.S. Constitution providing that no person shall be deprived of "life, liberty, or property, without due process of law."

POLICE POWER The power of a government to impose restrictions on the rights of private persons, so long as those restrictions are reasonably related to the promotion and protection of public health, safety, morals and the general welfare.

■━■

Dennis v. United States

Communist party leaders (D) v. Federal government (P)

341 U.S. 494 (1951).

NATURE OF CASE: On writ of certiorari to review convictions of conspiracy to overthrow the government by force or violence.

FACT SUMMARY: Dennis (D) and other Communist Party leaders were convicted for violation of the Smith Act, which is directed at conspiracy to teach or advocate the overthrow of the government by force or violence.

🏛 RULE OF LAW
Where an offense is specified by a statute in nonspeech or nonpress terms, a conviction relying upon speech or press as evidence of violation may be sustained only when the speech of publication created a clear and present danger of attempting or accomplishing the prohibited crime.

FACTS: The Smith Act made it unlawful to advocate or teach the overthrow of the government by force or violence, or to organize people to teaching and advocating. It also prohibited a conspiracy to do any of the above. Dennis (D) and other Communist Party leaders were convicted of conspiracy to overthrow the government by force or violence. The evidence showed that the Communist Party was a highly disciplined organization, adept at infiltration into strategic positions, use of aliases, and double-meaning language. The Party was rigidly controlled and tolerated no dissension. The Party literature and statements advocated a successful overthrow of the government by force and violence.

ISSUE: Does the Smith Act, which punishes advocacy of the overthrow of the government by force or violence and conspiracy to so advocate, violate the First Amendment, inherently or as applied to Communist Party leaders?

HOLDING AND DECISION: (Vinson, C.J.) No. In determining the constitutionality of a statute which restricts First Amendment rights, the test is: where the offense is specified in nonspeech on nonpress terms, a conviction relying upon speech or press as evidence of violation may be sustained only when the speech or publication created a clear and present danger of attempting or accomplishing the prohibited crime. Here, the Smith Act seeks to protect the government from overthrow by force or violence. This is certainly a substantial enough interest for the government to limit speech. Now it must be determined whether a clear and present danger existed. Success or probability of success of an attempt to overthrow the government is not a criterion of whether that attempt constitutes a clear and present danger. The question is whether the gravity of the evil, discounted by its improbability, justifies such an invasion of free speech as is necessary to avoid the danger. Here, the formation by Dennis (D) and

the others of such a highly organized conspiracy with rigidly disciplined members subject to call when the leaders felt the time had come, coupled with the inflammable nature of world conditions, similar uprisings in other countries, and our relations with Communist countries convince us that a clear and present danger existed here.

CONCURRENCE: (Frankfurter, J.) The validity of the statute depends on a balancing of competing interests, such as the nature of the speech and the nature of the advocacy. This balancing should be done by the legislatures not by the courts. The courts can overturn a statute, including statutes dealing with First Amendment rights, only if there is no reasonable basis for it.

DISSENT: (Black, J.) First Amendment rights should have a preferred position in a free society. Laws restricting those rights should not be sustained by the courts on the grounds of mere reasonableness.

DISSENT: (Douglas, J.) A restriction of First Amendment rights can only be sustained where there is plain and objective proof of danger that the evil advocated is imminent. This was not shown here, where it is inconceivable that Dennis (D) and other Communists advocating the violent overthrow of the government have any chance of success.

▶ ANALYSIS

After *Dennis*, the government brought Smith Act cases against a number of Communists who were lower echelon rather than leaders. In *Yates v. U.S.*, 354 U.S. 298 (1957), the Court reversed the reversed the convictions of 14 defendants. It distinguished and explained *Dennis* on the ground that it had involved group indoctrination toward future violent action, under circumstances that reasonably justified the apprehension that violence would result. In *Scales v. U.S.*, 367 U.S. 203 (1961), the Court sustained the membership clause of the Smith Act, making it clear that to be convicted under that clause one must have had knowledge of an organization's illegal advocacy and must have joined the group with the specific intent of furthering its illegal aims.

■=■

Quicknotes

CLEAR AND PRESENT DANGER TEST Doctrine that restraints on freedom of speech are permissible if the speech incites persons to engage in unlawful conduct.

SMITH ACT Federal law prohibiting the violent overthrow of government.

■=■

Brandenburg v. Ohio

Ku Klux Klan leader (D) v. State (P)

395 U.S. 444 (1969).

NATURE OF CASE: Appeal from conviction for violation of the Ohio criminal syndicalism statute.

FACT SUMMARY: Brandenburg (D) was convicted under a state statute that proscribes advocacy of the duty, necessity, or propriety of crime, sabotage, violence, or unlawful methods of terrorism as a means of accomplishing reform.

🏛 RULE OF LAW
The constitutional guarantees of freedom of speech and freedom of press do not permit a state to forbid or proscribe advocacy of the use of force or of law violation except where such advocacy is directed to inciting or producing imminent lawless action and is likely to produce or incite such action.

FACTS: Brandenburg (D), a Ku Klux Klan leader, was convicted under Ohio's (P) criminal syndicalism statute. The statute prohibited advocacy of the duty, necessity, or propriety of crime, sabotage, violence, or unlawful methods of terrorism as a means of accomplishing reform, and the assembling with any group formed to teach or advocate the doctrine of criminal syndicalism. The case against Brandenburg (D) rested on some films. One film showed 12 hooded figures, some carrying firearms, gathered around a wooden cross, which they burned. Scattered words could be heard that were derogatory to Jews and blacks. Brandenburg (D) made a speech and stated, "We are not a 'revengent' group, but if our President, our Congress, and our Supreme Court, continues to suppress the White, Caucasian race, it's possible that there might have to be some 'revengence' taken."

ISSUE: Does a statute that proscribes advocacy of the use of force, where such advocacy is directed to inciting or producing imminent lawless action, and is likely to produce or incite such action, violate the rights guaranteed by the First and Fourteenth Amendments?

HOLDING AND DECISION: (Per curiam) No. The constitutional guarantees of free speech and free press do not permit a state to forbid or proscribe advocacy of the use of force or of law violation except where such advocacy is directed to inciting or producing imminent lawless action and is likely to incite or produce such action. The mere abstract teaching of the moral propriety or even moral necessity for a resort to force and violence is not the same as preparing a group for violent action and steering it to such action. A statute that fails to draw this distinction impermissibly intrudes upon the freedoms guaranteed by the First and Fourteenth Amendments. It sweeps within its condemnation speech that the Constitution has immunized from governmental control. The Ohio statute purports to punish mere advocacy and to forbid assembly with others merely to advocate the described type of action. Hence, it cannot be sustained.

▶ ANALYSIS

This case demonstrates that imminence of danger is an essential requirement to the validity of any statute curbing freedom of speech. This requirement was reiterated in *Bond v. Floyd*, 385 U.S. 116 (1966), in which the Court reversed a state legislature's resolution excluding Bond from membership. The exclusion was based on the ground that Bond could not take the oath to support the state and U.S. Constitutions after his endorsement of a Student Non-violent Coordinating Committee (SNCC) statement and his remarks criticizing the draft and the Vietnam war. The Court found no incitement to violation of law in Bond's remarks.

■■■

Quicknotes

FIRST AMENDMENT RIGHTS Rights conferred by the First Amendment to the U.S. Constitution prohibiting Congress from enacting any law respecting an establishment of religion, prohibiting the free exercise of religion, abridging freedom of speech or the press, the right of peaceful assembly and the right to petition for a redress of grievances.

■■■

Chaplinsky v. New Hampshire

Criminal defendant (D) v. State (P)

315 U.S. 568 (1942).

NATURE OF CASE: Appeal from criminal conviction.

FACT SUMMARY: Chaplinsky (D) was convicted of violating a state criminal statute that prohibited a person from addressing so-called fighting words to another person in public.

🏛 RULE OF LAW
A statute that makes it a crime to address so-called fighting words to a person in public does not violate the Fourteenth Amendment right to free speech.

FACTS: Chaplinsky (D), on a public sidewalk near the entrance to a city hall, during a heated altercation, called another person a "damn Fascist" and a "damn racketeer." He was prosecuted and convicted of violating a state criminal statute that prohibited a person from addressing so-called fighting words to another person in public. Specifically, the statute made it illegal, in any street or public place, to call a person by any offensive or derisive name.

ISSUE: Does a statute that makes it a crime to address so-called "fighting words" to a person in public violate the Fourteenth Amendment right to free speech?

HOLDING AND DECISION: [Judge not stated in casebook excerpt.] No. A statute that makes it a crime to address so-called "fighting words" to a person in public does not violate the Fourteenth Amendment right to free speech. It is well understood that there are certain well-defined and narrowly limited classes of speech, the prevention and punishment of which does not raise any constitutional problem. These include the lewd and obscene, the profane, the libelous, and the insulting or "classical fighting words" which are those that by their very utterance inflict injury or tend to incite immediate breach of the peace, as in this case. Such utterances are no essential part of any expression of ideas and are of such slight social value as a step to truth that any benefit that may be derived from them is clearly outweighed by the social interest in order and morality. Here, the statute was narrowly drawn and limited to define and punish specific conduct lying within the domain of state power.

▶ ANALYSIS

The Court here indicates two situations in which speech constitutes fighting words: (1) speech likely to cause a violent response against the speaker and (2) speech that is an insult likely to cause immediate emotional harm.

Quicknotes

FREEDOM OF SPEECH The right to express oneself without governmental restrictions on the content of that expression.

■=■

Gooding v. Wilson

Criminal defendant (D) v. State (P)

405 U.S. 518 (1972).

NATURE OF CASE: Appeal from criminal conviction.

FACT SUMMARY: The Defendant was convicted of violating a state criminal statute that prohibited a person from saying of another in their presence opprobrious words or abusive language.

> ## 🏛 RULE OF LAW
> A statute that makes it a crime to say of another in their presence opprobrious words or abusive language violates the Fourteenth Amendment right to free speech.

FACTS: Defendant was convicted of using opprobrious words and abusive language in violation of a state statute that prohibited a person from saying to another in their presence, "White son of a bitch, I'll kill you," and "You son of a bitch, I'll choke you to death."

ISSUE: Does a statute that makes it a crime to say of another in their presence opprobrious words or abusive language violate the Fourteenth Amendment right to free speech?

HOLDING AND DECISION: (Brennan, J.) Yes. The constitutional guarantee of freedom of speech forbids states from punishing the use of words or language not within narrowly limited classes of speech. The statute here does not withstand Fourteenth Amendment attack. Dictionary definitions of "opprobrious" and "abusive" give the words a greater reach than "fighting" words. Words that are opprobrious or abusive may not necessarily lead to a breach of the peace. In every Fourteenth Amendment case, the power to regulate must be so exercised as to not, in attaining a permissible end, unduly infringe the protected freedom. Reversed.

DISSENT: (Burger, C.J.) Nothing demonstrates that the narrow language of the state statute has any significant potential for sweeping application to suppress or deter important protected speech.

DISSENT: (Blackmun, J.) The language of the statute was not overbroad but rather was concise.

▶ ANALYSIS

The majority noted that even as to the "narrowly limited classes of speech" that may be regulated, the line between speech unconditionally guaranteed and speech that may legitimately be regulated, suppressed, or punished is finely drawn.

R.A.V. v. City of St. Paul, Minnesota

Teenager (D) v. Municipality (P)

505 U.S. 377 (1992).

NATURE OF CASE: Appeal from reversal of dismissal of "hate crime" prosecution.

FACT SUMMARY: When R.A.V. (D) was charged with allegedly burning a cross inside the fenced yard of a black family, the City of St. Paul (P) charged R.A.V. (D) under the Bias-Motivated Crime Ordinance.

🏛 RULE OF LAW
Where content discrimination in an ordinance is not reasonably necessary to achieve a city's compelling interests, the ordinance cannot survive First Amendment scrutiny.

FACTS: R.A.V. (D) and several other teenagers allegedly assembled a crudely made cross and burned it inside the fenced yard of a black family. This conduct could have been punished under any of a number of laws, but the City of St. Paul (P) chose to charge R.A.V. (D) under the Bias-Motivated Crime Ordinance, which made criminally punishable conduct known as "hate crimes." R.A.V. (D) moved to dismiss on the ground that the ordinance was substantially overbroad and impermissibly content-based and therefore facially invalid under the First Amendment. The trial court granted this motion, but the Minnesota Supreme Court reversed because the modifying phrase "arouses anger, alarm or resentment in others" limited the reach of the ordinance to conduct that amounted to "fighting words," and therefore the ordinance reached only expression "that the First Amendment does not protect." The court also concluded that the ordinance was not impermissibly content-based because it was a narrowly tailored means toward accomplishing the compelling governmental interest of protecting the community against bias-motivated threats to public safety and order.

ISSUE: Where content discrimination in an ordinance is not reasonably necessary to achieve a city's compelling interests, can the ordinance survive First Amendment scrutiny?

HOLDING AND DECISION: (Scalia, J.) No. Where content discrimination in an ordinance is not reasonably necessary to achieve a city's compelling interests, the ordinance cannot survive First Amendment scrutiny. Assuming that all of the expression reached by the ordinance is proscribable under the fighting words doctrine, the ordinance is nonetheless facially unconstitutional in that it prohibits otherwise permitted speech solely on the basis of the subjects the speech addresses. Some areas of speech can, consistent with the First Amendment, be regulated because of their constitutionally proscribable content, namely, obscenity, defamation, and fighting words. Although the Minnesota Supreme Court construed the modifying phrase in the ordinance to reach only those symbols or displays that amount to fighting words, the remaining, unmodified terms make clear that the ordinance applies only to fighting words that insult, or provoke violence, on the basis of race, color, creed, religion, or gender. The First Amendment does not permit St. Paul (P) to impose special prohibitions on those speakers who express views on disfavored subjects. Burning a cross in someone's front yard is reprehensible, but St. Paul (P) has sufficient means at its disposal to prevent such behavior without adding the First Amendment to the fire.

CONCURRENCE: (White, J.) The judgment of the Minnesota Supreme Court should be reversed. However, this case could easily be decided under First Amendment law by holding that the ordinance is fatally overbroad because it criminalizes not only unprotected expression but expression protected by the First Amendment. The Court's new "underbreadth" creation serves no desirable function.

CONCURRENCE: (Blackmun, J.) The result of the majority opinion is correct because this particular ordinance reaches beyond fighting words to speech protected by the First Amendment. However, by its decision today, the majority appears to relax the level of scrutiny applicable to content-based laws, thus weakening the traditional protections of speech.

▶ ANALYSIS

The text of the St. Paul Bias-Motivated Crime Ordinance provides that: "Whoever places on public or private property a symbol, object, appellation, characterization or graffiti, including, but not limited to, a burning cross or Nazi swastika, which one knows or has reasonable grounds to know arouses anger, alarm or resentment in others on the basis of race, color, creed, religion or gender commits disorderly conduct and shall be guilty of a misdemeanor." The flaw in the wording of the ordinance was that it required the person who committed the hateful act to discern the reaction of the victim to the perpetrator's conduct. It is likely that hate crime ordinances that are worded to punish conduct intended by the perpetrator to frighten, anger, etc., on the basis of race, religion, etc., would be upheld. Even if no hate crime ordinance could be upheld, the hateful conduct could still be punished under criminal trespass, arson, battery, homicide statutes, etc.

■=■

Continued on next page.

Quicknotes

CONTENT BASED   Refers to statutes that regulate speech based on its content.

FIRST AMENDMENT RIGHTS   Rights conferred by the First Amendment to the U.S. Constitution prohibiting Congress from enacting any law respecting an establishment of religion, prohibiting the free exercise of religion, abridging freedom of speech or the press, the right of peaceful assembly and the right to petition for a redress of grievances.

■═■

Feiner v. New York

Public speaker (D) v. State (P)

340 U.S. 315 (1951).

NATURE OF CASE: Appeal from conviction for disorderly conduct.

FACT SUMMARY: Feiner (D) gave an open-air speech before a racially mixed audience. The crowd that gathered forced pedestrians into the street. Feiner (D) urged black people to rise up in arms against whites and fight for equal rights. He refused to stop when asked to do so by a police officer and was arrested.

🏛 RULE OF LAW
When clear and present danger of riot, disorder, interference with traffic on the streets, or other immediate threat to public safety, peace, or order, appear, the state has the power to punish or prevent such disorder.

FACTS: Feiner (D) addressed an open-air meeting. A racially mixed crowd of about eighty people gathered. The crowd forced pedestrians walking by into the street. In response to a complaint about the meeting, two police officers arrived. They heard Feiner (D) urge black people to take up arms and fight against whites for equal rights. The remarks stirred up the crowd a little, and one person commented on the police's inability to control the crowd. Another threatened violence if the police did not act. The officers finally "stepped in to prevent it from resulting in a fight." They asked Feiner (D) to stop speaking twice. He ignored them, and they arrested him.

ISSUE: May a speaker be arrested because of the reaction engendered by his speech?

HOLDING AND DECISION: (Vinson, C.J.) Yes. When clear and present danger of riot, disorder, interference with traffic on the streets, or other immediate threat to public safety, peace, or order, appears, the state has the power to punish or prevent such disorder. Here, the crowd's behavior and Feiner's (D) refusal to obey the police requests presented a sufficient danger to warrant his arrest and to persuade the Court that Feiner's (D) conviction for violation of public peace, order and authority does not exceed the bounds of proper state police action. Feiner (D) was neither arrested nor convicted for the making or the content of his speech. Rather, it was the reaction it engendered. The community's interest in maintaining peace and order on its streets must be protected.

DISSENT: (Black, J.) "I will have no part or parcel in this holding which I view as a long step toward totalitarian authority." Disagreement, mutterings, and objections from a crowd do not indicate imminent threat of a riot, nor does one threat to assault the speaker. Even assuming that a critical situation existed, it was the police's duty to protect Feiner's (D) right to speak, which they made no effort to do. Finally, a person making a lawful address is not required to be silent merely because an officer so directs. Here, Feiner (D) received no explanation as to why he was being directed to stop speaking. This decision means that the police have the discretion to silence minority views in any city as soon as the customary hostility to such views develops.

▶ ANALYSIS

As *Feiner* demonstrates, free speech is not an absolute right. The conflicting interest of community order must also be considered. *Feiner* points out the question of whether the boundaries of protected speech depend on the content of the speech and the speaker's words or on the environment, the crowd reaction or potential crowd reaction. This question arose again in *Gregory v. Chicago*, 394 U.S. 111 (1969), which reversed convictions of disorderly conduct. There, participants in a "peaceful and orderly procession" to press their claims for desegregation were arrested when, after the number of bystanders increased, and some became unruly, they were asked to disperse and did not. The majority asserted that this was a simple case as the marchers' peaceful conduct was a protected activity within the First Amendment. The concurring opinion saw *Gregory* as involving some complexities, since, as the judge noted, both the demonstrators and the officers had tried to restrain the hecklers but were unable to do so. He concluded that "this record is a crying example of a need for some narrowly drawn law," rather than the sweeping disorderly conduct law.

■═■

Quicknotes

CLEAR AND PRESENT DANGER TEST Doctrine that restraints on freedom of speech are permissible if the speech incites persons to engage in unlawful conduct.

■═■

Beauharnais v. Illinois

Criminal defendant (D) v. State (P)

343 U.S. 250 (1952).

NATURE OF CASE: Appeal from criminal conviction.

FACT SUMMARY: Beauharnais (D) produced and distributed leaflets defaming the Negro race and urging whites to unite to stop Negro aggressions, rapes, robberies, and similar acts. Under criminal libel legislation, Beauharnais (D) was prosecuted and convicted for distributing these leaflets.

🏛 RULE OF LAW
The Due Process Clause does not prevent a state from punishing a criminal libel directed at designated collectives and flagrantly disseminated.

FACTS: Beauharnais (D) produced and distributed leaflets setting forth a petition calling on the mayor and city council of Chicago "to halt the further encroachment, harassment, and invasion of white people" and calling for white people to unite, saying that if whites do not unite, "then the aggressions, rapes, robberies, knives, guns, and marijuana of the [N]egro, surely will." Beauharnais (D) was prosecuted and convicted for distributing these leaflets under a state criminal libel statute that essentially made it unlawful to libel any "class of citizens" of any race, color, creed, or religion, which might result in breach of the peace or riots.

ISSUE: Does the Due Process Clause prevent a state from punishing a criminal libel directed at designated collectives and flagrantly disseminated?

HOLDING AND DECISION: (Frankfurter, J.) No. The statute here was not a catchall enactment but rather a law specifically directed at a defined evil, its language drawing from history and practice in many jurisdictions, to ease racial violence and destruction. In the face of a violent racial history in Illinois and extreme racial and religious propaganda, made in public places and by means calculated to have a powerful emotional impact, the scope of the statute was not so broad as to violate constitutionally protected rights.

DISSENT: (Black, J.) No legislature is charged with the duty or vested with the power to decide what public issues Americans can discuss. In a free country, that is the individual's choice, not the state's. State experimentation in curbing freedom of expression is a startling and frightening doctrine in a country dedicated to self-government by its people.

▶ ANALYSIS

The majority stated that if an utterance directed at an individual may be the object of criminal sanctions, the Court could not deny to a state the power to punish the same utterance directed at a defined group, as here.

Quicknotes

DUE PROCESS CLAUSE Clauses found in the Fifth and Fourteenth Amendments to the U.S. Constitution providing that no person shall be deprived of "life, liberty, or property, without due process of law."

Virginia v. Black

State (D) v. Convicted cross burner (P)

538 U.S. 343 (2003).

NATURE OF CASE: Constitutional challenge to statute banning cross burning.

FACT SUMMARY: The state of Virginia (D) passed a statute criminalizing cross burning and treated any cross burning as prima facie evidence of intent to intimidate. Black (P) was convicted under the statute and challenges the constitutionality of the statute on First Amendment grounds.

> 🏛 **RULE OF LAW**
> A statute prohibiting cross burning with the intent to intimidate a person or group of persons is unconstitutional when it treats any cross burning as prima facie evidence of intent to intimidate.

FACTS: The state of Virginia (D) passed a statute prohibiting cross burning done to intimidate a person or group of persons. The Virginia statute treated any cross burning as prima facie evidence of the requisite intent to intimidate. Black (P) was convicted under the statute when he led a Ku Klux Klan (KKK) rally and coordinated burning a cross at the end of the rally. The rally was held on private property and was attended by the property's owner. Neighbors chose to watch the rally from their property, but the cross burning was not directed at any one person or group of persons in particular. The cross was burned as a symbol of the KKK. Black (P) appealed his conviction and challenged the constitutionality of the statute on First Amendment grounds.

ISSUE: Is a statute prohibiting cross burning with the intent to intimidate a person or group of persons unconstitutional when it treats any cross burning as prima facie evidence of intent to intimidate?

HOLDING AND DECISION: (O'Connor, J.) Yes. A statute prohibiting cross burning with the intent to intimidate a person or group of persons is unconstitutional when it treats any cross burning as prima facie evidence of intent to intimidate. The statute is prohibiting a form of free speech and must be evaluated under First Amendment considerations. Cross burning has a long, evil history in this country and is forever associated with the intimidating tactics of the KKK. States may absolutely prohibit certain conduct that reaches such a level of invidiousness. The issue arises, however, when the proscribed conduct is also considered prima facie evidence of intent to intimidate. The state should have to meet its burden of establishing such intent. In the case of Black (P), the cross burning occurred as a symbol of the KKK solidarity and not as a form of intimidation directed toward any one person or group. His conviction must be reversed. The Virginia statute is unconstitutional as far as the prima facie section is concerned.

CONCURRENCE AND DISSENT: (Souter, J.) No exception should save the statute from unconstitutionality because its content-based distinction was invalid from the start.

DISSENT: (Thomas, J.) The fact that the statute permits a jury to draw an inference of intent to intimidate from the cross burning itself presents no constitutional problem. The plurality fears a chill on expression. First, it is unclear that the inference comes into play prior to the instructions stage of an actual trial. Second, the inference is rebuttable, and Virginia law still requires the jury to find each element of the crime, including the intent to intimidate, beyond a reasonable doubt. I would uphold the validity of this statute.

▶ *ANALYSIS*

It is arguable that punishing the "speech" element of cross burning results in eliminating the intended message of hate. States must try to curb such inciting speech, however, and such statutes may be the best way to do so if they meet the burden of constitutionality. Critics argue, however, that no matter how offensive or profane the expression, the First Amendment should protect it.

■══■

Quicknotes

FIRST AMENDMENT RIGHTS Rights conferred by the First Amendment to the U.S. Constitution prohibiting Congress from enacting any law respecting an establishment of religion, prohibiting the free exercise of religion, abridging freedom of speech or the press, the right of peaceful assembly and the right to petition for a redress of grievances.

■══■

Roth v. United States

Publisher (D) v. Federal government (P)

354 U.S. 476 (1957).

NATURE OF CASE: Appeal from criminal conviction under an obscenity statute.

FACT SUMMARY: Two defendants were convicted under obscenity statutes for selling obscene material. Roth (D) was convicted under a federal statute, Alberts (D) under a state statute.

> ## 🏛 RULE OF LAW
> Obscenity is not a constitutionally protected expression.

FACTS: Roth (D) was a publisher and seller of books, magazines, and photographs. He was convicted under a federal statute for mailing obscene circulars and advertising and an obscene book. Alberts (D) was convicted under a California (P) statute that prohibited the keeping for sale of obscene and indecent books or the writing, composing, and publishing of an obscene advertisement therefor.

ISSUE: Is obscenity outside the protection of the First Amendment freedom of expression guarantees?

HOLDING AND DECISION: (Brennan, J.) Yes. Obscenity is not a constitutionally protected expression. The apparently unconditional phrasing of the First Amendment has been held by this Court not to protect every utterance. However, all ideas having even the slightest degree of socially redeeming value are fully protected unless they encroach upon the limited areas of more important interests. Obscenity has been held to carry no socially redeeming value and is, therefore, outside the protection of the First Amendment. A properly drawn and enforced statute outlawing obscenity will withstand the test of constitutionality. The portrayal of sex is not obscenity per se, as is evidenced by the large range of classic presentations in art, literature, and scientific works.

DISSENT: (Douglas, J.) The First Amendment is expressed in absolute terms and any law that purports to regulate material that can only produce thoughts is a clearly impermissible encroachment on these absolute guarantees. While the state and federal governments can regulate conduct, they should not be allowed to regulate the thought that precedes the conduct.

▌ ANALYSIS

The standard of the *Roth* case soon became a thorn in the side of the Court. As Justice Harlan had predicted, the Court was reduced to a case-by-case review of obscenity convictions. In each case, the Court was forced to make a factual analysis of the material to determine if it was obscene, despite the fact that the same determination had already been made in every lower court. One clarification of the *Roth* standard came in *Jacobellis v. Ohio*, 378 U.S. 184, in 1964. In that case, a split Court stated the "community standard" was a national standard since a national constitution was being applied. The other noteworthy concept to come from that case was from Justice Stewart. He stated that the Court was attempting to deal with "hard core" pornography. While he admitted he could not define that term, he stated he knew it when he saw it, and the motion picture involved in that case was not it.

■══■

Quicknotes

FIRST AMENDMENT RIGHTS Rights conferred by the First Amendment to the U.S. Constitution prohibiting Congress from enacting any law respecting an establishment of religion, prohibiting the free exercise of religion, abridging freedom of speech or the press, the right of peaceful assembly and the right to petition for a redress of grievances.

■══■

Paris Adult Theatre I v. Slaton

Criminal defendant (D) v. State (P)

413 U.S. 49 (1973).

NATURE OF CASE: Civil proceeding to enjoin continued showing of two adult films.

FACT SUMMARY: Two adult films were shown at theaters (D) that advertised the nature of the films and required proof that all patrons were over 21.

RULE OF LAW

A state can forbid the dissemination of obscene material to consenting adults in order to preserve the quality of the community and to prevent the possibility of resulting antisocial behavior.

FACTS: Two movie theatres (D) in Atlanta showed "adult" films exclusively. The State of Georgia (P) sought to enjoin the showing of sexually explicit movies in these theatres under an obscenity statute. It was determined that the exterior advertising was not obscene or offensive, but that there were signs at the entrance stating that patrons must be 21 years of age and able to prove it. There was a further warning that those who would be offended by nudity should not enter. However, the films in question included, in addition to nudity, various simulated sex acts.

ISSUE: Can a state prohibit the dissemination of obscene material if the material is distributed only to consenting adults?

HOLDING AND DECISION: (Burger, C.J.) Yes. A state has a valid interest in preventing exposure of obscene material to consenting adults. Even if exposure to juveniles and unwilling observers is prevented, the state has a further interest in preserving the quality of life, the community environment, and possible threats to public safety, which will allow the regulation of obscenity. Here, even though only consenting adults are involved, the state can make a judgment that public exhibition of obscenity has a tendency to injure the community and can, therefore, enjoin the distribution of obscenity.

DISSENT: (Brennan, J.) Prior obscenity standards have proved unworkable because they fail to give adequate notice of the definition of obscenity, producing a chilling effect on constitutionally protected speech. Because of the vague nature of these standards, every case is marginal, producing a vast number of constitutional questions that create institutional stress in the judicial system. States do have a valid interest in protecting children and unconsenting adults from exposure to allegedly obscene material, but other possible state interests, as discussed in the majority opinion, are vague, speculative, and cannot be proven. Therefore, in the absence of threat of exposure to juveniles or unconsenting

adults, material cannot be suppressed, but the state can regulate the manner of distribution.

DISSENT: (Douglas, J.) Art and literature reflect tastes; and tastes, like musical appreciation, are not reducible to precise definitions; hence, "obscenity" should not be deemed an exception to the First Amendment. Matters of taste, like matters of belief, turn on the idiosyncrasies of individuals.

ANALYSIS

Interestingly, Justice Douglas in his dissent notes that he never reads nor sees the materials coming to the Court under charges of obscenity on the theory that "I have thought the First Amendment made it unconstitutional for me to act as a censor."

Quicknotes

FIRST AMENDMENT RIGHTS Rights conferred by the First Amendment to the U.S. Constitution prohibiting Congress from enacting any law respecting an establishment of religion, prohibiting the free exercise of religion, abridging freedom of speech or the press, the right of peaceful assembly and the right to petition for a redress of grievances.

OBSCENITY Indecency, lewdness or offensive behavior in appearance or expression.

Miller v. California

Bookseller (D) v. State (P)

413 U.S. 15 (1973).

NATURE OF CASE: Criminal prosecution for knowingly distributing obscene matter.

FACT SUMMARY: Miller (D) sent out advertising brochures for adult books to unwilling recipients.

🏛 RULE OF LAW

Material is obscene and not protected by the First Amendment if: (1) the average person, applying contemporary community standards, would find that the work, taken as a whole, appeals to the prurient interest; (2) the work depicts in a patently offensive way sexual conduct specifically defined by the applicable state law; and (3) the work, taken as a whole, lacks serious literary, artistic, political, or scientific value.

FACTS: Miller (D) conducted a mass mailing campaign to advertise the sale of adult books. The advertising brochures were themselves found obscene. These brochures were sent to unwilling recipients who had not requested the material. Miller (D) was convicted of violating a statute that forbade knowingly distributing obscene matter.

ISSUE: Is the *Memoirs* requirement (383 U.S. 413 [1966]) that material must be "utterly without redeeming social value" to be considered obscene, a proper constitutional standard?

HOLDING AND DECISION: (Burger, C. J.) No. Material is obscene and not protected by the First Amendment if: (1) the average person, applying contemporary community standards, would find that the work, taken as a whole, appeals to the prurient interest; (2) the work depicts in a patently offensive way sexual conduct specifically defined by the applicable state law; and (3) the work, taken as a whole, lacks serious literary, artistic, political or scientific value. If material meets this definition of obscenity, then the state can prohibit its distribution if the mode of distribution entails the risk of offending unwilling recipients or exposing the material to juveniles. The burden of proof of the *Memoirs* test, that the material be utterly without redeeming value, is virtually impossible for the prosecution to meet and must be abandoned.

▎ *ANALYSIS*

The *Miller* test of obscenity is the most current test. If the three requirements are met, then the material in question is considered obscene and outside the protection of the First Amendment. *Miller* is a turnaround from *Memoirs* for many reasons: the *Memoirs* standard was too difficult to prove: the lower courts had no clear-cut guidelines because *Memoirs* was a plurality opinion; the Court decided

to use local community standards to allow greater jury power; and the Court was beginning to feel institutional pressures, since every obscenity question was a constitutional question. Therefore, *Miller* was an attempt by the Court to decentralize decision-making.

■=■

Quicknotes

FIRST AMENDMENT RIGHTS Rights conferred by the First Amendment to the U.S. Constitution prohibiting Congress from enacting any law respecting an establishment of religion, prohibiting the free exercise of religion, abridging freedom of speech or the press, the right of peaceful assembly and the right to petition for a redress of grievances.

OBSCENITY Indecency, lewdness or offensive behavior in appearance or expression.

■=■

New York v. Ferber

Criminal defendant (P) v. State (D)

458 U.S. 747 (1982).

NATURE OF CASE: Appeal from criminal conviction.

FACT SUMMARY: Ferber (P) was convicted under a New York statute that prohibited persons from knowingly promoting sexual performances by children under the age of 16 by distributing material that depicts such performances.

🏛 RULE OF LAW
The government may prohibit the exhibition, sale, or distribution of child pornography even if it does not meet the test for obscenity.

FACTS: At issue was the constitutionality of a New York criminal statute that prohibited persons from knowingly promoting sexual performances by children under the age of 16 by distributing material which depicts such performances.

ISSUE: May the government prohibit the exhibition, sale, or distribution of child pornography even if it does not meet the test for obscenity?

HOLDING AND DECISION: (White, J.) Yes. The exploitive use of children in the production of pornography is a serious national problem, resulting in legislation directed at its production by the federal government and 47 states. Such materials constitutionally may be prohibited even though they may not necessarily always be deemed obscene because (1) a state's interest in safeguarding the physical and psychological well-being of a minor is "compelling"; (2) the distribution of such material is intrinsically related to child abuse; (3) child pornography provides an economic motive for such materials; (4) any value in such materials is modest, if not de minimis; and (5) classifying such material as a category of material outside First Amendment protection is not incompatible with earlier Supreme Court decisions.

CONCURRENCE: (Brennan, J.) While the state has a special interest in protecting the well being of its youth, the application of child pornography legislation to depictions of children that in themselves do have serious literary, artistic, scientific, or medical value, would violate the First Amendment.

▶ ANALYSIS

The majority pointed out that there are limits on the category of child pornography that, like obscenity, is unprotected by the First Amendment. As with all legislation in this sensitive area, noted the Court, the conduct to be prohibited must be adequately defined by the applicable state law, as written or authoritatively construed.

Quicknotes

COMPELLING STATE INTEREST Defense to an alleged Equal Protection Clause violation; that a state action was necessary in order to protect an interest the government is under a duty to protect.

FIRST AMENDMENT RIGHTS Rights conferred by the First Amendment to the U.S. Constitution prohibiting Congress from enacting any law respecting an establishment of religion, prohibiting the free exercise of religion, abridging freedom of speech or the press, the right of peaceful assembly and the right to petition for a redress of grievances.

OBSCENITY Indecency, lewdness or offensive behavior in appearance or expression.

Ashcroft v. Free Speech Coalition

U.S. Attorney General (D) v. First Amendment supporter group (P)

535 U.S. 234 (2002).

NATURE OF CASE: Constitutional challenge to federal statute.

FACT SUMMARY: A federal anti-child-pornography statute purported to ban possessing or distributing images, however created, of minors engaging in sexual activity. The minors may or may not be real because the images could be computer-generated or of adults resembling minors. Plaintiffs challenged the constitutionality of a federal anti-child-pornography statute as a violation of the First Amendment guarantee of freedom of speech.

🏛 RULE OF LAW
Speech that is neither obscene nor child pornography although related cannot be abridged as a means to categorically suppress illegal child pornography speech.

FACTS: The Child Pornography Prevention Act of 1996 (CPPA) extended the federal prohibitions against child pornography to include images of minors engaging in sexual activity even where the minors were not real children. *New York v. Ferber*, 458 U.S. 747 (1982), prohibits child pornography and *Miller v. California*, 413 U.S. 15 (1973), prohibits obscene speech, but this statute goes even further to suppress all speech related to the mere possibility of child pornography. The CPPA prohibits images that do not actually include children. Adults resembling minors and computer-generated images fall under the auspices of the CPPA. Any person found creating or possessing such images is subject to serious criminal sanctions, including up to 15 years' imprisonment for a first offense.

ISSUE: Can speech that is neither obscene nor child pornography, although related, be abridged as a means to categorically suppress illegal child pornography speech?

HOLDING AND DECISION: (Kennedy, J.) No. Speech that is neither obscene nor child pornography, although related, cannot be abridged as a means to categorically suppress illegal child pornography speech. If the images do not fall under the prohibitions of *Ferber* or *Miller*, then this is an entirely new universe of speech. While the goal of the statute is laudable—to stamp out child pornography and its insidious consequences—the First Amendment does not allow the suppression of an entire universe of speech in order to accomplish the suppression of a limited portion of illegal speech. The CPPA broadly implicates images of minors that "appear to be" minors engaging in sexual activity. Such language literally includes creations such as Shakespeare's "Romeo and Juliet" and classic portraits of children in various states of undress. Allowing the loss of this type of artwork to protect against

potential abuse is contrary to the purpose of the First Amendment. Additionally, the criminal penalties for violating the CPPA are severe. Its penalties result in a chilling effect on any artists that would have chosen to depict images of minors engaging in sexual activity even when it is not done for pornographic purposes or even with actual minors. *Ferber* allowed for computer-generated images as a viable alternative to images employing actual minors and certainly provides no support for the CPPA's ban against the images. The Government argues that virtual child pornography and actual child pornography are nearly indistinguishable, but that is difficult to accept given that producers would then cease to use actual children completely in exchange for lack of fear of the criminal sanctions. Lawful speech, however close to the unlawful sort, may not be suppressed in an attempt to rid the world of the unlawful speech. The statute here is overbroad and unconstitutional.

CONCURRENCE IN PART AND DISSENT IN PART: (O'Connor, J.) Outright bans on virtual child pornography protect actual minors from the whetted appetites of sexual predators. The majority is correct, though, in finding fault with the language "appears to be" when the statute should read that it bans images that are "virtually indistinguishable" from actual children. Youthful-adult pornography differs significantly from child pornography and the ban should stand regarding the latter.

DISSENT: (Rehnquist, C.J.) Congress has a compelling interest in prohibiting child pornography and that should include virtual images. The majority's view that the statute would include Shakesperian images is a stretch without indication that such an interpretation was intended. In fact, the movies mentioned by the majority were made after the CPPA was enacted, so the chill on speech does not seem to have occurred.

▶ ANALYSIS

Supporters of the statute argued that the virtual child pornography images were just as dangerous as images of actual children because of the way in which the virtual pornography was employed. If pedophiles were aroused and abused more often because of virtual porn, it seems worth the loss of speech rights to protect the new child victims. Nothing indicates, however, any connection between virtual child pornography and a dangerous reaction in a predator. Critics of the statute had the unenviable task of seeking to protect basic freedom of speech rights by defending the production of images depicting

Continued on next page.

children engaged in sex acts. The fear, though, was that one universe of language would be sacrificed for the better of society, and then other demands for freedom of speech sacrifices would follow.

■══■

Quicknotes

COMPELLING STATE INTEREST Defense to an alleged Equal Protection Clause violation; that a state action was necessary in order to protect an interest the government is under a duty to protect.

FIRST AMENDMENT RIGHTS Rights conferred by the First Amendment to the U.S. Constitution prohibiting Congress from enacting any law respecting an establishment of religion, prohibiting the free exercise of religion, abridging freedom of speech or the press, the right of peaceful assembly and the right to petition for a redress of grievances.

OBSCENITY Indecency, lewdness or offensive behavior in appearance or expression.

■══■

Young v. American Mini Theatres, Inc.

Theater owners (P) v. Zoning board (D)

427 U.S. 50 (1976).

NATURE OF CASE: Determination of constitutionality of zoning ordinance.

FACT SUMMARY: The City of Detroit (D) adopted zoning ordinances for "adult" theaters.

🏛 RULE OF LAW
The First Amendment is not violated by a zoning classification that differentiates between motion picture theaters that exhibit sexually explicit "adult" movies and those that do not.

FACTS: The City of Detroit (D) adopted zoning ordinances. Instead of concentrating "adult" theaters in limited zones, the ordinances required that such theaters be dispersed. Specifically, an adult theater could not be located within 1,000 feet of any two other "regulated uses" or within 500 feet of a residential area. The term "regulated uses" included ten different kinds of establishments in addition to adult theaters.

ISSUE: Is a zoning classification that differentiates between motion picture theaters that exhibit sexually explicit "adult" movies and those that do not unconstitutional because it is based on the content of communication protected by the First Amendment?

HOLDING AND DECISION: (Stevens, J.) No. Although adult motion picture theaters must satisfy a locational restriction not applicable to other theaters, the 1,000-foot restriction does not, in itself, create an impermissible restraint on protected communication. The city's interest in planning and regulating the use of property for commercial purposes is clearly adequate to support that kind of restriction applicable to all theaters within the city limits. Even within the area of protected speech, a difference in content may require a different governmental response. As to whether the line drawn by the zoning ordinance was justified by the city's interest in preserving the character of its neighborhoods, a city's interest in attempting to preserve the quality of urban life is one that must be accorded high respect. Moreover, a city must be allowed a reasonable opportunity to experiment with solutions to admittedly serious problems.

DISSENT: (Stewart, J.) This case does not involve a simple zoning ordinance, or a content-neutral time, place, and manner restriction, or a regulation of obscene expression or other speech that is entitled to less than the full protection of the First Amendment. The kind of expression at issue here is no doubt objectionable to some, but that fact does not diminish its protected status.

▶ ANALYSIS

The majority noted that even though the First Amendment protects communication in this area from total suppression, a state may legitimately use the content of these materials as the basis for placing them in a different classification from other motion pictures.

Quicknotes

CONTENT BASED Refers to statutes that regulate speech based on its content.

CONTENT NEUTRAL Refers to statutes that regulate speech regardless of its content.

FIRST AMENDMENT RIGHTS Rights conferred by the First Amendment to the U.S. Constitution prohibiting Congress from enacting any law respecting an establishment of religion, prohibiting the free exercise of religion, abridging freedom of speech or the press, the right of peaceful assembly and the right to petition for a redress of grievances.

ZONING Municipal statutory scheme dividing an area into districts in order to regulate the use or building of structures within those districts.

City of Erie v. Pap's A.M.

Municipality (D) v. Nude bar (P)

529 U.S. 277 (2000).

NATURE OF CASE: Complaint seeking declaratory relief and a permanent injunction against enforcement of a municipal ordinance.

FACT SUMMARY: Pap's (P), a nude dancing establishment, brought suit against the City of Erie (D) for enacting an ordinance prohibiting public nudity, seeking declaratory relief and a permanent injunction against enforcement of the ordinance.

🏛 **RULE OF LAW**

If the government's purpose in enacting a regulation is unrelated to the suppression of expression and meets the four-factor test set forth in *United States v. O'Brien*, 391 U.S. 367 (1968), then it is a valid content-neutral regulation. Nudity is not an inherently expressive condition.

FACTS: Erie (D) passed an ordinance banning public nudity. Pap's (P) operated a nude dancing establishment in Erie, featuring totally nude dancing performed by women. Pap's (P) filed a complaint seeking declaratory relief and a permanent injunction against the enforcement of the ordinance. The Pennsylvania Supreme Court concluded that the public nudity provisions of the ordinance violated Pap's (P) right to freedom of expression under the First and Fourteenth Amendments.

ISSUE: If the government's purpose in enacting a regulation is unrelated to the suppression of expression and meets the four-factor test set forth in *O'Brien*, is it a valid content-neutral regulation?

HOLDING AND DECISION: (O'Connor, J.) Yes. If the government's purpose in enacting a regulation is unrelated to the suppression of expression and meets the four-factor test set forth in *O'Brien*, then it is a valid content-neutral regulation. If the governmental purpose in enacting a regulation is unrelated to the suppression of expression, then the regulation need only satisfy the "less stringent" standard of *O'Brien*. If the government regulation is related to the content of the expression, then the regulation must be justified under a more demanding standard. Government restrictions on public nudity, such as the ordinance at issue here, should be evaluated under the framework set forth in *O'Brien* for content-neutral restrictions on symbolic speech. Pap's (P) argues that the ordinance is nonetheless related to suppression of expression because language in the ordinance's preamble suggests that its actual purpose is to prohibit erotic dancing. This Court has noted that the government's interest in combating prostitution and other criminal activity is not inherently related

to expression. Pap's (P) argues that the ordinance is aimed at suppressing expression suggesting that the city counsel had an illicit motive in enacting the ordinance. This Court will not strike down an otherwise constitutional statute on the basis of an alleged illicit motive. The state's interest in preventing the harmful secondary effects of nude dancing establishments is not related to the suppression of the erotic message conveyed by nude dancing. Thus the ordinance is a content-neutral restriction on conduct.

CONCURRENCE: (Scalia, J.) It is the communicative nature of nude dancing that should be the subject of the ban. Suppressing nude dancing itself does not suppress what the nude dancing communicates, so the ban is unsuccessful. The First Amendment allows government to foster good morals by banning nude dancing anyway.

DISSENT IN PART: (Souter, J.) I agree with the analytical approach employed, but do not agree that the city (D) made a sufficient showing to sustain the regulation. Intermediate scrutiny requires a regulating government to make some demonstration of an evidentiary basis for the harm it claims to flow from the expressive activity. The record here does not support the conclusion that the ordinance is reasonably designed to mitigate concrete harms.

DISSENT: (Stevens, J.) The Court concludes that the "secondary effects" may justify the total suppression of protected speech.

▶ *ANALYSIS*

Nudity is not an inherently expressive condition. Nude dancing, such as the type involved here, though constituting expressive conduct, does not fall within the core of First Amendment protection.

■▬■

Quicknotes

CONTENT BASED Refers to statutes that regulate speech based on its content.

CONTENT NEUTRAL Refers to statutes that regulate speech regardless of its content.

FIRST AMENDMENT RIGHTS Rights conferred by the First Amendment to the U.S. Constitution prohibiting Congress from enacting any law respecting an establishment of religion, prohibiting the free exercise of religion, abridging freedom of speech or the press, the right of peaceful assembly and the right to petition for a redress of grievances.

■▬■

Stanley v. Georgia

Criminal defendant (D) v. State (P)

394 U.S. 557 (1969).

NATURE OF CASE: Appeal from criminal conviction.

FACT SUMMARY: Stanley (D) was prosecuted for private possession of obscene materials found in his home during a police search.

🏛 RULE OF LAW
An obscenity statute, insofar as it punishes mere private possession of obscene matter, violates the First Amendment.

FACTS: While police were executing a search warrant in Stanley's (D) home, based on bookmaking, they found three reels of eight-millimeter allegedly obscene films. Stanley (D) was prosecuted for knowing possession of obscene matter in violation of state law.

ISSUE: Does an obscenity statute, insofar as it punishes mere private possession of obscene matter, violate the First Amendment?

HOLDING AND DECISION: (Marshall, J.) Yes. It is well established that the Constitution protects the right to receive information and ideas. This right, regardless of the social worth of the information received, is fundamental to our free society. Moreover, in the context of this case—a prosecution for mere possession of printed or filmed matter in the privacy of a person's own home—that right takes on an added dimension. Fundamental is the right to be free, except in very limited circumstances, from unwanted governmental intrusions into one's privacy. If the First Amendment means anything, it means that a state has no business telling a person, sitting alone in their own house, what books they may read or what films they may watch.

▶ ANALYSIS

The Court noted that there was no empirical basis for any assertion that exposure to obscene materials may lead to deviant sexual behavior or crimes of sexual violence.

∎≡∎

Quicknotes

FIRST AMENDMENT RIGHTS Rights conferred by the First Amendment to the U.S. Constitution prohibiting Congress from enacting any law respecting an establishment of religion, prohibiting the free exercise of religion, abridging freedom of speech or the press, the right of peaceful assembly and the right to petition for a redress of grievances.

∎≡∎

Cohen v. California

Defendant (D) v. State (P)

403 U.S. 15 (1971).

NATURE OF CASE: Criminal prosecution for violation of disturbing the peace statute.

FACT SUMMARY: Cohen (D) wore a jacket with the words "Fuck the Draft" on it in a courthouse corridor and was arrested and convicted under a disturbing the peace statute.

🏛 RULE OF LAW
A state cannot bar the use of offensive words either because such words are inherently likely to cause a violent reaction or because the state wishes to eliminate such words to protect the public morality.

FACTS: Cohen (D) was arrested in a courthouse because he was wearing a jacket bearing the words, "Fuck the Draft." Cohen (D) did not engage in any act of violence or any other unlawful act. There was also no evidence that anyone who saw the jacket became violently aroused or even protested the jacket. Cohen (D) testified that he wore the jacket to inform people of his feelings against the Vietnam war and the draft. He was convicted under a statute prohibiting "maliciously and willfully disturbing the peace or quiet . . . by offensive conduct." The state court held that "offensive conduct" meant conduct that had a tendency to provoke others to disturb the peace.

ISSUE: Can a state constitutionally prevent the use of certain words on the ground that the use of such words is offensive conduct?

HOLDING AND DECISION: (Harlan, J.) No. A state cannot constitutionally prohibit the use of offensive words either because such words are inherently likely to cause a violent reaction or because the state wishes to eliminate such words to protect the public morality. Here, Cohen (D) could not be punished for criticizing the draft, so the statute could be upheld, if at all, only as a regulation of the manner, not the substantive content, of his speech. Cohen's (D) speech does not come within any of the exceptions to the general rule that the form and content of speech cannot be regulated: (1) this is not a prohibition designed to protect courthouse decorum because the statute is not so limited; (2) this is not an obscenity case because Cohen's (D) words were not erotic; (3) this is not a case of fighting words which are punishable as inherently likely to provoke a violent reaction because here the words were not directed as a personal insult to any person; and (4) this is not a captive audience problem since a viewer could merely avert his eyes, there is no evidence of objection by those who saw the jacket, and the statute is not so limited. The state tries to justify the conviction because the words are inherently likely to cause a violent reaction, but this argument cannot be upheld because these

are not fighting words and there is no evidence that words that are merely offensive would cause such a response. Next, the state justifies the conviction on the ground that the state is guardian of the public morality. This argument is unacceptable because "offensive" is an unlimited concept and forbidding the use of such words would also cause the risk of suppressing the accompanying ideas. Therefore, there is no valid state interest that supports the regulation of offensive words in public.

DISSENT: (Blackmun, J.) Cohen's (D) immature action was conduct, not speech, so the First Amendment evaluation was unnecessary.

▶ ANALYSIS

This case reasserts the *Chaplinsky* [315 U.S. 568 (1942)] holding that fighting words are not protected by the First Amendment. Fighting words, then, are only those words that are likely to cause an immediate breach of the peace by another person, and are not just offensive words. More importantly, this case holds that a state has no valid interest in preventing the use of offensive words when there is no competing privacy interest. Here, the public in general has no right to protection from hearing either offensive words or offensive ideas.

■═■

Quicknotes

FIRST AMENDMENT RIGHTS Rights conferred by the First Amendment to the U.S. Constitution prohibiting Congress from enacting any law respecting an establishment of religion, prohibiting the free exercise of religion, abridging freedom of speech or the press, the right of peaceful assembly and the right to petition for a redress of grievances.

■═■

Federal Communications Commn. v. Pacifica Foundation

Federal agency (P) v. Broadcasting company (D)

438 U.S. 726 (1978).

NATURE OF CASE: Appeal from a Federal Communications Commission (FCC) disciplinary order.

FACT SUMMARY: The FCC (P) disciplined Pacifica (D) for broadcasting "indecent language" over the radio airwaves.

RULE OF LAW
Government may validly regulate speech that is indecent but not obscene.

FACTS: Pacifica (D) broadcasted a monologue performed by comedian George Carlin over its radio station. The monologue sought to express Carlin's view of the public perception of "obscene" language, and included the use of certain words that were considered "indecent" by a listener of the station. This listener filed a complaint with the FCC (P), contending he was harmed by being exposed to Carlin's monologue. The FCC (P) found the words "indecent" and issued an order that would be considered when the station's license came up for renewal. The court of appeals overturned the order as in violation of the First Amendment freedom of speech. It held that because the FCC (P) specifically found the speech not to be obscene, it had no power to regulate it. The Supreme Court granted certiorari.

ISSUE: May government regulate speech that is indecent but not obscene?

HOLDING AND DECISION: (Stevens, J.) Yes. Government may regulate speech which is indecent yet not obscene. Government may regulate the content of speech where such speech, in context, is vulgar, offensive, and shocking. Patently offensive speech is not entitled to complete constitutional protection. It may be limited under time and place restrictions. As a result, the order was properly issued. Broadcast media receives limited First Amendment protections because prior warnings of upcoming vulgar content are often insufficient to listeners tuning in and out. Broadcasting is also available to children, even though too young to read.

ANALYSIS

Justice Stevens, in this plurality decision, was careful to point out that if there had been any basis for concluding that the FCC (P) characterization of Carlin's monologue rested upon its political content, First Amendment protection might be required. If it is the speaker's opinion being expressed which gives offense, constitutional protection is mandated. In this case, the objection was not to Carlin's expressing his opinion, but to the manner in which it was expressed.

Quicknotes

FREEDOM OF SPEECH The right to express oneself without governmental restrictions on the content of that expression.

OBSCENITY Indecency, lewdness or offensive behavior in appearance or expression.

Sable Communications of California, Inc. v. Federal Communications Commn.

Communications company (P) v. Federal government (D)

492 U.S. 115 (1989).

NATURE OF CASE: Appeal by federal government from district court's holding of the unconstitutionality of Section 223(b) of the Federal Communications Act.

FACT SUMMARY: Sable Communications (P) offered "dial-a-porn" prerecorded telephone messages through the Pacific Bell telephone system. The district court held unconstitutional legislation that placed an outright ban on indecent as well as obscene interstate commercial telephone messages.

🏛 RULE OF LAW
The Federal Communications Act's outright ban on indecent as well as obscene interstate commercial telephone messages constitutes a First Amendment violation.

FACTS: Sable Communications (P) began offering sexually oriented prerecorded telephone messages ("dial-a-porn") through the Pacific Bell telephone network through special phone lines requiring access codes and scrambling so that only subscribers could obtain the messages. Those who called the adult message number were charged a special fee. Section 223(b) of the Communications Act of 1934, as amended in 1988, imposed an outright ban on indecent as well as obscene interstate commercial telephone messages. The district court held that Section 223(b) was not sufficiently narrowly drawn, and thus violated the First Amendment.

ISSUE: Does the Federal Communications Act's outright ban on indecent as well as obscene interstate commercial telephone messages constitute a First Amendment violation?

HOLDING AND DECISION: (White, J.) Yes. Sexual expression that is indecent but not obscene is protected by the First Amendment. The private telephone communications here at issue are substantially different from public radio broadcasts. In contrast to public displays, unsolicited mailings, and other means of expression that the recipient has no meaningful opportunity to avoid, the dial-in medium requires the listener to take affirmative steps to receive the communication. There is no "captive audience" here; callers will generally not be unwilling listeners. Placing a telephone call is not the same thing as turning on a radio and being taken by surprise by an indecent message.

▶ ANALYSIS

The Court noted that credit cards, access codes, and scrambling rules were a satisfactory solution to the problem of keeping indecent dial-a-porn messages out of reach of minors.

Quicknotes

FIRST AMENDMENT Prohibits Congress from enacting any law respecting an establishment of religion, prohibiting the free exercise of religion, abridging freedom of speech or the press, the right of peaceful assembly and the right to petition for a redress of grievances.

OBSCENITY Indecency, lewdness or offensive behavior in appearance or expression.

Reno v. American Civil Liberties Union

U.S. Attorney General (D) v. Civil liberties organization (P)

521 U.S. 844 (1997).

NATURE OF CASE: Review of judgment striking down provisions of the Communications Decency Act of 1996 (CDA).

FACT SUMMARY: The American Civil Liberties Union (ACLU) (P) challenged the constitutionality of provisions of the CDA that purported to protect minors from harmful transmissions over the Internet.

🏛 RULE OF LAW
Content-based government regulations on speech are unconstitutional unless the government can demonstrate that it has a compelling interest for the regulation and that the regulation is the least restrictive means of achieving that interest.

FACTS: The CDA contained provisions designed to protect minors from "indecent" and "patently offensive" communication on the Internet. The "indecent transmission" provision prohibited the knowing transmission of obscene or indecent messages to any recipient under eighteen years of age. The "patently offensive display" provision prohibited the knowing sending or displaying of patently offensive messages to a person under eighteen years of age. The ACLU (P) filed an action alleging that the CDA abridged freedom of speech protected by the First Amendment. The district court found in its favor and enjoined the enforcement of the "indecent" communications provisions, but expressly preserved the government's right to investigate and prosecute the obscenity or child pornography activities prohibited by the provision. The court also issued an unqualified injunction against the enforcement of the "patently offensive displays" provision because it contained no separate reference to obscenity or child pornography.

ISSUE: Are content-based government regulations on speech unconstitutional unless the government can demonstrate that it has a compelling interest for the regulation and that the regulation is the least restrictive means of achieving that interest?

HOLDING AND DECISION: (Stevens, J.) Yes. Content-based government regulations on speech are unconstitutional unless the government can demonstrate that it has a compelling interest for the regulation and that the regulation is the least restrictive means of achieving that interest. Although the congressional goal of protecting children from harmful materials is a legitimate and important one, the CDA provisions at issue here are so broad and imprecise that they cannot be upheld. The definitions within the CDA are imprecise and would certainly lead to a chilling effect on speech and expression over the Internet. Persons communicating over the Internet using even innocuous terms would hesitate to do so rather than risk criminal penalties imposed by a vague statute. It unquestionably deserves the highest level of First Amendment protection. The breadth of the CDA's coverage is wholly unprecedented and would undoubtedly impact adult as well as minor access to such materials. It does not limit its restrictions to commercial speech or entities, but encompasses anyone posting messages on a computer, regardless of time of day, website, or any other factor. The current provisions cannot stand as they are more likely to interfere with the free exchange of ideas than to encourage it.

▶ ANALYSIS

Issues surrounding speech, pornography, and access to the Internet will undoubtedly be revisited often in the next several years. The issues are extremely complex because the technology is so novel, and are further complicated by the fact that the Internet extends worldwide. The Court was appropriately cautious in striking down the provisions and leaving the issue in the hands of parents until further developments evolve.

■==■

Quicknotes

CONTENT BASED Refers to statutes that regulate speech based on its content.

■==■

Ashcroft v. American Civil Liberties Union

U.S. Attorney General (D) v. Civil liberties organization (P)

524 U.S. 656, 124 S. Ct. 2783 (2004).

NATURE OF CASE: Appeal from entry of preliminary injunction.

FACT SUMMARY: Congress passed the Child Online Protection Act (COPA) and the American Civil Liberties Union (ACLU) (P) obtained a preliminary injunction to prevent its enforcement. The Attorney General (D) appealed, arguing that the statute did not violate First Amendment rights.

🏛 RULE OF LAW
Less restrictive alternatives should be employed when the government seeks to restrict content-based speech.

FACTS: Congress sought to protect minors from sexually explicit content on the Internet and passed the COPA to accomplish this goal. COPA imposed criminal penalties for posting material "harmful to minors" for "commercial purposes." What constituted harm to minors was broadly defined in the statute. The ACLU (P) challenged the constitutionality of the statute on First Amendment grounds and obtained a preliminary injunction to prevent Attorney General Ashcroft (D) from enforcing it. Under COPA, adults had to prove age through the use of one of several software screens prior to accessing commercial pornography. The ACLU argued that this was an unconstitutional restriction on speech. Ashcroft (D) appealed and the court of appeals affirmed the entry of preliminary injunction. The Supreme Court granted certiorari.

ISSUE: Should less restrictive alternatives be employed when the government seeks to restrict content-based speech?

HOLDING AND DECISION: (Kennedy, J.) Yes. Less restrictive alternatives should be employed when the government seeks to restrict content-based speech. Content-based restrictions are presumed invalid unless the government can justify them by meeting the burden of proving constitutionality. The government has not been able to meet that burden here because it cannot justify the statute in the face of several less restrictive alternatives. Filters, for example, could be installed on computers allowing adults to monitor the Internet content for their children rather than the government monitoring the Internet content for everyone. As the government cannot meet its burden, the district court did not err in granting the preliminary injunction.

DISSENT: (Scalia, J.) Commercial pornography is not entitled to First Amendment strict scrutiny. COPA is constitutional.

DISSENT: (Breyer, J.) Congress could not have achieved its goal through less restrictive means. The material regulated is not entitled to First Amendment protections, so the less restrictive means are not required. COPA imposes a minor burden on adults seeking access to commercial pornography. The majority ignores the fact that the less restrictive alternative, filtering software, already exists and does not accomplish the stated goal of protecting children from commercial pornography. If that system is ineffective, as it is, COPA is an appropriate response.

▶ ANALYSIS

The ACLU feared that a restrictive minority could affect the Internet content for the entire nation if a national standard was imposed. Defining "harmful to minors" could result in too sweeping restrictions. The government disagreed with the notion that parents should monitor the Internet for children because that was currently not working. Protecting children from commercial pornography is a compelling governmental interest, but overly restricting lawful speech is not going to succeed.

■=■

Quicknotes

COMPELLING STATE INTEREST Defense to an alleged Equal Protection Clause violation; that a state action was necessary in order to protect an interest the government is under a duty to protect.

CONTENT BASED Refers to statutes that regulate speech based on its content.

STRICT SCRUTINY Method by which courts determine the constitutionality of a law, when a law affects a fundamental right. Under the test, the legislature must have had a compelling interest to enact the law and measures prescribed by the law must be the least restrictive means possible to accomplish its goal.

■=■

Virginia State Board of Pharmacy v. Virginia Citizens Consumer Council, Inc.

State board (D) v. Residents (P)

425 U.S. 748 (1976).

NATURE OF CASE: Action for declaratory judgment.

FACT SUMMARY: The State Board (D) was charged with enforcing a state law that made it illegal for a pharmacist to advertise the prices of his prescription drugs.

🏛 RULE OF LAW

The First Amendment guarantee of freedom of speech extends to the recipients as well as the sources of the speech, and, as such, the consumer's interest in the free flow of advertising information brings such "commercial speech" within the protection of the First Amendment.

FACTS: Virginia law provides that licensed pharmacists are guilty of "unprofessional conduct" if they advertise "in any manner whatsoever, any amount, price, fee, premium, discount, rebate or credit terms ... for any drugs which may be dispensed only by prescription." Consumer Council (P) is comprised of Virginia residents who require prescription drugs. Citing statistics that show that drugs vary in price strikingly from outlet to outlet (e.g., from $2.59 to $6.00 for one drug), they filed this action to have the advertising ban declared an unconstitutional infringement on their First Amendment right to free speech. From a judgment for the Council (P), the State Board (D) appealed contending that "commercial speech" such as this is not protected by the First Amendment.

ISSUE: Does the First Amendment protect "commercial speech" as manifested in price advertising by professional groups?

HOLDING AND DECISION: (Blackmun, J.) Yes. The First Amendment guarantee of freedom of speech extends to the recipients as well as the sources of the speech, and, as such, the consumer's interest in the free flow of advertising information brings such "commercial speech" within the protection of the First Amendment. The traditional rule that "commercial speech" is not protected has been gradually eroded by the court and today, it is set to rest. Advertising, however tasteless, is information nevertheless and entitled to constitutional deference thereby. To be sure, the holding today does not prevent reasonable regulation as to "time, place, and manner" or prevent illegal or misleading speech. It only recognizes the legitimacy of commercial speech for First Amendment purposes.

DISSENT: (Rehnquist, J.) The Court's decision today is troublesome for two reasons. First, it extends standing to sue to a group not asserting their right to receive information but rather the right of third parties to publish it. Second, the majority opinion today extends First Amendment protections to commercial speech previously discouraged so long as the speech is not misleading or promoting anything illegal. This usurps the legislative right and duty to regulate the promotion of health care products.

▶ ANALYSIS

This case has brought many observers to the conclusion that advertising bans on professionals are no longer constitutional. Indeed, the American Bar Association and several state bar associations have begun to promulgate standards for advertising by attorneys that will protect the public from the perceived evils of a competitive bar. *Consumer Council* claims to overrule the 1951 case of *Breard v. Alexandria*, 341 U.S. 662 (1951).

Quicknotes

COMMERCIAL SPEECH Any speech that proposes a commercial transaction, or promotes products or services.

FIRST AMENDMENT RIGHTS Rights conferred by the First Amendment to the U.S. Constitution prohibiting Congress from enacting any law respecting an establishment of religion, prohibiting the free exercise of religion, abridging freedom of speech or the press, the right of peaceful assembly and the right to petition for a redress of grievances.

Bolger v. Youngs Drug Products Corp.

Federal government (P) v. Drug product corporation (D)

463 U.S. 60 (1983).

NATURE OF CASE: Challenge to prohibition of unsolicited mailings.

FACT SUMMARY: Youngs Drug Products (D) sought to make unsolicited mailings of advertisements for contraceptives in violation of a federal statute.

🏛 RULE OF LAW
A sweeping statutory prohibition against mailing unsolicited advertisements for contraceptives violates the First Amendment.

FACTS: Youngs Drug Products (D), which manufactures, sells, and distributes contraceptives, undertook a campaign to publicize the availability and desirability of its product by various methods, including unsolicited mass mailings to members of the public. The advertising took the form of multipage, multi-item flyers, promoting prophylactics. 39 U.S.C. § 3001(e)(2) prohibited the mailing of unsolicited advertisements for contraceptives.

ISSUE: Does a sweeping statutory prohibition against mailing unsolicited advertisements for contraceptives violate the First Amendment?

HOLDING AND DECISION: (Marshall, J.) Yes. The mere fact that these informational pamphlets were conceded to be advertisements clearly did not compel the conclusion that they are commercial speech. Similarly, the reference to a specific product did not by itself render the pamphlets commercial speech. Finally, the fact that the company had an economic motivation for mailing the pamphlets was insufficient by itself to turn the materials into commercial speech. This "combination of characteristics," however, provides strong support for the conclusion that these informational pamphlets were properly characterized as commercial speech. These mailings are entitled to the qualified but nonetheless substantial protection accorded to commercial speech, and here the justifications offered by the government were insufficient to warrant the sweeping prohibition of the mailing of unsolicited advertisements.

▶ ANALYSIS

The Court observed that advertising that links a product to a current public debate is not thereby necessarily entitled to the constitutional protection afforded noncommercial speech.

Quicknotes

COMMERCIAL SPEECH Any speech that proposes a commercial transaction, or promotes products or services.

FIRST AMENDMENT RIGHTS Rights conferred by the First Amendment to the U.S. Constitution prohibiting Congress from enacting any law respecting an establishment of religion, prohibiting the free exercise of religion, abridging freedom of speech or the press, the right of peaceful assembly and the right to petition for a redress of grievances.

Central Hudson Gas & Electric Corp. v. Public Service Commn. of New York

Gas company (P) v. Federal agency (D)

447 U.S. 557 (1980).

NATURE OF CASE: Action challenging the constitutionality of a federal regulation.

FACT SUMMARY: Central Hudson Gas (P) claimed the First Amendment prohibited the Public Service Commission's (PSC) (D) regulation completely banning promotional advertising by an electrical utility.

🏛 RULE OF LAW
Where there is a substantial governmental interest, a restriction on commercial speech protected by the First Amendment is constitutional if it directly advances that interest and is not more extensive than is necessary to serve that interest.

FACTS: The PSC (D) banned all promotional advertising by an electrical utility as contrary to the national policy of conserving energy. Central Hudson Gas (P) challenged the regulation on First Amendment grounds.

ISSUE: Can the government place a restriction on commercial speech protected by the First Amendment if it directly advances a substantial governmental interest and is not broader than is necessary to serve that interest?

HOLDING AND DECISION: (Powell, J.) Yes. Commercial speech that concerns lawful activity and is not misleading is protected under the First Amendment, although at a lesser level than other speech. However, this protection prevents governmental restrictions on covered commercial speech unless they advance a substantial governmental interest and are not more extensive than is necessary to serve that interest. These principles produce a four-step analysis which, when applied to this case, indicates the regulation at issue is unconstitutional. It satisfies all the requirements except the last. It is so broad that it suppresses speech about electrical devices or services that would cause no increase in total energy usage and thus be unrelated to the energy conservation interest of the state.

▶ ANALYSIS

Historically, the Court had always held that commercial speech was not within the protections of the First Amendment. In the mid-1970s, however, a new trend began in which the Court recognized that the First Amendment did encompass certain commercial speech and offered it protection, although of a more limited sort than other speech. In recent years, though, there is evidence that the enthusiasm among the justices for including commercial speech within the First Amendment is waning.

■■■

Quicknotes

COMMERCIAL SPEECH Any speech that proposes a commercial transaction, or promotes products or services.

FIRST AMENDMENT RIGHTS Rights conferred by the First Amendment to the U.S. Constitution prohibiting Congress from enacting any law respecting an establishment of religion, prohibiting the free exercise of religion, abridging freedom of speech or the press, the right of peaceful assembly and the right to petition for a redress of grievances.

■■■

Friedman v. Rogers

Optometrist (P) v. State (D)

440 U.S. 1 (1979).

NATURE OF CASE: Appeal from judgment that upheld legislation prohibiting optometrists from advertising and practicing under trade names.

FACT SUMMARY: Friedman (P), an optometrist, sought to advertise and practice under a trade name in violation of a Texas statute.

🏛 RULE OF LAW
Legislation that prohibits optometrists from advertising and practicing under trade names does not violate the First Amendment.

FACTS: Optometrists sought to be permitted to advertise and practice using trade names, arguing that Texas legislation that prohibited optometrists from advertising and practicing under trade names constituted a violation of their First Amendment rights.

ISSUE: Does legislation that prohibits optometrists from advertising and practicing under trade names violate the First Amendment?

HOLDING AND DECISION: (Powell, J.) No. Here, the state of Texas was concerned with a form of commercial speech that has no intrinsic meaning. A trade name conveys no information about the price and nature of the services offered by an optometrist until it acquires meaning over a period of time by association formed in the minds of the public between the name and some standard price or quality. Because these ill-defined associations of trade names with price and quality, information can be manipulated by the users of trade names, there is a significant possibility that trade names will be used to mislead the public, and the possibilities for deception are numerous. The use of a trade name is "strictly business." The use of trade names in connection with optometric practice, then, is a form of commercial speech and nothing more. Affirmed.

▶ ANALYSIS

The Court observed that the concerns of the Texas legislature about the deceptive and misleading uses of optometrists' trade names were not speculative or hypothetical, but were based on experience in Texas with which the legislature was familiar; hence, this legislation was a constitutionally permissible state regulation in furtherance of its interest.

Quicknotes

COMMERCIAL SPEECH Any speech that proposes a commercial transaction, or promotes products or services.

Linmark Associates, Inc. v. Township of Willingboro

Realtor (P) v. Municipality (D)

431 U.S. 85 (1977).

NATURE OF CASE: Appeal from judgment of district court, which struck down municipal ordinance.

FACT SUMMARY: Linmark (P), a realtor, challenged an ordinance prohibiting the posting of "For Sale" or "Sold" signs, on First Amendment grounds.

RULE OF LAW
The First Amendment does not permit a municipality to prohibit the posting of "For Sale" or "Sold" signs to stem what it perceives as the flight of white homeowners from a racially integrated community.

FACTS: To stem what it perceived as the flight of white homeowners from a racially integrated community, a municipality (D) enacted an ordinance prohibiting the posting of "For Sale" or "Sold" signs. Linmark (P), a realtor, challenged the ordinance on First Amendment grounds.

ISSUE: Does the First Amendment permit a municipality to prohibit the posting of "For Sale" or "Sold" signs to stem what it perceives as the flight of white homeowners from a racially integrated community?

HOLDING AND DECISION: (Marshall, J.) No. The First Amendment does not permit a municipality to prohibit the posting of "For Sale" or "Sold" signs to stem what it perceives as the flight of white homeowners from a racially integrated community. The township (D) here acted to prevent its residents from obtaining certain information pertaining to sales activity in the town, which information was of vital interest to the residents since it could bear on one of the most important decisions they have a right to make: where to live and raise their families. The municipality's (D) concern here was not with any commercial aspect of the "For Sale" signs but with the "substance of the information communicated" to the town's residents. Furthermore, the record demonstrated that the municipality (D) failed to establish that such an ordinance was needed to assure an integrated community since there was no evidence of any panic selling by white homeowners, and nor did the record show that proscribing the signs would reduce public awareness of realty sales and thereby decrease public concern over selling.

ANALYSIS

The Court stressed that the societal interest in the free flow of commercial information is in no way lessened by the fact that the subject of the commercial interest here is realty rather than abortion or drugs.

Quicknotes

FIRST AMENDMENT RIGHTS Rights conferred by the First Amendment to the U.S. Constitution prohibiting Congress from enacting any law respecting an establishment of religion, prohibiting the free exercise of religion, abridging freedom of speech or the press, the right of peaceful assembly and the right to petition for a redress of grievances.

44 Liquormart, Inc. v. Rhode Island

Liquor distributor (P) v. State (D)

517 U.S. 484 (1996).

NATURE OF CASE: Appeal of decision upholding a state law prohibiting alcohol advertising.

FACT SUMMARY: Rhode Island (D) banned the advertising of retail prices of alcoholic beverages.

 RULE OF LAW
Complete bans on truthful commercial advertising are unconstitutional.

FACTS: In 1956, Rhode Island (D) enacted a prohibition against advertising the retail price of any alcoholic beverage offered for sale in the state. The law also proscribed the news media from publishing this information. Rhode Island (D) claimed that the law was enacted to reduce market-wide consumption of alcohol. The law was challenged as an unconstitutional abridgement of free speech. The district court concluded that the ban was unconstitutional because liquor price advertising had no impact on levels of alcohol consumption in Rhode Island (D), and thus the ban did not directly advance the State's (D) interest. The court of appeals reversed. The Supreme Court granted certiorari to decide the issue.

ISSUE: Are complete bans on truthful commercial advertising unconstitutional?

HOLDING AND DECISION: (Stevens, J.) Yes. Complete bans on truthful commercial advertising are unconstitutional. Traditionally, commercial messages have provided consumers with information about the availability of goods and services. The common law prohibited fraudulent and misleading advertising. However, prior cases have recognized that regulation of commercial advertising is not protected to the same degree as core First Amendment speech. In *Central Hudson v. Public Service Commission of N.Y.*, 447 U.S. 557 (1980), this Court held that regulation of commercial speech had to be related to a significant state interest and that more limited alternatives are not available. When a state entirely prohibits the dissemination of truthful advertising for reasons unrelated to protecting consumers, strict scrutiny of the law is applicable. In the present case, Rhode Island (D) could reduce alcohol consumption by other methods, such as taxes, rather than through speech regulation. Thus, there is no reasonable relationship between the regulation and state objective. Accordingly, Rhode Island's (D) law is unconstitutional. Reversed.

CONCURRENCE: (Thomas, J.) The government's manipulation of consumers' choices by keeping them ignorant is per se illegitimate. Thus, the balancing test of *Central Hudson* is not appropriate. Accurate commercial speech is entitled to full protection.

CONCURRENCE: (O'Connor, J.) Because Rhode Island's (D) regulation fails even the less stringent standard set out in *Central Hudson*, nothing here requires adoption of a new analysis for the evaluation of commercial speech regulation.

ANALYSIS

The Court also overruled the case of *Posados de Puerto Rico Associates v. Tourism Co. of P.R.*, 478 U.S. 328 (1986), in which the Court held that a ban on casino advertising was valid since the state could choose to ban casinos themselves entirely. The decision correctly points out that banning speech may be more intrusive than banning conduct and that the speech ban is not necessarily a lesser included state power. The Court also rejected any "vice" exception that *Posados* may have implied.

Quicknotes

COMMERCIAL SPEECH Any speech that proposes a commercial transaction, or promotes products or services.

STRICT SCRUTINY Method by which courts determine the constitutionality of a law, when a law affects a fundamental right. Under the test, the legislature must have had a compelling interest to enact the law and measures prescribed by the law must be the least restrictive means possible to accomplish its goal.

Lorillard Tobacco Co. v. Reilly

Smokeless tobacco company (P) v. Massachusetts Attorney General (D)

533 U.S. 525 (2001).

NATURE OF CASE: Constitutional challenge to advertising restrictions.

FACT SUMMARY: Smokeless tobacco and cigar companies objected to their inclusion in the advertising restrictions imposed upon cigarette companies.

🏛 RULE OF LAW
Excessively strict regulations on companies' advertising violate their commercial free-speech rights under the First Amendment.

FACTS: Massachusetts passed stringent restrictions on tobacco companies' advertising, specifically prohibiting any outdoor advertising within 1,000 feet of playgrounds or schools. Particularly in the metropolitan areas of Massachusetts, this resulted in a near shut-out of tobacco company outdoor advertising. The Lorillard Tobacco Co. (Lorillard) (P) manufactures smokeless tobacco and joined forces with cigar manufacturers to challenge the validity of the application of the advertising laws to them. Lorillard conceded that the Attorney General (D) has identified a correlation between cigarette advertising and underage smoking, but argued that no such correlation exists between smokeless tobacco advertising and underage use. Lorillard also argued that the Attorney General's (D) restrictions were overly broad.

ISSUE: Do excessively strict regulations on companies' advertising violate their commercial free-speech rights under the First Amendment?

HOLDING AND DECISION: (O'Connor, J.) Yes. Excessively strict regulations on companies' advertising violate their commercial free-speech rights under the First Amendment. Commercial speech regulation is evaluated according to the framework handed down in *Central Hudson Gas & Electric Corp. v. Public Service Commission of New York*, 447 U.S. 557 (1980). The Attorney General's (D) regulations here meet the first three elements, but do not meet the fourth because the restrictions are too excessive. The 1,000-foot barrier substantially eliminates outdoor tobacco advertising in major metropolitan areas in Massachusetts. In addition, indoor advertising visible from outside the store falls under the restriction, which severely curtails store-owners' ability to offer onsite advertising. This speech restriction violates the commercial free-speech rights of the tobacco companies and is thus invalid.

CONCURRENCE: (Thomas, J.) The advertising restrictions should be evaluated with strict scrutiny because the intent of the restrictions is to regulate the content of the expressed commercial speech. Smoking does pose serious risks, but tobacco advertising does not require the suspension of First Amendment protections. Other advertisers promote equally harmful products, such as alcohol or fatty foods, with impunity. Tobacco advertising should be treated no differently.

CONCURRENCE IN PART AND DISSENT IN PART: (Stevens, J.) The regulations effectively achieve the ends sought, but the 1,000-foot rule is not an appropriately tailored means. Whether a child-directed location restriction goes too far in regulating adult speech is a question to be remanded for trial.

▶ *ANALYSIS*

The Court supported Massachusetts's finding that cigarette advertising affected underage smoking, but the sweeping regulations on the tobacco company advertising simply went too far. Massachusetts stopped just short of banning all tobacco advertising. As Justice Thomas notes in his concurrence, other products are just as insidious if not more dangerous to minors, and it is absurd to abandon the First Amendment for tobacco products. Suspending constitutional protections for even one admittedly fatal product could lead to other "distasteful" products being regulated out of existence and everyone's opinion could significantly differ on what constitutes "distasteful."

◼■◼

Quicknotes

COMMERCIAL SPEECH Any speech that proposes a commercial transaction, or promotes products or services.

STRICT SCRUTINY Method by which courts determine the constitutionality of a law, when a law affects a fundamental right. Under the test, the legislature must have had a compelling interest to enact the law and measures prescribed by the law must be the least restrictive means possible to accomplish its goal.

◼■◼

New York Times Co. v. Sullivan

Newspaper publisher (D) v. Public official (P)

376 U.S. 254 (1964).

NATURE OF CASE: Appeal of defamation judgment.

FACT SUMMARY: New York Times (D) published an editorial advertisement in which false statements were made which concerned Sullivan (P).

🏛 RULE OF LAW
The First Amendment requires that a public official may not recover damages for defamatory false-hoods relating to his official conduct unless he proves that the statement involved was made with "actual malice—that is, with knowledge that it was false or with reckless disregard of whether it was false or not."

FACTS: Sullivan (P) was a commissioner in the city of Montgomery, Alabama, charged with supervision of the Police Department. During a series of civil rights demonstrations in that city in 1960, the New York Times (D) published an editorial advertisement entitled, "Heed Their Rising Voices," in which several charges of terrorism were leveled at the Police Department. The falsity of some of these statements was uncontroverted. The advertisement charged that nine students at a local college had been expelled for leading a march on the state capitol when, in fact, the reason had been an illegal lunch counter sit-in. The advertisement charged that the police had padlocked the dining hall of the college to starve the demonstrators into submission when, in fact, no padlocking had occurred. Other false statements also were made. Sullivan (P) brought a defamation action against New York Times (D) for these statements and recovered $500,000. Under Alabama law, a publication is libel per se (no special damages need be proved—general damages are presumed), whenever a defamatory falsehood is shown to have injured its subject in his public office or impute misconduct to him in his office. New York Times (D) appealed the Alabama judgment, challenging this rule.

ISSUE: Are defamatory falsehoods regarding public officials protected by constitutional guarantees of freedom of speech and press?

HOLDING AND DECISION: (Brennan, J.) Yes. The First Amendment requires that a public official may not recover damages for defamatory falsehoods relating to his official conduct unless he proves that the statement involved was made with "actual malice—that is, with knowledge that it was false or with reckless disregard of whether it was false or not." First Amendment protections do not turn upon the truth, popularity, or social utility of ideas and beliefs that are involved. Rather, they are based upon the theory that erroneous statements are inevitable in free debate and must be protected if such freedom is to survive. Only where malice is

involved do such protections cease. Here, the Alabama rule falls short of this standard and the evidence at trial was insufficient to determine its existence.

▶ ANALYSIS

New York Times is the landmark case in constitutional defamation law. The subsequent cases have expanded this concept even further. In *Rosenblatt v. Baer*, 383 U.S. 75 (1966), the Court defined "public official" as anyone having substantial responsibility for conduct of government affairs. In *Curtis Publishing v. Butts*, 388 U.S. 130 (1967), *New York Times* was extended to "public figures" as well as officials. In *Gertz v. Welch*, 418 U.S. 323 (1974), however, the Court retreated a bit by stating that, "As long as they do not impose liability without fault, the states may define for themselves the appropriate standard of liability for publisher . . . of defamatory falsehood injurious to a private individual." Note that the Court has also taken steps to toughen the *New York Times*'s recklessness standard. In *St. Amont v. Thompson*, 390 U.S. 727 (1968), the Court ruled that recklessness was not to be measured by the reasonable man standard, but rather by the subjective standard of whether or not the defendant in the case subjectively entertained serious doubts about the truth of his statements.

◼══◼

Quicknotes

DEFAMATION An intentional false publication, communicated publicly in either oral or written form, subjecting a person to scorn, hatred or ridicule, or injuring him in relation to his occupation or business.

LIBEL A false or malicious publication subjecting a person to scorn, hatred or ridicule, or injuring him or her in relation to his or her occupation or business.

◼══◼

Gertz v. Welch

Attorney (P) v. Publisher (D)

418 U.S. 323 (1974).

NATURE OF CASE: Action for defamation.

FACT SUMMARY: Gertz (P) sued Welch (D), a publisher of a John Birch Society newsletter, when Welch (D) published an article calling Gertz (P) a long-time Communist who helped frame a Chicago policeman's conviction for murder, all of which was untrue.

RULE OF LAW
In an action for defamation, a private individual must show the publisher to be at fault and may recover no more than actual damages when liability is not based on a showing of knowledge of falsity or reckless disregard for the truth.

FACTS: Welch (D) published *American Opinion*, a monthly newsletter of the John Birch Society. An article appeared in that publication purporting to illustrate that the conviction of Nuccio, a Chicago policeman, for the murder of Nelson, a young man, was a communist frameup led by Gertz (P). It was said further that Gertz (P) had a criminal record, was an official of the Marxist League, a Leninist, and an officer of the National Lawyers Guild, which was falsely described as a communist organization in the forefront of the attack on Chicago police during the 1968 Democratic Convention. The only element of truth was that 15 years earlier Gertz (P) had been a National Lawyers Guild officer. Actually, he was a reputable lawyer whose only connection with the Nuccio case was to represent the Nelson family in civil litigation against Nuccio. Gertz (P) attended the coroner's inquest into Nelson's death and filed an action for damages, but did not discuss the matter with the press or play any part in the criminal proceedings. At trial, the evidence showed that *American Opinion*'s managing editor knew nothing of the defamatory content but had belief in the reputation and accuracy of the author. The jury found the matter libelous per se and not privileged, and awarded a $50,000 judgment, but the judge applied *the New York Times* standard as pertaining to any discussion of a public issue wihout regard to the status of the person defamed. Judgment n.o.v. was entered for Welch (D). The court of appeals affirmed, and Gertz (P) appealed.

ISSUE: In an action for defamation, must a private individual show the publisher to be at fault and recover no more than actual damages when liability is not based on a showing of knowledge of falsity or reckless disregard for the truth?

HOLDING AND DECISION: (Powell, J.) Yes. In an action for defamation, a private individual must show the publisher to be at fault and may recover no more than actual damages when liability is not based on a showing of knowledge of falsity or reckless disregard for the truth. The *New York Times* standard applies to public figures and public officials, but the state interest in compensating injury to reputation of private individuals requires that a different rule should apply to them. A public figure or official has greater access to the media to counteract false statements than private individuals normally enjoy. Being more vulnerable to injury, the private individual deserves greater protection and recovery. As long as the states do not impose liability without fault, the states themselves may define the appropriate standard of liability for a publisher of defamatory matter injurious to a private person. And the states may not permit the recovery of presumed or punitive damages, at least when liability is not based on a showing of knowledge of falsity or reckless disregard for the truth. Here, Gertz (P) was not publicly involved. The public figure question should look to the nature and extent of an individual's participation in the controversy giving rise to the action. Reversed and remanded for new trial as the jury was allowed to impose liability without fault and presume damages without proof of damages.

DISSENT: (Brennan, J.) "We strike the proper accommodation between avoidance of media self-censorship and protection of individual reputations only when we require states to apply the *Times*'s 'knowing-or-reckless falsity' standard in civil libel actions concerning media reports of the involvement of private individuals in events of public or general interest."

DISSENT: (White, J.) Federalizing major aspects of libel law is a radical change and a severe invasion of the prerogatives of the states not shown to be necessitated by present circumstances or required by the First Amendment. Neither *New York Times* nor the First Amendment should deprive this private citizen of his historic recourse to redress damaging falsehoods. The risk of falsehood here is shifted to the victim. While a statement may be wholly false, wrong and unjustified, a defamation case will be dismissed if the victim cannot prove negligence or other fault.

ANALYSIS

The majority advances the view that it is necessary to restrict victims of defamation who do not prove knowledge of falsity or reckless disregard for the truth to compensation for actual injury alone. Actual injury is not limited to out-of-pocket loss. Actual harm includes impairment of

Continued on next page.

reputation and standing in the community, personal humil-
iation, and mental anguish and suffering. While the court
noted the fact that juries in the past were tempted to
award excess damages, there was no proof that trial
judges have failed to keep judgments within reasonable
bounds.

■══■

Quicknotes

DEFAMATION An intentional false publication, communicated publicly in either oral or written form, subjecting a
person to scorn, hatred or ridicule, or injuring him in
relation to his occupation or business.

JUDGMENT NOTWITHSTANDING THE VERDICT A judgment
entered by the trial judge reversing a jury verdict if the
jury's determination has no basis in law or fact.

PUNITIVE DAMAGES Damages exceeding the actual injury
suffered for the purposes of punishment of the defendant, deterrence of the wrongful behavior or comfort to
the plaintiff.

■══■

Dun & Bradstreet, Inc. v. Greenmoss Builders, Inc.

Credit reporting agency (D) v. Contractor (P)

472 U.S. 749 (1985).

NATURE OF CASE: Appeal from an award of damages for defamation.

FACT SUMMARY: Dun & Bradstreet (D) contended Greenmoss (P) could not recover punitive damages for defamation even though the subject was not one of public concern.

🏛 RULE OF LAW
In defamation cases involving subjects that do not involve public concern, no actual malice need be shown to support an award of punitive damages.

FACTS: Dun & Bradstreet (D) circulated a false and defamatory credit report on Greenmoss (P) that injured the latter in its business relations. The report had been prepared negligently, and no action had been taken to verify the contents. Greenmoss (P) sued and received an award for compensatory and punitive damages. Dun & Bradstreet (D) appealed, contending that even though the subject of the defamation was not one of public concern, the constitutional limits on recoverable damages based on a showing of actual malice applied to deny recovery. The Supreme Court granted certiorari.

ISSUE: Must actual malice be shown in cases where the defamatory statements do not involve a subject of public concern?

HOLDING AND DECISION: (Powell, J.) No. In defamation cases involving subjects that are not of public concern, actual malice need not be shown to support a recovery of punitive damages. The requirement of actual malice relates to constitutional guarantees of free press. Public figures or events of public concern generate enough media exposure to allow both parties an opportunity to present their views publicly. However, where a private entity is defamed in a matter that is not of concern to the general public, this opportunity to rebut the defamation does not exist. As a result, a less stringent standard must apply to allow recovery in this case. Affirmed.

DISSENT: (Brennan, J.) *Gertz* requires that actual malice must be shown to support a jury award for presumed and punitive damages. Even if it can be accepted that a distinction must be drawn between matters of public and private concern, the credit reporting at issue here is certainly of public concern and deserving of *Gertz* protections.

▶ ANALYSIS

This case represents a refusal of the Court, in the plurality, to extend its holding in *New York Times v. Sullivan*, 376 U.S. 254 (1964), and *Gertz v. Robert Welch, Inc.*, 418 U.S. 323

(1974). In those cases, the Court developed rules whereby public figures and issues of public concern were given constitutional requirements for recovery in defamation. More than mere negligence was required to be shown. Actual malice or a reckless disregard for the truth was made an element of the cause of action.

■━■

Quicknotes

ACTUAL MALICE The issuance of a publication with knowledge of its falsity or with reckless disregard as to its truth.

DEFAMATION An intentional false publication, communicated publicly in either oral or written form, subjecting a person to scorn, hatred or ridicule, or injuring him in relation to his occupation or business.

NEGLIGENCE Conduct falling below the standard of care that a reasonable person would demonstrate under similar conditions.

PUNITIVE DAMAGES Damages exceeding the actual injury suffered for the purposes of punishment of the defendant, deterrence of the wrongful behavior or comfort to the plaintiff.

RECKLESSNESS The conscious disregard of substantial and unjustifiable risk.

■━■

Hustler Magazine v. Falwell

Magazine publisher (D) v. Minister (P)

485 U.S. 46 (1988).

NATURE OF CASE: Review of a diversity action alleging invasion of privacy, libel, and intentional infliction of emotional distress.

FACT SUMMARY: Jury ruled in favor of Falwell (P) on intentional infliction of emotional distress claim.

🏛 RULE OF LAW
Recovery for the tort of intentional infliction of emotional distress must meet the New York Times standard.

FACTS: Hustler Magazine (D) published a parody of a Campari Liqueur ad featuring Jerry Falwell (P), a nationally known minister. The parody was a play on a Campari ad campaign that featured interviews with celebrities about their "first time" partaking of Campari Liqueur. The "first time" nature of the ad campaign had strong sexual undertones. The caption on the Hustler Magazine (D) fictional ad read: "Jerry Falwell talks about his first time." The ad went on to detail a fictional interview with Jerry Falwell (P) in which he states that his "first time" was during a drunken incestuous rendezvous with his mother in an outhouse. In small print on the bottom of the page, the ad contained the disclaimer "ad parody—not to be taken seriously." The magazine's (D) table of contents also listed the ad as "Fiction; Ad and Personality Parody." Following publication of this ad, Falwell (P) brought this diversity action alleging invasion of privacy, libel and intentional infliction of emotional distress.

ISSUE: May public figures and public officials recover for the tort of intentional infliction of emotional distress by reason of publications such as the one at issue here?

HOLDING AND DECISION: (Rehnquist, C.J.) Yes, but only if the public figure or public official can demonstrate that the publication contains a false statement of fact that was made with "actual malice." The *New York Times* standard as applied in this area reflects a First Amendment limitation upon a state's authority to protect its citizens from intentional infliction of emotional distress.

▶ ANALYSIS

The *Hustler Magazine* decision upholds the right and prerogative of the American citizenry to criticize public figures and measures.

Quicknotes

ACTUAL MALICE The issuance of a publication with knowledge of its falsity or with reckless disregard as to its truth.

DEFAMATION An intentional false publication, communicated publicly in either oral or written form, subjecting a person to scorn, hatred or ridicule, or injuring him in relation to his occupation or business.

Cox Broadcasting Corp. v. Cohn

Broadcaster (D) v. Rape victim's parent (P)

420 U.S. 469 (1975).

NATURE OF CASE: Appeal involving First and Fourteenth Amendment challenge to liability under the tort of public disclosure of private facts.

FACT SUMMARY: State of Georgia extended a cause of action for damages for invasion of privacy caused by the publication of a deceased rape victim's name.

🏛 RULE OF LAW
The First Amendment prevents liability for public disclosure of private facts if the information was lawfully obtained from public records and is truthfully reported.

FACTS: In August 1971, Cohn's (P) 17-year-old daughter was the victim of rape and did not survive the incident. Six youths were indicted for the murder and rape. There was substantial press coverage of the crime, but the identity of the victim was not disclosed largely due to a Georgia law making it a misdemeanor to publish or broadcast the name of a rape victim. In April 1972, the six defendants appeared in court. In the course of the proceedings, a reporter covering the incident learned the name of the rape victim from an examination of the indictments made available for his inspection in the courtroom. Later that same day, the reporter broadcast the rape victim's name over a TV affiliate of Cox Broadcasting Corporation (D). Cohn (P) brought this action under the Georgia statute and the common-law tort of public disclosure of private fact.

ISSUE: May a state extend a cause of action for damages for invasion of privacy caused by the publication of a deceased rape victim?

HOLDING AND DECISION: (White, J.) No, not if the name of the deceased rape victim was lawfully obtained from the public records and is truthfully reported. Great responsibility is placed on the news media to report fully and accurately the proceedings of government, and official records and documents open to the public provide basic reports of government activity. The media must be free to report such publicly available information to ensure that the people are an informed judge of government activity.

▌ ANALYSIS

The Court in *Cox Broadcasting* stopped short of imposing a rule that, despite making public records available to the media, would forbid publication of the information contained therein if offensive to the sensibilities of the reasonable man. Such a rule would invite timidity and self-censorship on the part of the media, potentially leading to the suppression of many items that should be made available to the public.

Quicknotes

PUBLIC DISCLOSURE OF PRIVATE FACTS A form of invasion of privacy involving the disclosure of private facts regarding a person with which the public has no concern.

Florida Star v. B.J.F.

Newspaper publication (D) v. Rape victim (P)

491 U.S. 524 (1989)

NATURE OF CASE:
Review of a First Amendment challenge to a statutory invasion of privacy claim.

FACT SUMMARY:
In finding that the Florida Star (D) violated the Florida invasion of privacy statute, jury awarded compensatory and punitive damages to B.J.F. (P).

🏛 RULE OF LAW
Where a newspaper publishes truthful information that it has lawfully obtained, punishment may lawfully be imposed only when narrowly tailored to a state interest of the highest order.

FACTS:
Florida Statute § 794.03 (1987) makes it unlawful to "print, publish, or broadcast . . . in any instrument of mass communication" the name of the victim of a sex offense. B.J.F. (P) reported to the Duval County, Florida Sheriff's Department ("Department") that she had been robbed and sexually assaulted by an unknown assailant. The Department prepared a report on the incident that identified B.J.F. (P) by her full name. The Department then placed the report in an unrestricted pressroom. A Florida Star (D) reporter-trainee entered the pressroom, copied the report and presented it to a Florida Star (D) reporter. The Florida Star (D) reporter then drafted an article including B.J.F.'s (P) full name for publication. B.J.F. (P) filed suit in Circuit Court of Duval County against the Department and the Florida Star (D), alleging violations of Florida Statute § 794.03.

ISSUE:
May a newspaper be held civilly liable for publishing the name of a rape victim that it had obtained from a publicly released police report?

HOLDING AND DECISION:
(Marshall, J.) Yes. A newspaper may be held civilly liable for publishing the name of a rape victim that it had obtained from a publicly released police report, but only if there is a state interest of the highest order justifying liability. No such interest, however, is served by imposing liability under § 794.03 to the Florida Star (D) in this case. Three considerations support the principle that if a newspaper lawfully obtains truthful information about a matter of public significance then state officials may not constitutionally punish publishers of that information: (1) the formulation only protects the publication of information "lawfully obtain[ed]"; (2) punishing the press for dissemination of information that is already publicly available is relatively unlikely to advance the state interest in protecting confidential or inaccessible information; and (3) subjecting the media to sanctions for the publication of certain truthful information may lead to unnecessary self-censorship.

DISSENT:
(White, J.) Jury award of damages below in this case is not at odds with the First Amendment. By holding that a rape victim's right to privacy is not among those state interests of the highest order, the majority obliterates the tort of publication of private facts.

▶ ANALYSIS

The majority in *Florida Star* distinguished *Cox Broadcasting*, 420 U.S. 469 (1975), limiting the *Cox Broadcasting* holding to the public disclosure of private facts during the course of adversarial criminal proceedings.

■═■

Quicknotes

PUBLIC DISCLOSURE OF PRIVATE FACTS A form of invasion of privacy involving the disclosure of private facts regarding a person with which the public has no concern.

■═■

Bartnicki v. Vopper

Cell phone user (P) v. Radio commentator (D)

532 U.S. 514 (2001).

NATURE OF CASE: Appeal from decision that provisions of federal anti-wiretapping laws that prohibit disclosure of illegally intercepted communications violate the First Amendment when applied to disclosures relating to matters of public concern.

FACT SUMMARY: The cell phone conversation between two union representatives, Bartnicki (P) and Kane (P), was illegally intercepted and recorded during a period of collective-bargaining negotiations in which the union representatives were involved. Vopper (D), a radio commentator, played a tape of the intercepted conversation on his radio show in connection with news reports about the settlement. Bartnicki (P) and Kane (P) filed suit for damages, alleging, among other things, that Vopper (D) and others had repeatedly published the conversation even though they knew or had reason to know that it had been illegally intercepted. Vopper (D) claimed that the disclosures were protected by the First Amendment.

🏛 RULE OF LAW
Provisions of anti-wiretapping laws that prohibit disclosure of illegally intercepted communications violate the First Amendment when applied to disclosures of information that has been legally obtained from the intercepting party and that relates to matters of public concern.

FACTS: An unidentified person intercepted and recorded a cell phone conversation between Bartnicki (P), the chief negotiator for a local teacher's union, and Kane (P), the union president. In the conversation, Bartnicki (P) threatened violence (at least as a matter of speaking) if the union's demands were not met. After the parties accepted a proposal favorable to the teachers, Vopper (D), a radio commentator, played a tape of the intercepted conversation on his show in connection with news reports about the settlement. Vopper (D), however, had nothing to do with the interception and did not know who the responsible party was. Also, the tapes themselves had been obtained legally. Bartnicki (P) and Kane (P) filed a damages suit under federal wiretapping laws, which, under § 2511(1)(a) prohibited intercepting cell phone calls, and under § 2511(1)(c) prohibited disclosure of the contents of any illegally intercepted material. The Supreme Court granted review on appeal.

ISSUE: Do provisions of anti-wiretapping laws that prohibit disclosure of illegally intercepted communications violate the First Amendment when applied to disclosures of information that has been legally obtained from the intercepting party and that relates to matters of public concern?

HOLDING AND DECISION: (Stevens, J.) Yes. Provisions of anti-wiretapping laws that prohibit disclosure

of illegally intercepted communications violate the First Amendment when applied to disclosures of information that has been legally obtained from the intercepting party and that relates to matters of public concern. First, the Court accepts Vopper's (D) assertion that he played no part in the illegal interception, that his access to the information was obtained lawfully, and that the conversations dealt with a matter of public concern. Generally, state action that punishes the publication of truthful information is usually unconstitutional. The issue here is whether a publisher of information who has obtained the information in a lawful manner from someone who has obtained it unlawfully may be punished for the ensuing publication. The government's first asserted interest served by the statute—removing an incentive for parties to intercept private conversations—does not justify applying the statute to an otherwise innocent disclosure of public information. The normal method of deterring unlawful conduct is to punish the person engaging in it. It would be remarkable to hold that speech by a law-abiding possessor of information can be suppressed in order to deter conduct by a non-law-abiding third party. The Government's second interest—minimizing the harm to persons whose conversations have been illegally intercepted—is considerably stronger. Privacy of communication is an important interest. However, in this suit, privacy concerns give way when balanced against the interest in publishing matters of public importance. One of the costs associated with participation in public affairs is an attendant loss of privacy. It is clear that a stranger's illegal conduct does not suffice to remove the First Amendment shield from speech about a matter of public concern.

CONCURRENCE: (Breyer, J.) The Court's holding is limited to the particular facts of this case and does not extend beyond these present circumstances. These facts are that (1) the broadcasters acted lawfully up to the time of final disclosure; and (2) the information involved a matter of unusual public concern—a threat of potential physical harm to others.

DISSENT: (Rehnquist, C.J.) In an attempt to prevent egregious violations of privacy, the federal and state governments have enacted laws prohibiting the intentional interception and knowing disclosure of electronic communications. The majority holds that all of these statutes violate the First Amendment insofar as the illegally intercepted conversation touches upon a matter of "public concern," a concept the majority does not even attempt to define. But the majority's decision diminishes, rather than enhances, the

Continued on next page.

purposes of the First Amendment, and chills the speech of the millions of Americans who rely upon electronic technology to communicate. The statutes are content neutral, applying only to illegally obtained information. It is hard to imagine a more narrowly tailored prohibition of the disclosure of illegally intercepted communications, and, therefore, it goes contrary to precedent to review these laws under strict scrutiny. These laws should be upheld under intermediate scrutiny because they further the substantial government interest in protecting privacy; the Constitution should not be used to protect the involuntary disclosure of private conversations.

▶ ANALYSIS

The issue in this case was one of first impression and enabled the Court to expand its jurisprudence in this area. Before this case, the Court had held that the First Amendment prevents liability for public disclosure of private facts if the information was lawfully obtained from public records, unless there was a state interest of the "highest order" justifying liability. The result in this case can be explained by the majority's emphasis on the relatively "public" nature of the communication involved, which consequently did not rise to the "highest order" that a purely private communication would have risen to.

■══■

Quicknotes

CONTENT NEUTRAL Refers to statutes that regulate speech regardless of its content.

FIRST AMENDMENT Prohibits Congress from enacting any law respecting an establishment of religion, prohibiting the free exercise of religion, abridging freedom of speech or the press, the right of peaceful assembly and the right to petition for a redress of grievances.

■══■

United States v. O'Brien

Federal government (P) v. Draft card burner (D)

391 U.S. 367 (1968).

NATURE OF CASE: Appeal from conviction for draft-card burning.

FACT SUMMARY: O'Brien (D) was convicted of a violation of a federal statute after he publicly burned his draft card during a demonstration against the compulsory draft and the war in Vietnam.

🏛 RULE OF LAW
When both speech and nonspeech elements are combined in the same conduct, a sufficiently important governmental interest in regulating the nonspeech element can justify incidental limitations of First Amendment freedoms.

FACTS: During a public demonstration directed against the compulsory draft and the war in Vietnam, O'Brien (D) and several others burned their Selective Service Registration Certificates. His act was witnessed by several FBI agents, who arrested him. The arrest was for violating a federal statute prohibiting the knowing destruction or knowing mutilation of a Selective Service Certificate. The act also prohibited any changes, alterations, or forgeries of the Certificates. O'Brien (D) was convicted and now appeals, contending a violation of his First Amendment right to free speech.

ISSUE: May the government incidentally limit First Amendment rights where it seeks to regulate the nonspeech aspect of conduct composed of both speech and nonspeech elements where that regulation is supported by a vital governmental interest?

HOLDING AND DECISION: (Warren, C.J.) Yes. The Court considered two aspects of O'Brien's (D) appeal. First, that the statute was unconstitutional in its application to him, and secondly, that the statute was unconstitutional as enacted. Where conduct is composed of speech and nonspeech elements, the speaker can invoke his freedom of speech rights to defend against unwarranted governmental interference. What must be determined is whether the attempted regulation of the nonspeech element also impermissibly inhibits the speech aspect. An incidental restriction on speech can be justified where the government can show a substantial interest in furthering a constitutional power that is not directed at the suppression of speech. In order to facilitate the implementation of its power to raise and support armies, Congress has enacted a system for classifying individuals as to eligibility for military service. The Selective Service cards provide an efficient and reasonable method for identifying those persons previously deemed fit for military service should a national emergency arise. The Court found

the requirement that the card be in the possession of the holder to be a valid requirement. The Court also found an independent justification for both the possession requirement and the prohibition against mutilation or destruction. While admitting some overlap, the possession requirement was intended for a smooth functioning of the draft system while the prohibition against mutilation was a sabotage prevention measure. A person could destroy another's card while retaining his own intact. The statute was intended as a necessary and proper method to carry out a vital governmental interest. No reasonable alternative is apparent and the narrow construction of the statute indicates it was not intended to suppress communication.

▶ ANALYSIS

Many articles written about this decision have been critical of the Court's superficial analysis of the interests involved on both sides of this case. The commentators felt that O'Brien's (D) contention that the draft card was not a vital document was dismissed out of hand. They also felt there should have been a more probing analysis of the operation of the Selective Service System and an examination of the actual, not supposed, importance of the draft card in that system. The strongest criticism of this case has been that the Court justified the suppression of expression, not on the basis of a compelling interest, but on a bureaucratic system designed for convenience. There was no analysis of alternative systems. Finally, some observers saw in this decision a desire to counterbalance the long string of cases decided by the Warren Court upholding individual rights in the face of much stronger governmental interests.

■■■

Quicknotes

FIRST AMENDMENT Prohibits Congress from enacting any law respecting an establishment of religion, prohibiting the free exercise of religion, abridging freedom of speech or the press, the right of peaceful assembly and the right to petition for a redress of grievances.

■■■

Texas v. Johnson

State (P) v. Flag owner (D)

491 U.S. 397 (1989).

NATURE OF CASE: Appeal of reversal of conviction for desecration of venerated object.

FACT SUMMARY: Johnson (D), who burned a U.S. flag as a means of political protest, was convicted under Texas (P) law of desecrating a venerated object.

🏛 RULE OF LAW
Burning a U.S. flag as a means of political protest may not be criminalized.

FACTS: Johnson (D) joined a protest at the site of the 1984 Republican National Convention. Except for some minor vandalism in which Johnson (D) took no part, the protest was peaceful. At one point Johnson burned a U.S. flag. He was convicted under a state law criminalizing the desecration of a venerated object. The state court of criminal appeals reversed, holding Johnson's (D) actions protected under the First Amendment. The Supreme Court granted review.

ISSUE: May burning the U.S. flag as a means of political protest be criminalized?

HOLDING AND DECISION: (Brennan, J.) No. Burning a U.S. flag as a means of political protest may not be criminalized. While the First Amendment literally only protects "speech," it has long been the rule that conduct that is meant to express an idea also raises First Amendment concerns. Johnson's (D) behavior undoubtedly was so meant, and Texas (P) conceded this. This being so, the prosecution of Johnson (D) could only be upheld if Texas (P) could show an interest therein unrelated to the suppression of ideas. Two have been offered, keeping the peace and preserving the flag as a symbol of national unity. Here, no breach of the peace occurred, and this court is unwilling to presume that symbolic conduct not directed at any person or group in particular constitutes such a danger to public tranquility that a state may proscribe such conduct. As to the latter justification, it is a core principle of the First Amendment that government may not prohibit expression of an idea because it finds the idea disagreeable. While the Court does not doubt that government is free to promote respect for the flag as a symbol of national unity, it may not compel how a flag, or any symbol, is used. All this being so, the conclusion must be that the law under which Johnson (D) was prosecuted constitutes an abridgement of expressive conduct for which no justification separate from such abridgement can be found, and the statute violates the First Amendment.

DISSENT: (Rehnquist, C.J.) The flag does not represent any idea or point of view. It is a unique symbol of our national heritage and deserves special protection. Beyond that, the acts of Johnson (D) did have a tendency to incite a breach of the peace. It is more likely to antagonize others than to communicate an idea.

DISSENT: (Stevens, J.) Due to the unique value of the flag as a symbol, government's interest in preserving that value is significant and legitimate.

▶ ANALYSIS

This was one of the most controversial decisions of the Supreme Court in decades. Almost immediately, calls for a constitutional amendment to overturn the decision were made. Within the year of its decision, Congress had passed a statute, rather than an amendment, in a response that was hoped would pass First Amendment scrutiny. The amendment movement faltered because never in history has the Bill of Rights been amended.

■━■

Quicknotes

FIRST AMENDMENT Prohibits Congress from enacting any law respecting an establishment of religion, prohibiting the free exercise of religion, abridging freedom of speech or the press, the right of peaceful assembly and the right to petition for a redress of grievances.

■━■

Buckley v. Valeo

Congressman (P) v. Federal government (D)

424 U.S. 1 (1976).

NATURE OF CASE: Action for declaration of unconstitutionality.

FACT SUMMARY: Senator Buckley (P) and others challenged the Federal Election Campaign Act's contribution and expenditure limitation, reporting and disclosure requirements, and public financing of presidential elections.

🏛 RULE OF LAW

Although "the First Amendment protects political association as well as political expression . . . a limitation upon the amount that any one person or group may contribute to (and associate with) a candidate or political committee entails only a marginal restriction on the contributor's ability to engage in free communication (and association)"; but, "a restriction on the amount of money a person or group can spend on political communication (as a whole) during a campaign (excessively) reduces the quantity of expression by restricting the number of issues discussed, the depth of their exploration, and the size of the audience reached."

FACTS: In order to curtail political corruption, Congress in the Federal Election Campaign Act of 1971, as amended in 1974, developed an intricate statutory scheme for the regulation of federal political campaigns. Inter alia, Congress imposed a $1000 limitation on individual contributions "to a single candidate" in § 608 (b)(1), a $5000 limitation on "contributions" to a single candidate by political committees in § 608(b)(2), a $25,000 limitation on total "contributions" by any individual in one year to political candidates in § 608(b)(3), a $1000 ceiling in "expenditures" relative to a known candidate in § 608 (e)(1), and similar ceilings on "expenditures" by the candidate and his family and on overall campaign "expenditures" § 608 (a) and (c). In addition, Congress required disclosure by candidates of all "contributions" greater than $10, and by individuals of all "contributions and expenditures" aggregating over $1000— § 434 (e). In a separate action, Congress provided for federal financing of presidential elections. Senator Buckley (P) and others, pursuant to a special section in the Act of 1971, brought this action to have all the above-mentioned sections declared an unconstitutional violation of their First Amendment rights of freedom of expression and association. This appeal followed.

ISSUE: Does the strong governmental interest in preventing election corruption justify imposition of substantial restrictions on the effective ability of any individual to express his political beliefs and engage in political association?

HOLDING AND DECISION: (Per curiam) No. Although "the First Amendment protects political association as well as political expression . . . a limitation upon the amount that any one person or group may contribute to (and associate with) a candidate or a political committee entails only a marginal restriction on the contributor's ability to engage in free communication (and association);" but, "a restriction on the amount of money a person or group can spend on political communication (as a whole) during a campaign (excessively) reduces the quantity of expression by restricting the number of issues discussed, the depth of their exploration, and the size of the audience reached." As such, the so-called "contribution" (i.e., to candidates) limitations here (§ 608(b)1-3) may be upheld as valid means for limiting political corruption by "fat cats." The so-called "expenditure" (on political expression) limitations (§ 608 a,c,e), however, places too broad a restriction on the individual's ability to speak out and must therefore be voided. As for the reporting and disclosure requirements, broad as they are, they are clearly upheld by the "compelling government interest" in deterring corruption by getting important information to the voters and providing records for enforcement of the law. Finally, the challenge to the public financing of presidential elections is simply unfounded since it entails no abridgment of speech whatsoever.

▶ ANALYSIS

In this case, the Court has identified one of the few "compelling governmental interests" that may be employed to justify congressional regulation of an area subject to strict judicial scrutiny. That interest is the interest in maintaining the integrity of the political process. Note, however, that even though the interest is held compelling, the Court does not automatically affirm its imposition. Note that the Court's decision left the Federal Election Campaign Act rife with loopholes. Perhaps the most exploited was that which permitted individuals to "expend" (i.e., separately from any candidate or his organization) large sums to endorse a vote for a particular candidate.

■■■■

Quicknotes

COMPELLING STATE INTEREST Defense to an alleged Equal Protection Clause violation; that a state action was necessary in order to protect an interest the government is under a duty to protect.

Continued on next page.

STRICT SCRUTINY Method by which courts determine the constitutionality of a law, when a law affects a fundamental right. Under the test, the legislature must have had a compelling interest to enact the law and measures prescribed by the law must be the least restrictive means possible to accomplish its goal.

■══■

Nixon v. Shrink Missouri Government PAC

State (D) v. Political Action Committee (P)

528 U.S. 377 (2000).

NATURE OF CASE: Review of Missouri statute imposing limits on contributions to state political candidates.

FACT SUMMARY: The Court of Appeals below took the state (D) to task for failing to back up its contributions limits with empirical evidence of actually corrupt practices or a perception among Missouri voters that unrestricted contributions have been exerting a covertly corrosive influence.

🏛 RULE OF LAW
Buckley v. Valeo, 424 U.S. 1 (1976), is authoritative for state limitations on contributions to state political candidates.

FACTS: Missouri (D) imposed campaign contribution limits on contributions to state political candidates. The contribution limits ranged from a high of $1,075 for contributions to candidates for statewide office (including state auditor) and for any office where the population exceeded 250,000, down to $275 for contributions to candidates for state representative or for any office for which there were fewer than 100,000 people represented. The Shrink Missouri Government PAC (P) raised a First Amendment challenge to this legislation for Missouri's (D) failure to present empirical evidence of actually corrupt practices or evidence of a perception among voters that unrestricted contributions have exerted a covertly corrosive influence.

ISSUE: Is *Buckley v. Valeo* authoritative for state limits on contributions?

HOLDING AND DECISION: (Souter, J.) Yes. The evidence introduced in this case by the Shrink Missouri Gov't PAC (P) and cited by the lower courts in this case is enough to show the substantiation of the congressional concerns reflected in *Buckley* has its counterpart supporting the Missouri (D) contribution limits. The state interest in this case is the interest in preventing corruption and the appearance of it. *Buckley* established the legitimacy of these concerns and is applicable here.

CONCURRENCE: (Stevens, J.) The right to use one's own money to fund "speech by proxy" merits significant constitutional protection; however, it does not merit the same protection as the right to say what one pleases.

DISSENT: (Kennedy, J.) This Court in *Buckley* and the majority in this case have paved the way for covert speech funded by unlimited soft money. A substantial amount of political speech has been forced underground as contributors and candidates devise even more elaborate methods of avoiding campaign contribution limits, making a mockery of the First Amendment. Further, a candidate cannot oppose

this system without selling out to it. "Soft money must be raised to attack the problem of soft money." The majority ruling thus immunizes itself from correction in the political process and forum of unrestrained speech; a fact that ought to caution hesitation here.

DISSENT: (Thomas, J.) By applying *Buckley*, the majority weakened the already feeble constitutional protection that *Buckley* afforded campaign contributions. Buckley was in error and should be overruled. In its stead, regulations imposing contribution limitations should be subject to strict scrutiny.

▎ *ANALYSIS*

Since *Buckley*, the Court has adhered to a distinction between contributions and expenditures. *Buckley* upheld contribution limitations and the *Nixon* Court reaffirmed. However, *FEC v. National Conservative PAC*, 470 U.S. 480 (1985), declared expenditure limits unconstitutional. Interestingly, the three dissenting justices in *Nixon* expressly called for overruling *Buckley*'s allowance of contribution limits and concurring Justice Stevens indicated a willingness to allow expenditure limits.

Quicknotes

STRICT SCRUTINY Method by which courts determine the constitutionality of a law, when a law affects a fundamental right. Under the test, the legislature must have had a compelling interest to enact the law and measures prescribed by the law must be the least restrictive means possible to accomplish its goal.

Randall v. Sorrell

[State legislator (P)] v. State (D)

548 U.S. 230 (2006).

NATURE OF CASE: Review of federal appeals court judgment.

FACT SUMMARY: [Plaintiff not identified in casebook excerpt.] Vermont (D) passed a campaign finance law imposing limitations on (1) the amount candidates for office could spend during the election cycle and (2) the amount individuals, political groups, and parties could contribute to a candidate's campaign.

🏛 RULE OF LAW
(1) Expenditure limits for political candidates violate the U.S. Constitution's First Amendment guarantee of freedom of speech.
(2) Vermont's contribution limits of $200-$400 per candidate for individuals, political groups, and political parties are unconstitutionally low under the First Amendment.

FACTS: [Plaintiff not identified in casebook excerpt.] Vermont (D) passed a campaign finance law imposing limitations on (1) the amount candidates for office could spend during the election cycle and (2) the amount individuals, political groups, and parties could contribute to a candidate's campaign. The contribution limits were set by the state at $200-$400 per candidate.

ISSUE:
(1) Do expenditure limits for political candidates violate the U.S. Constitution's First Amendment guarantee of freedom of speech?
(2) Are Vermont's contribution limits of $200-$400 per candidate for individuals, political groups, and political parties unconstitutionally low under the First Amendment?

HOLDING AND DECISION: (Breyer, J.)
(1) Yes. Expenditure limits for political candidates violate the U.S. Constitution's First Amendment guarantee of freedom of speech. In *Buckley v. Valeo*, 424 U.S. 1 (1976), the court held that spending money to influence elections is a form of constitutionally protected free speech, and that expenditure limits violate the First Amendment. That case is valid precedent, it will stand, and it controls here. There is no special justification requiring the court to overturn *Buckley*, and this case is indistinguishable from *Buckley*. The Vermont limits are not substantially different from those at issue in *Buckley*.
(2) Yes. Vermont's contribution limits of $200-$400 per candidate for individuals, political groups, and political parties are unconstitutionally low under the First Amendment. Some limits on political contributions

are constitutional, but Vermont's (D) exceptionally low limits could prevent candidates from campaigning effectively, and are "disproportionate to the public purposes they were enacted to advance." The conclusion is not based only on the low dollar amounts of the limits, but also on the statute's effect on political parties and on volunteer activity in Vermont elections.

CONCURRENCE: (Kennedy, J.) The judgment is correct, but not the reasoning, because the court has itself created and permitted the universe of campaign finance regulation. There is little basis to say that $200 is too restrictive a limit while $1,500 or some other amount is not.

CONCURRENCE: (Thomas, J.) The judgment is correct, but not the reasoning, because *Buckley* provides insufficient protection to political speech. *Buckley* should be overruled.

DISSENT: (Stevens, J.) *Buckley* should be overruled as it pertains to expenditure limits. While stare decisis is an important principal, overturning *Buckley* is justified because its holding on expenditure limits upset a long-established practice. In addition, candidates should be freed from the fundraising straightjacket.

DISSENT: (Souter, J.) The contribution limits should be upheld and the expenditure limits should be referred to the lower courts for a determination of whether they were the "least restrictive means" of accomplishing Vermont's (D) goals.

▶ ANALYSIS

The plaintiff in this case was Neil Randall, a Vermont state legislator. Note that *Buckley* does not categorically preclude the possibility of mandatory spending limits that might meet constitutional scrutiny. *Randall* does not change the legal status quo of expenditure limits. Most importantly, the court's decision does not affect the constitutionality of voluntary expenditure limitations contained in public financing systems.

■■■

Quicknotes

FREEDOM OF SPEECH The right to express oneself without governmental restrictions on the content of that expression.

STARE DECISIS Doctrine whereby courts follow legal precedent unless there is good cause for departure.

■■■

First National Bank of Boston v. Bellotti

Bank (P) v. State Attorney General (D)

435 U.S. 765 (1978).

NATURE OF CASE: Appeal from an action seeking a declaratory judgment.

FACT SUMMARY: The First National Bank of Boston (P) brought this action to challenge the constitutionality of a Massachusetts statute that forbids certain expenditures by banks and business corporations for the purpose of influencing the vote on referendum proposals.

🏛 RULE OF LAW
First Amendment freedom of speech embraces at least the liberty to discuss publicly all matters of public concern without previous restraint or fear of subsequent punishment regardless of whether the speaker is an individual or a corporation.

FACTS: The statute at issue prohibits the First National Bank of Boston (P) and other banking associations and business corporations from making contributions or expenditures for the purpose of influencing or affecting the vote on any question submitted to the voters other than one materially affecting any of the property, business, or assets of the corporation. The statute further specifies that no question submitted to the voters solely concerning the taxation of the income, property, or transactions of individuals shall be deemed materially to affect the corporation. First National Bank (P) and the other businesses wanted to spend money to publicize their views on a proposed constitutional amendment that was to be submitted to the voters. The amendment would have permitted the legislature to impose a graduated tax on the income of individuals. After Bellotti (P), the Attorney General of Massachusetts, informed First National (P) that he intended to enforce the statute against it, First National (P) and the others brought this action seeking to have the statute declared unconstitutional because it violated the First Amendment's guarantee of free speech. The Massachusetts Supreme Court upheld the statute and First National (P) appealed to the U.S. Supreme Court.

ISSUE: Does freedom of speech to discuss matters of public concern apply to corporations as well as individuals?

HOLDING AND DECISION: (Powell, J.) Yes. The freedom of speech and of the press guaranteed by the First Amendment embraces at least the liberty to discuss publicly all matters of public concern without prior restraint or fear of subsequent punishment regardless of whether the speaker is an individual or a corporation. The Massachusetts statute permits a corporation to communicate on certain referendum subjects—those materially affecting business—but not others. It also singles out one

kind of ballot question—individual taxation—as a subject about which corporations may never make their ideas public. In the realm of protected speech, the legislature is constitutionally disqualified from dictating the subjects that persons may speak about and the speakers who may address a public issue. The argument that such restrictions protect shareholders who may disagree with the corporate message must fail because the corporation would have to remain silent even if the shareholders unanimously support the speech. The statute is thus overinclusive. If the legislature may direct business corporations to "stick to business," it may also limit other kinds of corporations to their respective enterprises when addressing the public. Such power in government to channel the expression of views is unacceptable under the First Amendment. The decision of the Massachusetts Supreme Court is reversed.

DISSENT: (White, J.) A state should be able to prevent corporate management from using the corporate treasury to propagate views having no connection with the corporate business. The Court should not substitute its judgment for the Massachusetts legislature when those knowledgeable legislators have fashioned a proper balance to protect all parties' rights to free speech.

▶ ANALYSIS

In the case of *Thornhill v. Alabama*, 310 U.S. 88 (1940), the Supreme Court held that freedom of discussion, if it would fulfill its historic function in this nation, must embrace all issues about which information is needed or appropriate to enable the members of society to cope with the exigencies of their period. The referendum issue that the bank wishes to address in the present case falls squarely within this description. In the bank's view, the enactment of a graduated personal income tax would have a seriously adverse effect on the economy of the state.

■═■

Quicknotes

FREEDOM OF SPEECH The right to express oneself without governmental restrictions on the content of that expression.

■═■

Hague v. Committee for Industrial Organization

Director of Safety (D) v. Union (P)

307 U.S. 496 (1939).

NATURE OF CASE: Review of a city ordinance impinging on the right to use government property for speech purposes.

FACT SUMMARY: In determining whether the ordinance advanced a valid state interest, the district court found it void on its face.

🏛 RULE OF LAW
The privilege of a citizen of the United States to use streets and parks for communication of views on national questions may be regulated in the interest of all, but may not be abridged or denied.

FACTS: A Jersey City ordinance enabled the Director of Safety (D) to refuse a permit to assemble based upon his opinion alone that such refusal would prevent "riots, disturbances or disorderly assemblages." Agents for the Committee for Industrial Organization (P), acting to organize unorganized workers into a labor union, were restrained under this ordinance from passage upon the streets and access to the parks of the city. The union (P) brought the present action challenging the constitutionality of the ordinance.

ISSUE: May a citizen use some government property under some circumstances for speech?

HOLDING AND DECISION: (Roberts, J.) Yes. Streets and parks have, from time immemorial, been held in trust for use by the public for the purposes of assembly, communicating thoughts between citizens, and discussing public questions. The ordinance at issue in this case gives too much discretion to the Director of Safety (D) and can thus be made an instrument of arbitrary suppression of free expression.

▌ ANALYSIS

The *Hague* decision was crucial in recognizing the right to use some government property under some circumstances for speech and was decided against a backdrop of decisions upholding the government's ability to control its property however it wishes.

◼━◼

Quicknotes

FIRST AMENDMENT Prohibits Congress from enacting any law respecting an establishment of religion, prohibiting the free exercise of religion, abridging freedom of speech or the press, the right of peaceful assembly and the right to petition for a redress of grievances.

◼━◼

Schneider v. New Jersey

Jehovah's Witness (P) v. State (D)

308 U.S. 147 (1939).

NATURE OF CASE: Review of ordinance prohibiting the distribution and circulation of handbills.

FACT SUMMARY: Three municipalities—the City of Los Angeles, the City of Milwaukee, and the Town of Irvington—all enacted ordinances prohibiting the distribution and circulation of handbills.

🏛 RULE OF LAW
An ordinance aimed at the prevention of littering the streets may not abridge the individual liberties of those who wish to speak, write, print, or circulate information or opinion.

FACTS: Schneider (P) was arrested and charged with canvassing without a permit under a Town of Irvington (D) ordinance. Schneider (P) was a member of Watch Tower Bible and Tract Society and, as such, was certified by the society to be one of "Jehovah's Witnesses." As a Jehovah's Witness, Schneider (P) called from house to house at all hours to provide testimony. Together with Schneider's (P) case, the Court was presented with two other ordinances prohibiting the distribution and circulation of handbills.

ISSUE: May a municipality enact regulations in the interest of public safety, health and welfare or convenience that abridge constitutional individual liberties?

HOLDING AND DECISION: (Roberts, J.) No. A municipality may not enact regulations such as the ones at issue in this case that are designed to keep the streets clean and of good appearance but abridge constitutional individual liberties. However, this rationale is insufficient to justify an ordinance that prohibits a person rightfully on a public street from handing literature to one willing to receive it. Thus, the ordinances at issue in this case are void.

▶ ANALYSIS

As the Court in *Schneider* points out, a municipality has other options for achieving the goal of litter prevention that do not impinge on constitutionally protected rights. Additionally, the *Schneider* court suggests that certain aspects of hand-billing can be regulated. For example, a town/municipality can fix reasonable hours when canvassing may lawfully be done.

the free exercise of religion, abridging freedom of speech or the press, the right of peaceful assembly and the right to petition for a redress of grievances.

Quicknotes

FIRST AMENDMENT Prohibits Congress from enacting any law respecting an establishment of religion, prohibiting

Perry Education Assn. v. Perry Local Educators' Assn.

Union (D) v. Union (P)

460 U.S. 37 (1983).

NATURE OF CASE: Review of a right-of-access claim under the First and Fourteenth Amendments.

FACT SUMMARY: In reviewing plaintiff's right-of-access claim below, the court of appeals found that Perry School District's interschool mail system is not a traditional forum.

🏛 RULE OF LAW
The constitutionality of a regulation of speech depends upon the place and nature of the government's action.

FACTS: Perry Education Association (PEA) (D) is the duly elected exclusive bargaining representative for the teachers of the Metropolitan School District of Perry Township, Indiana. A collective bargaining agreement with the Board of Education provided that PEA (D), but no other union, would have access to the interschool mail system and teacher mailboxes in the Perry Township schools. Perry Local Educators Association (PLEA) (P), a rival teachers' union, brought this action, alleging that the denial of access to the interschool mail system and teacher mailboxes violated the First and Fourteenth Amendments.

ISSUE: Is the denial of access to an interschool mail system a violation of the First and Fourteenth Amendments?

HOLDING AND DECISION: (White, J.) No. Perry School District's interschool mail system is not a traditional public forum. The "normal and intended function [of the interschool mail system] is to facilitate internal communication of school-related matters to teachers." Further, the interschool mail system is not a "limited public forum." The periodic use of the interschool mail system by private nonschool connected groups does not transform it into a "limited public forum." Thus, because the interschool mail system is a nonpublic forum, the School District had no "constitutional obligation" to grant PLEA (P) access to it.

▶ ANALYSIS

Perry Education Assn. provides the clearest statement of the three forms of government property: public forums, limited public forums, and nonpublic forums. In quintessential public forums such as streets or parks, the state may enforce a content-based speech restriction only if it shows such regulation to be necessary to serve a compelling state interest and that it is narrowly drawn to that end. The state may also regulate content-neutral time-, place-, and manner-of-expression regulations if the same are narrowly tailored to serve a significant government interest and leave open ample alternative channels of communication. Limited public forums are public property that the state has opened for use by the public as a place of expressive activity. Although a state is not required to retain the open character of a facility, as long as it does so, it is bound by the same standards that apply in a traditional forum. In nonpublic forums such as the one at issue in *Perry*, the state has no constitutional duty to provide access.

■■■

Quicknotes

PUBLIC FORUM Public area so associated with freedom of speech so that restriction of access to it for that purpose is unconstitutional (e.g., sidewalks, streets, parks, etc.).

■■■

Police Department of the City of Chicago v. Mosley

Regulator (D) v. Picketer (P)

408 U.S. 92 (1972).

NATURE OF CASE: Review of a picketing ordinance under the First and Fourteenth Amendments.

FACT SUMMARY: Ordinance exempted peaceful labor picketing from its general prohibition on picketing next to a school.

🏛 RULE OF LAW
Under the First Amendment, the government has no power to restrict expression because of its message, ideas, subject matter, or content.

FACTS: The City of Chicago (D) enacted an ordinance exempting peaceful labor picketing from its general prohibition on picketing next to a school. Earl Mosley (P), a federal postal employee, peaceably demonstrated on the sidewalk adjacent to Jones Commercial High School for seven months prior to the enactment of the above-mentioned ordinance. Mosley mounted a First Amendment challenge to this content-based ordinance.

ISSUE: May the government grant a forum to those whose views it finds acceptable, but deny use to those wishing to express less-favored views?

HOLDING AND DECISION: (Marshall, J.) No. Under the First Amendment, the government has no power to restrict expression because of its message, ideas, subject matter, or content. The ordinance at issue in this case describes impermissible picketing not in terms of time, place and manner, but in terms of subject matter. The regulation slips from the neutrality of time, place and manner into a concern about content, which is never permitted.

▶ ANALYSIS

Government regulation of speech in public forums must be content neutral. At a minimum, this means that the government cannot regulate speech based on its viewpoint or its subject matter unless strict scrutiny is met.

Quicknotes

CONTENT BASED Refers to statutes that regulate speech based on its content.

CONTENT NEUTRAL Refers to statutes that regulate speech regardless of its content.

Hill v. Colorado

Counselors (P) v. State (D)

530 U.S. 703 (2000).

NATURE OF CASE: Suit challenging constitutionality of a state statute.

FACT SUMMARY: Petitioners challenged the constitutionality of a Colorado statute regulating speech-conduct within 100 feet of the entrance to any health care facility.

> ### 🏛 RULE OF LAW
> A statute may be upheld as a valid time, place and manner regulation where it serves governmental interests that are significant and legitimate, the restrictions are content-neutral and the statute is narrowly tailored to serve such interests, leaving open ample alternative channels for communication.

FACTS: [Facts not stated in casebook excerpt.]

ISSUE: May a statute be upheld as a valid time, place and manner regulation where it serves governmental interests that are significant and legitimate, the restrictions are content-neutral and the statute is narrowly tailored to serve such interests, leaving open ample alternative channels for communication?

HOLDING AND DECISION: (Stevens, J.) Yes. A statute may be upheld as a valid time, place and manner regulation where it serves governmental interests that are significant and legitimate, the restrictions are content-neutral, and the statute is narrowly tailored to serve such interests, leaving open ample alternative channels for communication. All of the lower court opinions upheld the statute as a valid content-neutral time, place and manner regulation. This is true for three reasons: (1) it does not regulate speech but rather some of the places where speech may occur; (2) it was not adopted because of disagreement with the message it conveys; and (3) the state's interests in protecting access and privacy and providing the police with clear guidelines are unrelated to the content of the demonstrators' speech. The petitioners argued that the statute is not content-neutral because it applies to some oral communication. The Court rejects this argument since the statute here places no restrictions on and does not prohibit either a particular viewpoint or any subject matter that may be discussed by a speaker. Furthermore, it is narrowly tailored to serve the state's interest and leaves open ample alternative channels for communication.

DISSENT: (Scalia, J.) The Court concludes that a regulation requiring speakers on the public streets bordering medical facilities to speak from a distance of eight feet is not a regulation of speech but a regulation of the places where some speech may occur, and that regulation of certain categories of speech (protection, education and counseling)

is not content-based. This decision represents a blatant distortion of First Amendment principles that the Court seems to invoke when abortion is involved.

DISSENT: (Kennedy, J.) The Court's holding contradicts well-established First Amendment principles, approving a law that bars a private citizens from peacefully communicating a message to a fellow citizen on a public sidewalk. The statute here imposes content-based restrictions and limits speech with respect to certain topics. Not only is the statute not content-neutral but it is not viewpoint neutral and prohibits only those persons who speak "against" certain medical procedures.

▌ ANALYSIS

The Court also rejects the petitioners' argument that the statute is overbroad because it protects too many people in too many places, rather than simply patients at medical facilities where confrontational speech has occurred. The Court rejects this argument on the basis that it fails to identify a constitutional defect and that it misinterprets the overbreadth doctrine. The Court maintains that the statute does not "ban" any message but merely regulates the places at which such communications can take place.

■=■

Quicknotes

CONTENT BASED Refers to statutes that regulate speech based on its content.

CONTENT NEUTRAL Refers to statutes that regulate speech regardless of its content.

■=■

Ward v. Rock Against Racism

Municipality (D) v. Concert promoter (P)

491 U.S. 781 (1989).

NATURE OF CASE: Certiorari from invalidation of New York City's regulation of Central Park concerts.

FACT SUMMARY: After New York City (D) required bands performing in the Central Park bandshell to use City (D)-approved amplification equipment and technicians, Rock Against Racism (P) argued that there were less intrusive means of regulating the volume.

🏛 RULE OF LAW
Valid time, place, and manner restrictions need not be the least restrictive alternative.

FACTS: In order to control the sound volume of concerts in Central Park, New York City (D) adopted regulations on the use of the bandshell. Bandshell performers were required to use sound amplification equipment and a sound technician provided by the City (D). The regulations were in response to prolonged difficulties with concerts by Rock Against Racism (P). Rock Against Racism (P) challenged the regulations as restricting its First Amendment rights.

ISSUE: Must valid time, place and manner restrictions be the least restrictive alternative?

HOLDING AND DECISION: (Kennedy, J.) No. Valid time, place and manner restrictions need not be the least restrictive alternative. Even in a public forum, the government may impose reasonable restrictions on the time, place, and manner of protected speech so long as the restrictions are content neutral, narrowly tailored to serve a significant government interest and leave open ample alternative channels for communication of the information. Here, the regulations are content neutral because the noise control is unrelated to content. Moreover, controlling noise pollution is a significant government interest. The requirement of narrow tailoring has been met since the regulation promotes the City's (D) interest in limiting sound, an interest that would not have been achieved without the regulations.

DISSENT: (Marshall, J.) The majority in effect abandons any sense that a time, place, and manner restriction must be narrowly tailored. By allowing a government entity to regulate speech in a public forum while ignoring a less restrictive satisfactory alternative, the majority reduces the burden to one of merely advancing the government's interest only in the slightest. In this case, it allows the government to control speech even in advance of its dissemination.

▶ ANALYSIS

The decision in this case is based upon the determination that New York City's (D) requirements were content neutral. While the court concluded that noise control was a goal unrelated to content, the means that the City (D) used were less obviously content neutral. There are two obvious criticisms of the characterization as content neutral: first, volume in and of itself may be part of the message because music played at one decibel level may be different from music at a different volume; second, the composition of the volume is almost certainly not content neutral because music performed with more or less bass, for example, could change its character substantially.

Quicknotes
CONTENT BASED Refers to statutes that regulate speech based on its content.

CONTENT NEUTRAL Refers to statutes that regulate speech regardless of its content.

Adderley v. Florida

Students (D) v. State (P)

385 U.S. 39 (1966).

NATURE OF CASE: Grant of certiorari after conviction on a charge of trespass with a malicious and mischievous intent upon the premises of another.

FACT SUMMARY: Adderley (D) and other students marched to the jail to protest segregation policies. They were told to leave. When they refused, they were arrested.

🏛 RULE OF LAW
Demonstrators do not have a constitutional right to expound their views whenever, wherever, and however they choose.

FACTS: Adderley (D) and 200 other students went to a jail to protest the arrest of other demonstrators and segregation policies. They stood or sat, singing, clapping, and dancing on a jail driveway that was normally used to transport prisoners and was not used by the public. They were blocking the driveway and, when the sheriff arrived, he told them they were trespassing on jail property and that they would be arrested if they did not leave. He warned them again, and arrested those who remained.

ISSUE: Does a state's conviction of demonstrators for trespass on jail property unconstitutionally deprive them of their rights to freedom of speech, press, assembly, or petition?

HOLDING AND DECISION: (Black, J.) No. In this case, Adderley (D) and the other demonstrators were convicted under a narrowly drawn statute aimed at one limited kind of conduct, trespass upon the property of another with a malicious intent. The statute does not suffer from overbreadth or vagueness. The state may control the use of its own property for its own lawful, nondiscriminatory purpose. There is no evidence that Adderley (D) was arrested because the sheriff objected to what was being sung or said. Rather, he objected to their presence on that part of the jail grounds. The assumption that demonstrators have a constitutional right to expound their views whenever, wherever, and however they please has been vigorously rejected and is rejected again here. Adderley's (D) conviction is affirmed.

DISSENT: (Douglas, J.) A trespass law is being used to penalize people for exercising their constitutional right. A seat of government, such as a prison, is an appropriate place for protesting, especially when other forms of protest have been shut off to citizens. For people who cannot afford to advertise in newspapers, for example, protesting as Adderley (D) did may be the only available, effective option.

▶ ANALYSIS

State statutes cannot be invoked arbitrarily to defeat First Amendment freedoms. State trespass convictions have been reversed where the only acts involved were the peaceable assembly at and refusal to leave a public facility or public place. The "sit-in demonstration" cases state that peaceful presence in a place held open to the public cannot be made a crime. In *Wright v. Georgia*, 373 U.S. 284 (1962), the Court found the distinguishing factor in *Adderley* to be that a jail is not a place held open to the public. In *Food Employees v. Logan Plaza*, 391 U.S. 308 (1968), private property that had been held open to public use was treated like a public place, meaning that neither state nor private trespass rules could be applied to limit the reasonable exercise of First Amendment rights. There, the Court reversed trespass convictions that arose out of union members' peaceful picketing of a grocery store in a privately owned shopping center.

■=■

Quicknotes

TRESPASS Unlawful interference with, or damage to, the real or personal property of another.

■=■

Greer v. Spock

Major General (D) v. Presidential candidates (P)

424 U.S. 828 (1976).

NATURE OF CASE: Review of a First Amendment challenge to military-base decision not to grant access to candidates for federal office.

FACT SUMMARY: Military base rejected candidates' request to campaign and distribute literature on the base.

🏛 RULE OF LAW
It is the business of a military base to train soldiers, not to provide a public forum.

FACTS: Benjamin Spock (P) and Julius Hobson (P) were candidates of the People's Party for the offices of President and Vice-President of the United States and Linda Jenness (P) and Andrew Pulley (P) were candidates of the Socialist Workers Party for the same offices. On September 9, 1972, Spock, Hobson, Jenness, and Pulley (P) wrote a joint letter to Major General Bert A. David (D), then commanding officer of Fort Dix, informing him of their intention to enter the reservation on September 23, 1972, for the purposes of distributing campaign literature and holding a meeting to discuss election issues with service personnel and their dependents. On September 18, 1972, General David (D) rejected the candidates' (P) request, relying on Fort Dix regulations.

ISSUE: Does a military base have a constitutional obligation to provide a public forum for political candidates?

HOLDING AND DECISION: (Stewart, J.) No. The State has the power to preserve property under its control for the use to which it was lawfully dedicated. Fort Dix is lawfully dedicated to the use of providing basic combat training for newly inducted Army personnel. This Court has recognized on numerous occasions the special constitutional function of the military in national life. A military base need serve no other function than that of housing and training soldiers. It need not provide a public forum for political candidates.

DISSENT: (Brennan, J.) "The First Amendment does not evaporate with the mere intonation of interests such as national defense, military necessity, or domestic security." The majority errs in finding that the training of soldiers necessitates the exclusion of those who would publicly express their views from streets and theatre parking lots open to the general public.

▶ *ANALYSIS*

Professor Erwin Chemerinsky notes that "[n]on-public forums are government properties that the government can close to all speech activities. The government may prohibit or restrict speech in nonpublic forums so long as the regulation is reasonable and viewpoint neutral." [Chemerinsky, Erwin, *Constitutional Law*, Third Edition, © 2009, Aspen Publishers, p. 1551.] In *Greer*, the Supreme Court found that military bases are nonpublic forums because their main functions are to "train soldiers, not to provide a public forum."

■━■

Quicknotes

PUBLIC FORUM Public area so associated with freedom of speech so that restriction of access to it for that purpose is unconstitutional (e.g., sidewalks, streets, parks, etc.).

■━■

Lehman v. City of Shaker Heights

Candidate for state office (P) v. City (D)

418 U.S. 298 (1974).

NATURE OF CASE: Review of city policy limiting advertising space on public transit to ads by purveyors of goods and services.

FACT SUMMARY: Lehman (P), a candidate for state office, was denied access to ad space on public transit vehicles for political campaign ads.

🏛 RULE OF LAW
The government, when acting in a proprietary capacity, may validly take action that may limit expression unless such action is unreasonable or is "arbitrary, capricious or invidious" in nature.

FACTS: Lehman (P), a candidate for state office, attempted to purchase ad space for paid political ads on vehicles of the Shaker Heights Rapid Transit System. Metromedia, Inc., the exclusive advertising agent for the system, refused Lehman (P) the space on the basis of a contract with the system prohibiting acceptance of political advertisements. Lehman (P) brought this action, alleging that the City of Shaker Heights (D) is prohibited under the First Amendment as applicable to the states through the Fourteenth Amendment from refusing space for political ads on transit system buses.

ISSUE: Is a city operating a public transit system required by the First and Fourteenth Amendments to accept paid political ads on behalf of a candidate for office?

HOLDING AND DECISION: (Blackmun, J.) No. The government, when acting in a proprietary capacity, may validly take action that may limit expression unless such action is unreasonable or is "arbitrary, capricious or invidious" in nature. The car cards at issue here are not a public forum protected by the First Amendment. The City (D) must provide rapid, convenient, pleasant, and inexpensive service to the commuters of Shaker Heights, but the car card space is really part of a commercial venture. The City's (D) limitation on ads, which is aimed at minimizing the chances of abuse, the appearance of favoritism and the risk of imposing on a captive audience is not arbitrary or capricious, but a reasonable legislative objective.

CONCURRENCE: (Douglas, J.) Lehman (P) has no right to force his message upon an audience incapable of declining to receive it.

DISSENT: (Brennan, J.) By accepting commercial and public service advertising, the City (D) effectively waived any argument that advertising in its transit cars is incompatible with the City's (D) primary function of providing transportation. A forum for communication was voluntarily established when the city installed the physical facilities for the ads and created the administrative machinery for regulating access to the forum.

▶ ANALYSIS

The majority in *Lehman* seems to suggest that no public forum is created where the City (D) is engaged in commercial activities.

Quicknotes

PUBLIC FORUM Public area so associated with freedom of speech so that restriction of access to it for that purpose is unconstitutional (e.g., sidewalks, streets, parks, etc.).

United States v. Kokinda

Federal government (D) v. National Democratic Policy Committee advocate (P)

497 U.S. 720 (1990).

NATURE OF CASE: Review of a First Amendment challenge to a postal regulation prohibiting solicitation.

FACT SUMMARY: Kokinda (P) was found to be in violation of a United States Postal Service regulation for soliciting contributions and distributing literature on behalf of the National Democratic Policy Committee on postal premises.

🏛 RULE OF LAW
The standard of review for nonpublic fora is reasonableness.

FACTS: Marsha Kokinda (P) and Kevin E. Pearl were volunteers for the National Democratic Policy Committee. Kokinda (P) and Pearl set up a table on the sidewalk near the entrance of a Bowie, Maryland, post office to solicit contributions, sell books and subscriptions, and distribute literature addressing a variety of political issues. A United States Postal Service regulation prohibits "soliciting alms and contributions" on postal premises. Kokinda (P) brought this action alleging that the Postal Service regulation violates the First Amendment protection of solicitation as a recognized form of speech.

ISSUE: Does a postal regulation prohibiting solicitation violate the First Amendment?

HOLDING AND DECISION: (O'Connor, J.) No. The Postal Service's sidewalk is not a public thoroughfare, but simply provides access to and from for persons engaged in postal business. Additionally, the postal service has not dedicated its sidewalks to any expressive activity. Thus, the Postal Service's sidewalk is a nonpublic forum. As a result, the regulation relating to the sidewalk is subject to the standard of review applicable to nonpublic fora, the reasonableness standard. The Postal Service contends that it is reasonable to regulate solicitation because it is inherently disruptive to the Post Office's constitutional purpose. In its experience, opening up postal premises to solicitation leads to a number of competing demands for the space and distracts Postal Service employees from their primary jobs. To ensure effective and efficient distribution of the mails, the Post Office has imposed this regulation and it is reasonable.

CONCURRENCE: (Kennedy, J.) It is not necessary to determine whether the Postal Service's sidewalk at issue here is a traditionally a public or a nonpublic forum. The Postal Service regulation in this case meets the traditional standards applicable to time, place and manner restrictions of protected expression. The regulation is narrowly drawn to serve an important government interest, does not discriminate as to content, and permits citizens to engage in a wide range of activity to express their views.

DISSENT: (Brennan, J.) The Postal Service's sidewalk at issue here is clearly a public forum. However, even if it were not a public forum, the Postal Service's regulation draws an unreasonable distinction between solicitation and all other kinds of speech and thus is invalid.

▶ ANALYSIS

As *Kokinda* makes eminently clear, it will be very difficult to find that any government property is a public or a limited public forum. The plurality states that sidewalks on Post Office property are not even limited public forums because they were not dedicated to speech activities. By this criterion, virtually no property ever would be a public forum or a limited public forum.

■══■

Quicknotes

PUBLIC FORUM Public area so associated with freedom of speech so that restriction of access to it for that purpose is unconstitutional (e.g., sidewalks, streets, parks, etc.).

■══■

International Society for Krishna Consciousness, Inc. v. Lee

Religious organization (P) v. State agency (D)

505 U.S. 672 (1992).

NATURE OF CASE: Appeal of ruling upholding solicitation ban.

FACT SUMMARY: The Krishna (P) sought to overturn a regulation of the Port Authority of New York and New Jersey (D) prohibiting solicitation and leafletting in airport terminals.

🏛 RULE OF LAW
A ban on solicitation in airport terminals, which are not public forums, is reasonable and does not violate the First Amendment.

FACTS: The Krishna (P) perform a religious ritual by going into public places to disseminate religious literature and solicit funds. The Port Authority (D) issued a regulation prohibiting sale of merchandise, sale or distribution of written material, and solicitation and receipt of funds inside terminals at the three main New York City airports. The activities were allowed on the sidewalks outside the terminals. The Krishna (P) sued the Port Authority (D), including police superintendent Lee (D), claiming the regulation violated the First Amendment. The district court granted summary judgment for the Krishna (P). The court of appeals affirmed in part and reversed in part, upholding the ban as to solicitation but not as to leafletting. The Krishna (P) appealed the solicitation ruling in this case [and the Port Authority (D) appealed the leafletting decision in a companion case, *Lee v. International Society for Krishna Consciousness*, Inc., 505 U.S. 830 (1992)].

ISSUE: Does a ban on solicitation in airport terminals violate the First Amendment?

HOLDING AND DECISION: (Rehnquist, C.J.) No. A solicitation ban in airport terminals is reasonable and does not violate the First Amendment. Regulation of speech on government property is subject to the highest scrutiny only where the property traditionally has been available for public expression. Airports are recent developments, with an even shorter history of use for religious and speech activities. Airports are commercial enterprises dedicated to the facilitation of air travel and do not have a primary purpose of "promoting the free exchange of ideas." Since airports are not public forums, the speech restrictions only must be reasonable. Solicitation disrupts airport traffic. Airport users are often in a hurry, and a missed flight creates major inconvenience. Face-to-face soliciting presents risks of duress and fraud, and airport travelers on tight schedules are unlikely to report such activity.

▶ ANALYSIS

This case and its companion upheld the ban on solicitation while striking down the leafletting ban. A per curiam opinion in the companion case held the leafletting ban invalid for reasons expressed in the opinions of Justices O'Connor, Kennedy, and Souter in this case. In dissent in the companion case, Chief Justice Rehnquist found leafletting to present risks of congestion similar to solicitation. Additionally, leaflets may be dropped, creating an eyesore, a safety hazard, and additional cleanup efforts for airport staff.

Quicknotes

PUBLIC FORUM Public area so associated with freedom of speech so that restriction of access to it for that purpose is unconstitutional (e.g., sidewalks, streets, parks, etc.).

Arkansas Educational Television Commn. v. Forbes

Broadcaster (D) v. Political candidate (P)

523 U.S. 666 (1998).

NATURE OF CASE: Review of a ruling applying strict scrutiny to a claim that First Amendment rights were violated when one speaker was excluded from a televised public debate.

FACT SUMMARY: A television broadcaster's (D) decision to exclude Forbes (P), a candidate for public office, from a televised debate was challenged as a violation of his First Amendment rights.

🏛 RULE OF LAW
A televised debate offering candidates for public office selective access to air time is not a public forum for constitutional analysis purposes.

FACTS: The Arkansas Educational Television Commission (AETC) was a state agency that owned and operated noncommercial television stations and whose staff exercised broad editorial discretion in planning the network's programming. When Forbes (P), an independent candidate running for office, was denied permission to participate in a scheduled debate on AETC (D), Forbes (P) sued AETC (D), claiming that both his First Amendment rights and his rights under a statute affording political candidates a limited right of access to television air-time had been violated. The district court dismissed Forbes's (P) action for failure to state a claim. The court of appeals affirmed the dismissal of the statutory claims since Forbes (P) had failed to exhaust all his administrative remedies, but reversed and remanded Forbes's (P) First Amendment claim. On remand, the district court found as a matter of law that the debate was a nonpublic forum. After a trial, the jury found that AETC's (D) decision had not been influenced by political pressure and that Forbes's political views were not the basis for his exclusion from the debate. The court of appeals again reversed because it found that AETC (D) had made the debate a public forum when it opened its facilities to candidates for office and AETC (D) could not meet the court's strict scrutiny test.

ISSUE: Is a televised debate offering candidates for public office selective access to air time a public forum for constitutional analysis purposes?

HOLDING AND DECISION: (Kennedy, J.) No. A televised debate offering candidates for public office selective access to air time is not a public forum for constitutional analysis purposes. To be consistent with the First Amendment of the Constitution, the exclusion of a speaker from a nonpublic forum must not be based on the speaker's viewpoint and it must be otherwise reasonable in light of the purpose of the property. Although public broadcasting does not lend itself to scrutiny under the forum doctrine as a general rule, candidate debates present the narrow exception to the rule. A designated public forum is not created when the government allows selective access for individual speakers rather than general access for a class of speakers. AETC's decision to exclude Forbes (P) was a reasonable, viewpoint-neutral exercise of journalistic discretion.

DISSENT: (Stevens, J.) The decision of the court of appeals should be affirmed since the First Amendment will not tolerate arbitrary definitions of the scope of the forum.

▶ ANALYSIS

The three categories of speech fora are the traditional public forum, the public forum created by government designation, and the nonpublic forum. The parties in the above case had agreed that the AETC (D) debate was not a traditional public forum. Under earlier case precedents, the AETC (D) debate was not a designated public forum either.

Quicknotes

PUBLIC FORUM Public area so associated with freedom of speech so that restriction of access to it for that purpose is unconstitutional (e.g., sidewalks, streets, parks, etc.).

STRICT SCRUTINY Method by which courts determine the constitutionality of a law, when a law affects a fundamental right. Under the test, the legislature must have had a compelling interest to enact the law and measures prescribed by the law must be the least restrictive means possible to accomplish its goal.

Parker v. Levy

Military superior (P) Military physician (D)

417 U.S. 733 (1974).

NATURE OF CASE: Review of an overbreadth challenge to imprecise language in certain articles of the Uniform Code of Military Justice.

FACT SUMMARY: Levy (D) was court-martialed for statements made in violation of Articles 90, 133, and 134 of the Uniform Code of Military Justice.

🏛 RULE OF LAW
The different character of the military community and of the military mission requires a different application of the protections granted by the First Amendment.

FACTS: Howard Levy (D) was a physician and a captain in the Army stationed at Fort Jackson, South Carolina. Levy (D) made several statements to enlisted personnel discouraging them from supporting the war effort in Vietnam, detailing the discrimination enlisted men of color face in the United States and abroad in combat situations. On June 2, 1967, Levy (D) was court-martialed under Articles 90, 133, and 134 of the Uniform Code of Military Justice and sentenced to dismissal from service, forfeiture of all pay and allowances, and confinement for three years of hard labor. Levy (D) raises this overbreadth challenge to Articles 90, 133, and 134, alleging violations of his rights to speak freely under the First Amendment.

ISSUE: Should Articles 90, 133, and 134 of the Uniform Code of Military Justice be struck down as a result of Levy's overbreadth challenge?

HOLDING AND DECISION: (Rehnquist, J.) No. The fundamental necessity of obedience and the consequent necessity for the imposition of discipline may render permissible within the military that which is impermissible in civilian society. There is a wide range of activities to which Articles 133 and 134 may be applied without infringement of the First Amendment. Levy's conduct as a commissioned officer urging enlisted men to refuse to obey orders that might send them into combat was unprotected under the most expansive notions of the First Amendment.

DISSENT: (Douglas, J.) Congress should not, under the "different character of the military" argument, have the power to empower the military to suppress conversations at a bar, ban discussions of public affairs or prevent enlisted men or women or draftees from meeting in discussion groups at times or places and for such periods of time that do not interfere with the performance of military duties.

DISSENT: (Stewart, J.) The military articles at issue here are unconstitutionally vague under the standards normally applied by this Court. Such vague laws can only hamper the military's distinct objectives of high morale and esprit de corps with their propensity for arbitrary and discriminatory enforcement.

▶ ANALYSIS

In *Brown v. Glines*, 444 U.S. 348 (1980), the Court went even further than *Parker* and upheld an Air Force regulation that amounted to a prior restraint on speech.

■■■

Quicknotes

FIRST AMENDMENT RIGHTS Rights conferred by the First Amendment to the U.S. Constitution prohibiting Congress from enacting any law respecting an establishment of religion, prohibiting the free exercise of religion, abridging freedom of speech or the press, the right of peaceful assembly and the right to petition for a redress of grievances.

■■■

Thornburgh v. Abbott

Parties not identified.

490 U.S. 401 (1989).

NATURE OF CASE: Review of a First Amendment challenge to a penal statute authorizing prison officials to reject certain incoming publications.

FACT SUMMARY: Prison officials rejected certain publications requested by inmates.

🏛 RULE OF LAW
Government may censor certain publications requested by inmates if the action is reasonably related to a legitimate penological interest.

FACTS: The Federal Bureau of Prisons broadly permits federal prisoners to receive publications from the "outside," but authorizes prison officials to reject incoming publications found to be "detrimental to the security, good order, or discipline of the institution or if it might facilitate criminal activity." Under this regulation, prison officials suppressed 46 publications. Prisoners mounted a First Amendment challenge to this regulation.

ISSUE: May government censor certain publications requested by inmates if the action is reasonably related to a legitimate penological interest?

HOLDING AND DECISION: (Blackmun, J.) Yes. Government may censor certain publications requested by inmates if the action is reasonably related to a legitimate penological interest. The Federal Bureau of Prisons regulation is facially valid under the reasonableness standard. The regulation at issue here is directed at protecting prison security. Once in prison, prisoners may observe particular material in possession of a fellow prisoner, draw inferences as to that fellow's beliefs, sexual orientation, or gang affiliations from that material, and cause disorder by acting accordingly. Prison security is "central to all other corrections goals." The broad discretion accorded to prison wardens in reviewing publications is rationally related to these security interests, partly because of the kind of security risk presented by incoming publications and partly because of the individualized nature of the determinations required by the regulations.

CONCURRENCE AND DISSENT: (Stevens, J.) The majority errs in prematurely approving the Bureau's regulations. This decision threatens to strip inmates of all but a vestige of free communication with the world beyond the prison gate.

▶ ANALYSIS

Most regulations of prisoner speech have been upheld under the reasonableness test.

■■■

Quicknotes

FIRST AMENDMENT RIGHTS Rights conferred by the First Amendment to the U.S. Constitution prohibiting Congress from enacting any law respecting an establishment of religion, prohibiting the free exercise of religion, abridging freedom of speech or the press, the right of peaceful assembly and the right to petition for a redress of grievances.

■■■

Shaw v. Murphy

Prison official (D) v. Inmate law clerk (P)

532 U.S. 223 (2001).

NATURE OF CASE: Appeal from conviction for violation of prison rules.

FACT SUMMARY: Murphy (P), an inmate acting as a law clerk, provided legal assistance to another inmate in violation of prison rules. Upon conviction for the violations, Murphy (P) argued that his communication to the other inmate carried additional First Amendment protections.

> 🏛 **RULE OF LAW**
> Inmates do not have a First Amendment right to provide legal assistance to other inmates.

FACTS: Murphy (P) was an inmate serving as a law clerk. In violation of prison rules, he assigned himself to another inmate's legal matter and sent the inmate a letter containing legal advice. That letter was intercepted and reviewed by Shaw (D), a prison official, in accordance with prison regulations regarding inmate correspondence. The letter revealed Murphy's (P) rule violations and Murphy was convicted of violating two prohibitions. He appealed, arguing that his letter was entitled to additional First Amendment protections because it contained legal advice. The court of appeals reversed his conviction on the basis that letters containing legal assistance should be entitled to greater constitutional protections than other inmate correspondence. Shaw (D) appeals.

ISSUE: Do inmates have a First Amendment right to provide legal assistance to other inmates?

HOLDING AND DECISION: (Thomas, J.) No. Inmates do not have a First Amendment right to provide legal assistance to other inmates. In *Turner v. Safley*, 482 U.S. 78 (1987), this Court held that inmate communications could be constitutionally restricted to achieve legitimate penological interests. *Turner* did not require prison officials to determine the value of the communications on a constitutional level, but simply to determine whether the communication fell within appropriate prison regulations. To afford greater constitutional protections to a prison communication simply because it contained legal assistance would unnecessarily involve the federal court system in prison administrative affairs as each missive would have to be evaluated for its First Amendment content. Turner does not require this and this Court declines to cloak the provision of legal assistance with any protection beyond that normally accorded prisoners' speech.

> ▶ **ANALYSIS**
>
> The Court was not impressed with inmates' abilities or decisions to provide legal advice to others, characterizing such advice as "sometimes a menace to prison discipline."

The Court noted a concern that prisoners use legal correspondence as a method to pass contraband items and that heightened constitutional protections could encourage this practice. The Supreme Court has historically been reluctant to encourage prisoners' attempts to obtain additional constitutional protections while in prison.

■═■

Quicknotes

FIRST AMENDMENT RIGHTS Rights conferred by the First Amendment to the U.S. Constitution prohibiting Congress from enacting any law respecting an establishment of religion, prohibiting the free exercise of religion, abridging freedom of speech or the press, the right of peaceful assembly and the right to petition for a redress of grievances.

■═■

Tinker v. Des Moines Independent Community School District

Student (P) v. School district (D)

393 U.S. 503 (1969).

NATURE OF CASE: Suit challenging the constitutionality of a student's suspension from school.

FACT SUMMARY: Tinker (P), a student, was suspended from high school for wearing a black armband protesting the war in Vietnam despite a school regulation prohibiting such armbands.

🏛 RULE OF LAW

Absent a showing of material and substantial interference with requirements of appropriate discipline, school officials may not constitutionally prohibit the expression of a particular opinion by students.

FACTS: Tinker (D), a high school student in Des Moines, Iowa, along with his parents and several other students, strongly objected to the war in Vietnam. To publicize their feelings, the group decided to wear black armbands for a specified period. Tinker (P) wore his armband to school " . . . and was suspended when he refused to remove it." He did not return to school until the end of the specified period of protest. The district court determined that the school authorities acted constitutionally in attempting to prevent school disturbances. Tinker's (P) position was that the armbands represented constitutionally protected speech.

ISSUE: May school officials restrict a student's right of expression without showing that the expression constituted a material and substantial interference with the requirements of appropriate discipline in the operation of the schools?

HOLDING AND DECISION: (Fortas, J.) No. Students, along with all others, are afforded the guarantees of the First Amendment. The guarantees extend onto the schoolhouse grounds. While obviously nonverbal, the wearing of the armbands was intended to communicate an idea. It was a passive act that was not aggressive or disruptive. The court concluded the wearing of the armbands was essentially "pure speech." Before the school authorities could constitutionally attempt to restrict Tinker's (P) expression, they must show a compelling and substantial interest in so doing. The expressed justification was a fear that the wearing of armbands would cause a disturbance and distract from the orderly process of learning. However, the only reaction occurred after school, off the grounds, when several students made hostile remarks. A memorandum prepared after the suspension indicated the officials were as much concerned with the content of the expression as they were with its supposed effect. A major part of the student's development must come from individual assertion of opinion and interaction with other students. The school may not confine this expression to a dogma laid down by its officials. This does not mean that expressions that cause actual disturbance may not be prohibited. But no such action was demonstrated in this case. The school officials unconstitutionally infringed on Tinker's (P) right of expression.

DISSENT: (Black, J.) This decision thrusts the courts into the classroom and administration of education in a manner that will seriously undermine the ability of school officials to maintain order in the schools. The majority determined that the armbands were a passive expression that caused no disruption of the learning process. Yet the armbands were intended to draw specific attention to one of the most divisive issues in our country's history. If the expression was as innocuous as the majority holds, why did the students hold so steadfastly to their intent to wear them if not to draw attention to what they symbolized?

▶ ANALYSIS

In a later case, Justice Fortas found that student demonstrations accompanied by violence were not protected activity. He determined that the student's conduct was aimed more at destruction than at expressing ideas. It is interesting to note that the strongest dissent came from Justice Black, normally a staunch defender of First Amendment guarantees. But it is an example of the distinction he made between speech, which was to be absolutely protected, and conduct, which could be subjected to reasonable controls. While these distinctions were clear in his mind, they were not so clearly delineated in the minds of the other Justices, much less members of the public.

■■■

Quicknotes

COMPELLING STATE INTEREST Defense to an alleged Equal Protection Clause violation; that a state action was necessary in order to protect an interest the government is under a duty to protect.

FIRST AMENDMENT RIGHTS Rights conferred by the First Amendment to the U.S. Constitution prohibiting Congress from enacting any law respecting an establishment of religion, prohibiting the free exercise of religion, abridging freedom of speech or the press, the right of peaceful assembly and the right to petition for a redress of grievances.

■■■

Bethel School District No. 403 v. Fraser
School district (D) v. Student (P)

478 U.S. 675 (1986).

NATURE OF CASE: Challenge to public school's regulation prohibiting lewd speech.

FACT SUMMARY: Fraser (P) was suspended for making sexual innuendos during a student election speech at a school assembly.

RULE OF LAW
A public school may prohibit the use of sexually explicit language at school-related functions.

FACTS: At an assembly convened pursuant to student government elections, Fraser (P) delivered a nominating speech replete with sexual innuendos. He had been warned prior to making the speech that it would violate school rules prohibiting the use of vulgar language. The school district (D) suspended Fraser for three days. Fraser (P) brought an action against the district (D), alleging that the district's (D) actions violated his freedom of speech. The district court found such a violation and held for Fraser (P). The Ninth Circuit affirmed.

ISSUE: May a public school prohibit the use of sexually explicit language at school-related functions?

HOLDING AND DECISION: (Burger, C.J.) Yes. A public school may prohibit the use of sexually explicit language at school-related functions. While students maintain their constitutional guarantees of freedom of expression while at school, the right is not absolute. Schools have a right, indeed a duty, to instruct their students in proper societal values, and the proscription of indecent behavior is included. The right of others not to be exposed to that which many consider offensive must also be taken into account. Here, the language/behavior being proscribed was not a communication of political ideas, which would have been entitled to greater protection.

CONCURRENCE: (Brennan, J.) The language used by Fraser (P) comes nowhere near the threshold of unprotected obscene speech, and only in a narrow set of circumstances could it be proscribed. A school assembly is one such circumstance.

DISSENT: (Marshall, J.) The district (D) failed to show Fraser's (P) remarks were disruptive.

ANALYSIS
The Court stressed the fact that there was no political content to Fraser's speech. The Court distinguished *Tinker v. Des Moines Independent Community School District*, 393 U.S. 503 (1969). In that action, school regulations prohibiting the wearing of armbands were struck down. One wonders what the result would have been if Fraser's (P) speech had mixed sexual innuendo with a political message?

Quicknotes
FIRST AMENDMENT RIGHTS Rights conferred by the First Amendment to the U.S. Constitution prohibiting Congress from enacting any law respecting an establishment of religion, prohibiting the free exercise of religion, abridging freedom of speech or the press, the right of peaceful assembly and the right to petition for a redress of grievances.

Hazelwood School District v. Kuhlmeier

School district (D) v. Student (P)

484 U.S. 260 (1988).

NATURE OF CASE: Review of appellate order striking down school student-newspaper content regulation.

FACT SUMMARY: Reynolds (D), principal of Hazelwood East High School, refused to permit the publication of certain articles in a newspaper published by the journalism class.

🏛 RULE OF LAW
School authorities may restrict the content of school-sponsored expressive activities so long as the restriction promotes legitimate pedagogical concerns.

FACTS: The journalism class at Hazelwood East High published a newspaper. School policy required that the content be approved by the principal. The class teacher submitted the proposed articles to Reynolds (D), the principal. He refused to permit the publication of an article dealing with birth control and another article dealing with divorce, believing the subject matter inappropriate and expressing right-to-privacy concerns. Hazelwood (P), a student writer, along with two other student writers, challenged the editorial policy as violative of the First Amendment. A district court upheld the policy, but the Court of Appeals for the Eighth Circuit reversed. The Supreme Court granted review.

ISSUE: May school authorities restrict the content of school-sponsored expressive activities so long as the restrictions promote legitimate pedagogical concerns?

HOLDING AND DECISION: (White, J.) Yes. School authorities may restrict the content of school-sponsored expressive activities so long as the restrictions promote legitimate pedagogical concerns. While students do have First Amendment rights, the rights of students are not coextensive with those of adults in other settings. A school need not tolerate speech inconsistent with its basic educational function. Further, what is and is not so inconsistent is a decision best left to school authorities. A school must be able to set standards for work it sanctions and refuse to disseminate speech not meeting those standards. The education of the young is properly the realm of teachers and parents, not the federal judiciary, and only when a restriction has no valid educational purpose may the courts intervene. Here, certain articles perceived as inappropriate to the high school educational environment were deleted, and this Court sees no reason to second-guess the judgment of the appropriate school authorities.

DISSENT: (Brennan, J.) The censorship in this instance should be subjected to a strict scrutiny test, not one of reasonableness. Under strict scrutiny, the censorship in this case must fail as it was not narrowly tailored to promote the interests of protecting privacy and preventing disruption.

▶ ANALYSIS

The Supreme Court's most notable decision favoring free student speech was *Tinker v. Des Moines Independent Community School District*, 393 U.S. 503 (1969). However, the Court has, in recent years, begun to narrow the scope of student expression. Examples include the present case and *Bethel School District No. 403 v. Fraser*, 478 U.S. 675 (1986), which upheld the disciplining of a student for an allegedly offensive student council election speech.

■══■

Quicknotes

FIRST AMENDMENT RIGHTS Rights conferred by the First Amendment to the U.S. Constitution prohibiting Congress from enacting any law respecting an establishment of religion, prohibiting the free exercise of religion, abridging freedom of speech or the press, the right of peaceful assembly and the right to petition for a redress of grievances.

STRICT SCRUTINY Method by which courts determine the constitutionality of a law, when a law affects a fundamental right. Under the test, the legislature must have had a compelling interest to enact the law and measures prescribed by the law must be the least restrictive means possible to accomplish its goal.

■══■

Morse v. Frederick

Student (P) v. School principal (D)

127 S. Ct. 2618 (2007).

NATURE OF CASE: Review of federal appeals court judgment.

FACT SUMMARY: Joseph Frederick (P), a student, was suspended by Principal Deborah Morse (D) after Frederick (P) held up a banner with the message "Bong Hits 4 Jesus," a slang reference to marijuana smoking, at a school event that was televised. He sued her.

🏛 RULE OF LAW
Public schools may prohibit students from displaying messages promoting the use of illegal drugs at school-supervised events.

FACTS: Public school student Joseph Frederick (P) held up a banner with the message "Bong Hits 4 Jesus," a slang reference to marijuana smoking, at a school event that was televised. Principal Deborah Morse (D) took away the banner and suspended Frederick (P). The school had a policy against the display of material that promotes the use of illegal drugs. Frederick (P) sued, arguing that his right to freedom of speech under the Constitution's First Amendment was violated. The district court found no constitutional violation, holding that even if there were a violation, the principal (D) had qualified immunity. The Court of Appeals for the Ninth Circuit reversed, citing *Tinker v. Des Moines Independent Community School District* (1969), which extends First Amendment protection to student speech except where the speech would cause a disturbance.

ISSUE: May public schools prohibit students from displaying messages promoting the use of illegal drugs at school-supervised events?

HOLDING AND DECISION: (Roberts, C.J.) Yes. Public schools may prohibit students from displaying messages promoting the use of illegal drugs at school-supervised events. The speech rights of public school students are not as extensive as those adults normally enjoy, and that the highly protective standard set by *Tinker* would not always be applied. Students have some right to political speech even while in school, but the right does not extend to pro-drug messages that may undermine the school's important mission to discourage drug use. Frederick's (P) message, though "cryptic," was reasonably interpreted as promoting marijuana use. The question of Morse's (D) immunity need not be reached.

CONCURRENCE: (Thomas, J.) The right to free speech does not apply to students and *Tinker* should be overturned altogether.

CONCURRENCE: (Alito, J.) The decision should apply only to pro-drug messages and not to broader political speech.

DISSENT: (Stevens, J.) The principal should have had immunity from the lawsuit, but the majority opinion ignores the constitutional imperative to allow unfettered debate, even among high-school students. The school's interest in protecting students from exposure to speech that is reasonably regarded as promoting illegal drug use cannot justify disciplining Frederick (P) for an attempt to make an ambiguous statement to a television audience simply because it contained an "oblique" reference to drugs.

▶ *ANALYSIS*

This case was a 5-4 decision, and the court remains deeply divided as to the parameters of a student's rights to free speech under the First Amendment. *Tinker*, 393 U.S. 503 (1969), stands for the proposition that students do not "shed their constitutional rights to freedom of speech or expression at the schoolhouse gate," but *Hazelwood School District v. Kuhlmeier*, 484 U.S. 260 (1988), limits *Tinker* by holding that the rights of students must be applied in the context of the particular school environment, as did *Bethel School Dist. No. 403 v. Fraser*, 478 U.S. 675 (1986), which held that the rights of students in public school are not automatically coextensive with the rights of adults in other settings.

■=■

Garcetti v. Ceballos

Government (D) v. Government employee (P)

126 S. Ct. 1951 (2006).

NATURE OF CASE: Review of federal appeals court judgment.

FACT SUMMARY: The government (D) disciplined Richard Ceballos (P) when his communications ran counter to the interests of the government (D), and Ceballos (P) sued, claiming the First Amendment protected his speech.

🏛 RULE OF LAW
Speech by a public official is only protected if the official speaks as a private citizen, and not as part of the official's public duties.

FACTS: After Richard Ceballos (P), an employee of the Los Angeles District Attorney's office, found that a sheriff misrepresented facts in a search warrant affidavit, he notified the attorneys prosecuting the case. They all agreed that the affidavit was questionable, but the D.A.'s office (D) refused to dismiss the case. Ceballos (P) then told the defense he believed the affidavit contained false statements, and defense counsel subpoenaed him to testify. Ceballos (P) then sued his employer, alleging that D.A.s in the office retaliated against him for his cooperation with the defense. Ceballos (P) argued that the First Amendment of the Constitution protected his cooperation. The district court held that the D.A.s were protected by qualified immunity, but the Court of Appeals for the Ninth Circuit reversed, holding that qualified immunity was not available because Ceballos (P) had been engaged in speech that addressed matters of public concern and was thus protected by the First Amendment.

ISSUE: Is speech by a public official only protected if the official speaks as a private citizen, and not as part of the official's public duties?

HOLDING AND DECISION: (Kennedy, J.) Yes. Speech by a public official is protected only if the official speaks as a private citizen, and not as part of the official's public duties. When public employees make statements pursuant to their official duties, the employees are not speaking as citizens for First Amendment purposes and their speech is not insulated by the Constitution from employer discipline. Ceballos's (P) employers were justified in taking action against him based on his testimony and cooperation with the defense, because it occurred as part of his official duties.

DISSENT: (Stevens, J.) The First Amendment sometimes protects a government employee from discipline based on speech made in the course of his duties. The distinction between speaking as a citizen and speaking in the course of one's employment is false.

DISSENT: (Souter, J.) Private and public interests in addressing official wrongdoing and threats to health an safety can outweigh the government's interest in the efficient implementation of employer policy, and when they do, public employees speaking contrary to employer policy in the course of their duties should be protected by the First Amendment.

DISSENT: (Breyer, J.) The First Amendment protects a government employee's speech that both (1) involves a matter of public concern and (2) takes place in the course of ordinary job-related duties when in the presence of augmented need for constitutional protection and diminished risk of undue judicial interference with governmental management of the public's affairs.

▌ ANALYSIS

Ceballos extends the rule of *Pickering v Board of Education*, 391 U.S. 563 (1968). In *Pickering*, the court held that the government can discipline or fire government employees speaking about public concerns if the government can show that office efficiencies justify the action. In *Ceballos*, the court held that the speech of a government employee is not protected if it occurs on the job and as part of the employee's duties.

■=■

Quicknotes

FIRST AMENDMENT RIGHTS Rights conferred by the First Amendment to the U.S. Constitution prohibiting Congress from enacting any law respecting an establishment of religion, prohibiting the free exercise of religion, abridging freedom of speech or the press, the right of peaceful assembly and the right to petition for a redress of grievances.

■=■

NAACP v. State of Alabama, ex rel. Patterson

Association (D) v. State (P)

357 U.S. 449 (1958).

NATURE OF CASE: Appeal from conviction for contempt for failure to obey state court order to produce records.

FACT SUMMARY: The National Association for the Advancement of Colored People (NAACP) (D), in a hearing initiated by the State of Alabama (P) to oust it from the state for failure to comply with incorporation requirements, refused to obey a state court order to produce its membership lists.

🏛 RULE OF LAW
A state must demonstrate a controlling justification for the deterrent effect on the free enjoyment of the right to associate that disclosure of membership lists is likely to have.

FACTS: Alabama (P) brought proceedings against the NAACP (D) to oust it from the state for failure to comply with a state statute setting forth requirements governing foreign corporations. The NAACP (D) claimed it was exempt. A state court issued an order restraining the NAACP (D) from continuing to engage in further activities or to attempt to qualify itself while the action was pending. Before the hearing began, the state moved for the production of the NAACP's (D) membership lists, alleging that the documents were necessary for adequate preparation for the hearing. The court granted the motion and issued an order to that effect. The NAACP (D) thereupon complied with the requirements of the statute but did not produce the lists. The NAACP (D) was held in civil contempt, fined, and prevented from obtaining a hearing on the merits of the ouster action until it produced the records.

ISSUE: May a state, consistent with the Due Process Clause of the Fourteenth Amendment, compel an organization to reveal to the state's Attorney General the names and addresses of all its state members and agents without demonstrating a controlling justification for the deterrent effect on free association disclosure would involve?

HOLDING AND DECISION: (Harlan, J.) No. A state must demonstrate a controlling justification for the deterrent effect on the free enjoyment of the right to associate that disclosure of membership lists is likely to have. Group association is an effective means to further advocacy of both public and private viewpoints. The fact that Alabama (P) has taken no direct steps to interfere with the Association's (D) freedom of association does not end the question for it may have engaged in more subtle intimidation. There is a vital relationship between the freedom to associate and privacy in one's associations. Here, there is a good possibility that disclosure would expose members to economic reprisal, loss of employment, and threat of physical coercion, thus having a deterrent effect on continued membership and discouraging others from joining. Having found the potential for deterrence, the next inquiry is whether the state was justified in seeking the lists. The disclosure of the lists has no substantial bearing on the issue of compliance with the state statute.

▶ ANALYSIS

At the same time that state investigations seeking public disclosure were prevailing over countervailing claims of First Amendment freedoms in other contexts, the Court, as evidenced in *NAACP v. Alabama* and *Shelton v. Tucker*, 364 U.S. 479 (1960), required the state to produce a relevant justification for its probe and the collateral effect of disclosure on First Amendment freedoms. *NAACP v. Alabama* thus portends a shift in the Court's focus to greater scrutiny of reasons for state inquiries that have deterring, or "chilling" effects, on freedom of speech, association, or expression. The new approach would gain wider application in the 1960s, when the state's interest in seeking information was pitted against the individual's right to privacy.

■■■

Quicknotes

DUE PROCESS CLAUSE Clauses found in the Fifth and Fourteenth Amendments to the U.S. Constitution providing that no person shall be deprived of "life, liberty, or property, without due process of law."

FREEDOM OF ASSOCIATION The right to peaceably assemble.

■■■

Board of Regents of the University of Wisconsin System v. Southworth

University (D) v. Students (P)

529 U.S. 217 (2000).

NATURE OF CASE: Review of constitutional challenge to student fees.

FACT SUMMARY: University students (P) alleged their student fees could not be used to support speech they found objectionable.

🏛 RULE OF LAW
When a university requires its students to pay fees to support the extracurricular speech of other students, it may not prefer some viewpoints to others.

FACTS: Southworth and other students (P) paid student fees that the University of Wisconsin (D) used to support student organizations engaging in political or ideological speech. Southworth (P) claimed that the mandatory fees violated the First Amendment. The district court and appellate court invalidated the student fee program and the University (D) appealed. The Supreme Court granted certiorari.

ISSUE: When a university requires its students to pay fees to support the extracurricular speech of other students, may it prefer some viewpoints to others?

HOLDING AND DECISION: (Kennedy, J.) No. When a university requires its students to pay fees to support the extracurricular speech of other students, it may not prefer some viewpoints to others. The viewpoint neutrality requirement of the University (D) is sufficient to protect the rights of students (P). The student referendum aspect of the program appears to be inconsistent with the viewpoint neutrality requirements.

▶ *ANALYSIS*

The referendum aspect of the University's program was found to be violative of the First Amendment. By majority vote of the student body, a given registered student organization could be funded or defunded. There seemed to be no protection for viewpoint neutrality in this process.

■══■

Quicknotes

FIRST AMENDMENT RIGHTS Rights conferred by the First Amendment to the U.S. Constitution prohibiting Congress from enacting any law respecting an establishment of religion, prohibiting the free exercise of religion, abridging freedom of speech or the press, the right of peaceful assembly and the right to petition for a redress of grievances.

■══■

Roberts v. United States Jaycees

State (D) v. Professional organization (P)

468 U.S. 609 (1984).

NATURE OF CASE: Appeal from judgment requiring a professional organization to admit women as members.

FACT SUMMARY: The court of appeals held that the Minnesota Human Rights Act violated the Jaycees' (P) rights to free association guaranteed by the First and Fourteenth Amendments by requiring them to allow women to become members.

🏛 RULE OF LAW
The right to associate for expressive purposes may be limited by regulations adopted to serve compelling state interests, unrelated to the suppression of ideas, that cannot be achieved through means significantly less restrictive of associational freedoms.

FACTS: The U.S. Jaycees (P) sued for a declaratory judgment, contending the Minnesota Human Rights Act violated its right to freely associate by requiring it to allow women to become members. The Jaycees (P) contended their right to associate with whom they chose was protected expressive conduct under the First Amendment. The State (D) defended, contending the statute served the compelling state interest in ending sexual discrimination. The district court denied declaratory relief, upholding the constitutionality of the statute. The court of appeals reversed, and the State (D) appealed.

ISSUE: May the right to freely associate be limited by restrictions serving compelling state interests?

HOLDING AND DECISION: (Brennan, J.) Yes. The right to associate for expressive purposes may be limited by regulations adopted to serve compelling state interests, unrelated to the suppression of ideas that cannot be achieved through means significantly less restrictive of associational freedoms. The restriction here does not regulate speech. It directly promotes the state's compelling interest in prohibiting and correcting injustices based on sexual discrimination. Further, no less restrictive means of achieving this end was shown to exist by the Jaycees (P). As a result, the statute was constitutional. Reversed.

▶ ANALYSIS

There are two distinct senses in which the freedom of association has been protected by the Court. The first recognizes the freedom of association as a fundamental element of personal liberty. In another line of cases, the Court places the freedom to associate within freedom of speech, characterizing it as expressive conduct. The Court recognized in this case that these two characterizations may coincide.

Quicknotes

FREEDOM OF ASSOCIATION The right to peaceably assemble.

Hurley v. Irish-American Gay, Lesbian, and Bisexual Group of Boston

Parade sponsor (D) v. Permit applicants (P)

515 U.S. 557 (1995).

NATURE OF CASE: Review of order mandating parade permit.

FACT SUMMARY: The sponsors of a parade in Boston contended that a law compelling them to issue a permit to an organization they found repugnant violated the First Amendment.

RULE OF LAW

Private citizens organizing a parade may not be forced to include groups whose message they do not wish to convey.

FACTS: Since 1947, Boston's annual St. Patrick's Day parade had been organized by the South Boston Allied War Veterans Council (D). In 1983 the Irish-American Gay, Lesbian and Bisexual Group of Boston (the Group) (P) applied for and was refused a permit. It filed suit. The trial court held that the parade was a public accommodation subject to Massachusetts antidiscrimination laws and ordered the Group (P) admitted. The state supreme court affirmed. The U.S. Supreme Court granted review.

ISSUE: May private citizens organizing a parade be forced to include groups whose message they do not wish to convey?

HOLDING AND DECISION: (Souter, J.) No. Private citizens organizing a parade may not be forced to include groups whose message they do not wish to convey. A parade is a collection of marchers who make a collective point. A parade's dependence on watchers is so extreme that a parade without spectators and media coverage is arguably not a parade at all. Consequently, a parade is without question a form of expressive conduct protected by the First Amendment. Expression in the context of a parade is more than banners and speeches; the type of participants is also part of the overall message. Free speech in the demonstration/parade context necessarily involves the right on the part of the parade organizer to not include those whose inclusion would send a message the organizer does not wish said. Here, the Veterans Council (D) was of the opinion that inclusion of the Group (P) in its parade conveyed an unwanted message. It was therefore acting within its rights not to allow the Group (P) to march. Reversed.

▶ ANALYSIS

A conceptually similar case, which came out differently, was *Turner Broadcasting Systems, Inc. v. FCC*, 512 U.S. 622 (1994). In that case, FCC regulations mandated that cable operators include certain types of programming. This was held constitutional.

Quicknotes

FIRST AMENDMENT RIGHTS Rights conferred by the First Amendment to the U.S. Constitution prohibiting Congress from enacting any law respecting an establishment of religion, prohibiting the free exercise of religion, abridging freedom of speech or the press, the right of peaceful assembly and the right to petition for a redress of grievances.

Boy Scouts of America v. Dale

Nonprofit organization (D) v. Member of organization (P)

530 U.S. 640 (2000).

NATURE OF CASE: Review of the constitutionality of a private organization's membership policies.

FACT SUMMARY: Dale's (P) membership in the Boy Scouts (D) was revoked when the Boy Scouts (D) learned that he is an avowed homosexual and gay rights activist.

🏛 RULE OF LAW

A group may constitutionally exclude an unwanted person if forced inclusion would infringe the group's freedom of expressive association by affecting in a significant way the group's ability to advocate public or private viewpoints.

FACTS: James Dale (P) entered scouting in 1978 at the age of eight by joining Monmouth Council's Cub Scout Pack 142. Dale (P) became a Boy Scout in 1981 and remained a Scout until he turned 18. During this time, Dale (P) was an exemplary Scout. In 1988, he achieved the rank of Eagle Scout, one of scouting's highest honors. In 1989, Dale (P) applied for adult membership in the Boy Scouts (D). His application was approved and he was appointed assistant scoutmaster of Troop 73. At this time, Dale (P) began his studies at Rutgers University. Dale (P) became involved with and later became copresident of the Rutgers University Lesbian/Gay Alliance. In 1990, Dale (P) attended a seminar addressing the psychological and health needs of lesbian and gay teenagers. A newspaper covering the event interviewed Dale (P) about his advocacy of gay teens' need for homosexual role models, and published the interview with his photo. Later that same month, Dale (P) received a letter from Monmouth Council Executive James Kay revoking his adult membership in the Boy Scouts (D). Dale (P) wrote to Kay, requesting the reason for the decision to revoke his membership. Kay responded that the Boy Scouts (D) "specifically forbid membership to homosexuals." Dale (P) filed this suit, alleging that the Boy Scouts (D) had violated New Jersey's public accommodations statute and its common law by revoking his membership.

ISSUE: May a group constitutionally exclude an unwanted person if forced inclusion would infringe the group's freedom of expressive association by affecting in a significant way the group's ability to advocate public or private viewpoints?

HOLDING AND DECISION: (Rehnquist, C.J.) Yes. A group may constitutionally exclude an unwanted person if forced inclusion would infringe the group's freedom of expressive association by affecting in a significant way the group's ability to advocate public or private viewpoints.

The New Jersey Supreme Court held that the state's public accommodations law requires that the Boy Scouts (D) admit Dale (P). Application of the law in this way, however, violates the Boy Scouts' First Amendment right of expressive association. The statute prohibits in part discrimination on the basis of sexual orientation in places of public accommodation. The Supreme Court held that the Boy Scouts (D) was a place of public accommodation subject to the law, that the organization was not exempt from the law under any of its express exemptions, and that the Boy Scouts violated the law by revoking Dale's (P) membership based on his homosexuality. The forced inclusion of an unwanted person in a group infringes the group's freedom of expressive association if that person's presence affects in a significant way the group's ability to advocate public or private viewpoints. However, the freedom of expression is not absolute. It may be overridden by regulations enacted to serve compelling state interests, unrelated to the suppression of ideas that cannot be achieved through means significantly less restrictive of associational freedoms. In determining whether a group is protected by the First Amendment's expressive associational right, it must first be determined whether the group engaged in "expressive association." Given that the Boy Scouts (D) engages in expressive activity, it must be determined whether the forced inclusion of Dale (P) as assistant scoutmaster would significantly affect the Boy Scouts' (D) ability to advocate public or private viewpoints. The Boy Scouts (D) asserts that homosexual conduct is inconsistent with the values instilled in the Scout Oath, "To keep myself physically strong, mentally awake, and morally straight." The Boy Scouts (D) assert that it does not wish to promote homosexual conduct as a legitimate form of behavior. Thus we must determine whether Dale's (P) presence as an assistant scoutmaster would significantly burden this goal. The court must give deference both to an association's assertions regarding the nature of its expression as well as the association's view of what would impair its expression. Dale's (D) presence would force the organization to send a message that it accepts homosexual conduct as a legitimate form of behavior.

DISSENT: (Stevens, J.) The law does not impose any serious burdens on the Boy Scouts' (D) "collective effort on behalf of its shared goals," nor does it force the Boy Scouts (D) to communicate any message that it does not wish to advocate. Thus it does not infringe any constitutional right of the Boy Scouts (D).

Continued on next page.

▶ *ANALYSIS*

Public accommodation laws, such as the one here, were initially promulgated in order to prevent discrimination in public places of accommodation. Such laws have gradually expanded to include many other forms of accommodation.

■═■

Quicknotes

FIRST AMENDMENT RIGHTS Rights conferred by the First Amendment to the U.S. Constitution prohibiting Congress from enacting any law respecting an establishment of religion, prohibiting the free exercise of religion, abridging freedom of speech or the press, the right of peaceful assembly and the right to petition for a redress of grievances.

■═■

Minneapolis Star and Tribune Co. v. Minnesota Commissioner of Revenue

Newspaper publisher (P) v. State (D)

460 U.S. 575 (1983).

NATURE OF CASE: Action for a refund of use taxes paid.

FACT SUMMARY: The Minneapolis Star (P) contended that Minnesota had acted unconstitutionally in imposing a four percent use tax on the cost of ink and paper consumed in the production of any publication and then enacting an exemption that effectively resulted in only a few of the biggest newspapers having to pay any such use tax.

🏛 RULE OF LAW
Differential taxation of the press places such a burden on the interests protected by the First Amendment that it cannot pass constitutional muster unless the state asserts a counterbalancing interest of compelling importance that cannot be achieved without differential taxation.

FACTS: Under the tax scheme set up by the Minnesota legislature, newspapers were exempt from the four percent sales tax. However, a four percent use tax on the costs of ink and paper consumed in the production of any publication was imposed. In addition, an exemption was provided for the first $100,000 worth of ink and paper consumed by a publication in any calendar year, which amounted to giving each publication an annual tax credit of $4,000. Only 11 papers, one of them the Tribune (P), used sufficient quantities of ink and paper to become liable for payment of use taxes beyond the amount of the tax credit in 1974. Only 13 papers had to pay actual use tax in 1975. In challenging the constitutionality of the use tax and seeking a refund of the use taxes it had paid, the Tribune (P) argued that there had been a violation of the guarantees of freedom of the press and equal protection found in the First and Fourteenth Amendments. The Minnesota Supreme Court upheld the tax against this constitutional challenge.

ISSUE: In order to be constitutionally permissible, must any differential taxation of the press be necessary to the achieving of a state interest of compelling importance?

HOLDING AND DECISION: (O'Connor, J.) Yes. Because differential taxation of the press places such a burden on the interests protected by the First Amendment, it is not constitutionally permissible unless the state asserts a counterbalancing interest of compelling importance that cannot be achieved without differential taxation. By creating this special use tax, Minnesota singled out the press for special tax treatment. It justifies such by its need to raise revenue. Yet, that goal could be attained by taxing businesses generally, thus avoiding the censorial threat implicit

in a tax that singles out the press. Minnesota offers the counterargument that the use tax actually favors the press. However, the very selection of the press for special treatment threatens the press not only with the current differential treatment, but with the possibility of subsequent differentially more burdensome treatment. Thus, this Court would hesitate to fashion a rule that automatically allowed the state to single out the press for a different method of taxation as long as the effective burden on the press was lighter than that on other businesses. Such a rule should also be avoided because the courts as institutions are poorly equipped to evaluate with precision the relative burdens of various methods of taxation. Minnesota's ink and paper tax would not survive anyway because it violates the First Amendment for another reason other than its singling out of the press. It also violates the First Amendment because it targets a small group of newspapers. Recognizing a power in the state not only to single out the press but also to tailor the tax so that it singles out a few members of the press presents such a potential for abuse that no interest suggested by Minnesota can justify the scheme. When, as in this case, a tax exemption operates to select such a narrowly defined group to bear the full burden of the tax, the tax begins to resemble more a penalty for a few of the largest newspapers than an attempt to favor struggling smaller enterprises. There having been no satisfactory justification offered for this tax on the use of ink and paper, it must be held to violate the First Amendment.

DISSENT: (Rehnquist, J.) The $1,224,747 the Tribune (P) actually paid in use taxes over the years in question is significantly less burdensome than the $3,685,092 that it would have had to pay were the sales of its newspapers subject to the sales tax. Thus the tax scheme, which allowed newspapers to pay a use tax in return for being free of sales tax, actually benefitted, not burdened, the freedom of speech and the press. If there was no burden, there was no "abridgment" of these freedoms of speech and the press. Without such an "abridgement" there is no violation of the First Amendment.

▶ ANALYSIS

In *Washington v. United States*, 460 U.S. (1983), the Court was dealing with a state tax that singled out federal contractors as a separate category. It did not evidence any reluctance in that case to assess the impact of the tax, finding it was not impermissibly discriminatory on the United States because it imposed a tax burden no greater than

Continued on next page.

what the contractors would have had to otherwise pay in state taxes were they treated the same as everyone else.

■═■

Quicknotes

EQUAL PROTECTION CLAUSE A constitutional provision that each person be guaranteed the same protection of the laws enjoyed by other persons in like circumstances.

FREEDOM OF THE PRESS The right to publish and publicly disseminate one's views.

■═■

Cohen v. Cowles Media Co.

Confidential informant (P) v. Media company (D)

501 U.S. 663 (1991).

NATURE OF CASE: Review of a First Amendment challenge to liability under state promissory estoppel law.

FACT SUMMARY: Newspaper revealed the name of a confidential source of information after promising the source that his identity would be kept confidential.

🏛 **RULE OF LAW**
The press is not exempt under the First Amendment from general laws.

FACTS: Dan Cohen (P), an active Republican associated with the Wheelock Whitney Independent-Republican gubernatorial campaign, approached reporters from the *St. Paul Pioneer Press Dispatch* (D) and the *Minneapolis Star and Tribune* (D) and offered to provide documents relating to a candidate in the upcoming election. Cohen (P) made clear to the reporters that he would provide the information only if he was given a promise of confidentiality. Reporters from both papers (D) promised to keep Cohen's (P) identity anonymous and Cohen (P) turned over copies of two public court records concerning the Democratic-Farmer-Labor candidate for Lieutenant Governor. After consultation and debate, the editorial staffs of the two newspapers independently decided to publish Cohen's (P) name as part of their stories concerning the Democratic candidate.

ISSUE: Is the press exempt from general laws under the First Amendment?

HOLDING AND DECISION: (White, J.) No. Generally applicable laws do not offend the First Amendment simply because their enforcement against the press has incidental effects on its ability to gather and report the news. Thus, Cohen (P) can maintain a cause of action for promissory estoppel here.

DISSENT: (Souter, J.) A state's interest in enforcing a newspaper's promise of confidentiality is insufficient to outweigh the interest in unfettered publication of the information revealed in this case.

▸ *ANALYSIS*

The Supreme Court consistently has refused to find that the protection of freedom of the press entitles it to exemptions from general regulatory laws.

PROMISSORY ESTOPPEL A promise that is enforceable if the promisor should reasonably expect that it will induce action or forbearance on the part of the promisee, and does in fact cause such action or forbearance, and it is the only means of avoiding injustice.

Quicknotes

FREEDOM OF THE PRESS The right to publish and publicly disseminate one's views.

Branzburg v. Hayes

News reporters (D) v. State and federal governments (P)

408 U.S. 665 (1972).

NATURE OF CASE: Appeal from contempt citations for failure to testify before state and federal grand juries.

FACT SUMMARY: Newsmen refused to testify before state and federal grand juries, claiming that their news sources were confidential.

🏛 RULE OF LAW
The First Amendment's freedom of the press does not exempt a reporter from disclosing to a grand jury information that he has received in confidence.

FACTS: Branzburg (D), who had written articles for a newspaper about drug activities he had observed, refused to testify before a state grand jury regarding his information. Pappas (D), a television newsman, even though he wrote no story, refused to testify before a state grand jury on his experiences inside Black Panther headquarters. Caldwell (D), a reporter who had interviewed several Black Panther leaders, and written stories about the articles, refused to testify before a federal grand jury which was investigating violations of criminal statutes dealing with threats against the President and traveling interstate to incite a riot. Branzburg (D) and Pappas (D) were held in contempt.

ISSUE: Does the First Amendment protect a reporter from revealing his sources before a grand jury that has subpoenaed him to testify, even if the information is confidential?

HOLDING AND DECISION: (White, J.) No. The First Amendment's freedom of the press does not exempt a reporter from disclosing to a grand jury information that he has received in confidence. The First Amendment does not invalidate every incidental burdening of the press that may result from the enforcement of civil or criminal statutes of general applicability. Newsmen cannot invoke a testimonial privilege not enjoined by other citizens. The Constitution should not shield criminals who wish to remain anonymous from prosecution through disclosure. Forcing newsmen to testify will not impede the flow of news. The newsman may never be called. Many political groups will still turn to the reporter because they are dependent on the media for exposure. Grand jury proceedings are secret and the police are experienced in protecting informants. More important, the public's interest in news flow does not override the public's interest in deterring crime. Here, the grand juries were not probing at will without relation to existing need; the information sought was necessary to the respective investigations. A grand jury is not restricted to seeking information from non-newsmen—it may choose the best method for its task.

CONCURRENCE: (Powell, J.) The newsman always has resort to the courts to quash subpoenas where his testimony bears only a remote and tenuous relationship to the subject of the investigation.

DISSENT: (Stewart, J.) After today's decision, the potential source must choose between risking exposure by giving information or avoiding the risk by remaining silent. When neither the reporter nor his source can rely on the shield of confidentiality, valuable information will not be published and the public dialogue will inevitably be impoverished.

▶ ANALYSIS

Thirty-one states have laws allowing reporters to protect sources' confidentiality and identities. With no equivalent federal law, a federal judge sentenced reporter Judith Miller to jail in July 2005 for refusing to divulge the name of her source for an article that revealed the identity of CIA agent Valerie Plume. The American public clamored for justice for the compromised safety of Agent Plume, but also recognized the struggle for Ms. Miller. First Amendment protections for reporters and their sources are not absolute. Some reporters may be forced to divulge sources' identities when testifying before grand juries, which contravenes the duty reporters argue is owed to confidential sources. The federal judge in Miller's case noted that the prosecution exhausted other avenues before issuing subpoenas to Miller and others, but reporters contend that nothing should require the revelation of a confidential source's identity as it chills the sharing of information. As it presently stands, the test to determine the necessity of forcing a reporter to divulge a confidential source's identity recommends that the judge determine whether the information sought is "essential to a successful investigation" and whether non-press sources could provide the information.

■=■

Quicknotes

FREEDOM OF THE PRESS The right to publish and publicly disseminate one's views.

GRAND JURY A group summoned to investigate, inform, and accuse persons of crimes when sufficient evidence exists to do so.

■=■

Red Lion Broadcasting Co. v. Federal Communications Commn.

Broadcasting company (P) v. Regulatory agency (D)

395 U.S. 367 (1969).

NATURE OF CASE: Review of a First Amendment challenge to the fairness doctrine and an FCC rulemaking.

FACT SUMMARY: The Federal Communications Commission (FCC) declared that a radio broadcast constituted a personal attack and ordered the station to provide reply time to the victim of the attack.

🏛 **RULE OF LAW**
The government may require the media to make broadcast time available to respond to personal attacks without violating the First Amendment freedom of the press.

FACTS: The Red Lion Broadcasting Co. (P) is licensed to operate a Pennsylvania radio station, WGCB. On November 27, 1964, WGCB carried a 15-minute broadcast by the Reverend Billy James Hargis as part of a "Christian Crusade" series. A book by Fred J. Cook entitled "Goldwater—Extremist to the Right" was discussed by Hargis, who said that Cook was fired by a newspaper for making false charges against city officials, that Cook worked for a Communist-affiliated publication, that he defended Alger Hiss and attacked J. Edgar Hoover and the Central Intelligence Agency, and that he had now written a "book to smear and destroy Barry Goldwater." When Cook heard of the broadcast, he concluded that he had been personally attacked and demanded free reply time. The station refused. After an exchange of letters between Cook, Red Lion (P) and the FCC (D), the FCC (D) concluded that the broadcast constituted a public attack, that Red Lion (P) had failed to meet its obligation under the fairness doctrine to send a tape, transcript, or summary of the broadcast to Cook and offer him reply time, and that the station must offer Cook reply time whether or not he paid for it. Subsequently, the FCC (D) issued a rulemaking with an eye toward making the personal attack aspect of the fairness doctrine more precise and more readily enforceable. Red Lion (P) challenges the specific application of the fairness doctrine in this case and the rulemaking as abridging freedoms of speech and the press protected by the First Amendment.

ISSUE: May the government require the media to make broadcast time available to respond to personal attacks?

HOLDING AND DECISION: (White, J.) Yes. The Federal Communications Commission has for many years imposed on radio and television broadcasters the requirement that discussion of public issues be presented on broadcast stations, and that each side of those issues be given fair coverage. This doctrine is known as the fairness doctrine. In view of the scarcity of broadcast frequencies, and the legitimate claims of those unable without government assistance to gain access to those frequencies for expression of their views, we hold the regulations and ruling at issue here are both authorized by statute and constitutional. It is the right of the viewers and listeners, not the right of the broadcasters, that is paramount to ensure the means and ends of the First Amendment.

▶ **ANALYSIS**

Just five years after *Red Lion*, the Court unanimously declared unconstitutional a right to reply law as applied to newspapers.

■■■

Quicknotes

FAIRNESS DOCTRINE Requires broadcasters to provide free time for presentation of opposing views on public issues.

FREEDOM OF THE PRESS The right to publish and publicly disseminate one's views.

■■■

Miami Herald v. Tornillo

Newspaper publishing company (D) v. Candidate (P)

418 U.S. 241 (1974).

NATURE OF CASE: "Right of reply" statute.

FACT SUMMARY: The Miami Herald Publishing Co. (D) appealed from a decision validating a statute which required newspapers to give political candidates equal space to reply to criticisms and attacks in the press.

🏛 RULE OF LAW
Newspapers cannot be compelled by statute to publish "replies" to editorial opinions with which certain persons (including the subject of the editorial) may disagree.

FACTS: The Miami Herald Publishing Co. (MHPC) (D) published editorials critical of Tornillo's (P) candidacy for the Florida House of Representatives. Tornillo (P) demanded that MHPC (D) print his verbatim replies. MHPC (D) declined to do this, and Tornillo (P) sued for declaratory and injunctive relief under a "right of reply" statute. The "right of reply" statute granted a political candidate a right to equal space to reply to criticism and attacks on his record by a newspaper. The circuit court found the statute unconstitutional as an infringement on the freedom of the press under the First and Fourteenth Amendments. On appeal, the Florida Supreme Court reversed, found the statute constitutional, and entered a judgment for Tornillo (P). MHPC (D) appealed.

ISSUE: Can newspapers be compelled by statute to publish "replies" to editorial opinions with which certain persons (including the subject of the editorial) may disagree?

HOLDING AND DECISION: (Burger, C.J.) No. Newspapers cannot be compelled by statute to publish "replies" to editorial opinions with which certain persons (including the subject of the editorial) may disagree. The statute is void on its face because it purports to regulate the content of a newspaper in violation of the First Amendment. The choice of material to go into a newspaper is an exercise of editorial control and judgment. It has yet to be demonstrated how governmental regulation of this editorial process can be exercised consistent with First Amendment guarantees of a free press. Reversed.

▶ ANALYSIS

The basic concept that the First Amendment prohibits the government from dictating to the press the contents of its news columns or the slant of its editorials was established in such landmark cases as *N.Y. Times v. Sullivan*, 376 U.S. 254 (1964) and *N.Y. Times Co. v. U.S.*, 403 U.S. 713 (1971).

This statute would have resulted in self-censorship by the press in an effort to avoid printing political replies.

■=■

Quicknotes

FREEDOM OF THE PRESS The right to publish and publicly disseminate one's views.

■=■

Richmond Newspapers v. Virginia

Newspaper (P) v. State (D)

448 U.S. 555 (1980).

NATURE OF CASE: Action to overturn a closure order.

FACT SUMMARY: At the behest of the criminal defendant and without objection by the prosecutor, a trial judge closed a criminal trial to the public and press, including Richmond Newspapers (P).

🏛 RULE OF LAW
Absent an overriding interest articulated in findings, the trial of a criminal case must be open to the public.

FACTS: A defendant on trial for murder had suffered a conviction that was reversed on appeal and two subsequent mistrials. His attorney moved that the trial be closed to the public, and neither the prosecutor nor the two Richmond Newspapers (P) reporters present in court objected. Later that day, the reporters requested a hearing on a motion to vacate the order, claiming closure should not be ordered absent a court finding that there was no other way to protect the defendant's rights. The trial judge denied the motion, and the Virginia Supreme Court dismissed the mandamus and prohibition petitions of Richmond Newspapers (P) and denied its petition for appeal from the closure order.

ISSUE: Must the trial of a criminal case be open to the public absent an overriding interest articulated in findings?

HOLDING AND DECISION: (Burger, C.J.) Yes. The right to attend criminal trials is implicit in the guarantees of the First Amendment and requires that a criminal trial be open to the public (including the press) absent an overriding interest articulated in findings. Without the freedom to attend such trials, which people have exercised for centuries and which is part of the presumption of openness that inheres in our system of justice, important aspects of freedom of speech and of the press could be eviscerated. A trial courtroom is a public place where the people have a right to be present and where a vital government function about which they enjoy freedom of communication takes place. Closing the courtroom is unconstitutional absent an overriding interest articulated in findings, and there was no such articulation in this case.

CONCURRENCE: (Brennan, J.) Resolution of First Amendment public access claims in individual cases must be strongly influenced by the weight of historical practice and by an assessment of the specific structural value of public access in the circumstances. As to the case at bar, the ingrained tradition of public trials and the importance of public access to the broader purposes of the trial process tips the balance strongly in favor of the rule that trials be open. What countervailing interests might be sufficiently compelling to reverse this presumption of openness need not concern the Court now, for the statute at stake here authorizes trial closures at the unfettered discretion of the judge and parties and is thus in violation of the First and Fourteenth Amendments.

DISSENT: (Rehnquist, J.) Neither the First nor Sixth Amendment requires that a state's reasons for denying public access to a trial, where both the prosecuting attorney and the defendant have consented to an order of closure by the judge, are subject to any additional constitutional review at our hands.

▶ ANALYSIS

In the case of *Gannett Co. v. DePasquale*, 443 U.S. 368 (1979), the Court had faced the question of the right of public/press access to hearings on pretrial motions as opposed to trials. It refused to decide whether such a right existed under the Sixth Amendment, although broadly hinting that that Amendment conferred a right only upon the defendant. Even if public access right did exist, the Court said, the circumstances of the case showed that the defendant's right to a fair trial required closure in that particular case. The decision left legal commentators and journalists confused as to the posture of the Court in this whole area of public access to criminal proceedings.

■=■

Quicknotes

FIRST AMENDMENT Prohibits Congress from enacting any law respecting an establishment of religion, prohibiting the free exercise of religion, abridging freedom of speech or the press, the right of peaceful assembly and the right to petition for a redress of grievances.

SIXTH AMENDMENT Provides the right to a speedy and public trial by impartial jury, the right to be informed of the accusation, the right to confront witnesses, and the right to have the assistance of counsel in all criminal prosecutions.

■=■

Pell v. Procunier

Reporter (P) v. Prison warden (D)

417 U.S. 817 (1973).

NATURE OF CASE: Review of the constitutionality under the First and Fourteenth Amendments of a California Department of Corrections manual provision.

FACT SUMMARY: Reporters (P) were denied access to a California prison to conduct individual interviews with specified inmates.

🏛 RULE OF LAW
Newsmen have no constitutional right of access to prisons or their inmates beyond that afforded the general public.

FACTS: Eve Pell (P), Betty Segal and Paul Jacobs sought permission to interview three inmates of a California prison. In addition, the editors of a certain periodical wished to speak with an inmate about the possibility of publishing his writings concerning prison conditions. All these requests were denied in accordance with § 415.071 of the California Department of Corrections Manual, which provides that "press and other media interviews with specific individual inmates will not be permitted." The reporters in this case, along with the prospective interviewees, brought this action seeking to enjoin the continued enforcement of this regulation.

ISSUE: Does the media have a constitutional right of access to prisons or their inmates beyond that afforded to the general public?

HOLDING AND DECISION: (Stewart, J.) No. The regulation in question seeks to achieve a valid goal for prisons—maintaining security. In practice, it was found that the practice in place prior to the promulgation of § 415.07 had resulted in press attention being concentrated on a relatively small number of inmates who, as a result, became virtual "public figures" within the prison society and gained a disproportionate degree of notoriety and influence among their fellow inmates. These inmates often became the source of severe disciplinary problems. Additionally, the press is not denied all access to prisons. The press is able to take public tours of prisons, visit maximum security and minimum-security sections of institutions and stop and speak on any subject with any inmate they come across, sit in on group meetings of inmates, and interview inmates selected at random by the guards. The First and Fourteenth Amendments do not guarantee the press access to any information that is not available to the general public. Thus, the regulation at issue here is constitutionally valid.

▶ ANALYSIS

Pell points out the alternative methods available to the press for gathering information from prisons and inmates in support of its contention that limiting one method, individual interviews, is not constitutionally infirm. If there were no alternative information-gathering methods available, might the Court have decided differently?

■■■

Quicknotes

FIRST AMENDMENT Prohibits Congress from enacting any law respecting an establishment of religion, prohibiting the free exercise of religion, abridging freedom of speech or the press, the right of peaceful assembly and the right to petition for a redress of grievances.

■■■

Houchins v. KQED

County Sheriff (D) v. Broadcaster (P)

438 U.S. 1 (1978).

NATURE OF CASE: Review of a First Amendment challenge to a county jail policy.

FACT SUMMARY: Permission to inspect and take pictures in a county jail was denied to a broadcaster.

🏛 RULE OF LAW
The media has no special right of access to a county jail different from or greater than that accorded to the public generally.

FACTS: KQED operates licensed television and radio stations that have frequently reported newsworthy events relating to penal institutions in the San Francisco Bay area. On March 31, 1975, KQED reported the suicide of a prisoner in the Greystone portion of the Santa Rita jail. The report included a statement by a psychiatrist that the conditions at Greystone facility were responsible for the illnesses of his patient-prisoners there. KQED requested permission from County Sheriff Houchins to inspect and take pictures within the Greystone facility. Houchins refused permission and KQED filed this suit, alleging First Amendment violations in their denial of access.

ISSUE: Does the media have a special right of access to a county jail different from or greater than that accorded to the public generally?

HOLDING AND DECISION: (Burger, C.J.) No. *Pell* is dispositive in this case. This Court has never intimated a First Amendment guarantee of a right of access to all sources of information within government control. Additionally, there exist a number of alternatives to preventing problems in penal facilities from escaping public attention. The media may learn about prison conditions by receiving letters from inmates, they may interview those who provide legal representation to the inmates, and they are free to seek out former inmates, visitors to the facility public officials, and institutional personnel.

CONCURRENCE: (Stewart, J.) KQED was entitled to some form of preliminary injunctive relief. Terms of access that are reasonably imposed on individual members of the public may, if they impede effective reporting without sufficient justification, be unreasonable as applied to journalists who are there to convey to the general public what the visitors see.

DISSENT: (Stevens, J.) KQED has previously taken cameras and recording equipment into a number of other correctional facilities without disturbing the conditions within the same facilities. Denying access the press here inhibits the free flow of information to the general public

guaranteed by the First Amendment. Thus, information gathering by the press ought to be afforded some measure of constitutional protection.

▌ *ANALYSIS*

In *Houchins*, as in *Pell v. Procunier*, 417 U.S. 817 (1973), the media had other alternatives available for gathering information concerning prison conditions.

■═■

Quicknotes

FIRST AMENDMENT Prohibits Congress from enacting any law respecting an establishment of religion, prohibiting the free exercise of religion, abridging freedom of speech or the press, the right of peaceful assembly and the right to petition for a redress of grievances.

■═■

First Amendment: Religion

Quick Reference Rules of Law

United States v. Seeger

Federal government (D) v. Conscientious objector (P)

380 U.S. 163 (1965).

NATURE OF CASE: Constitutional challenge to an armed forces exemption.

FACT SUMMARY: Seeger (P) claimed an exemption from the armed forces based on his claimed exemption as a conscientious objector. The United States (D) rejected his exemption application because Seeger (P) did not claim an objection to war based on a belief related to a Supreme Being, as required by the statute.

> ### 🏛 RULE OF LAW
> Where a given belief occupies a place in the life parallel to that filled by the orthodox belief in God, it clearly qualifies the possessor for conscientious-objector status.

FACTS: Section 6(j) of the Universal Military Training and Service Act allows conscientious objectors to apply for an exemption from service in the armed forces based upon "religious training and belief," which is defined as "an individual's belief in a relation to a Supreme Being." Seeger refused to be inducted into the armed forces and was convicted for his refusal. Seeger (P) applied for the exemption, but his application was denied because he did not profess a belief in a Supreme Being. Seeger (P) truly opposed participation in war and the court found his objection to be made in good faith, but Seeger (P) was skeptical about the existence of God and could not claim a belief in relation to a Supreme Being as required by the statute. Seeger's objection, however, was an expression of "religious faith" after much study in religious fields and was not based purely on a personal moral code. When his application for exemption was denied solely on the basis of his disbelief in a specific Supreme Being, Seeger (P) challenged the constitutionality of that section.

ISSUE: Where a given belief occupies a place in the life parallel to that filled by the orthodox belief in God, does it clearly qualify its possessor for conscientious-objector status?

HOLDING AND DECISION: (Clark, J.) Yes. Where a given belief occupies a place in the life parallel to that filled by the orthodox belief in God, it clearly qualifies the possessor for conscientious objector status. Section 6(j) requires the applicant's objection to be based on religious belief rather than "political, sociological, or philosophical views." The United States has over 250 religious groups within its borders. Putting a name to the focus of the varied and intricate faiths in our country must have been daunting for Congress. Rather than using the designation "God," Congress used "Supreme Being" as a descriptive term to encompass all expressions of faith and to differentiate such expressions from those more closely related to political, sociological or philosophical views. Seeger's (P) beliefs legitimately fall within those related to an expression of faith and qualify for the exemption. The statute is constitutional.

▶ ANALYSIS

The Court is to decide only whether an applicant's beliefs are religious and not whether the applicant's religion is legitimate. With the rich and varied tradition of religious freedom in this country, determining the validity of an applicant's religion would be overwhelming to the judicial system and a practical impossibility. Simply determining that an applicant's expression of faith is sincere is difficult enough. Critics question courts' abilities to distinguish between religious and philosophical beliefs. Perhaps the definition of "religious" should be expanded or perhaps an overly expansive definition would erode the effectiveness of the test at all.

Quicknotes

FIRST AMENDMENT RIGHTS Rights conferred by the First Amendment to the U.S. Constitution prohibiting Congress from enacting any law respecting an establishment of religion, prohibiting the free exercise of religion, abridging freedom of speech or the press, the right of peaceful assembly and the right to petition for a redress of grievances.

United States v. Ballard

Federal government (P) v. Religious organizer (D)

322 U.S. 78 (1944).

NATURE OF CASE: Appeal from an indictment for fraud in the promotion of a religious sect.

FACT SUMMARY: In instructing the jury, the district court withheld all questions concerning the truth or falsity of the religious beliefs or doctrines of the defendants.

🏛 RULE OF LAW
The judiciary can determine only if religious beliefs are sincerely held beliefs, not whether they are true or false.

FACTS: Ballard (D) organized and promoted the "I AM" movement, covering his religious beliefs and doctrines. Ballard (D) claimed that he had a supernatural power to heal persons of ailments and diseases. To spread word of his powers, Ballard (D) formed corporations, distributed and sold literature, solicited funds and sought memberships in the "I AM" movement. Ballard (D) was subsequently indicted on 12 counts of mail fraud. The truth or verity of Ballard's (D) claims was not submitted to the jury.

ISSUE: May the judiciary constitutionally determine the truth or verity of religious beliefs?

HOLDING AND DECISION: (Douglas, J.) No. "The law knows no heresy, and is committed to the support of no dogma, the establishment of no sect." Freedom of thought, which includes freedom of religious belief, is basic to American society. Persons may believe what they cannot prove. The district court ruled properly when it withheld from the jury all questions concerning the truth or verity of the religious beliefs or doctrines of the respondents.

DISSENT: (Jackson, J.) Religious leaders may be convicted of fraud for making false representations on matters other than faith or experience. However, inviting prosecutions of religious leaders for fraud based on false representations on matters of faith could easily degenerate into religious persecution. The indictment below ought to have been dismissed altogether.

▶ ANALYSIS

Because religion is inherently personal and the sincerely held beliefs of an individual may depart from the dogma of the individual's religion, the Court has stated that the dominant views in a faith are not determinative in assessing whether a particular belief is religious.

Quicknotes

ESTABLISHMENT CLAUSE The constitutional provision prohibiting the government from favoring any one religion over others, or engaging in religious activities or advocacy.

Employment Division, Department of Human Resources of Oregon v. Smith

State (P) v. Applicant for unemployment compensation (D)

494 U.S. 872 (1990).

NATURE OF CASE: Appeal from judgment declaring unconstitutional an Oregon statute prohibiting the sacramental use of peyote.

FACT SUMMARY: After Smith (D) ingested peyote during a ceremony of the Native American Church, he was terminated from his job as a drug counselor.

🏛 RULE OF LAW
An individual's religious beliefs do not excuse noncompliance with an otherwise valid law prohibiting conduct that the state is free to regulate.

FACTS: Smith (D) was fired from his job with a private drug rehabilitation organization because he ingested peyote for sacramental purposes during a ceremony of the Native American Church. Oregon law classifies peyote as a controlled substance. Persons convicted of possessing peyote are guilty of a felony. Smith (D) was deemed ineligible for unemployment compensation benefits after it was determined he was discharged for "misconduct." The Oregon Court of Appeals and the Oregon Supreme Court reversed that determination on the basis that the Oregon prohibition of the sacramental use of peyote violated Smith's (D) free exercise of religion. The U.S. Supreme Court granted certiorari.

ISSUE: Do an individual's religious beliefs excuse noncompliance with an otherwise valid law prohibiting conduct that the state is free to regulate?

HOLDING AND DECISION: (Scalia, J.) No. An individual's religious beliefs do not excuse noncompliance with an otherwise valid law prohibiting conduct that the state is free to regulate. The free exercise of religion means the right to believe and profess whatever religious doctrine one desires. The exercise of religion often involves not only belief and profession but the performance of physical acts. A state would be prohibiting the free exercise if it seeks to ban acts that are only engaged in for religious reasons. Smith (D) contends that his religious motivation for using peyote places its use beyond the reach of a criminal law not specifically directed at religious practice even though the law is constitutional when applied against nonreligious use of a controlled substance. This Court's decisions have consistently held that the right of free exercise does not relieve an individual of the obligation to comply with a valid and neutral law of general applicability on the ground that the law proscribes conduct that his religion prescribes. Smith (D) contends that rejection of his claim for religious exemption for peyote use may only be justified by a balancing compelling state interest. The compelling state interest test is inapplicable to validate challenges to criminal prohibitions on a particular form of conduct. Application of the compelling interest standard in this context would open the prospect of constitutionally required religious exemptions from civic obligations of almost every conceivable kind—ranging from compulsory military service to the payment of taxes.

CONCURRENCE: (O'Connor, J.) The majority errs in allowing government prohibitions that prohibit conduct mandated by an individual's religious beliefs solely because the prohibitions are generally applicable. A person is barred from freely exercising his religion regardless of whether the law prohibits the conduct only when engaged in for religious reasons, only by members of that religion, or by all persons. If the First Amendment is to have any vitality, it ought not to be construed to cover only the extreme and hypothetical situation in which a state directly targets a religious practice. The Court ought to follow a course where it engages in case-by-case balancing, to examine if the generally applicable regulation that burdens religious conduct is "essential to accomplish an overriding government interest" or represents "the least restrictive means of achieving some compelling state interest."

DISSENT: (Blackmun, J.) The courts should not turn a blind eye to the severe impact of a state's restrictions on the adherents of a minority religion. A statute interfering with the free exercise of religion is presumed unconstitutional unless the state meets its burden of demonstrating a narrowly tailored means to achieve a compelling interest. The majority today ignores this settled principle and characterizes the free exercise of religion to be a "luxury." The Founders would be surprised at such a characterization. Oregon's interest in enforcing its drug laws against religious use of peyote is not sufficiently compelling to outweigh Smith's (D) right to the free exercise of religion.

▶ ANALYSIS

The holding in this case can be distinguished from the line of cases absolving conscientious objectors opposed to war from complying with selective service laws, an otherwise valid law like the one in this case. Selective service laws have traditionally exempted from military service conscientious objectors opposed to war in any form on religious grounds. But the Court has traditionally held that the exemption is a product of the legislature rather than compelled by the constitutional prohibition on the free exercise of religion. See for example *Selective Draft Law Cases*, 245 U.S. 366 (1918).

■■■■■

Continued on next page.

Quicknotes

COMPELLING INTEREST TEST A standard employed by the court under strict scrutiny review to determine the constitutionality of a statute, whereby the proponent of the statute must demonstrate that classifications drawn therein serve a compelling interest and are necessary for the furtherance of a state objective.

FREE EXERCISE CLAUSE The guarantee of the First Amendment to the U.S. Constitution prohibiting Congress from enacting laws regarding the establishment of religion or prohibiting the free exercise thereof.

Sherbert v. Verner

Applicant for unemployment compensation (P) v. Commission (D)

374 U.S. 398 (1963).

NATURE OF CASE: Action arising out of the Employment Security Commission's (D) denial of Sherbert's (P) claim for unemployment-compensation benefits.

FACT SUMMARY: Sherbert (P) was discharged by her employer because she would not work on her religion's sabbath.

🏛 RULE OF LAW
It is an unconstitutional burden on a worker's free exercise of religion for a state to apply eligibility requirements for unemployment benefits so as to force a worker to abandon her religious principles respecting her religion's Sabbath.

FACTS: Sherbert (P) was discharged by her employer because she refused to work on Saturday, her religion's Sabbath. The Employment Security Commission (D) found Sherbert (P) ineligible for benefits because her refusal to work on Saturday was failure without good cause to accept available work. [The state law provides that no employee shall be required to work on Sunday.]

ISSUE: Is it unconstitutional for a state to refuse unemployment benefits to a worker who was discharged because of her refusal to work on her religion's Sabbath?

HOLDING AND DECISION: (Brennan, J.) Yes. It is an unconstitutional burden on a worker's free exercise of religion for a state to apply eligibility requirements for unemployment benefits so as to force a worker to abandon her religious principles respecting her religion's Sabbath. Sherbert (P) was forced to choose between following her religion or obtaining unemployment benefits. Such a choice puts the same kind of burden on her free exercise of religion as would a fine imposed for Saturday worship.

DISSENT: (Harlan, J.) The purpose of unemployment benefits was to tide people over while work was unavailable. It was not to provide relief for those who for personal or religious reasons became unavailable for work. The exercise of religion only requires special treatment in a select few cases and this is not one of them.

▌ *ANALYSIS*

The Court has encountered many situations unlike *Sherbert*, in which the individual's right to freedom of religious belief and practices is subordinated to other community interests. Freedom of religion is not absolute, and does not extend to situations where its practice would jeopardize public health, safety, or morals, or the rights of third persons. Hence, laws prohibiting polygamy and bigamy have been upheld, as well as those requiring compulsory vaccination and X-rays, in spite of allegations that such laws required action in violation of the Mormon and Christian Science religions. The conscientious objector's right to avoid military service has been said to rest upon legislative grace rather than constitutional right.

■=■

Quicknotes

FREE EXERCISE CLAUSE The guarantee of the First Amendment to the U.S. Constitution prohibiting Congress from enacting laws regarding the establishment of religion or prohibiting the free exercise thereof.

■=■

Church of the Lukumi Babalu Aye, Inc. v. City of Hialeah

Church (P) v. Municipality (D)

508 U.S. 520 (1993).

NATURE OF CASE: Review of decision upholding an ordinance prohibiting ritual animal sacrifice.

FACT SUMMARY: The Church of Lukumi Babalu Aye, Inc. (P), which performed the sacrificial killing of animals as required by the Santeria religion, challenged various Hialeah (D) ordinances prohibiting such killings as a violation of the Free Exercise Clause of the First Amendment.

🏛 RULE OF LAW
If a law's object is to infringe upon or restrict religious practices, it must be justified by a compelling interest and be narrowly tailored to advance that interest.

FACTS: The Church of the Lukumi Babalu Aye, Inc. (P) (Church) and its members practiced the religion of Santeria. An integral part of the religion was the sacrificial killing of animals for certain events. In 1987, the Church (P) leased land in the city of Hialeah (D) on which it planned to build various structures including a house of worship. Distressed by the Church's (P) plans, Hialeah (D) called an emergency public session during which it passed various ordinances that essentially prohibited the type of sacrifices required in Santeria. The Church (P) thereafter filed suit, arguing that the ordinances violated the Free Exercise Clause of the First Amendment by targeting its religious practices. The district court disagreed and upheld the ordinances with the court of appeals affirming. The Supreme Court granted review.

ISSUE: Must a law be justified by a compelling interest and be narrowly tailored to advance that interest if its object is to infringe upon or restrict religious practices?

HOLDING AND DECISION: (Kennedy, J.) Yes. If a law's object is to infringe upon or restrict religious practices, it must be justified by a compelling interest and be narrowly tailored to advance that interest. Neutral and generally applicable laws need not meet this higher level of scrutiny. The ordinances at issue, however, were not neutral and generally applicable. They restricted the practices because of their religious motivation. Though not evident on the face of the ordinances, their non-neutrality is clear from the expressed concerns of residents and citizens, the expressed motive of council members, and the ordinances' operation. Practically the only conduct prohibited by the ordinances is that exercised by Santeria church members. In addition, the ordinances in no way promoted the legitimate concerns of public morals, peace, or safety advanced in their support. Thus, since the ordinances were not neutral and were not narrowly tailored to serve compelling interests, they were unconstitutional.

▌ ANALYSIS

Though a majority of the Court agrees that the correct result was reached, the concurring opinions evidence the hostility of many justices to the rule announced in *Employment Div., Dept. of Human Resources of Oregon v. Smith*, 494 U.S. 872 (1992) just one year earlier. *Smith* held that neutral laws of general applicability are not subject to a high level of scrutiny. Thus, its continued viability is questionable as the makeup of the Court changes.

■═■

Quicknotes

COMPELLING INTEREST TEST A standard employed by the court under strict scrutiny review to determine the constitutionality of a statute, whereby the proponent of the statute must demonstrate that classifications drawn therein serve a compelling interest and are necessary for the furtherance of a state objective.

FREE EXERCISE CLAUSE The guarantee of the First Amendment to the U.S. Constitution prohibiting Congress from enacting laws regarding the establishment of religion or prohibiting the free exercise thereof.

■═■

Cutter v. Wilkinson

Prison inmates (P) v. State prison (D)

544 U.S. 709 (2005).

NATURE OF CASE: Review of federal appeals court judgment.

FACT SUMMARY: Prisoners in Ohio (P) alleged that prison officials (D) violated a federal law by failing to accommodate the inmates' (P) exercise of their "non-mainstream" religions, including Satanism, Wicca, and Asatru. The prison officials (D) argued that the act allowed government to advance religion and therefore violated the First Amendment's establishment clause.

🏛 RULE OF LAW
A federal law prohibiting government from burdening prisoners' religious exercise does not violate the First Amendment's establishment clause.

FACTS: The Religious Land Use and Institutionalized Persons Act of 2000 (RLUIPA) prohibited prisons and their officials from imposing a substantial burden on prisoners' religious exercise, unless the burden furthered a "compelling government interest." Prisoners in Ohio (P) alleged in federal district court that prison officials (D) violated RLUIPA by failing to accommodate the inmates' exercise of their "non-mainstream" religions, including Satanism, Wicca, and Asatru. The prison officials (D) argued that the act allowed government to advance religion and therefore violated the First Amendment's establishment clause. The district court rejected that argument and ruled for the inmates (P). The Sixth Circuit Court of Appeals reversed, holding that RLUIPA violated the Establishment Clause.

ISSUE: Does a federal law prohibiting government from burdening prisoners' religious exercise violate the First Amendment's establishment clause?

HOLDING AND DECISION: (Ginsburg, J.) No. A federal law prohibiting government from burdening prisoners' religious exercise does not violate the First Amendment's establishment clause. On its face, RLUIPA made an accommodation for the free exercise of religion, which is allowed by the First Amendment. The law was an effort to alleviate the "government-created burden" on religious exercise that prisoners faced, and does not discriminate between mainstream and non-mainstream religions. Constitutional problems could arise if RLUIPA were enforced improperly and religious prisoners received favored treatment, or if religious exercise and security concerns were not properly balanced, but that's not the issue. Reversed and remanded.

▶ ANALYSIS

The court unanimously reversed the Sixth Circuit, which held that under traditional First Amendment doctrine, the law would be subject to "rational relationship" review.

Under that test, the law would be unconstitutional unless there were a "valid, rational connection" between the prison regulation and a legitimate government interest, or the prisoners had an alternate means of free exercise. But RLUIPA set a higher standard; under that law, the restriction is given "strict scrutiny," which requires prison officials, not the inmate, to prove that the regulation furthers a compelling interest and is the least restrictive means of satisfying this interest. The court found that in practice, RLUIPA imposes a switch from a scheme of deference to prison officials to one in which the regulation is presumptively unconstitutional. According to the Sixth Circuit, such heightened scrutiny impermissibly advances religion by giving greater protection to religious rights than to other constitutionally protected rights.

■══■

Quicknotes

COMPELLING INTEREST TEST A standard employed by the court under strict scrutiny review to determine the constitutionality of a statute, whereby the proponent of the statute must demonstrate that classifications drawn therein serve a compelling interest and are necessary for the furtherance of a state objective.

FREE EXERCISE CLAUSE The guarantee of the First Amendment to the U.S. Constitution prohibiting Congress from enacting laws regarding the establishment of religion or prohibiting the free exercise thereof.

■══■

Locke v. Davey

Party not identified (D) v. Theology student (P)

540 U.S. 714 (2004).

NATURE OF CASE: Constitutional challenge to state scholarship program.

FACT SUMMARY: Davey (P) qualified for a state scholarship but elected to earn a degree in theology. Devotional degrees are excluded under the program, so Davey did not receive scholarship funds.

RULE OF LAW

Excluding devotional degrees from an otherwise inclusive scholarship program does not violate the Religion Clauses of the Constitution.

FACTS: The state of Washington established the Promise Scholarship Program for postsecondary students who qualified under set income, academic, and enrollment requirements. Students could attend any accredited university or college, but could not seek a devotional degree. Religious courses were acceptable, but a degree was not. Davey (P) qualified for the Promise scholarship funds and chose to attend a small, private, Christian college. He intended to earn dual degrees in business and theology because he wanted to become a church pastor after graduation. He soon learned that he had to certify to the scholarship officials that he was not intending to major in theology or he would not receive the scholarship funds. Davey (P) refused to sign the certification and did not receive the funds. Davey (P) challenged the constitutionality of the scholarship program, arguing that it violates the Religion Clauses of the First Amendment.

ISSUE: Does excluding devotional degrees from an otherwise inclusive scholarship program violate the Religion Clauses of the Constitution?

HOLDING AND DECISION: (Rehnquist, C.J.) No. Excluding devotional degrees from an otherwise inclusive scholarship program does not violate the Religion Clauses of the Constitution. Washington could allow scholarship recipients to earn devotional degrees without violating the Establishment Clause. Washington's constitution, however, is more stringent than the federal constitution and does not allow even indirect funding of religious instruction. This could be construed as violating the Free Exercise clause of the federal constitution, but nothing in the scholarship program suggests an animus toward religion. Students may attend religious institutions and participate in religious classes. Washington simply places great import in separating government funds from solely religious training. The program is constitutional.

DISSENT: (Scalia, J.) This scholarship program facially discriminates against religious training and nothing in the state's argument justifies doing so. Several program alternatives exist to facial discrimination, including providing funds only for students to attend public universities without theology degree offerings, but the majority allows this unconstitutional program to remain.

ANALYSIS

The Ninth Circuit below sided with Davey (P) and held that the scholarship program blatantly singled him out solely because of the exercise of his religious preferences. Critics argue that the government is not remaining neutral in religious matters when it singles out people of faith for discriminatory treatment. Proponents agree with the Court that singling out devotional degrees simply supports the separation of church and state.

Quicknotes

ESTABLISHMENT CLAUSE The constitutional provision prohibiting the government from favoring any one religion over others, or engaging in religious activities or advocacy.

FREE EXERCISE CLAUSE The guarantee of the First Amendment to the U.S. Constitution prohibiting Congress from enacting laws regarding the establishment of religion or prohibiting the free exercise thereof.

County of Allegheny v. American Civil Liberties Union, Greater Pittsburgh Chapter

County (D) v. Union (P)

492 U.S. 573 (1989).

NATURE OF CASE: Review of order mandating the removal of certain religious symbols from public property.

FACT SUMMARY: Challenge was made to the placement of religious symbols on public property.

🏛 RULE OF LAW
Religious symbols may not be put on public property if they have the effect of promoting religion.

FACTS: The County of Allegheny (D) in Pennsylvania permitted the erection, in different locations, of a nativity scene and a menorah. The nativity scene was placed alone; the menorah was placed in conjunction with a Christmas tree and a sign entitled "Salute to Liberty." The American Civil Liberties Union (ACLU) (P) sued to force removal of the scenes, claiming them to be in violation of the Establishment Clause. The district court denied the injunction, but the court of appeals reversed. The County (D) petitioned for certiorari.

ISSUE: May religious symbols be put on public property if they have the effect of promoting religion?

HOLDING AND DECISION: (Blackmun, J.) No. Religious symbols may not be put on public property if they have the effect of promoting religion. The Establishment Clause prohibits governments from appearing to endorse a religion or religion in general. To permit the erection of religious symbols if they promote religion cannot be countenanced. Whether a symbol promotes religion depends on its context. Here, the nativity scene is particularly indicative of Christianity and sits by itself. This improperly promotes religion. The menorah, however, symbolizes not only the Jewish religion but Jewish culture as well. Also, its placement with secular objects dilutes any religious overtones it may have, which is sufficient to conclude it is permissible under the Establishment Clause.

CONCURRENCE: (O'Connor, J.) The menorah's placement is permissible because it sends a secular message of pluralism.

CONCURRENCE AND DISSENT: (Brennan, J.) The display of the menorah and Christmas tree implies favoritism of Christianity and Judaism, which is impermissible.

CONCURRENCE AND DISSENT: (Stevens, J.) The Establishment Clause prohibits not only a national religion but multiple religious establishments as well, which is what the menorah and Christmas tree constitute.

CONCURRENCE AND DISSENT: (Kennedy, J.) Establishment Clause jurisprudence must differentiate between impermissible establishment of religion and permissible accommodation therewith. To permit the erection of traditional religious symbols is an accommodation, not an establishment.

▶ ANALYSIS

The Court has traditionally had trouble with the Establishment Clause, and this fragmented opinion demonstrates this. The "meat" of Justice Blackmun's analysis was joined only by Justice Stevens. Thus, the value of this analysis as a precedent is suspect at best. This opinion leaves little by way of guidance for future decision-makers.

■=∎

Quicknotes

ESTABLISHMENT CLAUSE The constitutional provision prohibiting the government from favoring any one religion over others, or engaging in religious activities or advocacy.

FREE EXERCISE CLAUSE The guarantee of the First Amendment to the U.S. Constitution prohibiting Congress from enacting laws regarding the establishment of religion or prohibiting the free exercise thereof.

■=∎

Larson v. Valente

Minnesota government official (D) v. Church follower (P)

456 U.S. 228 (1982).

NATURE OF CASE: Constitutional challenge to validity of a registration statute.

FACT SUMMARY: Valente (P) challenged the constitutionality of a Minnesota statute requiring charitable organizations to register with the Minnesota Department of Commerce if the organization received less than 50 percent of its financial contributions from members.

🏛 RULE OF LAW
Governmental preferential treatment for one religion over another is a violation of the Establishment Clause of the Constitution.

FACTS: A Minnesota statute required charitable organizations to register with the Minnesota Department of Commerce if the organization received less than 50 percent of its financial contributions from members. John R. Larson, Commissioner of Securities (D), was charged with implementing the statute. Valente (P), a member of the Unification Church, challenged the statute on constitutional grounds as a violation of the Establishment Clause. Specifically, Valente (P) argued that the statute gave preferential treatment to those religions receiving over 50 percent of financial support from members because those religions did not have to register with the state.

ISSUE: Is governmental preferential treatment for one religion over another a violation of the Establishment Clause of the Constitution?

HOLDING AND DECISION: (Brennan, J.) Yes. Governmental preferential treatment for one religion over another is a violation of the Establishment Clause of the Constitution. Requiring only certain religions (i.e., those receiving less than 50 percent of financial contributions from members) to register serves to grant denominational preference. Such a preference clearly violates the Establishment Clause unless the statute is narrowly tailored to effect a compelling governmental interest. The governmental interest here is to protect its citizens from abusive solicitation practices, even by religious organizations. The state's argument, however, that the 50 percent rule is narrowly tailored to achieve that interest fails. The state assumes that members pay closer attention to an organization's use of their donations and have easier access to an organization's financial records. No substantial evidence exists in the record to support these assumptions. The 50 percent rule simply results in some denominations receiving preferential treatment over others. The statute is unconstitutional.

▶ ANALYSIS

The statute in this case targeted those "nontraditional" religions that solicited funds from strangers in public places such as airports and parks. "Traditional" religions simply passed the collection plate during Sunday services and purportedly received more of their money from members. The statute clearly preferred the traditional religious collection methods, which is in direct conflict with the Establishment Clause. Greater government oversight, registration with a state department, for example, cannot be imposed on minority religions unless it is equally imposed on traditional religions.

■■■

Quicknotes

ESTABLISHMENT CLAUSE The constitutional provision prohibiting the government from favoring any one religion over others, or engaging in religious activities or advocacy.

■■■

Lemon v. Kurtzman

Parties not identified.

403 U.S. 602 (1971).

NATURE OF CASE: Review of an establishment-clause challenge to state statutes providing aid to church-related elementary and secondary schools.

FACT SUMMARY: Statutes at issue provided financial support to nonpublic elementary schools.

🏛 RULE OF LAW
Statutes providing financial support to church-related elementary and secondary schools foster an impermissible degree of government entanglement with religion.

FACTS: Pennsylvania and Rhode Island both enacted statutes providing financial aid to church-related elementary and secondary schools. Pennsylvania adopted a statutory program providing financial support to nonpublic elementary and secondary schools by way of reimbursement for the cost of teachers' salaries, textbooks, and instructional materials in specified secular subjects. Rhode Island adopted a statute under which the state pays directly to teachers in nonpublic elementary schools a supplement of 15 percent of their annual salary. Under each statute, state aid was given to church-related educational institutions. The statutes were challenged under the Establishment Clause of the First Amendment.

ISSUE: Do statutes providing financial support to church-related elementary and secondary schools trigger Establishment Clause violations?

HOLDING AND DECISION: (Burger, C.J.) Yes. A three-part test may be gleaned from Establishment Clause precedent: (1) the statute must have a secular legislative purpose; (2) the statute's principal or primary effect must be one that neither advances nor inhibits religion; and (3) the statute must not foster "an excessive entanglement with religion." In order to determine whether government entanglement with religion is excessive, we must examine the character and purposes of the institutions that are benefited, the nature of the aid that the state provides, and the resulting relationship between the government and the religious authority. In this case, church-related schools are benefited by financial support of the state, leaving the state entangled in the details of administration of the same schools.

▶ ANALYSIS

The *Lemon* test has been frequently used by the Court. It is favored by justices taking the strict separationist approach to the Establishment Clause. Justices favoring the accommodationist approach, however, urge the overruling of the *Lemon* test.

Quicknotes

ESTABLISHMENT CLAUSE The constitutional provision prohibiting the government from favoring any one religion over others, or engaging in religious activities or advocacy.

■═■

Rosenberger v. Rector and Visitors of the University of Virginia

Students (P) v. University (D)

515 U.S. 819 (1995).

NATURE OF CASE: Appeal from a judgment upholding the denial of a request for payment of printing charges for a university student newspaper.

FACT SUMMARY: When a student publication dedicated to philosophical and religious expression was denied reimbursement for its printing costs under the state University (D) guidelines prohibiting reimbursement for religious activities, students publishing the paper filed suit, alleging violation of their rights of free speech and of the Establishment Clause.

> **RULE OF LAW**
> Government may not regulate speech based on its substantive content or the message it conveys.

FACTS: Rosenberger (P) and other undergraduates at the University of Virginia (D), a state university, formed Wide Awake Productions (WAP) to publish a student magazine of philosophical and religious expression. WAP qualified as a Contracted Independent Organization, thus making it eligible to submit bills from its outside contractors for payment by the Student Activities Fund (SAF). WAP's request that the SAF pay its printing costs was denied under University (D) guidelines prohibiting reimbursement for "religious activities." Rosenberger (P) and others filed suit, alleging violation of their rights to freedom of speech, free exercise of religion, and equal protection of the law. The district court ruled for the University (D). The court of appeals affirmed, holding that while the guidelines discriminated on the basis of content, the judgment was justified under the Establishment Clause. Rosenberger (P) appealed.

ISSUE: May government regulate speech based on its substantive content or the message it conveys?

HOLDING AND DECISION: (Kennedy, J.) No. Government may not regulate speech based on its substantive content or the message it conveys. Viewpoint discrimination is the proper way to interpret the University's (D) objections to Wide Awake. The University (D) does not exclude religion as a subject matter but selects for disfavored treatment those student journalistic efforts with religious editorial viewpoints. The prohibited perspective resulted in the refusal to make third-party payments, for the subjects discussed were otherwise within the approved category of publications. Having offered to pay the third-party contractors on behalf of private speakers who convey their own messages, the University (D) may not silence the expression of selected viewpoints. Thus, the regulation invoked to deny SAF support is a denial of Rosenberger's (P) right of free speech guaranteed by the First Amendment. Furthermore, any benefit to religion is incidental to the University's (D) provision of secular services for secular purposes on a religion-neutral basis. To obey the Establishment Clause, it was not necessary for the University (D) to deny eligibility to student publications because of their viewpoint.

▶ ANALYSIS

According to the majority opinion, the guideline invoked by the University (D) to deny third-party contractor payments on behalf of WAP effects a sweeping restriction on student thought and student inquiry in the context of University-sponsored publications. The prohibition on funding on behalf of publications that "primarily promote or manifest a particular belief in or about a deity or an ultimate reality," in its ordinary and common sense meaning, has a vast potential reach. However, were the dissent's view to become law, it would require the University (D) to scrutinize the content of all student speech, lest the expression in question contain too great a religious content.

■==■

Quicknotes

ESTABLISHMENT CLAUSE The constitutional provision prohibiting the government from favoring any one religion over others, or engaging in religious activities or advocacy.

■==■

Santa Fe Independent School District v. Doe

School district (D) v. Parents (P)

530 U.S. 290 (2000).

NATURE OF CASE: Suit challenging constitutionality of a school policy.

FACT SUMMARY: The Does (P) challenged the constitutionality of a school district (D) policy permitting student-led religious invocations prior to its football games.

🏛 RULE OF LAW
A school policy permitting student-led, student-initiated prayer at football games violates the Establishment Clause.

FACTS: Before 1995, the Santa Fe High School student who occupied the elective office of student council chaplain delivered a prayer over the public address system before each varsity football game for the entire season. This practice was challenged in district court and the Does (P) moved for a temporary restraining order to prevent the school district (D) from violating the Establishment Clause at the upcoming graduation exercises. The district court entered an interim order permitting nondenominational prayer to be presented. In response, the school district (D) adopted a series of policies dealing with prayer at school functions. The district court entered an order precluding enforcement of the open-ended policy concluding that delivering a prayer over the school's public address system prior to each football game coerces student participation in religious events. Both parties appealed. The court of appeals held that the policy violated the Establishment Clause. The school district (D) petitioned for certiorari.

ISSUE: Does a school policy permitting student-led, student-initiated prayer at football games violate the Establishment Clause?

HOLDING AND DECISION: (Stevens, J.) Yes. A school policy permitting student-led, student-initiated prayer at football games violates the Establishment Clause. In *Lee v. Weisman*, 505 U.S 577 (1992), this Court held that a prayer delivered by a rabbi at a middle school graduation violated the Establishment Clause. The principle annunciated in that case is applicable here. The constitution requires, at a minimum, that government may not coerce anyone to support or participate in religion or its exercise, or otherwise act in a way that establishes a state religion. The district (D) argued that *Lee* was inapplicable since the message being conveyed is private student speech, not public speech. While this distinction is important, the speech at issue here is not private. The invocations are authorized by government policy and take place on government property at government-sponsored school events. Moreover, the district's (D) student election system ensures that only those messages deemed appropriate

may be delivered; that is, the majority's views will always be expressed. The district (D) does nothing to separate itself from the religious content in the invocations, but rather its policy involves both perceived and actual state endorsement of religion. The district (D) also argued that its football policy is distinguishable from *Lee* in that it does not coerce students to participate in religious observances. First it claims there is no government coercion since the pre-game messages are the result of the student's choices, and second that there is no coercion at all because attendance at an extracurricular event is voluntary. The purpose of the Establishment Clause is to remove debate over this type of issue from government control. The student elections authorized by the policy impermissibly invade that private sphere, encouraging separation along religious lines in a public-school setting. Even if the decision to attend the extracurricular football game were purely voluntary, the delivery of a pre-game prayer has the improper effect of coercing those present to participate in religious worship. Last, the district (D) argued that the Does (P) made a premature facial challenge to the October policy that must fail since no student has yet actually delivered a religious message under the policy. However, the Court may invalidate a statute if it lacks a secular legislative purpose. Thus it is proper to examine the purpose of the October policy. The text of the policy alone reveals that it has an unconstitutional purpose. The selective process of the policy and other content restrictions show that it is not a content-neutral regulation.

DISSENT: (Rehnquist, C.J.) The fact that a policy might operate unconstitutionally under a conceivable set of standards is not sufficient to render it invalid.

▶ *ANALYSIS*

One problem with the policy here was that it implemented the majority view at the expense of the minority. Viewpoint neutrality requires that minority views be treated with the same respect as majority views so that the former is neither silenced nor isolated.

■═■

Quicknotes

CONTENT NEUTRAL Refers to statutes that regulate speech regardless of its content.

ESTABLISHMENT CLAUSE The constitutional provision prohibiting the government from favoring any one religion over others, or engaging in religious activities or advocacy.

■═■

McCreary County v. ACLU of Kentucky

Kentucky county (D) v. Civil liberties group (P)

545 U.S. 844 (2005).

NATURE OF CASE: Establishment Clause challenges to postings of the Ten Commandments in county courthouses.

FACT SUMMARY: Two Kentucky counties posted the Ten Commandments in their respective courthouses.

RULE OF LAW

Government action that has the ostensible and predominant purpose of advancing religion violates the Establishment Clause.

FACTS: Two Kentucky counties, McCreary County (D) and Pulaski County (D) (Counties), placed gold-framed copies of the Ten Commandments in their respective courthouses; each display contained only the Ten Commandments and included a citation to the Book of Exodus. The American Civil Liberties Union of Kentucky (ACLU) (P) sued the Counties (D), [seeking injunctive relief and] alleging violations of the Establishment Clause. Counties (D) then altered their displays to include a statement that the Ten Commandments served as a foundation for the civil and criminal codes of Kentucky. The trial court ordered that the displays be removed. Counties (D) then altered their displays a second time, this time putting up new displays in their respective courthouses that included the Ten Commandments within a group of documents presented under the title of "Foundations of American Law and Government." [The trial court granted the ACLU's (P) request to supplement the original injunction to include the third display, and the intermediate appellate court affirmed.] Counties (D) petitioned the Supreme Court for further review.

ISSUE: Does government action that has the ostensible and predominant purpose of advancing religion violate the Establishment Clause?

HOLDING AND DECISION: (Souter, J.) Yes. Government action that has the ostensible and predominant purpose of advancing religion violates the Establishment Clause. Government action for a predominant religious purpose violates the cardinal principle of Establishment Clause jurisprudence—that government must maintain neutrality toward religion, that is, between one religion and another and between religion and irreligion. In any given case, details in the record are crucial in determining the government's purpose in the Establishment Clause analysis. Here, the first display of the plainly religious Ten Commandments, with the Commandments standing apart from any secular context, clearly furthered a religious purpose. The second display also demonstrated a religious purpose because the statement about the Commandments' foundational status for Kentucky law was based on the Commandments' religious content. The

third display, with the Ten Commandments included in and among several other documents, still demonstrates a religious purpose in this case, given the full context of Counties' (D) repeated efforts to post the Ten Commandments. This holding should not be interpreted as prohibiting all integrated displays of the Ten Commandments; this decision is only that this particular integrated display violates the Establishment Clause on this case's specific facts. Affirmed.

CONCURRENCE: (O'Connor, J.) As a nation, we have no reason to trade a system based on government neutrality toward religion for a system like so many others around the world that cause so much strife. Counties' (D) displays in this case clearly violated the Establishment Clause because the displays unmistakably endorsed religion. The Framers did not foresee the multiplicity of religious belief in today's America. They did see, though, that choosing between religions is an enterprise that government should avoid.

DISSENT: (Scalia, J.) The Constitution has never required the complete exclusion of religion from public life. The founding generation made multiple official references to and recognitions of religion. That generation believed that morality was crucial for the social order, and that fostering religion promoted morality. In the United States, government can favor religion over irreligion. It also can favor one religion—specifically, monotheistic religion—over another. Today's opinion thus only increases this Court's hostility toward religion by now requiring that a secular purpose must "predominate" in government action. The displays in this case were constitutional, though, even under the majority's misguided analysis. The third, integrated "foundations" display served precisely the secular purpose that Counties (D) have advanced: to show that the Ten Commandments have influenced our system of law. The Court has no basis for conflating the purposes for the first two displays into the analysis of the purpose behind the third display.

▶ ANALYSIS

As the *McCreary County* majority notes, a government's purpose in actions involving religion is a firmly developed part of the Court's Establishment Clause jurisprudence. Regardless of the general understanding of the Establishment Clause held by some individual members of the founding generation, it is worth noting that none of Justice Scalia's examples from the founding period arose in a specifically framed case or controversy in which a litigant sought to enforce the Establishment Clause against the

Continued on next page.

actions that Justice Scalia recites. In the case or controversy in *McCreary County,* the majority correctly saw through Counties' (D) belated defenses of their efforts to do nothing more than to promote the plainly religious Ten Commandments.

■═■

Quicknotes

ESTABLISHMENT CLAUSE The constitutional provision prohibiting the government from favoring any one religion over others, or engaging in religious activities or advocacy.

INJUNCTION A court order requiring a person to do, or prohibiting that person from doing, a specific act.

INJUNCTIVE RELIEF A court order issued as a remedy, requiring a person to do, or prohibiting that person from doing, a specific act.

■═■

Van Orden v. Perry

User of state capitol grounds (P) v. Governor of Texas (D)

545 U.S. 677 (2005).

NATURE OF CASE: Establishment Clause challenge to the placement of a Ten Commandments monument in an integrated display of monuments and historical markers on the grounds of the Texas State Capitol.

FACT SUMMARY: The State of Texas (D) created a display, on the grounds of its State Capitol, of monuments and historical markers to commemorate "Texan identity." One of the monuments was a large monolith depicting the Ten Commandments.

🏛 RULE OF LAW
Government action that has religious content or that promotes a religious message does not necessarily violate the Establishment Clause.

FACTS: On the 22 acres surrounding the Texas State Capitol, the State of Texas (D) placed 17 monuments and 21 historical markers to honor various aspects of "Texan identity." One of the 17 monuments was a six-feet-by-three-feet monolith of the Ten Commandments. Van Orden (P) was offended by the monolith when he had to walk past it to reach the Texas Supreme Court Library. He sued the State of Texas (D), alleging that the use of the Ten Commandments violated the Establishment Clause.

ISSUE: Does government action that has religious content or that promotes a religious message necessarily violate the Establishment Clause?

HOLDING AND DECISION: (Rehnquist, C.J.) No. Government action that has religious content or that promotes a religious message does not necessarily violate the Establishment Clause. The three-factor test announced in *Lemon v. Kurtzman*, 403 U.S. 602 (1971), does not apply here because the case is more appropriately analyzed by considering the nature of the Ten Commandments monument and American history. The Ten Commandments are religious, but the person whom Judeo-Christians believe to have delivered the Commandments, Moses, was also a lawgiver. Here, Texas (D) has treated the display involving the Ten Commandments as an expression of the state's (D) political and legal history. That display therefore does not violate the Establishment Clause.

CONCURRENCE: (Thomas, J.) The original understanding of the Establishment Clause means that the clause should not be incorporated against the states at all. Even if it is incorporated, we should adopt the original meaning of "establishment," a term that the Framers understood to mean "necessarily [to] involve actual legal coercion." Under that correct understanding of establishment, Texas's (D) use of the Ten Commandments here clearly comports

with the Establishment Clause because Texas (D) has not compelled Van Orden (P) in any way.

CONCURRENCE: (Breyer, J.) This borderline case requires an exercise of legal judgment more than it requires a legal test. The key inquiry here is how the Ten Commandments are used, and that consideration in turn requires the further consideration of the context in which the Commandments appear. The circumstances suggest that the State of Texas (D) intended a predominantly secular purpose. That no one has challenged the Commandments in 40 years, until this case, only buttresses the conclusion that visitors to the grounds themselves have seen a predominant secular purpose. Invalidating Texas's (D) use of the Ten Commandments in this case, merely because the Ten Commandments are religious, could well lead to the very religious strife that the Establishment Clause was adopted to avoid.

DISSENT: (Stevens, J.) Texas (D) has placed the Ten Commandments on its Capitol grounds solely for the Decalogue's religious content. The State's (D) message is therefore clear: Texas (D) endorses the "Judeo-Christian" God. Texas (D) can use secular means to legitimately combat juvenile delinquency (which was one purpose that informed the original decision to place the Ten Commandments on the grounds 40 years ago). The message in the monument, however, is a plainly religious text, indeed an inherently sectarian text, and Texas's (D) use of the monument is therefore unconstitutional. The beliefs of the individual members of the founding generation are irrelevant; it is also easy to contradict views of Founders who favored fusing church and state with, for example, the views of Jefferson and Madison, who advocated strictly separated church and state. Regardless of individual Framers' beliefs, though, this Court is bound, not by the Framers' individual expectations, but by the text of the Constitution that they adopted and ratified. That text prohibits Texas's (D) use of the Ten Commandments in this case.

DISSENT: (Souter, J.) Neutrality can be reconciled with a government's display of an indisputably religious text only if the display's predominant purpose is not to promote the religious message. The Ten Commandments can be depicted with a predominant secular purpose, as in their depiction, and the depictions of Moses, in and around this Court. In this case, though, people strolling through the Texas State Capitol grounds would be hard pressed to find a nonreligious reason for Texas's (D) use of the Ten Commandments: there is no readily discernible theme linking the Ten Commandments to the other displays

Continued on next page.

scattered across the 22 acres of the grounds. A state's Capitol, however, should represent all the state's citizens, not only the ones who agree with a religious perspective promoted by the state.

▶ *ANALYSIS*

An important point to note in this difficult, intensely fragmented decision is that five members of the Court applied some form of the "predominant purpose" test used in *McCreary County v. ACLU of Kentucky,* 545 U.S. 844 (2005). The four dissenters here use that test (with Justice O'Connor using the "endorsement" language that she long preferred in Establishment Clause cases). Despite his protestations that he favors legal judgment over a legal test in this case, Justice Breyer, in his concurrence, also examines Texas's (D) predominant purpose in its use of the Ten Commandments. Even after *Van Orden,* then, some form of the "predominant purpose" test still seems to be the law.

■══■

Quicknotes

ESTABLISHMENT CLAUSE The constitutional provision prohibiting the government from favoring any one religion over others, or engaging in religious activities or advocacy.

■══■

Engel v. Vitale

Parties not identified.

370 U.S. 421 (1962).

NATURE OF CASE: Constitutional challenge to state composed prayer in public school.

FACT SUMMARY: A school district composed a prayer to be recited daily in its public schools. Petitioners challenged the constitutionality of the statute giving the district such authority.

🏛 RULE OF LAW
Government-composed or official prayer for recitation by the American public violates the Establishment Clause of the Constitution.

FACTS: The New York State Board of Regents (the Board) has broad authority over the state's public school system. The Board recommended that school districts encourage the daily recitation of a certain Board-composed prayer acknowledging dependence on and requesting blessings from "Almighty God." The school district permitted students to leave the room or simply stand in silence rather than participate in the prayer, if they so desired. Petitioners challenged the statute granting the Board the authority to institute an official prayer in public schools. Petitioners claimed the statute violated the Establishment Clause of the Constitution.

ISSUE: Does government-composed or official prayer for recitation by the American public violate the Establishment Clause of the Constitution?

HOLDING AND DECISION: (Black, J.) Yes. Government-composed or official prayer for recitation by the American public violates the Establishment Clause of the Constitution. The separation of church and state at least prevents government officials from imposing the recitation of a government-composed prayer onto the American public. The U.S. government may not establish a religion and the Board's prayer unequivocally establishes religious beliefs for an "Almighty God." The Board argues that it deliberately composed a "nondenominational" prayer and that students are not required to participate, but those arguments ignore the blatant unconstitutionality of establishing an official prayer in the first place. Government-composed and imposed prayer is the very reason many of our early colonists left England to seek religious freedom in America. The state should stay out of the business of providing religious instruction and allow that to remain the American public's private decision. The statute is unconstitutional.

DISSENT: (Stewart, J.) Students may choose not to participate in the daily prayer. Allowing those who wish to begin their day with a nondenominational prayer is not "establishing a religion" in violation of the Establishment Clause. Many governmental bodies, including this Court, begin sessions with an invocation to God. Religious practice is a deeply engrained part of our society and the majority's decision today is incorrect.

▶ ANALYSIS

The majority dismissed the school district's argument that students could opt out of the prayer. Much support has been generated for that decision because it is difficult for students to make the choice to not participate in a teacher-led activity. Critics of the decision, however, point to the many instances of hostility in this country toward any religious expression and add this opinion to the list. It is difficult to determine what religious freedom should mean in a country with so many religious groups. Some argue that religious freedom means that no religion of any kind should be present in any governmental or official sense. Others argue that religious freedom gives people the right to choose not to participate when religion is brought up in a governmental or official sense, but that this country was founded on religious principles. The debate certainly rages on because, as the dissent points out, many U.S. governmental bodies begin sessions with prayer or religious invocations.

▪■▪

Quicknotes

ESTABLISHMENT CLAUSE The constitutional provision prohibiting the government from favoring any one religion over others, or engaging in religious activities or advocacy.

▪■▪

Lee v. Weisman

School officials (D) v. Parent (P)

505 U.S. 577 (1992).

NATURE OF CASE: Appeal of permanent injunction.

FACT SUMMARY: Daniel Weisman (P), father of student Deborah (P), sought a permanent injunction barring the Providence public school officials (D) from inviting clergy to deliver invocations and benedictions at graduation ceremonies.

🏛 RULE OF LAW
Religious invocations and benedictions may not be given at a public primary or secondary school graduation ceremony.

FACTS: As allowed by the Providence School Committee (D), Principal Lee (D) invited Rabbi Gutterman to give the invocation and benediction at Lee's (D) middle school's graduation. Attendance at graduation exercises at Providence public schools is voluntary. Following school procedure, Lee (D) gave Rabbi Gutterman written guidelines for nonsectarian prayers. David Weisman (P), on behalf of himself and his daughter Deborah (P), sought a TRO against school officials (D) to prevent Rabbi Gutterman from delivering prayers at Deborah's (P) graduation. The TRO was denied, and Deborah (P) went through ceremonies. The students stood for a few minutes while Rabbi Gutterman delivered prayers. The Weismans' (P) suit continued since Deborah (P) was a student at a Providence public high school and would likely face the same situation at high school graduation. The district court held the prayers violated the Establishment Clause and permanently enjoined school officials (D) from inviting clergy to give invocations and benedictions at future graduations. The court of appeals affirmed.

ISSUE: May religious invocations and benedictions be given at a public primary or secondary school graduation ceremony?

HOLDING AND DECISION: (Kennedy, J.) No. Religious invocations and benedictions may not be given at a public primary or secondary school graduation ceremony. Here, state officials (D) directed the performance of a formal, explicit religious exercise at public school graduation. Principal Lee (D) decided which prayers should be given, selected the cleric, and gave written guidelines for the prayer. Even for students who objected to religious exercise, attendance and participation was in every practical sense obligatory. High school graduation is one of life's most significant occasions. To say that attendance is "voluntary" is formalistic in the extreme. Such prayers in public schools carry a particular risk of coercion. There is public and peer pressure on attending students to stand as a group, or maintain respectful silence. A dissenter is injured by his reasonable perception that others view his standing as approval, and that he is being forced by

the state to pray. The First Amendment protects the objector from having to take unilateral, private action to avoid compromising religious principles at a state function. The fact that the prayer was "nonsectarian" does not make government involvement acceptable.

CONCURRENCE: (Blackmun, J.) The Establishment Clause not only prohibits government coercion, but also any government engagement in religious practices. The simple issue is whether the state placed a stamp of approval on a religious activity. Here, it did.

DISSENT: (Scalia, J.) Nonsectarian prayers at graduations and other public celebrations are a longstanding American tradition. From the Framers to our current President, Congress, and Supreme Court, government leaders have opened public functions with prayer. Deborah (P) was not forced to pray. Standing is not necessarily a sign of approval; more likely it is a sign of respect for religious beliefs of others, a civic virtue that our schools should cultivate. The Establishment Clause only bars state religious activity backed by threat of penalty for nonparticipation.

▶ ANALYSIS

The dissent claimed that the Court's failure to apply the three-part test of *Lemon v. Kurtzman*, 403 U.S. 602 (1971), means the test is no longer good law. However, Justice Kennedy in his opinion for the Court expressly declined to reconsider *Lemon*. Justices Kennedy and Souter both cited *Lemon* with approval, though they did not apply the test. Justice Blackmun's concurrence, joined by Justices Stevens and O'Connor, expressed the view that *Lemon* still applies in all Establishment Clause cases.

Quicknotes

ESTABLISHMENT CLAUSE The constitutional provision prohibiting the government from favoring any one religion over others, or engaging in religious activities or advocacy.

TEMPORARY RESTRAINING ORDER A court order preserving the status quo pending a hearing regarding injunctive relief.

Mitchell v. Helms

Parties not identified.

530 U.S. 793 (2000).

NATURE OF CASE: Review of constitutionality of a school aid program.

FACT SUMMARY: As part of a school aid program, Chapter 2, the federal government distributes funds to state and local governmental agencies that in turn lend educational materials and equipment to public and private schools based on enrollment.

> ## 🏛 RULE OF LAW
> In determining whether government aid has the effect of advancing religion, the court must consider the following criteria: (1) whether the statute results in governmental indoctrination; (2) whether the statute defines its recipients by reference to religion; and (3) whether the statute creates an excessive government entanglement.

FACTS: Chapter 2 of the Education Consolidation and Improvement Act of 1981 is a vehicle to deliver federal funds to elementary and secondary school students. Aid to private schools is restricted to nonreligious aid and can only be in the form of a "loan" of applied-for materials, equipment, and the like. In Jefferson Parish, the private schools tend to use their loans for materials and equipment. Most of the private schools are religiously affiliated. The question presented here is whether Chapter 2, as applied in Jefferson Parish, Louisiana, is a law respecting an establishment of religion since many of the private schools receiving such aid are religiously affiliated.

ISSUE: In determining whether government aid has the effect of advancing religion, must the court consider the following criteria: (1) whether the statute results in governmental indoctrination; (2) whether the statute defines its recipients by reference to religion; and (3) whether the statute creates an excessive government entanglement?

HOLDING AND DECISION: (Thomas, J.) Yes. In determining whether government aid has the effect of advancing religion, the court must consider the following criteria: (1) whether the statute results in governmental indoctrination; (2) whether the statute defines its recipients by reference to religion; and (3) whether the statute creates an excessive government entanglement. In *Agostini v. Felton*, 521 U.S. 203 (1997), this Court overruled two anomalous precedents and consolidated some previously disparate considerations under a revised test, modifying the test set forth in *Lemon v. Kurtzman*. There the Court set out revised criteria for determining whether government aid has the effect of advancing religion: (1) whether the statute results in governmental indoctrination; (2) whether the statute defines its recipients by reference to religion; and (3) whether the statute creates an excessive government entanglement.

Here we need only examine the statute's effect since respondents do not challenge the district court's holding that the statute has a secular purpose. Moreover, the Court only need consider the first two criteria, since there is no question as to whether the statute creates an excessive government entanglement. The Court concludes that Chapter 2 neither results in religious indoctrination nor defines its recipients with respect to religion. Thus, Chapter 2 is not a law respecting the establishment of religion. The issue of whether governmental aid to religious schools results in governmental indoctrination is whether any religious indoctrination that occurs in those schools could reasonably be attributable to government action. In making this determination, the Court has upheld aid offered to a broad range of persons without regard to their religion. The second criterion of the *Agostini* test requires a court to consider whether an aid program defines its recipients be reference to religion. This requires an inquiry as to whether the criteria allocating the aid create a financial incentive to undertake religious indoctrination.

CONCURRENCE: (O'Connor, J.) The plurality announces a rule of unprecedented breadth for the evaluation of Establishment Clause challenges to government school-aid programs. The plurality's rule holds that government aid to religious schools does not have the effect of advancing religion so long as the aid is offered on a neutral basis and the aid is secular in content. The plurality also rejects the distinction between direct and indirect aid, thereby allowing actual diversion of secular aid by a religious school to the advancement of its religious mission.

DISSENT: (Souter, J.) The Court errs in failing to recognize the divertibility of funds to serve religious objectives. The Court breaks fundamentally with Establishment Clause jurisprudence and with the established methodology.

▶ ANALYSIS

Prior to this case, the applicable test in determining whether a statute respected an establishment of religion was that set forth in *Lemon v. Kurtzman*, 403 U.S. 602 (1971). That test involved a three-part inquiry to determine whether the statute: (1) has a secular purpose; (2) has a primary effect of advancing or inhibiting religion; or (3) creates an excessive entanglement between the state and religion.

■=■

Quicknotes

ESTABLISHMENT CLAUSE The constitutional provision prohibiting the government from favoring any one religion over others, or engaging in religious activities or advocacy.

■=■

Zelman v. Simmons-Harris

School superintendent (D) v. Taxpayers (P)

536 U.S. 639 (2002).

NATURE OF CASE: Appeal from affirmance of injunction against a school voucher program that can be used for parochial school education.

FACT SUMMARY: To address the dismal performance of the Cleveland public school system, Ohio enacted a school voucher program that enabled parents to choose to send their children to participating private schools. An overwhelming number of the private schools participating in the program had a religious affiliation, and Ohio taxpayers (P) challenged the voucher program as a violation of the Establishment Clause.

> 🏛 **RULE OF LAW**
> A school voucher program that gives parents the choice to send their children to a private school does not violate the Establishment Clause where the overwhelming number of participating private schools is comprised of religiously affiliated parochial schools.

FACTS: Ohio's Pilot Project Scholarship Program gave educational choices to families in any Ohio school district that was under state control pursuant to a federal court order. The program provided tuition aid for certain students in the Cleveland City School District, the only covered district because of its dismal performance as compared to most other districts in the nation, to attend participating public or private schools of their parent's choosing and tutorial aid for students who chose to remain enrolled in public school. Both religious and nonreligious schools in the district could participate, as could public schools in adjacent school districts. Tuition aid was distributed to parents according to financial need, and where the aid was spent depended solely upon where parents chose to enroll their children. The number of tutorial assistance grants provided to students remaining in public school had to equal the number of tuition aid scholarships. In the 1999-2000 school year, 82 percent of the participating private schools had a religious affiliation, none of the adjacent public schools participated, and 96 percent of the students participating in the scholarship program were enrolled in religiously affiliated schools. Sixty percent of the students were from families at or below the poverty line. Cleveland schoolchildren also had the option of enrolling in community schools, which were funded under state law but run by their own school boards and received twice the per-student funding as participating private schools, or magnet schools (public schools emphasizing a particular subject area, teaching method, or service). Ohio taxpayers (P) sought to enjoin the program on the ground that it violated the Establishment Clause. The district court granted them summary judgment, and the court of appeals affirmed. The Supreme Court granted review.

ISSUE: Does a school voucher program that gives parents the choice to send their children to a private school violate the Establishment Clause where the overwhelming number of participating private schools is comprised of religiously affiliated parochial schools?

HOLDING AND DECISION: (Rehnquist, C.J.) No. A school voucher program that gives parents the choice to send their children to a private school does not violate the Establishment Clause where the overwhelming number of participating private schools is comprised of religiously affiliated parochial schools. Because the program here was undisputedly enacted for the valid secular purpose of providing educational assistance to poor children in a demonstrably failing public school system, the question is whether the program nonetheless has the forbidden effect of advancing or inhibiting religion. The Court's jurisprudence [see, e.g., *Mueller v. Allen*, 463 U.S. 388 (1983), and its progeny] makes clear that a government aid program is not readily subject to challenge under the Establishment Clause if it is neutral with respect to religion and provides assistance directly to a broad class of citizens who, in turn, direct government aid to religious schools wholly as a result of their own genuine and independent private choice. The Ohio program is one of true private choice, and is thus constitutional. It is neutral in all respects towards religion, and is part of Ohio's general and multifaceted undertaking to provide educational opportunities to children in a failed school district. It confers educational assistance directly to a broad class of individuals defined without reference to religion and permits participation of all district schools—religious or nonreligious—and adjacent public schools. The only preference in the program is for low-income families, who receive greater assistance and have priority for admission. Rather than creating financial incentives that skew it towards religious schools, the program creates financial disincentives: Private schools receive only half the government assistance given to community schools and one-third that given to magnet schools, and adjacent public schools would receive two to three times that given to private schools. Families, too, have a financial disincentive, for they have to copay a portion of private school tuition, but pay nothing at a community, magnet, or traditional public school. Thus, no reasonable observer would think that such a neutral private choice program carries with it the imprimatur of government endorsement. Even though 46 of the 56 private schools participating in the program are religious schools, the Establishment Clause question whether Ohio is coercing parents into sending their children to religious schools must be answered by evaluating all options Ohio

Continued on next page.

provides Cleveland schoolchildren, only one of which is to obtain a scholarship and then choose a religious school. Eighty-two percent of Cleveland's private schools are religious, as are 81 percent of Ohio's private schools. To attribute constitutional significance to the 82 percent figure would lead to the absurd result that a neutral school-choice program might be permissible in parts of Ohio where the percentage is lower, but not in Cleveland, where Ohio has deemed such programs most sorely needed. The taxpayers (P) additionally argue that constitutional significance should be attached to the fact that 96 percent of the scholarship recipients have enrolled in religious schools. However, a closer look at the 96 percent figure reveals that if over 1,900 Cleveland children enrolled in alternative community schools, 13,000 children enrolled in alternative magnet schools, and 1,400 children enrolled in traditional public schools with tutorial assistance are factored in, the percentage drops to 20 percent. In sum, the Ohio program is entirely neutral with respect to religion. It provides benefits directly to a wide spectrum of individuals, defined only by financial need and residence in a particular school district. It permits such individuals to exercise genuine choice among options public and private, secular and religious. The program is therefore a program of true private choice. Reversed.

CONCURRENCE: (O'Connor, J.) This case does not depart from precedent. It is different from prior indirect aid cases because a significant portion of the funds appropriated for the voucher program reaches religious schools without restriction on the use of these funds. The share of public resources that reach religious schools is not as significant as the taxpayers (P) suggest (82 percent of participating schools are religious; 96 percent of participating students are enrolled in religious schools) because the statistics on which these assertions are based do not take into account all of the reasonable educational choices that may be available to students in the district. When one considers the option to attend community schools, the percentage of students enrolled in religious schools falls to 62.1 percent. If magnet schools are included in the mix, this percentage falls to 16.5 percent. In addition, the state spent $1 million more on students in community schools than in religious schools although one-half as many students attended community schools than attended religious schools. Moreover, the amount spent on religious private schools ($8.2 million) was minor compared to the $114.8 million spent on students in magnet schools. Although $8.2 million is no small sum, it pales in comparison to the billions of dollars that federal, state, and local governments already provide religious institutions in the form of different tax breaks, public health programs, educational programs, and other social welfare programs. These funds, like the voucher program funds, typically are unaccompanied by restrictions on subsequent use. The Court's decision does not mark a dramatic break with the Court's prior Establishment Clause jurisprudence. Here, the Court clarifies that the Establishment Clause requires that state aid going to religious organizations through the hands of beneficiaries must do so

only at the discretion of those beneficiaries. The parents have a genuine nonreligious choice when all the choices available are considered, and, therefore, the voucher program is consistent with the Establishment Clause.

CONCURRENCE: (Thomas, J.) Although the voucher program easily passes muster under the Court's stringent test, this test should not be applied to the states. On its face, the Establishment Clause does not apply to the states; originally, it protected states and their citizens from the imposition of an established religion by the federal government. The use of the Fourteenth Amendment to protect religious liberty rights is acceptable, but to oppose neutral programs of school choice through the incorporation of the Establishment Clause is unacceptable. Religious schools, like other private schools, achieve far better educational results than their public counterparts. But, the success of religious and private schools is in the end beside the point, because the state has a constitutional right to experiment with a variety of different programs to promote educational opportunity. That Ohio's program includes successful schools simply indicates that such reform can in fact provide improved education to underprivileged urban children.

DISSENT: (Stevens, J.) The voluntary character of the private choice to prefer a parochial education to a public one is irrelevant to the question whether the government's choice to pay for religious indoctrination is constitutionally permissible. The removal of any safeguard of the separation between religion and government weakens the foundation of our democracy.

DISSENT: (Souter, J.) The dismal condition of Cleveland's public schools is no excuse for giving short shrift to the Establishment Clause. Most of the money spent under the program the majority approves will be spent not only on teaching students secular subjects but will also be spent on teaching religion in schools that are founded to teach religious doctrine and to imbue all subjects with a religious dimension. Under the Court's precedent, neutrality conceived of as evenhandedness toward aid recipients has never been treated as alone sufficient to satisfy the Establishment Clause. However, under the majority's decision, the substantial character of government aid has no significance, and the criteria of neutrality in offering aid and private choice in directing it, are nothing but examples of verbal formalism. The Court's logic could lead to a finding that there is "neutrality" in a voucher scheme where there are no secular private schools at all. This, indeed, is the only way the majority can gloss over the very non-neutral feature of the total scheme covering "all schools": public tutors may receive from the state no more than $324 per child to support extra tutoring, whereas the tuition voucher schools (which turn out to be mostly religious) can receive up to $2,250. If, contrary to the majority, the question is posed in terms of

Continued on next page.

choice regarding how to use the vouchers, the answer here is that something is influencing choices in a way that aims the money in a religious direction. It is not the particular religion of the school that is responsible for this effect, because two out of three families chose religious schools, the religion of which they did not embrace. The fact is that nonreligious private schools are more expensive than the religious schools, and can afford to accommodate only a few voucher students. The obvious fix to this problem would be to increase the value of the vouchers. However, to get to the point where true choice is available would require such massive funding of religion as to disserve every goal of the Establishment Clause even more than the scheme here does.

DISSENT: (Breyer, J.) The Establishment Clause's concern for protecting the nation's social fabric from religious conflict outweighs the goals of the well-intentioned voucher program at issue here.

▶ *ANALYSIS*

The Court has traditionally been satisfied that a law has a neutral primary effect if the religious impact of the law is remote, indirect, and incidental. Here, the dissent seems to argue that the voucher program's impact was not remote or incidental, because by its very design, given the demographic realities of the school district, it encouraged enrollment in religious schools. The case leaves several constitutional questions unanswered, including whether provisions in voucher programs that prohibit discrimination by recipient schools are now constitutionally mandated, and whether state laws that expressly prohibit the use of aid for religious schools are themselves unconstitutional.

■══■

Quicknotes

ESTABLISHMENT CLAUSE The constitutional provision prohibiting the government from favoring any one religion over others, or engaging in religious activities or advocacy.

■══■

Glossary

Common Latin Words and Phrases Encountered in the Law

A FORTIORI: Because one fact exists or has been proven, therefore a second fact that is related to the first fact must also exist.

A PRIORI: From the cause to the effect. A term of logic used to denote that when one generally accepted truth is shown to be a cause, another particular effect must necessarily follow.

AB INITIO: From the beginning; a condition which has existed throughout, as in a marriage which was void ab initio.

ACTUS REUS: The wrongful act; in criminal law, such action sufficient to trigger criminal liability.

AD VALOREM: According to value; an ad valorem tax is imposed upon an item located within the taxing jurisdiction calculated by the value of such item.

AMICUS CURIAE: Friend of the court. Its most common usage takes the form of an amicus curiae brief, filed by a person who is not a party to an action but is nonetheless allowed to offer an argument supporting his legal interests.

ARGUENDO: In arguing. A statement, possibly hypothetical, made for the purpose of argument, is one made arguendo.

BILL QUIA TIMET: A bill to quiet title (establish ownership) to real property.

BONA FIDE: True, honest, or genuine. May refer to a person's legal position based on good faith or lacking notice of fraud (such as a bona fide purchaser for value) or to the authenticity of a particular document (such as a bona fide last will and testament).

CAUSA MORTIS: With approaching death in mind. A gift causa mortis is a gift given by a party who feels certain that death is imminent.

CAVEAT EMPTOR: Let the buyer beware. This maxim is reflected in the rule of law that a buyer purchases at his own risk because it is his responsibility to examine, judge, test, and otherwise inspect what he is buying.

CERTIORARI: A writ of review. Petitions for review of a case by the United States Supreme Court are most often done by means of a writ of certiorari.

CONTRA: On the other hand. Opposite. Contrary to.

CORAM NOBIS: Before us; writs of error directed to the court that originally rendered the judgment.

CORAM VOBIS: Before you; writs of error directed by an appellate court to a lower court to correct a factual error.

CORPUS DELICTI: The body of the crime; the requisite elements of a crime amounting to objective proof that a crime has been committed.

CUM TESTAMENTO ANNEXO, ADMINISTRATOR (ADMINISTRATOR C.T.A.): With will annexed; an administrator c.t.a. settles an estate pursuant to a will in which he is not appointed.

DE BONIS NON, ADMINISTRATOR (ADMINISTRATOR D.B.N.): Of goods not administered; an administrator d.b.n. settles a partially settled estate.

DE FACTO: In fact; in reality; actually. Existing in fact but not officially approved or engendered.

DE JURE: By right; lawful. Describes a condition that is legitimate "as a matter of law," in contrast to the term "de facto," which connotes something existing in fact but not legally sanctioned or authorized. For example, de facto segregation refers to segregation brought about by housing patterns, etc., whereas de jure segregation refers to segregation created by law.

DE MINIMIS: Of minimal importance; insignificant; a trifle; not worth bothering about.

DE NOVO: Anew; a second time; afresh. A trial de novo is a new trial held at the appellate level as if the case originated there and the trial at a lower level had not taken place.

DICTA: Generally used as an abbreviated form of obiter dicta, a term describing those portions of a judicial opinion incidental or not necessary to resolution of the specific question before the court. Such nonessential statements and remarks are not considered to be binding precedent.

DUCES TECUM: Refers to a particular type of writ or subpoena requesting a party or organization to produce certain documents in their possession.

EN BANC: Full bench. Where a court sits with all justices present rather than the usual quorum.

EX PARTE: For one side or one party only. An ex parte proceeding is one undertaken for the benefit of only one party, without notice to, or an appearance by, an adverse party.

EX POST FACTO: After the fact. An ex post facto law is a law that retroactively changes the consequences of a prior act.

EX REL.: Abbreviated form of the term ex relatione, meaning upon relation or information. When the state brings an action in which it has no interest against an individual at the instigation of one who has a private interest in the matter.

FORUM NON CONVENIENS: Inconvenient forum. Although a court may have jurisdiction over the case, the action should be tried in a more conveniently located court, one to which parties and witnesses may more easily travel, for example.

GUARDIAN AD LITEM: A guardian of an infant as to litigation, appointed to represent the infant and pursue his/her rights.

HABEAS CORPUS: You have the body. The modern writ of habeas corpus is a writ directing that a person (body) being detained (such as a prisoner) be brought before the court so that the legality of his detention can be judicially ascertained.

IN CAMERA: In private, in chambers. When a hearing is held before a judge in his chambers or when all spectators are excluded from the courtroom.

IN FORMA PAUPERIS: In the manner of a pauper. A party who proceeds in forma pauperis because of his poverty is one who is allowed to bring suit without liability for costs.

INFRA: Below, under. A word referring the reader to a later part of a book. (The opposite of supra.)

IN LOCO PARENTIS: In the place of a parent.

IN PARI DELICTO: Equally wrong; a court of equity will not grant requested relief to an applicant who is in pari delicto, or as much at fault in the transactions giving rise to the controversy as is the opponent of the applicant.

IN PARI MATERIA: On like subject matter or upon the same matter. Statutes relating to the same person or things are said to be in pari materia. It is a general rule of statutory construction that such statutes should be construed together, i.e., looked at as if they together constituted one law.

IN PERSONAM: Against the person. Jurisdiction over the person of an individual.

IN RE: In the matter of. Used to designate a proceeding involving an estate or other property.

IN REM: A term that signifies an action against the res, or thing. An action in rem is basically one that is taken directly against property, as distinguished from an action in personam, i.e., against the person.

INTER ALIA: Among other things. Used to show that the whole of a statement, pleading, list, statute, etc., has not been set forth in its entirety.

INTER PARTES: Between the parties. May refer to contracts, conveyances or other transactions having legal significance.

INTER VIVOS: Between the living. An inter vivos gift is a gift made by a living grantor, as distinguished from bequests contained in a will, which pass upon the death of the testator.

IPSO FACTO: By the mere fact itself.

JUS: Law or the entire body of law.

LEX LOCI: The law of the place; the notion that the rights of parties to a legal proceeding are governed by the law of the place where those rights arose.

MALUM IN SE: Evil or wrong in and of itself; inherently wrong. This term describes an act that is wrong by its very nature, as opposed to one which would not be wrong but for the fact that there is a specific legal prohibition against it (malum prohibitum).

MALUM PROHIBITUM: Wrong because prohibited, but not inherently evil. Used to describe something that is wrong because it is expressly forbidden by law but that is not in and of itself evil, e.g., speeding.

MANDAMUS: We command. A writ directing an official to take a certain action.

MENS REA: A guilty mind; a criminal intent. A term used to signify the mental state that accompanies a crime or other prohibited act. Some crimes require only a general mens rea (general intent to do the prohibited act), but others, like assault with intent to murder, require the existence of a specific mens rea.

MODUS OPERANDI: Method of operating; generally refers to the manner or style of a criminal in committing crimes, admissible in appropriate cases as evidence of the identity of a defendant.

NEXUS: A connection to.

NISI PRIUS: A court of first impression. A nisi prius court is one where issues of fact are tried before a judge or jury.

N.O.V. (NON OBSTANTE VEREDICTO): Notwithstanding the verdict. A judgment n.o.v. is a judgment given in favor of one party despite the fact that a verdict was returned in favor of the other party, the justification being that the verdict either had no reasonable support in fact or was contrary to law.

NUNC PRO TUNC: Now for then. This phrase refers to actions that may be taken and will then have full retroactive effect.

PENDENTE LITE: Pending the suit; pending litigation underway.

PER CAPITA: By head; beneficiaries of an estate, if they take in equal shares, take per capita.

PER CURIAM: By the court; signifies an opinion ostensibly written "by the whole court" and with no identified author.

PER SE: By itself, in itself; inherently.

PER STIRPES: By representation. Used primarily in the law of wills to describe the method of distribution where a person, generally because of death, is unable to take that which is left to him by the will of another, and therefore his heirs divide such property between them rather than take under the will individually.

PRIMA FACIE: On its face, at first sight. A prima facie case is one that is sufficient on its face, meaning that the evidence supporting it is adequate to establish the case until contradicted or overcome by other evidence.

PRO TANTO: For so much; as far as it goes. Often used in eminent domain cases when a property owner receives partial payment for his land without prejudice to his right to bring suit for the full amount he claims his land to be worth.

QUANTUM MERUIT: As much as he deserves. Refers to recovery based on the doctrine of unjust enrichment in those cases in which a party has rendered valuable services or furnished materials that were accepted and enjoyed by another under circumstances that would reasonably notify the recipient that the rendering party expected to be paid. In essence, the law implies a contract to pay the reasonable value of the services or materials furnished.

QUASI: Almost like; as if; nearly. This term is essentially used to signify that one subject or thing is almost analogous to another but that material differences between them do exist. For example, a quasi-criminal proceeding is one that is not strictly criminal but shares enough of the same characteristics to require some of the same safeguards (e.g., procedural due process must be followed in a parole hearing).

QUID PRO QUO: Something for something. In contract law, the consideration, something of value, passed between the parties to render the contract binding.

RES GESTAE: Things done; in evidence law, this principle justifies the admission of a statement that would otherwise be hearsay when it is made so closely to the event in question as to be said to be a part of it, or with such spontaneity as not to have the possibility of falsehood.

RES IPSA LOQUITUR: The thing speaks for itself. This doctrine gives rise to a rebuttable presumption of negligence when the instrumentality causing the injury was within the exclusive control of the defendant, and the injury was one that does not normally occur unless a person has been negligent.

RES JUDICATA: A matter adjudged. Doctrine which provides that once a court of competent jurisdiction has rendered a final judgment or decree on the merits, that judgment or decree is conclusive upon the parties to the case and prevents them from engaging in any other litigation on the points and issues determined therein.

RESPONDEAT SUPERIOR: Let the master reply. This doctrine holds the master liable for the wrongful acts of his servant (or the principal for his agent) in those cases in which the servant (or agent) was acting within the scope of his authority at the time of the injury.

STARE DECISIS: To stand by or adhere to that which has been decided. The common law doctrine of stare decisis attempts to give security and certainty to the law by following the policy that once a principle of law as applicable to a certain set of facts has been set forth in a decision, it forms a precedent which will subsequently be followed, even though a different decision might be made were it the first time the question had arisen. Of course, stare decisis is not an inviolable principle and is departed from in instances where there is good cause (e.g., considerations of public policy led the Supreme Court to disregard prior decisions sanctioning segregation).

SUPRA: Above. A word referring a reader to an earlier part of a book.

ULTRA VIRES: Beyond the power. This phrase is most commonly used to refer to actions taken by a corporation that are beyond the power or legal authority of the corporation.

Addendum of French Derivatives

IN PAIS: Not pursuant to legal proceedings.

CHATTEL: Tangible personal property.

CY PRES: Doctrine permitting courts to apply trust funds to purposes not expressed in the trust but necessary to carry out the settlor's intent.

PER AUTRE VIE: For another's life; during another's life. In property law, an estate may be granted that will terminate upon the death of someone other than the grantee.

PROFIT A PRENDRE: A license to remove minerals or other produce from land.

VOIR DIRE: Process of questioning jurors as to their predispositions about the case or parties to a proceeding in order to identify those jurors displaying bias or prejudice.

Casenote Legal Briefs